Lodge of the
Double-Headed Eagle

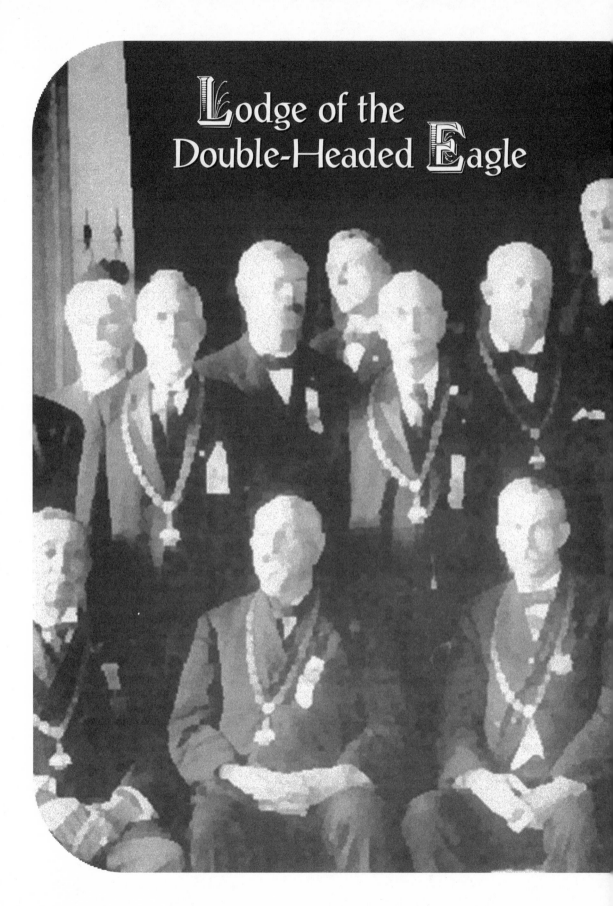

Lodge of the Double-Headed Eagle

*Two Centuries
of Scottish Rite
Freemasonry in
America's Southern
Jurisdiction*

WILLIAM L. FOX

The UNIVERSITY *of*
ARKANSAS PRESS
1997

01   00   99   98   97   5   4   3   2

Design by A. G. Carter

⊛ The paper used in this publication meets the minimum
requirements of the American National Standard for Perma-
nence of Paper for Printed Library Materials   Z39.48-1984.

LIBRARY OF CONGRESS CATALOGING-IN-PUBLICATION DATA

Fox, William L., 1953–
      Lodge of the Double-Headed Eagle : two centuries
of Scottish Rite Freemasonry in America's Southern
Jurisdiction / William L. Fox.
            p.   cm.
      Includes bibliographical references and index.
      ISBN 1-55728-477-6 (alk. paper)
      1. Scottish Rite (Masonic order). Southern Masonic
Jurisdiction—History.   2. Scottish Rite (Masonic order).
Southern Masonic Jurisdiction—Biography.   I. Title.
   HS765.F69   1997
   366'.1'0975—dc21   97-14064
                                                    CIP

To the Memory of

William Lloyd Fox
1921–1993

Master of the historian's craft

Ever present coauthor in the work of his namesake

Contents

		Foreword	IX
		Preface	XI
CHAPTER	I	The Scottish Rite's Prehistory *The Genesis and Genius of Freemasonry*	3
CHAPTER	II	First Light, 1801–1826 *Mitchell, Dalcho, and Auld*	25
CHAPTER	III	Keepers of the Flame, 1826–1858 *Holbrook, McDonald, and Honour*	39
CHAPTER	IV	Exodus from Charleston, 1859–1870 *Albert Pike*	57
CHAPTER	V	The Washingtonian Pike, 1870–1891	89
CHAPTER	VI	A Fragile Interim, 1891–1900 *Batchelor, Tucker, and Caswell*	121
CHAPTER	VII	New Century, New Age, New Temple, 1900–1914 *James D. Richardson*	141
CHAPTER	VIII	Forerunner of Americanism, 1915–1921 *George F. Moore*	171
CHAPTER	IX	Prosperity to Depression, 1921–1935 *John H. Cowles*	201
CHAPTER	X	Steel Helmets and Iron Curtains, 1936–1952 *Later Years of John H. Cowles*	237
CHAPTER	XI	Stretched Nerves, 1950s *Harkins and Smith*	269
CHAPTER	XII	The Moon Above, Perplexity Below, 1959–1969 *Luther A. Smith*	293
CHAPTER	XIII	When the Waves Went High, 1969–1985 *Henry C. Clausen*	319
CHAPTER	XIV	Continuity and Opportunity, 1985 and Forward *C. Fred Kleinknecht*	347
CHAPTER	XV	The Scottish Rite and the American Right, 1990s *Religious Prejudice as a Source of Anti-Masonry*	381
		Epilogue	411
		Notes	421
		Bibliographical Note	475
		Index	479

Foreword

The origins of Freemasonry are a subject for discussion and occasional dispute. What seems beyond contention is that the Order experienced a great leap in vitality and appeal in the eighteenth century, a period in European history when a social and political system based on authority was giving way to one in which individual choice and personal initiative were increasingly seen as the basis for stability and prosperity.

William Fox's admirably thorough and honest history traces the process that brought the Masonic drama first to the point of focus represented by the Southern Jurisdiction of the Scottish Rite, and then down to our own days, in which the Scottish Rite is seeking to cope with a period of challenge and outright crisis—one even more serious, perhaps, than that of the Great Depression.

In the eighteenth century, Freemasonry represented an amazing act of adaptation. The traditional rituals of European society—religious and political—were suddenly being under-mined by the outlook summarized in a figure like Voltaire, who was capable of wielding skep-ticism and outright satire against the sacred truths of an earlier time. Those who laughed at the products of his pen still felt the inner emptiness that such laughter implied. To them, the Masonic Ritual offered a new and yet deeply rooted possibility: that of linking with one's fellow human beings in a community based on choice rather than compulsion—but one as rich in symbolism and emotion as the rituals of an earlier time.

In this sense, a marriage was fated between Freemasonry and what eventually became the new American republic, similarly based on conscious choice rather than thoughtless conti-nuity. The marriage was sealed by the most fundamental fact about the order: its identification with an ancient craft and that craft's rich freight of symbolism. The choice of stonemasons as paradigms of human accomplishment was a remarkable way of defining Freemasonry as an ultimately open system that could adapt even to the new order of democracy, and to the growth of a nation based on commerce rather than feudal privilege. It also connected those who chose to be Masons with the intellectual and ideological currents of a century that was bracketed at one end by the Russian Tsar, Peter the Great, who labored as an apprentice in the shipyards of Holland as a prelude to his development of a powerful modern navy; and at the other end by the great encyclopedia produced in France by Denis Diderot and his colleagues, with its insatiable curiosity about human industry and its countless products and processes.

To identify with the trade of masonry, in other words, was an act of imagination that could only be perceived as threatening by those still dedicated to the suppression rather than the cultivation of human choice. No wonder the enemies of Freemasonry in the twentieth century have included such a roster of tyrants and oppressors. And no wonder the Scottish Rite has expended such major efforts in the struggle to rescue those, both Masons and non-Masons, whose lives have been threatened by these aficionados of compulsion.

What the Masonic ethic also predicted, in a sense, was the deep involvement of the Scottish Rite with education in general and public education in particular. My own school, George

Washington University, has experienced this involvement, in a very positive way, over a period of many years. Education has proven a liberating force of the first order in modern societies. It has provided those born in humble and unpromising circumstances with the leverage they needed to gain full access to their local, regional, and national economies. Today it provides full access to the most dynamic (because of its being truly global) economy our planet has ever seen.

No one can read Mr. Fox's history without asking—more than once—a crucial question: Does Freemasonry have a future as well as a past, and, if so, what form is that future likely to take? The decline in membership experienced by the Scottish Rite in recent years, a decline which Mr. Fox connects with the whole spirit of the 1990s, is not necessarily terminal. A rebound, such as has occurred before in the Scottish Rite's experience, can be called a good possibility. And the recent renewal of interest in the Ritual may point us in the direction that such a rebirth is likely to take.

That which our species as a whole is passing through right now has many parallels with what Western Europe and its American extensions were passing through two centuries ago. Then, the forces of skepticism and satire, as they targeted what we might call the poetry of faith, practically guaranteed the enormous spiritual revival that became known as Romanticism or the Romantic Movement. Above all, the use of prose for analytic purposes—and prose's capacity for tearing down any assertion not based on measurable fact—saw to it that poetry and music would try to fill the resulting vacuum in the human heart. Today, there are many who fear that our new fascination with computers and the world of "the electronic" is similarly reducing us to creatures who only live in the abstract, hypnotized by images and representations rather than grounded in tangible realties.

In today's world as in the eighteenth century, therefore, Freemasonry and the Scottish Rite may have a future as well as a past. What could be more appropriate for our age than the devotion to tangibility communicated by the mason's craft, utterly preoccupied as it is with the handling of solid rock? We live in a time, after all, when tens of millions of people find in gardening or a variety of crafts the literally manual activities that make their otherwise abstract lives tolerable. For those who stare at computer screens all day, what can be more deeply fulfilling than a successfully cultivated flower? And for those who measure their lives in words, what can have a more effective appeal than the tools with which masons go about shaping otherwise impenetrable stone?

Mr. Fox's history, focused on the Scottish Rite, is also a history of the human spirit, in its quest for the values of community and equality. How that spirit has coped with the challenges of first the industrial and then the information age is his ultimate subject. His history can be recommended to all those who care about the past, present, and future of our very remarkable species.

Stephen Joel Trachtenberg
President of George Washington University
and Professor of Public Administration

Preface

My reasons for wanting to write this book changed in the course of my labors. It was not my first choice for a new project after completing and publishing a doctoral dissertation on the Harvard theologian Willard L. Sperry. And I was not the first one to attempt the history of an organization two hundred years old, though no professional historian had paid much attention to its record in the twentieth century—a period of American history in which I had concentrated.

I entered the work of this book because the proposed author of it died. He was my father. At the time of his death, I had recently returned to my hometown, Washington, D.C., from California, where I was the senior minister of Pilgrim Congregational Church in Pomona and adjunct professor of church history at the Claremont School of Theology. Once back on the east coast, I departed slightly from my church orientation, which for me had been fast rising and rewarding. I began to teach history full time and enjoy, at a different pace, an itinerant ministry with regular preaching opportunities. This was a reversal of my California vocational life.

Simultaneously, as my father's cancer progressed to the inevitable state, some of the college courses I taught were the same ones he had covered more than forty years before my own presence in the classroom. Moreover, I was teaching on the same faculty from which my father had retired in 1976. (Meanings in coincidence typically stump theologians, too.) At this point, I had also become happily attached to the community of scholars at the Howard University School of Divinity. In the lecture hall, I experienced a reassuring continuity by being placed in a setting so loved and honored by my father. To be a teacher in a family of teachers whose chalk-dust lines ran back four generations seemed fitting and fair.

My life was rich enough professionally without adding a Masonic dimension. But then, when my father died there was all this raw material he left behind pertaining to the history of the Supreme Council of the Scottish Rite of Freemasonry, Southern Jurisdiction of America. Our family and my father's friends lamented the "waste" of the book dying with him. Apparently, C. Fred Kleinknecht, Sovereign Grand Commander of the Supreme Council, also shared their sense of acute privation.

When I was first summoned to discuss the problem of what to do about the excavated foundation of a project that might never have a building over it, I had determined in advance that the answer would be a negative one. Fred Kleinknecht and the late Lynn G. Fox, my mother, who survived my father by only eighteen months, knew differently and better. Thus, I began this book out of love that was labor; then it became a labor of love.

At first, I spent hours and days in the main reading room of the Library of Congress, reviewing the published material on fraternal orders. I was struck by the similarity of their structures and purposes to those of the Medieval monastic culture that I was enthusiastically presenting to Divinity students in my lecturing responsibilities. Both fraternities and monasteries exhibit a similar "love of learning," in the phrase of medievalist Jean Leclercq. Also, I realized there was a gap in the historical literature about the Masons. In particular, the Scottish Rite was relatively unknown in the typical bibliographies I was consulting and was not much of a presence in the public's awareness of Masonry. Further, little discussion had occurred, except in the tame, propagandistic ways of fraternal publications, about Masonic history in the larger context of American social and cultural developments.

To make this book more than an "in-group" or merely celebratory history, I set up a framework by reference to other events in American and sometimes international life. I have tried to select illuminating details of Americana so that my consideration of one branch of the Masonic family tree is not only a narrow history of an institution but also an interwoven story that has bearing on how American culture as a whole has cohered. There is a forest surrounding the tree I am writing about.

The strategy has been to put forward the case that Scottish Rite Freemasonry, where it was strongest and most influential, grew out of the prevailing cultural and social arrangements of the United States and, subsequently, influenced those nearby fraternal and public institutions profoundly. My tactics have been simply to show that the institutional history at hand is best understood in light of the men who superintended the organization.

This book is, therefore, an administrative and institutional history of the headquarters of the Scottish Rite's Southern Jurisdiction, built around the biographies of its chief executives. Geographically, the Southern Jurisdiction is the largest Masonic jurisdiction in the world; it is the oldest Scottish Rite establishment and is numerically the most significant. When local occurrences cross the stage in the narrative, they do so as they impinge upon developments at headquarters. But the main focus is on the Grand Commanders as they embody both the direction and spirit of the movement in American Freemasonry which tended toward the Scottish Rite variety.

The web of regional and local history woven into larger national trends, while important and sometimes quantifiable, is beyond the mission of this book. Who, for instance, were the Scottish Rite members in Houston in 1930, and who were they in San Francisco, and were they the same "type"? Answers to these questions may have important things to tell us, but not in this book. Instead, the story is centered on two cities only—Charleston, South Carolina, for about seventy years, and Washington, D.C., for the balance of time after the Civil War. This has explicit limitations; but as an institutional history, focusing on official actions of the Supreme Council as well as the personalities, leadership, and decisions of its Grand Commanders, there is no better way available.

Whenever possible, however, I have tried to extend the reach of the book beyond an exclusive focus on the council. Besides the obvious chronological expansion of the history, this "insider-outsider" analysis is what separates it from earlier Supreme Council histories, notably by Charles S. Lobingier, Ray Baker Harris, and James A. Carter. In other words, while preparing this book, a non-Masonic audience was as much in mind as the audience of the fraternity.

For this reason, since the book is designed with a biographical accent that includes both the "life and times" of a man, it invites one to dip into the story at points of specific interest. Reading a chapter as a stand-alone entry is in keeping with the plan. I hope, however, that by reading the book in its entirety the comprehensiveness of a few integral themes will be self-evident and convincing.

I have traced the organizational history from a time before the Supreme Council's inception in 1801 to the point where that tidal ripple finally strikes the beaches of the present. Despite its high pretensions, the Supreme Council of the Southern Jurisdiction was almost entirely a local Charleston, South Carolina, operation until Albert Pike took over on the eve of the Civil War.

Pike is the fulcrum of the story. His leadership for more than thirty years (1859–1891) transformed the Scottish Rite from being fraternally landlocked—trapped in the self-imposed isolation of Charleston society, caused in large part by a rigid plantation culture that was increasingly on the defensive—to being broadly popular throughout the American South and Far West. He did it not only by the force of his charismatic personality but also by developing a much more portable and understandable ritual than the original founders had used.

The appeal of the ritual was intrinsic, meeting a growing need for all sorts and conditions of Victorian men to experience lyrically cadenced ceremonies inside imaginary historical settings, reminiscent of the adult "Ever-Ever Land" described by the quintessential Victorian G. K. Chesterton. Remarkably, the particular experience offered by the Scottish Rite to thoughtful men who were already Master Masons was not available anywhere else; at least it was not presented satisfactorily enough for them in their religious and civic associations. Then, Pike's ritual became greatly enhanced by theatrical presentations, and the growth of the Scottish Rite was practically Malthusian. From the Scottish Rite's peak in census returns, which occurred when baby boomer men became eligible to join Masonry around 1968, the history turns next to the erosion of membership down to the present-day rate of continuing decline.

Meanwhile, as this history comes to its close, there are many capable minds at work on the question of "reinventing" the Scottish Rite for the first decades of the twenty-first century. Its recent history cannot be ignored, and it heartens me as an author that this work may somehow be useful to the endeavors of those younger men contemplating the future of an intellectual and philanthropic brotherhood.

■ ■ ■

Authors, because they work in solitude for such long stretches at a time, often have the self-pitying thought of being out there all alone in a small boat upon the open sea. They are, of course, joined by many salt-water oarsmen, the obliging hands who have encouraged them just at the right moment or helped in some specific task so that the adventure could stay on course. My gratitude is a debt beyond repaying.

It begins with C. Fred Kleinknecht, who recognized, long before he knew me, that a history of the Scottish Rite in the Southern Jurisdiction was overdue. He sensed, before any professional historian evaluated the Scottish Rite's rich past, that there was an important story waiting to be brought forward. And he was right. Fiercely determined, it seemed as long as he was Grand Commander, the book's future was never in doubt, which meant also that the Supreme Council's wonderful support never wavered. For me, he was the model of cooperation and dispassion. All records, papers, and archives were open to me. Moreover, Fred Kleinknecht never once asked me what I was writing, never asked to read a single word, and never "volunteered" to straighten me out on fine points. He left me entirely alone to make independent judgments and to consult whomever I chose for advice.

In the end, the interpretations are mine and do not in any way represent an official position. That kind of scholarly freedom, as I learned, was an inviolable Masonic principle. For his belief in the book coupled with his discipline to keep away from its progress, Fred Kleinknecht was a gentleman in the highest possible way that term can be used.

When I began this project, I was not a member of the Masonic fraternity. In part due to Fred Kleinknecht's example, but also in large measure because of my own wide-ranging exploration of its nature and purpose, which ultimately gave my decision historical warrant, I became a Scottish Rite member along the way. My reasons, in the end, were personal, as they always must be; but I based my decision on the question: If I were a member, would I be compromised by conflicting loyalties? Could I be trusted by a non-Masonic readership?

Finally, I decided that it would make little difference to me professionally, but that I could make a perceptible difference for the benefit of a good institution that had been bypassed and written off by so many of my generation and professional background. After all, I had previously addressed a similar question about conflict of interest as an ordained minister teaching religion, history, and philosophy courses at a public college.

I convinced myself at that point in my teaching career that one did not have to surrender his private practice of faith in order to teach the history of Christianity—an issue of academic freedom put to rest at most American universities. It seemed to me, furthermore, that one did not have to be an atheist to teach "objectively" about the role of religion in human societies and civilizations. So, too, one does not sacrifice himself by using the tools of his training in the conduct of work that involves him personally at some level. No historian can be that clinical and still write a lively tale.

Whatever obvious or unintended forms of admiration for Masonry are evident in the book, they are weighted by the heavier principle of trying to get the story right. My bias, however mild or strong, is on the table; but once known, it has actually granted me a sense of greater caution and, consequently, the earnest resolve to aim for the highest standards of honesty and intellectual integrity. The advantages of being a historian with some personal connection to the subject at one's elbow has actually increased my access to sources, particularly in interviewing men who take their Masonry quite seriously. As a result of this accommodation, I have tried to portray the deficiencies of the brotherhood with a consideration equal to that which I have given to the merits.

Among my many Masonic advisors, I wish to thank John W. Boettjer and W. Gene Sizemore for their constancy and countless ways of being helpful. John Boettjer read every sentence of the early drafts. As a former professor of English, his editorial scrutiny has saved me from many embarrassments that I might have otherwise had to endure. Gene Sizemore, a retired Rear Admiral in the U.S. Navy, is simply one of the finest "skippers" I have ever observed. The trustworthiness of his advice saved me from many moments of dead reckoning. My admiration for them both is genuine.

The late Reynold J. Matthews, Archivist of the Supreme Council, never failed to answer my first questions born of blushing ignorance. Arturo deHoyos, Rex Hutchens, Jim Tresner, Harry Echols, Dick Fletcher, Brent Morris, Forrest Haggard, Duane Anderson, Alain Bernheim, David Broad, and Lowell Dyson—all Freemasons, five of them PhDs—contributed with exceeding generosity to the successful completion of this work. They either read chapters or discussed with me sticky points in the text, but whatever connection each one had with the project, they always were kind, but also firmly forthright in telling me where I was going astray. And their opinions were almost always faultless.

The staff at the Northern Masonic Jurisdiction's Museum of Our National Heritage in Lexington, Massachusetts, at times saved me much trouble. I wish to thank John Hamilton, Tom Leavitt, Catherine Swanson, and Tim Frankel for the pleasant way my requests were always handled. Also, through this book I befriended William D. Moore of the Livingston Library in New York; he has contributed to my increasing sense that the Masonic story matters greatly.

In Washington, D.C., the competence of several offices at the Supreme Council, Southern Jurisdiction, made many buckling loads much lighter. I thank Joan Kleinknecht and Sandy Fennell for reference assistance; and before they took charge of the library and museum, Inge Baum was always eager to help. Others on the staff who pitched in occasionally include Russ Stogsdill, Ray Bunnell, Frank Simpkins, Beverly Jeffries, Martha Bell, Carol Acotto, Michele Massey, Frances Johnson, Mary Jiron, and Dana Osterndorf. Special mention of Linda S. Janetis is made because of the stenographic assistance she rendered my father in the beginning. Jay Naughton and John White also helped me escape more than one deep hole when computer equipment failed. Also, I wish to thank Susan Carroll for compiling the index.

Historians may not admit it without many discursive qualifications, but they are by nature a fraternal lot. I was encouraged by two friends and teaching colleagues whose conversation never failed to stimulate. Tom Walker is still an all-star lineman and Kurt Borkman has a mind like a sixty-yard arm. I caught more passes in the "end zone" than I would have believed possible had it not been for them.

Mark C. Carnes and Steven C. Bullock earned much deserved national reputations in Masonic history before I arrived on the scene. Neither of them are members of the craft, which made their impressions of my work especially valuable. They read the entire manuscript, providing not only critical commentary but also the kind of confidence an author needs from such well-respected authorities.

Dewey D. Wallace also read the full text with a scrutiny that resembled the Puritan discipline of his own intellectual heroes who lived about four hundred years ago in England. Dewey is a master teacher, premier scholar, and, most importantly, a wonderful friend. His wise counsel on matters of scholarship and life abide as a major influence.

I wish further to acknowledge the useful suggestions made in the early stages of publication by Miller Williams, Debbie Self, and Kevin Brock. To Karen Johnson I owe particular gratitude for sifting out of the text the annoying inconsistencies every author dreads discovering after the bindery has finished its task. Many others offered advice and encouragement along the way, but to list them all here would begin to encroach on the business at hand. They know my feelings.

A personal word is in order, too, about my most loving and exacting critics, for I am not the kind of worker who can leave his tasks outside the front door when the day is over. All aspects of this book lived at home with my family, sometimes as a guest who stayed too long. Home and workplace are not usually separate spheres for writers, a condition that Lynn, my wife, and Hallie, my daughter, have never begrudged.

Lynn Smith Fox grew up in a world where Masonic activities were an integral segment of her parents' lives. Both are now gone but were never far from the picture in my mind of how this book might capture a part of their story. Lynn and I enjoy a richly blessed partnership. And I am wise enough to yield to its sources of strength, without which this book would surely have come to grief in more ways than one. Her love, too, for my parents is in the mortar of this book's binding in equal portions to my own.

Arguably, this kind of book rarely occurs, for its essence and drive originate as the product of a family. It certainly seems unusual for scholarship to be a form of patrimony. The exchange between fathers and sons, when death makes a bigger man out of the younger one of them, is often represented by the passing down of a family heirloom such as a gold pocket watch. This and more was true in my case.

There is, assuredly, precedent for father-son historians in the world. There have been two Arthur Schlesingers in American historiography. In Britain, the last of the great Whig historians, G. M. Trevelyan, followed the vocational route of his father and his famous uncle, Thomas Babbington Macauley. Some historians come by their calling as a natural outcome of genetic predisposition. The renowned broadcast journalist David Brinkley, for example, sired two outstanding American historians.

In my own experience, I attribute much to the light I absorbed over the years around the family dinner table presided over by my father. Therefore, this uncommon piece of inheritance in the form of a book is a tribute to the man who during my youth lit the candles every night before dinner. And afterwards, as the dishes were cleared, he would rest a cup of tea on the end of the family piano, play songs from a time before I was born, and announce with predictable whimsy, "And then I wrote. . . ."

Lodge of the
Double-Headed Eagle

CHAPTER I

The Scottish Rite's Prehistory

The Genesis and Genius of Freemasonry

᠄᠄᠄᠄᠄᠄᠄᠄᠄᠄

Freemasonry is the oldest fraternity in the United States, being comfortably and publicly established in all of the English seaboard colonies of North America by the time of the War of Independence.[1] Its origins have been sought in antiquity, the ancient world of Egypt, Greece, and Rome and, on more certain ground, in the guilds of stonemasons who built the great cathedrals of England, Scotland, and the continent during the late Medieval era, a remarkable period for the soaring achievements in philosophy and architecture. "In tracing the direct line of descent of modern freemasonry, the starting point undoubtedly lies in England, in the documents known as the 'Old Charges' or 'Old Constitutions.' Like other medieval trades the masons had their craft organizations or guilds, and their mythical histories stressing antiquity and importance of the crafts, closely linking them with religious and moral concepts."[2]

In time, these operative masons developed some manner of protocol for those entering the guild initiatory ceremonies whereby they imparted secrets related to their work. By the fifteenth century, according to British historian David Stevenson, English masons were different in their emphasis on geometry, especially its association with King Solomon's Temple and the monumental buildings of ancient Egypt such as the great Temple of Karnak.[3] As Masonry evolved with its rich symbolism, spirit of brotherhood, and secret rituals, it is not surprising that men other than stonemasons, particularly distinguished men of the community, who were perhaps antiquarians interested in architectural history, found themselves drawn to guilds or lodges and were accepted as "honorary" members, thus Accepted Masons. They became over the years, during an unknown interim, the seedbed for speculative Masonry, or Freemasonry as it became known in modern times.[4]

The guild lodges attracted gentlemen intellectuals by the time of the Restoration of 1660. This subtly changed male institution provided a cloistered vehicle for the working out and transmission of radical to moderate Enlightenment ideas. The results of seventeenth- and eighteenth-century gentlemen being introduced to lodge practices and discussions, therefore, came to have measurable cultural significance.

Masonry was propelled by an upward social mobility that began curiously from a lower rung on the ladder and not within the advantaged ranks. It would not only help define what a gentleman is, but how gentlemen resolve disputes and how they are best governed. Euclidean geometry and the stonemason's craft helped formulate balanced, symmetrical constitutional charges. And yet, the actual means by which the transfer of purpose occurred are obscure. What is certain is that the Masons went from being a primitive labor organization to a modern genteel academy of brothers in a relatively short span.

Several scholars, including Margaret C. Jacob, have noticed that the aura of late Renaissance hermeticism, moved forward by vague impulses from marginalized Rosicrucians and Familist mystics, was one seedbed of Masonry's ultimate diffusion into the philosophical realm.[5] This is possible because these movements gathered themselves around shared notions of alchemy, metaphysics, and some astrology. They were all linked with a long past in folk traditions constructed on the premise that the earth's basic elements, including stone, the material of the mason's craft, were endowed with transforming powers. Invested with more than its geological reality, the stone had secret properties of interpretation unlocking ideas about the universe and human nature.

More specifically, David Stevenson has pushed back the source documents of speculative Masonry to the late sixteenth century, offering a strong case that the philosophical lodges began in the low country of Scotland and, thence, spread cautiously into England in the last half of the seventeenth century.[6] A decidedly English bias, however, has prevailed in the historiography built up around the question of Masonic taproots.[7]

Perhaps on a firmer foundation, because of a later and larger body of evidence, Steven C. Bullock suggests "the cultural moment of early Masonry can be more closely defined" by examining the impact of the seminal genius of Isaac Newton on the Masonic fraternity. According to Bullock, Newton was immersed in "the mysteries of alchemy and biblical prophecy even as he forged many of the concepts that underlay the later mechanistic science" which simultaneously and contradictorily stood at odds against "these occult connections." Newton is pivotal because "Masonry's founders largely came, not from Newton's generation, but from his immediate heirs."[8] Margaret Jacob comments,

"[G]radually the Hermetic lore would be replaced by the 'magic' of Newtonian science, just as the artisans would be displaced from this 'speculative' institution."[9]

The general process by which the lodges of workingmen lost their operative character and were converted into lodges of speculative Masons, who translated the working tools of the operatives into symbols inculcating moral lessons, nevertheless, is traceable up to a point. It is known, for instance, that philosophical meaning was assigned to the fundamental tools of a laboring craftsman, so that the square with which the stonemason tries and adjusts rectangular corners of buildings represented the teaching of morality, the level denoted equality, and the plumb rule stood for uprightness in life's thought and actions. "Within this egalitarian atmosphere the aristocratic leadership of the lodges became embourgeoised, while the illusion of equality must have pleased the largely mercantile rank and file, some of whom probably had artisan and 'mechanick' origins."[10] This transition inside the lodges—whether principally from hermetic or enlightened catalysts—somehow went from hand to mind, from the building of physical structures to the conceptual world of moral building blocks; it was evident both in England and Scotland during the seventeenth century, until it culminated in the public establishment of the Grand Lodge of England in 1717.

■   ■   ■

Long before 1717 nonoperative, gentlemen Masons were admitted to the craft on the basis of their fellowship and high-mindedness, not their ability to chisel, cut, or lay stone. A reliable record exists, for instance, that on June 8, 1600, John Boswell, Laird of Auchinleck (a village in East Ayrshire, Scotland), was present at a meeting of the Lodge of Edinburgh. On that occasion, as was the custom of the operative members present, he attested the minutes by his mark. Then, also a later document shows that Sir Robert Moray, who served as quartermaster-general of the Scottish army which occupied Newcastle in 1641, was admitted into Masonry that year at Newcastle by some members of the Lodge of Edinburgh who were also despatched to the army.

In England, the earliest proof of the existence of speculative Freemasonry is presented in the records of the Masons Company of London, from which it is obvious that prior to 1620 certain members of the company and others gathered periodically to form a lodge for the purposes of speculative or symbolical Masonry. These men were called "Accepted" Masons. Still another important matter of the English record is the diary of Elias Ashmole, the famous antiquarian and founder of the Ashmolean Museum at Oxford. Ashmole indicates that he was made a Freemason at Warrington in Lancashire in 1646; his journal entry lists the names of other lodge members, none of whom were working stonemasons. Ashmole's lodge brothers, accordingly, were men of established social position.[11] John Hamill claims confidently "that Accepted Masonry was sufficiently known to the public by 1676."[12]

What these noncraftsmen discovered as new initiates "seemed exciting, for their experiences matched learned beliefs about antiquity." The historical accomplishments of ancient builders, memorialized by artisans themselves in a craft organization's ceremonies and signs, formed an intersection with a widening outside interest to speculate about antiquity. Much of the educated classes and most of British popular culture accepted Masonic lore as having a likely connection with Judeo-Christian, Graeco-Roman, and Afro-Asiatic (i.e., the Nile and Euphrates valleys) antiquity. Coincidentally and gradually, at a moment in genteel culture that "venerated the distant past, Masonry's intimations of antiquity allowed a new stage of Masonic history, the appropriation of the builders' forms and activities by noncraftsmen."[13]

Most importantly, the membership transition from worker to thinker within the Masons' craft indicated powerful cultural themes. First, the genealogy preserved in their Medieval constitutions made these men historically conscious and, as carriers of esoteric knowledge (that is, trade secrets), they believed themselves to be living in an unbroken chain of continuity with great discoverers, such as Euclid.

Secondly, political ideas were bred in the bone of the stonemasons' craft guild. The importance of regulating a specialized trade and protecting "intellectual property," such as craft knowledge, was not lost on men afraid of losing wages due to unfair competition or devious labor practices. Consequently, these local guilds served as protective associations, extending charitable aid and necessary fellowship to members who formed a fictive family. This strength in numbers also gained them economic and political privileges of full citizenship. As skilled laborers who were "free of the city," they were enfranchised freemen who were, thus, known as Freemasons. Early on, before Locke's theories of human understanding and government, they represented a common man's sense of rights and happiness.

Thirdly, anything with honorable ancient origins in post–Restoration England commanded nearly unassailable respect. The quality of modern achievements were arguably superior to the world lost when the Middle Ages closed. And yet, the eighteenth century constantly measured itself against the standards of classical and Biblical antiquity. Bullock points out, "law, religion, and politics all believed precedent the primary means of asserting present legitimacy. . . . Connection with the past seemed so significant partly because of the continuing belief that the ancients possessed secret wisdom of great, even occult, power."[14] Masonic forms, accordingly, through symbolic language and secret ceremonies, were identified with knowledge the ancient world was still conveying to the modern one. In an age that revered the remote, mysterious past, the assumption grew that Masonry was a well-preserved pass door into ancient wisdom.

With the development of Freemasonry into its proximate and current fraternal form have come countless definitions of the institution, including the well-known one in the English Lectures to the effect that "Freemasonry is a peculiar institution of morality veiled in allegory and illustrated by symbols."[15] None is better or more encompassing than that of Roscoe Pound, a distinguished Masonic scholar, active Scottish Rite member of the Northern Masonic Jurisdiction (NMJ), and for twenty years (1916–1936) dean of the Harvard Law School. He defines Freemasonry as:

> The *art* and *mystery* of the Freemasons or Free Accepted Masons, a universal religious, charitable and benevolent fraternal organization. It is religious in requiring belief in God as a prerequisite of initiation and insisting on such belief as one of its unalterable fundamental points. Beyond this and belief in immortality it has no religious dogma but expects the brother to adhere to some religion and obligates him upon the sacred oath of the religion he professes. For the rest it seeks to promote morals by ceremonies, symbols and lectures, inculcating life measured by reason and performance of duties toward God, one's country, one's neighbor and oneself. It relieves needy Brothers, cares for their dependents, educates orphans, and insists upon duties of charity and benevolence.[16]

The institution of modern Freemasonry, it may be said, began with the establishment of the Grand Lodge of England at the Apple-Tree Tavern in February 1717, when four Lodges of London met for the purpose of reviving the fraternity and putting it on a sound footing. On the following St. John the Baptist's Day, June 24, 1717, the Grand Lodge was formally established at the Goose and Gridiron Alehouse; "and the Brethren by a majority of Hands elected Mr. Anthony Sayer, Gentleman, Grand Master of Masons (Mr. Jacob Lamball, Carpenter, Capt. Joseph Elliot, Grand Wardens) who being forthwith invested with the Badges of Office and Power by the said oldest Master, and install'd, was duly congratulated by the Assembly who paid him the Homage."[17] This quotation is a part of the only existing record pertaining to the founding of the Grand Lodge of England, the Mother Grand Lodge of the World, that exists. Six years later, with the recording of a meeting of the Grand Lodge in London (June 24, 1723), the earliest minute book of that body was begun.

The founding of the first Grand Lodge indicated a shift in the winds and tides of modern culture as the emphasis on hermetic lore in Masonry was supplanted by Enlightenment rationalism.[18] As John C. Brooke points out, the formation of the English Grand Lodge was led by one of the central players in London's moderate Enlightenment, Jean Theophile Desaguliers, a Huguenot who, while seeking asylum, "absorbed sanitized Newtonianism at Oxford and became a leading figure in the Royal Society after 1714." Brooke explains the significance of the Newton-Desaguliers axis to the evolving public life of Freemasonry:

> Although leading English intellectuals were caught up in the hermetic millennialism of the 1640s, they backed away from its associations with sectarian occultism in the 1650s. With the formation of the Royal Society in 1661, they pursued a hierarchical view of nature that would allow for divine intervention from the invisible to the visible world. Humanity and matter were simply inert substances, acted on by a divine force. By the eighteenth century that divine force had been reduced to a rational plan at Creation: Newton without his alchemy. In sum, the Freemasonry of the eighteenth-century London Grand Lodge was fundamentally a bastion of Enlightenment deism.[19]

In the ensuing decades, however, other (perhaps deeper) Masonic springs began to surface again. Modern speculative Masonry has always held in tension the dynamic, polar forces of rationalism and mysticism. It is not surprising, therefore, that a Free-masonry of Newtonian cosmology would diverge and gain expression in the 1730s as a compound of hermetic theology and Christian millenarianism. Its chief proponent was Andrew Michael Ramsay (1686–1743), a Scottish Jacobite exiled in France. Ramsay traveled extensively in Germany and Holland, coming into contact with representatives of pietist, mystical, and quietist traditions. In 1715, Ramsay converted to Catholicism, having been born a Protestant, but the faith he practiced was hardly conventional from the perspective of either side of the Reformation divide. He expounded a new hermetic religion, universal salvation for pre-existent souls, and the compatibility of revelation with Newtonian naturalism.[20]

It is doubly ironic that a Frenchman (Desaguliers) was instrumental in the formal-ization of English Freemasonry and that a British subject (Ramsay) was a key figure in the development of Freemasonry in France. If Desaguliers' mind was a product of Newtonian scientific precision,[21] then Ramsay let his imagination run free, unfettered from Aristotelian reason. As a result, "he conjured up a knightly mythology of Masonic origins that ran through the medieval Templars to Scottish lodges" where the persecuted Knights found sanctuary. Brooke explains the significance of Ramsay's influence: "From these beginnings, Freemasonry in France and throughout continental Europe evolved into a proliferation of competing institutions and rituals in the decades following Ramsay's death in 1743, broadly denominated as following a 'Scottish Rite,' in deference to Ramsay's influence and the legends of the Scottish refuge of the medieval Templars."[22] To a great extent the progress of continental Masonic orders, from which the Scottish Rite of Freemasonry descends, signaled a departure from the Masonry in the British Isles and Colonies where a constituency of "gentleman scientists" was served. Instead, the particular manifestation of Masonry in France supplied a counterweight to the Enlightenment; even though it started in aristocratic French circles, it anticipated the later Romantic correction to cool-headed Newtonian physics that European and North American culture required.

■ ■ ■

Nearly thirty-five years after the establishment of the Grand Lodge of England, a rival was founded under the name Grand Lodge According to the Old Institutions, which attacked the older lodge for its alleged waywardness, thus causing the older lodge to be known as the Modern Grand Lodge and its members "Moderns." The newer Grand Lodge, formed by unattached Irish Masons,[23] paradoxically, came to be called the Ancient and its supporters "Antients"—all of which is somewhat Masonically con-fusing. In 1813, sixty-two years after the Ancient Grand Lodge was established, a union of the two Grand Lodges was achieved.

Both the Modern and Ancient Grand Lodges warranted lodges in the English Colonies prior to the American Revolution; the latter, however, did not at first establish as many lodges as did the Modern or senior Grand Lodge. Yet as Conrad Hahn notes, "that handicap was considerably overcome by its proselyting zeal and revolutionary fervor."[24] By the 1770s, moreover, the Antients had overtaken the Moderns in developing new lodges.[25] Gordon Wood confidently states, "it would be difficult to exaggerate the importance of Masonry for the American Revolution. . . . [because] it was a major means by which [Americans] participated directly in the Enlightenment."[26]

The division between the Antients and the Moderns explains the confusing difference at the close of the twentieth century between lodges which are called "F & A M" and those identified as "A F & A M." Grand Lodges in the United States which trace their charters to the Moderns are known as Free and Accepted Masons. Those possessing charters from the Antients are known as Ancient Free and Accepted Masons. The distinction is one of name and genealogy only, for there is no significant difference in their Masonic practices.

The "importance of Masonry" for an understanding of American colonial and early national history cannot be grasped, however, without taking fuller account of what the rupture between Antients and Moderns implied. Generally, it was the aspiring upper middle class prying open the doors of aristocratic gentility and refinement. It was a minor social revolution that changed notions of class and fraternity. Perhaps through substantive subliminal influences, when members of the colonial middle class learned how to rebel against the society of cosmopolitanism, they already had in place mental patterns of how to form the backbone of a political revolution, too.

It is a critical juncture that had been overlooked until the publication of Steven C. Bullock's *Revolutionary Brotherhood* (1996). Bullock illustrates how social elites could become democratic while at the same time retaining qualities of exclusivity. The implicit mild hypocrisy of this formula had major implications for Masonry, for the American Revolution, and for the post-Revolutionary society. Bullock sees the rapid expansion of the Antients in the seaboard cities from the 1750s as the breeding ground for future "Revolutionary developments in society and culture that accompanied the fight for Independence."

From Bullock's fresh perspective, "by opening Masonry to social groups outside the elites . . . and by preserving the Modern identification of the fraternity with genteel cosmopolitan culture, Ancient Masons created an organization of extraordinary appeal." The progressive (Ancient) lodges "offered a way to assert a new importance—a concrete example of Revolutionary equality and participation." Put inversely, Bullock also argues, "the same upheaval that shaped the new political geography of post-Revolutionary America also created Ancient Masonry."[27]

■ ■ ■

It was only natural for English, Scottish, and Irish immigrant Masons to bring their Masonry with them to the American colonies. John Skew, according to general agreement among Masonic scholars, may well have been the "first" known Mason in the colonies, having been made a Mason in Aberdeen, Scotland, in 1682 shortly before departing for Burlington, New Jersey. The first native American colonist to become a Mason, it is thought, was Governor Jonathan Belcher of Massachusetts and New Hampshire (1730–1741), who received his degrees while visiting London in 1704.[28]

Such American luminaries as Benjamin Franklin, George Washington, and Joseph Warren joined the Masonic fraternity during the stable colonial years of the eighteenth century. Franklin became a Mason in a lodge that met in Tun Tavern in Philadelphia around 1730 and 1731 and later served as Deputy Grand Master of Pennsylvania. (There is some dispute as to whether he was ever Grand Master of Pennsylvania.)[29]

Washington was "Initiated, Passed, and Raised" in the Fredericksburg, Virginia, lodge in 1752 and 1753. Thirty-five years later he was elected Worshipful Master of Alexandria No. 22. Dr. Joseph Warren, a physician and major general of the Massachusetts militia who was killed in the battle of Bunker Hill, was made a Mason in Boston's St. Andrew's Lodge in 1761. Eight years later the Grand Master of Scotland deputized Warren Provincial Grand Master "at Boston and within 100 miles of the same." A second deputation from the Grand Master of Scotland in 1772 extended Warren's jurisdiction to the American continent.

By the outbreak of the American Revolution in 1775, Freemasonry had become international in character with Grand Lodges established not only in England but also in France, Germany, Holland, Italy, Poland, Scotland, Spain, Sweden, and Switzerland. The growth of Freemasonry triggered a denunciatory response from Pope Clement XII in the form of his bull, *In Eminenti* of April 28, 1738, by which he strongly condemned the fraternity and threatened Catholics with excommunication should they join or assist it. What concerned Clement XII was Masonry's expansion, its secrecy underscored by oaths, and its development outside the precincts of the Church. Clement's assault was but the first of more than a dozen papal bulls and encyclicals attacking Freemasonry. It is worth noting that anti-Masonry, Catholic and otherwise, has paralleled historically the development of the fraternity and is still in evidence in some measure at the end of the twentieth century, both in the United States and abroad.

A little over a generation after Clement XII's bull of 1738, the American War of Independence broke out, producing a division within the colonial ranks of Masonry with some brothers taking up the patriot cause and others siding with the Crown. Thirty-three of the general officers of the American forces were Masons, including Israel Putnam, Richard Montgomery, Henry Knox, Lafayette, von Steuben, and, of course, George Washington. Of particular note, too, Benedict Arnold's betrayal was perhaps more painful to Washington's general staff because he was a Masonic brother. Military or traveling Masonic Lodges were established in both the British and American armies, there being no less than ten such lodges attached to the American army, including the renowned American Union Lodge in the Connecticut Line.[30]

On July 2, 1776, more than fourteen months after the war broke out, Congress by the adoption of Richard Henry Lee's motion declared the independence of the United States. Two days later Congress adopted the Declaration of Independence, Thomas Jefferson's immortal statement justifying such action, which was ultimately signed by fifty-six members of the Continental Congress, several of whom were Masons, including John Hancock, the president of the Congress, Benjamin Franklin, Joseph Hewes, William Ellery, William Hooper, Robert Treat Paine, Richard Stockton, George Walton, and William Whipple. A little more than seven years later, the Treaty of Paris was signed, thus formally ending the war with recognition of the independence of the United States. As American minister to France, Franklin had a key role in negotiating the treaty.

The outcome of the war had a decided effect on the direction that Freemasonry was to take in the new nation. During the conflict when the American army was in winter quarters (1779) at Morristown, New Jersey, the American Union Lodge, at a meeting on December 15, proposed that General Washington become General Grand Master of the United States. "Although the action by American Union may not be surprising because its members knew Washington well," notes Masonic author Allen E. Roberts, "the same proposal by the Grand Lodge of Pennsylvania five days later was because it was willing to give up its sovereignty."[31] Nothing ever came of these proposals, presumably in large part because Washington gave no encouragement to them. Instead of one Grand Lodge for the United States with one Grand Master, American Masonry developed along federal lines with each state having its own Grand Lodge. Thus, Massachusetts (1775) was the first to have a Grand Lodge and Virginia (1777) the second, the latter now being the oldest continuing Grand Lodge in the United States.[32]

At the town or village level, in contrast with the later practice of Masonic Lodges meeting in temples or halls designed for such purpose, meetings of lodges during the eighteenth century "were generally held in taverns, where the 'merry Masons' spent the evening proposing toasts and singing songs."[33] Drinking was very much a part of Masonic meetings with lodges requiring their members to pay the tavern keepers what they owed before their departure. Some lodges, rather than paying tavern keepers, designated "closet stewards" to provide beer and wine punches.[34] Such bibulous practices continued into the early 1800s, eventually being replaced through the influence of the temperance movement and the campaign tactics of the Anti-Masonic Party by a strict prohibition of any form of alcoholic beverage in Masonic temples.

■ ■ ■

For the new nation the years immediately following the War of Independence were difficult, both politically and economically. Jealousy and boundary squabbles among the states were common. An inflated currency that produced problems of taxation and foreclosures resulted in pockets of unrest such as that manifested by Shays's Rebellion (1786–1787) in central and western Massachusetts that was led by Daniel Shays, a Masonic brother as well as a veteran of Bunker Hill, Saratoga, and Ticonderoga. Another instance of discontent arose over rival state's interests: in order to resolve differences over navigation rights on the Potomac River, Virginia and Maryland, on invitation of General Washington, sent commissioners to Mount Vernon to try to resolve their problems. This meeting prompted a call to all of the states for a meeting in Annapolis in September 1786, for the purpose of discussing their trade disputes; however, only five states sent delegates (not even Maryland).

The one and only important accomplishment of the Annapolis Convention was to issue a call for a convention of the states to meet in Philadelphia the following May for the sole and express purpose of revising the Articles of Confederation, the country's first constitution that permitted less than minimal national government. National defense and national road building were impossible under the Articles of Confederation.

What turned out to be the Constitutional Convention was delayed in opening on May 14, 1787, because of foul weather and bad roads. Finally, on May 25, a quorum of seven states was obtained, and Washington was promptly and unanimously elected president of the body. Early in their deliberations the delegates agreed to abandon the proposal for revising the Articles of Confederation and, instead, to draft a new constitution behind closed doors, secrecy being the only possible way of achieving this end. Four months later, after much heated debate and necessary compromise, the Constitution of the United States was completed, engrossed on parchment, and ready for signing. Forty-two delegates were present on September 17; thirty-nine signed the document, and of that number, fourteen (more than one-third) were known to have been Masons. George Mason, a member of the fraternity, refused to sign. The fact that Masons had been familiar with constitution making and had lived by constitutional principles (governing Grand Lodges) since 1723 was no little point of precedence or assurance for the Masonic participants in Philadelphia.

The process of ratification was arduous, and the suspenseful outcome of the state-by-state conventions was uncertain for a long time. The seventh and final article of the Constitution required the ratification of nine states before the new government could be established. Before the battle for ratification closed, Rufus King, the Massachusetts Federalist, advised James Madison, "Our prospects are gloomy, but hope is never entirely extinguished."[35] On June 21, 1788, New Hampshire became the ninth state to ratify the Constitution, Delaware having been the first six months before.

Five of the states' ratifying conventions had emphasized the need for the prompt amending of the Constitution so as to correct omissions, and the promise of introducing these amendments had been a means of securing ratification. Six months after the new government was launched, James Madison introduced in the House of Representatives twelve amendments that the states had proposed. By mid-December 1791, three-fourths of the states, as required by the Constitution, had ratified ten of these amendments, which collectively are known as the Bill of Rights.

Meanwhile, the Congress of the Confederation, in bringing its business to a close, set the seat of the new government in New York, the dates for the appointment of the presidential electors and their balloting as January 7 and February 4 respectively, and the meeting of the first Congress under the Constitution as March 4, 1789. Inclement weather, just as it had two years before with the opening of the Constitutional Convention, caused a delay in launching the new government. Finally on April 1 the House of Representatives had a quorum that permitted it to organize and, in turn, to elect the Lutheran minister Frederick A. Muhlenburg of Pennsylvania, a Mason, as Speaker. His brother, John Peter, also a clergyman and a Mason, who had raised and led the 8th Virginia Regiment during the Revolutionary War, was also in the first Congress. Five days later the Senate followed suit, promptly counting the presidential electoral ballots. Washington was unanimously elected president with sixty-nine votes, and John Adams, vice president, with thirty-four votes.

Not until April 14 did Washington learn of his election. Two days later he set out for New York, the temporary capital, and arrived there a week later, having been honored and feted on the way. Congress then set the date of his inauguration for April 30. Standing on the balcony of Federal Hall with his hand on a Bible that General Jacob Morton, Worshipful Master of St. John's Lodge No. 1, had hastily secured from the lodge altar, Washington was administered the oath by Robert R. Livingston, Chancellor of the State of New York and Grand Master of Masons of New York. The president then delivered his inaugural address in the Senate chamber located in Federal Hall.

From the coming to the North American English Colonies in the early part of the eighteenth century to the establishment of the United States government under the Constitution, members of the Masonic fraternity had played a significant role in the unfolding of American social, miliary, and political history. By the close of the century, American Masonry was on a sound footing with the establishment of a system of state Grand Lodges. Whether or not it would have been better had one national Grand Lodge been established, instead of allowing state boundaries to determine autonomous Grand Lodge jurisdictions, is a matter of conjecture.

■　■　■

A fascinating aspect of the history of Freemasonry is the plethora of degrees or lessons written for the purpose of seeking further enlightenment, that is, a light that would illumine the truth for thinking about life and the wisdom for living it. More than eleven hundred degrees were generated by the Masonic orders over four centuries. "By a degree," notes Henry Wilson Coil, "we mean some esoteric ceremony, no matter how brief, which advances the member or candidate to a higher rank, including the communication to him of particular distinguishing words, signs, grips, tokens or other esoteric matter, those of each degree being denied to members of lower degrees as firmly as they are denied to complete strangers."[36]

Afterwards, the term *rite* in Masonry developed essentially into two meanings: it may refer to a particular degree such as the Fellow Craft Rite in the symbolic or blue lodge or it may denote, as Coil indicates, "a collection of degrees" that over a period of time is considered as a body with "a common government" or is linked in a working relationship to a continuum of degree conferrals.[37] It was in France during the early part of the eighteenth century that *rite,* in the collective sense, began to be used with reference to the Rite of Perfection, the immediate forerunner of the Scottish Rite.

The lineage of the Scottish Rite is somewhat obscure, beginning perhaps with the establishment of the Chapter of Clermont in 1754 outside Paris by the Chevalier de Bonneville. Honoring the Duc de Clermont, then Grand Master of the English Grand Lodge of France, the chapter, which may have worked in seven degrees or possibly as many as twenty-five, lasted for about four years. Emanating evidently from the chapter's demise came the Knights of the East and Emperors of East and West, the former of the bourgeoisie or middle class, the latter, of the second estate or nobility. The Knights and Emperors apparently fought each other, with the aristocratic Emperors emerging victorious in 1761.[38]

There are earlier allusions to "Scottish" Masonry that can be documented. A pamphlet published in 1744, entitled *Le Parfait Maçon,* claimed to offer "the true secrets of the four degrees of Apprentice, Companion, Master Ordinary, and Scottish." The author of the tract confidently states: "It is reported among Masons that there are still other degrees above the Master's of which I am about to speak. Some say six, others seven. Those who are called Scottish Masons claim to constitute the Fourth Degree. As this Masonry, differing from the other in certain particulars, is beginning to gain favor in France, the public will only be informed that I have given it what I have read in the same manuscripts which permit the Scottish to be ranked above Apprentice, Companion, and Ordinary Master."[39]

In light of the subsequent formation of the Scottish Rite, it is interesting to note that the full name of the Emperors who emerged in the 1750s via Germany, but in continuity with the Chapter of Clermont, was "Emperors of the East and West, Sovereign Prince Masons, Substitutes General of the Royal Art, Grand Surveillants and Officers of the Grand Sovereign Lodge of St. John of Jerusalem."[40] The Emperors were also known as the Heredom of Perfection or Kilwinning. After the formation of the Emperors, the Rite of Perfection was established, comprising twenty-five degrees, twenty-two of which were what the French called the *haut grades* (high degrees) and which were added to the three degrees of the symbolic lodge.[41] The highest of these degrees was that of Sublime Prince of the Royal Secret, a precursor in name at least of the Scottish Rite's thirty-second degree. A document pertaining to the Rite of Perfection, which came to be known as the *Secret Constitutions of 1761* (a dubious date of authorship),[42] designated officers as Inspectors General Thirty-third Degree.

At the time of the *Secret Constitutions*'s emergence, Etienne (Stephen) Morin, a merchant, received a patent (August 27, 1761) from the Grand Lodge of France and the Emperors of the East and West, signed by the same men who had agreed to the *Secret Constitutions*—a question remains as to which Masonic body granted the patent—for the purpose of propagating the Rite of Perfection in the Americas. Morin, who belonged to a Masonic Lodge in Bordeaux, France,[43] subsequently appeared in Santo Domingo and Jamaica, but not before the British captured him at sea and took him to London where his acquaintanceship with Count Ferrers, Grand Master of the Grand Lodge of England, may have been instrumental in his release. Morin's capture occurred during the Seven Years' War (1756–1763) that was fought not only on the high seas between England and France but in Europe (Third Silesian War), in America (French and Indian War) and in India—a mid-eighteenth-century world war and a harbinger of another Anglo-French clash in the American War of Independence twenty years later.

The patent of 1761 granted Morin, with the title of Inspector General (no mention of thirty-third degree), the authority to create other inspectors and to "establish a Lodge in order to admit to and multiply the Royal Order of Masons in all the perfect and sublime degrees . . . to rule and govern the members who should compose his Lodge under the title of Lodge of St. John and surnamed 'Perfect Harmony'."[44]

"For years it was taken for granted," notes Harold Van Buren Voorhis in *The Story of the Scottish Rite*, "that Morin was the first to bear the title 'Inspector.' Now we have come upon many original documents which show that there were at least two others before him—Lamoliere de Feuillard [Feuillas is the correct spelling] was appointed a Deputy Inspector in France, July 24, 1752, and he appointed (evidently) one Bertrand Barthomieu, a Deputy for the West Indies in 1753."[45] Apparently, Feuillas and Morin were at cross-purposes in the West Indies, so that Morin wanted the matter resolved. This was done by the patent he received in 1761.

A little more than a year after Morin had received the patent to proselytize for the Rite of Perfection in the Western Hemisphere, the *Grand Constitutions of 1762* were issued at Paris supposedly by representatives of the Council of the Emperors of the East and West and the Council of Princes of the Royal Secret at "B," the "B" possibly, if not probably, referring to Bordeaux. Made up of thirty-five articles, this document, which included the *Secret Constitutions* of the previous year, dealt with the twenty-five degrees of the Rite, including the three degrees of craft or blue Masonry and gave the Inspectors General and their Deputies governing authority over the symbolic lodges.[46] The *Grand Constitutions of 1762* provided for a Sovereign Grand Lodge with the authority to charter Lodges of Perfection and other councils as well as the establishment of such officers of the Sovereign Grand Council as Sovereign Grand Commander, Lieutenant-Commander, Grand Warden, Grand Secretary, Grand Treasurer, and Grand Orator or Minister of State. This document was yet another step in the evolution leading to the establishment of the Scottish Rite.

Sometime in 1762 or 1763 Etienne Morin arrived in the West Indies; and within the next five years he conferred at Kingston, Jamaica, the Degrees of the Rite of Perfection on Henry Andrew Francken, a naturalized French citizen of Dutch origin, employed as a customs officer, and made him a Senior Deputy Inspector General.[47] Morin subsequently granted Francken, about whom there is scant information, a patent to establish at Kingston a Grand Chapter of the Rite (1770). This event was the last known activity of Morin who died in Jamaica and was buried there.[48]

With the authority he had received from Morin, Francken journeyed to New York where he conferred the Degrees of the Rite on William Gamble and Francis Joseph von Pfister, both of Albany, and granted them a patent, dated December 26, 1767, to establish there a Lodge of Perfection. The records of this lodge show that Francken was a visitor on St. John's Day, June 24, 1768. His presence in New York marked the first time that the Degrees of the Rite of Perfection were presented in one of the thirteen British colonies of North America. This lodge worked eleven of the ineffable degrees, from the fourth (Secret Master) to the fourteenth (the Perfection).[49] Significantly, the minutes of this Lodge of Perfection, dating from 1767 to 1774, when it apparently ceased to exist (until it was revived about thirty years later in Schenectady), are still extant.[50]

In establishing "firsts," however, it is widely assumed that New Orleans, as a French possession, was the earliest site of the sublime degrees of Freemasonry being conferred on the North American continent. This legitimate claim is based on the April 12, 1764, opening of the Lodge de Parfaits d'Éccose, four years prior to Francken establishing the first Ineffable Lodge at Albany. Freemasonry in Louisiana, however, was short-lived once the terms of the 1763 Treaty of Paris were in force, whereby France ceded New Orleans to Spain, whose crown was a major Catholic bulwark historically hostile to Freemasonry. Documented Masonic activity returned to Louisiana in the 1790s.[51]

When he was in New York, Francken also communicated these degrees to Moses Michael Hays (1739–1805), a Jew who later moved to Boston where he became wealthy as an enterprising businessman. Francken, moreover, appointed him a Deputy Inspector General for the West Indies and North America on December 6, 1768.[52] Subsequently, Hays in early 1781 made eight Deputy Inspectors General at Philadelphia, four of whom were important in South Carolina Masonry and, therefore, in the history of the Scottish Rite: Isaac Da Costa, Deputy Inspector General for South Carolina; Abraham Forst, Deputy Inspector General for Virginia; Joseph M. Myers, Deputy Inspector General for Maryland; and Barend M. Spitzer, Deputy Inspector General for Georgia. The patent that Hays issued to Forst, a Philadelphia merchant, on April 4, 1781, "is the second oldest Scottish Rite document in the Pennsylvania Grand Lodge archives."[53]

One of Hays's appointees, Isaac Da Costa Sr., had refused to take the oath of allegiance to the Crown after the British capture of Charleston in May 1780, resulting in the confiscation of his property and his banishment from South Carolina. He thereafter departed for Philadelphia where Hays, as noted, made him a Deputy Inspector General and "where he presided over a meeting called to provide funds for the building of a syna-gogue in the city during 1782."[54] After the British evacuation of Charleston in mid-December, 1782, Da Costa returned and shortly established the "Sublime Grand Lodge of Perfection" in February 1783; he died there the following November.

Later, Hays appointed Joseph M. Myers as Da Costa's successor. Joined in Charleston by Abraham Forst, Deputy Inspector for Virginia, and Barend M. Spitzer, Deputy Inspector for Georgia, Myers opened on February 20, 1788, a Grand Council of Princes of Jerusalem which, under the Rite's system of governance at that time, "had jurisdiction over Lodges of Perfection."[55] While there is no record of the total number of bodies of the Rite of Perfection in this country before 1801, Masonic scholars know of eight, three of which were located in Charleston and five of which were "dark" when the Supreme Council of the Scottish Rite (Mother Council of the World) was formed. Only the Council of the Princes of Jerusalem, mentioned above, and the Sublime Grand Council, Princes of the Royal Secret, established in Charleston in 1797, were active in 1801.

■ ■ ■

In the intricate drama leading to the establishment of the Scottish Rite under the governance of the Supreme Council, a document known as the *Grand Constitutions of 1786* is of considerable importance because it deals with the Rite of Thirty-three Degrees and, thus, gives a legal underpinning to it and the Supreme Council. The origins, issuance, and date of the *Grand Constitutions* have generated considerable dispute among Masonic scholars.

Who were the authors of the document, if indeed there were more than one? Was it really prepared in Berlin? Did it have "the approval" and "the sanction" of Frederick the Great, King of Prussia? Was it actually drawn up in 1786? Both Albert Pike and Henry C. Clausen, noted Grand Commanders of the Supreme Council, Southern Jurisdiction, and, more recently, Jean-Pierre Lassalle of the faculty in the University of Toulouse-lemirail, accepted the historicity of the document as to its date, origin, and royal approval if not its authorship, in their respective writings on the subject. Others such as Robert B. Folger, M.D., Harold V. B. Voorhis, and R. S. Lindsay thought otherwise.[56]

The resolution of these questions may never be satisfactorily achieved. Taking a dis-passionate position concerning authorship, Charles Lobingier notes that "there is no direct statement in the Constitutions themselves as to who their author was, and it seems futile at this late date to seek a determination."[57] Regardless of the enigma that the *Grand Constitutions of 1786* present, an understanding of their nature is essential for what was to follow. Supposedly prepared in Berlin, "with the approval, in the presence, and with the sanction of His August Majesty Frederic (Charles) the Second, King of Prussia" on May 1, 1786, "the Grand Supreme Universal Inspectors, in constituted Supreme Council . . . determined and ordained the Decretals hereunder written, which are and forever shall be their CONSTITUTIONS, STATUTES and REGULATIONS, for the government of the Consistories and other Masonic Bodies placed under the jurisdiction of the said Grand Inspectors."[58]

The *Grand Constitutions of 1786* are, in effect, divided into two parts. The first part consists of the New Secret Institutes, which should not be confused with the *Secret Constitutions of 1761* but rather describes the degrees from one to thirty-three "united under the titles of The Ancient and Accepted Scottish Rite."[59] In the latter part of the New Secret Institutes, a description of the purpose and responsibility of the thirty-third degree and the Supreme Council is set forth: "Let the first degree be subordinated to the second, that to the third and so in regular order to the Sublime Degree—the thirty-third and last—which will exercise vigilance over them, will correct their errors and govern them; and an association or body whereof will be a SUPREME GRAND COUNCIL, which it will govern and administer, in accordance with the present Constitutions, and those that may hereafter be enacted."[60]

The Princes of the Royal Secret were to place themselves in the thirty-second degree immediately below the Sovereign Grand Inspectors General, "the thirty-third and last degree of the Order."[61] There followed in inverted order the titles of the degrees from the thirty-first through the twenty-third.

The second part of the *Grand Constitutions of 1786* is composed of eighteen articles, in contrast with the thirty-five articles in the *Grand Constitutions of 1762*. Article I of the *Constitutions of 1786* provided that the terms of the earlier document made "by the Nine Delegates from the Grand Councils of Prince-Masons of the Royal Secret" and not in conflict with those of 1786 were to be "in force."[62]

In the next article the duties and responsibilities of the thirty-third degree, together with the organization of the Supreme Council, were set forth in greater detail than in the New Secret Institutes. The thirty-third degree Masons, or Sovereign Grand Inspectors General, were to teach and enlighten the brethren and cause "the Dogmas, Doctrines, Institutes, Constitutions, Statutes and Regulations of THE ORDER and especially those of the Sublime Masonry, to be reverently regarded."[63] Men of this degree were to be organized as "a Council of the Thirty Third, or of Puissant Grand Inspectors" as follows: the Inspector "who has been longest admitted" was "to elevate to that Degree of Dignity (33°) another Brother . . . and shall receive the oath of the person so elected." In turn, these Grand Inspectors General could "jointly confer the same degree upon another person in the same manner," thus establishing a Supreme Council. "But of the subsequent Candidates, no one is to be admitted, unless he shall have in his favor a unanimous vote, given by each member *viva voce*, beginning with the youngest of the voters, that is, with the one last received."[64]

Provision was made in Article III for "the first two officials of the Supreme Council; to wit, the Most Puissant Monarch Grand Commander, and the Most Illustrious Lieutenant Grand Commander." If the Grand Commander were to die, abdicate, or leave the council's jurisdiction, the Lieutenant Grand Commander would succeed him and would in turn appoint another brother of the thirty-third degree to the second post. The Grand Commander was given the authority to "select the Illustrious Minister of State of the Holy Empire, the Illustrious Grand Master of Ceremonies, the Illustrious Captain of the Guards" and to "appoint persons to the other offices" that may be vacant.[65] Of course, as one might expect, the office of the "Most Illustrious Treasurer of the Holy Empire" (Article IV) was specified in the *Grand Constitutions*. He was to receive payments of ten Frederics-d'or (Prussian) or ten Louis-d'or (French) or equivalent money for a particular place or country for not only the thirty-third degree but for each of the thirtieth, thirty-first, and thirty-second degrees. The writer(s) of the *Grand Constitutions* wished obviously to underscore the need of compensation for receiving the higher degrees.

According to Article V, each Supreme Council was to consist of "nine Grand Inspectors General, of the 33d degree"; at least four of them, according to Albert Pike's version, were to "profess the prevailing religion [Christian]." Dr. Frederick Dalcho, however, the first Lieutenant Grand Commander of the Mother Supreme Council, in his English-language version of the *Grand Constitutions,* "undoubtedly" the text of "the Grand Constitutions used by the Founders," stated that at least five Grand Inspectors General (i.e., a majority) were to be members of the prevailing religious belief.[66]

Another provision of Article V allowed in each country of Europe the establishment of a "single" Supreme Council whereas in North America there would be two councils, "one at as great a distance from the other as may be possible";[67] and a similar arrangement (i.e., two councils) for South America was also included. The provision for two Supreme Councils in North America (what would later be the Southern and Northern Masonic Jurisdictions) has been difficult to reconcile in point of chronology (1786) and American history for some Masonic scholars. But generally, dual organizational structures were not in place until 1813, though the idea perhaps predated the Southern Council's beginning in 1801.

In a later article (XIII), the means by which a new council could be established, "in any of the Countries mentioned in these Statutes," called for one or more Sovereign Grand Inspectors General of a given council "to found, constitute and establish a Council of the same degree [33°]."[68] For the acts of the Sovereign Grand Inspectors General in a Supreme Council to be invested "with lawful authority," a majority vote was necessary (Article XVII).

Another feature of the *Grand Constitutions of 1786* that deserves mentioning was a provision for a Grand Consistory as set forth in Article VIII. This was the earliest reference to a Grand Consistory in association with the Rite of Perfection-Scottish Rite, the Grand Consistory being composed of "Prince Masons of the Royal Secret, of the 32nd degree" whose acts were to have no force "without the previous sanction of the Supreme Council of the 33d degree."[69]

In Masonic history this document of 1786 is important because the thirty-three degrees of the Scottish Rite (which included the initial three craft lodge degrees) are set forth as distinguished from the twenty-five degrees of the Rite of Perfection; and the rank of Sovereign Grand Inspector General (SGIG) or thirty-third degree, together with the eight degrees[70] that were added to those of the Rite of Perfection, are noted for the first time. Prior to this, Inspector General or Deputy Inspector and Prince Mason or Prince of the Royal Secret, twenty-fourth and twenty-fifth degrees respectively, were the highest ranks. More than a century and a quarter later, Grand Commander John H. Cowles summed up the importance of the Sovereign Grand Inspectors General, as reflected in the *Grand Constitutions of 1786*, by declaring "that it is the duty of members of the degree to watch over all the others, correct their errors and govern them."[71]

■   ■   ■

With the appearance of the *Grand Constitutions of 1786*, the stage was set for the subsequent establishment of the Scottish Rite in the United States and what was to be the first Supreme Council, the "Mother Council of the World." "No one knows when 'Mother Council of the World' was first used," according to former Scottish Rite historian James D. Carter.[72] As noted earlier, a Lodge of Perfection had been established in Albany, New York, in 1767, followed by a second in Philadelphia in 1782, and a third in Charleston, South Carolina, the following year. Five years later a Council of the Princes of Jerusalem was also established in Charleston as was a Grand Chapter of the Princes of the Royal Secret in 1797. Meanwhile, a Lodge of Perfection was also founded in Baltimore in 1792 and a Chapter of Rose Croix at New York City in 1797.[73]

Two years before, Barend M. Spitzer, Deputy Inspector of the Rite of Perfection for Georgia, with the departure of Joseph M. Myers, the Deputy Inspector General for South Carolina from the back waters, appointed Colonel John Mitchell of Charleston, South Carolina, a Deputy Inspector General on April 2, 1795, and granted him a patent bearing that date. According to the *Circular throughout the Two Hemispheres*, more commonly known as the Scottish Rite *Manifesto of 1802*, which will be discussed later, "Brother Mitchell was restricted from acting until after Brother Spitzer's death which took place in the succeeding year."[74] Thus, Mitchell assumed the office of Deputy Inspector General for South Carolina in 1796, five years before the founding of the Supreme Council.

Born in Antrim County, Ireland, about 1741, Mitchell, who was to become the first Grand Commander of the Scottish Rite, came in the spring of 1769 to America where he joined a brother in Philadelphia in a mercantile business. During the War of Independence he served as Deputy Quarter Master General of the American army. Interestingly, "sometime in the latter half of 1778 a correspondence began between George Washington and John Mitchell," dealing, among other things, with securing lodgings for Mrs. Washington in Philadelphia during the fall of 1779.[75]

During President Washington's administration and a few years before John Mitchell became Deputy Inspector General for South Carolina, three significant events involving the Masonic Fraternity occurred in the fledgling city of Washington, D.C. They included the laying of cornerstones for the boundary of the District of Columbia, "The President's House," later to be known, in succession, as the Executive Mansion and the White House, and the United States Capitol. On April 15, 1791, two years after the new federal government under the Constitution had been organized in New York City, the cornerstone of the District of Columbia was laid "with elaborate Masonic ceremonies" at Jones Point on the Potomac River,[76] the southernmost tip of the constitutionally mandated ten-mile square for the seat of government, by Alexandria Lodge No. 22 (Virginia), now Alexandria-Washington Lodge No. 22.[77]

A year and a half later, on October 13, 1792, Lodge No. 9 of Maryland, in Georgetown, which is now Potomac Lodge No. 5 of the District of Columbia, laid the cornerstone of the President's House, the architect of which was James Hoban, a young Irish immigrant and a Mason. Over 150 years later when the White House underwent a major renovation during President Harry S. Truman's administration, it was learned that the cornerstone with the brass plate placed beneath it was located in the southwest corner. "Curiosity thereafter prompted many suggestions that the cornerstone be removed and examined. President Truman, fully aware of the Masonic symbolism of a cornerstone, made it known that he did not wish to have the cornerstone removed merely to satisfy curiosity. It was to be removed only if the normal progress of the work required this to be done."[78]

In the third event, at the Laying of the Cornerstone of the United States Capitol on September 18, 1793, the Grand Lodge of Maryland officiated with the two previously mentioned lodges participating, together with Lodge No. 15 of Maryland, recently chartered and presided over by James Hoban, the architect of the White House and one of the supervising architects of the Capitol. President Washington attended as a Mason, wearing his Masonic apron, and participated with trowel and gavel in laying the cornerstone. "The precise location of the 1793 stone is not known for certain today. There are records which reveal that some time after the cornerstone laying one of the assistant superintendents was dismissed for having made unauthorized changes in the location of the original wall. Whether this work involved a relocation of the stone and its silver plate is not known."[79]

▪   ▪   ▪

By 1796 when John Mitchell became Sovereign Grand Inspector in South Carolina, Charleston was a thriving seaport with a slave-dependent economy based on the successful cultivation of rice, indigo, and cotton, as well as a fast-developing shipbuilding industry. The population of the city was ethnically and religiously diverse, numbering among its inhabitants Scottish Presbyterians, who had arrived early, French Huguenots, Anglicans, Baptists, Congregationalists, German Protestants, Methodists, Jews, Unitarians, and Roman Catholics, including a large number of refugees from the slave revolt in Haiti (1794–1804). This diversity of population was reflected in the cultural life of the city that "had a free public library as early as 1698, a free school by 1710, and a professional theatre in 1735."[80] Charleston's cosmopolitan character, moreover, encouraged the establishment of Masonic lodges with no less than nine of them meeting routinely by the mid-1790s.

As a flourishing city of ethnic and religious junctions, it is not surprising that Charleston, five years after Colonel Mitchell became the Sovereign Grand Inspector General in South Carolina, was in 1801 the place where the Supreme Council of the Scottish Rite was founded, "the home of the only complete organization of French Rite bodies in North America."[81] Meanwhile, how had Mitchell received the thirty-third degree of what was to be the Scottish Rite, which he in turn conferred on May 25, 1801, on Dr. Frederick Dalcho, a Charleston physician, in keeping with the *Grand Constitutions of 1786*? Years later, Dalcho, in response to a query of Moses Holbrook, who became the fourth Grand Commander of the Scottish Rite, Southern Jurisdiction (1826–1844), replied that he could not remember but that Mitchell, in Holbrook's words, "had signed some obligation in French for it. He [Dalcho] thinks it came from some Prussian who was in Charleston, who was authorized to communicate it to him."[82] Perhaps so; however, there is no documentary evidence to prove it.

Expeditiously, Dalcho's patent, dated May 25, 1801, the same day on which Mitchell conferred the degree upon him, not only designated him a Sovereign Grand Inspector General but, according to Article III of the *Grand Constitutions,* Lieutenant Grand Commander as well. Born in London in 1770, the son of a retired officer of Frederick the Great's army, Frederick Dalcho came to Baltimore when he was seventeen in order to acquire an education and to study medicine with his uncle, Dr. Charles Frederick Wiesenthal, a distinguished physician and Mason. Later, Dalcho served as a surgeon's mate in the army and was subsequently promoted to the rank of lieutenant in the Artillery and Engineers. Following his military service, he settled in Charleston where he operated an apothecary's shop along with his medical practice. He became active in the cultural and professional life of the city, serving for some years as the secretary of the South Carolina Medical Society.

In the meantime, Thomas Jefferson was inaugurated on March 4, 1801, as the third President of the United States, his inauguration being the first to be held in Washington where the permanent capital had been established the previous summer. A little less than three months after Jefferson's inauguration, John Mitchell and Frederick Dalcho opened the Supreme Council, the governing body of the Scottish Rite, for the first time. According to a long tradition, the opening occurred on May 31, 1801, in a building located at the corner of Church and Broad Streets in Charleston. This building is not mentioned in the *Manifesto of 1802*, and there is no contemporary evidence, such as newspapers, to show that the founding occurred there.[83] "If the tradition is correct, it is not surprising.

It was in this building that Da Costa organized and held the first meeting of the Sublime Grand Lodge of Perfection in 1783, and it was there that the first symbolic lodge met and organized in 1736 when the building was known as 'Mr. Shepheard's Tavern.'"[84] So Mitchell and Dalcho may have wanted to establish the Supreme Council in a building closely associated with Freemasonry. This would seem logical, but there is no historical documentation concerning the location of that inaugural meeting.

The first Supreme Council of the Scottish Rite had quietly opened "with the high honors of Masonry" that spring of 1801.[85] Now the two builders, the Sovereign Grand Commander and the Lieutenant Grand Commander, were confronted with the task of expanding the Supreme Council to its constitutional limits by finding qualified prospective leaders.

At this time and afterwards, the Scottish Rite was fitting itself to a certain select segment in seaboard corners of American society. In this instance, these efforts coincided with the influential era of Thomas Jefferson, who set a national tone not only as president, but "as the chief patron of science and learning, whose interest extended to everything that bore on human knowledge or well-being and whose universality of spirit transcended all boundaries."[86]

Similarly, the increasing appeal of Jefferson, as a symbol of freedom and the elegance of the human spirit, created an atmosphere in America that somehow promoted fresh outlets for experimentation in the social order. Thus, the Scottish Rite of Freemasonry came to represent a degree of experimentation with some of those minor transforming values in Jeffersonian society.

Grand titles and exalted names of offices and degrees may have seemed at odds with the leveling ideas embodied by Jeffersonianism that concerned class and social rank. After all, Article I of the U.S. Constitution specified without ambivalence, "No state shall . . . grant any title of nobility." But in its worldly outlook and through its French sensibilities (apart from overlapping British Masonic sources), the Scottish Rite attempted its own distinctive mix of the democratic values expressed as liberty, equality, and fraternity. The Rite was just getting organized after almost seventy-five years of one kind of Masonic presence in America. For the next half century, while developing its forms of governance and honing its distinctive appeal, without becoming in the slow process an easily defeated rival of other fraternal organizations, the Scottish Rite was a superfluous part of American Freemasonry. This fact provided it a protective interim. Nevertheless, as a fraternal testing station for ritual, governance, and international sodality, the Scottish Rite presented a fresh view of Freemasonry at a turning point for a growing organization. The intra-fraternal relationships hold significance in the long run because Masonry was already a window on some of the awkward ordering of an American society unsure of how democracy could achieve brotherly harmony.

CHAPTER II

First Light
1801–1826

Mitchell, Dalcho, and Auld

When the Supreme Council opened in May 1801, there was presumably no reference to the "Scottish Rite"; in fact, there are no minutes of that first meeting to indicate that this appellation was used or whether others besides Mitchell and Dalcho were present. The word "Scottish" was added several decades later, its origins being generally considered obscure. "The use of the word 'Scottish' has led many Masons to believe that the Rite originated in Scotland and that Scotland remains the fountainhead of its activity. Such is not the case."[1] As was noted earlier, the *haut grades* or higher degrees—those beyond the three degrees of the symbolic or blue lodge—of the Rite of Perfection originated in France. In the late seventeenth and eighteenth centuries Scottish immigrants settled in France, some of whom were "Jacobites," or supporters of the restoration of the Stuarts to the English throne after the Glorious Revolution (1688). Perhaps these Scottish immigrants had some influence in the formulation of the degrees of the Rite of Perfection such as that of St. Andrew.

Rex R. Hutchens, a popular Scottish Rite author, believes inferentially that Andrew Michael Ramsay, a prominent Scottish Mason of the eighteenth century and supporter of the House of Stuart, was "responsible for the addition of the word 'Scottish' to the name of the Rite, despite its French origin." In support of this assertion, Hutchens adds that Scottish was derived from what is often considered a fable: the Knights Templar, wishing to avoid death at the hands of Pope Clement V (1305–1314) and Philip the Fair of France (1285–1314), "actually took refuge in Scotland and eventually founded Freemasonry as a cover to protect their activities which were condemned by the Catholic Church."[2]

John Hamill, among other authorities, asserts that "the suppression of the Templars and the death of Jacques deMolay . . . in 1314 . . . continued to have a romantic appeal," but had no bearing whatsoever on the derivation of Craft or Scottish Rite Freemasonry.[3] And Arnold Whitaker Oxford, an English Mason writing in *The Origin and Progress of the Supreme Council of the Ancient and Accepted (Scottish) Rite for England, Wales, The Dominions and Dependencies of the British Crown*, suggested with perhaps tongue in cheek that "Scotland has always been the fairyland of foreign Freemasonry. Scottish was a good term to apply to any new degree."[4] It appears that there is no clear evidence as to the origin of the term Scottish Rite, and there may never be.

. . .

Following the opening of the Supreme Council late in May 1801, Colonel Mitchell and Dr. Dalcho set about to enlarge the body to its constitutional limits of nine. As there are no minutes of that first meeting, it is not known whether others were present. In the register of Dr. Dalcho,[5] listing the members of that first Supreme Council, the name of Abraham Alexander, Senior (1743–1816), is third between those of Dalcho and Emanuel De La Motta. Alexander, who was born in London, arrived in Charleston in 1764 to begin service as Rabbi of the Congregation Beth Elohim, a position he held for the rest of his life. In his later years, as noted in the Charleston city directories between 1802 and 1813, he was listed as "Auditor in the Custom House." According to family tradition, "he was Collector of the Port of Charleston at the time of his death; was accorded a public funeral, with flags of the shipping in the harbor and of the Custom House at half mast."[6] Among his Masonic offices Rabbi Alexander served as the first Grand Secretary General of the Supreme Council, presumably until his death.

On June 15, 1801, a little over two weeks after the opening meeting of the Supreme Council, Emanuel De La Motta (1760–1821) received the thirty-third degree. Born at St. Croix in the Danish West Indies (later the Virgin Islands) of Sephardic Jewish parentage, he settled in the late 1790s in Charleston where he was a commission merchant, auctioneer, and active member of Beth Elohim Synagogue.[7] He served as the first Grand Treasurer General of the Supreme Council for some ten years.

The fifth person listed in Dalcho's register of the founders was Major Thomas Bartholomew Bowen (1742–1805) who was born in Ireland and who arrived in America before the Revolution. He served with Pennsylvania units during the war, after which he moved to Charleston where he became a printer. In 1792 Bowen was elected Grand Master of the Ancient Grand Lodge of South Carolina. He also served as a Grand Master of the Sublime Grand Lodge of Perfection. On July 5, 1801, a little over a month after the establishment of the Supreme Council, he was among three who were elected to it.

In turn, Major Bowen became the Grand Master of Ceremonies of the council. His death four years later was the first among the founders.[8]

The name of Israel De Lieben (1740–1807) follows that of Bowen in Dalcho's register. Born in Prague, Bohemia (now the Czech Republic), De Lieben spent some time in Dublin, Ireland, where he became a Mason. "In view of the speculation upon the influence of Irish Masonry in the degree[s] of the Rite, it is interesting to note that among the founders only De Lieben is known to have had Masonic associations while in Ireland."[9] He subsequently settled in America, first in Northumberland County, Pennsylvania, next in Philadelphia, later in Savannah, and finally in Charleston where he was employed as a commission merchant and was a member of Beth Elohim Synagogue, along with De La Motta and Alexander. In 1797 he joined Orange Lodge No. 4 in Charleston and became the Hospitaller of the Grand Lodge. His other Masonic offices included Grand Treasurer of the Grand Council and Keeper of the Seals and Archives of the Consistory. It is not surprising that De Lieben, highly regarded by friends and neighbors in Charleston, was made a Sovereign Grand Inspector General by the Supreme Council.

Next on Dalcho's list of founders was "Doctor Isaac Auld" (1770–1826), born in Pennsylvania of Scottish Jacobites who had fled to France and later sailed to America. Auld came by his Masonic affiliation naturally as his father, a successful businessman and one-time excise collector for Montgomery County, Pennsylvania, was a Mason and a frequent visitor to Lodge No. 8 in which his son was a member. Possibly Isaac received his medical education in nearby Philadelphia at the first medical school in America, but there is no record of his attendance.[10] By the late 1790s he had settled in Charleston, although he was to spend much of his time on Edisto Island, about fifty miles south of the city. On April 1, 1801, Auld was elected "the 65th member of the South Carolina Medical Society preceding Dr. Dalcho (the 66th member) by three months. Dalcho and Auld were within a few months of being the same age, and the two men had a number of mutual interests to draw them together,"[11] including a strong attraction to botany that led to their establishment of Charleston's Botanical Gardens.

When or where Auld received the Scottish Rite degrees is not known, "but presumably in Charleston."[12] As Grand Secretary of the Sublime Grand Lodge of Perfection, he was present when Dr. Dalcho delivered an oration dedicated to John Mitchell, "President of the Supreme Council of Masons in the United States," before it and the Grand Lodge of Ancient York Masons. On January 10, 1802, he was elected to the Supreme Council and served as the Senior Warden in the Lodge of Perfection as well as Junior Warden in the Chapter of Rose Croix. Years later Dr. Auld succeeded Dalcho as Grand Commander, contributing continuity and practicality at a delicate moment in the council's formative progress.

The eighth and ninth members of the Supreme Council, as noted in Dalcho's register, Le Comte Alexandre Francois Auguste de Grasse (1765–1845) and Jean Baptiste Marie Delahogue (1744–1822), respectively, were related by marriage. Auguste de Grasse was the only son of Admiral Francois Joseph Paul, Comte de Grasse, whose French West Indian fleet together with 3,000 troops helped greatly in the American siege and British surrender at Yorktown (1781). It is for Admiral de Grasse that a river in New York's North Country was named. In August 1793, young de Grasse with his wife, one of his daughters, and his father-in-law, Jean Baptiste Delahogue, fled from the island of San Domingo, then in French hands, to Charleston. This was during the height of the French Revolution. Three years later de Grasse and Delahogue founded in Charleston the Loge La Candeur, "composed exclusively of French Roman Catholics. A tableau of the Lodge lists De Grasse as its Master in 1798."[13] The following year he became a naturalized American citizen, not an easy accomplishment under the Alien and Sedition Acts, but he was apparently waiting for "the next opportunity to resume the military life to which he had been born and trained."[14] He subsequently resumed a military career and was still a major in the French army at the time of his death at the age of eighty.

On February 21, 1802, the Supreme Council appointed de Grasse a Grand Inspector General as well as Grand Commander of the French West Indies and at the same time made Delahogue a Grand Inspector General and Lieutenant Grand Commander "of the same islands."[15] Like his son-in-law, Delahogue became a naturalized American citizen on August 6, 1804, as the records indicate, in New Orleans. The city, having been a part of the Louisiana Purchase (1803), was now within the United States. Shortly after he acquired his American citizenship, he returned to France where he was employed in the Ministry of War and the Bureau of Military Police.

It was also in 1804 that, with the establishment of the Supreme Council for France in Paris, de Grasse became its Grand Commander. This became an awkward development in the peevish French Masonry of the time. (De Grasse's situation is further discussed in the epilogue.) In turn, Delahogue succeeded his son-in-law as Grand Commander of the Supreme Council for the French West Indies "in what we would describe today as a Supreme Council in Exile."[16] Next to the Mother Supreme Council these two were the oldest councils in the Scottish Rite, the French West Indian Council being the second and now extinct.

Surprisingly, the names of de Grasse and Delahogue were omitted from the Supreme Council's roster in the *Annual Register for the Year 1802*, published by the Grand Lodge of Perfection at Charleston, from which both had meanwhile left. To maintain the constitutional requisite number of nine members, the Supreme Council replaced them with Moses Clava Levy (1749–1839) who became an Active Member on May 9, 1802, and Dr. James Moultrie (1766–1836) who was made an Active Member three months later (August 3). Both men were distinguished citizens of Charleston when the thirty-third degree was conferred upon them.

Born in Cracow, Poland, Moses Levy lived for awhile in London before migrating to Charleston where he became the owner of a dry-goods store as well as treasurer and later president of Beth Elohim Congregation. He was listed as Treasurer General of the

Supreme Council when it was incorporated by the South Carolina legislature in December 1823.

Of the eleven founders of the Supreme Council, James Moultrie Sr., was the only one born in South Carolina. He followed his father and grandfather in studying medicine at the renowned University of Edinburgh, from which he graduated in 1788. Shortly thereafter, Moultrie returned to Charleston to practice medicine, becoming an enthusiastic member of the South Carolina Medical Society and subsequently its president. Besides being a Sovereign Grand Inspector General, Moultrie served as the Grand Orator and Keeper of the Seals in the Sublime Grand Lodge of Perfection, Grand Minister of State in the Consistory, and later, Grand Secretary General and Acting Lieutenant Grand Commander of the Supreme Council when Isaac Auld was Grand Commander.

With the admission of Moultrie and Levy to the Supreme Council, the roster of the founders was completed. *The Eleven Gentlemen of Charleston*, as Ray Baker Harris called them, were a happy amalgam of Protestants, Jews, and Catholics, of diverse occupations, including business, medicine, the military, and differing national origins, only two of them being American-born. It is hard to imagine a more stunning example of American assimilation in the early national period than that which occurred in the Supreme Council. As a result of his research, Harris confirmed

> that [Albert] Pike was very right when he wrote that we had no reason to be ashamed of the parentage of our Supreme Council. They were a remarkable group of men. One thing especially impressed me; between the eleven founders not a single piece of evidence indicates the slightest dissension between them. Everything indicates the closest friendship existed between all of them, and although quarrels and troubles arose later with the Cerneauists and others, none of this ever touched the relations between the founders themselves—and they were of a half dozen different religions, backgrounds and professions. In the Rite they all had a single-minded devotion.[17]

■ ■ ■

Sometime during the early weeks of October 1802, the Grand Lodge of Perfection at Charleston published its *Annual Register for the Year 5802* (1802) which listed the members of the Supreme Council, omitting the names of the Comte de Grasse and Jean Delahogue, as previously mentioned, and substituting for them the names of Moses Levy and Dr. James Moultrie. Two months later, on December 4, the Supreme Council adopted a seven-page report, prepared by Dr. Dalcho, Dr. Auld, and Emanuel De La Motta, bearing the title *Circular throughout the Two Hemispheres* that was to be sent "to the different Symbolic Grand Lodges and Sublime Grand Lodges and Councils throughout the two Hemispheres, explanatory of the origin and nature of the Sublime Degrees of Masonry, and their establishment in South Carolina."[18] The *Circular*, in time, was commonly referred to as the Supreme Council's *Manifesto of 1802*. At the top of its first page it bore the Latin inscriptions *Deus Meumque Jus* (God and My Right) and *Ordo Ab*

Chao (Order Out of Chaos), the former becoming a motto of the Supreme Council and the latter an appropriate precept for the formation of the Council and its issuance of the *Circular*, announcing the creation of "the Grand and Supreme Council of the Most Puissant Sovereign Grand Inspectors General"[19] and the *Grand Constitutions* as the source of its authority and powers.

Moreover, the *Circular* or *Manifesto* included "the list of the thirty-three degrees substantially as we have them today."[20] The committee which prepared this document noted that most of the Inspectors General also possessed "a number of detached degrees, given in different parts of the world," as for example, "Compagnon Ecossais [Scottish Companion], Le Maitre Ecossais [Scottish Master] & Le Grand Maitre Ecossais [Grand Scottish Master]."[21]

Undoubtedly in response to the publication of the *Circular* and the presence of the high degrees in Sweden before 1800, the Grand Lodge of Sweden became the first Masonic body to recognize formally the Supreme Council at Charleston and to exchange representatives with it. In time, the Supreme Council was recognized by and exchanged representatives with many grand bodies of both the symbolic and the sublime degrees.

Besides the recognition of the Supreme Council by the Grand Lodge of Sweden, another important event in its early life was the transfer of the Louisiana Territory from France to the United States, thereby roughly doubling the size of the young nation and increasing the territorial jurisdiction of the infant council. Not long after Napoleon sold the Louisiana Territory to the United States for approximately $15 million, New Orleans became "a greater center of Scottish Rite Masonic activity than Charleston, and this was a situation that later developed into jurisdictional difficulties."[22] In fact, the rivalry is easily explicable once it is considered that "the earliest known ancestor of Scottish Rite Masonry in North America was an Ecossais Lodge constituted on November 12, 1763, at New Orleans."[23] In 1804 the Supreme Council provided for the establishment of Scottish Rite bodies in the former French provincial city.

Two years later a jurisdictional struggle arose in New York that centered on two French Masons and that affected the five-year old council at Charleston. Antoine Bideaud, who was an Active Member of the Comte de Grasse's Supreme Council for the West Indies landed in New York on his way to Bordeaux. He wasted no time in profitably conferring degrees and establishing the "Sublime Consistory 30°, 31°, and 32°,"[24] in violation of Article XVII of the *Grand Constitutions of 1786* that stated "an Inspector General possesses no power individually in a country where a Supreme Council is established, because a majority of votes is necessary to legalize his proceedings, except by virtue of patents especially granted by the Council."[25] Bideaud had no permission from the Supreme Council at Charleston to do what he did. He had, however, a patent from his Supreme Council in the West Indies that allowed him to confer degrees and to establish bodies such as consistories but only in conformity with the *Grand Constitutions*.

Inspector General Emanuel De La Motta, as Treasurer General of the Supreme Council, investigated the New York situation that involved not only the Bideaud group but other rival bodies, including one established by Joseph Cerneau, whose activities would prove to be threatening and vexing in years to come.

Meanwhile, Bideaud had conferred the thirty-second degree on five officers of Lachelle's Scottish Sovereign Chapter of Rose Croix de H-R-D-M of Kilwinning, at forty-six dollars apiece, and had established, as mentioned above, a "Sublime Grand Consistory" in New York City. Finding "that the Bideaud group was the only one with any semblance of claim to recognition," De La Motta, by authority of the Supreme Council at Charleston, issued a certificate, dated August 5, 1813, for the establishment of a Supreme Council for the Northern Jurisdiction and designated Governor Daniel Decius Tompkins of New York as Sovereign Grand Commander, Samson Simson as Lieutenant Grand Commander, John Gabriel Tardy as Grand Treasurer General, John James Joseph Gourgas as Grand Secretary General, Richard Riker as Grand Master of Ceremonies, and Moses Levi Maduro Peixotto as Captain of the Life Guards.[26] The following June, Jacob De La Motta, the son of the organizer of this new Supreme Council, was made a Sovereign Grand Inspector General and an Active Member of the Northern Jurisdiction.

There is archival significance in these developments, that with the establishment of the Northern Supreme Council, Emanuel De La Motta gave Gourgas, its first Grand Secretary General and later Grand Commander, a copy of the *Grand Constitutions of 1786*, which is one of the earliest known copies of this document and is now in the council's archives in Lexington, Massachusetts.[27] Some years later Gourgas sent copies of the *Grand Constitutions* and all the Rite's rituals to the Supreme Council at Charleston after three fires had destroyed its oldest records.

In the interim, the Charleston Council issued on January 7, 1815, almost a year and a half after the certificate, a charter or "Letters of Constitution" to the Northern Supreme Council, which "seem really to have been Letters of Ratification."[28] The Northern Council, at last, was an officially recognized body of the Scottish Rite.

With the establishment of two Supreme Councils in the United States, there immediately arose a question of territorial jurisdiction. On February 7, 1814, the "Administrative and Executive Commission" for the Northern District (Jurisdiction) sent a letter to Colonel Mitchell and Dr. Dalcho as "Supreme Chiefs of the Thirty-third Degree at Charleston" requesting that they "be so good as to specify the states you have been pleased to put in and under our Northern Jurisdiction."[29] Apparently, the request was never acknowledged and nothing was done about the matter until 1827. Territorial jurisdiction between the two Supreme Councils continued to be an irritant for many years.

■ ■ ■

In the meantime, a second jurisdictional nettle for the Charleston Supreme Council reached New York some months after Bideaud's arrival. The appearance of Joseph

Cerneau, a French jeweler, expelled from Cuba in 1806 (after fleeing there from the unpleasant repercussions of the slave rebellion in Haiti in 1802), meant that criteria for Scottish Rite regularity needed form and specificity. Sometime in the 1780s he had left France for San Domingo where he was involved in Masonic activity other than the ephemeral Supreme Council for the West Indies. Because of the slave revolt on the island of Haiti, Cerneau hastily left Port-au-Prince for Cuba in 1802. Four years later Antoine Mathieu du Potet, allegedly Grand Provincial of San Domingo, appointed him a Deputy Inspector General in the Rite of Perfection; but Cerneau's patent was more restricted "in its power than any known to have been granted to a Deputy Inspector General."[30] Cerneau was authorized in patent from du Potet to confer the Lodge of Perfection degrees only (i.e., up to the 24°). Peculiarly, he was permitted to offer the twenty-fifth degree to one candidate only per year, but not outside of Cuba.

In November 1806, Cerneau reached New York where he promptly ignored the limitations of his patent (conferral of degrees from fourth through the twenty-fifth—Rite of Perfection). Since he held the twenty-fifth or Prince Mason/Prince of the Royal Secret Degree and, under the system perfected by the Supreme Council at Charleston, that degree had become the thirty-second, he decided that he should do likewise and confer the thirty-second degree. This was questionable, but even more so was his establishment, in October of the following year, of the Most Puissant Sovereign Grand Consistory of Sublime Princes of the Royal Secret, Supreme Chiefs of Exalted Masonry, according to the Ancient Constitutional Rite of Heredom for the United States of America, its territories and dependencies.

In addition, he proclaimed himself a Sovereign Grand Inspector General, later including the thirty-third degree among his several Masonic titles. Not satisfied with the name of the Grand Consistory, Cerneau changed it in 1812 to "The Grand Consistory of the United States of America" and again the next year to "Sovereign Grand Consistory." Apparently his Grand Consistory was a façade, for his other activities included the establishment of a Supreme Council which never met. And, therefore, it never "conferred the 33rd Degree other than by issuing a certificate, never adopted any Constitutions [1762 and 1786], and quite obviously existed only on paper."[31] He operated what would be later called a Masonic "diploma mill."

Furthermore, Cerneau did not confine himself to an intrusion on the Scottish Rite. Noting that the York Rite was prospering, he established a "Grand Encampment of New York" in 1814 "and began conferring Knights Templar Degrees, although never himself having been initiated in that Order."[32]

Cerneau's activities also spilled over into politics. In the formation of his Grand Consistory, he enlisted DeWitt Clinton, who was then mayor of New York City and, later, governor of the state during the Morgan affair and the opening of the Erie Canal. Clinton was a bitter rival of Governor Daniel Tompkins of the Bideaud group; Tompkins was the first Grand Commander of the Northern Jurisdiction of the Scottish Rite (1813–1825).

There was expansive political rivalry as well among other members of the respective groups. The atmosphere recalled the intensity of New York State politics that got Alexander Hamilton killed in a duel with Aaron Burr in 1804, a highly charged moment that projected upon the Clinton-Tompkins period, too.

By the time Cerneau returned to France in 1827, several subordinate bodies of his Scottish Rite had supposedly been established in Louisiana, Massachusetts, Pennsylvania, South Carolina, and abroad in Brazil, Colombia, Cuba, Puerto Rico, and Venezuela. "With the exception of the body in New Orleans, all expired during the anti-Masonic fever in 1832–1840."[33] Just before Cerneau's departure, his Sovereign Grand Consistory met for the last time. Its responsibilities were assumed by an activated Supreme Council under the leadership of Elias Hicks who was unable to sustain even a pretense of organization in the face of anti-Masonic feelings cutting across the New York landscape and beyond after the disappearance of William Morgan. The impact of Cerneauism was nevertheless annoying, and the confusion it caused in regular Masonry, especially in the Northern Supreme Council, was felt for years to come, even well beyond the Union of 1867.[34] The continuing pressure of this competition helped in solidifying the Scottish Rite in the Northeast and the Ohio River valley.

■ ■ ■

The last years of Grand Commander Mitchell's administration in Charleston saw the United States, for the second time in a generation, involved in a conflict with Great Britain —the War of 1812—which ended with the signing of the Treaty of Ghent on Christmas Eve, 1814, negotiated by Henry Clay, Albert Gallatin, James A. Bayard, Jonathan Russell, and John Quincy Adams. While peace was restored as the absence of war, none of the issues that had brought on the war were resolved. President James Madison's cabinet at this time was also notable for "the disproportionate political influence of Masons." Worth mentioning is that seven out of the thirteen members of Madison's cabinet during the War of 1812 were Masonic brothers.[35] Thirteen months later—January 25, 1816—Colonel Mitchell died at his home in Charleston at the age of seventy-five.

During his fifteen years as the first Grand Commander of the Supreme Council, Mitchell had successfully introduced the thirty-third degree and the *Grand Constitutions of 1786* as the foundation stones of the Rite. Over his signature the *Manifesto of 1802* was sent to Masonic bodies throughout the world. At Charleston the Rite's bodies were activated, and its Grand Council of the Princes of Jerusalem established a Lodge of Perfection in Savannah, Georgia. Moreover, Inspector General Delahogue was given the authority to form bodies at New Orleans. Efforts by Mitchell were made to resolve the clash in South Carolina between contending Grand Lodges (Antients and Moderns) which was successfully decided through merger in 1817.

Charleston, South Carolina, for example, was fairly typical in its Masonic divisions which occurred during the Revolutionary War. Taking advantage of the Patriot-Loyalist split within the Modern lodges of Charleston, the Antients began forming lodges during the war.[36] Repairing the old political disorder within Modern lodges and healing the newer breach between Moderns and Antients was interconnected with the larger pattern of class loyalties taking shape in post-Revolutionary society. The prestige of the fraternity achieved by the Charlestonian brothers (Mitchell among them) is demonstrable. The editor of Charleston's city directory, for instance, listed the officers of the South Carolina Grand Lodge among high public officials, instead of placing their names in the expected section devoted to societies of benevolent and charitable purposes.[37]

Mitchell, together with Dr. Frederick Dalcho, the Lieutenant Grand Commander, directed and supported Emanuel De La Motta's efforts in refuting Cerneau and his Masonic bodies in New York and in his (De La Motta's) establishment of the Northern Jurisdiction of the Scottish Rite. With the help of others, notably Dr. Dalcho, John Mitchell had effectively brought into existence and modest prominence the Supreme Council of the Scottish Rite, which later came to be known as "the Mother Council of the World."[38]

The day following Mitchell's death his widow received a curious request. Thomas W. Bacot, Grand Master of the Grand Lodge of South Carolina and not a member of the Supreme Council or other Charleston bodies of the Rite, dispatched a servant to Mrs. Mitchell for the purpose of obtaining all of her husband's "masonic papers." She readily complied with Bacot's request, as her husband considered him the regular Grand Master in the existing clash between the Grand Lodges. As a result, Bacot acquired Mitchell's voluminous correspondence, the minutes of the Supreme Council, and copies of charters. Dr. Dalcho may have tried to retrieve the Mitchell papers. Unfortunately for the history of the Supreme Council, they were never recovered. Except for Jean Baptiste Marie Delahogue's manuscript copy of Mitchell's *33rd Degree, Constitutions, Regulations*, by 1826, ten years after his death, Mitchell's correspondence as Grand Commander, his copies of minutes and charters seemed entirely lost.[39] Fires in 1819 and 1838 were also responsible for the near total destruction of Supreme Council records, books and papers documenting the early years of its organization.

■ ■ ■

With the death of Colonel Mitchell, Dr. Dalcho became the Grand Commander. Under the *Grand Constitutions* no election was then necessary. At the beginning of the new administration, the Supreme Council was composed of the following officers: Frederick Dalcho, Grand Commander; Isaac Auld, Lieutenant Grand Commander; Moses Clava Levy, Treasurer General; and James Moultrie, Secretary General. Besides these officers, Emanuel De La Motta may have been a member, but there is no certainty that he was.

During Dalcho's administration the Scottish Rite bodies in Charleston numbered about seventy members, which was rather considerable for those times. While the

Cerneau bodies at Charleston were an annoyance to the Supreme Council, they never achieved any significant membership and disappeared "within the decade though they caused trouble throughout their existence."[40]

In the meantime, Dr. Dalcho had given up the practice of medicine in order to enter the ministry of the Episcopal Church. Ordained a deacon in the early months of 1814, he served parishes at Stono and Radcliffie before becoming an assistant minister of St. Michael's Church in Charleston in February 1819. While a cleric he published, among other things, a history of the Protestant Episcopal Church in South Carolina, "the first published history of any diocese in America."[41]

Five months after Grand Commander Dalcho had been installed as assistant minister of St. Michael's, fire destroyed the building in which the Charleston Sublime Bodies met (July 6, 1819). All the furnishings and records, including those of the Supreme Council, were lost.

That same year the United States acquired from Spain additional territory with the cession of East Florida and the Spanish renouncement of all claims to West Florida. Simultaneously, the United States renounced its claims to Texas and assumed the claims of American citizens against Spain to a maximum of $5 million. With the acquisition of Florida, the territorial jurisdiction of the Supreme Council at Charleston was correspondingly enlarged. Eventually, Florida became "one of the most important Scottish Rite strongholds in the Southern Jurisdiction."[42]

On the heels of the Spanish cession of Florida came the Missouri Compromise (1820), an issue that brought to the surface the whole slavery question (deferred by the framers of 1789), a portent of the sectional conflict forty years later. Late in 1819 when Missouri and Maine applied for admission to statehood, the Union was composed of twenty-two states—eleven free, eleven slave. After considerable congressional maneuvering, a major compromise was achieved by Henry Clay, the principal sponsor, who was, incidentally, elected Grand Master of Kentucky in August 1820. Maine was admitted as a free state, Missouri as a slave state, and slavery was prohibited from the Louisiana Purchase north of the latitudinal line of 36° 30', which is the southern boundary of Missouri. "This momentous question, like a fire bell in the night," wrote Thomas Jefferson to a friend, "awakened and filled me with terror. I considered it at once as the knell of the Union. It is hushed, indeed, for the moment. But this is a reprieve only, not a final sentence."[43]

In the summer of 1821, shortly after the occurrence of the notable national events— the Treaty of Ghent and the Missouri Compromise—several Masons in Charleston, having been made aware that "many valuable Masonic papers were scattered abroad in the hands of different persons," became interested in retrieving them.[44] Eleven of these Masons, later to be known as "The Associators," came together in order to acquire these papers, which were essentially documents and rituals of the Supreme Council, some of which related to the New York Scottish Rite situation and had once belonged to Emanuel De La Motta.

The Cerneau group in Charleston, having learned of the efforts of "The Eleven," demanded that the papers be turned over to them. Possibly, the papers would have been transferred to the Cerneau group but for Dr. Dalcho, who told this group that it was an irregular Masonic organization and that the papers should be turned over to the Supreme Council. "The Eleven" agreed to yield the papers of the Supreme Council, but on condition that they be "healed" (i.e., the process to overcome Masonic individual or group illegality or irregularity) and made members of the regular Rite to the thirty-second degree. Dalcho objected vociferously as some of these men had been involved with Cerneau. The issue, however, did not remain merely an intra-fraternal matter but was publicly aired in Charleston's newspapers. The Grand Commander was urged by friends to fight Cerneauism but, following customary Masonic reticence and cheek-turning, refused to go beyond what he had already declared.

Meanwhile, Dalcho had withdrawn from his post as Grand Commander early in February 1822 but had not resigned as a Sovereign Grand Inspector General of the Supreme Council. The following year he gave up his position as Grand Chaplain of the Grand Lodge. There is no evidence to suggest that he was disillusioned with the Supreme Council or with Masonry in general. Rather, he probably wished to devote his energies completely to his ministerial calling. Further, he may have realized that by staying in his post an unavoidably public and potentially embarrassing controversy would probably materialize.

Once De La Motta had acquired the documents held by "The Eleven," a request of the Supreme Council for the conferral of the thirty-second degree upon the Cerneauists was received. Dalcho had a number of personal friends, such as Peter Javain, who were Cerneauists. To continue as Grand Commander under these awkward circumstances perhaps placed him on a collision course with his own Supreme Council which had stood totally unyielding to Cerneauism. Dalcho wished to avoid standing in a no-win crossfire and, therefore, retired from office in quiet dignity.[45]

With Dr. Dalcho's departure after serving six years as Grand Commander, Dr. Isaac Auld became Acting Grand Commander, and took immediate steps to publish new Letters of Constitution for the Council of Princes of Jerusalem at Charleston, which had been dormant since the fire three years before. Curiously, he initiated over the next ten months six men of "The Eleven" into the Rite. By the end of 1822, Dr. Auld had become the third Grand Commander.

In summary, during the Dalcho administration membership in the Charleston bodies reached about seventy; a disastrous fire in 1819 resulted in the destruction of the Supreme Council's records; and, as has been seen, the Grand Commander stood up to the demands of the Cerneauists, insisting upon "regularity" and consistency in the Rite. "No act of Dr. Dalcho detracted from the dignity of the Supreme Council or Sublime Masonry. In the end, the Cerneau group in Charleston died from lack of support and, it may be concluded, from lack of respect."[46]

After Dr. Auld finally became Grand Commander, having demurred at first from interfering with Dr. Dalcho's possible resumption of the office, he appointed Dr. James Moultrie as Acting Lieutenant Grand Commander. Apparently, Moultrie was reluctant to continue in that position; and so Dr. Auld turned to Dr. Moses Holbrook, another physician, to fill the office of Lieutenant Grand Commander. Willingly, Auld let Holbrook handle most of the Supreme Council's business during his relatively brief administration.

Late in 1822, the Supreme Council took an important step in moving to acquire incorporation. Not until December of the following year did the South Carolina legislature enact the necessary legislation whereby the Supreme Council, now that it was a legal entity, "could exercise control over its properties and records. The need for this had been taught by bitter experience."[47]

Largely through the efforts of Dr. Holbrook, the Supreme Council, on August 13, 1824, issued letters patent for the establishment of a Supreme Council of the thirty-third degree for Ireland and named the Duke of Leinster as its Grand Commander. This was the first instance of the Supreme Council at Charleston establishing directly by letters patent a Supreme Council.

Two days after the Supreme Council's issuance of letters patent to a Supreme Council for Ireland, the Marquis de Lafayette (1757–1834), the beloved French officer of the American Revolution and a distinguished Mason, arrived in New York City for what turned out to be a celebrated tour of the United States, starting first in Boston and, thence, moving slowly southward. On March 14, 1825, Lafayette was enthusiastically greeted in Charleston. The *Charleston Courier* reported that

> The Supreme Council of the Thirty-third Degree of the United States of America, located in Charleston, having passed a resolution on the 16th day of September 1824, that on arrival of their illustrious Brother, General La Fayette, in this city, they would, as a mark of the respect they entertain for his virtues, and gratitude for his service to this country during the Revolutionary War, offer to confer on him the thirty-third, together with all the appendant degrees; but find[ing] that his stay would be too short to admit, they did not convene for this purpose.[48]

Much to the disgust of the Charleston Supreme Council, the Cerneau group in New York had conferred the thirty-third degree upon Lafayette, who subsequently learned of the dubious honor he had received from the Cerneauists in New York and refused to meet with the Cerneau Consistory in Charleston. His Masonic reception in Charleston was thus muted, being confined to the Knights Templar.[49]

Ten days before Lafayette arrived in Charleston, John Quincy Adams, the son of the second president, was inaugurated as the sixth president of the United States after a heated four-way contest that was decided in the House of Representatives because no candidate had a majority of the electoral vote. An avowed skeptic of Masonry, Adams[50] defeated William H. Crawford, Henry Clay, and Andrew Jackson—the latter two were Masons and at one time Grand Masters of their respective states, Kentucky and

Tennessee. Although Adams did not much care for Clay—nor Clay for him—he found it expedient to appoint him secretary of state. Clay had given Adams lukewarm support in the contest in the House. Although no deal was made between the two men, the charge of "corrupt bargain" dogged them both during the ensuing four years.[51]

A little over a year and a half after Adams became president, Dr. Auld died of "country fever" (likely malaria) at his home on Edisto Island, South Carolina, on October 17, 1826. With his death the era of the founders of the Supreme Council of the Scottish Rite, Southern Jurisdiction, had come to an end, even though Moses Levy and James Moultrie still continued to serve as members. While Auld had not played a very active role as Grand Commander, he had provided continuity at a difficult time following Dalcho's withdrawal. During Auld's administration the Supreme Council had been incorporated and had been instrumental in the establishment of the Supreme Council for Ireland. Interestingly, the Charleston Supreme Council added two members from outside the city, Joseph Eveleth of Massachusetts and Giles F. Yates of New York, as a means of extending its authority beyond its jurisdiction, although they may not have been considered to be a part of the constitutional nine composing the council.

With the elevation of Dr. Moses Holbrook as Grand Commander, the Supreme Council enjoyed a relatively smooth transition from the two and half decades of its founders to the demanding, crucible days ahead when Freemasonry in America faced an enormous challenge to its survival in a "non-elitist," democratic society.

CHAPTER III

Keepers of the Flame
1826–1858

Holbrook, McDonald, and Honour

𐂷𐂷𐂷𐂷𐂷𐂷𐂷𐂷𐂷𐂷

On the night of September 12, 1826, five weeks before the death of Grand Commander Auld, an incident occurred in the town of Canandaigua in upstate New York that rocked the institution of Freemasonry in the United States. Four men abducted William Morgan, a stonemason and presumably a member of the Masonic fraternity, from the town jail because he was about to publish an exposé of Masonic rituals entitled *Illustrations of Masonry: By One of the Fraternity Who Has Devoted Thirty Years to the Subject.* (There is a question whether Morgan ever took the craft or blue lodge degrees—Entered Apprentice, Fellow Craft, Master Mason—as there are no records that he did, though the absence of such records is not unusual; many lodge records from the period have not survived.)[1] In May 1825, he was initiated a Royal Arch Mason at Le Roy, New York, and shortly signed a petition requesting that a Royal Arch Chapter be established at Batavia, New York, where he lived. Unpopular with some of the Batavian Masons, Morgan was irritated by the elimination of his name from the petition and possibly by the denial of employment on the construction of a new Masonic Temple at Le Roy. Motivated by more than revenge, he was anxious to make considerable money from the sale of *Illustrations of Masonry* as he had a family to support and he suffered from alcoholism and indigence.[2]

What happened to Morgan following his abduction remains an unsolved mystery. No trace of his corpse was ever found. Some sixty-nine Masons involved in his removal had, by several accounts, arranged with Canadian brothers to set him up on a farm in Ontario where he would quietly remain for the rest of his life. This was one proposal (among many suggestions in later accounts) that appeared benign enough. Perhaps viewed much later, it might appear to be a kind of prototype of the Federal Witness Protection Program of the late twentieth century, except that the people who wished to move Morgan to "safety" were also the same people who might have harmed him in the first place.

On September 26, two weeks after his abduction, "he was allegedly bound with weights and thrown into the Niagara River (below the falls), near the place where the river sluggishly flows into Lake Ontario. Of course, this account is conjecture, for authorities never located Morgan's body, and although his abduction was ultimately proved in court, his murder was not."[3] Victor Birdseye, the state of New York's third special counsel for the related case in 1831, believed that Morgan was in all likelihood murdered by Masons who with the collapse of the Canadian plan decided in panic to get rid of him as a means of forestalling the publication of *Illustrations of Masonry*, which, to their embarrassment, was published three months after his disappearance.[4]

The news of the Morgan affair generated a pronounced reaction against Masonry not only in New York but in New England, Pennsylvania, and Ohio. The trials of those charged covered a period of five years and helped to keep the Anti-Masonic cauldron boiling. "Some twenty grand juries were called, fifty-four Masons were indicted, thirty-nine brought to trial, and ten received convictions and jail terms from thirty days to twenty-eight months."[5] Of the ten Masons who were convicted, six actually participated in Morgan's dispatch.

In order to understand the Anti-Masonic outburst following the Morgan affair, which served as its immediate cause, several developments must be considered. To begin with, Anti-Masonry was not a new phenomenon; for as William Preston Vaughn trenchantly observed: "Antimasonry is as old as Masonry itself and actually predates organization of the Grand Lodge of England in 1717."[6] Masonry had been satirized in Boston as early perhaps as the 1740s by the witty Harvard graduate Joseph Green, who was not a Mason but enjoyed the friendship of many gentlemen who were.[7]

Evidence of Anti-Masonic activity in the eighteenth century can be found, for example, in the publication of Samuel Pritchard's *Masonry Dissected* (1730), which was the first of several exposés detailing the Rituals of the Craft Degrees. And also, toward the end of the century, it was alleged that there were Masonic plots against the New England Congregational Church and the Federalist Party. The longstanding intolerance for and irritation with secret organizations, particularly Masonry, were certainly contributing causes to the eruption of Anti-Masonic activity beginning in 1826. American historians recall that the secrecy of the Constitutional Convention in 1789 disturbed a wide range of people; further, Madison's detailed notes and journal of the convention were not published until 1840. And, not to be overlooked, "a silent and unorganized Antimasonry among women," as Dorothy Ann Lipson notes, "accounted for part of the power of public opinion that crippled Masonry."[8]

Ideas associated with Masonic chivalry, which simultaneously protected and excluded women, at times came into conflict with emerging ideas that women had about themselves as society's moral leaven. Women in the antebellum period were often viewed as the premier guardians of family godliness, the teachers and arbitrators of duty and happiness. Some of these attitudes were shared by men and women alike who adopted the belief in the "purity of women" as an article of faith, posited in part on the grounds that men by their nature are "coarse." Meanwhile, just as women had discovered affirmation in the "sorority of church-related activities," Masons turned to the fraternity for similar needs. Men wanted their lodges to be acceptable agents of social virtue. Some women, therefore, saw in the lodge a rival. They often had a view of Masons as being part of that culture which was outside the mainstream currents of religion and reform, associating lodges with the tavern culture. Particularly, some women were convinced of the implicit argument that if men were serious about becoming god-fearing gentlemen they could not possibly exclude women, the exemplars of gentle virtue.[9] Being left out, they concluded that Masons were not serious instruments of social improvement.

Women were, therefore, a natural constituency for Anti-Masons. And yet, "only a single reference to women's participation in public organized Antimasonry survives."[10] Rather, many women "surrounded the political movement," opposing Freemasonry through church-related, familial, and private spheres. Anti-Masonry for various reasons failed as a political movement but succeeded as a social movement. In each case it had to do with the influence of women. Perhaps if the Anti-Masonic phenomenon had been timed to occur after women had tasted political success and acceptance in abolitionism, the balance might have shifted away from Masonry's ultimate survival. As it was, "social Antimasonry was strong enough to deal Masonry a blow from which even incomplete recovery took a generation."[11]

Steven Bullock summarizes the rapid acceleration of an untapped popular skepticism toward the fraternity: "The transformation of reaction to a small-town crime into an assault upon a worldwide fraternity took less than two years. Over the next five years, this new opposition to Masonry spread throughout virtually the entire northern United States. Newspapers played a key role in spreading this message . . . . The fraternity's huge size and power caused particular alarm. Opponents recognized how quickly American Masonry had grown after the Revolution."[12]

Some of the Anti-Masonic anger was directed specifically at the higher degrees, represented in Royal Arch and Scottish Rite Masonry. It is often forgotten that the "novelty of Morgan's enterprise lay in its threat to reveal the newer York Rite rituals [as] lower-degree ceremonies had long been publicly available in America." From the malleable public perception, the higher degrees were characteristic of Masonry's incipient threat— the special advantages and privileges of belonging to a lodge not open to everybody, not to mention the claimed relationship between the fraternity and Christian faith. Bullock offers an overlooked nuance, "[T]he Antimasonic emphasis on the higher degrees suggests that its quarrel was ultimately, not with the fraternity in the abstract, but the particular shape Masonry had taken after the Revolution."[13]

The Anti-Masonic Movement that began with the Morgan affair in the Burned-over District or "that portion of New York State lying west of the Catskill and Adirondack Mountains"[14] (in the first half of the 19th century an area which had figuratively been "burned over" several times by fervent religious enthusiasm reflected in millennialism, revivalism, the Mormon Church, etc.)[15] had essentially two phases. The first phase being religious, it centered on Masonry as an evil force and an unacceptable substitute for the church, but it had to compete with the growing temperance movement and evangelism. The second or political phase of the movement quickly superceded the religious phase in New York.

Beginning with state organizations, political Anti-Masonry developed a national convention system as a means of nominating presidential and vice-presidential candidates. The national Anti-Masonic Party held a convention in Philadelphia on September 11, 1830, the fourth anniversary of William Morgan's abduction. After considerable debate over the question of nominations, it was decided that a second convention be held in Baltimore on September 26, 1831, at which time former Attorney General William Wirt of Maryland, a one-time Mason, was nominated for president and Amos Ellmaker of Pennsylvania, for vice president. An unenthusiastic candidate, Wirt won only Vermont in the election of 1832, his opponents being Senator Henry Clay, the National Republican candidate and a former Grand Master of Kentucky (1820–1821), and President Andrew Jackson, the Democratic Party's victorious candidate and a former Grand Master of Tennessee (1822–1824). That President Jackson was a Mason provided the Anti-Masonic Party with considerable ammunition in its campaign.

As a matter of precedence, the Anti-Masonic Party, which gave up the ghost in 1838, was the first third party in American politics. It was also the first party to employ a nominating convention for the selection of a presidential candidate, and the two major parties promptly followed its example for this and future elections. Thus Anti-Masonry or the Blessed Spirit, as it was frequently called by its supporters, left its mark on the United States, being particularly "felt throughout the Northeastern, Northwestern, and mid-Atlantic states."[16]

There was, of course, a set of deeper contradictions in American society that created a long-term irony for Freemasonry. Anti-Masonry was a forerunner of "grass-roots" American democratic impulses expressed later as populism. So, in terms of improving participatory democracy, defining political parties, and modeling forms of social protest, it served an enormously important function. But the cost of those positive democratic consequences is found in the irony that Masonry, as a kind of "peoples'" movement itself, helped create the very "monster" that tried to destroy it: "In assailing a group that had embodied the central social tensions of the post-Revolutionary period, Antimasonry acted as a precursor of later nineteenth-century changes. Like Jefferson, the fraternity had attempted to repudiate a formal and closed aristocracy without denying the need for leaders of republican virtue and talents. For Antimasons and others who sought a society where all possessed an equal say in public affairs, such a compromise now seemed, not the Revolution's embodiment, but its opposite."[17]

The one section of the country in which Anti-Masonry had little support was the South, which was combatting abolition, defending its way of life, and highly suspicious of a movement that originated north of the Mason-Dixon line.[18] Yet it should be noted that Masonry in Maryland, the District of Columbia, Alabama, and Georgia (the Grand Lodge of the last named did not meet in 1833 and 1834) felt the hot breath of contentious rhetoric. In a letter of early March 1830, Dr. Moses Holbrook, the Grand Commander of the Charleston Supreme Council, observed to J. J. J. Gourgas, the Grand Secretary General of the Scottish Rite's Northern Jurisdiction, that "it is really ebb tide in Masonry in this state at present—not from Anti Masonry but for the alarming want of cash."[19]

The demise of the Anti-Masonic Party and the expiration of the Anti-Masonic Movement (1826–1843) did not, of course, mean the end of Anti-Masonry in the United States. It would briefly appear again with the National Christian Association after the Civil War and with the continued antipathy of certain Christian denominations, such as the Church of Jesus Christ of Latter-day Saints (Mormon),[20] the Lutheran Church Missouri Synod, the Assemblies of God, and the Roman Catholic Church. More than likely Anti-Masonry will continue as long as Masons do, but, as twentieth-century brothers believed (naively), perhaps with diminishment through greater awareness of the nature and purpose of Freemasonry. Meanwhile, Bullock sees the larger meaning of the transition as the point where "the Jacksonian-era assault on Masonry domesticated it—pushing it further into private life and taming its power as a very public symbol of the Republic and its values." In an odd twist, the "humbling" of Freemasonry emanated from the larger social transformation it had helped to bring about in the first place as a midwife.[21]

．．．

On October 27, 1826, six weeks after the abduction of William Morgan, Dr. Moses Holbrook, whom Dr. Auld had appointed Lieutenant Grand Commander, became automatically upon Auld's death the Sovereign Grand Commander of the Supreme Council,[22] Southern Jurisdiction—what came to be referred to as the "Mother Council of the World."[23] Born in Massachusetts in 1783, Holbrook, who enjoyed a large medical practice in Charleston, was an enthusiastic Mason. He served as Master of Washington Lodge No. 7 in Charleston as well as Corresponding Grand Secretary and Grand Treasurer of the Grand Lodge of South Carolina and Grand Secretary of the Grand Chapter of Royal Arch Masons.

One of the first problems requiring the attention of the new Grand Commander was a jurisdictional question raised in a balustre[24] (a statement or declaration of a Scottish Rite Supreme Council) by the Supreme Council of the Northern Jurisdiction, which had been inactive since 1815. Through its Grand Secretary, J. J. J. Gourgas, the Northern Supreme Council wanted to know the division of states and territories between the two councils. In response the Supreme Council at Charleston adopted a report on January 22, 1827, suggesting that for "friendly discussion" the Northern Jurisdiction should "consist of the states of Maine, New Hampshire, Vermont, Massachusetts, Rhode Island, Connecticut, New York, New Jersey, Pennsylvania, Ohio, Michigan, Indiana, Illinois, and perhaps Delaware."[25] The Northern Jurisdiction, in its reply, accepted the proposal but added "unless you have any special objection to the contrary, we would like the State of Delaware to be included therein."[26] This inclusion was readily agreed to by the Southern Council. The Northern Council accepted the terms in a balustre of October 21, 1827, signed by Gourgas, in which it recognized that the Southern Jurisdiction embraced "all the other States and Territories" and that this division was "fully accepted, firmly settled and confirmed, at least until some change for the better, and the general good of the order in this country may be mutually deemed necessary."[27]

Five months later, the Supreme Council at Charleston formally approved the jurisdiction of the Northern Supreme Council (March 20, 1828). This, however, did not settle for all time the question of territorial jurisdiction. It was the first item of business Albert Pike took up as Grand Commander in 1859; and, even then, it was not fully resolved until 1878. Aspects of the dispute were again revisited shortly after results of the Spanish-American War (1898) were known; in this instance, American imperialism provided new territories for potential Scottish Rite development that both jurisdictions wanted to pursue.[28] Generally, with westward expansion the issue of jurisdictional boundaries was reopened episodically, as it would be for Protestant denominations, such as the Presbyterians and Congregationalists who had developed a Plan of Union in 1801.

The "Oregon controversy" regarding the boundary between Great Britain and the United States in the Oregon Territory (1846), the Mexican cession of California by the Treaty of Guadalupe Hidalgo (1848) following the Mexican War, the California Gold Rush (1849) with its attendant influx of population, and the acquisition of Alaska from Russia (1867) induced the Northern Supreme Council to suggest in 1875 "that the boundary lines established by the concordat of 1827 were outdated, and that the Northern Jurisdiction had a territorial right to the northern half of the Western United States."[29] This produced a decided strain in the relations between the two councils, which was ultimately resolved but whose outcome must be deferred till a later chapter.

Meanwhile, in keeping with the harmonious efforts to decide the limits of territorial control between the two councils during Holbrook's administration, the Southern Council relinquished on March 27, 1827, its jurisdiction over the consistory at Albany, New York, which it had chartered only three years before, and over its bodies in Boston, Massachusetts, inasmuch as they were located in states now assigned to the Northern Jurisdiction.

At this time both councils reflected considerable parochialism. All the Active Members of the Southern Supreme Council were residents of Charleston with the exception of John Barker who traveled as agent of the council. The situation was about the same for the Northern Council in New York. "The system of Orients, with a resident Inspector General also an Active Member of the Supreme Council, did not then exist."[30]

During the late 1820s and early 1830s there was considerable correspondence between Holbrook and Gourgas, which, besides the thorny jurisdictional question, covered such topics as the Cerneau problem in South Carolina and elsewhere, organization of the councils, fees charged to candidates, and, as mentioned earlier, the prevalence of Anti-Masonry.[31] With the cordial relations that this correspondence reflected between Gourgas and Holbrook, it is not surprising that the Northern Supreme Council on May 1, 1830, elected Holbrook an Honorary Member and its representative to the Southern Council.

For both Gourgas and Holbrook the Cerneau problem was a chronic distraction. The two men kept their distance from the Hicks–St. Laurent union. Joseph Cerneau had returned to France in 1827. His successor was Elias Hicks, Grand Secretary of the Grand Lodge of New York, who "picked up the Cerneau pieces and aided by a Count St. Laurent, a Masonic soldier of fortune, who claimed to be Sovereign Grand Commander over North America, tried to form,"[32] by issuance of a *Manifesto* in April 1832, a "United Supreme Council for the Western Hemisphere of the Grand Inspectors General 33d Degree of the Ancient and Accepted Scottish Rite." In all likelihood this council, which recognized the *Grand Constitutions of 1786* presumably to strengthen its status, ceased four years later, but it formally dissolved in 1846 with a division of property among the four remaining members. The employment of the term "Ancient and Accepted Scottish Rite" was the first instance of using this name, as neither the Northern nor Southern Councils had used it heretofore, nor would they until both councils came back to life in 1844 and 1845.[33]

Just a few weeks prior to the establishment of the Hicks–St. Laurent Supreme Council, Gourgas became Sovereign Grand Commander of the Northern Supreme Council on March 7, 1832, a post he was to hold for nineteen years.[34] He had clearly shown during the previous nineteen years as Grand Secretary General that he was the linchpin of the Northern Council.

Three months later, in a letter of June 5, 1832, Gourgas expressed to Holbrook his frustrations and troubles with the condition of the Northern Supreme Council, admitting it had "remained in a profound sleep" since around 1815. It was also in trouble because of Anti-Masonry. Looking back later, with the receipt of Holbrook's five circulars in January 1826 regarding the North's languor, Gourgas was appreciative of a timely catalyst. Gourgas wrote that it was a turning point in his taking charge: "I was then called upon . . . to say what I thought was best to be done. My answer was plain: answer the circulars and either let go [i.e., quit] or go on."[35] Thanks in part to Holbrook's prodding efforts, Gourgas decided to "go on," fortunately for the future of the Northern Supreme Council.

Shortly after Gourgas's candid letter reached Holbrook, an epidemic of deadly Asiatic cholera from which more than 2,200 people died occurred in New York City. Other cities were stricken as well, with the notable exception of Boston and Charleston. "New Orleans was probably the most severely visited. Cholera claimed five thousand lives in the Crescent City."[36] Fifty years lapsed before Robert Koch, a German bacteriologist, discovered the cause of this disease, which is *vibrio comma*, a motile, comma-shaped bacterium.

For the next ten years, from 1832 to 1842, following this epidemic of cholera, the Supreme Council at Charleston was as inactive as it was after 1816 when Dalcho became Grand Commander. Anti-Masonry had also infected the South, but because it was not as organized or concentrated there as in the North, the effects were less crippling. Nevertheless, the Grand Lodge of South Carolina could not recruit an ordained minister to serve as Grand Chaplain from 1827 to 1840.[37]

Further, South Carolina was not immune to other ill-feelings, as national constitutional issues preoccupied its cities in lieu of cholera. The nullification crisis of late 1832, precipitated by John C. Calhoun's understanding of states' rights within a federal system, was a close call for the coherence of the Union. Also during this period, Texas acquired its independence from Mexico (1836) under the leadership of General Samuel Houston, a Mason; the Panic of 1837 the next year stemmed from, among other things, reckless speculation with cotton prices and resulted in the fall of cotton commodities by almost half on the New Orleans market and, in addition, bank foreclosures and unemployment; and an immense fire destroyed almost a third of the major part of Charleston, including Seyle's Hall where the Grand Lodge as well as some subordinate lodges met. The fire claimed, too, the almost finished new Masonic Temple. Records and paraphernalia of Subordinate Sublime bodies together with those of the Supreme Council were destroyed.

By the early 1840s Dr. Holbrook was ready to leave Charleston and give up his responsibilities as Grand Commander. The enactment of the U.S. Armed Occupation Act (August 4, 1842), which provided homesteads in East Florida "to any settlers who could maintain their property against hostile Indians for a period of seven years,"[38] afforded Holbrook such an opportunity. He applied for and received a homestead on April 16, 1843, in what is now Ankona, overlooking the Indian River. No record of concluding action by Holbrook as Grand Commander, including the appointment of a Lieutenant Grand Commander, has been found. By the time of his departure the Supreme Council was reduced to four members: Holbrook, Joseph McCosh, Alexander McDonald, and Horatio G. Street. Albert G. Mackey, according to his own statement, became the next new member in May 1844.[39] He was to have an active role in the development of the Supreme Council and, moreover, was to make substantial contributions to the literature of Freemasonry.

About a month after Holbrook received his homestead permit, an important Masonic meeting was held in Baltimore for the object and purpose of producing "uniformity of Masonic work" and recommending "such measures as shall tend to the elevation of this Order to its due degree of respect throughout the world at large."[40] The Baltimore Convention of May 8 through 17, 1843, to which all the Grand Lodges had been invited although some were not represented, sought uniformity in the degree work as the dissipation of the Anti-Masonic Movement in the early 1840s stimulated innovations in the ritual among the various Grand Lodges. Oddly, "six months later those who attended could not agree on what had been decided."[41] Perhaps there was a fear among some of those in attendance that a uniformity in the rituals would lead to a united Grand Lodge of the United States and thus end the sovereignty that the Grand Lodges of the respective states enjoyed.[42]

By the time of the Baltimore Convention, a pronounced effort was apparent to replace with sobriety the bibulousness of an earlier day in Masonic Lodges. The fraternity "also insisted upon a waiting period to determine whether new members were worthy of higher degrees."[43]

When Holbrook left for Florida in April 1843 to take up his homestead claim, there was no immediate successor to him as Grand Commander. Dr. Jacob De La Motta (son of Supreme Council founder, Emmanuel De La Motta), who may have become an Active Member of the Supreme Council at Charleston before Holbrook's departure or who may have affiliated at a meeting in May 1844, became Lieutenant Grand Commander, possibly by Holbrook's appointment. It is open to conjecture. In the meantime, Holbrook died in Florida on December 1, 1844. Two weeks later the Supreme Council at Charleston met and passed a resolution of bereavement and condolence at which Dr. De La Motta presided. Following this action he apparently assumed at that meeting the role of Grand Commander and appointed Dr. Albert Mackey as Grand Secretary General, "perhaps having first appointed Alexander McDonald as Lieutenant Grand Commander."[44] Dr. De La Motta's service as Grand Commander was brief as he died two months later at the age of fifty-five on February 13, 1845.

It should be recalled that as the *Grand Constitutions of 1786* made no provision for the election of a Grand Commander—this would not be done until Albert Pike became Grand Commander—the Lieutenant Grand Commander succeeded to that position upon the death or resignation of the Grand Commander, who in turn had appointed him, leading to a potentially awkward election process. Hence, because officers were installed by appointment, not election, the question surfaced over the legitimacy of Dr. De La Motta's actions unless somehow (there is no record) Dr. Holbrook had appointed him Lieutenant Grand Commander before he left Charleston. More than likely, Masonic historians shall never know.

■ ■ ■

With the death of Dr. Jacob De La Motta, Alexander McDonald, who had been made a Sovereign Grand Inspector General on November 17, 1822, became Grand Commander. A Charleston merchant, whom Mackey described as a man "of much intelligence, of great masonic experience and of retentive memory,"[45] McDonald had served as Senior Grand Deacon, Junior Grand Warden, Senior Grand Warden, and Corresponding Secretary of the Grand Lodge of South Carolina. In 1830 he was captain of the "Irish Volunteers" and, fifteen years later, an alderman of the city of Charleston. Upon becoming Grand Commander, McDonald appointed John Henry Honour as Lieutenant Grand Commander, in keeping with the *Grand Constitutions of 1786.*

During the first half year of his administration McDonald moved quickly to reassert the dominion and power of the Supreme Council in the Southern Jurisdiction after its dormant decade of 1832 to 1842. To underscore this activity the Supreme Council issued on August 2, 1845, a printed *Manifesto*, which "assumes an importance second only to the Manifesto of 1802."[46] This second *Manifesto* included a brief restatement of the history of the Scottish Rite and the Supreme Council, a declaration of "the exclusive right" to confer the fourth through the thirty-third degrees, a renewed acknowledgement of the Northern Supreme Council and its territorial jurisdiction "distributed over the northern, northwestern and northeastern parts of the United States," a solicitation on behalf of the Northern and Southern Supreme Councils for "the sympathy and fraternal kindness" of other Masons, and a strong "protest against the false and scandalous statements made by J. F. B. Clavel in his 'Histoire Pittoresque de la Franc Maconnerie' (Pictorial History of French Masonry)—statements which exhibit, on the part of their author, either a deplorable ignorance of the true history of our order, or a wanton violation of the grand characteristic of Freemasonry—Truth."[47]

In addition to the publication of the *Manifesto*, another notable event of Masonic lore that occurred in 1845 was the publication of Mackey's first of more than a dozen books about the craft, *A Lexicon of Freemasonry*, which later was republished in numerous editions. Born in Charleston, South Carolina, on March 12, 1807, Albert Gallatin Mackey was the eighth child of Dr. John and Abigail Miles Mackey. Albert Gallatin, for whom Mackey was named, served as Secretary of the Treasury under Presidents Jefferson and Madison. Young Mackey graduated from Charleston Medical College in 1832 (Coil indicates 1834); ten years later he scaled back his practice of medicine in order to devote more time to his activity in Freemasonry, especially expanding his interest in its origins and history; and in 1854, he gave up the practice altogether so as to concentrate on Masonic studies and diverse antiquities. Mackey's medical background placed him on common ground with the lengthening list of Active Members of the Supreme Council who, during the early decades of the nineteenth century, were physicians.

At the time his *Lexicon of Freemasonry* was published, Mackey was serving as the Grand Secretary of the Grand Lodge as well as its Grand Lecturer. He was already a member of the Royal Arch, becoming High Priest, and of the Knights Templar, in which he served as Commander of the South Carolina Encampment No. 1 in 1844, the same year he became an Active Member of the Supreme Council. Five years later Mackey published his second book, *The Mystic Tie*, the title of which is derived from an old term of the craft for the bond of brotherhood in Freemasonry, a term rarely used today. Probably one of Mackey's greatest accomplishments in Masonry was introducing Albert Pike to the Scottish Rite in 1853. This connection alone merits special interest in nineteenth-century American Masonry.

Meanwhile, about a year and a half after he assumed office, Grand Commander McDonald abruptly left Charleston in the second week of August 1846, "never to return."[48] The suddenness of his departure has never been explained, and the date and place of his death remain unknown.

■ ■ ■

Following McDonald's exodus the Reverend John Henry Honour became the new Grand Commander. With his elevation, Honour became the sixth Grand Commander of the Southern Supreme Council. Early in his administration he appointed as Lieutenant Grand Commander Charles M. Furman, who had been made an Active Member the previous year.

A distinguished citizen of Charleston, where he was born on December 20, 1802, Honour began a banking career with the Charleston Insurance and Trust Company in 1837 and became its president nine years later. He had a keen interest in religious affairs, having served as a Sunday school teacher, a founder of the Methodist Protestant Church in Charleston in 1834, and, upon ordination in 1836, as a minister. Moreover, switching denominations later in life, he served as president of the Lutheran Synod, was editor of its magazine, the *Lutheran Visitor*, and in 1871 and 1872 was pastor of St. John's Lutheran Church until a cataract condition forced him to resign.

Busy as he was with his career in business and the church, Honour was able to participate in civic affairs, serving variously on the city council, as acting mayor, and as a trustee of the Charleston library, among other offices. And in Masonry he served for twenty years as Grand Treasurer of the Grand Lodge and was also at one time the Grand High Priest of Royal Arch Masons in South Carolina. Besides his Masonic activity, Honour was an Odd Fellow (I.O.O.F.), becoming the first Grand Master of that fraternity in South Carolina.

Under this distinguished Charlestonian, the Supreme Council adopted in 1847 a fresh policy of bringing in new Active Members from other areas of the Southern Jurisdiction, which was indeed a significant departure from the practice of drawing the council's membership from South Carolina, almost exclusively from Charleston. Only one of the next five members elected to the Supreme Council was from the Palmetto State, and this policy was even more prevalent under the next Grand Commander, Albert Pike. Not until some years later was the Southern Jurisdiction divided by states into orients and by cities into valleys with a Sovereign Grand Inspector General or Active Member being the highest officer in an orient (state); and in orients where there were no Inspectors General, Deputies of the Supreme Council served as the highest officers.[49] In 1847 the Active Members were still elected at large as they had been since 1801.

When Honour became Grand Commander in August 1846, the Mexican War was already three months old and the Senate had meanwhile ratified a treaty with Great Britain (June 15) that settled the Oregon boundary dispute. The treaty called for the extension of the boundary line along the forty-ninth parallel to the middle of the channel between the mainland and Vancouver and then southward through the Strait of Juan de Fuca to the Pacific, free navigation of the channel and strait by both countries, and free navigation of the Columbia River below the forty-ninth parallel by the British.

A little more than a year and a half later, James W. Marshall discovered gold in the mill race of John Augustus Sutter's sawmill (January 24, 1848) on a branch of the American River, about forty miles from present-day Sacramento. Word of this quickly spread; and President James K. Polk, a Mason and member of Columbia Lodge No. 10, Columbia, Tennessee, confirmed the discovery in his annual message of December 5, 1848. As a result of the Gold Rush that followed, California's population increased by 100,000 within a year. Moreover, by the terms of the Treaty of Guadalupe Hidalgo, which ended the Mexican War and was signed on February 2, 1848, Mexico ceded to the United States California, New Mexico, and parts of the present states of Utah, Nevada, Arizona, and Colorado, and relinquished its claim to Texas north of the Rio Grande. Texas had joined the Union as a state in 1845. Although the victor, the United States agreed to pay Mexico $15 million and to assume the adjusted claims of American citizens amounting to $3.25 million against the Mexican government. Just as the Louisiana Purchase increased considerably the size of the Southern Jurisdiction of the Scottish Rite, so likewise did the Mexican cession. As was mentioned earlier, westward expansion of the United States was to cause recurring irritation between the Northern and Southern Jurisdictions.

On July 4, 1848, five months after the treaty ending the war with Mexico was signed, the cornerstone of the Washington Monument in Washington, D.C., was laid in due Masonic form by Benjamin B. French, the Grand Master of the Grand Lodge of the District of Columbia and a future Lieutenant Grand Commander of the Southern Supreme Council. Among the Masons on hand for this ceremony was General John A. Quitman, an Active Member of the Southern Supreme Council.

Strikingly, the original plan for the Washington Monument was an equestrian statue of the first president, which he turned down. More than a generation later the Washington National Monument Society, a private organization, was formed in 1832. It raised money and obtained "tribute blocks" (which included Masonic and other inscriptions on the inside walls) for a Greek temple that Robert Mills, an American architect, designed. Political quarreling in the 1850s and the ensuing Civil War, however, inter-rupted work on the project. Finally, Congress took over the construction in 1876 and proceeded to fund the operation. The base was completely changed from Mills's origi-nal design; the monument became an obelisk, inspired by the growing American fasci-nation with Egyptian building and decorative forms. Remarkably, too, it was built by the Army Corps of Engineers and dedicated in 1885.

About six months after the beginning of the Washington Monument, early in 1849, several Masons in Washington, D.C., who were interested in the establishment of the Scottish Rite in the capital asked the Northern Supreme Council in New York to con-sider their request. They knew nothing of the boundaries between the jurisdictions; and apparently, Giles F. Yates, the Lieutenant Grand Commander of the Northern Supreme Council and at that time acting on its behalf, did not either. He thought the Potomac River was the boundary between the two jurisdictions and continued to think so even after he was told that by the terms of the agreement of 1827 the Mason-Dixon line was the boundary. Yates was stubborn, believing that the agreement reached twenty-two years before was temporary. In fact, he persisted in advocating the inclusion of Maryland and the District of Columbia in the Northern Jurisdiction. This issue was not resolved until sometime later during the administration of Grand Commander Albert Pike.[50]

Sectional friction was not confined to the Scottish Rite's two American jurisdictions. Mounting irritation between the North and South over the slavery-abolition question, conflicting economic issues, and problems arising from the Mexican cession, including the admission of states with or without slavery, had been building for twenty years or more. The increasingly acrimonious debates infiltrated the national religious denomi-nations and, when they were splitting apart in the 1840s and 1850s over the morality of slavery, a more ominous house divided was prefigured.[51] Thus, as Samuel Eliot Morison, the distinguished American historian, has observed, "The state of the American union in 1848 may be compared with that of Europe in 1913 and 1938. Political and diplomatic moves become frequent and startling. Integrating forces win apparent victories, but in reality grow feebler. The tension increases until some event that, in ordinary times, would have little consequences, precipitates a bloody conflict."[52]

A fratricidal conflict was avoided in 1850 when Henry Clay, recently returned to the Senate after a long absence, introduced on January 29 a series of resolutions that called for the admission of California as a free state, the organization of the remainder of the territory acquired from Mexico without a prohibition of slavery, an adjustment of the Texas–New Mexico boundary, the assumption of the pre-annexation Texas debt (pro-viding Texas relinquished its claim to any part of Mexico), noninterference with slavery in the District of Columbia, a prohibition of the slave trade in the District of Columbia, and a strengthened provision for the return of fugitive slaves. A great debate followed in the Senate, certainly one of the most famous in the annals of that body, which included

Daniel Webster's oft-recited March 7 oration. Finally, Clay's resolutions were drawn together in five acts that became law between September 9 and 20. Later, they would be known collectively as the "Compromise of 1850." It has been argued that the Compromise forestalled civil war for ten years, a veritable firewall of the Union that ultimately collapsed.

By the time of this momentous Congressional action, the Cerneauists in Charleston were inactive; and in 1850 their bodies were dissolved, the few survivors taking an oath of allegiance to the Mother Supreme Council. Meanwhile, the council was establishing subordinate bodies outside South Carolina; as for example, a Grand Consistory was established at New Orleans "to regularize the Rite in Louisiana." Grand Secretary Mackey issued a warrant on August 21, 1852, "to open and hold a Consistory of Sublime Princes of the Royal Secret in the State of Kentucky at Louisville."[53] Under later organization of the Supreme Council with an augmentation from nine to thirty-three members, the Grand Consistories were replaced as the administrative body in each state by a Sovereign Grand Inspector General or a Deputy, except for Kentucky and Louisiana, which were allowed to keep the Grand Consistory in name and body but which gave up their authority as Deputies of the Supreme Council.

Besides the establishment of subordinate bodies in the early 1850s beyond South Carolina, the Supreme Council was blessed in 1853 by a fortuitous meeting of Albert Mackey and Albert Pike, both of whom were respectively the Grand High Priests of Royal Arch Masonry in South Carolina and Arkansas. Their common labors for this York Rite body and their meeting set the stage for Pike's lifelong involvement with the Supreme Council of the Southern Jurisdiction. Years later, Pike declared, "I never heard of the Scottish Rite until 1853."[54] On March 20 of that year Mackey communicated the Sublime Degrees from the fourth to the thirty-second to Pike at Charleston. What is more, he urged Pike to study the rituals in some detail and in turn to become actively involved in the Scottish Rite. Later Pike recalled: "I found all [old rituals] at Charleston when I received the degrees. I took most of them home with me the year afterwards, and had the rest sent to me, and copied the whole of them, from beginning to end, in a book now in the archives of the Supreme Council."[55]

In his *Allocution* of 1878 to the Supreme Council, Pike was brusque in his assessment of the Rite's condition and its rituals when he began work on the latter, "The truth is that the Rite was nothing, and the Rituals almost nought, for the most part a lot of worthless trash, until 1855."[56] Writing to Mackey on September 13 of that year from Little Rock, Arkansas, Pike reported that he had finished work on "the 21°, 22°, 23°, 25°, 26°, 27°, 28°, 29° and 30°" and that an abstract would explain what he had done with each degree. He added that if he dealt with any other degree, he might "take up and spiritualize the 32° to harmonize with what I have done in the 30°."[57] Pike was to continue this work on the rituals for some years.

Earlier in 1855 the Supreme Council had reached an agreement with the so-called Supreme Council at New Orleans that resulted in the latter's merger with the Mother Council. Although Pike was living in New Orleans at the time, he apparently was not involved in the negotiations leading to the *Concordat of 1855* as he was busy with his law practice and revising the Scottish Rite rituals.

A little over a month after the *Concordat* had been signed, the Supreme Council adopted at its session on March 20, 1855, the *Revised Statutes for the Government of The Supreme Council.* Inasmuch as these were the first *Statutes* for which there is any record, the word "revised" must not be taken literally. The document provided that "the active members of the Supreme Council shall never exceed nine," a carry-over from the *Grand Constitutions of 1786* and the *Manifesto of 1802;* that "an active member, who, by reason of age or infirmity, shall resign his seat, will become an Emeritus member"; and that "Honorary members may be elected from such Sovereign Inspectors as have removed into this jurisdiction from the jurisdiction to which they originally belonged." The *Statutes* also specified that in each state there was to be only one consistory which was to act as the Deputy of the Supreme Council; that for the charters of subordinate bodies specific fees were set, as for example, fifty dollars for a consistory and forty dollars for a chapter of Rose Croix; and that set minimum fees for the degrees conferred were established. Where the *Statutes* remained silent, the *Grand Constitutions of 1786* were in force.[58]

As Pike was not a member of the Supreme Council when the *Revised Statutes* were adopted, he had nothing to do with their preparation or enactment. In fact, he had not gone beyond the thirty-second degree, so he was not elegible for a seat on the council.

A year and a half after the Supreme Council's adoption of the *Revised Statutes,* Pike was elected to receive the thirty-third degree, the Deputies of the council in Louisiana having been authorized to confer the degree upon him and several others. Pike, however, was in Washington at the time on legal business. Two months later, on April 25, 1857, at an adjourned session, the degree was conferred upon him at New Orleans. On March 20 of the following year he was elected an Active Member of the council, thus beginning an association with that body until his death thirty-three years later.

Shortly before the thirty-third degree was conferred upon him, Pike wrote from Washington (March 31, 1857) to Mackey that he had finished the first revision of the rituals, 100 copies of which he had printed, having "paid $1,168.98 for the printing—it and other expenses over-running $1,200." He added that "if the Supreme Council will adopt the work and pay me $1,100 at its *leisure,* I will ship the whole edition at once." He urged "speedy action" by the Supreme Council as he had given "two years' labor and $100" and felt "that is liberal enough."[59]

Upon receiving his copy of the revised rituals, Mackey labeled it his friend's *Magnum Opus.* He was no doubt pleased with what Pike had accomplished as he had urged Pike to undertake the revisions and had been instrumental in the creation of a Committee on Ritual Revision which included Grand Commander Honour, Pike, and himself. But for Mackey there was also cause for embarrassment; for as Walter Lee Brown, one of Pike's biographers, has observed, "If Pike had any enemies on the Supreme Council they must have burned with rage at his display of nerve not only in revising the rituals without authorization but also in ordering them printed, without permission, at the expense of the order. But there was apparently no serious opposition to what he had effected."[60]

Four years later, a committee of three that had been appointed to consider Pike's recommendations responded with "a full endorsement of everything he had done regarding the rituals [April 3, 1861]."[61] The Supreme Council, in turn, accepted the committee's report and adopted a resolution of thanks to Pike. And that was all the recognition the council bestowed upon him. It could not, even in the years to come, reimburse him for the cost of the initial printing of the rituals. Apparently, for the next thirty years the Supreme Council was content to let Pike handle the revisions of the rituals and their printing.[62]

No doubt his original work on the rituals and Albert Mackey's encouragement, even more insistence, set the stage for his becoming Grand Commander upon Honour's retirement. Only on July 7, 1858, did Mackey at last write to Pike about his election as an Active Member of the council on March 20. The Rite, he declared, "must be resuscitated" and, he insisted, "*You must and shall be its head* [emphasis is his]." Mackey continued by noting that if William S. Rockwell declined the office, as he thought he would, Pike would be next in line; and, to underscore his feelings about Pike becoming the next Grand Commander, he added: "I waive, *absolutely* [emphasis his], my own claims as the oldest member now living."[63]

Mackey already knew that Honour would be resigning shortly, as the Grand Commander had been suffering from cataracts that ultimately led to almost total blindness. On August 13, 1858, Honour submitted his resignation to Mackey with a request that the Inspectors General take steps to elect his successor. The *Revised Statutes* of 1855 made no provision for officers, let alone their election. Honour did not mention Charles M. Furman, the Lieutenant Grand Commander, who under the *Grand Constitutions of 1786* was in line to become Grand Commander. Perhaps Furman had also resigned. If that were so, Honour could have then appointed Pike as Lieutenant Grand Commander, making it possible for him to become Grand Commander when Honour resigned. (Honour did not give up his seat on the Supreme Council as an Active Member.) In any event, Pike was nominated by Inspector General McDaniel and in turn was elected, it appears, by correspondence. No minutes of the Supreme Council regarding Pike's election have been found.

Seemingly, between Honour's resignation and Mackey's proclamation of Pike's election on January 1, 1859, the council was in adjournment awaiting the new Grand Commander to assume the responsibilities of that high office. With Honour's retirement the Supreme Council had completed nearly sixty years of its life as the Mother Council of the World, a very inflated claim, given its provincial reality. During the Holbrook, McDonald, and Honour administrations, the territorial question between the jurisdictions was settled, at least for awhile; the *Manifesto of 1845* was adopted; subordinate bodies were established; and the *Revised Statutes* of 1855 were enacted. These Grand Commanders had been keepers of the flame. It was time for new and more dynamic leadership. Albert Pike's entrance on the stage was viewed immediately as the right man appearing on cue.

CHAPTER IV

Exodus from Charleston
1859–1870

Albert Pike

🔲🔲🔲🔲🔲🔲🔲🔲🔲🔲

When Albert Pike learned of his election as Sovereign Grand Commander (official date: January 2, 1859), he wrote a few days later to Secretary General Mackey his heartfelt acceptance: "I shall accept the office of Sovereign Grand Commander with reluctance, since I know that, if the duties of the office are well performed, they involve both labor and responsibility. But I have the advancement of the Scottish Rite too much at heart to decline to accept an office, how responsible soever, conferred on me by so flattering a vote; and I can only promise that I will omit no exertion to propagate and extend the Scottish Rite, and also to make it *worthy* to be propagated and extended among Masons of intellect and learning."[1]

The new Grand Commander had just turned forty-nine and had only been a Mason for the previous nine years. He had already lived a fascinating and varied life by the time he became Grand Commander. Within months of his Scottish Rite election to the Supreme Council's highest office, Harvard conferred on him the honorary degree of A.M. (Master of Arts), at the same ceremony that the future philosopher of pragmatism Charles Sanders Peirce and the future architect Henry Hobson Richardson received their bachelor's degrees. Other distinguished public figures receiving honorary degrees that year included Charles Sumner and Henry Wadsworth Longfellow.[2]

Born in Boston, Massachusetts, on December 29, 1809, the same year of Abraham Lincoln's birth, Pike was the son of Benjamin, a shoemaker, and Sarah Andrews Pike.

The Pike family came from old English stock, descendants of John Pike, who had emigrated to Massachusetts with his wife, Dorothy Daye, and five offspring in 1635. Benjamin Pike acquired the reputation of a hard-drinking rounder, while his wife was known in the community as a long-suffering churchwoman. She read the Bible daily and hoped her only son in a family of girls would one day enter the ministry.

When young Albert was about the age of four, his family moved to Newburyport where he received his primary and grammar schooling. A precocious scholar in adolescence, he received tutoring in Framingham, Massachusetts, while living with an uncle, perhaps a maternal tactic to obviate the effects of his father's licentious habits. Pike was admitted to Harvard College in 1824 at the age of fifteen but never enrolled, though after his death it was widely assumed and reported that he had been a student and graduate of Harvard College.[3]

However, there is no official record of his attendance at the university. Pike's own testimony the year before he died puts to rest any confusion about his Harvard ambitions or status:

> I am not a graduate of Harvard. I passed examinations successfully for the purpose of entering, in 1825, presented myself a year afterward for the purpose of entering the Junior Class, having completed the Freshman and Sophomore Studies during my year at home; declined to pay the *two* years tuition required of me; and so never was a student for even a day, at the University. A diploma of A.B. [*sic*] was sent me, unsolicited about 1859, which I lost during the War.[4]

Since he could not pay all at once the tuition for two years that the college required, Pike felt terribly disheartened and, consequently, left Cambridge for good.[5]

While continuing to teach school in order to cover his modest living expenses, he actually taught himself privately the subjects covered in Harvard's junior and senior years. From 1824 to 1831 much of his time was devoted to acquiring by his own efforts a firm foundation in the classical languages and literature. At this time, also, he began writing poetry in the style of Byron and Shelley. Some of this verse appeared in local newspapers and literary journals.

As a teacher he was under contract at various times with schools in Gloucester, Fairhaven, and Newburyport. A twentieth-century biographer notes that in this period of his life "he had unbounded physical energy, an avid mind, an adventurous disposition, marked independence, and great determination."[6] One Sunday the young schoolmaster was heard playing the violin through an open window. Sometimes Pike and his father played duets on Sundays at the Episcopal Church in Newburyport. In fact, the younger Pike was apt enough on the violin to have once played privately with the principal violinist of the Philharmonic Society of Boston, Louis Ostinelli, who with his equally renowned wife, the pianist and singer Sophia Hewitt Ostinelli, was passing through the North Shore area on a concert tour of Maine and New England in 1822. None of this mattered, however, when Pike was challenged for fiddling on the Sabbath. The school board, upon learning of his breach in Sabbath decorum, charged him with being impious and demanded a formal apology. Pike refused and therefore was discharged immediately.[7]

Though his mother was disappointed at the turn of events, she already had heard stories of her son's experienced social prowess, which made the firing less shocking. Albert Pike was clearly at odds with the remnants of the strict Calvinist culture still present in New England. In remarking about Pike's formative years, Robert Lipscomb Duncan surmised that Albert Pike "was destined to be forever torn between the two extremes [of his parents], between the penchant for moral order, which would eventually lead him into the bizarre religions of the ancient world, and the ungovernable appetites of the flesh, which he would satisfy in unusual ways."[8]

Pike's climactic dismissal from teaching in 1831 prompted him next to go west. At the invincible age of twenty-two, he joined a band of hunters and traders heading from St. Louis, Missouri, via the trailhead at Independence, for Santa Fe, New Mexico. After a little less than a year in Santa Fe and nearby Taos, Pike, in the company of like-minded adventurers, headed for New Orleans. They traveled through present-day Oklahoma, met friendly Indians—an experience that left Pike with a life-long favorable opinion of Native Americans—took at one point the wrong road, and thus wound up at Fort Smith, Arkansas.[9] For a brief time Pike taught school in the northern part of the state, Pope County, where he met the editor of the *Little Rock Advocate*. The newspaper became an outlet for Pike's love of writing, and he subsequently bought it and then ran it for about two and a half years.

Standing "some six feet two inches in height, magnificently proportioned, and crowned with a head of commanding aspect and strikingly attractive features,"[10] Pike was always an imposing figure, a man who, with the added attraction of cultural graces, had no difficulty in attracting women. Pike's leonine features never left him, as he was later described as being "of large frame and Jovian countenance, with flowing locks reaching to his shoulders, and a long beard," so that he "presented an impressive appearance."[11] Later in life it was estimated he tipped the scales at 300 pounds.

Shortly after he settled in Little Rock, he met Mary Ann Hamilton, an attractive brunette and the daughter of James and Drusilla Hamilton of Arkansas Post, a village one hundred miles below Little Rock. After an ardent courtship they were married in Arkansas Post in the fall of 1834 at the home of Colonel Terence Farrelly, Mary Ann's guardian, by Judge James Lucas. She brought into the marriage some modest property, which permitted him to buy a partnership in the *Advocate*, of which in 1835 he became the sole editor and proprietor. There were ten children born of this union, only three of whom, two sons and a daughter, survived their father.

By the mid-1850s Mary Pike was mentally ill. The nature of the illness may have been manic depression or a form of schizophrenia. In this regard, Pike's life and marriage may have resembled some of the tensions in the family and home of Abraham and Mary Todd Lincoln of Springfield, Illinois. She made the lives of her husband and children miserable; consequently Pike obtained an official separation in 1857, leaving her in a special trust their lovely home and household slaves.[12] As a devout Episcopalian and as a product of a society committed to romantic marriage as a once and for all settled matter, that is, "until death us do part," he was opposed to divorce and so never pursued that legal avenue. They shared quarters, nevertheless, during a period of temporary reclusiveness not long after Pike resigned his command in the Confederate army. Most of the time, however, Mary Ann Pike lived alone until her death in 1876.

Meanwhile, Pike, having been admitted to the Arkansas bar, gave up the *Advocate*. He developed a successful law practice yet found the time to edit five volumes of the Arkansas Supreme Court Reports for the years 1837 to 1844. Pike's most lucrative legal work involved land cases with the U.S. government in behalf of the Cherokee Nation. In one instance he received a fee from the Cherokees of $100,000.

In the spring of 1846 the Mexican War began. Pike, although a Whig—the Whig Party, for the most part, was opposed to the war (e.g., Congressman Abraham Lincoln, a fairly typical Northern Whig, questioned its necessity)—raised a squadron of cavalry and served with distinction as its captain in the battle of Buena Vista. Years later, "Pike's son went to Washington and Lee University with a letter from his father to General Lee [then president of Washington College], who asked the boy, 'Did your father ever tell you he gave me a horse at the Battle of Buena Vista? My horse was shot from under me and your father dismounted and made me take his while he found another for himself.'"[13]

The Mexican War formally ended with the signing of the Treaty of Guadalupe Hidalgo, in the village of that name just outside Mexico City, on February 2, 1848. One of the results of the war was the renewal of interest in building a transcontinental railroad to the Pacific. Such a proposal was first made in 1832 and then twelve years later by Asa Whitney, a New York merchant, who thought of linking Oregon with the Great Lakes. Other proposals followed, influenced by westward expansion and the growing sectional tension. Pike was the author of one of these proposals, which he called a "National Plan for an Atlantic and Pacific Railroad." On November 21, 1849, he set forth his plan before a large audience at Memphis, Tennessee. Rather than an exclusive northern or southern route to the Pacific, he proposed that the route

> should start at one and the same time from two points on the Mississippi, one at St. Louis, or some other point in the northern states, connected or to be connected by railroad with the northern Atlantic states, and one at Memphis, or some other point in the southern states, connected or to be connected by railroad with the southern Atlantic states; that these two roads should be carried forward simultaneously, unite at some point west of Missouri or Arkansas, and one of them thence proceed to the Pacific by such route . . . as shall afford equal facilities and advantages to the South and North, and to the southern and northern Atlantic states, and that whenever, therefore, another branch shall be built from a terminus in the North, one shall be built simultaneously from a terminus in the South.[14]

The Memphis audience adopted Pike's proposal and drew up a petition to Congress in support of it, but the proposal foundered. "The approaching session of Congress was to be too busy with the great emotional debate over slavery expansion (leading to the Compromise of 1850) to have time to devote attention to the Pacific railroad."[15]

. . .

It was during this time of heated national and congressional debate that Pike became a Mason. Already a member of the Independent Order of Odd Fellows, he was raised in 1850 to a Master Mason in Western Lodge No. 1 of Little Rock. Two years later he helped organize Magnolia Lodge No. 60 in Little Rock, and he became its Worshipful Master in 1853.

During these years he took all ten degrees of the York Rite of Freemasonry, served as High Priest of Union Chapter No. 2 of Royal Arch Masonry (1852) in Little Rock, and helped to establish in 1851 the Arkansas Grand Chapter of Royal Arch Masonry, serving two terms as its Grand High Priest (1853–1855). Pike was also a founder of Occidental Council No. 1 of the Council of Royal and Select Masters in Little Rock and was its Illustrious Master. Moreover, he participated in the organization of the Hugh de Payens Commandery No. 1, Knights Templar, also in Little Rock, and became its first Eminent Commander.[16] By the time he received from Albert G. Mackey the Scottish Rite degrees in March 1853, Pike had been an enthusiastic, dedicated Mason for only three years.

Besides his law practice and recent interest in Masonry, he was much involved in Arkansas politics. But after a hard-fought congressional election in 1851, he dropped out of active involvement in the Whig Party of the state, although he continued to consider himself a national Whig until the following year. For many years the Whig economic program proposing federal sponsorship of growth and development of natural resources had been losing momentum. Once prosperity followed the opening of the California gold fields in 1848, the party's policy was moribund. Nor did the Whigs have any new ideas about political policies after they united with the Democrats in favoring the Compromise of 1850 with a sense of finality. Pike, up until the early 1850s, embraced the views of Chief Justice John Marshall about a strong federal government asserting its full delegated and implied powers in behalf of an indivisible nation. He held "faith without inquiry in the doctrines of [Daniel] Webster."[17] The differences between the two major parties after the Compromise of 1850 became indistinguishable. Party loyalties began to fracture.

Pike was disappointed with the Whig Party's nomination of General Winfield Scott for president in 1852, preferring either former President Millard Fillmore or Senator Daniel Webster, who, as it turned out, died that fall. He could not bring himself to vote for either Winfield Scott or Franklin Pierce, the victorious Democratic candidate. With the decline and ultimate demise of the Whig Party, Pike was a man in need of a new political party. Former Congressman Abraham Lincoln was in a similar dilemma. Lincoln remarked in his eulogy of the Whig statesman Henry Clay that "the man who is of neither party, is not—cannot be, of any consequence."[18] Further down the Mississippi Valley, Pike also struggled to define his position through the changing political structures.

While in Washington, D.C., pursuing Indian claims in the spring of 1854, a time of intense debate over the Kansas-Nebraska issue, Pike "first became interested in the American Party, popularly labeled the 'Know-Nothing Party' because of the supposed common response, 'I know nothing,' with which the members met inquiries about the principles and objects of the order."[19] The American Party received impetus from "The Supreme Order of the Star-Spangled Banner" or the "Sons of the Sires of '76," a secret organization "of descendants of at least two generations of Americans."[20] Pike was attracted to a party whose slogan was "America for the Americans" as he was fearful of the large influx of immigrants that had occurred during the past three decades. "He resented the manners, habits, tastes, and usages of the foreigners with whom he came in contact in Boston, New York, Philadelphia, and other Eastern cities, and he had a genuine fear that allowing so many aliens and naturalized citizens to vote and to hold office was a serious threat to American institutions."[21] As a Southerner by assimilation, but not by birth, he feared the North's desire for immigrants (i.e., free labor) and consequently wanted immigration restricted. He never had much interest, however, in the American Party's anti-Catholic stand. "Religious intolerance was certainly no part of his belief."[22]

Pike's interest in and support of the American Party were reflected in his serving as president of a provisional state council in Arkansas in the spring of 1855, the party having achieved a considerable membership there. He also served as a delegate to the national council which drew up a platform and to the national convention which nominated respectively for president and vice president ex-President Millard Fillmore (New York) and Andrew J. Donelson (Tennessee) for the election of 1856. The adopted platform omitted a plank supporting slavery. Pike felt that the plank supporting slavery was essential because "the 'only safety' for the South 'consisted in placing our candidates upon the platform as it was.'"[23] Consequently he did not support the platform or vote for the Fillmore-Donelson ticket, although he had no objection to Fillmore, whom he had earlier supported. By then he had abandoned the national ideology of Webster and was "self-converted to the theory of [John C.] Calhoun, as to the origin and nature of the Constitution," that left the states the right to decide the issue of slavery.[24]

James Buchanan, a Pennsylvania Democrat and Mason who was secretary of state in Polk's administration, won the election, carrying all the Southern states except Maryland, which gave its electoral vote to the Know-Nothing Party's Millard Fillmore. Besides the appearance of a third party, this election witnessed the emergence of the Republican Party and its presidential candidate, the colorful Colonel John C. Frémont, who had played a leading but controversial part in the acquisition of California.

"In the years between 1856 and 1860," writes biographer Walter Lee Brown, "Pike was torn between his love for the Union and his love for the South, much of the time undecided and confused over what went on about him."[25] During the height of the Kansas controversy he wrote and anonymously published in 1856 "a series of *Letters to the People of the Northern States* [italics supplied] in which he attempted to look impartially at the slavery controversy and to see where it was leading." In this series, which was distributed north of the Mason-Dixon line, Pike emphasized that he was not "one of those who believe slavery a blessing." While he granted that it was an evil, it was not the "great outrage upon humanity" that some had portrayed it to be.[26] Pike's conservative position was not too dissimilar from Lincoln's in the late 1850s. Lincoln stated frequently and explicitly that as much as he abhorred slavery in moral terms, he "would consent to the extension of it rather than see the Union dissolved." Instead of condemning the South for the immorality of slavery, Lincoln expressed patience and understanding in search for a resolution, as so many central Illinois Whigs had Southern roots.[27]

Although a Unionist, Pike was, in effect, also an apologist for the institution of slavery. Unlike Lincoln, who became committed to doing something about slavery, Pike, like many Southerners, did not believe slavery a positive good; but he could never find the right time to end it or even do anything more serious than coexist with it uncomfortably.[28] As the Kansas ("bleeding Kansas" as it was called) issue heated up between the free-state advocates and the pro-slavery group, Pike considered himself a "Southern State Rights Democrat," despite his profession of neutrality in national politics after he left the American or Know-Nothing Party in 1856.[29] Four years later, in the fateful election of 1860, he voted his conviction by supporting John C. Breckinridge (Kentucky), the candidate of the apostates taking flight from the Charleston convention of the Democratic Party. Breckinridge ran with Joseph Lane (Oregon) on a pro-slavery platform. In a four-way national race, Lincoln won with less than 40 percent of the popular vote.

■ ■ ■

Despite his political involvements, Pike maintained his active interest in the Scottish Rite, particularly through his borrowed copy of Mackey's Scottish Rite rituals. Sometime between 1854 and 1855 he copied the whole ritual into his manuscript book, *Formulas and Rituals*, the original title of which appeared in cipher. His appointment to a committee charged with revising the rituals occurred on March 21, 1855, and from that position he acquired his reputation as a formidable ritualist. By the spring of 1857 he completed the first polished revision of the rituals, ordered the printing of 100 copies, as was mentioned earlier, and received the thirty-third degree.[30] This publication is considered to be Pike's *magnum opus*. A year later, he was elected an Active Member of the Supreme Council, thirty-third degree. With Grand Commander Honour's resignation and Grand Secretary Mackey's persistent efforts, the stage was set for Pike to be elected Grand Commander. He assumed the responsibilities of that office early in 1859. Reflecting some two decades later on the condition of the Supreme Council when he assumed the high office, he recalled:

> The Supreme Council, when I became Grand Commander . . . had a Treasurer General and no Treasury. I do not suppose that Brother [Achille] LePrince, who was called Treasurer

General, ever in his life received or paid out a dollar of moneys of the Supreme Council. He kept no books; the Secretary General kept none; and whatever came into [his] hands, for degrees, was his. If any bodies had made returns for twenty years back, I could not find them. There were no records. The Supreme Council had not a printed volume, nor any property of any kind to the value of a dollar, nor credit enough to buy a book.[31]

It must be emphasized that when Pike became Grand Commander there were no existing records, minutes, or documents for the first fifty-eight years of the Supreme Council. This was certainly a depressing situation for the new leader, but one which he was determined to overcome. He wasted no time in calling a meeting of the Supreme Council for March 25, 1859. Four years before, the council had adopted the so-called *Revised Statutes*. Pike felt that much more had to be done in order to make the Supreme Council of the Southern Jurisdiction more effective, and so fifty-one articles making up the 1859 *Statutes* were adopted.

The first sentence of Article I provided for a drastic change in the Supreme Council's composition: "The number of active members of the Supreme Council is hereby increased and enlarged to, and forever fixed at, thirty-three [remains unchanged], including therein the nine existing members."[32] Article II set forth the apportionment of the thirty-three Active Members thus: "Maryland, 1; District of Columbia, 1; Virginia, 2; North Carolina, 1; South Carolina, 5; Georgia, 2; Florida, 2; Alabama, 2; Mississippi, 2; Louisiana, 3; Tennessee, 2; Kentucky, 2; Texas, 1; Arkansas, 2; Missouri, 2; Iowa, 1; Minnesota, 1; and California, 1."[33] The practice of one Active Member or Deputy from each state was established later.

Of the twenty-four new seats thus created, six Active Members were elected at the session of March 1859, raising the membership of the council to fifteen. Apparently some of the new members were elected as an honor or as recognition of service rendered rather than at the prospect of future service since several of them never attended later sessions of the Supreme Council.[34]

Provision was made in Articles IV, XXXIV, and XXXV for the establishment and authority of Grand Consistories, with one for each state, each consistory being composed of at least nine members. Each of these bodies was to serve as "the Deputy of this Supreme Council, and the governing power of the Ancient and Accepted Rite in the State wherein it is organized."[35] Not all states in the Southern Jurisdiction had Grand Consistories. By March 1860 there were five: Arkansas, Kentucky, Louisiana, Mississippi, and Virginia. According to John H. Cowles, who was Sovereign Grand Commander of the Supreme Council of the Southern Jurisdiction from 1921 to 1952,

> The original form of organization of the Scottish Rite was to have one Grand Consistory in each state or Orient or sub-jurisdiction, whatever you want to call it. Then these Grand Consistories would issue the charters for the Lodges of Perfection, 4°–14°; for the Councils of Princes of Jerusalem, 15°–16°; for the Chapters of Rose Croix, 17°–18°; for the Councils of Kadosh, 19°–30°, but the Grand Consistories retained the 31° and 32°. The subordinated

bodies would be scattered over the state, but the members would have to come to the Grand Consistories to get the 31° and 32°. Originally, the Grand Consistory membership was limited to 81 Active Members [not the Active Members of the Supreme Council], and if anyone of them, who only had the right to vote, was absent (if I remember rightly) two or three meetings of the Grand Consistory, then he was dropped from the Active Membership and a 32nd Degree Mason elected to take his place.[36]

While Pike was interested in seeing the Scottish Rite extended in all areas of the Southern Jurisdiction and wanted at that time a Grand Consistory in each state, he stressed the importance of careful selection of new members. "In his view, extension of the Rite was not to be synonymous with popularizing it."[37] The Scottish Rite, in other words, was not for every Mason.

Besides the provisions made for the enlargement of the Supreme Council and for the establishment of Grand Consistories, the *Statutes* of 1859 also called for the election of the Grand Commander, Lieutenant Grand Commander, Secretary General, and Treasurer General by majority vote of the council as stated in Article VII. This was a significant departure from the long-established way these offices had been filled, which had heretofore been by appointment.

Another noteworthy facet of the *Statutes* of 1859 was the appearance of the name "Ancient and Accepted Scottish Rite" in several places. It was the first time that the appellation using the modifier "Scottish" had appeared "in official documents of the Southern Jurisdiction."[38] A similar, if somewhat ambiguous, name had been employed prior to this latter change when "Ancient and Accepted Rite" was the nomenclature of the *Manifesto of 1851* and the *Revised Statutes of 1855*. The distinctive interpolation of "Scottish," however, was not adopted before 1859.

In addition to the adoption of the *Statutes* just discussed, the Supreme Council also adopted resolutions calling for exchanges of Grand Representatives and recommended that a convention of two delegates from each Supreme Council meet in London on the first Monday of July 1861. Such a meeting had earlier been proposed by the Supreme Council for England and Wales in 1856, but nothing came of it. However, the resolutions pertaining to the exchange of representatives among the Supreme Councils and an international convention of these bodies ultimately bore fruit. Printed nine months later as a folio circular in English and French and bearing the signatures of Pike and Mackey, copies of the resolutions were sent to the various Supreme Councils. The resolutions included six proposals for the projected convention to consider: (1) to improve "the system of representation and intercommunication" among Supreme Councils; (2) to neutralize the power of "all spurious and illegitimate Bodies pretending to be Powers of any regular Rite of Masonry"; (3) to revise "the Rituals for all the Degrees of the Ancient and Accepted Rite from the 4th to 33d inclusive" so that they become connected and coherent; (4) to consider changes "in the ancient Constitutions, *Statutes* and Regulations" and to provide "one consistent code" for all Supreme Councils; (5) to suggest ways of extending and propagating the Scottish Rite and "to persuade the intellectual and learned Masons of the Symbolic Degrees to seek admission"; and (6) "to provide regular Sessions of such Conventions" at different places in Europe and America and at stated times.[39]

The international convention, as proposed for July 1861, never occurred as civil war in the United States broke out in April of that year; and only a few of the Supreme Councils, meanwhile, had acted on the proposal. Four years later, with the war ended, Pike still hoped that such a meeting would be held, perhaps three years hence.[40]

Shortly after the session of the Supreme Council in the spring of 1859, Pike wrote to James C. Batchelor, the Deputy of the Grand Consistory at New Orleans (Pike was still commander in chief of this body), that he had prepared ceremonies of inauguration and installation for the Lodges of Perfection, chapters of Rose Croix, councils, and consistories, as well as ceremonies for funeral, baptism, adoption (making a woman an associate of the Scottish Rite), and for the reception of a louveteau (French term for lewis, a special stonemason's tool, that became the symbolic term for the son of a Mason).[41] Pike's restoration of these ceremonies was but another instance of his desire to provide organization and stability for the Scottish Rite and to ensure its survival.

■ ■ ■

Between the time of Pike's correspondence with Batchelor in the spring of 1859 and the following January when the Supreme Council was to meet again, a dramatic event occurred at Harper's Ferry, Virginia (now West Virginia), that jarred the nation: John Brown's raid on the little town at the confluence of the Potomac and Shenandoah Rivers wherein he led a band of eighteen of the twenty-one men he had gathered at the Kennedy farmhouse on the Maryland side of the Potomac (three remained behind to guard the house) in order to instigate a slave insurrection in Virginia. The radical abolitionist wanted to establish a free state in the southern Appalachians and stimulate rebellion southward among the bondsmen. Brown and his men seized the Federal arsenal and armory located in the town, but no slaves came to their aid.

After a two-day battle (October 16–18), a detachment of U.S. Marines from Washington, under the command of Colonel Robert E. Lee, an Army Corps of Engineers officer, took Brown and the five other survivors prisoner. The Commonwealth of Virginia wasted no time in indicting them for treason against the state and criminal conspiracy to incite a slave insurrection. At Charles Town, Virginia (now West Virginia), Brown was tried, convicted, and on December 2 hanged. He was entombed at North Elba, New York, south of Lake Placid, where he once had a farm. Later, the others were sent to the gallows. The South's reaction to Brown's raid was one of alarm, the blame being directed at the abolitionists and the so-called "Black Republicans." The North's reaction was mixed; conservatives deplored it, but abolitionists and anti-slave organizations mourned Brown's death and considered him a hero and a martyr to the cause of emancipation.

Ralph Waldo Emerson, using hyperbole, eulogized Brown in the prediction that his execution "will make the gallows as glorious as the cross."[42]

Brown's foray on Harper's Ferry underscored what Senator William H. Seward (New York), a former leader in the Anti-Masonic Party and a leading Republican contender for the nomination in 1860, had avowed regarding the sectional clashing a year before the raid: "It is an irrepressible conflict between opposing and enduring forces and it means that the United States must and will, sooner or later, become either entirely a slaveholding nation or entirely a free-labor nation."[43] Seward was right: the growing division between North and South became an inevitable and unavoidable sundering. That realistic view probably cost him the Republican nomination, whereas Lincoln's similar prediction of "a house divided" was carefully downplayed while he emerged as a national candidate.

Three months after John Brown's raid, the Supreme Council met in Charleston (January 9, 1860). Enough members were in attendance to allow business to be conducted under the provisions of the *Grand Constitutions*. However, Pike felt that it was time to resolve the issue of attendance. Consequently he stated that in the absence of a quorum of membership no business could be taken up, and he adjourned the session, to meet again on March 28, 1860, at Washington, D.C. On that day the formerly adjourned session was called to order at the Masonic Hall with most of the Active Members on hand or their absence justified by written explanations. After the meeting was under way, a committee was formed to consider the factors involved in members' absences. It later reported that seven members had provided satisfactory reasons for being absent, "but that four had failed to appear or send any explanation."[44] This underscored Pike's strong feeling that Active Members should regularly attend the meetings of the Supreme Council and is reflected today in Article IV, Section 20, of the *Statutes of The Supreme Council*, which states: "Any Sovereign Grand Inspector General absent from two successive regular Sessions of the Supreme Council without excuse adjudged sufficient may, at the close of the second Session, be deemed to have resigned his Membership in the Supreme Council."[45]

In what came to be known as the Grand Commander's *Allocution*[46] or address to the Supreme Council, Pike set forth in detail all the business with which it was involved and in turn asked the members to share in the consequent labor. At one point the Grand Commander gave a reasoned review for the need to enlarge the membership of the council, noting that

> The Ancient and Accepted Rite has heretofore, in our country, been viewed by the large body of Masons with somewhat of doubt and distrust. It is very generally imagined to be Masonry in little more than the name. It is supposed to deal too much in speculation, to encourage innovation, to teach heresies in Masonry, if not elsewhere, to be arrogant and exclusive, to desire power, and to be fond of high-sounding titles. Its degrees being too

generally communicated in private, and the recipient really instructed in not more than three or four of the whole series, going at a stride or two, and in a day, from the 4th to the 32nd, the Fraternity at large had some warrant for looking upon them as a sort of *side* degrees, of little or no value, containing little or no instruction, and invented only in order to confer on those who could afford to pay for them, certain inflated and pompous titles.

To extend and propagate the Rite in the face of these prejudices, it was indispensable to enlist in each State one or more of those Masons who by long service had deserved well of the Order and were held by universal consent to possess and to deserve to possess weight, authority, and influence. Their acceptance of Dignities in the Rite is a guarantee to the Fraternity in which they occupy the first place, of the excellence and value, of that to which they thus give their countenance and approval.[47]

This clearly revealed Pike's justification for having in each state a Sovereign Grand Inspector General or Deputy who enjoyed respect and prestige within the fraternity and who would provide leadership and visible representation for the Rite in a particular state.

In this 1860 *Allocution* Pike also dealt with the question of division of the Southern Jurisdiction, such as regional Supreme Councils respectively for the southwestern and Pacific coast states or, as recommended by the Scottish Rite Masons of Louisiana, a Supreme Council "for *each* State in the Jurisdiction."[48] Pike concluded that such multiplication of Supreme Councils "would have given just cause of censure on the part of the Supreme Councils of great nations; and would have left the Rite in the United States without any central authority or national character whatever."[49] These proposals were not pursued any further.

Later in his *Allocution* Pike submitted the rituals of the eighteenth, thirtieth, thirty-first and thirty-second degrees, which he had revised and combined with the revisions of Charles Laffon de Ladebat of Louisiana, who had been made an Active Member in 1859. The council adopted them, as it did Pike's recommendation for four permanent committees for finance, correspondence, jurisprudence and legislation, and the doings of subordinates.

Inasmuch as the Northern Jurisdiction of the Scottish Rite had attempted to exercise its hegemony over the District of Columbia, Pike reasserted in the *Allocution* the territorial division agreed upon in 1827, with all the states north of the Mason-Dixon line, including Delaware, and east of the Mississippi constituting the Northern Jurisdiction.

On the recommendation of the Grand Commander, the Supreme Council adopted a resolution to print its *Transactions*. This was indeed an important step as the minutes or records of previous sessions, except for that at New Orleans in 1857, had never been published "and the handwritten records were either lost or destroyed during ensuing years."[50] Macoy, the Masonic publishing firm of New York, published the *Transactions* of 1860 that same year; and the council's *Transactions* have been regularly published without interruption since then.

During the historic session of 1860, Pike requested Grand Secretary Mackey to arrange a ceremonial visit of the Supreme Council to the grave of Brother George Washington at Mount Vernon, thus inaugurating a practice that the council later followed at its meetings in Washington, D.C.

Two days after Pike had delivered his *Allocution*, which as Harris and Carter noted, "opened the door upon a new era for the Southern Jurisdiction,"[51] a committee of three Active Members brought in twenty resolutions of endorsement or acceptance of his proposals. Approval followed. Because of these far-seeing revisions, there is no question that the session of March 1860 was one of the most transforming moments in the annals of the Supreme Council.

Less than a year later, another session was called, to meet in January in Charleston. When no quorum was present, Pike tried again in February with the same result. He then summoned the council to meet at New Orleans on April 1. The lack of a quorum in January and February underscored the problem of rousing council members to attend the sessions and the importance of Pike's insistence that they either attend or yield their titles and seats.

On April 2, 1861, the day following the opening of the Supreme Council's session in New Orleans' Masonic Hall, Pike delivered his *Allocution*, taking note at the beginning, "There is a world of significance in the fact, that this Body, which only a few short months ago was the Supreme Council, in name, for the Southern, and in fact for the Southern and Western Jurisdiction of the United States of America, is now the Supreme Council for the Southern and Western United States, and for the Confederate States of America."[52]

■　■　■

Two months before the Supreme Council's 1861 meeting, the seceding slave-holding states called a convention which gathered in Montgomery, Alabama, drew up a constitution stressing the "sovereign and independent character" of each state,[53] established a provisional government, and elected Jefferson Davis of Mississippi as provisional president of the Confederacy and Alexander H. Stephens of Georgia as provisional vice president. Despite such a national rupture, Pike insisted in his *Allocution* "that the convulsions which rock the outer world, severing the bonds that have heretofore tied State to State, and creating new Republics, do not shake the firm foundations of our Masonic governments and institutions, nor cut asunder the ligaments that make Masons dwell together in unity."[54] But since the national churches had not held together, dividing in two over the various theological implications of slavery in the 1840s,[55] it was hard to imagine what Pike had in mind with regard to unity. Surely the Masonic fraternity, despite the strength of its "ligaments," would also be affected by the repercussions of a society ripping apart. In anticipation of the ultimate failure of national politics to resolve moral differences, these denominational schisms, as much as anything else, prefigured the script of political secession.[56]

At the time that Pike uttered his words affirming the firm moorings of "Masonic governments and institutions," Fort Sumter in Charleston Harbor was under siege; and one week after the adjournment of the Supreme Council on April 5, the fort was bombarded for thirty-four hours by Confederate shore batteries while the Union fleet languished offshore unable to help. The Civil War had begun.

The tortuous day and a half of being under sustained fire required Major Robert Anderson, the commanding officer and a Mason, to surrender the fort to General Pierre G. T. Beauregard, a former student of his at West Point who was also a Mason. The Confederate attack galvanized Northern determination to preserve the Union. President Abraham Lincoln, in turn, on April 15, issued a call for 75,000 volunteers for an enlistment of three months. About six weeks before Lincoln's call, President Davis had called for and readily obtained 100,000 volunteers for one year. With the siege and surrender of Fort Sumter, there was no turning back either for the Union or the Confederacy. During the three months that followed this opening event, there was a lull with only a few skirmishes before the first, major battle of the war was fought at Bull Run on July 21.

Before the Supreme Council adjourned its session in New Orleans on April 5, it provided that honorary membership in that body was to be limited to no more than two "from any State or Territory,"[57] that it was to meet triennially on the third Monday of February at Charleston beginning in 1862, and that no alteration or amendment of the *Statutes* could be made "unless it be proposed at one regular Session of the Supreme Council, and adopted at a subsequent one; unless notification be made to all Active Members of the Supreme Council, through the Secretary-General, twelve months previous to action on the same."[58]

Although Pike in his *Allocution* urged that the Supreme Council "as soon as possible rid" itself of all control of the degrees of the Councils of Royal and Select Masters,[59] the only action taken by the Southern Council in this regard was to relinquish, on his recommendation, any dues from the subordinate councils to the Grand Council of Royal and Select Masters in Arkansas. The Supreme Council's complete relinquishment of control of the Council of Royal and Select Masters, which became subsequently a York Rite body, was to come later.

Other actions taken in the session of 1861 included the election of James Penn of Tennessee, an Active Member since 1859, as Lieutenant Grand Commander and a request to Mackey "to act as the special agent of the Supreme Council in extending the Rite into the States of North Carolina and Florida."[60]

On the afternoon of April 5, the Supreme Council concluded its deliberations, agreeing "to meet again on the 3d Monday of February 1862, in the city of Charleston, South Carolina."[61] As there was no quorum present for this wartime session, the meeting adjourned.

At the close of the session of 1861, there were twenty-six Active Members (seven vacancies to be filled), two Emeriti Members (John H. Honour, Past Sovereign Grand Commander, and Charles M. Furman, Past Lieutenant Grand Commander), and sixty-four

Sovereign Grand Inspectors General Honorary, certainly an indication that under Pike the Supreme Council was not standing still. But the Civil War precluded its further official activity and meeting until the cessation of national hostilities four years later.

■   ■   ■

Some three and a half weeks after the surrender of Fort Sumter, Arkansas joined the Confederacy, thus focusing Pike's attention on "a problem that was of vital concern to the safety of his state. This was to secure [the] Indian Territory for the Confederate States. By the end of the first week of May all the United States posts in the Territory had been abandoned."[62] In Pike's judgment the Confederacy should take possession of the territory before Federal troops were ordered to regarrison the evacuated posts. He shared his views with Robert Toombs, the Confederate secretary of state, and Robert W. Johnson, the Arkansas delegate to the provisional Congress then meeting at Montgomery, Alabama. Shortly thereafter, the provisional Congress enacted legislation annexing the Indian Territory to the Confederacy and thereby putting the tribes of the territory under its protection.

Although Pike may have hoped for the military command of the territory, he was quite satisfied that Brigadier General Benjamin McCulloch, a Texas Ranger, was selected. Pike, in recognition of his legal experience in Indian affairs, was appointed commissioner of the Confederate States to the Indians west of Arkansas.[63] As commissioner he negotiated treaties of alliance and military support with the so-called Five Civilized Tribes (Cherokee, Choctaw, Comanche, Creek, and Seminole). "Pike did a magnificent job," as W. Craig Gaines notes in *The Confederate Cherokees*, "in bringing the Five Civilized Tribes, into the Confederate camp."[64] Part of his success was due to the bitter memory held by the Cherokees of the Trail of Tears, the harsh relocation program initiated in 1838 by the government in Washington. Chief John Ross's wife, sometimes called Elizabeth but also known as Quatie Martin Ross, died on the trip to Indian Territory. She was buried in 1839 at Little Rock, Arkansas, in a cemetery lot owned by Pike.[65] To the Indians the tacit appeal of the Confederacy in 1861 was essentially that "an enemy of my enemy is my friend."

The following October while at Fort Smith, Arkansas, Commissioner Pike received word from Richmond, which had meanwhile become the Confederate capital, "that he had been commissioned a brigadier general in the Provisional Army of the Confederate States to command the Indian troops raised under his treaties."[66] As it turned out, his military service lasted less than a year, during which time his troops fought in the battle of Pea Ridge in Arkansas.

It was important to the Confederacy's western strategy that Arkansas and Texas be secure and that the Indian Territory not be used for Federal forces to stage an invasion of the two states. Pike's agreement with each major tribe was that it should raise a regiment for Confederate service, but only as a defensive measure. They would not be used, without their consent, in any offensive operation. Brigadier General Pike, commander of the Confederate Department of Indian Territory, generally ignorant of a planned "all-or-nothing campaign" into Missouri, was ordered to bring his entire force of white and Indian troops into Arkansas. Two Indian regiments stayed behind, but later changed their minds and arrived too late to make any difference. Nevertheless, Pike led a "ragtag" force.[67]

The Indian troops were engaged in fighting at Leetown on March 7, the first day of the Pea Ridge battle. Of the four field generals present that day, two had been killed, leaving Pike as the senior officer in command of bedlam, which the right wing had become. The Cherokees had not conducted themselves well. For Pike "it was not only a unique but also an uncertain command" right from the beginning.[68] He had no training or experience as a commander of a large corps of troops, no knowledge of the roads in the battle zone, hardly any information about the Confederate battle plan, no prior communications from the generals who were killed about the exact position of Confederate troops, and no idea about the strength of the opposing Union army.[69] It is a little unfair, therefore, to place all the blame on Pike for his "inglorious command."[70]

The legacy of Pea Ridge, "a battle of all kinds of surprises and accidents," in the words of the Union general Franz Sigel, had two important consequences. It was the only time during the Civil War that Indian troops would ever be used, for the atrocities that occurred at Leetown horrified both the North and the South. Pike did not learn of the scalpings, mutilations, and murders until after his return to the Indian Territory. He was never able to fully dissociate himself from the reports in both the Northern and Southern press. But of larger importance strategically, the battle of Pea Ridge, won by the Union army, was one recognizable turning point in the course of the Civil War. In short, it has sometimes been defined with a tinge of overstatement as "the Gettysburg of the West." The battle's "direct military results were enormous: the loss of Missouri, the end of the Confederate plan for outflanking and turning back the Federal advance into Tennessee, the beginning of the end for the Confederate hope of retaining control of the Mississippi."[71] Sherman maintained that Union victories at Pea Ridge, Donelson, and Shiloh "gave the keynote to all subsequent events of the war."[72]

After the battle, Pike "learned with the utmost pain and regret that one, at least, of the enemy's dead was scalped upon the field."[73] When word of this atrocity was made public, General Pike was denounced by several newspapers, including the *Boston Evening Transcript* that "called its native son 'the meanest, the most rascally, the most malevolent of the rebels. It is not presumed that a more venomous reptile than Albert Pike ever crawled the face of the earth.'"[74] The New York *Daily Tribune* editorialized sensationally about Pike "who led the Aboriginal Corps of Tomahawkers and Scalpers," for "as his name indicates, he is a ferocious fish, and has fought duels enough to qualify himself to be the leader of the savages."[75]

Despite his issuance after the atrocity of a special order to the troops under his command condemning such brutal behavior and his sending a copy of it under a flag of truce to Brigadier General Samuel Curtis, his Federal opponent, Pike was never able to live down what became "a source of frequent embarrassment, even bitterness, in his later life. His best friends at the North probably never believed that he could have condoned, much less encouraged the perpetration of atrocities by anyone."[76] To others he was left to explain repeatedly his innocence. Curtis, for example, never mentioned Pike's nearly instantaneous gesture of remorse in his official report. And there were, inevitably, accounts "of how Pike maddened his Indians with whiskey and sent them against the Federals at Pea Ridge" to fight "in their own fashion," using bow and arrow and tomahawk.[77]

Pike's service in the Confederate army was further burdened by problems with his superiors, including quarrels with Major General Thomas C. Hindman and Major General Theophilus N. Holmes, which ultimately led to his resignation. He subsequently bought a small farm on the Little Missouri River in an area called Greasy Cove, had a cabin built there, and settled down with his books to continue the revision of the Scottish Rite rituals.[78] Later, when Federal troops advanced into the area, Pike moved to Washington, Arkansas, where he was joined by his wife and three of their daughters, who were refugees from Little Rock. One son, Hamilton, was a private in an Arkansas regiment nearby; and another son, "Walter Lacy, promoted to the rank of captain, had been killed in Missouri on April 7, 1864. Pike always said he was robbed and murdered after having been wounded in an engagement with Federal cavalry; an obituary in the *Washington [Arkansas] Telegraph*, June 8, 1864, supports Pike's statement."[79]

• • •

Early in June 1864, Governor Harris Flanagin appointed Pike an associate justice of the Arkansas Supreme Court, a position he held until the end of the year or the early weeks of 1865 when with his family he left Washington, Arkansas, which was then overcrowded and lacking food, for a place on Big Creek in Lafayette County, "six miles from the village of Rondo."[80] Pike arranged for his library to be moved to Washington, Arkansas, while he was sitting on the state supreme court; and then, in turn, it was moved to Big Creek. There, he continued working on the Scottish Rite rituals and presumably finished *Morals and Dogma*, a project he had begun at Washington, Arkansas, and which he referred to as "lectures of all the degrees."[81]

Pike's *Morals and Dogma* originally included the published lectures accompanying the degrees of the *magnum opus*, the Pike ritual. Subsequent ritual revisions omitted these lectures. Technically, Pike's 1865 work, *Morals and Dogma*, was mainly a task of amending and editing material he had already tried out in published form. It was all of a piece, not a stand-alone, original discourse.

In the preparation of the rituals "Pike followed Zoroaster in believing that truth emerged from opposition and conflict. Men should strive not to efface the contradictions of life but to internalize them. Ritual, similarly, should teach purity and contemplation as well as aggression and heroism."[82] Persian dualism, for instance, was inherent in the revisions Pike proposed. The "royal secret," for example, is based on the concept of equilibrium, which makes no sense without a belief that opposing forces create a balance. With his literary gifts, his knowledge of ancient religions and mysteries, and his sense of the dramatic, Pike shaped himself into a superb ritualist.

It needs noting, however, that Pike's intellectual sources for his ritual revisions came to him in second-hand form. He was constantly disadvantaged by the deficiencies of the authors whom he read. Pike was influenced, for instance, by the dated work of William Stukeley, an eighteenth-century English Masonic writer and antiquarian who promoted, among many ideas, the Druids as kindred forerunners of the speculative craft. Pike read *about* ancient myths and religions, but not in their original languages. He came to Eastern philosophy through Thomas Maurice (*Indian Antiquities*, 1800) and Godfrey Higgins (*Anacalypsis*, 1836). Like Emerson, Pike kept up with French and English translations of the Persian poets and pursued the commentary of European writers such as F. Max Müller, Sir William Jones, and possibly Ernest Renan.

Pike read in French the works of the occultist Eliphas Levi (*Doctrine of Transcendental Magic*, 1855; *Key of the Grand Mysteries*, 1861; and *History of Magic*, 1860). Early in his career, Pike had learned French so he could practice law in New Orleans. While Levi was a prolific author, his scholarship on ancient mystery religions was riddled with errors and infelicities. Pike's rituals and subsequent commentary on craft and Scottish Rite degrees in *Morals and Dogma*, however, show the heavy footprints of Levi. Pike covers much ground wearing Levi's boots.

Pike, nevertheless, read widely, seriously, and deeply in accomplishing the necessary overhaul of the rituals. When completed, it would gradually transform the Rite in several subtle ways. Unlike the York Rite with its emphasis on a precision that insists on exact words and the learning of complex march steps, Pike gave the Scottish Rite poetic license. He was more concerned with ideas than the exact words, more with being understood than perfecting the details.

One of those main ideas centered on duty, "a stern voice of the daughter of God." This fits Victorian culture with obvious ease, recalling Tennyson, Kipling, and other poets of the time who examined duty as a virtue. The ethical value of duty fitted Masonry in every respect, too, since obligations were taken by the initiate as part of each degree. But Pike's rituals moved the concept of duty way beyond that which is owed to a brother Mason.

Pike made duty a social construct for Masonry to follow. This alteration of emphasis in the Scottish Rite rituals was a departure from Craft Masonry with its all-for-one and one-for-all sense that the lodge will take care of its own. This modification led, consequently, to a major transformation in American Freemasonry. Pike's rituals at some level provided the brotherhood with a social conscience; the Scottish Rite tread past traditional fraternal boundaries to become mindful of society as a whole. While it has seemed convenient to offer less noble reasons for the expansion of Masonic philanthropies in the twentieth century, such as the need for a more polished public image, it was Pike's idealism and gradual influence expressed in the degree work, as much as anything else, that served as an impetus for later fraternal outreach.

Pike, nevertheless, struggled in the challenge of setting the rituals and, therefore, the Rite on a new course. His preparation was laborious and rigorous: "After I had collected and read a hundred rare volumes upon religious antiquities, symbolism, the mysteries, the doctrines of the gnostics and the Hebrew and Alexandrian philosophy, the Blue degrees and many others, our Rite still remained as impenetrable enigmas to me at first. The monuments of Egypt with their hieroglyphics gave me no assistance."[83]

Morals and Dogma, a work of some 861 pages, which was not published until 1871, was a logical companion to Pike's work on the Scottish Rite rituals. He never claimed it "to be an entirely original production."[84] In fact, he noted in the preface that he had been "about equally Author and Compiler" and that he had "extracted quite half its contents from the works of the best writers and most philosophic or eloquent thinkers."[85] His extractions were later criticized for not complying with the canons of scholarship in failing to acknowledge sources, but the demands for proper citation were not as strong then as they were subsequently.

Pike's *Morals and Dogma* is the work of synthesis, not analysis. The book traces many abstract ideas by jumping around from religion to religion, not in the interest of tight systematic coherence, but in trying to demonstrate by a common-sense method that all human experience is basically the same. Pike was a capacious thinker who revealed a preference in *Morals and Dogma* for intuition as a desirable starting point from which he searched for evidence of a great principle.

His method of thought was inductive, an inversion of the scientific method of deduction which approached a body of evidence with the sharp tools of objective analysis. Pike, who was also an authority on comparative law, might be better understood as one who preferred the reasoning of common law (formed on precedents) over that of civil law (formed on codified principles). In Arkansas during Pike's time there, English common law was a more typical basis of conducting trials than the tradition of Roman civil law, as prescribed by Napoleonic legal reforms, which was the form followed in the courts of Louisiana.

Pike's exploration of world religions and philosophies may seem initially disjointed, but there is an underlying theory holding *Morals and Dogma* together. Before Carl Jung named the common themes of religious experience "archetypes"—themes which transcend all human communities regardless of time or location—Pike was thinking along the same lines. He was fascinated with detecting shared patterns in the varieties of religion. Wherever he could, he lifted up the similarities as evidence of a sameness in all human experience.

Pike believed there was a fundamental equivalency in all belief systems from pre-history and primitive societies to the Abrahamic faiths and Eastern philosophies. These common threads of belief made up Pike's "unity concept," the evidence of which rested for him within the fabric of linguistic exchanges, the shared words of Indo-European language families. Pike saw whole cloth woven as cultures came into contact with each other.[86] At the time Pike was working on *Morals and Dogma*, he likely became familiar with one of the pioneering works in comparative philology, F. Max Müller's *Science of Language* (1861, 1863).

Müller, an authority on Sanskrit and Eastern religions, taught at Oxford. Through his lectures and writings Müller was the foremost scholar to popularize philology and mythology. When Emerson sailed on his last trip abroad in 1872, he stopped in Paris, Naples, and Egypt. During his time in England on the return trip home, Emerson, the most famous American man of letters of the day, visited William Gladstone, John Ruskin, and F. Max Müller.[87] Emerson's homage to Müller was an indicator of how important the *Science of Language* was in America and how acceptable some of the derivative ideas from Müller were, ideas that showed up in Pike's work.

The organizing premise of the Pike rituals of the Scottish Rite and his *Morals and Dogma* was, according to Rex Hutchens, "religious cross-fertilization," so that knowledge of the ancients, whether from Jewish mysticism, Christian Platonism, or medieval hermeticism and alchemy (nourished specifically by a seventeenth-century sect of German mystics called Rosicrucians), was funneled into Freemasonry "along many diverse paths."[88] Divided into thirty-two chapters—one for each degree—*Morals and Dogma* became in time a source for ritualists of various fraternal orders "hoping to find," notes Mark Carnes, "fresh ritualistic motifs or bibliographical sources; the Scottish Rite had become the standard for ritualistic excellence."[89]

■ ■ ■

In the spring of 1865 while Pike was working on the rituals and *Morals and Dogma* at Big Creek, the Civil War came to an end with the surrenders of General Robert E. Lee to General Ulysses S. Grant at Appomattox Courthouse on April 9; General Joseph E. Johnston to General William T. Sherman near Durham Station, North Carolina, on April 26; General Richard Taylor to General Edward R. S. Canby at Citronelle, Alabama, on May 4; and, finally, General Kirby Smith to General Canby at New Orleans on May 26. This four-year struggle bearing various names—Civil War, War between the States, War of the Rebellion, War for Southern Secession, War for the Union, Second American Revolution—has been referred to as the last of the old wars and first of the new.

It was certainly new in American history with regard to the tremendous size of enlistments and the field armies, and the approximate 600,000 battle-incurred and disease-related deaths.[90] The dead and wounded of the Union and Confederate armies totaled more than in all other American wars combined, including World War II. Expenditures amounted perhaps to about $5 billion for both sides. It was, however, like older wars in the immeasurable pain and heartbreak that war inevitably brings. It radically transformed lives, Albert Pike's in particular. And what ultimate effect did this momentous clash of arms have on the nation? A perceptive response appears in the vivid words of Henry Seidel Canby, "The Civil War is a sword cut across American history. Before it there is one United States, and after it another, and yet there is only one body, and the arteries run through."[91] After the assassination of Abraham Lincoln, whose qualities of patience made him the South's best friend in the minds of many Union soldiers, a sentiment born of grief gave way to a national faith expressed by the view that the South had "slain Mercy, and now must abide by the sterner master, Justice."[92]

■ ■ ■

At the end of the war, Pike was left in legal limbo as he was excluded from the general amnesty granted to Confederate soldiers and officials by President Andrew Johnson's Amnesty Proclamation of May 29, 1865. Possibly his successful efforts in securing the allegiance of the Five Civilized Tribes to the Confederate States, Northern remembrance of the Pea Ridge scalping atrocities, and, as James Carter suggests, "the hatred of all Masons and all things Masonic by some leaders of the Anti-masonic movement still in the United States Congress"[93] (such as Thaddeus Stevens, a leader of the Radical Republicans) were causes for his exclusion from the general amnesty. Pike's problems with qualifying for a pardon were not likely related to his Masonic affiliations. In fact, his counterpart at Pea Ridge to whom he sent a copy of his order prohibiting scalping, Union General Samuel Ryan Curtis, was a Mason. It was not Masonry that was held against Pike.

Fearing that he might be arrested, Pike apparently headed for Mexico with his family but stopped for whatever reason in Boston, Texas, where he left his sixteen-year-old son Yvon in charge and headed for Shreveport. He then boarded a steamboat for New Orleans and, in turn, went up river to Memphis. There he made arrangements to open a law office with General Charles W. Adams, who, like Pike, was not only a native Bostonian but had migrated to Arkansas in the mid-1830s and had become a brigadier general in the Confederate army. While in Memphis, Pike also asked John Jennings Worsham, an Honorary Member of the Supreme Council and other (possibly Masonic) friends to petition for his pardon. On June 26, 1865, a petition with eighteen signatures was sent to Benjamin B. French, commissioner of public buildings in Washington, D.C., and a member of the Supreme Council, who in turn sent it on to Andrew Johnson, who upon the assassination of Lincoln had become the seventeenth president of the United States.

These efforts, together with a letter that Pike sent, through Benjamin French, to President Johnson "asking for special pardon under the President's proclamation of amnesty and pardon of May 26,"[94] ultimately bore fruit but not before the Grand Commander found it expedient to go to Canada. He spent about two months in Ottawa under trying conditions, noting irritably to Charles C. McClenachen, a Masonic friend, that he did not "expect Masonry to have energy or influence enough to obtain [him] a pardon."[95] The Grand Commander was anxious to have his rights of citizenship restored so that, as he told Samuel M. Todd, a future Sovereign Grand Inspector for Louisiana, he might "set vigorously to work extending the Rite."[96] Finally, on September 11, he received word that President Johnson had signed an order on August 30 that allowed him to return without interference by civil or military authorities, provided that he take an oath of allegiance and conduct himself as a loyal citizen.

With that presidential assurance Pike left shortly for New York City where he was involved with the printing of the Ritual of the Lodge of Perfection, which he had finally and completely revised during the past year or two. While in New York he called for a meeting of the Supreme Council at Charleston on November 16, 1865, the council not having met in more than three and a half years.

When it met, it lacked a quorum and so adjourned until the next day when Pike delivered his florid *Allocution*. He began by noting, "At the close of the great harvest of that pitiless reaper, Death, and while having paused through mere weariness he rests, we assemble from States widely distant from each other and not long since mad with all the direful passions of civil war, to kneel together once more around the altar of Scottish Masonry, to lament the dead, and to labour for the benefit of society, our country and humanity."[97]

The Grand Commander reported that he had completed all the rituals from the first through the thirty-second degree and that they had either been or were ready to be printed. "Ten years ago," he noted, "they were a heterogeneous and chaotic mass, in many parts of incoherent nonsense and jargon, in others of jejuneness; in some of the degrees, of absolute nothingness."[98]

Later in the 1865 *Allocution* Pike expressed concern about the membership of the Supreme Council, pointing out that there were no Inspectors General for seven states and vacancies existed in four others, too. He urged that the vacancies be filled; "and if the person elected for any State does not appear, in order to be qualified, we shall at once put him aside and select another."[99]

Before the Supreme Council adjourned to meet again on April 16, 1866, in Charleston, King Christian IX of Denmark, King Charles XV of Sweden, Prince Oscar of Sweden, and Grand Duke Constantine of Russia were unanimously elected to receive the thirty-third degree and rank of honorary membership in the Mother Council. Taliaferro P. Shaffner was authorized to confer the degree on these Masons of royal lineage. Given the uncertain status of the council, some may view this gesture as affrontery. Pike acted boldly by calculating the wise saying "Honors change manners and the prestige of the bestower."

A little over a month after the Supreme Council session of November 1866, Pike submitted his oath of allegiance and parole of honor to Secretary of State William H. Seward as required by President Johnson's order of August 30, 1865. He had not sought, meanwhile, a full pardon, believing that with the presidential order he was safe from arrest and prosecution for treason related to the Pea Ridge atrocities (he had been earlier indicted in the Federal Circuit Court for the Eastern District of Arkansas).[100] At the time he submitted his oath and parole to Seward he also asked the indictment for treason be dismissed. He was worried that he might lose more than his Little Rock property which had been seized and sold under the Confiscation Act of 1862. "Whether the indictment for treason against Pike and the proceedings against his other property were dropped by presidential order is not known."[101] Pike's position was that Johnson's order of August 30 was essentially a full pardon.

When the Supreme Council met in a seven-day session in April 1866, acting on a motion of Grand Secretary Mackey, it "proceeded [one morning] to the White House in a body and paid their respects to the President of the United States, who received them in a very courteous and fraternal manner,"[102] Johnson being a Mason and a member of Greeneville Lodge No. 119 (now No. 3) at Greeneville, Tennessee. Thus began the Supreme Council's custom, lasting into the middle of the twentieth century, of calling on the president during its sessions in Washington, D.C. In the course of the council's first social call at the White House, Johnson gave Pike his pardon, which "his Scottish Rite brethren, and perhaps others, secured" for the Grand Commander. But "Pike refused to accept the pardon because it required that he should pay $300 in costs in the suits by which his property had been confiscated and that he should never claim any property or proceeds from that seized and sold under the confiscation laws of the United States."[103] Pike believed that the court costs had already been deducted from the proceeds and that if he were to accept the pardon, it would imply his guilt of treason. Consequently, as Brown concludes, Pike's "conscience and conviction told him that he would do well enough without a pardon, and so it was to be."[104]

Not only was the Supreme Council's session of April 1866, which was a continuation of a meeting held the previous November, important for the initial call upon the president but for several decisions that were taken. Thirteen Active Members were on hand for this session, indeed an encouraging sign. (Five had submitted acceptable excuses.) To aid in the advancement of the Scottish Rite, the council authorized the Grand Commander to appoint Deputies. It also provided that Active Members should retain as compensation for their services, besides their expenses, 25 percent of the fees received for degrees. As a reflection of the expanding operation of the council, it authorized the purchase of office furniture and stationery for the Grand Commander and the Secretary General.

In response to Pike's request for a council of administration, "composed of the Chief Dignitaries, to be convened by the Grand Commander as frequently as circumstances may require,"[105] the council subsequently approved such a body as described in Article

XX of the *Statutes and Institutes of The Supreme Council, 33d for the Southern Jurisdiction of the United States* (1866). "The Council of Administration, or, if the title is preferred, the Executive Council," stated Pike in his *Allocution*, "should consist of the Grand Commander, the Lieutenant Grand Commander, the Secretary-General, the Grand Chancellor, the Grand Minister of State and the Treasurer-General."[106] Also, on Pike's recommendation, the Chamber of Deputies for Louisiana was abolished. The council requested the Grand Commander to prepare a manual for the degrees and to go ahead with the publication of *Morals and Dogma*.

Other actions taken by the council in this session of 1866 included the establishment of a committee to provide "a suitable Jewel" for the Grand Commander as "a token of appreciation of his services and his worth";[107] the unanimous election, on Pike's motion, of Albert Mackey as Lieutenant Grand Commander, which he promptly declined, preferring to continue as Secretary General but ranking as third officer of the council for life; and the approval of a motion requesting "an Act of Incorporation"[108] by the South Carolina legislature so that the council could hold real estate.

Besides these actions, the Supreme Council gave considerable attention to the internal feud that had been going on in the Northern Masonic Jurisdiction of the Scottish Rite. Suffice it to say that in May 1867 a union of the competing Supreme Councils of this jurisdiction was achieved. For over thirty years the presence of the Cerneau Supreme Council badly confused the Scottish Rite prospects in the northern states. Pike was consulted in May 1861 by two of the three contending councils, each seeking final, sole authority in the Northern Jurisdiction, while a sort of "Great Schism" ensued similar to the late-fourteenth-century crisis in the Christian Church when three papal claimants vied for the see and staff of St. Peter.[109]

Josiah H. Drummond, the new Grand Commander of the Northern Jurisdiction, a capable administrator as well as Masonic historian, informed Pike of the resulting compromise and asked that fraternal relations between the jurisdictions be reestablished.[110] Although Drummond was appreciative of Pike's labors in helping to resolve the schism in the Northern Jurisdiction, they strongly differed on constitutional grounds concerning the territorial division between the Northern and Southern Jurisdictions, a question that, as noted earlier, periodically caused friction between the jurisdictions. However, Pike in 1868 shared his recently overhauled thirty-third degree with the North.[111]

When the Supreme Council "closed in Ample Form and with the Sacred Numbers"[112] in 1866 to meet again in biennial session in 1868 at Charleston, Pike returned to Memphis, his law practice, and the continued work of the Scottish Rite. Two months later the Report of the Joint Committee of Fifteen, chaired by Senator William P. Fessenden of Maine, recommended that the former Confederate states were not entitled to representation and declared that the authority of Congress, rather than that of the president, was paramount in matters of Reconstruction. The Radical Republicans in

Congress and President Johnson were clearly on a collision course, which ultimately resulted in Johnson's impeachment by the House of Representatives and his trial by the Senate (February 24 to May 16, 1868). Johnson won acquittal by one vote.

■ ■ ■

Another disturbing result of Radical Reconstruction appeared in the form of the Ku Klux Klan, first organized as a young men's social club at Pulaski, Tennessee, in 1866. The six original founders, young, bored Confederate veterans, planned initially a social fraternity. According to most accounts, they were all from fine families, as each was properly educated and active in local church life. The Klan's name was derived from the Greek word "kuklos," meaning circle. Its real purpose, in the end, was to intimidate the southern black freedmen through nighttime rides by hooded, white-robed "Knights." The high-water mark of its activity was the period between 1868 and 1870.

From modest beginnings the Klan spread throughout Tennessee as an assertive opponent of the Union League, the Republican Party, and congressional Reconstruction policy. Because of its popularity, the Klan was reconstituted in 1867 at Nashville, with a high-sounding moral agenda of protecting southern whites from the indignities of Federal occupation, aiding impoverished survivors of Confederate casualties, defending the U.S. Constitution, and supporting laws commonly deemed valid. By 1871, because of the strict application of congressional legislation known as Force Laws, the Klan was practically effaced from the landscape, though small isolated pockets of it somehow survived.

Long before these strong congressional measures were enacted, "a public outcry against the Klan . . . began rising from the very Southern aristocracy whose interests the Ku Klux Klan had been organized to protect."[113] Nathan Bedford Forrest, the renowned Confederate cavalier, had resigned as Imperial Grand Wizard and officially dissolved the original Klan by 1869. Forrest spent the rest of his life denouncing the remnants of the Ku Klux Klan he had tried to deactivate once the guerilla tactics had crossed over the proprieties of the order's original purpose (and began damaging, too, Forrest's own business interests in railroads and insurance). Forrest appeared before a congressional hearing in June 1871, revealing very little of the Klan's membership or secrets. In spite of his cagy evasions during the interrogation and testimony, he insisted that the organization was "broken up in 1868, and never has existed since that time as an organization . . . and [was] to be no longer countenanced."[114]

Whether or not Albert Pike was ever involved with the Klan is a matter of conjecture. Walter Brown, in his definitive biography of Albert Pike, states that "one might reasonably surmise that Pike, considering his strong aversion to the Negro suffrage and his frustration at his own political impotence, would not have stood back from the Klan."[115] And in what appears to be an unreliable and discredited history of the Klan, as it is a 1920s apology for it, Susan Lawrence Davis flatly states without documentation that "General

Pike organized the Ku Klux Klan in Arkansas after General [Nathan Bedford] Forrest [the Grand Wizard] appointed him Grand Dragon of that Realm at the convention at Nashville, Tenn."[116] No documentation, such as diaries, correspondence, minutes of meetings, federal investigative reports, or testimony, has ever materialized to support the Davis claim.

Further, Pike never admitted, nor did Forrest ever reveal, that he was a member of the notorious Klu Klux Klan. Many men came forward years later to admit their former involvement in the Klan of early Reconstruction, almost as a proud badge of honor, but Pike never said or intimated a word. He seemingly had nothing to admit because he had probably nothing to hide. In the judgment of Walter Brown it is more likely that Pike was never a member of the Klan.[117] Pike's other major biographer offers a judicious comment: "Whether Pike played any part in the formation of the Klan will probably never be known. But even if he could have sympathized with the policy of passive resistance characterizing the organization in the beginning, he could never have countenanced the resultant terror and bloodshed that became the heritage of the Klan."[118]

The most exhaustive historical studies of the Klan's earliest incarnation, conducted by university scholars such as Allen W. Trelease (1971) and David M. Chalmers (1965, revised 1981),[119] either make little to no mention of Albert Pike as having a founding role in it during his years in Memphis or the mention is from the unsubstantiated Davis book. Trelease comments that much has been written about the Klan's organization at the top levels, but so much of it turns out to be "fictitious" and lacks proof. He says that because the Klan was sanctified by the "Lost Cause" myth (i.e., "the South shall rise again!") which was embraced by many Southerners down through the 1960s, the tendency was "to make it more widespread, more fully organized, more highly connected, and more noble than it actually was."[120] Charles Reagan Wilson explains that "the Ku Klux Klan had crucial Confederate connections that made it a part of the religion of the Lost Cause . . . so the Confederate link was a vital organizational factor."[121] Meanwhile, Pike was under suspicion and close scrutiny in both the North and the South at the time in question. Pike boasted no positive experience with the Confederacy as President Jefferson Davis had once informed him that charges of treason against the Arkansan might be preferred because of the line of military honor allegedly breached at Pea Ridge by the misconduct of the Cherokee troops.[122]

After 1862 Pike was practically *persona non grata* in the Confederate hierarchy, especially in the wake of his bad press and the question of his command that was widely aired in the aftermath of Pea Ridge. Pike held no sympathy with nor expressed any sentimentality for the Lost Cause myth. Furthermore, he was not likely to jeopardize his intense and cautious efforts to be restored in his rights as a U.S. citizen by flirting very earnestly with a militant rear guard such as the Klan.

Wilson offers a broad overview of the Klan as representing "the mystical wing of the Lost Cause, as the most passionate organization associated with this highly ritualized civil religion. Its mysticism was attained not through a disciplined meditation, but through the cultivation of a mysterious ambience, which fused Confederate and Christian symbols and created unique rituals."[123] Pike, even when portrayed as an authority on fraternal ritual, does not fit the profile of a rabid southern patriot or a Christian chauvinist. His own mystical interests were already long past the narrow definitions of southern cavalier myth-making.[124]

One of Nathan Bedford Forrest's biographers, Jack Hurst, discusses the role of Democratic Clubs (a local parallel organization to the Democratic Party) in the 1868 national election. Hurst explains that "Democratic Clubs often were virtually indistinguishable from the Klan in many Southern towns, and this appears to have been true in Memphis."[125]

In reporting a public meeting of the Democratic Club on July 7, 1868, Pike's newspaper, the *Appeal*, featured an article strongly disavowing a rumor that the Democratic Club was "a secret conclave." Moreover, Pike himself had been identified by another newspaper as the Club's president. As editor of the *Appeal* Pike published a casual refutation of the charge that he or the Democratic Club were doing anything underhanded, such as supplanting the established party apparatus.[126] If he thought differently about the accusation, thereby taking the matter seriously, it would more than likely have been answered with a weightier defense than his published breezy reply, for Pike was, after all, an experienced lawyer.

■   ■   ■

While these activities of national import were going on, the Supreme Council assembled for another biennial session on May 4, 1868, at Charleston. Pike reported in his *Allocution* that "after ten years, my long labor for the Rite is completed. The Rituals, from the 4th to the 32nd degree are printed and in the possession of the Brethren."[127] He had also prepared rituals for the three "Blue Degrees, degrees according to the Scottish Rite revised"[128] (for men who had these degrees according to the York Rite but were applying for admission to the Lodge of Perfection). He had finished also the ceremonies for funerals, the Lodge of Sorrow, Masonic baptism, louveteau, and adoption. He reported that *Morals and Dogma* was ready for publication in two volumes and that he was submitting a revision of the thirty-third degree to the council for adoption, which it subsequently did.

In his *Allocution* Pike devoted some attention to the Rite of Memphis, which he felt was "undoubtedly entitled to be called a Masonic Rite"[129] because some of its degrees were borrowed from the Scottish Rite. The Rite of Memphis came about after Napoleon Bonaparte's Egyptian campaign, and this "Oriental Rite" was instituted at Paris in 1814. By 1856 it offered ninety-seven degrees but had been "legally terminated both by governmental decree and by the edict of the highest Masonic authority in France" four years earlier, which is why it surfaced in America and England.[130] While the Rite of Memphis was quite active in some areas of the North, it had not made much progress in the South, nor was it likely to do so, in Pike's opinion. The Scottish Rite had no quarrel with this organization; for, as the Grand Commander felt, the world was big enough for them both.[131] Though an on-going feeble presence in American Masonry, it caused some minor agitation in the North after 1881 when two new Supreme Councils appeared again, one of which (Seymour-Peckham Council) was based on the Rite of Memphis; the other was known as the Thompson-Folger Council and more closely resembled the older Cerneau forms. Pike blasted them conjointly as "twin-headed" Cerneauism.[132]

An unpleasant subject which Pike took up in his *Allocution* and which the council dealt with later during the session centered on George Frank Gouley, the Grand Commander of the Knights Templar in Missouri and a thirty-second degree Mason of the Southern Jurisdiction. Gouley had taken exception to some features of the Scottish Rite, including what he thought were revelations of certain secrets of the York Rite in the twenty-ninth and thirtieth degrees as revised by Pike. He wanted the Supreme Council "to make it the law of our Rite that no one should receive the degree of Perfection who had not the American Royal Arch, and no one the degree of Rose Croix who had not that of American Masonic Templar."[133] Gouley forbade Missouri Knights Templar to be present for Scottish Rite degree conferrals unless the candidates were already members of the Royal Arch and the Commandery. Through the periodical *Freemason* he launched an attack on the Scottish Rite, to which Pike responded in *The Morning Herald*.[134] Moreover, at the council's session Pike preferred four separate charges against Gouley, including "Maligning the Ancient and Accepted Scottish Rite, in publications free to be read by the Profane [non-Masons]" and "Wilful and deliberate violation of his vows and obligations as a Knight Kadosh and Prince of the Royal Secret."[135]

A special committee on the charges recommended a tribunal, as called for by the *Statutes*, to try Gouley. Once formed, the tribunal found him guilty of all the charges. His punishment was the "Deprivation of all Rights and Privileges of the Masonry of the Ancient and Accepted Scottish Rite."[136] A year later Pike sent out to all Scottish Rite Masons of the Southern Jurisdiction a mandate detailing the case against Gouley.[137] "The York Rite in Missouri was in opposition to the adopted Ritual of the Scottish Rite, and the quarrel had all the possibilities of creating a breach between the two great Masonic orders of the nation."[138]

By 1872 Pike realized that steps should be taken to resolve this "family" quarrel. A committee of three, who were also Knights Templar, came forth with a recommendation to alter the passages in the twenty-ninth and thirtieth degrees to which Gouley had objected. Pike readily agreed. With the resolution of this problem, Gouley petitioned the Supreme Council for reinstatement and was thus restored to membership. In 1876, by action of the council he was invested with the rank and decoration of Knight Commander of the Court of Honor, an honor established as a Southern Jurisdiction innovation in 1870.[139]

■   ■   ■

Before the Supreme Council reassembled the following September (1868) in special session, primarily for the purpose of conducting a Lodge of Sorrow for several illustrious brothers, including Benjamin B. French, Grand Chancellor and former Grand Master of the District of Columbia, Pike was faced with hardship in Memphis. His law practice was not doing well; and the *Daily Appeal*, a newspaper he owned and edited, was barely keeping afloat. He finally found buyers who were willing for him to stay on as editor. However, he required a higher salary than they were willing to pay, and so his connection with the paper abruptly ended. Upon leaving he warned the new owners of the *Daily Appeal* about the dangers of black suffrage and cautioned against the Democrats' bid for the freedmen's vote vis-à-vis the Radical Republicans' competition for the same new constituents.[140]

The presidential campaign was already underway, and the freedmen's vote was important. The Republicans for the fourth time in American history selected a military hero, General Ulysses S. Grant, while the Democrats nominated former governor Horatio Seymour of New York. Although Grant won the electoral vote by 214 to 80, his popular majority was only 306,000 out of 5,715,000 votes cast. The black vote of more than 700,000 had decided the election. Pike's prediction had been borne out that the Republicans had a lock on new beneficiaries of suffrage.

Meanwhile, the Grand Commander went to St. Louis shortly after his leaving the *Daily Appeal* to attend the triennial convocation of the General Grand Chapter of Royal Arch Masons and the Grand Encampment of the Knights Templar as well as the adjourned session of the Supreme Council which followed. While in St. Louis he attended a banquet that the Grand Royal Arch Chapter of Missouri gave the General Grand Chapter. Several of the companions in attendance urged him to speak, and so "in response he thanked the Northern Masons for the magnanimity they had shown the Southern delegates"[141] and proposed that they mutually pledge to put aside all ill feelings and animosity. Two days later the Supreme Council met to conduct a Lodge of Sorrow and some minor business. Its next biennial session was planned for the early days of May 1870 in Baltimore, Maryland.

About two months after the St. Louis session, Pike went to Washington, D.C., to join his law partner Robert W. Johnson, a former United States and Confederate States senator from Arkansas. Pike's son Hamilton and General Charles W. Adams agreed to handle the local cases of the firm in which Pike was the senior partner while the Grand Commander and Johnson, who agreed to settle permanently in Washington, would deal with cases before the Supreme Court and claims before Congress and the executive departments. That both Pike and Johnson were "Rebel" lawyers proved a handicap to their Washington practice. The Grand Commander had not intended to make Washington his permanent home, but the sudden death of his favorite daughter, Isadore ("Issy"), on July 6, 1869, changed his mind. It would be too painful to remain at the family home in

Memphis. Thus he decided to start over, once again, and make Washington his steadfast home.

Along with his settlement in the capital came a decision "to move the Secretary General's office; to employ a full time secretary for the Secretary General's office; to 'leave Mackey the Secy. Gen., however.'"[142] For some time Pike had been frustrated by the lack of adequate fiscal and membership records for the Southern Jurisdiction. On several occasions during the previous ten years he had recommended to the Supreme Council that something needed doing to correct this problem. The stumbling block was Dr. Albert G. Mackey; though having practiced medicine for twenty years before devoting his full-time attention to Masonic writing, Mackey was afflicted with acutely anemic management skills. As the Secretary General, he was simply indifferent to the importance of accurate record-keeping.

Pike's patience with this annoying situation was exhausted by the summer of 1869. As a result, the headquarters of the Supreme Council, including the offices of the Grand Commander and Secretary General, were relocated in Washington where they have remained to the present. Interestingly, no evidence exists in the Supreme Council's official records or in Pike's correspondence to explain why the administrative offices were moved from Charleston to Washington, D.C., in 1870. Besides the Grand Commander's frustration with Mackey, as noted above, other factors that may have contributed to the decisive move north included Pike's establishment of a law office in Washington, a concern for the Northern Jurisdiction's thrusts into the District of Columbia and Maryland, the South's dimming prospects of national importance, and the prestige of the relocation at the seat of federal government.

■ ■ ■

The decade from 1859 to 1869, Pike's first ten years as Grand Commander, proved to be momentous for the nation and for the Supreme Council of the Scottish Rite, Southern Jurisdiction. A great civil war had been fought during these years with decisive results: the preservation of the Union, the destruction of slavery, the northern domination of the economy and the government, the temporary "economic chaos and social revolution"[143] in the former Confederate states, and the staggering loss of life and property.

Not only did the Supreme Council survive the war years and the war's bitter aftermath, but under Pike's superb leadership its organization, administration, and membership were remarkably strengthened. The size of the council was increased from nine to thirty-three in order to overcome parochialism; the rituals were completely revised and published; *Morals and Dogma*, a series of lectures on the degrees, was prepared for publication, eventually becoming a Masonic classic; a council of administration, to advise and support the Grand Commander, was established; assistance to the Northern Supreme Council in its reorganization was rendered; *Statutes* (1866) pertaining to organization and operation were adopted; and membership throughout the Southern Jurisdiction was increased to some degree. James D. Richardson referred to Albert Pike as "the Moses of the Rite."[144] In so far as the image of Moses is that of a leader and liberator, Pike similarly took the Scottish Rite out of the bondage of poverty and depressed morale into a better land of its seeking. Pike, as the Rite's "Moses," deliverer of a new law, leader of an exodus, did not stand still, for his deeper conviction insisted that "it is the motionless and stationary that most frets and impedes the current of progress." The Masons who hesitate to labor for the order's improvement are like "the solid rock or stupid tree, rested firmly on the bottom, and around which the river whirls and eddies."[145] Pike crossed the Potomac mindful of a new day for himself and the Scottish Rite.

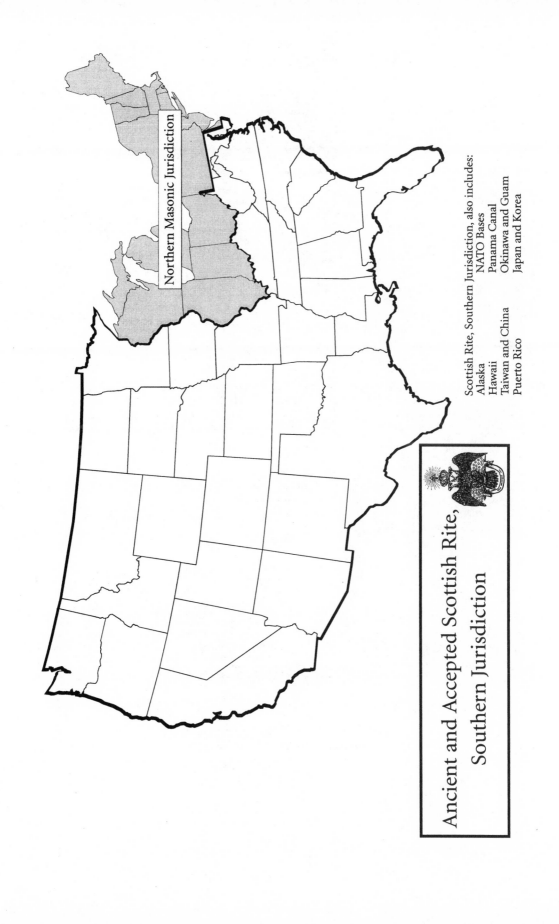

Northern Masonic Jurisdiction

Scottish Rite, Southern Jurisdiction, also includes:
Alaska   NATO Bases
Hawaii   Panama Canal
Taiwan and China   Okinawa and Guam
Puerto Rico   Japan and Korea

Ancient and Accepted Scottish Rite,
Southern Jurisdiction

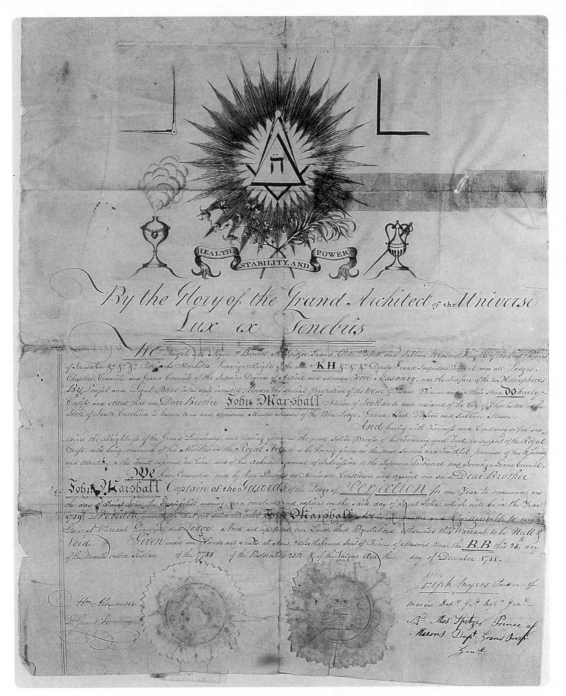

Patent for Charleston Lodge of Perfection for
John Marshall of Scotland, December 1788

Frederick Dalcho patent, 1801

Circular throughout the two Hemiſpheres·

———— •✦✦✦✦✦• ————

UNIVERSI TERRARUM ORBIS ARCHITECTONIS GLORIA AB INGENTIS.

Deus Meumque Jus.

ORDO AB CHAO.

F ROM the Eaſt of the Grand and Supreme Council of the moſt Puiſſant Sovereigns, Grand Inſpectors General, under the Celeſtial Canopy of the Zenith, which anſwers to the 32 deg. 45. Min. N. L.

To our Illuſtrious, moſt Valiant and Sublime Princes of the Royal Secret, Knights of K. H. Illuſtrious Princes and Knights, Grand Ineffable and Sublime, Free and Accepted Maſons of all degrees, Ancient and Modern, over the ſurface of the two Hemiſpheres.

To all thoſe to whom theſe Letters ſhall come :

Health, Stability and Power·

At a meeting of Sovereign Grand Inſpectors General in Supreme Council, of the 33d. degree, duly and lawfully eſtabliſhed and congregated, held at the Grand Council Chamber, on the 14th day of the 7th Month, called 5563, Anno. Lucis. 5802, and of the Chriſtian Æra, the 10th day of October, 1802·

Union, Contentment and Wisdom·

The Grand Commander informed the Inſpectors, that they were convened for the purpoſe of taking into conſideration, the propriety of addreſſing circular Letters to the different Symbolic Grand Lodges, and Sublime Grand Lodges and Councils throughout the two Hemiſpheres, explanatory of the origin and nature of the Sublime Degrees of Maſonry, and their eſtabliſhment in South-Carolina·

When a reſolution to that effect was immediately adopted, and a committee, conſiſting of the Illuſtrious Brethren, Doct. Frederick Dalcho, Doctor Iſaac Auld and Emanuel De La Motta, Eſqr. Grand Inſpectors General, was appointed to draft and ſubmit ſuch letter to the Council at their next meeting.

At a meeting of the Sovereign Grand Inſpectors General, in Supreme Council of the 33d. &c. &c. &c. on the 10th day of the 8th Month called Chiſleu, 5563. A, L. 5802, and of the Chriſtian Æra, this 4th day of December, 1802.

The

Manifeſto of 1802, firſt page

Free Masons throughout the two Hemispheres, may form but one band of Brotherhood. "Be-
" hold how good, and how pleasant it is for Brethren to dwell together in unity."

They respectfully salute your Supreme Council, by the *Sacred Numbers*.

Charleston, South-Carolina, the 10th day of the 8th Month, called Chisleu, 5563, A. L. 5802,
and of the Christian Æra, this 4th day of December, 1802.

> FREDERICK DALCHO, K. H—P. R. S. Sovereign Grand
> Inspector General of the 33d, and Lieu-
> tenant Grand Commander in the United
> States of America.
>
> ISAAC AULD, K. H—P. R. S. Sovereign Grand Inspector
> General of the 33d.
>
> E. DE LA MOTTA, K. H—P. R. S. Sovereign Grand In-
> spector General of the 33d, and Illustri-
> ous Treasurer General of the H. Empire.

The above report was taken into consideration, and the Council was pleased to express the highest approbation of the same.

Whereupon Resolved, that the foregoing report be printed and transmitted to all the Sublime
and Symbolic Grand Lodges, throughout the two Hemispheres.

> *[signature]* K. H—P. R. S. Sovereign Grand
> Inspector General of the 33d, and Grand
> Commander in the U. States of America.

True Extract from the deliberations of the Council.

> *[signature] Ab: Alexander*
>
> K. H—P R. S Sovereign Grand
> Inspector General of the 33d, and Illustrious
> Secretary General of the H. Empire.

Deus Meumque Jus.

Manifesto of 1802, last page

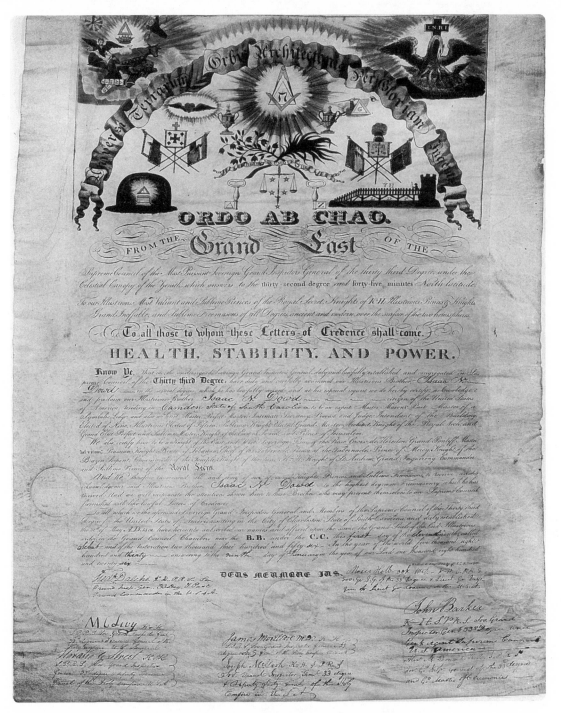

Patent of Issac N. Dowd, January 9, 1826, signed by
Dalcho, Holbrook, Levy, Moultrie, and Barker

List of the Most Illustrious and Puissant Sovereign Grand Inspectors General composing the Grand & Supreme Council of the 33° Degree, duly and lawfully organized and constituted under the C.C. of the zenith answering to 33 47 North Latitude and to the Meridian of 2.30 West Longitude.

No	Names	Under Military Quality Masonic Quality	Grade	Initiation	Native Birth	Place of Birth	Present Residence	Avocation	Religious Persuasion	Remarks
1	Isaac Auld	M.D. M.S.G.J.S. Grand Commr 33 & S.P.R.S.	33° & S.P.R.S.	May 10. 1802	1770	Pennsylvania	Edisto Island	Physician	Congregational	Senior 1808 & 1814
2	Frederick Dalcho	M.D. M.S.G.J.S. Past. Dr. Commr.	33 & S. & S.L.	May 28. 1801	1770	Maryland	Charleston. S. No.	Protestant Epis. priest	Episcopalian	
3	Hanns Kloss	M.D. M.S.G.J.S. St. Commr.	33° S.G.J.C.	24 y 9el 1722	1729	Wetstein Mass	Ditto	Physician	Presbyterian	
4	Moses C. Levy		32. 2. 1m y 8 16	May 7. 1802	1729	John, Holland	Ditto	Merchant	Hebrew	
5	James Moultrie	M.G. M.J.C. & Me.	33. S.G.J.C.	August 3. 1802	1742	Charleston S. Ca.	Ditto	Physician	Episcopalian	
6	Emanuel de la Motta		32. S.G.J.C.	July 9. 1822	1760	Sandston Conn.	Ditto	Merchant	Presbyterian	
7	Alexander McDonald		33. S.G.J.C.	July 9. 1823	1769	Hampton. McCa.	Ditto	Merchant	Catholic	
8	Joseph McCosh		33. S.G.J.C.	July 9. 1835	1756	Lisbon, Holland	Ditto	Resident	Presbyterian	
9	John Barker	Esq. D.M. & J.P.	33. S.J.C.	May 13. 1823	1798	Wallingford Conn.	Ditto	Farmer	Presbyterian	
10	John Rech		33° S.G.J.C.	March 30. 1823	1762	Lisbon, Holland	Ditto	Greek	Catholic	
11			32. S.J.C.	Oct. 31. 1794	1794	City of N.Y.	Ditto	Printer	Presbyterian	

A true extract from the Records, Grand Book of the date, 33°——
day of 12th month, Anno... A.M. 5731... A.M. 5731.

Signed Jno Carter, S.P.R.S.

Since the explt died. 33° Degree & Chl. in the United States of America.

Albert Pike, ca. 1850

Albert Pike on the eve of the Civil War, ca. 1859

The Supreme Council relocated in 1870 from Charleston, South Carolina. The first House of the Temple was at 433 Third Street, NW, in Washington, D.C., which became Albert Pike's home in his final years.

Vinnie Ream (Hoxie), ca. 1870s, sculptor of the full-scale statue of Abraham Lincoln in the U.S. Capitol. Albert Pike confided in her and conferred upon her the degrees of the French Rite of Adoption. Courtesy of the Library of Congress.

*Albert Pike, ca. 1875, as Grand Commander, in
the Matthew Brady studio of Washington, D.C.*

Albert Pike Monument, dedicated October 23, 1901, in what is currently called Judiciary Square

Double-headed eagle pendant of the 33°,
Scottish Rite Jewel belonging to
Grand Commander Albert Pike

Scottish Rite jewel belonging to
Grand Commander Albert Pike

*Masonic chart of the Scottish Rite,
1874, in possession of the Scottish
Rite Museum of Our National
Heritage, Lexington, Massachusetts*

President Theodore Roosevelt visits Scottish Rite Temple in Little Rock, Arkansas, October 25, 1905

Supreme Council under Grand Commander James D. Richardson, seated center, *ca. 1908. Note George Flemming Moore,* pictured furthest back in arch.

*Original House of
the Temple at Third
and E Streets, NW,
Washington, D.C.,
ca. 1910. Note spit-
toons on sidelines.*

Breaking ground for the House of the Temple, 1911. Left to right: Stirling Kerr Jr., the Reverend William Tayloe Snyder, James D. Richardson, Francis J. Woodman, William L. Boyden.

Preparing cornerstone for Mason's ceremony at the House of the Temple, Washington, D.C., October 1911

*Theodore Roosevelt in the East, holding gavel and wearing
apron, collar, and jewel of Worshipful Master, 1912*

Sept 30, 1912.

House of the Temple
under construction,
September 30, 1912.
Note boy on roller
skates on north side
of building.

House of the Temple under construction, April 7, 1913, view from south-east corner of building. Note blacksmith's shop, right, James A. Meyers Horse Shoeing.

HARRIS & EWING
WASHINGTON, D.C.

JUNE 30, 1913.

House of the Temple under construction, June 30, 1913. Note horse-drawn wagon and teamsters, and portable furnace.

JOHN RUSSELL POPE
ARCHITECT
527 FIFTH AVENUE

SUBJECT FILE:
House of the Temple

SPECIAL
STATEMENT

NEW YORK 12/19/16

SCOTTISH RITE TEMPLE, WASHINGTON, D.C.

Recalc. OK Net cost of Exterior and Interior contracts - $1,301,581.75 •

Recalc. OK Net cost of Furniture, carpets, Hangings, etc. 75,330.57 •

Total contracts....... 1,376,912.32 •

1-1/4% •

$ 17,211.40 . OK

This statement ~~and~~ if correct as to items extensions and additions on which commission is based is correct and payable in accordance with Resolution and authority of Executive Committee.

Rosenbaum
Chairman

To
Chas. E. Rosenbaum, Esq., 33°,
Chairman, Executive Committee,
c/o Harris & Ewing, Washington, D.C.

Received payment
Jan 8 1917
John Russell Pope

John Russell Pope's statement and architectural commission, December 19, 1916

*Aerial perspec-
tive of the
House of the
Temple, by
Lieutenant
William J.
Jacobi, Air
Service, U.S.
Army, 1920*

Costumed Scottish Rite degree team, ca. 1917. Center, seated, *Charles S. Lobingier with ceremonial mace in hand.*

CHAPTER V

The Washingtonian Pike
1870–1891

᠌᠌᠌᠌᠌᠌᠌᠌᠌᠌

In 1869—the off year between the biennial sessions of the Supreme Council, which had met the preceding year in Charleston and Washington, D.C., and was already in preparation for the session approaching in Baltimore—the first transcontinental railroad (central route) in the United States was completed on May 10; and six months later, the Suez Canal, a 104-mile, sea-level waterway connecting the Mediterranean and the Red Seas, was opened. Both were milestones in the history of modern transportation; the former held enormous consequences for the development of the Scottish Rite in the Southern Jurisdiction, which embraced all the region west of the Mississippi River, and the latter engineering feat shortened the water route between Europe and the Far East by several thousand miles.

The selection of Baltimore as the site of the biennial session, which began on May 2, 1870, came about in order to reduce objection to the presence of the Scottish Rite in Maryland's most burgeoning port city. Carter suggests that the opposition to the Rite there was perhaps because Pike and other members of the Supreme Council had once been prominent in the Confederate forces.[1] Possibly so, though sympathies in Baltimore tended not to favor the Union. Undoubtedly, another reason for holding this session in Baltimore was to underscore the fact that Maryland lay within the Southern Jurisdiction, since the Northern Jurisdiction of the Scottish Rite had signaled its desire for expansion into the Old Line State.

The session, which met at the Masonic Hall for six days, dealt with several important items of business, including a provision that "on condition that the office of the Secretary General be moved to Washington, D.C., a salary was fixed at $1,000 per annum plus 10% of money collected from the sale of publications in addition to the fees already established by law."[2] The Committee of Jurisprudence's report, which was adopted, provided that the Supreme Council could confer the thirty-third degree upon anyone Masonically eligible, but only those Masons who were at least thirty-five years old could be elected as Active Members. Other resolutions that were approved called for the Secretary General "to prepare a roll of all Active and Honorary Members of the Supreme Council from its organization with pertinent data included" and the appropriation of $300 "for the transcription of records in a 'Book of Gold.'"[3]

In his "Alloquium" (*Allocution*), which was the first time the term was used for the Grand Commander's report, Pike proposed the joint publication of an official bulletin for both the Northern and Southern Jurisdictions and the establishment of a Court of Honor. As it turned out, the *Official Bulletin* was confined to the Southern Jurisdiction, and the first issue was finished one month after the session. In "Prefatory to No. 1" of the *Official Bulletin*, the Grand Commander stated the nature and purpose of the new publication:

> The Bulletin of the Supreme Council for the Southern Jurisdiction of the United States, is intended to be published at intervals of not more than four months, and as much oftener as may be found necessary, to furnish official information of the acts of that Body, of the Council of Administration, and of the Grand Commander.
>
> It will be strictly official and historical, containing information of the actions of the Supreme Council at its sessions, the important reports made to it, the statutes adopted, the resolutions, edicts, and decisions of the body, the acts and decisions of the Council of Administration, and the mandates and rulings of the Grand Commander.
>
> Each number will contain also the latest information in regard to the doings of Foreign Supreme Councils and Grand Orients.
>
> It will not be a vehicle for essays, discussions or disputations; but in regard to domestic matters, will furnish under the head of "Unofficial," the current information in regard to Consistories and Subordinate Bodies of the obedience, and such extracts from Foreign Bulletins, and other documents, Official and Historical, as may be interesting and valuable.
>
> The Bulletin will be published at the expense of the Supreme Council.[4]

During the first two years of its publication, Pike, as editor, "without compensation," brought out five numbers comprising a volume of 660 pages. Each number of the *Official Bulletin* was divided into five sections: "1st. *Official.* 2d. *Domestic Unofficial.* 3d. *Foreign.* 4th. *Historical.* 5th. *Miscellaneous.*"[5] For the first volume there were some 100 subscribers and for the first two numbers of the second, only 60. These well-intended endeavors badly miscalculated the depth of members' pockets and interests.

At the session in Baltimore the Supreme Council was supposed to act on a proposed statute for the establishment of a Court of Honor but postponed consideration until the next biennial session. However, several Active Members requested earlier action, and so

Pike submitted a written ballot to the council, which was to be returned to the Secretary-General at "1418 F Street, Washington City." He announced on June 8, 1870, that the statute had been unanimously approved, thereby establishing "a Court of Honour, of those who have deserved well of the Ancient and Accepted Scottish Rite, to be composed of Sublime Princes of the Royal Secret."[6] Two ranks of the Knights of the Court of Honor were established: Knight Commanders and Grand Crosses of Honor. They were to be elected by a three-fourths majority vote of those present at a meeting of the Supreme Council. Section 6 of the statute contained the significant proviso regarding a Scottish Rite Mason's request for an honor: "The Rank and Decoration of Knight Commander of the Court of Honour shall never be asked or applied for by any person; and if asked or applied for, shall be refused. And no fee or charge shall ever be made for the said Rank and Decoration, or those of the Grand Cross of the Court of Honour."[7] In another section of this statute the Grand Commander was designated Praefect of the Court of Honor and the Lieutenant Grand Commander, Pro-praefect.

With the institution of the Knight Commander of the Court of Honor, a means of honoring those who had contributed to the Scottish Rite of the Southern Jurisdiction was not only created but a screening process for candidates for the thirty-third degree was in effect established. Henceforth, candidates for the thirty-third degree were drawn only from the pool of Knights Commander of the Court of Honor. These honors reflected what Carter has considered "one of the major problems in the propagation of the Rite," namely, "the finding of the right man in a given territory to do the work. Pike was constantly looking for such men."[8]

Notable, too, general membership in the Southern Jurisdiction during the transitional decades of the 1870s and '80s, when the headquarters was moved from Charleston to Washington, was puny. It is probable that at no time before 1860 did the Scottish Rite exceed five hundred members for the entire United States. Statistical reports did not appear before 1880, so the estimates remain vague, but even during Albert Pike's most productive years as Grand Commander, the Southern Jurisdiction never counted much more than several thousand total members. The trajectory of expansion headed upward under Pike, but the increments were small and, when compared to other fraternal groups, the numbers made the Rite borderline in its influence until the twentieth century:

MEMBERSHIP IN THE SOUTHERN JURISDICTION[9]

Year	Members
1880	1,150
1885	1,519
1890	2,658
1895	5,819
1900	10,570
1905	23,473

■　■　■

But not all of the Grand Commander's attention during his early years in Washington was directed to the work of the Supreme Council, the need for finding able men to provide leadership in the council, or his law practice. Rather, he also enjoyed the companionship of his family and "the affection of women, both young and old, one of his maxims being that it was 'no small thing to have the good opinion of good women.' He thought it absolutely absurd that people often said it was hard for an old man to love the young ardently because the young could not return love to the old."[10] In Vinnie Ream he found such a young woman; she was only nineteen when they first met in 1866 at the Capitol in Washington.

Attractive and vivacious, she was a budding sculptor who had rendered busts of several senators and was working on a statue of President Lincoln at the time of his assassination. Her figure of the martyred president, which was unveiled in 1871, was her principal claim to fame.[11] Apparently, the only bust from the life of Pike in the possession of the Supreme Council is a fine likeness that Vinnie had sculpted in plaster.[12]

Vinnie Ream was born September 25, 1847, in a log cabin out on the frontier of Madison, Wisconsin. With the hope of increasing their financial prospects, her family moved to western Missouri when she was ten. Her father was a government surveyor who ended up in Fort Smith, Arkansas, in the real estate business at the moment the Civil War began. The family of five (Vinnie had a brother and a sister) made their way with considerable difficulty through Confederate lines into the city of Washington. Her father, now partially disabled with rheumatism, obtained a government job, while Vinnie secured a clerkship in the post office.

Sometime in 1863 she visited the studio of the sculptor Clark Mills in a wing of the Capitol. On the spur of the moment she auditioned for him, working up on the spot a clay model of an Indian chief's head. Mills agreed to accept her as a part-time art student and from there she was soon making busts of members of the Congress and the Senate. "Her work found such favor that late in 1864 Congressional friends arranged for her to model a bust of President Lincoln." Lincoln wanted no part of the project, but "on hearing that she was a poor girl making her own way he granted her half-hour daily sittings for five months."[13] The artist and her subject started and remained on good terms. One of her prized possessions was a partial draft of the Emancipation Proclamation given her by Lincoln.[14]

Vinnie Ream was working on the Lincoln bust when he was assassinated. After the president's death she was awarded a large federal commission, despite Mary Todd Lincoln's disapproval on the grounds that Vinnie was much too young, to create a full-scale marble statue of Lincoln to stand in the Capitol rotunda. She was the first woman to win such a government contract. In January 1871, with much public attention and in a grand ceremony, the completed Carrara marble statue was unveiled. It was instantly acclaimed.

While Pike loved her, he realized the handicap of their considerable difference in age (38 years) and early on stated that "as I am not so insane to expect the love which you could feel for one far younger . . . I am not in danger of misunderstanding you: and I shall try not to come to love too much and so make love a misery."[15] Pike's love for Vinnie blossomed privately but was declared publicly. Their abiding friendship, perhaps resembling aspects of Shaw's *Pygmalion* (subsequently made into the Broadway musical *My Fair Lady*), was reflected in a privately-printed book of poems, *Hymns to the Gods and Other Poems*, that he dedicated to her.[16] Another instance of his strong affection for her was shown in part in a letter of October 20, 1877: "To all Freemasons in all Countries, to whom this Letter may come: Miss Vinnie Ream, Daughter by adoption of the Sovereign Grand Commander of the 33° of the Ancient and Accepted Scottish Rite of Freemasonry for the Southern Jurisdiction of the United States, has received at his hands the degrees of the Ancient French Rite of Adoption; and is by virtue of the same entitled to the generous and kindly consideration and brotherly regard of all genuine Freemasons, wheresoever she may be in any Country where Masonry is."[17]

About twelve years after the Grand Commander and Vinnie met, she married young Lieutenant Richard L. Hoxie, U.S. Army Corps of Engineers, a wealthy West Point graduate. The Hoxies, in time, became socially prominent in Washington while she continued her career as a sculptor, rendering, among several works, an impressive statue of Admiral David Farragut of Civil War fame which was placed in Farragut Square in the center of the city. The Hoxies "established themselves in a brick mansion on Farragut Square in which she presided over one of Washington's best known political salons."[18]

During the twenty-five years of what Brown has called "a beautiful friendship that lasted until Pike's death,"[19] Vinnie and he kept in touch mainly through correspondence as they were often separated because of Pike's extensive travels and her own career with its increasing social demands. Her marriage was apparently no obstacle to their long-lasting companionship, which, for him, with the growing afflictions of body, including rheumatic gout, and the perpetual inadequacy of purse, must have been a source of some happiness.[20]

■ ■ ■

In the early 1870s Pike not only found Washington "a hard world for a rebel to live in"[21] but experienced, among several problems, the difficulty of payment of printing bills owed by the Supreme Council, a part of which involved the cost of publishing *Morals and Dogma,* whose first two dozen copies Macoy, the Masonic publisher, sent to the Grand Commander on March 2, 1872. Robert Toombs, the distinguished Georgia lawyer and former Confederate secretary of state and later a brigadier general, offered to loan Pike $3,000 to meet the printing expenses, $2,000 of which he received in installments of $1,000 apiece.

Despite these frustrations, the Grand Commander, while improving the translations of words and symbols of the revised Scottish Rite rituals, undertook the study of the religions of the ancient Hindus and the ancient Persians as found respectively in the

Rig-Veda and the Zend-Avesta. "Because of these studies a legend has grown up that Pike was a Sanskrit scholar; he was not, and he did not claim to be."[22] Rather, he made use of translations by well-known scholars, just as the New England lecturer and essayist Ralph Waldo Emerson had done thirty years before Pike.[23]

The Grand Commander was well into these studies by the spring of 1872 when the biennial session, which had originally been scheduled to convene in San Francisco, met in the "Orient of Louisville," Kentucky, on May 6. (The designation of states as orients appeared later.) Prior to this session, Pike informed the Active Members that they each could nominate for Knight Commander of the Court of Honor two Sublime Princes of the Royal Secret and that each consistory could nominate one. Thus, twenty-two thirty-second degree Masons received "the decoration of Knight Commander of the Court of Honour," as did twelve "Honorary Inspectors-General."[24] Later in the session three Honorary Members and seven Princes of the Royal Secret were also elected to receive the rank and decoration of the Knight Commander of the Court of Honor. In addition the council unanimously elected William Edward Leffingwell of Iowa to receive the Grand Cross of the Court of Honor. He was the first to receive this high honor.

In his *Allocution* for this session Pike spoke of a desire to have the rituals translated into French, German, and Spanish and recommended that the Supreme Council plan to build a "Sanctuary" or headquarters in Washington, D.C., and to institute a charity fund that would draw interest for widows and orphans, all of which slowly came to pass. Every one of these fresh ideas were prescient innovations. He reported that he had visited during the previous summer Illinois, Michigan, and Wisconsin in the Northern Jurisdiction, met the Deputies of those states, and attended "a Session of the Council of Deliberation of Illinois."

Wherever he went, Pike was hospitably received with fraternal affection "by hundreds who a few years ago, had held me enemy and rebel, and invaded the land which my sons aided to defend. The sons and brothers of many of them had fallen in that war, as one of my sons had; and they, no doubt, thought, when the war ended at last, that they could never forgive us, as we thought we could never forgive them." He added, "but Masonry, like a white-robed angel of Peace and Love, had taught me and them alike another Lesson—that to love is better than to hate; and that forgiveness is wiser than revenge."[25]

Somewhat in that spirit, the Amnesty Act, removing disabilities from all but the most prominent (some 500) former Confederates, became law about ten days after the Supreme Council's session of 1872 ended. Six months later President Grant had no trouble in winning reelection over Horace Greeley. Greeley was the Liberal-Republican-Democratic nominee (having been a leader in a political coalition formed by Radical Republican reactions toward the South and corruption in the Grant administration) and renowned editor of the *New York Tribune*, who died one month after the election, after the exhausting national campaign schedule.

About six weeks after this election, Pike sent out a letter proposing that a Congress of the Supreme Councils of the Scottish Rite should meet in Washington, D.C., on the second Monday in May 1874, for the purpose of discussing problems, ideas, and relations with each other and with other Masonic bodies. For some time he had felt there was a need for such a meeting; and in April, prior to the session of 1872, he had received a letter from Antonio De S. Ferreira, Sovereign Grand Commander of the Supreme Council of Peru, calling on him "as the head of 'the oldest [Supreme Council] in the Masonic world,'"[26] to request a Congress of the Supreme Councils.

But the proposal fell on deaf ears, for no such meeting took place in 1874; however, a year later one was attempted in Lausanne, Switzerland, for which Pike drafted "Articles of Confederation between the several Supreme Councils," which were adopted by the southern council. Ironically, the "Articles" were not represented at the Lausanne Congress, as its delegate, Ebenezer S. Shaw, was taken ill. The eighteen Supreme Councils, which attended in response to the invitation of the Supreme Council of France, reached agreement on protecting each other's jurisdictions and on acting in unison in recognition of other Supreme Councils.

• • •

Meanwhile, the country was stricken by a depression that began with the Panic of 1873, when the great banking house of Jay Cooke and Company of Philadelphia closed its doors. A combination of forces had brought this about: wild speculation in railroad construction, widespread watering of corporate stock, overexpansion in industrial and agricultural development attended by an unfavorable balance of trade, and European investors calling in their American loans as the depression became worldwide in nature. The inevitable results for the United States were foreclosures on farms and factories and widespread unemployment.

Added to these distressing developments were the revelations of corruption at all levels of government. From the bilking of New York City by the Tweed Ring of upwards of $200 million; the Treasury Department's farming out of uncollected taxes to J. D. Sanborn, who then proceeded to collect and keep about one-half of some $425,000 from corporations; the wholesale "buying" of entire state legislatures by corporate interests and political machines; to the defrauding of the federal government of millions of dollars in taxes on distilled whiskey by the "Whiskey Ring" in St. Louis—all made for a dismal political picture of the country in the 1870s.

"The general atmosphere was one of profound discouragement," as Carter notes, "when the Supreme Council opened its Session in Washington, D.C., on May 4, 1874."[27] Only seven of the twenty Active Members and only four of the Honorary Members were on hand. The report of the "Committee on the Doings of Subordinate Bodies" showed a deplorable lack of information. No totals were given concerning the membership at large, the number of candidates admitted, or the income from fees and dues collected per year. This led the Supreme Council to adopt a resolution calling on the Secretary-General to "present a tabular abstract of the returns received by him."[28]

In his *Allocution* for this session (1874), Pike expressed his view as guardedly optimistic about the future of the Southern Jurisdiction of the Rite, believing that its condition was not "sound or healthy," but that it was "becoming so."[29] But he realized "that of the 32ds in our jurisdiction there is not one in every ten, if there is one in every twenty, who really knows anything about the Rite."[30] Moreover, he felt that both the thirty-second and thirty-third degrees were being cheapened by their high rate of conferment.

Further in his *Allocution* the Grand Commander unleashed his disappointment that little had been done towards providing funds for the building of a "Sanctuary" in the nation's capital and the creation of a charity fund. He had had stock certificates for the "Sanctuary" printed up and had distributed some of them among the Active Members and other Scottish Rite Masons. From their prospective offer of investment, the Supreme Council could have purchased a corner lot at Delaware Avenue and C Street, NE, which was near the Capitol. No doubt the current depression created an adverse effect on the purchase of the certificates and the expected contributions to the charity fund, but by the next session the council was installed in a sanctuary at the corner of Seventh and D Streets, NW, "over the Bank of the Republic."[31]

The session of 1876 opened on May 29 so as to coincide with the seventy-fifth anniversary of the Supreme Council, and on the evening of the thirty-first a "social meeting" was held to celebrate its founding in Charleston. In his *Allocution*, Pike "regretted that so little which is authentic is known as to the founders, and so little as to the history, for a half century of our Supreme Council."[32]

Elsewhere in the *Allocution* he noted that three of the founders—Emanuel de la Motta, Israel de Lieben, and Moses Levy—who were "conscientious Hebrews" and Knights Rose Croix (eighteenth degree) "in accordance with the old Rituals" would have found that degree, as exemplified in the Northern Jurisdiction, "a strictly and intensely Christian degree." He felt that "if our Rituals of any degree were such a Hebrew or Mohammedan residing here could not conscientiously receive that degree by them [a particular Supreme Council], he could go elsewhere and obtain it."[33] Grand Commander Josiah H. Drummond of the Northern Jurisdiction considered it law that a brother who was resident in one jurisdiction could not seek degrees in another without the former's consent. Pike agreed with him in principle but said there was no such law.[34]

Later in the *Allocution*, the Grand Commander reported that the Grand Master of Masons in Georgia wanted to adopt the Pike ritual for the three symbolic degrees. Pike "advised against it, suggesting rather that the Lodges be chartered to work in the ritual, if they requested it, as was done in Louisiana."[35] The Grand Commander went on to make a sharp criticism of American Masonry:

Our American Masons generally have heretofore seemed to imagine that there is no Masonry entitled to the name, in the world, outside of the United States; and that there is but one legitimate Rite of Masonry, the "York Rite." There neither is nor ever was a York Rite. The very name asserts a falsehood. There never was any Grand Lodge at York. Our American Blue Masonry is not like any other in the world, not because it is purer, but because it was adulterated early in the present century, by men of little capacity or knowledge on this side of the Atlantic. In solemnity and impressiveness the work does not approach that of the Scottish and French Rites; nor does it give the means of recognition and of obtaining aid in danger, as these are known even in England.[36]

Pike added that when American Masons were virtually isolated from worldwide Masonry, such provincialism and "absurd self-conceit" were understandable. But with thousands of American Masons then visiting Europe annually, these views were ludicrous. Here was yet another instance of Pike's outspoken criticism when he felt it was justified. Pike's mind on the nature of Masonry blended the purist-conservative with the adaptive-progressive.

In the course of this session, the Supreme Council rejected the position of the Supreme Council of France concerning French claims of jurisdiction in Hawaii and continued the support of the Scottish Rite bodies that were organized under the Southern Jurisdiction in the island kingdom. The French insisted that they had established a Masonic presence in Honolulu as of 1846 with the Progress of Oceanica Lodge No. 124, which offered the first three degrees. Pike responded "with astonishment" that the "Sandwich Islands are not of the Dependencies of France. If they had been, we should have established no bodies there, whether the Supreme Council of France had done it or not."[37]

Meanwhile, the Supreme Council of France continued its protest by presenting its claim to the convention of Supreme Councils meeting in 1875 at Lausanne. Since the Southern Jurisdiction was not represented at the Lausanne meeting, the French pleading was easily sustained, which soon brought Pike's comment that the decision was "contrary to well-settled and universally acknowledged Masonic law." Pike, with the unanimity of the Supreme Council, informed the leadership of the Lausanne convention that the Southern Jurisdiction would "not accede to the alliance formed at Lausanne" and, therefore, believed the matter of Hawaii was settled in favor of the Americans.[38] Hawaii was not stabilized for the Southern Jurisdiction's purposes, however, until 1919, when it was attached to the jurisdiction of northern California.

Other grounds existed for the Southern Jurisdiction's reluctance to abide by the international alliance and confederation of the Lausanne meeting. The Southern Jurisdiction's council refused membership in the confederation of Supreme Councils not only because the alliance supported the French Supreme Council's position concerning Hawaii but also because it included potentially atheistic language in the prerequisites for membership. The confederation's Declaration of Principles "proclaimed from the beginning, the existence of a *Principe-Createur* [Creative Principle or Superior Force]" rather than "faith in a personal God."[39] While the conference did not reject the name "Great Architect of the Universe," and was careful about being on record as opposed to atheism, it tended toward a redefinition of what Freemasonry meant by the term God. The difference was between Aristotle's philosophy of causation that begins with a Prime Unmoved Mover and the knowable God of the Abrahamic faiths. This contrast, which also serves as a short-hand comparison between eighteenth-century Enlightenment Masonry and nineteenth-century Romantic Masonry, became a source of tension for English-speaking and continental Masonic bodies. Even though Pike did not attend, he lined up enough opposition to the Lausanne decisions afterwards to "nullify the results" so that "the work of the conference apparently came to naught."[40] However, the Supreme Council in time approved the establishment of and membership in a new confederation of Supreme Councils.

In response to the perennial demand of the Northern Supreme Council for greater territorial jurisdiction west of the Mississippi, the council turned it down on the basis of the original agreement of 1827. Within the southern council's own structure, the geographical representation was broadened with the increasing importance of the American West. As the Supreme Council of Canada had been recently established by warrant of the Supreme Council of England and Wales, the Mother Council happily established fraternal relations with the Canadian body. And while the council endorsed most of the Grand Commander's recommendations for reform of the fiscal system and reorganization of the Secretary-General's office, it felt that time and deliberation were needed "to perfect such statutes and regulations as may be necessary."[41]

With the adjournment of the session of 1876, some problems, particularly of a financial nature, remained unsettled. The building of a "Sanctuary" and the establishment of a charity fund were among those needed projects deferred indefinitely. As this was a time of economic depression, it is quite understandable why the Supreme Council could not readily address these plans for expansion. And it must be remembered that the membership in the Southern Jurisdiction was then very modest, perhaps no more than a thousand. A more effective propagation of the Rite was clearly in order.

■ ■ ■

Not only did the year 1876 mark the 75th anniversary of the Supreme Council, it was the 100th anniversary of the United States of America, which was appropriately celebrated with the opening of the Centennial Exposition in Philadelphia's Fairmont Park in May, the same month of the session. Some ten million visitors came that summer to Philadelphia to see the many exhibits—from huge dynamos to paintings of the Old and New World masters—and the many buildings of varied architecture, Renaissance, Moorish, Japanese, Victorian Gothic. "America's first world exposition, it was designed to dramatize cultural independence as much as to celebrate political: Bayard Taylor wrote an ode for the occasion, the venerable Whittier composed a Hymn, Sidney Lanier provided a cantata, and Richard Wagner composed a special march."[42]

The year 1876 also marked the opening of the Johns Hopkins University in Baltimore under the leadership of Daniel Coit Gilman. Drawing upon the model of the German university system, Hopkins became a trailblazer in American graduate education. On March 10, a little over two weeks after the inauguration of Gilman as president of Johns Hopkins, Alexander Graham Bell gave the first practical demonstration of his magneto-electric telephone in Boston.

Besides these important events, 1876 was also significant for the highly disputed presidential election held that fall. At their convention in Cincinnati the Republicans nominated Governor Rutherford B. Hayes of Ohio for president over Speaker James G. Blaine of Maine, the favorite, whose reputation was badly tarnished by the revelation of the "Mulligan Letters" and the disclosure of his corrupt dealings. The Democrats, in turn, nominated Samuel J. Tilden of New York, who in the general election received 250,000 more votes than Hayes. The Republicans, however, refused to concede Tilden's election on the basis that the returns from Florida, Louisiana, South Carolina, and Oregon were being contested. Without these electoral votes Tilden was one vote short of the necessary majority in the electoral college.

The election was ultimately decided by an electoral commission in a vote of eight to seven along party lines. It was the first and only time that a presidential election was decided in this manner. In order to gain the support of southern Democrats for the electoral commission's decision, the Republicans promised the withdrawal of the remaining federal troops from the South, the appointment of at least one southerner to the Cabinet, and substantial appropriations for internal improvements in the South, such as levees along the Mississippi River to check floods. President Hayes subsequently appointed David M. Key of Tennessee as postmaster general; the last federal troops were withdrawn from the South in April. The southern states, however, were much less successful in obtaining the promised internal improvements, even though Hayes in his inaugural address suggested that the federal government ought to give immediate attention to the economic demands of the South.

While the Hayes-Tilden presidential campaign moved into its closing weeks, Pike completed the first visit of a Grand Commander of the Southern Jurisdiction to the Pacific Coast, returning to Washington, D.C., about October 23. Pike's travels covered the states of Nevada, California, Oregon, and the Washington Territory and cost $875 in gold and $325 in currency. He had in turn received for his labors on behalf of the Supreme Council in the West $1,250 in gold. Of the tour he remarked simply that it was "pleasant," and he later reported confidently that "we have the affectionate loyalty of all the Brethren on that coast."[43]

Upon returning to Washington, Pike moved his living quarters into the Supreme Council's building at 602 D Street, NW, because of his impecunious condition, resulting from his law firm's lack of clients and the prevailing prejudice against former "rebels." Until his death fifteen years later, Pike lived in the Supreme Council's residential quarters, first on D Street, NW, later at 218 Third Street, NW (an address apparently renumbered around 1883 as 433 Third Street).

About a month after the Grand Commander moved into the council's quarters on D Street, he wrote to Frederick Webber of Kentucky, the Treasurer General of the Supreme Council, to complain that Secretary General Mackey had written to him "only once in six mos." and in that instance to object that, as Pike continued his letter to Webber,

> [I] had said in a printed letter that the income of the Sup. Council had *heretofore* been no more than sufficient to pay his salary and current expenses. I had said nothing of the kind, but spoke of *the present* only. I told him so in my reply with surprise that he could have so *misrepresented* what was too plain to be misunderstood: and I have no answer. I urged him to make his returns, telling him that I had nothing to do with the money he had received, but that I *was* bound by the Statutes to see that returns were made regularly by all members, of *work* done. He has made no report nor returns of any sort since he went away, nor said anything about the business of the Secretary's office.[44]

Later in this letter to Webber, Pike suggested that if Mackey would employ Webber as an assistant at $500, this would help the Supreme Council, as its revenues were declining "in consequence of neglect in the office of the Secretary General." Mackey, according to the Grand Commander, had taken $3,000 for two years' salary and had done nothing; to Pike this was "simply monstrous."[45] He felt that Mackey really did not care for the Scottish Rite "as a Rite" and that the Secretary General was much more involved with the blue lodge and Royal Arch Masonry. "That's the trouble—and the *work* and *teaching* of the Rite have never had much interest for him."[46]

It was difficult enough for Pike, without the burden of Mackey's indifference or inadequacy, to lead a small Masonic organization of slow development. After all, as he noted, "It costs money, it requires thought and study, it is above the comprehension of the mass of Masons. It does not display itself in fuss and feathers, receptions and pilgrimages and other fooleries, which captivate the mass of men. It has not many offices to which ignorance can elect the ambitious: and every one who comes into it is already engaged in other bodies that take up enough of his time."[47]

Pike hoped that in the future someone would work for the Rite besides himself and would do it without "fear of losing caste among Blue Masons and Templars."[48] Despite the discouraging tone of his comments about the Rite, there were some encouraging signs: a new Scottish Rite Temple of the Grand Consistory of Kentucky was dedicated late in February 1877; the Albert G. Mackey Lodge of Perfection was established at about the same time at Deep Creek in Norfolk County, Virginia; and a report from Hawaii spoke of growth of the Rite there.

At the biennial session of the Supreme Council, which met in Washington in May 1878, the notable accomplishments included the completion of the revision of the *Statutes*, an improvement in the system of record-keeping, and the establishment of a library for the Supreme Council, which Pike in his *Allocution* reported he had begun "without purchasing books." He encouraged further book donations and a modest annual appropriation for the purchase of books. By resolution the Supreme Council established the library and provided for an annual appropriation of $100 "for the purchase of books, papers, pamphlets, documents, etc., and bindings."[49] The library, which was to be placed in the rooms of the council and under the Grand Commander's control, was largely for reference. Books were to contain bookplates listing the library's rules, and the seal of the Supreme Council was to be stamped on a leaf of each volume.

What were the objectives that Pike had in mind for establishing the library of the Supreme Council? Unfortunately, there is no documentation concerning his specific aims. From the *Catalogue of the Library of the Supreme Council, 33d, for the Southern Jurisdiction of the United States* (Jan. 1, 1880), "numbering over a thousand volumes,"[50] it appears that he was interested in the establishment of a general public library that would include an excellent collection of Masonic material. Years later, in 1941, Ray Baker Harris, the librarian of the Supreme Council, noted that this library was "the oldest as well as the first free public library in the District of Columbia."[51] From a collection of over 1,000 volumes in 1880, the library grew to about 250,000 volumes by the early 1990s. Two-thirds of the collection today is non-Masonic in character (ranging broadly in the fields of history, literature, philosophy, religion, etc.) while the remaining third of the inventory is devoted to the vast subject matter of Freemasonry.[52]

A few days after the close of the session of 1878, John Robin McDaniel, the Sovereign Grand Inspector in Virginia and the Lieutenant Grand Commander, died. Shortly thereafter Secretary General Mackey submitted ballots by mail to the Active Members for the election of a successor to McDaniel. Pike announced on July 22, 1878, that James Cunningham Batchelor of Louisiana had been elected Lieutenant Grand Commander and that he (Pike) had appointed Thomas H. Caswell, the Sovereign Grand Inspector in California, as "Grand Constable or Marshal of the Ceremonies of the Supreme Council."[53] Both of these men, in turn, would later serve briefly as Sovereign Grand Commander, but meanwhile, in the biennial session of 1880, Batchelor was (again) unanimously elected Lieutenant Grand Commander.

In looking back at the efforts of Pike and the Supreme Council during the 1870s, one is struck by their accomplishments: the completion, printing, and distribution of the rituals; the publication of *Morals and Dogma;* the publication of the *Official Bulletin;* the establishment of a library; the successful defense of territorial jurisdiction against the Northern Jurisdiction; the improvement of the council's fiscal accounting; the involvement in the establishment of an international confederation of Supreme Councils; the creation of a printing fund; and a modest growth in the membership.[54]

Notably, the chief financial supporter of the Supreme Council and its activities in the 1870s—actually dating back to the end of the Civil War—was California. This was due in large part to the gold mining in the state and to the overall increase in new wealth there. On this point, one observer believes that "Pike's ritual of the Fifteenth Degree proves beyond any question of doubt that he was aware of the possible degrading power of gold. Hence, his criticism of the rapid expansion of the Rite, for that period of time, in California which he had expressed in his *Allocution* at the Session [of] 1874."[55]

. . .

Among the *Revised Statutes* which the Supreme Council adopted during the session of 1878 was a measure designating the fixed time for future sessions as "the Third Monday in October."[56] Thus, the council next met on Monday, October 18, 1880, with twelve of the current twenty-five Active Members in attendance. Most of the business of this session was routine; the one important exception was the decision to buy a building for the executive offices and to establish a committee of three members, appointed by the Grand Commander, "to consider and suggest a scheme for raising the amount necessary for such purchasing by the issuing of certificates of stock or otherwise."[57]

The committee wasted no time in obtaining a "Home" at 218 Third Street, NW, a spacious house of four stories and a basement, the monthly rent for which was $83.33. This was the first House of the Temple. Pike was delighted to be out of the council's "miserable quarters" and into "a fine large house,"[58] which the council would later purchase.

In his *Allocution* for the session of 1880, the Grand Commander reported that since the session of 1878 he had been away from home nine and a half months and had traveled "in all 20,000 miles" on behalf of the Supreme Council.

During this session, Pike also dealt with the matter of Masonic and Scottish Rite law, noting that Scottish Rite Masons who were tried for Masonic offenses in symbolic lodges ought not to be tried on the same charges in Scottish Rite bodies. Decisions of symbolic lodges, he affirmed, were binding on the Scottish Rite. Furthermore, "any judgment or decree of a Civil or Criminal Court of the Country adjudging that a person has been guilty of crime or fraud, must be given full effect to in Masonry, without rehearing or re-examination, upon the production and filing of an exemplification of the record or the judgment or decree."[59] In other words, Masonic jurisprudence abided by the prohibition against double-jeopardy and the binding decision of blue lodge hearings or the independent findings of the civil courts. One cannot be simultaneously a convicted felon and a Mason in good standing.

In addition to the published *Allocution* for the session of 1880, Pike prepared a confidential *Allocution* which was essentially a depressing review of the Rite's failure in promoting its program and development.[60] He considered that, among other things, the Grand Consistories had proven "worse than useless, doing nothing to build up Subordinates, unnecessary as Governing Powers, in some States of two or three Subordinates only, and rendering the Inspector of the State powerless to effect anything."[61]

Perhaps the confidential *Allocution* reflected Pike's momentary frustration with the Rite. After all, he had often said that Scottish Rite Masonry was for the intellectual and scholarly elite of the fraternity. In previous sessions he had indicated satisfaction with the modest growth of the Rite and had criticized those who wished to accelerate its growth.[62]

Before the Supreme Council adjourned in 1880, it responded to the Grand Commander's financial plight, about which he had confidentially reported, by "voting him an annuity of $1,800 a year from October, 1879, for the remainder of his life. They made the salary retroactive for one year to enable him to pay all his indebtedness except that which he owed to the treasury of the Supreme Council."[63] Despite this act of generosity, Pike somehow thought that the council regarded him as "a pensioner on the bounty of the Order."[64] This was apparently the motivation for his transferring by letter to a confidential session in 1882 all of his personal property. This included his library, which he valued at $25,000, an organ, some paintings, and furniture, to be given over to the council. The Grand Commander requested that "the conveyance be accepted in full repayment of all monies ever received by me from the Supreme Council . . . and that I have a home in which I have bought and paid for the right to live."[65] At last, Pike achieved some security for the autumn years of his life.

Meanwhile, the Supreme Council suffered the loss of its Secretary General, Albert Mackey, who, having been ill for some time, died at Ft. Monroe, Virginia, on June 20, 1881. Pike, who had known Mackey for thirty years and was quite aware of his strengths and limitations, observed in a eulogy that "Masonry will not soon lose as great a man, and she may put dust upon her head and wear sackcloth in her Lodges, where in Masonry, his heart always was."[66]

Twelve days after Mackey's demise, President James A. Garfield was shot at a Washington railroad station while on his way to a Williams College commencement in Massachusetts. The assassin was identified as Charles J. Guiteau, a disappointed office seeker. Garfield, who was a York Rite and fourteenth degree Scottish Rite Mason, lingered for three and a half months before he died at Elberon, New Jersey, where it was hoped the sea air would be beneficial to his survival. He was buried in Lakeview Cemetery in Cleveland, Ohio, not far from his birthplace. Garfield was the second of four American presidents who have been assassinated.

Only five days after Mackey's death, Grand Commander Pike appointed William M. Ireland, who had been serving as Deputy for Washington, D.C., as Acting Secretary General. Ireland had also recently been Assistant Grand Auditor and had accompanied Pike on his western tour of 1878 and on later tours as well. In view of the Grand Commander's age and rheumatic gout, Ireland's assistance on these journeys was invaluable. At the biennial session of 1882, Ireland was elected Sovereign Grand Inspector General in North Carolina and Secretary General of the Supreme Council. Pike was enthusiastic about the new Secretary General, noting emphatically that "there was never any real Secretariat of the Supreme Council, until Ireland was put in charge of it. He is *indespensable* [*sic*, emphasis is Pike's]."[67]

The 1882 session showed encouraging signs for the Rite's future. The new Secretary General's annual salary was set at $1,800 and the Treasurer General's at $500. In his *Allocution*, Pike reported that there were now ninety-six subordinate bodies of the Southern Jurisdiction, thirty published volumes of rituals, ceremonies, and other works, one volume of music for the Scottish Rite, and a library of over 5,000 volumes, "the whole worth at least twenty-five thousand dollars."[68]

Not only was the year 1882 significant in the life of the Supreme Council but it marked an important new era in the demographic history of the United States. That year saw a shift in the preponderance of immigrants coming from northern and western Europe—the so-called "old" immigration—to those arriving from southern and eastern Europe—Italians, Hungarians, Poles, Russians, Ukrainians, Jews, et cetera—what came to be known as the "new" immigration that was a source of cheap labor for America's mines, mills, and factories. "An influx of immigrants facilitated the triumph of industry. In depression years the numbers fell, but in the boom year 1882 almost 800,000 came in, a record which was not surpassed until 1905."[69] The Italians were the largest group of the "new" immigration; some 4 million of them, particularly from Sicily and southern Italy, reached American shores between 1881 and 1917.

Historian Oscar Handlin offers a sensitive picture of the human scale within the mass Atlantic transmigration involving 35 million people:

> There was no slack to the peasant situation. Without reserves of any kind these people were helpless in the face of the first crisis. The year the crops failed there was famine. The alternative to flight was death by starvation . . . . Who would help now? The empty weeks went by, marked by the burial of the first victims . . . . So much striving had come to no end . . . . Now the count was mounting. The endless tolling of the sexton's bell, the narrowing family circle, were shaping an edge of resolution. The tumbled huts, no longer home to anyone, were urging it. The empty road by pointing its form . . . For all about was the evidence of the consequences of staying . . . . Across the Atlantic the accumulation of immigrants created a magnetic pole that would for decades continue to draw relatives and friends in a mighty procession.[70]

While 1882 was a turning point between the "old" and the "new" patterns and sources of immigration, it was also the year which witnessed the first instance of pro-active governmental discrimination against a racial group with the enactment of the Chinese Exclusion Act. This measure stemmed from the Chinese immigrants' low standard of living, their "strange" appearance, manners, and customs. By the terms of the act, Chinese laborers (known as "coolies") were excluded from entering the United States for ten years while no restrictions were placed on the admission of Chinese businessmen and students.

A little more than nine months after the passage of the Chinese Exclusion Act, Congress, in reaction to Garfield's assassination and Democratic victories in the fall election of 1882, passed, and President Chester A. Arthur signed, the Pendleton Act on January 16, 1883. It was the first civil service reform legislation. This was a major milestone in the history of the federal government as it established a merit system for government employees based upon competitive examination and a three-man, bipartisan Civil Service Commission to oversee it.

Two months later on a matter of fraternal importance, Grand Commander Pike announced through a circular letter (March 19, 1883) that "the Ancient and Accepted Scottish Rite in the Southern Jurisdiction of the United States has at last a House of the Temple and a Home."[71] The council paid $17,000 for the property at the corner of Third and E Streets, NW, in Washington. It had paid in cash $10,000 and had borrowed $9,000 on a one-year mortgage on the property. Shortly the council was to add a library room to the house that would cost between $1,500 and $2,000. As often happens, the final cost of the library addition was in excess of the anticipated expenditure. When Pike left Washington on April 1, 1883, on an extended tour of the Southern Jurisdiction, a tour of some 11,450 miles and six months' duration, he was unaware that the addition to the House of the Temple would cost more than he had projected. The cost overran to a considerably higher figure, $3,950.

Reluctantly the Grand Commander agreed to the increased expenditure for the library, which was to be of brick and was to have a connecting cistern. His irritation was reflected in a letter he wrote from San Francisco to Ireland consenting to the higher cost: "For God's sake let the work begin."[72] As it turned out, the total cost for this first House of the Temple amounted to $25,210, all of which was paid by February 6, 1884. While on his long tour, Pike, with the help of Inspectors General and Deputies, raised some $15,225, which went into the Home Fund.[73] Pike's tour was a remarkable achievement when one considers the Grand Commander's age (73), his health problems, the times, and transportation conditions, including travel in hot weather without the comfort of air conditioning.

About two months after Pike had returned from his long journey, he believed that he was suffering from an ulcerated stomach from drinking "alkali water," and, at the same time, he reported a considerable weight loss amounting to fifty or sixty pounds.[74] Despite such fluctuating health and obvious discomfort, Pike carried on indefatigably in his responsibilities as Grand Commander.

An instance of this determination under trying circumstances occurred shortly after Pike completed his tour; he had to make an important decision regarding the fraternal "black ball," a potentially divisive ruling made on October 7, 1883, "that a member of the Rite had no right to ask another member to cast a black ball against a petition for degrees."[75]

Pike also announced that after January 1, 1884, certificates were to be available as a service to wives, mothers, daughters, and sisters of Scottish Rite Masons of the Southern Jurisdiction for one dollar each. These ladies' certificates, which a hundred years later were still obtainable, were designed to provide an attractive identification for families whose male members were Scottish Rite Masons. The gesture's origin probably had the hidden intention of shoring up occasionally tenuous public relations with women who felt left out of some important part of their husbands' fraternal lives when the men went out at night to lodge meetings.

The pressure on Masonry to share the degree work with women grew from such direct appeals as the couplet from 1870: "If the Masons to us will their secrets impart, / We'll embrace the dear Rite with all our heart."[76] The Scottish Rite never went so far as to develop a formal auxiliary with the attachments of female degrees. The Order of Eastern Star had from 1869 absorbed most of those demands in behalf of all Masonry, taking the higher degree bodies off the hook. Nevertheless, the Rite perpetuated a mild "deception" with the ladies certificates, a good faith act that had become widespread within Masonry in order to maintain a favorable public image, particularly in gaining the necessary support of women (one very good reason for the expansion of Masonic philanthropy in the 1920s, coincidental with women's suffrage). As the role of women in American society shifted into new possibilities throughout the twentieth century, dramatically at times, what the Scottish Rite offered women in small tokens of recognition was just enough without giving away too much, such as introducing them to the ritual.[77]

■   ■   ■

In the spring of 1884 the Masonic world was jolted by a strong attack from Pope Leo XIII in his encyclical *Humanum Genus* (the Human Race). This was but the latest in a series of papal bulls and encyclicals condemning Freemasonry; condemnation that had extended over a century and a half. No less than seven previous popes had denounced the Masonic fraternity. In his encyclical Leo XIII charged that "in a century and a half the sect of Masons grew beyond expectation; and, creeping audaciously and deceitfully among the various classes, of the people, it grew to be so powerful that now it seems the only dominating power in the States [i.e., nations or governments]. From this rapid and dangerous growth have come into the Church and into the States those evils which our predecessors had already forseen [*sic*]."[78]

Elsewhere in his encyclical Leo XIII argued that "the sect of the Masons aims unanimously and steadily also at the possession of the education of children."[79] This charge was inaccurate as to Masonic aims. What it came to represent, since Masonry was often a convenient focal point of an otherwise formless and ubiquitous American Protestant culture, was the Catholic conviction that religious neutrality in public education was virtually impossible. For instance, Catholics were indignant that the King James Version of the Bible, the chief symbol of Protestantism, was read in public school classes down to the middle of the twentieth century; they erected their own parallel system of parochial schools to deflect the influence of Protestant culture among Catholic children in America. This strong impulse helped the Catholic Church develop, according to Jaroslav Pelikan, "the most integrated and comprehensive educational system in the world."[80]

Whereas Masonic leaders had heretofore ignored the attacks of Leo XIII's predecessors, Pike wasted no time in responding with a powerful rejoinder to *Humanum Genus* on July 1, 1884, followed by a revision of this response a month later, and the inclusion of a response, though not the same as the preceding ones, in his *Allocution* given at the biennial session of the Supreme Council the following October. In his "Reply of the Supreme Council of the Ancient and Accepted Scottish Rite" that was a part of his *Allocution*, Pike set forth in the first paragraph why he found it necessary to answer Leo XIII:

If the Encyclical Letter of Leo XIII, entitled, from its opening word, 'Humanum Genus,' had been nothing more than a denunciation of Free-Masonry, I should not have thought it worth replying to. But under the guise of a condemnation of Free-Masonry, and a recital of the enormities and immoralities of the Order, in some respects so absurdly false as to be ludicrous, notwithstanding its malignity, it proved upon perusal to be a declaration of war, and the signal for a crusade, against the rights of men individually and of communities of men as organisms; against the separation of Church and State, and the confine of the Church within the limits of its legitimate functions; against education free from sectarian religious influences; against the civil policy of non-Catholic countries in regard to marriage and divorce; against the great doctrine upon which, as upon a rock, not to be shaken, the foundations of our Republic rest, that 'men are superior to institutions, and not institutions to men'; against the right of the people to depose oppressive, cruel and worthless rulers; against the exercise of the rights of free thought and free speech, and against, not only republican, but all constitutional government.[81]

The Grand Commander closed his energetic reply to Leo XIII's encyclical with a rather eloquent flourish, declaring that Freemasonry cannot by its essential nature attack religion, particularly Catholicism:

Free-Masonry makes no war upon the Roman Catholic religion. To do this is impossible for it, because it has never ceased to proclaim its cardinal tenets to be the most perfect and absolute equality of right of free opinion in matters of faith and creed. It denies the right of one Faith to *tolerate* another. To tolerate is to permit; and to permit is to refrain from prohibiting or preventing; and so a right to tolerate would imply a right to forbid. If there be a right to tolerate, every Faith has it alike. One is in no wise, in the eye of Masonry, superior to the other; and of two opposing faiths each cannot be superior to the other, nor can each tolerate the other.

Rome does claim the right to prohibit, precisely now as she always did. She is never tolerant except from compulsion. And, Masonry, having nothing to say as to her religious tenets, denies her right to interfere with the free exercise of opinion.[82]

Nine years later, in the biennial session of 1895, the Supreme Council approved resolutions calling for the distribution of Pike's reply and *Humanum Genus* in the original Latin, together with an English translation, to candidates for the degrees of the Lodge of Perfection. Thus, Pike's response to Leo XIII's anti-Masonic attack set a standard for Masonic apologetics for many years and was distributed to a wider audience than it otherwise would have found if left untouched in Pike's voluminous literary estate.

The inflammatory rhetoric of both sides, Catholic and Masonic, needs placement in a larger historical context to understand what occurred between 1880 and 1920 in American society when the tensions between them were in sharpest relief. The residual forces of these strong differences, however, continued to the end of the twentieth century. The mutual anger and suspicion reflected in the letter of Leo XIII and Pike's reply caused the polemics of each to cross the lines of calm reason and enter into the realm of exaggeration. The papal document of 1884 and the unofficial Masonic response to it created, in fiery combination, a pair of off-setting monsters that wrestled to an impasse. The question for each was fundamentally psychological: What was it that threatened the welfare of either of them that could move them to the point of irreconcilable antagonism?

For the Roman Catholic Church major changes in its global political status transpired under the longest pontificate in the Church's history, that of Pius IX (1846–1878). As the papacy lost its temporal power, particularly over the papal states, in the unification process of consolidating Italy (1870), while at the same time Bismarck in Germany took measures against the church's political ambitions (an example followed by other European states), Pius IX was not willing to suffer further indignities. After the revolution of 1848, for example, he had been expelled from the city of Rome, but was later restored to his see due to French intervention. Following these events, Pius IX developed and promulgated the doctrine of papal infallibility, thereby breaking new ground for the claims of the church's authority.[83]

Clearly, then, Pius IX found most disturbing the liberal, republican political ideas circulating in Europe and America. In 1864, Pius IX had issued the encyclical *Quanta cura*, accompanied by the *Syllabus of Errors* that listed eighty restrictive propositions. Under the terms of the *Syllabus*, faithful Catholics were supposed to deny a variety of modern ideas widely accepted in Western nations or risk being at odds with Rome.[84]

During the last decades of the nineteenth century, therefore, the papacy was officially and openly opposed to such liberal, Enlightenment innovations as the separation of church and state, freedom of worship, the right of free speech, and free public education under state supervision. Papal infallibility was defined and disseminated by Pius IX on July 18, 1870, as Rome was on the verge of surrendering to the armies of the Kingdom of Italy. It was this state of affairs that Leo XIII inherited.[85]

Following his predecessor's strategy of mounting a counteroffensive, Leo XIII reacted to the political conditions in Rome by declaring that Catholics should not vote in Italian elections, a prohibition that extended into the twentieth century.[86] Even though Leo XIII worked out some conciliatory agreements in the face of anti-Catholic policies in Germany and France, he nevertheless issued in the 1880s the papal bull *Immortale Dei*, which declared democracy incompatible with Catholicism. To his credit, however, he was not always bucking the overwhelming political trends that went against his own preferences. Leo XIII was, in fact, the first Pope to express concern for "the working classes" in industrial societies, giving tacit endorsement of the modern Catholic trade union movement. Pike, too, in *Morals and Dogma* had denounced the abuses of the wage system which had undermined the dignity of labor.

With generally hostile signals being broadcast in the face of rapid change in the Western world, both Pius IX and Leo XIII confused American Catholics (and Protestants) concerning their situation in a heterogeneous culture. Within American Catholicism itself, conflict brewed between conservatives and the more liberal assimilationists who were called Americanizers. The internal debate was burning hot in 1884 (the year of *Humanum Genus*) when the Third Plenary Council of Baltimore instructed all Catholic parishes to build parochial schools, as a higher priority than building churches. At the same time, the founding of the Catholic University of America (1884) by Catholic liberals was divisive, as conservatives feared the liberal enthusiasm of the Americanizers.

In another instance of breaking new ground in behalf of Catholics in the United States, the archbishop of Baltimore, James Cardinal Gibbons (1834–1921), successfully convinced Rome not to condemn the Knights of Labor as a fraternal "secret society." The Catholic conservatives in America were agitated by Cardinal Gibbons's Americanist tendencies because they viewed "labor unions in the same light as the secret anti-clerical organizations such as Freemasons who were out to subvert true religion and good order."[87]

Albert Pike could hardly be blamed if he overreacted in his reply to *Humanum Genus*. After all, Catholics themselves were unclear about what all the Vatican's pronouncements really meant. For Catholics in personal transition, it was a time of testing rationales and pushing the limits of old ideas within the new circumstances of Europe and America. This was especially true for recent immigrants to America who were still unsure about the democratic franchise there. Pike's language, while colorful, attempted not to overstep the lines of decency. His message was mild when compared with the torrent of anti-Catholic tracts that were published in America through the 1880s and '90s.

In one of many instances, a Baptist minister in Brooklyn fulminated against the Catholic priesthood in his 1889 diatribe entitled *The Fight with Rome*: "They pass from the brothel to the altar and celebrate the mass, and from a state of utter inebriety to perform the most solemn sacraments; and all this is borne with because they are Romanists. . . . Parents are compelled to take their children out of the public schools or have the sacraments withheld."[88]

Pike maintained sincerely that "Freemasonry makes no war upon the Roman Catholic religion," that "Freemasonry opens its doors to men of all religions alike."[89] He took the criticism of the Pope seriously enough to question how Masonry itself was at fault in the deepening misunderstanding. Pike admitted that Masonry had been done "incalculable harm" by illegitimate Rites whose "agents traverse the country soliciting men to receive the counterfeit Degrees. . . . [Further,] new Orders called Masonic spring up like mushrooms." He did not fault Rome for all of Masonry's problems with how it was perceived. But such a fine distinction between regular and bastardized Masonry, Pike realized, would "neither placate the Papacy nor win for it respect anywhere."[90]

Pike shared with the Pope a concern about Masonic belief in God. He assured Leo XIII that Masonry in the United States was absolutely theistic and that "atheism [was] a dreary unbelief" which was not relevant at all to English-speaking countries. He cautioned Catholic leaders against lumping all Masonry into one monolithic entity. Pike might have said that Masonry was more accurately a plural term, that there were varieties of Masonic practice, or even that there were "masonries." Masonry in France and Belgium, for example, was a culprit that Pike and the Pope both had in mind because atheists or skeptics were admitted to Masonic lodges in both those countries.[91]

Furthermore, Pike admitted that as far as he was personally concerned, Catholics and Masons shared the same values about the sanctity of marriage. Leo XIII's bull denounced the changing civil nature and status of marriage that made divorce easier to obtain in some countries. The Grand Commander insisted that Leo XIII had made another false accusation, for "very many Freemasons everywhere agree to a great extent with the Church of Rome in its views of marriage and divorce. Of these I am one."[92] Pike, in spite of a failed marriage, never sought the avenue of divorce to remedy his unhappy circumstances.

Despite Pike's willingness to concede some small points to Leo XIII, the poison arrows from both sides remained as the overall effect. Later, a Catholic apologist, after Pike's death, admitted a similar problem in the bitter dispute that obstructed civil discourse: "[S]ince 1896, when the writings of the infamous Leo Taxil [who attributed to Pike endorsements of Satan worship] were shown to be rank impostures . . . Catholic authors had in good faith quoted from his pages in their warfare against Masonry; and thus their works, excellent in other respects, have lost some of their authority."[93]

A century later the relationship between Catholicism and Masonry remained on uncertain, though mostly undisturbed, ground. Since many of the issues became moot points, one might rightly assume that the ensuing softer rhetoric indicated a higher ground of coexistence between the two. Not much ground, however, had been given.

The inconclusive results of the Vatican-Pike controversy have stayed fixed in a pattern of stalemate. It is a debate shelved indefinitely, except on occasion a conservative bishop or misinformed Masonic spokesman invokes the old polemical taunts. In any case, by the end of the twentieth century Masonic membership in American lodges and Rites included many Catholics.

Ironically, Freemasonry and the Roman Catholic Church in the twentieth century shared a common enemy—Soviet communism. This fact should have driven them to explore closer mutual ends. But instead of capitalizing on an opportunity to get over past differences or, at least, enter into useful dialogue, the biases and wrong assumptions were not entirely put aside. The bombastic words of the 1880s had their desired effect—to inflict wounds, as if they had been sticks and stones.

■ ■ ■

Not only was the biennial session of 1884 significant because of Pike's prompt retort to the Pope's assault on the Masonic fraternity; it was also noteworthy for the dedication of the House of the Temple on October 22; the establishment of a board of trustees for the temple with the Lieutenant Grand Commander serving as the president; the statutory creation of "A Fund of Fraternal Assistance" to aid "decayed Brethren" of the Rite and "the widows and orphans of Brethren thereof," with "one full third" of all of the Supreme Council's total revenues being earmarked for the fund;[94] and the approval of the *Revised Statutes*, composed of eighteen articles, as set forth by the Grand Commander.

During this session the council granted to fifteen bodies of the Rite, operating under letters temporary, their "Charters Perpetual." This constituted the largest number given by the Southern Jurisdiction from its establishment in 1801 to 1884. By that time, there was a demonstrable growth in membership and new bodies. Moreover, the Supreme Council, with the acquisition of the House of the Temple, now had a headquarters that it not only owned but held debt free.

While the Supreme Council gathered for its 1884 session, the country was experiencing another presidential campaign, one of the dirtiest in American history. James G. Blaine, on his third attempt, received the Republican nomination for president, with John A. Logan, a founder and former commander in chief of the Grand Army of the Republic (the powerful Union veterans organization), as the party's nominee for vice president. In turn, the Democrats nominated for president Stephen Grover Cleveland, who had successively served as the sheriff of Erie County, mayor of Buffalo, and governor of New York. For his running mate the Democratic Convention chose Thomas A. Hendricks of Indiana.

Blaine did not have the full support of his party, as the Stalwart wing was lukewarm towards his candidacy and the Independent Republicans, or Mugwumps as they came to be called, supported Cleveland. The Republicans used as political ammunition the fact that Cleveland, as a young bachelor in Buffalo, had fathered an illegitimate son—a charge that Cleveland readily acknowledged. The Democrats, besides reminding the public of Blaine's questionable operations as revealed in the Mulligan Letters, also took advantage of an incident in the campaign that may have cost Blaine the election. Blaine was on the platform in New York when a Protestant clergyman referred to the Democrats as the party of "Rum, Romanism, and Rebellion," an insult to the Irish and other Catholics; he made no attempt to deflect the Reverend Samuel Burchard's offensive remarks. Cleveland needed New York in order to win; the Democrats used the incident there to gain votes. As it turned out, Cleveland carried his home state by a small margin. His popular majority for the whole country was only 60,000 votes, and his electoral majority, merely 37. For the first time in more than a quarter of a century, a Democrat occupied the White House on Inauguration Day in 1885. The electorate preferred a man of impeccable public integrity, though flawed personally, over a man of sterling private scruples who was tainted with graft in public office.

Less than three months after Grover Cleveland had been inaugurated as the twenty-second president of the United States, Grand Commander Pike and Secretary General Ireland set out on another western tour of the Southern Jurisdiction. En route Pike twice fell ill with malarial fever, spending a total of twelve days in bed. Ireland and he traveled as far as Helena, Montana, and were back in Washington, D.C., on August 26, 1885. "It appears that the total money secured for work done on the trip was $1,968.74, a sum that, under the circumstances," according to Carter, "was more than to be expected."[95] Pike and Ireland went as marketing agents, offering Scottish Rite books and degrees to qualified candidates.

Meanwhile, Pike had been receiving complaints that the Secretary General and he were not acknowledging their correspondence. At first, Pike was defensive toward these criticisms. He even went so far as to suggest in a letter which was also signed by Ireland that letters addressed to the Supreme Council "had been taken by some knave belonging to the Cerneau Consistory here, and employed in the distributing department of the City Post Office in the hope that they might be found to contain information that could be profitably used by those who occupy themselves in disseminating lies throughout the prostituted 'Masonic' column of a Sunday paper here."[96] Pike was in error. His reference to a "Cerneau knave" was a reflection of his nervous concern with the spread of Cerneau Masonry in the 1880s. Comically, the real scoundrel was Ireland, who, as Pike later learned, had "neglected everything but [had] not appropriated money to his own use."[97]

In a letter to the Active Members on February 16, 1886, regarding Ireland's dereliction of duty, the Grand Commander reported that among the missing papers, "in letters opened and unopened, were drafts, money-orders, postal notes and bank notes, to the amount of more than eighteen hundred dollars, received by him for the Supreme Council and flung aside; many of the money-orders having been issued in 1882 and 1884."[98] Perhaps a cause—maybe *the* cause—for Ireland's irresponsible behavior was the constant attention he was giving "to a charming widow across the street."[99]

In response to Pike's summons to a special meeting of the council on February 24, 1886, several Active Members attended and, thence, addressed a letter to Ireland calling for his prompt resignation, which he in turn submitted the same day. Pike then appointed Frederick Webber, who had been serving as Treasurer General, as Acting Secretary General until the biennial session the following October, when he was unanimously elected Secretary General. After Ireland's resignation and through Webber's efforts, a decided improvement was achieved in the conduct of the Secretary General's office.

For more than a few years the Supreme Council had labored under the burden of two incompetent Secretaries General, Albert Mackey and William Ireland. Their combined negligence of office was undoubtedly Pike's most annoying as well as frustrating problem in his more than thirty years of service as Grand Commander. Pike's romantic and philosophical disposition perhaps impaired his judgment of others to whom was delegated the efficiency of administrative tasks.

Six months after Ireland was forced to resign from office, a violent earthquake struck Charleston, South Carolina, on August 31, 1886, with a considerable loss of life and with about 90 percent of the city destroyed or severely damaged. Early in September Pike issued a call for donations to aid the city in its distress. More than $2,400, including $50 from the Supreme Council treasury, was collected from the Southern Jurisdiction and sent to Charleston as a result of Pike's appeal. A report concerning the disbursement of these funds was made a few weeks later at the biennial session.

This session of 1886 produced little serious action. The *Statutes* were amended, as proposed by the Grand Commander, to provide for three Scottish Rite feast days: "15th Tisri [*sic*], day of the Dedication of the First Temple," "13th January, the day of the Confirmation of the Order of the House of the Temple as a Military Order," and "Feast-day, 31st May in each year, anniversary of the establishment of the Supreme Council."[100]

In his *Allocution* Pike declared that

> The chief purpose of the Supreme Council, formed at the beginning and steadily pursued ever since, has been to make the Ancient and Accepted Scottish Rite of Free-masonry which the man of intellect and the scholar might find it profitable to devote himself to; to embody in its teachings all the great truths taught by wise and good men in all ages; to comment upon and give the true interpretation of the symbols of the Blue Lodge; to ascertain and fully develop the special idea embodied in the beginning in each of its own degrees; to appeal to the intellectual and the moral sense only of its Initiates, leaving display and parade to other branches of the great Order; to indulge in no scenic pomp or theatrical representation; to so arrange the work of its degrees that they may be conferred at small expense, and that Lodges and Chapters may prosper wherever a Blue Lodge could be decently and creditably maintained.[101]

While these thoughts were not original with Pike, they had never been better stated. For him the Scottish Rite was striving "to become one of the agencies of our Father in Heaven for the dissemination of truth among men; to teach such doctrine in regard to Deity and the human soul, and the existence of sin and wrong and evil in the world, as reasonable men can believe, and so to make men wiser as well as better."[102] He offered the higher degrees of Masonry as a kind of vitamin supplement to an individual's professed religious faith and chosen place of worship.

These lofty ideas were reflected in the growth of the Scottish Rite of the Southern Jurisdiction during the 1880s. It is estimated that there were in 1880 about forty active bodies, and in 1886, almost 170. There was, of course, a corresponding increase in membership from an estimated 1,200 in 1880 to approximately 3,000 six years later.[103]

During this period the Library of the Supreme Council had grown from about 1,000 volumes to 8,000 in 1886; Pike estimated their a value at over $40,000. As a life-long bibliophile, Pike, while still residing in Arkansas thirty years before, was reputed to have "had the largest and most costly Library in the South."[104] He noted in the *Allocution* that the Supreme Council's library was "open to the public" and that books could be borrowed by "respectable and decent" people for thirty days without a charge or advance deposit. "The newspapers have not spoken of it," he added with a touch of wry humor, "because they are occupied with the more important matters of party-politics, base-ball, and scandal, and we have made no effort to call attention to it."[105]

It was remarkable that the Mother Council had accomplished as much as it had by 1886 despite the breakdown in Secretary General Ireland's office with a consequent estimated loss of about $8,000 to $10,000.[106] Most of the accomplishments of the council, it is safe to say, were the result of Pike's tireless efforts; he was both the fireman and the engineer of the Rite's locomotive.

On the heels of the biennial session of 1886, the Grand Commander, as a follow-up to a reference in his *Allocution*, sent out a letter to the Inspectors General and Deputies in which he outlined a plan for the development of the Fund of Fraternal Assistance, noting that "only one thing remains to be accomplished to ensure the perpetuity of the Order and to entitle it to live, because its life is useful and beneficial to Humanity."[107] He observed that he could not work for the fund as he had done "for other purposes" because he was "too old." It was up to the Active Members and Deputies to strive to raise $22,500 by the biennial session of 1888, in order to "fulfill the promise of the Supreme Council that it should be regularly increased by a sum equal to one full third of all its receipts of money."[108] The response to the Grand Commander's urgent appeal was quite disappointing. In the months following his appeal, the fund received remittances for $112.00 and $319.35, a miserably poor showing to say the least. This was not a personal rebuke but rather a reflection of a time in America before widespread voluntary philanthropic commitments were commonplace.

While Pike was busy dealing with such internal problems as gaining support for the Fund of Fraternal Assistance and handling Ireland's mismanagement of the Secretary General's office, he also faced during this period the proselytizing activity of the Cerneau Scottish Rite. This Rite, it will be recalled, dated back to Joseph Cerneau's efforts early in the century to establish his "brand" of Scottish Rite Masonry. The Southern and the Northern Councils had rejected the Cerneau Scottish Rite and deemed it irregular, causing it to pass into a state of suspended animation. An exception was its New Orleans body, during the anti-Masonic furor of the 1830s.

By the mid-1880s the Cerneauists were again active, this time in several quarters of the Southern Jurisdiction. As an example, "the renewal of Cerneau activity in 1881 appears to have caused Pike to give considerable attention to Maryland as one of the vulnerable spots in the Southern Jurisdiction."[109] Former members of the Grand Consistory of Maryland had been instrumental in the creation of the Cerneau Consistory in Baltimore. In 1884 Pike showed his anger and disgust with the fifty men involved by having their names inscribed, one to a page, in a special section of an innovative Masonic bill of indictment called *The Book of Infamy*.[110] It was a list of those censured for having sold themselves cheaply to the Cerneau "heresy."

Shortly, Edward W. Atwood, the Grand Commander of the Cerneau Scottish Rite, sought international recognition and, at the same time, launched attacks on Pike, who countered with incisive circular letters. The vigorous activity of Cerneauism came to a head in Iowa when the Grand Lodge adopted resolutions early in June 1889 that reaffirmed its recognition of the "Supreme Council of the Ancient and Accepted Scottish Rite, Southern Jurisdiction" as having "*exclusive jurisdiction in this state*."[111] It thereby denied recognition of the Cerneau Rite. Several hundred Iowa Masons petitioned the courts for orders prohibiting the Grand Lodge from such interference. They lost their suits and in turn their appeal to the Iowa Supreme Court. The thirteen brothers who led the legal attack against the Grand Lodge of Iowa initially suffered suspension of their Masonic rights and privileges and ultimately were expelled from the fraternity. Other Grand Lodges—Florida, Maryland, Minnesota, and Nebraska—followed with similar action. "The question of Grand Lodge supremacy in the Masonic organizational structure was no longer an academic subject; it was now a reality supported not only by Masonic jurisprudence but by the civil law."[112]

Meanwhile, the Supreme Council met on October 15, 1888, for its biennial session. Only a little more than half of the Active Members were present, and more than half of the Inspectors General and Deputies had failed to submit reports of the work in their respective states. Added to these disappointments, Pike lamented the dismal state of the Fund of Fraternal Assistance, showing only a balance of about $1,500, and delays of Inspectors General in submitting on time nominations for the rank and decoration of Knight Commander of the Court of Honor and for Inspectors General Honorary (the thirty-third degree).

In his *Allocution* for this session, Pike observed that twelve years from the following spring the Supreme Council would celebrate its 100th anniversary and the beginning of its second century. "That will be a fit occasion," he declared, "if then it shall be worthy to wear the crown of laurel." He charged the council to avoid becoming "indifferent, apathetic or inert!"[113] Later in the *Allocution* the Grand Commander spoke with pride of the Library of the Supreme Council and the service it was rendering to the community. "The life of an Order," he stressed, "consists of what it does. It lives by doing good; and if it sends out no rays of beneficence on any side, its life is only the life of a fungus."[114] Perhaps "mushroom" might have been a better metaphor.

Pike felt that the library had now reached a point where the Secretary General, while designated as the librarian, could no longer assume the responsibility for its day-to-day operation of cataloging books, indexing the volumes of the *Bulletin*, and making copies of "official letters." The services of a gentleman who would be responsible for these matters had been secured. Moreover, Pike thought that there should be a committee on the library, which would be accountable for its operation. He concluded his remarks about the library by averring that if he had "any hobby,—and few men are without one, nor will any man effect much who has not one,—it is the building up of a library, in which the lover of books may find delight and the student profit."[115]

With the absence of a substantial number of the Active Members from the 1888 session and a lack of reports from more than half of the Inspectors General and Deputies, it is not surprising that this biennial meeting was relatively inactive. During a senatorial (executive) session, the Supreme Council elected Thomas Hubbard Caswell (California), who could not be present, as Grand Chancellor, and Erasmus Theodore Carr (Kansas), as Grand Minister of State. At this same session it also dropped from its rolls former Secretary General William Ireland as a result of his unacceptable conduct in office.

While the Supreme Council gathered for its 1888 session, the country was experiencing another presidential campaign with the incumbent Grover Cleveland heading the Democratic ticket against the Republican nominee, Benjamin Harrison of Indiana, who was a brevet brigadier general in the Union army during the Civil War and later a United States senator (1881–1887). A high protective tariff was the chief plank in the Republican platform. This campaign marked the first time in American history that a high tariff was the central issue.

The Democrats received a costly blow from the publication of the so-called "Murchison letter," which involved Sir Lionel Sackville-West, the British minister in Washington, and "Charles F. Murchison," posing as a naturalized Englishman, who was actually George A. Osgoodby, a California Republican. Murchison/Osgoodby sought the British minister's advice on how to vote in the presidential election. Sackville-West replied in a letter that by voting for the low-tariff candidate (Cleveland) the inquirer would render assistance to the cause of Great Britain's free-trade policy. The Republicans immediately publicized this indiscreet letter, and the administration in turn handed the British minister his passport. But the damage had been done to Cleveland's campaign among the Irish voters. While the president received almost 100,000 votes more than Harrison, he lost in the electoral college by 233 to 168 as the result of the Republicans' decisive efforts to carry New York and other key states.

Four years later, former President Cleveland and President Harrison were again the respective Democratic and Republican candidates. But in the 1892 election, which included General James B. Weaver of Iowa, the People's (Populist) Party candidate, Cleveland won convincingly by more than 360,000 popular votes over Harrison, and by 279 electoral votes to President Harrison's 145 and Weaver's 22. The third party's effect, however, is deceiving if judged only in the numerical framework of a low electoral count.

A little more than three months after Grover Cleveland was inaugurated for the second time (March 4, 1889), one of the worst natural catastrophes in American history occurred: the Johnstown Flood (May 31) in which some 2,200 people lost their lives as the result of an earthen dam giving way and sending down a great wall of water that inundated the town. Grand Commander Pike immediately appealed to all the bodies of the Southern Jurisdiction for aid to the flood victims; and a warrant of June 6 in the amount of fifty dollars was sent from the Supreme Council for relief to the stricken Pennsylvania town.

By the time of the Johnstown Flood, Albert Pike had to face the infirmity of his advanced years. He was in continuously declining health. Trouble with gout persisted, and in a letter to Vinnie Ream some five months later, he reported that he had the painful discomfort of "neuralgia in his 'left eye and upper and lower jaw.'"[116] A life-long user of tobacco, he may have developed esophageal cancer, as had cigar-loving President Grant. When the Supreme Council met on October 20, 1890, for its biennial session, Pike was suffering from "a severe affection [sic] of the throat," an illness which had not been reported before.[117] In view of his throat condition, Pike asked Inspector General Odell Squier Long, the Grand Constable, to read his *Allocution* to the Supreme Council. Pike began his biennial address with his usual references to approaching death and a necrology of distinguished Scottish Rite Masons, here and abroad, who had died during the past biennium. In an early paragraph of the *Allocution* he offered the Active Members what might be considered a lovely benediction: "May that part of the voyage of life which is yet in the future for each of you be long and fortunate, over restful seas and under indulgent skies; and the accomplishment of no desire bring after-evil or self-reproach."[118]

The Grand Commander reported that the Rite had been making steadfast progress and that with the recent admission of several new states to the Union the Supreme Council could "fill some of the vacancies in our membership."[119] The council then had twenty-eight members. Pike noted that with the collection of historical materials he had assembled, "a history of the Rite and of our Supreme Council" should be undertaken, but it was "too late" for him to do it.[120] With regard to his beloved hobby, the library, he indicated that he had appointed, by the terms of a statute enacted in the 1888 session, members for the Committee on the Buildings and Library, including his son, (Luther) Hamilton Pike. And he expected to send to press by the first of the year "a complete catalogue of the Library, upon which much work has been done during the past year."[121] In the report of the Committee on the Buildings and Library, the value of the library was listed as of September 30, 1890, at $70,386.31; and the contents included some 15,000 volumes.[122]

With what turned out to be the last words of this, his last, *Allocution*, Pike closed simply but with a sublime feeling: "We have taken upon ourselves the charge of this Free-Masonry here; and we and they who had it before us have faithfully kept the charge to the best of our lights and gifts. On the whole, I think we may be content with our work."[123]

Five months after the biennial session of 1890 had ended, Pike, who had meanwhile turned eighty-one years old in December, wrote on March 23, 1891, to Lieutenant Grand Commander James C. Batchelor:

> I hereby make officially known to you that I have now been confined to my bed by sickness during almost five months and am totally disabled to perform the duties of Grand Commander, and have not the slightest ground to hope that I shall ever leave my bed alive. My work is ended.
>
> I hope you will, as soon as your health will permit, come to Washington, occupy rooms, ready to receive you, in the House of the Temple, and assume the place of Acting Grand Commander.[124]

Batchelor arrived in Washington on March 27. Anticipating that his days were numbered, Pike had taken steps to have the Active Members polled on March 7 concerning
the provision of a salary of $2,400 per year for Batchelor when he became the Acting
Grand Commander. Two days after Batchelor's arrival, Pike began to fail. At 8:00 P.M.
on April 2, he died, having passed, in Masonic parlance, *ad astra* (to the stars). With
him at the time of his death were his children, Hamilton, Lillian, and Yvon; his servant,
Edward Kenney; and nine Masonic friends. Among many last personal gestures, Pike
bequeathed his ring to Trevelyan William Hugo of Duluth, Minnesota. Hugo had
prepared the index to *Morals and Dogma*.[125]

"For five days he lay in state in the House of the Temple, while Masonic dignitaries
met with the family to make arrangements for a funeral."[126] His body was then taken
under escort of the Albert Pike Consistory of the District of Columbia to the Scottish
Rite Cathedral at 1007 G Street, NW, where it lay in state for two more days. The Albert
Pike Consistory then performed at midnight on April 9 the Scottish Rite Kadosh funeral
service at the First Congregational Church, the historic location where Howard
University had been founded in 1867. The availability of the New England–style church,
housing a congregation with a strong abolitionist history, for the funeral of the leader of
the Southern Jurisdiction and former Confederate general holds peculiar symmetry.
Convenience and coincidence worked together in an unplanned instance of spiritual
clemency. The following day an Episcopal burial service was held at the (pro-Cathedral)
Church of the Ascension in the presence of his children, the Active Members of the
Supreme Council, and many others.

Pike's body was then taken to Oak Hill Cemetery where it was temporarily placed in
a vault. A little less than a week later Hamilton, Yvon, and Acting Grand Commander
Batchelor had the body interred in a hillside grave in the cemetery. Twenty-six years later
Yvon placed a stone at his father's grave. Ironically, "Pike had left directions on Feb. 28,
1891, that his body should be cremated and his ashes placed around two acacia trees in
front of the House of the Temple; but his children refused to comply with them."[127]

• • •

Pike's legacy to the Scottish Rite was inestimable: superb rituals, *Revised Statutes*,
Morals and Dogma, a stronger and much improved system of organization, slow but
steady growth of membership (about 4,000 in the whole Southern Jurisdiction at the
time of his death), a successful defense of the territorial jurisdiction of the Supreme
Council against the periodic efforts of the Northern Masonic Jurisdiction or incursions
of Cerneauism, advocacy and support of international conferences of Supreme Councils
(although he never attended any), the Library of the Supreme Council, and a love of
Masonic learning and Freemasonry in general.

Pike's diverse talents, broad contacts, and varieties of experience make him impossible to comprehend fully. Many share the opinion of one Masonic commentator that it is "regrettable" his *Morals and Dogma* is inaccessible to the average reader, for it "has much valuable material embedded in obscure mystical verbiage."[128] And yet, Pike's accomplishments and insights are not entirely lost in "the matrix of mysticism," because his work was repeatedly mined by "degree writers for hundreds of orders . . . hoping to find fresh ritualistic motifs or bibliographic sources." On these grounds alone his work "had become the standard for ritualistic excellence."[129]

Furthermore, the significance of Albert Pike exceeds the claims of the Scottish Rite upon his extraordinary gifts and contributions to nineteenth-century fraternalism. He is captivating in American history because he is so representative of his times. Born the same year as Abraham Lincoln, his life, because of its wide span of four score years, provides an unparalleled case study for all the major themes and arguments of the century in which America came of age.

"Few men, whether in the nineteenth century or any other period, could have appreciated Pike's philosophy or understood his fascination for strange religions of antiquity."[130] He was the Scottish Rite's principal remodeler, like the ancient Nehemiah overhauling the bulwarks of Jerusalem. As an intellectual and literary figure, Pike's life is intriguing. But the extent of his life's journey in Federalist-Calvinist New England, the territorial American West, the slave-holding, antebellum South, and the evolving nation's capital establishes Albert Pike as an emblematic figure whose life speaks to the lives of many others and life in other times.

CHAPTER VI

A Fragile Interim
1891–1900

Batchelor, Tucker, and Caswell

When Albert Pike died in the early spring of 1891, the national press mentioned several possible successors as Grand Commander. The list of potential candidates included the surgeon general of the U.S. Navy, John Mills Browne; Thomas H. Caswell of California; and Thomas M. Dudley of Kentucky.[1] Why Acting Grand Commander James Batchelor was never mentioned in the public speculation is curious. Perhaps he was not viewed as Pike's equivalent in stature or, more probable, he was regarded as past his prime and, by acting honorably, might refuse to stand for election.

Whoever succeeded Pike would have to have a strong, confident personality to withstand the predictable comparisons and unavoidable criticism. What actually happened in the immediate line of Pike's succession, however, was a rapid turn-over in a condensed time of transition. While it was not the hoped for outcome, the accelerated change of leadership may have actually helped free the Rite of Pike's dominance and its dependence on the genius of one man. To the extent that a departure from Pike's shadow was necessary and desirable in order to promote the organization's growth and stability, the 1890s were a critical time for the Scottish Rite.

James Cunningham Batchelor, who had been elected Lieutenant Grand Commander of the Supreme Council in 1878, became the Acting Grand Commander during Pike's final days of life. Of English and Scottish descent, he was born in Quebec City, Canada, in 1818. Subsequently, his family moved to western New York and later to Montgomery,

Alabama, where in 1836 young Batchelor enlisted in the "Montgomery Blues" for service against the Florida Indians in the Seminole War. During this campaign he contracted a fever which caused a partial loss of hearing. After his discharge he studied medicine in Cincinnati and, in turn, as a physician and surgeon, he practiced near Selma, Alabama, until 1853 when he moved to New Orleans.

Active in several Masonic bodies in the Crescent City, Batchelor served as Grand Secretary of the Grand Lodge of Louisiana from 1867 to 1890, was coroneted an Inspector General Honorary of the thirty-third degree of the Scottish Rite on February 14, 1857, and was crowned an Inspector General in 1859, shortly after Pike became Grand Commander. During the Civil War Batchelor served as captain of a company in the Confederate army and while a prisoner of war for five months on Ship Island, which was off the coast of Mississippi, suffered severely from rheumatism that left him disabled for the rest of his life.

On April 18, 1891, a little more than two weeks after Pike's death, Dr. Batchelor sent out a circular letter announcing Pike's demise. The letter included Pike's autobiographical sketch, a supplement prepared by John Hallum, and an outline of the deceased Grand Commander's Masonic record. "There is no evidence in the files of the Supreme Council of any activity by Acting Grand Commander Batchelor after April 18, 1891, until December 16, 1891."[2] On the later date, the Acting Grand Commander, responding favorably to an appeal for help from the Grand Consistory of Japan because of a severe earthquake which struck late in October, published a circular letter to the Scottish Rite bodies soliciting jurisdiction-wide financial assistance. Together with the $500 which the Supreme Council contributed, a total of $855 was remitted for emergency aid to the affected Japanese region.

Ten months after the publication of Batchelor's second circular letter, the Supreme Council convened on October 17, 1892, for its biennial session. Batchelor, who had been ill for some time, asked Abraham Ephraim Frankland, an Emeritus Member, to read his *Allocution*, in which he noted that the reports of the Committees on the State of the Order, Subordinate bodies, and Finance showed "an improved condition of the Rite generally throughout our Jurisdiction. Financially, our receipts are greater than they have ever been."[3] Nothing else of importance was reported in the *Allocution*, though news of a positive cash position was an index of vitality.

Batchelor also gave a *Confidential Allocution* while the council was in executive session. There is no record of its contents. Perhaps in the *Confidential Allocution* Batchelor, who was in due course officially elected Grand Commander, dealt with two controversial issues that had surfaced after Pike's death: the election of the Supreme Council's officers for limited terms rather than for life and the union of the Southern and Northern Jurisdictions of the Scottish Rite. The former issue resulted in a Scottish Rite convention in Washington, D.C.; prior to the biennial session; and in the convention's petition to the Supreme Council, a change was proposed in the form of its government.

The leading proponent for these modifications in polity was Theodore Sutton Parvin of Iowa, who was an Active Member of the Supreme Council, a former Grand Minister of State, the first Grand Secretary of the Grand Lodge of Iowa from 1844 till his death in 1901, and the founder of the Iowa Masonic Library in 1844, which became in time one of the largest and best equipped Masonic libraries in the world. Parvin's views were reflected in resolutions he proposed on the first day of the biennial session of 1892. They were, not surprisingly, referred to the Committee on the State of the Order. Parvin believed that "the future success and best interests of the Rite" required "the union of the Southern and Northern (known as the Pike and [Henry L.] Palmer) Supreme Councils" and, following merger, the establishment of "a National Supreme Body of the Rite."

To effect this mammoth change, Parvin recommended that "a committee of five members be appointed to meet and confer" with a similar committee of the northern council, so as "to arrange the terms of such union upon a proper basis."[4] He was equally emphatic about "life tenure of office," which he considered "repugnant" to all American voluntary institutions. He argued it was an affront to democratic and Masonic principles, an anomaly that was wholly out of character with "the York Rite of Masonry upon which our Rite is based and exists." In its place he called for a representative, elected government, "similar to that observed in the York Rite."[5]

The Committee on the State of the Order and Unfinished Business, however, advised that Parvin's resolutions should not be adopted. Any dissenting opinion within the committee concerning the existing order was not recorded. Ultimately, the Supreme Council substituted the election of officers to a term of two years for elections *ad vitam* (i.e., for life), beginning with the regular session in October 1901. No union of the Northern and Southern Jurisdictions of the Scottish Rite was seriously considered or ever achieved after that one timely opening. The matter would return, though, at least in the abstract, to be discussed informally and unofficially at the end of the twentieth century by the two councils. The outcome of such deliberations on the eve of the Scottish Rite's (American) bicentennial remained far from certain.

These issues underscored the division within the Southern Jurisdiction between those who wanted change and, therefore, were attracted to Parvin and those who preferred the *status quo* and were drawn to Philip Crosby Tucker, the newly elected Lieutenant Grand Commander. "Both men were vigorous and determined in pursuit of their objectives. Parvin's support was drawn from subordinate bodies and the rank and file of the Rite, while that of Tucker came principally from the influential 'crowned heads' making up the Supreme Council."[6]

Among the proposals adopted by the council at the 1892 session were a half dozen minor policy adjustments which included (1) a reduction of the per capita tax;[7] (2) permission to establish State Councils of Deliberation in states where no Grand Consistories existed; (3) elimination of the office of Second Grand Auditor; (4) allowance of mileage and *per diem* expenses for Active Members at biennial sessions as a means of increasing attendance; (5) tightening of the procedure for amending the *Statutes;* and (6) termination of the *Official Bulletin,* as it failed to reach the membership at large and was too heavy a burden for the Grand Commander. The council also agreed to strike a commemorative bronze medal of Albert Pike, bearing his likeness on the obverse side and, on the reverse, the double-headed eagle of the Rite. On the last day of the biennial session, the Supreme Council voted to meet in St. Louis, Missouri, on the first Monday of October 1893, to mark the twenty-fifth anniversary of the last time that the council met there. By circular vote of the Active Members the date was changed to the third Monday of October as the earlier date conflicted with "Fair Week."[8] American film-goers many years later received a big-screen impression of how large an event the Missouri State Fair had been in this era from the 1944 Judy Garland classic, "Meet Me in St. Louis."

For Batchelor, the 1892 meeting was to be his only session as Grand Commander. After its adjournment he apparently never did anything more than call a meeting of the Council of Administration. Secretary General Frederick Webber, in addition to his own work, tried to handle the Grand Commander's incoming correspondence that did not require personal acknowledgment, but he could only do so much to compensate for the obvious operational deficiencies.[9] As Batchelor's state of health declined further, Lieutenant Grand Commander Tucker was asked at the end of June 1893 to take on the responsibilities of Acting Grand Commander. On July 28, a month after Tucker's arrival in Washington from Galveston, Texas, Batchelor died. He was buried in New Orleans with Masonic honors. The Supreme Council bore the cost of his funeral expenses ($569.25) as it had done for Pike's funeral.

■　■　■

As soon as Grover Cleveland was inaugurated as president on March 4, 1893, his second term after a four-year hiatus out of office, "he inherited a depression from his predecessor Benjamin Harrison, for which he was not responsible but for which he was bitterly blamed."[10] Seven weeks after his inauguration, the U.S. gold reserve dropped below the $100 million mark, thus helping to trigger a panic. This was followed two weeks later by the sudden fall of stocks on the New York Stock Exchange, and then the inevitable crash on June 27. Before the end of the year, nearly 500 banks and over 15,000 commercial institutions had failed. The winter of 1893 found the country engulfed in what was probably the worst depression of the nineteenth century with, of course, resulting mass unemployment and labor unrest, including the famous Pullman Strike (1894).

By the time of the Supreme Council's biennial session (October 16–20, 1893) in St. Louis, the depression was well under way. Twenty of the twenty-eight Active Members answered the roll call at the executive session on the afternoon of the opening day. Momentarily a constitutional question was raised about the election of officers at a second session within one year. It was settled in favor of proceeding with the elections on the basis of Sections 10 and 16 of Article I in the council's bylaws. Philip Crosby Tucker of

Texas was elected for life as the tenth Grand Commander, and Thomas Hubbard Caswell of California was elected as the Lieutenant Grand Commander, also *ad vitam.*

Tucker was born in Vergennes, Vermont, on February 14, 1826. He read law and was admitted to practice before moving to Galveston in 1852. "He was made a Mason in Dorchester Lodge of Vergennes during the exciting times of Morgan days."[11] This meant he entered the fraternity during the height of nineteenth-century American anti-Masonry, when many New England lodges had disbanded or were driven "underground." Active in the York bodies, Tucker became Grand Commander of the Grand Commandery of Knights Templar in 1864. Four years later he was elected a thirty-third degree Mason and was crowned shortly an Active Member. During the Civil War Tucker was in the Confederate army, like his predecessors Albert Pike and James Batchelor, and served on General John B. Magruder's staff with the rank of major.

In his relatively short inaugural *Allocution*, the new Grand Commander recommended that the Supreme Council adopt a resolution, for distribution among the bodies in the Southern Jurisdiction, "*condemning the unwise and unmasonic* public agitation of the repeal of the life tenure of office and membership in our Supreme Council."[12] This issue, together with the proposals for a union with the Supreme Council of the Northern Jurisdiction and a reduction of the tax on the subordinate bodies—all of which, as amendments to the *Statutes*, had been referred to the Committee on the Revision of the Statutes—were rejected by the Supreme Council on the recommendation of the committee. The party of change was blocked from getting any other "legislation" to the floor, so long as its ideas were stalled in the labyrinth buffer of a committee.

Among other actions taken by the council were the establishment of the armed forces as "a Masonic Jurisdiction" (army posts and naval stations and vessels) under the administration of the Supreme Council and the amending of the *Statutes* "by providing for annual election of officers of Subordinate Bodies and regulating the term of office in such subordinate body,"[13] an ironic contrast to the rejection of term limits for officers of the Supreme Council.

The library was a subject of concern during the council's deliberations, as it had been for the past decade and a half. Secretary General Webber, as librarian, reported that with his other responsibilities he could not handle the books, let alone the cataloguing and the reading room, especially since Mr. White, the assistant librarian, had retired the previous December. Dr. Thomas Edwards Hatch, a local Washington physician, retired government employee, and friend of Albert Pike, was to be employed as librarian at a salary of $1,000 per year. He was to catalogue the collection and establish rules for the library's operation. Dr. Hatch's service was unfortunately brief as he died the following summer.

In its executive session on the final day of the St. Louis session, the Supreme Council approved an annual budget which included, among other items, salaries for the officers: Grand Commander, $2,400; Secretary-General, $2,100; Treasurer-General, $500; Grand Auditor, $500. The council also allocated for contingent expenses $1,000 to the Grand

Commander, $1,200 to the Secretary-General, and $25 to the Grand Auditor, as well as $9,000 for alterations and repairs on the House of the Temple.

Upon returning to Washington from St. Louis, Tucker commissioned Robert J. Fleming, an architect, to draw up plans for the remodeling of the House of the Temple. The plans included doubling the size of the library, adding committee rooms, closets, lavatories, a lodge room with twice the seating capacity of its predecessor, and a new steam-heating system with radiators in all the rooms. A little over a month after the adjournment of the biennial session, the extensive work of renovating the temple was begun.[14]

Perhaps due to the strain of overseeing the remodeling of the temple and, at the same time, fulfilling his regular obligations, Tucker became ill during the winter of 1893 with "Washington malaria" and went home to Galveston to recover. He did not return to Washington until June 4, 1894, four months later, when he found the overhaul and redecorating of the House of the Temple almost finished. Five days after his arrival in the capital, Tucker called for a meeting of the Council of Administration to be convened on June 25, as the funds for the remodeling were exhausted, which meant additional money was necessary for the completion of the renovation. The construction proposed to create space in the library to house an additional 5,000 volumes still unshelved; a new council chamber; sidewalks along sides of the property sited at Third and E Streets, NW; a single flight of steps leading to the front entrance on E Street; and, above that entrance, a key-stone exhibiting "a double headed eagle, with the words and letters 'Supreme Council, A. & A. S. R. 1801–1894.'"[15]

The estimated cost of the additional work was a little more than $2,100, for which Tucker received authorization to proceed. The actual cost for the entire work was a few dollars less than $24,000, nearly $15,000 (or almost 166%) more than the amount originally allocated.

Within a few weeks after the Grand Commander had returned to Washington, he was again ill with a recurrence of "his poor spells, including chills."[16] Meanwhile, Thomas Hatch, the librarian, was seriously ill and was not expected to live. On July 9, Tucker started to prepare for Hatch's funeral, as his friend's death was imminent. At midday the Grand Commander decided that a bath might relieve his physical discomfort; but, while in the bathroom, he suffered an apoplectic stroke and died before a doctor could be summoned. As Thomas Hubbard Caswell, Lieutenant and Acting Grand Commander, observed in his *Allocution* of 1895, Tucker was "the third Grand Commander to pass away in the same building, and two in the same room, within a period of three years and three months."[17] Dr. Hatch died the following day.

Tucker's body was returned for burial to Galveston, Texas, where the Knight Kadosh service, which is no longer in general use, was conducted before a large assembly of Masons and the local citizenry.

Not only did the Supreme Council suffer the loss of its Grand Commander and its librarian in 1894 but also the loss of its Treasurer-General, John Mills Browne, a former surgeon general of the navy, who died on December 7 of the same year. Their deaths, occurring so close to one another, were dramatic and potentially devastating losses to the Rite. Sometimes, however, adversity in a community can draw out reserves of strength and cooperation that have been dormant. In a way, the crisis of leadership and threatened continuity may have been just the right impetus to accomplish a new sense of momentum.

■ ■ ■

Upon the death of Tucker, Judge Thomas Hubbard Caswell of California became the Acting Grand Commander. He was born in the lush Mohawk Valley, at the village of Exeter, Otsego County, New York, on August 10, 1825. He became, at age seventeen, a reporter for the *Freeman's Journal* of Cooperstown, New York. James Fenimore Cooper, author of *The Pioneers* and other popular novels set in and around Cooperstown, was established in his prominence at this time. A year later Caswell went to Arkansas, which he shortly left in order to attend St. Mary's College in Kentucky. Returning to Arkansas, he lived with an uncle, studied law, and was admitted to the bar in October 1848. Earlier that year, while political revolutions were transforming Europe, gold was discovered in California. The race to the gold fields soon began with rough-and-tumble abandon.

The cultural historian Kevin Starr offers a wide lens interpretation of how the population of California increased so rapidly with an odd mixture of dreamers, pikers, speculators, missionaries, and cardsharps: "As epic experience, the Gold Rush was both Iliad and Odyssey. It was an Odyssey in that it was a wandering away from home, a saga of resourcefulness, a poem of sea, earth, loyalty, and return. It was an Iliad in that it was a cruel foreign war, a saga of communal ambition and collective misbehavior, a poem of expatriation, hostile gods, and betrayal. At first impression, the years 1849-51 seem more burdened with suffering than victory, more Iliad than Odyssey. From the day sails were set for voyage around the Horn or oxen goaded on the first step of the transcontinental trek, the hardships of the enterprise were overwhelming."[18] In four years the California population of white settlers went from 14,000 to nearly a quarter million.

Thomas Caswell became one of the "forty-niners," leaving with a party from Fort Smith, Arkansas, on April 1, 1849. Upon reaching San Francisco, he worked for a short time as a stevedore and then returned to journalism before finally settling down in what became Nevada City, "where rich discoveries were reported and where he engaged in mining, merchandising and the practice of law."[19] It was not a genteel place in those formative, frontier years in California. John Steele, who was in Nevada City at the same time Caswell moved there, remembered once being present in a saloon around 1850. He was listening with pleasure to the tenor voice of a man singing Robert Burns's "Highland Mary." The crowd enjoyed the moment as a sweet violin accompanied the singer. Suddenly Steele dropped beneath the chairs as gun shots exploded. An instant later three men lay dead, a typical day's event.[20]

Shortly, Caswell was elected judge of Nevada County and, in turn, was reelected, serving for some eight years. By the outbreak of the Civil War, he was much involved with Masonry, especially in the York Rite. He became, in time, Grand High Priest of Royal Arch Masonry and Grand Commander of the Knights Templar in California. On October 17, 1867, he received the Scottish Rite degrees through the thirty-second, and the following July he was coroneted an Honorary Inspector General. His enthusiasm for the Scottish Rite was shown when he was crowned an Active Member of the Supreme Council on May 3, 1870. He subsequently served in several offices of the council before he was elected Lieutenant Grand Commander in 1893.

After Tucker's death, Caswell did not move immediately to Washington, D.C. Apparently, he did not arrive there until late summer or early fall. He was, however, in Washington by September 21, when he declared, as his "first official act of any importance," that a Master Mason who repudiated Cerneauism in compliance with the Grand Lodge of Georgia could become a candidate, if elected, for the Scottish Rite degrees in the Savannah bodies.[21] Eleven days later Caswell made the final payment to Robert J. Fleming, the architect, for his work on the renovation of the House of the Temple. Before the end of October, the Acting Grand Commander left Washington for San Francisco and apparently did not return until the biennial session of October 1895.

When this session opened on October 21, twenty-seven "Active Members were present; this was the first known time that all Inspectors General were recorded in attendance upon a Session of the Supreme Council."[22] Besides the election of Caswell as Grand Commander, Odell Squier Long of West Virginia as Lieutenant Grand Commander, Samuel Emery Adams of Minnesota as Grand Chancellor, and Gilmor Meredith of Maryland as Treasurer General in executive session, several significant measures were adopted.

In his *Allocution*, Caswell reported that during the past year in which he had served as Acting Grand Commander he had signed 1,000 "patents, briefs, &c." for new members of the Rite and that nine days before the opening of the session he had "secured, by an option, the right of the Supreme Council to purchase on or before November 1, 1895, the premises on E street, immediately adjoining the House of the Temple, for the sum of ten thousand dollars."[23] The council, on the recommendation of the Committee on Finance, appropriated $10,000 for this purchase, which would allow further expansion of the library and provide additional conference rooms for the nine standing committees. Already the library contained about 75,000 volumes in its collection; it was larger than the average college library and qualitatively on par with some of the best private collections in America.

During various stages of "alterations in the building," books had to be moved constantly from place to place in order to make room for the construction workers. Some concern about the security of the premises was, apparently, foremost in the mind of Frederick W. Webber, the librarian succeeding Hatch: "The building could not be left without someone to sleep in it, and Bro. [William L.] Boyden [who had been Hatch's stenographer] has to this time occupied it at night; but, being now a married man, on such nights as he desires to stay home with his wife and child I take his place and occupy his room in the building; for I do not consider it safe, for many reasons, to permit it to be unoccupied a single night."[24] Webber did not enumerate the specific danger he had in mind, though the valuable books and museum curios were a ready temptation for thieves. Webber's report, secondarily, leaves one to speculate about the stability of Boyden's marriage in its early days while the wife competed for attention against the night watch at the House of the Temple. Boyden, however, remained on duty for forty-six years, most of them as librarian of the Supreme Council.

The Supreme Council's acquisition of real estate, notably the prime location of the House of the Temple, prompted Caswell to question the title and the council's right to hold property in the District of Columbia. While he found the title was legally vested in the Supreme Council, four of the seven trustees who had received the deed of conveyance were now dead. Caswell recommended that "a special committee of three" be formed to examine the question of title, and if it felt under the circumstances that incorporation of the council was in order, to secure from Congress such a charter. "There is no record that he made the appointments to the committee."[25] However, Congressman James D. Richardson, an Active Member from Tennessee, introduced two months after the biennial session a bill for the incorporation of the Supreme Council, which was subsequently passed and signed into law by President Grover Cleveland on March 13, 1896. There was now no longer a question about the council's right to own property. At its biennial session of October 1897, the council adopted a resolution establishing a committee to draw up the necessary procedures for the ownership of property under the Federal Act of Incorporation.

Another recommendation that Caswell included in his *Allocution* was the appointment of a "Centennial Committee" as the 100th anniversary of the Supreme Council would be on May 30, 1901, "but five years and seven months hence."[26] Besides the Grand Commander, the committee included the Lieutenant Grand Commander, the Secretary General, the Treasurer General, and Inspector Nathaniel Levin of Georgia.

During this biennial session of 1895 Albert Pike's memory was honored by Caswell's announcement that he had purchased a large oil painting of the former Grand Commander for $400 and by two resolutions which have been in force ever since. The first provided

> that after the closing of each Session and before the dismissal of this Supreme Council, the Sovereign Grand Commander shall say, "And now to the memory of him who said: 'When I am dead, I wish my monument to be builded only in the hearts and memories of my brethren of the Ancient and Accepted Rite, and my name to be remembered by them in every country, no matter what language men speak, where the light of the Ancient and Accepted Scottish Rite shall shine and its Oracles of Truth and Wisdom be reverently listened.' He has lived; The fruits of his labor live after him."[27]

After the recitation of this "In Memoriam" paragraph, the assembled members were to give the mourning battery, a Masonic custom of uniform hand clapping which is done in rhythmic unison and in a special sequence to signal the solemnity of the hour.

The second resolution respecting Pike's memory provided that whenever a biennial session was held in Washington, D.C., the Supreme Council was to visit the Pike grave, where the current Grand Commander or a designated Inspector General was to deliver "a suitable address." On Friday morning, October 25, the Active Members with their wives assembled at the House of the Temple and then proceeded to Oak Hill Cemetery in Georgetown where Inspector Theodore S. Parvin of Iowa, an old friend of Pike's and the advocate of organizational reform, delivered a moving tribute to the Grand Commander and his work.

The day before Parvin gave his memorial address, he submitted a resolution requesting that all Supreme Council publications "not of a secret character" be sent as a courtesy to the Iowa Masonic Library at Cedar Rapids.[28] This resolution, which was easily adopted, represented not only a concern for the preservation of records but a tangible measure of foresight about the importance of Masonic history.

Before the council adjourned, it established a Committee on Rituals and authorized "the Grand Commander to publish his *Allocution* prior to Sessions of the Supreme Council."[29] All in all, the session of 1895 had been productive and allowed the Rite to recover some of its equilibrium after a rocky four years.

■ ■ ■

During the biennium that followed the session of 1895, a hard-fought national presidential campaign and election took place in 1896. In this time of national economic depression, the major issue of the campaign was the money question. The Republicans were campaigning for the single gold standard but promised also to advocate, by international agreement, a free-silver policy. On the same question the Democrats championed the free and unlimited coinage of silver at the rate of sixteen to one. That meant, specifically, "sixteen ounces of silver to one of gold, though the market ratio was about thirty-two to one."[30] In its convention at St. Louis (June 16), the Republican Party nominated Governor William McKinley of Ohio for president and Garret A. Hobart of New Jersey for vice president, both of whom were Masons. Meeting in Chicago three weeks later, the Democratic National Convention nominated for president William Jennings Bryan, a former Congressman from Nebraska and a future Mason (1902), and for vice president, Arthur Sewall, a Maine shipbuilder.

The dissimilarities between the campaign strategies of Bryan and McKinley, in addition to the differences in regional values each represented, were striking. Dubbed the "Boy Orator of the Platte," the thirty-six-year-old Bryan conducted a vigorous campaign covering some 13,000 miles in fourteen weeks and giving 600 speeches in twenty-nine states. By contrast, McKinley remained at his home in Canton, Ohio, at the behest of his friend Mark Hanna, the Cleveland industrialist and Republican campaign manager. McKinley conducted a front-porch campaign in which he would greet Republican delegations that came to see him.

This was a national campaign between creditor and debtor, the affluent, industrial East against the agrarian South and developing West. McKinley won by over a half million popular votes and by an electoral vote of 271 to 176. The Republicans also retained their control over both houses of Congress, control they had won in 1894. Undoubtedly, a major reason for the Republican victory during the depression was Hanna's effort to raise a much larger campaign fund than the Democrats. Also, Hanna employed the tactic of repeating the hyperbolic charge that Bryan was an anarchist and a revolutionist—hard to imagine given Bryan's sober reputation in his later role during the 1920s as the victor in the Scopes trial.

Despite the fact that the depression continued to be felt during the biennium that followed the session of 1895, the Scottish Rite of the Southern Jurisdiction enjoyed its greatest growth since its inception in 1801. In his report to the Supreme Council at the biennial session of 1897, Secretary General Webber stated that "the bodies have increased in numbers and also in membership."[31] Just why there was this growth at this time cannot be easily determined.[32] Both Caswell and the council felt that his extensive tour of some three months, beginning in September 1896 and comprising visitations to the bodies in such cities as Portland (Oregon), Seattle, Fargo (North Dakota), Minneapolis –St. Paul, St. Louis, Richmond, Baltimore, Charleston (South Carolina), Savannah, Montgomery (Alabama), New Orleans, Houston, Galveston, Tucson, Los Angeles, and Pasadena, was a significant cause of membership increase.[33]

Other reasons are perhaps broader. The Scottish Rite's successful growth coincided with changing cultural values in Victorian America that were endowed with revived chivalric sensibilities and gothic lyricism. The intrinsic appeal of fraternal ritual ran deep within these themes. Jackson Lears explains a vague, aesthetic phenomenon, which he named "the movement toward art and ritual," in terms of a general hunger in the middle class for "gardens of cool repose—therapeutic antidotes to feverish modern haste."[34] Scottish Rite Freemasonry, extending from the "art and artifice" of the lodge room, provided men with the means to discover "cool repose," an escape from modern demands.

Albert Pike years earlier admitted that when a man experienced the first three degrees of Masonry he may not have been entirely satisfied until a dazzling contrast could be drawn between the blue lodge and the Scottish Rite's fourth degree. The fourth degree was the first step to being transported, the "first step toward the inner sanctuary and heart of the temple"[35] whereby one entered the imagined world of King Solomon, his betrayed master builder Hiram Abiff, and the elite corps of Jewish high priests.

While it is difficult to ascertain the exact affect of the Scottish Rite ritual on the candidate's emotions, it is obvious that an experience of enchantment was a minimum benefit. As if through a looking glass, late Victorian America yielded magically to antiquity and a wondrous journey through time. Later degrees, especially enhanced by the use of painted scenery in the staging of Scottish Rite ritual, carried the candidate to the world of medieval knights encamped within view of cathedrals and castles. Through participation in the ritual, men transformed themselves into sages possessed of sacred wisdom or into heroes of ever honored memory for their combat in defense of principles.

As William D. Moore has realized, American Freemasonry provided men with several desirable, masculine vocations which were otherwise unattainable in normal walks of life. They were manly roles outside of common realms of experience, until they were entered into through the magic created by a degree. A man could feel what it was like to be a craftsman or artisan within the blue lodge; he could enter the life of a soldier as a Masonic Knight Templar; he could be a bon vivant or playful cutup as a Shriner; or he could don the mantle of a holy wise man in the Scottish Rite.[36]

Where else or where better could a man, without embarrassment in front of women or other men, experiment with his various natures? Masonry in the 1890s had become a form of moderate liberation from the lock-step world of industry and from the Victorians' unprecedented extension of the American Puritan ethic of self-control. As reference points of instruction, the degrees were, in combination, a school of personality development and character formation, giving participants outlets and affirmation. In other words, Masonry was, for many middle-class men, one kind of haven in a heartless world of market competition and another kind of haven from a world of all-heart in an increasingly feminized Victorian society (after all, the era was named for a long-reigning queen). As a source for archetypes of Victorian masculine identities, the fraternity's intangible offerings to men, beyond the obvious one of comradery, grew out of the prevailing cultural and social arrangements of the United States; much in that society happened privately, behind closed doors, so Masonry was not at odds with Victorian propriety. But in turn, Masonry helped to shape that workaday milieu in which it flourished by giving each individual a glimpse of more than one way to understand his manhood.

The phases of Masonic ritual experience, independent of fraternal fellowship and merriment, each of which represented masculine archetypes—the laborer, soldier, judge, and jester—seem to coincide, too, with deep cultural undercurrents of antimodernism. The American arts and crafts movement is one example of what Jackson Lears identified as a persistent theme of "psychic renewal" throughout the 1880s and '90s. Masonry has a claim on some portion of this important arts and craft leitmotif. Lears also points out the varieties of romantic activism that celebrated the martial ideal in "animated cults of strenuosity and military prowess." Here again, Masonry includes an expression of these values. The medieval knight, for example, was an avatar "of martial virtue in the late-Victorian imagination."[37] Knighthood is present in many forms of higher degree Masonry.

Scottish Rite ritual specifically exemplified themes of a dispersed Victorian culture in at least two ways. Just as Protestantism began to incorporate a more "theatrical" element into its worship, the Scottish Rite overcame a longstanding Masonic preference to adhere exclusively to the "communication" of austere moralism. In other words, reciting an obligation and listening to a lecture sufficed for Masonic ritual until the late Victorian period. Lears explains the phenomenon in larger terms: "the Protestant movement toward ritual may have been a recoil from habits of introspection which had lost supernatural sanction."[38] Within the fraternities, perhaps following American church trends of the time, the Scottish Rite broke new ground in how the lessons and texts of ancient wisdom were to be presented. This new enthusiasm for dramatic effect, which crossed into the church and fraternal worlds at select entry points, replaced the introspective with the scenic and confronted modern anxiety with decorative ritual.

Another way the Scottish Rite ritual was stitched to the seams of Victorian society was by a thread of fascination with pre-modern mysticism. Points along the journey of the Scottish Rite ritual, for instance, emphasize human mortality, even depicting skulls and skeletons in the regalia to remind the candidate of how democratic human destiny is. It was not surprising that the Scottish Rite degrees resonated with more and more men at a time when many Americans were stirred by "the ancient dread" and wanted a more appropriate response to death than the hollow pieties and sentimental perceptions common in the nineteenth century. There is evidence that in Victorian popular culture the revival of ghost stories as a best-selling genre reflected an interest in confronting directly the fear of death. Likewise, the Scottish Rite ritual did not sugarcoat death.

As the medieval mystics had once proposed a demanding self-denial, a final oneness with death and life, the Scottish Rite ritual offered a similar solution to the fear of being mortal. The ritual held up ascetic impulses, the contemplative study, and the fervent discipline of the mystic as countermeasures to the reality of death and, thereby, allowed a man's longing for intense experience to be legitimate. There was nothing banal about the ritual. Its message and presentation complemented an encompassing interest in and recovery of medieval values, giving hope over mere self-reliance by reaching for the infinite.

■   ■   ■

In his *Allocution* to the biennial session of 1897, the Grand Commander reported that between October 1, 1895, and October 1, 1897, he had signed "nearly three thousand patents, briefs &c., for newly-made members of the Rite."[39] Perhaps, as Reynold J. Matthews suggests, the perception among some Master Masons that the Scottish Rite could be of some help to them in those economically troubled times was an unspoken stimulus to its increased membership.[40] The increase in membership was reflected in the augmented bank balance of the Supreme Council which, as of October 1, 1897, stood at $55,598.07.

Among the changes that were taking place in the Scottish Rite of the Southern Jurisdiction was a request by the Grand Consistory of California to give up its charter with the proviso that it be rechartered as a particular consistory, San Francisco No. 1.

Caswell submitted this request on March 7, 1897, to the Active Members for a vote by mail, together with a recommendation, also from the Grand Consistory, for a particular consistory at Oakland. The council approved these requests. For both the orient and the Supreme Council, "the Grand Consistory had proven to be impractical as an administrative unit."[41] Perhaps the elimination of the Grand Consistory in California reflected a growing belief that a Sovereign Grand Inspector General ought to be "an active, working administrator in his Orient and not confined to actions in the Sessions of the Supreme Council."[42] Ultimately, the Supreme Council would discard altogether the Grand Consistory as an administrative entity.

At its biennial session the following October, Secretary General Webber reported that a granite monument, which had been ordered earlier for former Secretary General Albert Mackey's grave in Washington's Glenwood Cemetery, had been erected and that "Words Spoken of the Dead," which Pike originally prepared, was now ready for the printer. The council ordered Pike's work to be printed immediately. As librarian of the Supreme Council, through the Committee on Library and Buildings, Webber also reported that the card catalogue was virtually completed. About 50,000 library cards were used in the preparation of the catalogue, which was arranged by the Dewey Decimal System and was to be housed in an appropriate case so as to be free from dust (a major concern in a period of coal burning boilers).[43]

Among the important accomplishments of the 1897 session was the unanimous adoption of a resolution proposed by Inspector James Daniel Richardson calling for the erection of a statue of Albert Pike on a site in Washington, D.C., at a cost of "not less than ten thousand dollars."[44] A committee of five officers of the Supreme Council and four other Inspectors General were to appeal to the Scottish Rite brethren for donations while the council subscribed $5,000 for the project. The committee was to select the site for the statue, preferably "a public reservation." On April 9, 1898, an act of Congress, setting aside a site for the Pike monument, was approved through the efforts of two Scottish Rite members, Congressman James D. Richardson of Tennessee and Senator Henry M. Teller of Colorado.

The Committee for the Pike Monument then met with the superintendent of public buildings and grounds in the District of Columbia and the Joint Committee on the Library of the Senate and House of Representatives for the selection of a site at Third and D Streets, NW. In its choice of a statue design, the committee chose the proposal of Gaetano Trentanove, a sculptor from Florence, Italy. Among his many admired public works of art there are a few in Washington, D.C., including his James Marquette statue in Statuary Hall of the U.S. Capitol and a bronze monument of Daniel Webster on the west compass point of Scott Circle (a few blocks south of the present House of the Temple). He was issued a contract that called for completion in 1900. Meanwhile, the work on the statue, which was to be a standing figure of Pike, was carried on in Florence, Italy. When completed, the full monument would stand thirty feet high, the red granite pedestal being eighteen feet high and the bronze figure of Pike, twelve feet. A second decorative feature on the monument's base, a seated female figure "bearing aloft the Scottish Rite banner," was built of bronze, eight feet high.[45] Perhaps she is meant to be the "Mother" of the Supreme Council.

Another important action of the biennial session of 1897 was the Supreme Council's adoption of the *Revised Code of Statutes*. This was "a reaffirmation of the absolute sovereignty of the Supreme Council over the Rite in the Southern Jurisdiction," notes Carter, "based upon the Albert Pike translation and interpretation of the Grand Constitutions of 1786."[46] It resolved for some time the question of authority, including the election of officers for limited terms, a question which had been raised immediately after the death of Pike.

In addition to the measures just described, the council, acting on the Grand Commander's procurement of an option to buy the property on E Street next to that acquired two years before, appropriated $10,000 to purchase and renovate the desired building. The acquisition of this property reflected the growth in membership and the healthy purse of the Rite.

Among less important actions of this session was the council's approval of a suggestion from Inspector Nathaniel Levin of the Centennial Committee that the Northern Jurisdiction of the Scottish Rite be invited to join the Southern Jurisdiction in the centennial celebration and that "the Grand Commander of the Northern Jurisdiction be added to the Committee."[47] And, concerned over Masonic dignities, in an executive session Inspector George F. Moore of Alabama moved and the council approved that Active Members should bear the full ceremonial title of "Sovereign Grand Inspector General," as they once did before it was eliminated, and that Honorary Members of the Supreme Council should affix "Honorary" to their names.

On the last morning of the session (October 23, 1897), the Active Members were greeted by a story appearing in the *Washington Post* under the headline "Masons Leave the Temple." The account centered on two men belonging to the Scottish Rite from Wichita, Kansas, who wanted Colonel J. Jiles Smith of their city to be elected an Inspector General. The Supreme Council ignored their request and chose instead M. M. Miller. In anger the two campaigners left the House of the Temple and returned home. ·

The appearance of the embarrassing story in the *Washington Post* caused the Supreme Council to adopt promptly and unanimously a resolution calling on the Grand Commander to ascertain who was responsible for providing the information on which the story was based and, if found, to have the offender tried by a tribunal of the Rite or removed from the roll if it turned out he was an Honorary Member of the council.[48] Apparently Caswell never investigated the source of the account or took any action, as there are no records concerning the individual(s) who provided the leaked information. The council's resolution, however, underscored its serious concern about publicizing without permission its internal actions and problems.

About two months after the close of the 1897 session, Odell Squier Long, the Lieutenant Grand Commander, died at his home in Charleston, West Virginia. Grand Commander Caswell then appointed James D. Richardson, who had been serving as the First Grand Equerry of the Supreme Council, as the new Lieutenant Grand Commander *ad interim*, thus setting the stage for his election to that post at the next biennial session in 1899.

· · ·

In the meantime, the Spanish-American War began on April 20, 1898, when Congress adopted and President McKinley promptly signed a joint resolution recognizing the independence of Cuba, calling for the withdrawal of the Spanish military and naval forces from the island, authorizing the president to use the American armed forces to carry out this demand, and disclaiming any desire for the United States to assume control over Cuba after the Spanish colonial rule was overcome. (The Teller Amendment to the war resolution, whose sponsor was Senator Henry M. Teller, a Scottish Rite member, called for the independence of Cuba.) "The war itself was short (113 days), spectacular, low in casualties, and uninterruptedly successful—despite the disorganization."[49] With the signing of the Treaty of Paris (December 10, 1898), Spain relinquished her sovereignty over Cuba and ceded Puerto Rico, Guam, and, for a payment of $20 million, the Philippine Islands to the United States. Debate in the Senate over ratification was intense, carried on between the so-called imperialists and the anti-imperialists. Finally, by a margin of two votes, the Senate ratified the treaty on February 6, 1899. With the acquisition of the former Spanish possessions and, by a treaty of annexation, the Republic of Hawaii (July 7, 1898), the United States joined the ranks of the colonial powers of the world.

Naturally, the Spanish-American War had momentarily delayed the construction work on the House of the Temple. Though Caswell was on hand in October 1898 to launch the project, the contract was not signed until November 26. The war also affected the future of the Supreme Council through the subsequent establishment of Scottish Rite bodies in the Philippines and Puerto Rico. It should be recalled that jurisdictional extension of the Mother Supreme Council had been well established "long before the Spanish-American War,"[50] with the Louisiana Purchase, the acquisition of Florida, the annexation of Texas, the Mexican cession, and the Oregon settlement.

The territorial extension of the Supreme Council went hand in hand with its overall excellent standing at the opening of the last biennial session of the century on October 16, 1899. In his *Allocution*, Caswell declared "that the Rite generally was never in a more prosperous condition than it is today. Many new bodies have been established and dormant ones revived, and the seekers after the true light have been many and the material of the very best."[51] The Grand Commander noted there were about 10,000 Scottish Rite members out of a total of 340,000 Master Masons in the Southern Jurisdiction and consequently thought there was "a fruitful field for labor"[52] for a number of ambitious Inspectors General.

By the time of the 1899 session, the latest phase of remodeling work on the House of the Temple was completed. It was, in Caswell's judgment, "a grandly imposing edifice, with a frontage of sixty-eight feet on E street by one hundred and twelve feet on Third street," containing "spacious offices, committee rooms, library, museum, and banquet rooms, sufficient for all future wants or necessities." The major improvement also included a lavish council chamber or sanctuary.[53]

In another section of his *Allocution*, devoted to foreign relations, Caswell questioned the right of the Grand Lodge of Scotland to establish a symbolic lodge at Colon, Colombia, within the jurisdiction of the Supreme Council of New Granada (Colombia), as the latter had long exercised exclusive control over all Masonic degrees, from the first through the thirty-third. The Grand Commander felt that it was "wrong and should not be countenanced."[54] This was a startling departure from Pike's conviction that Supreme Councils had no authority to establish or govern symbolic lodges.

What is more, the Committee on Foreign Relations strongly endorsed Caswell's position, proposing "to apply the 'Monroe Doctrine' to Masonry, and say to the Grand Lodge of Edinburgh, and to all other grand bodies in Europe and the rest of the world, that the territorial jurisdiction upon either continent of the old or new world cannot be invaded without calling for the malediction of legitimate bodies elsewhere wherever located."[55] The Supreme Council concurred with the Grand Commander and the Committee on Foreign Relations in their noteworthy deviation from Pike's position and precedent. As an indirect result of the Spanish-American War, Caswell's bold move perhaps reflected, in a small symbolic way, the newfound American confidence to assume an expanding and dominant role in international affairs in general.

On Caswell's recommendation, one of the important accomplishments of the 1899 session was to correct and clarify many sections of the *Revised Statutes* that had been adopted two years before. A significant amendment to Article XI (Miscellaneous Provisions) provided for the semiannual publication of the *Official Bulletin*, which had been discontinued in 1892 after more than twenty years of publication. With the growth of the Southern Jurisdiction there was an obvious need for such a publication. It was to contain about 150 pages per number and was to be distributed—one copy each—to the Inspectors General, Deputies, Lodges of Perfection, and consistories.

Besides the approval of several changes in the *Revised Statutes*, the Supreme Council also adopted the report of the Committee on the Revision of the Ritual, which recommended the revision, correction, abbreviation, and reprinting of the rituals and their secret work. The publishing project would include an explanation of the placement of the lodge furniture, the pronunciation of the words, and the proper mode of communicating them.

Other actions at this session of the Supreme Council included a decision to make the American Security and Trust Company of Washington, D.C. (later American Security Bank, which would not survive under that name beyond the 1990s), its official depository, and it remained as such for many years into the twentieth century. On the recommendation of the Committee on the Centennial Celebration, the council gave approval for the observance of its 100th anniversary on May 31, 1901, at which time there would be a short ceremonial, an appropriate address, and the unveiling of the monument to Albert Pike.

To honor other dignitaries of the Supreme Council, the Scottish Rite bodies of the different states, as reported by Secretary General Webber, had presented portraits of their Inspectors General to the council, beginning with ones of Inspector Samuel E. Adams of Minnesota and Inspector Austin B. Chamberlin of Texas. Webber, in turn, had commissioned oil portraits of Grand Commander Caswell; Treasurer General Meredith; Lieutenant Grand Commander Richardson; Inspector Rufus E. Fleming of North Dakota, the Grand Constable; and Inspector W. Frank Pierce of California, the Grand Sword Bearer.[56] "This was the beginning of the collection of portraits in the House of the Temple which became so large that it was no longer possible to display all of the collection in that building."[57]

On a Sunday afternoon before the day of adjournment, the Supreme Council made a pilgrimage to former Grand Commander Pike's grave at Oak Hill Cemetery where five of the Supreme Council members paid tribute to his memory, where Lieutenant Grand Commander Richardson also read Pike's doleful poem "Every Year." This was followed by the singing of Lowell Mason's best known hymn, "Nearer, My God, to Thee," and the memorial service for feast days and obligatory meetings.

The next morning at the White House the Grand Commander was joined by more than thirty others on a fraternal appointment to see President William McKinley, also a Mason, who greeted each of them personally. At 11:20 A.M. the council met in senatorial session and finally closed the last biennial session of the century at about 10:30 that evening "with the Albert Pike memorial service."[58]

Afterward, Caswell returned to his home in San Francisco. There is no evidence of the Grand Commander taking any official action between the end of the session of 1899 and his death about a year later. After a three-month illness, Caswell died on November 13, 1900. Five days later he was buried in the Masonic Cemetery of San Francisco, "following the most impressive funeral ceremonies ever witnessed in the State."[59]

A California resident for more than fifty years, Caswell lived through the wild days of John C. Frémont in the early aftermath of the Bear Flag revolt; and he lived long enough to have known firsthand the mining camp stories of Bret Harte, the beauties of Yosemite experienced by John Muir, and the bohemia of San Francisco, which held such passing talent as Robert Louis Stevenson and Frank Norris. It was a period of California history and life depicted as "a confusion of unruliness with vigor, recklessness with style, and bravado with self-confidence."[60] If Masonry gave Caswell some personal perspective on his western surroundings, he returned to Masonry a confidence peculiar to the Californians of his time, who had such great possibilities before them.

For a little more than six years, including his service as Acting Grand Commander, Thomas Caswell had been the Sovereign Grand Commander. This was during a period of considerable growth and activity in the Rite, and Caswell had conducted much of the Supreme Council's business from his home in California. Upon Caswell's death, as prescribed by the *Grand Constitutions of 1786* and the *Statutes* of the Supreme Council, Lieutenant Grand Commander James D. Richardson became the Acting Commander until the biennial session of 1901.

■   ■   ■

The nine years between the death of Pike and the death of Caswell began as a troubled string of setbacks, yet concluded as heartening times for the Supreme Council, ready to begin its second century. Not counting Pike, three Grand Commanders in less than ten years does not usually result in growth and prosperity. The transition, rather than a time of calm seas and prosperous voyages, was an uncertain passage, as noted by the following conditions:

1. Internal tensions after Pike's death over the question of limited terms for officers of the council.
2. Constant remodeling and expansion of the House of the Temple.
3. Elimination of the *Official Bulletin* and its later reinstatement.
4. Expansion in membership and resources of the Rite in the Southern Jurisdiction despite deep economic depression nationwide.
5. Incorporation of the Supreme Council.
6. Enlargement of the library and completion of its card catalogue.
7. Revision of the *Statutes*.

Separately, each summary point is a small, minor transformation, barely making a dent on the longer history. Together, however, these were not idle changes, but mark the last decade of the nineteenth century as setting the agenda and the direction of the Rite for the next hundred years.

The mood of the country in general was mirrored within the Scottish Rite during the 1890s, as it would be throughout the twentieth century. It was vaguely the widespread sense that America was leaving behind forever the landscape of the past. New patterns in American society were inevitable and taking root. Major demographic changes were shaping the explosive growth of cities. In 1890, the Census Bureau announced that the great American frontier could now be viewed as nonexistent. All the arable land that had once attracted so many new settlers had been claimed.

The end of the frontier and the rise of the city in America signaled a major realization, which the historian Frederick Jackson Turner expressed ponderously: "the frontier is the line of most rapid and effective Americanization." He was asking his generation of the 1890s an existential question: Without the frontier how can we be and also make new Americans? The idea that the frontier could provide a safety valve for the personal and social discontent of Americans was turning out to be impermanent, even disposable.

Meanwhile, technological change generated commercial and industrial employment in the burgeoning cities, and inventions such as the Otis elevator, steel-frame construction, and street lights gave those cities a new face and a new density. Counterintuitively, during the great spurt of American industrialization between 1860 and 1900, farmland more than doubled and the number of those making a living in agriculture increased by nearly half.[61] Land and farm prices were still significant variables in the equation of the national economy, but psychologically the country had shifted itself toward the urban setting.

Clearly, by the 1890s the American people were becoming more numerous, more ethnically diverse, and more geographically concentrated. This was more true of the East and the mid-Atlantic states than the West; though perhaps more true of the West than the South, which was still rebuilding itself after the Civil War.

For middle-class Americans, the social structures of the Victorian decades were well fortified to guard against the disturbing effect of the rapid, incomprehensible changes already on the scene at the docks, in factories, and in tenements. As a means of protection, the Victorian ethos developed "a series of parallel dichotomies [that] became sharply etched in the American consciousness: male/female, work/home, power/purity, profane/sacred."[62]

Certain gender assumptions in American middle-class culture had profound implications for fraternal and organizational life. A living mythology developed in which women were ordained to conduct the sacred functions of home, such as nurturing the family. Men, correspondingly, were left to confront the profane realities of competition and work. Men now left home to go out into the world for their wages, whereas before, the habits of mind in rural America had insisted that the work was right at hand in a shop or on a farm.

The positive membership trend for the Scottish Rite during the 1890s, in spite of its fragile, aging, and changing leadership, may be accounted for partially in the implicit appeal of the "purification" that was offered to men who had new emotional needs and a need for moral assurance. Like the safety valve provided by the American frontier, the Scottish Rite, though not yet in any large-scale form, opened new horizons, fresh, imaginary spaces, and a new mental world to middle-class men in Victorian America who sometimes felt cutoff from the passing world of agrarian America. At this time, the usefulness of the Scottish Rite was in its intrinsic capacity to be a practical outlet for men feeling displaced by inevitable new realities. Notwithstanding the Supreme Council's modest initiatives of the 1890s, the larger fact was that the Scottish Rite fit the times and was well positioned to become more popular in the next century.

CHAPTER VII

New Century, New Age, New Temple
1900–1914

James D. Richardson

The year 1900 burned significance and hope into the American psyche. The sense of an invisible line dividing "before" from "after" was neither illusion nor artifice. The double-digit "ought-ought" of the year 1900, for Americans at the time, meant a new reality approached. A predominantly Protestant culture was geared to think of the last century of a millennium as suggestive of a final destiny, if not foreboding a doomsday. It was no ordinary change in the calendar. Actually, the first year of a new century begins with "01." But as Mark Sullivan, the well-known journalist, observed in *Our Times,*

> Throughout 1899 there had been much discussion as to what day and year marked the close of the nineteenth century and the beginning of the twentieth. It was recognized by everybody as a turning-point, a hundred-mile stone. There was a human disposition to sum things up, to say who had been the greatest men of the century just closed, what had been the greatest books, the greatest inventions, the greatest advances in science. Looking forward, there was a similar disposition to forecast and predict. This appealed to nearly everybody; and to find people disputing the correctness of the date you chose for harking back or looking forward was an irritation. Wherever men met they argued about it. Editorials dealt with it, seriously or factiously. Contentious persons wrote letters to the papers. School-children were set to figuring. It grew to the vogue of one of those puzzles "How old is Ann?"[1]

In 1900 there were forty-five states in the Union—Oklahoma, Arizona, New Mexico, Alaska, and Hawaii would be admitted later in the twentieth century—and the twelfth decennial census reported a population of nearly 76 million, which was 13 million more than that of the census of 1890. The influx of "new" immigration accounted for about a third of this increase. Moreover, during the 1880s and 1890s there was a vast migration to the cities as a result of industrialization, higher wages, and disenchantment with rural life and farm prices.

Not only was there an increase in population as reflected in the 1900 census, there was a growth in the membership of the Scottish Rite of Freemasonry, Southern Jurisdiction, to the unprecedented total of 10,570. It was the region west of the Mississippi River that reflected the largest gain of the Scottish Rite's Southern Jurisdiction in the last years of its first century. The increase in membership east of the Mississippi was quite modest and, indeed, was negligible in the states of the former Confederacy.[2] Despite the impressive growth in membership, a minority of the members, who reflected Pike's thought about the Scottish Rite as a Masonic elite, were apprehensive about this growth as they thought it would be inimical to the Rite's future. In contrast, for some six years Grand Commander Caswell had approvingly presided over the increase in membership and bodies, until his death on November 13, 1900, a week after the presidential election.

The Republicans at their convention in Philadelphia had nominated President William McKinley for another term and Colonel Theodore Roosevelt of New York—a Mason who had won renown during the Spanish-American War by leading the dismounted Rough Riders in the battle of San Juan Hill in Cuba two years earlier—for vice president. They ran on a platform which upheld the gold standard, supported the administration's expansionist foreign policy, and urged an American built and controlled Isthmian canal. In turn, the Democrats at their convention in Kansas City nominated William Jennings Bryan for president (a second time) and Adlai E. Stevenson of Illinois (vice president during Cleveland's second administration) for vice president on a platform of anti-imperialism. McKinley and Roosevelt won handily, and their party kept control of both houses of Congress.

With Caswell's death a week after the election, Lieutenant Grand Commander James D. Richardson became Acting Grand Commander. Born in Rutherford County, Tennessee, on March 10, 1843, he attended "Franklin College near Nashville, from which at the outbreak of the Civil War he enlisted in the Confederate Army and served until the close of the conflict, retiring as adjutant of the 45th Tennessee Volunteers."[3] After the Civil War, he was admitted to the bar and opened an attorney's office in Murfreesboro. He later was elected to the Tennessee legislature and in 1884 was elected to the U.S. House of Representatives where he served for twenty years.

In 1873 Richardson was elected for one term as Grand Master of Masons in Tennessee, an office once held by Andrew Jackson. Meanwhile, he had become a member of the York Rite bodies. Later, in 1881, he received the Scottish Rite degrees through the thirty-second; and at the end of December 1884, Richardson was coroneted an Inspector General Honorary. Two months later Grand Commander Pike crowned him an Active

Member of the Supreme Council. Parallel to Pike's Scottish Rite career, Richardson was also on the fast track because of his interest and talent.

Shortly after becoming the Acting Grand Commander, Richardson acted expeditiously on three important matters. He requested a recess vote of the council on his recommendation to combine the centennial celebration with the biennial session of October 1901 as a savings to the council and assurance of optimum attendance. The council, seeing the wisdom of Richardson's recommendation, unanimously agreed to the postponement of the celebration until the session.

In responding to a request for a decision on the requirement for a quorum in the subordinate bodies, Richardson answered that the presence of an Inspector General would constitute a quorum for opening and closing a lodge and that at least five members must be present for the conferral of degrees. As for the transaction of business of the lodge, it was necessary to have nine members in attendance, as the Regulations for the Government of Lodges of Perfection provided.

Richardson also ruled that "each body should adopt its own by-laws," committees should not be appointed by the presiding officer of one body from the other bodies, and a brother could not be expelled or suspended for the nonpayment of dues or other cause without giving him proper advance notice.[4]

Early the following spring, the Acting Grand Commander accepted on behalf of the Supreme Council "a magnificent bequest" of nearly 2,000 volumes "on occult and kindred literature, some of which were rare," from Dr. Leroy M. Taylor, of Washington, D.C. Taylor wished his gift to be kept separate from the rest of the library; he provided $500 for the cataloguing of "The Taylor Collection" and a portrait of himself, which was to be hung on the wall. As he explained to Richardson, he made "this donation as a stimulant to others, who are able to do something more than 'chin music' for our beloved order."[5] The Taylor Collection has still retained its integrity, as the donor requested.

On May 3, 1901, a little over a month after Richardson had acknowledged Taylor's impressive gift to the Library of the Supreme Council, a great fire destroyed most of the city of Jacksonville, Florida. Upon receiving a request for help from the Grand Master of Florida, Richardson promptly sent $500 to the Grand Master for disaster relief, another instance of and precedent for the Rite's extending help in a crisis.

Four weeks later, on May 31, a musical concert, which the Acting Grand Commander had arranged, was held at the House of the Temple as an observance of the Supreme Council's founding day in Charleston a century before, even though the official centennial celebration had been postponed until October at the biennial session.

■　■　■

When the biennial session opened on October 21, 1901, it was about six weeks after the assassination of President McKinley by Leon Czolgosz, an anarchist, at the Pan-American Exposition in Buffalo, New York. For the third time in thirty-six years, an

American president was the victim of an assassin's bullet. At the close of his *Allocution,* Richardson paid tribute to the martyred president and brother Mason.

As was customary, the Acting Grand Commander delivered his *Allocution* on the opening day of the biennial session. "There was never a time in the history of the Supreme Council," he noted, "when the Rite was more prosperous and buoyant with hope than it is to-day."[6] Between July 1, 1899, and July 1, 1901, there was an increase of 40 bodies in the Southern Jurisdiction for a total of 265. While this was gratifying, Richardson questioned whether the increase in membership and, therefore, in income was in the best interests of the Rite. He "warned that care must be exercised in accepting petitions, an admonition reminiscent of the words of Pike on the same subject."[7]

On the day after the delivery of his *Allocution,* the Supreme Council elected Richardson as Grand Commander for life and Samuel Emery Adams as Lieutenant Grand Commander for life. Later that day Grand Commander Henry L. Palmer of the Supreme Council of the Northern Masonic Jurisdiction installed them and the other officers. In turn, "a beautiful Loving Cup, handsomely and appropriately engraved," was presented to Palmer "as a visible token of the love and esteem" of the members of the Southern Jurisdiction's council.[8]

In view of the centennial of the Supreme Council, Richardson found it appropriate in his *Allocution* to note that for more than forty-five years none of the Grand Commanders of the Southern Jurisdiction were native southerners or, for that matter, natives of any state in the jurisdiction. John Mitchell and Frederick Dalcho, the first and second Grand Commanders were born respectively in Ireland and England, and Isaac Auld and Moses Holbrook, the third and fourth Grand Commanders, in turn, were natives of Pennsylvania and Massachusetts. Thus, observed Richardson, for about eighty-five years of the Supreme Council's first century the "Grand Commanders were all born outside of the jurisdiction."[9]

Other references to the history of the Supreme Council were made in the *Allocution.* Besides the Pike Monument that was to be unveiled two days later, Richardson reported that a memorial room for Pike had been established in the House of the Temple. It was the room in which both Pike and Batchelor had died.

The new Grand Commander also spoke of the need to acquire some manuscripts related to the early history of the Scottish Rite, including the register of Grand Commander Moses Holbrook, which the Archives of the Supreme Council now has in its possession. Richardson recommended that he "or some other suitable person" be given the authority "to procure all such manuscripts for preservation."[10] Later in the session, the council granted the Grand Commander the authority he had requested. No one knows how many of the early documents and Masonic records, presumably in Charleston since 1801, were lost during the Civil War.

The historical highlight of this biennial session occurred on October 23, 1901, with the unveiling of the statue of Albert Pike at Third and D Streets, NW,[11] at three o'clock.

At the unveiling ceremony Grand Master Harry Standiford of the Grand Lodge of the District of Columbia presided in the presence of the Active Members of both the Northern and Southern Supreme Councils, their Honorary Members, and other Masonic dignitaries. Standiford was assisted by the other Grand Lodge officers in the Masonic dedicatory ritual of finding the monument "to be mechanically perfect" with the aid of the square, level, and plumb. He then sprinkled the base of the statue with the customary corn, wine, and oil—the wages of a Fellow Craft—to the accompaniment of "a quartet rendering the regular Masonic chant for the occasion."[12]

Secretary General Webber, in turn, gave the dedicatory address, closing his remarks by presenting the statue to the government of the United States. H. B. F. Macfarland, one of the commissioners of the District of Columbia, in accepting the gift on behalf of the federal government, observed that "although Albert Pike was a soldier in the civil war, this statue will commemorate him rather as a victor in the honorable rivalries of peace,"[13] certainly a tactful comment about a former Confederate general.

At 7:30 that evening, Richardson delivered his Centennial Address before a large audience at the First Congregational Church, at Tenth and D Streets, NW, in the heart of the city. He began by noting that if his "narrative" fell short in interest and "entertainment," the fault would be due to a dearth of the "requisite materials,"[14] a matter which has been noted earlier in this history. In the course of his remarks, Richardson observed that inasmuch as the Supreme Council at Charleston was the first Supreme Council to be organized and had maintained without interruption its existence, "it justly claims to be the Mother Council of the World. This claim is not made arrogantly and with intent to give offense to other Supreme Councils, but only that the truth of history may be vindicated. Naturally we take pride in this fact, for it is something of which to be proud. But we indulge the hope that it is not of our years alone we may boast. The escutcheon of Scottish Masonry has been preserved untarnished throughout the century by the Southern Supreme Council."[15]

At the conclusion of the address, Richardson stated in a persuasive and memorable passage concerning the teaching purpose of the organization he was leading that "Scottish Rite Masonry has not attempted to propagate any creed, save its own simple and sublime one, of faith in God and of good works; no religion save the universal, eternal and immutable religion, a religion such as God planted in the heart of universal humanity. Its votaries may be sought and found alike in Jewish, Moslem and Christian temples. It is a teacher of the morals of all religions; it is the preacher of good and not of evil, of truth and not error."[16]

The Grand Commander then declared forcefully in his next paragraph, which has become the Scottish Rite Creed and has served as a de facto mission statement for the twentieth century, "The cause of human progress is our cause; the enfranchisement of human thought our supreme wish; the freedom of conscience our mission; and the guarantee of equal rights to all peoples everywhere the end of our contention."[17]

It is worth noting that many years later Ray Baker Harris, the librarian of the Supreme Council, told the then Grand Commander that he had reread Richardson's Centennial Address and felt that "it tells a great deal in very brief form." Harris gave the address high marks: "It again makes a strong appeal to me as being one of the finest, short accounts of the background history and the nature of the Scottish Rite."[18] Similarly perhaps, whole books have been devoted to the mere hundreds of words in the Gettysburg Address because of what it implies about the historical consciousness and national character of America.

At the conclusion of Richardson's address, the Active Members of the Supreme Council and their guests went to the "new" Willard Hotel for a large banquet. It was a fitting climax to the centennial celebration.

Later in the session, the members of the Supreme Council called on the new president of the United States, Theodore Roosevelt, at the White House. With the assistance of Secretary General Webber, Richardson, who was still a member of Congress, introduced the members to the president, who was a Mason though not a member of the Scottish Rite. Roosevelt, however, was a Scottish Rite "booster," as he attended, on September 18, 1902, the dedication ceremonies of the Masonic temple (later rebuilt and named the "Albert Pike Memorial Temple") in Little Rock, Arkansas. On that occasion, Roosevelt addressed his Scottish Rite audience with remarks about crimes against the state, particularly the corruption of officeholders. He said then, at the luncheon held in his honor, "I permit myself one particular bit of partisan discrimination. I am just a trifle more intent on punishing the Republican offender than the Democrat, because he is my own scoundrel."[19]

The day after the reception by President Roosevelt in Washington, the Supreme Council made its traditional biennial pilgrimage to the grave of Albert Pike in Oak Hill Cemetery where the usual tributes were rendered and the hymns "Nearer, My God to Thee" and "Rock of Ages" were sung.

Before the council adjourned, it elected Brigadier General Robert H. Hall as Sovereign Grand Inspector General for the army and navy of the United States. It also adopted some seventy amendments to the *Statutes* submitted by the Committee on Jurisprudence and Legislation, some of which only involved omitting or adding a word or two, and granted the Grand Commander the authority to approve changes in the rituals suggested by the Committee on Rituals. The council also granted him the authority to republish the rituals if he so desired. This was an important policy precedent, giving the Grand Commander wide discretionary powers, unlike other Masonic organizations and, for that matter, other public institutions.

By 1901, there was momentum already in place for a decided change in the way the Scottish Rite degrees were conferred, a move from the lodge room to an auditorium stage. Interestingly, the change did not originate with the Supreme Council but rather with the subordinate bodies and their officers. "In fact," as Carter notes, "the members of the Supreme Council, with exception of a very few, had objected to the change; however, they had not forbidden it."[20] Moreover, while Richardson cautioned "against changes in the Rituals for purposes of dramatization,"[21] he made no recommendation to terminate the staging of the degrees. Thus there was no turning back to an earlier day when the degrees were communicated. But the Supreme Council was uncertain about proposed alterations and changes which the Committee on Rituals had submitted. Richardson, as he noted in his *Allocution* of 1903, had not republished the rituals, believing that "no action was better than mistaken action."[22] Revision of the rituals has periodically been a subject of concern for the Supreme Council, but the greatest change came with their theatrical presentation.

C. Lance Brockman argues persuasively that the Scottish Rite's spectacular popular success in the first half of the twentieth century cannot be divorced from its "integration of theatrical techniques" in presenting degrees as stand-alone morality plays. The major shift away from traditional lodge room practices "served both to heighten the initiation experience, and more important, to provide the means of mass-producing members."[23]

Brockman points out that the "change from participatory to presentational space, or from lodge to theater, first occurred in 1884," in the Chicago Masonic Temple.[24] Scottish Rite classes or group initiations, however, probably began modestly in the early 1870s, not in a major city but in towns such as Lyons, Iowa.

Further, the Scottish Rite's need to restructure its degree presentation coincided with and, in part, may have been driven by the ambitious marketing of theater scenery and paraphernalia by commercial companies. In order to survive financially during frequent depressions and downturns, theater companies searched for new markets in which to peddle their merchandise. After all, the public would not support vaudeville if the price of tickets got in the way of buying daily bread. The market diversification of theater supply companies, therefore, had a role in how the Scottish Rite ritual was changed and enhanced. The companies may have helped create the market, but buyers were perhaps ready-made because of the demands placed on the Masonic fraternity to make room for new members.[25]

• • •

New ground was being broken internationally for Masonic relations. Among other subjects which the Grand Commander discussed in the *Allocution* of 1903 was the suggestion of Count Goblet D'Alviella, the Grand Commander of the Supreme Council of Belgium, in a letter of September 14, 1902, to establish in 1903 or 1904 an organization or bureau of Supreme Councils for the purpose of exchanging news and deciding "whom we have or ought to have inside our confederacy."[26] Richardson liked the proposal, and the Supreme Council, desiring international contact, readily endorsed it. In 1907, five years after D'Alviella's recommendation, the first in a series of international conferences of Supreme Councils met in Brussels. These conferences, which have continued to the present, have sometimes put a strain on amicable Masonic relations over such issues as "the legitimate functions" of such bodies, "their legal standing and, ultimately, all aspects of Foreign Relations between Supreme Councils—a wholly undeveloped phase of Scottish Rite policy and legislative activity which reopened all of the questions first raised by the Congress at Lausanne in 1875."[27] The Masonic fraternity may have been ahead of its time in this regard, because, with the exception of the Red Cross and YMCA, it was another fifty years before voluntary international organizations were earnestly tried.

There had been, to be sure, more than token efforts at international ecumenism, for example, in 1886 at the Lambeth Conference of Anglican Bishops, in 1910 at the famous World Missionary Conference at Edinburgh, in 1921 at the International Missionary Council, and in 1937 at the Conferences on Faith and Order (Edinburgh) and Life and Work (Oxford). But there was no worldwide organization to unify the many Christian bodies into a united purpose. The League of Nations was a failed experiment, but after 1945 the World Council of Churches and the United Nations were remedies whose time had come at long last. Masonry, however, had been thinking internationally at least as long as the Christian churches had.

Another issue, "a question of grave importance" which Richardson addressed in his 1903 *Allocution,* was "the use of intoxicants at the public banquets and functions of the Council, and in those of the subordinate bodies."[28] Although the major expense of the banquets held at reunions was the cost of liquor and wine, Richardson's main concern was overindulgence of "one or more present." This had an adverse effect on the Rite, he felt, and "nothing but injury results therefrom."[29] The Grand Commander recommended that no alcoholic beverages be served at any banquet or other affairs of the Supreme Council or the subordinate bodies within its jurisdiction. Later in the session, the council adopted a statute (Article XI, Section 21) stating "that the use of any spiritous, vinous or malt liquors by any body of the Ancient and Accepted Scottish Rite for the Southern Jurisdiction of the United States of America be, and the same is hereby, prohibited."[30]

Undoubtedly the Prohibition movement strongly influenced the Grand Commander and the Supreme Council. By 1900 the Prohibition Party, founded in 1869; the Women's Christian Temperance Union (WCTU), established in 1874; and the Anti-Saloon League, organized in 1893, were included in the growing movement that ultimately led to the ratification of the Eighteenth Amendment to the Constitution (1919), "prohibiting the manufacture, sale, or transportation of intoxicating liquors." The Prohibition movement underscores "the teaching of temperance in Freemasonry," even though moderate consumption at Masonic meetings had prevailed since well before the Civil War, dating to colonial America where lodges often met in the private rooms of taverns and inns.[31]

One of the most important actions of the Supreme Council during the biennial session of 1903 was the founding of "a literary monthly magazine" on the strong recommendation of Grand Commander Richardson, who believed "that some medium of communication between the brethren of the Rite throughout our vast jurisdiction is highly desirable, if not imperatively demanded."[32] The publication would not only be devoted to the interests and vitality of the Supreme Council but also to the objectives of Freemasonry and "the education of the people in the very highest sense."[33] The enabling resolution, which the council adopted, provided a board of directors for the magazine and an appropriation of $16,500 for the first year of its publication.

Having agreed to serve, the following group constituted the first board of directors: "James D. Richardson, Tennessee; H. L. Palmer, Wisconsin; Frederick Webber, Washington, DC; J. H. Codding, Pennsylvania; George F. Moore, Alabama; W. Frank Pierce, California; A. B. Chamberlin, Washington, DC; F. P. Elliott, New York; R. J. Nunn, Savannah, Georgia."[34] Worth noting was the inclusion of three directors from the Northern Masonic Jurisdiction of the Scottish Rite among the directors, an obvious gesture of goodwill, if not the first step to unification. Richardson expected that the magazine would reach thousands of Scottish Rite Masons of the Northern Jurisdiction, as it would be of interest to them, while of course every member of the Southern Jurisdiction would receive a copy.[35]

As a necessary concomitant to the establishment of the magazine, the Supreme Council repealed the statute authorizing the quarterly publication of the *Official Bulletin*. Its continuance would be a redundancy.

Shortly after the close of the biennial session of 1903, the Board of Managers (changed from "directors," as it appeared in the *Transactions* of 1903) of the new publication met and elected Richardson as president, Grand Commander Henry L. Palmer of the Northern Masonic Jurisdiction, vice president; Frederick Webber, secretary; and Allison Nailor Jr. of Washington, D.C., treasurer. The board chose as editors George F. Moore, Sovereign Grand Inspector General in Alabama, who had been elected at the 1903 session as Grand Minister of State of the Supreme Council, and Francis P. Elliott of New York, who was named managing editor. A thirty-second degree Mason, Elliott had been associated with Harper and Brothers and was editor of *Home* magazine for three years prior to his appointment by the Board of Managers. Elliott, however, was relieved of his responsibility as managing editor the following June. George F. Moore then became the sole editor, and George E. Howard, a Washington, D.C., publisher, became the business manager.

The first issue of *The New Age*, which appeared in June 1904, included 144 pages, 60 of which dealt with sketches, science, social service, poetry, stories, and an article on the House of the Temple. Thirty pages were devoted to Masonic material. Handsome in appearance, the new publication also had 36 pages of advertising, including the inside of the front cover and both sides of the back. The name was suggested to Moore by the ritual of the degree of Rose Croix (eighteenth degree) and was copyrighted in 1904. Five years later, Moore noted in *The New Age* that a Boston magazine, formerly known as *The New Theology*, "has recently assumed our name and is advertising itself in similar periodicals. The right of this magazine to enjoin the use of the name *The New Age* is undeniable."[36]

On August 1, 1904, Richardson sent a letter to all members of the Scottish Rite in the

Southern Jurisdiction, inviting them to subscribe to *The New Age* and pointing out that it was being sent free to all members in the Southern Jurisdiction for one year. As a result of his letter, a subscription list of 20,000 was obtained for the December 1904 issue. Apparently, the response from members of the Northern Masonic Jurisdiction was limited, and from the general public it was virtually nil, despite "a conscious effort" to appeal to that audience.[37] According to Richard J. Nunn—the Grand Almoner of the Supreme Council and a member of the new Board of Trustees, established at the biennial session in 1907 for *The New Age*—the magazine "was criticized because the articles 'are of too high a character to please [the] Brethren.'" Nevertheless, he wanted improvement in the "tone of literature with which the intellect of the Brethren is fed."[38] This tension, as Carter notes, has been "a problem universal with editors of Masonic publications."[39] It remains, too, a challenge for all forms of print communications of national scope.

Besides the founding of *The New Age* at the biennial session of 1903, the Supreme Council provided for the books of Albert Pike to be formed into a collection known as the Albert Pike Library. The council also approved Nunn's resolution endorsing the proposal of the Washington Monument Association of Alexandria, Virginia, to erect in Alexandria a monument honoring Washington as a citizen and Mason. Eight years later, the George Washington Masonic National Memorial Association was established at a meeting of twenty-seven jurisdictions.

Reflecting the substantial growth of the Rite, the total expenditures for the 1903 session, according to the unpublished minutes of its executive session of October 24, amounted to a sizeable figure of $119,070. Among the itemized expenditures were the salaries of the Grand Commander ($10,000), the Secretary General ($3,000), the assistant to the Secretary General ($2,000), the Treasurer General ($600), and the librarian ($2,000). For the early years of the twentieth century, the salary of the Grand Commander was indeed handsome, being the equivalent to a salary of about $140,000 in the early 1990s.[40]

■　■　■

During the biennium that followed the session of 1903, President Theodore Roosevelt won the Republican nomination for reelection by acclamation and went on to defeat the Democratic presidential nominee, Judge Alton B. Parker of New York, who was a Mason and a Past Master of Kingston Lodge No. 10, Kingston, New York. Roosevelt's triumph was by a large popular majority on November 8, 1904, and by an electoral vote of 336 to 140. "On the night of his election Roosevelt pledged that 'under no circumstances will I be a candidate for or accept another nomination.'"[41] Eight years later, in 1912, however, he accepted the nomination for president from a third party, the Progressive ("Bull Moose") Party, after he was unsuccessful in securing the Republican nomination.

On March 4, 1905, when Roosevelt was inaugurated in his own right as president, Grand Commander Richardson retired from Congress after twenty years of service, having declared his intention to do so in his *Allocution* of 1903 in order to devote his full attention to the Supreme Council. Perhaps an added inducement for retirement was the fact that as a Democratic congressman he could expect no further advancement in view of continued Republican control of both the Congress and the executive branch.[42] Further, he did not retire from Congress because of conflict of interest rules which would have forbidden accepting two salaries. Only later standards of propriety have made dual officeholding an ethical issue.

Besides his retirement from Congress in 1905, Richardson also published that year, at his own expense and with the permission of Congress, *A Compilation of the Messages and Papers of the Confederacy* in two volumes. An advertisement for the work was carried in the October 1904 issue of *The New Age*.

When the Supreme Council met in October 1905 for its biennial session, Richardson reported in his *Allocution* that as of July 1 there were 19,499 members of the thirty-second degree. This reflected an increase of 5,402 for the two previous years. Moreover, by mid-1905 the Southern Jurisdiction had 303 bodies, including 10 which had been added during the past two years.

As a reflection of the growth and prosperity of the Rite, Richardson stated in his *Allocution* that on May 14, 1904, he had taken a party of twenty—including Secretary General Webber, Inspector General Nunn of Georgia, Inspector General John W. Morris of West Virginia, and several Washington, D.C., Scottish Rite members—on a tour to Little Rock, Guthrie, Wichita, and St. Louis by a chartered Pullman car. They were gone eighteen days, traveled some 3,300 miles, attended four reunions, "and added about six hundred members to the Rite."[43] A little less than a year later, Richardson, together with Webber and J. A. Whitcombe of the Washington bodies, made another tour (April 17–May 12, 1905) that included visitations to Chicago, in the Northern Masonic Jurisdiction; Duluth, Minneapolis, and St. Paul, Minnesota; Fargo, Aberdeen, and Yankton, South Dakota; Sioux City, Iowa; Omaha, Nebraska; and Des Moines and Davenport, Iowa.

In addition to reporting on these peripatetic activities, Richardson made an ambitious proposal for charity to the Supreme Council concerning the education of a son or daughter of a Mason by means of scholarships in schools and colleges which advertised in *The New Age*. These institutions, in return for free advertising in the magazine, would provide free tuition to students, each Inspector General having the authority to appoint at least one from his state or jurisdiction. The council, in turn, would pay the cost of room and board. "In this way," said Richardson, "a free education would be given to the pupil."[44] The Grand Commander appointed a Special Committee on Education which reported at the biennial session of 1907 that it had agreed upon a general, but not a final, plan. Each Inspector General was to select from his jurisdiction a child of a deceased Scottish Rite Mason (later modified) and "place him or her in some school, within the same jurisdiction, which gives free tuition, or which will accept for tuition an advertisement in *The New Age* magazine."[45]

Among other actions taken by the Supreme Council at the 1905 session was the adoption of two recommendations of the Committee on Jurisprudence and Legislation. One authorized a payment of two dollars for each thirty-second degree conferred in a given orient, paid to the Inspector General or Deputy for expenses involved in the discharge of his responsibilities. Of added benefit in this provision was a quiet incentive to produce more candidates.

The other resolution empowered Richardson to negotiate "an amicable agreement" with the Grand Commander of the Northern Masonic Jurisdiction "by which the jurisdiction of the respective Council over the officers and men of the Army and Navy, the army posts, navy yards and ships of the United States,"[46] would be defined. An agreement was signed on August 28, 1909, whereby a Master Mason who was in the army or navy could petition a subordinate body of either the Northern or the Southern Jurisdiction regardless of his legal residence.

Besides the adoption of these resolutions, the Supreme Council approved a budget, which, among other items, set aside $10,000 for charity. This was a substantial sum for those days and another indication of the growth of the Rite. Discounting the budget for salaries and stipends, it was more than one tenth of the operating accounts.

In his Secretary General's report to the session of 1905, Webber stated that a small printing press had been acquired to print letterheads, notices, and other items. Furthermore, his office had purchased a camera to copy and enlarge photographs and a machine to make frames for pictures which had been given to the Supreme Council. All these practical devices streamlined administrative functions.

Another important announcement came in the report of William L. Boyden, the assistant librarian, who announced that a collection of Masonic medals had been started, to be housed in the library. In time, this would become a highly valuable museum asset.

Three months after the close of the biennial session of 1905, there took place in the First Baptist Church at Nashville, Tennessee, an open or public installation of the officers of the four bodies of the Scottish Rite (January 22, 1906) which had been recently established. "This may or may not have been the first such installation of officers but, so far as Supreme Council records reveal, it was the earliest installation outside of a tiled [i.e., private] meeting."[47]

■ ■ ■

In American history the year 1906 was notable not only for the disastrous San Francisco earthquake (April 18–19)—its effect was compounded by widespread fire and the use of dynamite to impede its spread, and it left 300,000 people homeless—but also for the enactment of three important statutes of the Progressive Era (1901–1917).

Without waiting for a request for help, the Supreme Council acted promptly in sending $25,000, together with contributions from individuals and subordinate bodies of the Rite, to Inspector General W. Frank Pierce in California. Hundreds of lives were lost and 28,188 buildings valued at more than $100 million were destroyed in the earthquake and its aftermath. Later, as conditions improved in San Francisco, Pierce returned the $25,000 to the Supreme Council and recommended that the council return pro rata the funds contributed by the Scottish Rite donors.

Two months after the San Francisco catastrophe, Congress passed and President Roosevelt promptly signed into law the Hepburn Act (June 29), the Food and Drugs Act (June 30), and the Meat Inspection Act (June 30). The Hepburn Act was named for Congressman William P. Hepburn of Iowa (1833–1916), who was chairman of the House Committee on Interstate and Foreign Commerce and a Mason; the act strengthened the Interstate Commerce Act (1887) by increasing the size of the Interstate Commerce Commission from five to seven members, granting the commission authority to set reasonable maximum railroad rates, and broadening its jurisdiction to include express and sleeping cars, ferries, terminal facilities, bridges, and oil pipelines. Along with Dr. Harvey W. Wiley,[48] the chief chemist of the United States Department of Agriculture, Hepburn was an author and leading advocate of the Food and Drugs Act, which prohibited the manufacture, sale, or transportation of adulterated or mislabeled food and drugs sold in interstate commerce. Helped by the recent publication of Upton Sinclair's widely read novel *The Jungle,* which depicted repulsive conditions in the meat-packing industry, the Meat Inspection Act called for the enforcement of sanitary regulations in the plants and for federal inspection of all companies shipping meats in interstate commerce. These measures and others that came under the banner of Progressivism were developed out of the American middle-class's response to the problems generated by industrialization and urbanization, including the growth of monopolies, concentration of wealth, worker poverty, and political corruption at all levels of government.

Conceivably, Freemasonry was a beneficiary of Progressivism's popularity, as reflected in "the multiplication of Masonic Bodies and increased membership" and in the fact that Richardson was deeply affected by the movement's ideology.[49] Americans inbued with middle-class values of hard work and fairness naturally found civic associations that reinforced their values to be necessary supports for a better society. Progressivism's demand for improved ethics in government and the correction of socioeconomic abuses undoubtedly appealed to many in the Masonic fraternity who, from lodge room training, embraced the goals of social equality.

About two weeks after President Roosevelt had approved the legislative program, Grand Commander Richardson received word from Bertram B. and Edwin R. Culver of St. Louis, Scottish Rite Masons whose father had founded the Culver Military Academy at Culver, Indiana, that they were providing "one perpetual scholarship" in their school to an orphan or son of a Scottish Rite Mason.[50] Confident that the council would not object, Richardson promptly accepted the scholarship and designated the son of a member of the Nashville bodies to receive the full-tuition scholarship. Culver's scholarship was in keeping with the declared interest of Richardson and the Supreme

Council regarding education and was a harbinger of the Rite's further concern for providing educational opportunities that would otherwise be unavailable. Scholarships (and professorial pensions) were not yet commonplace in American collegiate life.

■ ■ ■

In the spring of 1907, Richardson, in company with Moore and Pierce, left for Brussels to attend the International Conference of Supreme Councils of Scottish Rite Freemasonry. On their way to Brussels, they stopped in London for eight to ten days to attend a conference of the six English-speaking councils and to enjoy the hospitality of the English Scottish Rite Masons at two splendid dinners. The conference at Brussels, which Richardson considered "the most important Masonic incident of our day,"[51] met from June 10 to 15 with Count Goblet D'Alviella, the Grand Commander of the Supreme Council of Belgium, presiding. This set a precedent for the host Grand Commander to preside at future international conferences.

The work of the conference, at which twenty Supreme Councils were represented, was conducted in three sections of delegates: one devoted to questions pertaining to "legitimate and regular Supreme Councils, their definition and organization"; a second dealing with "protection against spurious and clandestine organizations"; and a third considering "all matters relative to the unity and uniformity of the Rite."[52] Agreement was reached on the publication in compact form of the complete English, French, and Latin versions of the *Constitutions of 1786* as the fundamental law; on the exchange of information, including the names of officers and titles of publications; on the need for uniformity of signs, words, and symbols as far as possible; and on the advisability of holding an international conference "at least once in five years,"[53] with the next one to be held at the invitation of the three English-speaking North American Supreme Councils.

At the biennial session of 1907, which opened on October 21, Richardson devoted considerable space in his *Allocution* to the international conference. The Supreme Council, on the recommendation of the Committee on Jurisprudence and Legislation, approved and ratified all of the resolutions and recommendations of the International Conference, which was probably "the most historically significant event of the session. It was diametrically opposed to the previously adopted policy of the Southern Jurisdiction,"[54] which had followed the words of President Washington's valedictory, to abstain from "foreign entanglements." Surprisingly, no objections came from the constitutional conservatives among the Active Members. The change from a provincial to a global outlook, which Richardson's initiative signaled, was in keeping with broader American horizons being shaped by President Theodore Roosevelt, who had long advocated the second Hague Peace Conference (1907) and the establishment of a world court.

In another part of his *Allocution* of 1907, Richardson dealt with the haphazard way Lodges of Perfection had distributed copies of *Morals and Dogma* to candidates receiving the fourteenth degree, resulting in some of them never obtaining their copies. He directed the masters and secretaries of the Lodges of Perfection, in a letter of March 28, 1906, to order copies and to include in lodge accounts the cost of one copy for each candidate.

The continued prosperity of the Southern Jurisdiction was reflected at the 1907 session in the reports on membership and receipts for the previous two years. For 1907, membership in the Lodges of Perfection and consistories was respectively 31,640 and 27,105, an increase of 8,167 for the lodges and 7,606 for the consistories since 1905. It was a phenomenal 34.7 percent increase over the two years. Receipts for the period amounted to $273,816.67 and expenditures, $202,786.27, leaving a balance of $71,030.40.

As further evidence of its fiscal soundness, the Supreme Council, by the time of the session of 1907, held $230,000 in U.S. government bonds. This indeed showed prudence, for on the day after the council first met there was a run on the Knickerbocker Trust Company of New York, triggering runs on other New York banks and causing a downward plunge of the stock market. Had the banking and currency system rested on a sounder foundation, the Panic of 1907 might have been avoided. As a consequence of this panic, the National Monetary Commission was established to study currency systems and to plan the reform of the American system, which was ultimately realized in the passage of the Federal Reserve Act of 1913.

■   ■   ■

A little more than a week after the adjournment of the biennial session of 1907, Secretary General Frederick Webber died at his home in Washington, D.C. At the time of his death on November 4, he was eighty years old and had had "the longest period of service in the Supreme Council by any Inspector General in the history of the Southern Jurisdiction, some 48 years and 7 months."[55] A friend and confidant of Albert Pike, Webber was one of the conservative members of the Supreme Council.

Richardson immediately appointed Allison Nailor Jr. of Washington, D.C., to succeed him as Secretary General, after having appointed Nailor less than a week before to the office of Grand Tiler. But Nailor's service as Secretary General was short lived as he died less than two months after his appointment. The Grand Commander next turned to Austin Beverly Chamberlin, the Sovereign Grand Inspector General in Texas, appointing him Secretary General pro tempore. Chamberlin's appointment, however, presented a legal but not insurmountable problem. At the biennial session of 1907, the *Statutes* were amended so that the Secretary General, after Webber's term ended, could not be an Active Member of the Supreme Council and would henceforth hold office at the pleasure of the council. Richardson requested and the council approved a suspension of the new provision with regard to his appointment of Chamberlin. Sixty years later similar maneuvering was required to permit C. Fred Kleinknecht Jr. a special "at-large" seat on the council while also serving in an administrative capacity.

The reason for this change in the *Statutes* stemmed from previous conflicts between Inspectors General who had served as Secretary General and the Grand Commander, the former believing that they were of "equal rank with the Grand Commander and would not allow him to supervise and direct the work of the Secretary General."[56] The tensions between these two offices were longstanding and did not end with the amendment to the *Statutes* adopted in 1907. Four years later at the biennial session of 1911, the Supreme Council restored the original statute that required the Secretary General to be an Active Member and at the same time reaffirmed that the Treasurer General must be an Active Member as well. Richardson recommended that the offices should each be provided with a paid assistant; thus no salary was necessary for either office, nor was it necessary for the occupants of those positions to live in Washington, D.C.[57] Apparently, however, the Supreme Council took no action on these recommendations.

During the biennium that followed the session of 1907, the White House Conservation Conference was held (May 1908) at the behest of President Roosevelt in order to point up the problem of depletion of the nation's natural resources. As a result of this conference, thirty-six state conservation commissions and the National Conservation Commission were established. On January 11, 1909, the latter submitted its first report, which was the first inventory of the nation's natural resources. Meanwhile, the introduction of the Model T car by Henry Ford (33°, N.M.J., 1940) at a price of $850 on October 1, 1908, reflected the growing popularity of the automobile. Perhaps proving the law of unintended consequences, the affordable automobile had a profound effect on the natural resources of the United States and resulted, over time, in such major American cultural phenomena as suburbs and motels.

A month later, on November 3, William Howard Taft, whom Theodore Roosevelt had in large part picked to be the Republican presidential nominee, decisively defeated William Jennings Bryan, the three-time, Democratic presidential candidate. About a year before he had become a presidential candidate, Taft, who was then Secretary of War, indicated a desire to become a Mason. His wish was realized two weeks before his inauguration on March 4, 1909, when the Grand Master of Masons of Ohio, Charles S. Hoskinson, made him a Mason "at sight" in Kilwinning Lodge No. 365, Cincinnati, Ohio.

Meanwhile, in the spring of 1908, the offices of *The New Age* were relocated to the Metropolitan Life Insurance Building in New York City by the precipitate action of the Board of Directors, composed of five Active Members who had been appointed at the biennial session of 1907. This was surprising because the expenses of publication would obviously increase in New York, and neither the Grand Commander nor the Secretary General had been consulted.

Besides his involvement as editor during the move of *The New Age* to New York, George F. Moore published an important article entitled "Recent Cerneauism" in the April 1908 issue of the magazine. In the article he discussed the efforts of Major W. Bayliss of Washington, D.C., to establish a lodge in Arkansas "under a body styled the Supreme Council for the United States, its Territories and Dependencies"[58] and to form Scottish Rite bodies in New Orleans. Moore noted that at the time there were "no less than three alleged Supreme Councils, each of which claims to be the true and lineal successor of that founded by Joseph Cerneau"[59] in the early 1800s.

Subsequently Bayliss sued the Grand Lodge of Louisiana for libel, charging that the Grand Master had characterized him as "a clandestine pretender" who had "peddled Masonic degrees."[60] Bayliss also sued the Supreme Council for statements published in *The New Age* in May 1908 that were, he averred, "false, scandalous, malicious, defamatory and libelous of and concerning the plaintiff."[61] He wanted $25,000 in damages and court costs. Despite several attempts to bring the case against the Supreme Council to trial, it was finally "ordered off calendar" on December 11, 1912. Two years and two months later Bayliss and his attorney asked the clerk of the Superior Court of the District of Columbia to "please enter this Cause discontinued."[62] Thus ended Bayliss's legal challenge to the Supreme Council.

Richardson summed up his attitude toward Cerneau Masonry when he observed in his *Allocution* of 1909 that "it only needs to be let alone to sink deeper into a richly merited oblivion."[63] For more than a century, Cerneau Masonry had been a periodic annoyance, not a real threat, to regular American Freemasonry. Bayliss's activity was but a residue of such past clandestine effort.

A little over a year after George Moore had published his article on "Recent Cerneauism," he announced in *The New Age* that *The Temple* would be published as a supplement to the magazine. The new publication would discuss the "purposes and objects" of *The New Age* and "matters of more personal nature" concerning why every member should support the magazine.[64] Curiously, no copies of *The Temple* have ever been located, which means it was never born or died instantaneously.

■ ■ ■

Meanwhile, on June 1, 1909, a recognizable breakthrough in the history of Freemasonry in the United States occurred: at the invitation of George B. Orlady, the Grand Master of Pennsylvania, a meeting of Grand Masters was held in Philadelphia. This was misinterpreted in several quarters as a call for the organization of a national Grand Lodge, a longstanding taboo among American Grand Masters. At that Grand Masters Conference, Thomas J. Shryock, the Grand Master of Maryland, who would become an Active Member two years hence, invited the Grand Masters to meet in Baltimore on November 16 through 17, 1909, for the dedication of the temple built by the Grand Lodge of Maryland. They could then discuss whatever topics dealing with Masonry they felt were important. The Grand Masters Conferences did not begin as annual meetings, but apparently from the mid-1920s on such gatherings happened annually.[65]

A month before the Grand Masters Conference in Baltimore, the Supreme Council met for its biennial session, beginning on October 18. It approved the Grand Commander's recommendation for dividing Japan and China into two jurisdictions. Although the council did not entirely eliminate the Grand Consistories (only two remained, Louisville and New Orleans), as Richardson had recommended in his *Allocution,* it did adopt resolutions that reduced them "to the status of Particular Consistories in every respect, except in name."[66] This was an obvious step towards the elimination of the Grand Consistories.

Other resolutions which the Supreme Council adopted included the forthcoming observance of the 100th anniversary of Albert Pike's birth on December 29; the allowance of each Inspector General to arrange the celebration of the event in his orient; the production and distribution of 200 bronze Albert Pike medals, one for each Inspector General, one for each Supreme Council, and the rest for dispersion at the discretion of the Grand Commander; the requirement that Deputies of an Inspector General should employ the title "Deputy of the Sovereign Grand Inspector General" and that Inspectors General Honorary should add the title "Inspector General Honorary" after thirty-third degree when signing their names; and the requirement that every Inspector General should wear at future sessions "the cap of his rank."[67] This was the first recorded reference to the cap, the Scottish Rite's most visible symbol.

Besides these resolutions at the 1909 session, the Supreme Council also provided, with reference to the Puerto Rican Scottish Rite bodies, for a translation of the rituals into Spanish. It also authorized that the purchase of an automobile, "a suitable standard machine of American make," be arranged, as it "would be very useful to the Supreme Council, at its meetings, and to the officers during the recess, and give great satisfaction and pleasure to the brethren during their visits to the House of the Temple."[68]

Without question the most important action taken by the Supreme Council at this session—and one of the most significant in its entire history—was that of calling "for the enlargement, or extension, of the present House of the Temple or for the erection of a new one" and for the Grand Commander to carry out this mandate.[69] Shortly after the close of the biennial session, Grand Chancellor William Frank Pierce, Inspector General in California, met with Richardson at the House of the Temple for a lengthy discussion about the question of expanding the temple or building a new one. Pierce had not been present at the session because of family illness. He felt strongly that it was foolish "to add to the present building and that it was necessary for us to buy ground elsewhere for a new Temple."[70] Pierce and Richardson then concluded that the best site was on Sixteenth Street between L and M, which was subsequently bought for $97,169 (presently where the National Geographic Society's headquarters are located). After consulting with several Active Members, the Grand Commander negotiated with the local Scottish Rite bodies to exchange the old temple at 433 Third Street for their property, a small yet valuable building at 1007 G Street, NW, which could be immediately sold.

By this arrangement the Supreme Council would take the Washington bodies' property, which was encumbered with a mortgage of about $33,000; the council would pay off the mortgage while the Washington bodies would repay it at the rate of $300 per month without interest. The local bodies would receive the House of the Temple, which would give them more space; but the Supreme Council would have all the room it needed in the temple while the new House of the Temple was under construction.

All of this was included in Richardson's letter of December 9, 1909, to the Active Members, in which was enclosed a ballot. Twenty-five members favored the proposal. Horatio C. Plumley of North Dakota was opposed to it, thinking it an unsafe proposal for various reasons: "lack of information," "loss of interest in this investment," the "precedent which troubles me most," and doubt that the Grand Commander had the authority to build a new House of the Temple.[71] It is highly noteworthy that, in response to Richardson's letter, eighteen of the returned votes lacked written endorsement or critique, which perhaps showed little interest in the project. The meaning of so many "abstentions" is far from clear but cannot be attributed to apathy or indifference. It may have been the only way to express doubts without challenging or offending the Grand Commander.

This did not deter Richardson, who went ahead with the plans with the enthusiastic support of the so-called "progressives" and "without the advice and assistance of the committee from the Supreme Council mentioned in the 1909 resolution."[72] Actually, the Executive Committee was not appointed until the biennial session of 1911 when by resolution five members were approved, with Richardson to be an ex-officio member of the committee. By that time the Grand Commander had made all the arrangements, including the approval of building design, appointment of the architect, and selection of a construction company. The progressives among the council had meanwhile told him "that we should make the Temple the most elegant, stately and superb ever built for Scottish Rite Masons."[73] Richardson eagerly accepted the monumental challenge.

. . .

The plans for the construction of a new House of the Temple were, of course, a reflection on the growth in membership and revenue of the Scottish Rite, Southern Jurisdiction, which had occurred in recent years. By 1910 there were over 40,000 members. Decidedly the Rite was urban oriented so that as municipal populations grew countrywide, so did membership in the order. Moreover, during the first decade of the twentieth century, the greatest increase in Scottish Rite membership occurred in orients that had the lowest percentages of illiteracy; and, by the same token, the least gain occurred in orients where illiteracy was relatively high. Thus, as Carter speculates, "there is a direct relationship between the educational level in a population and the growth of Scottish Rite membership."[74] With higher than average educational levels, too, the correlation of Scottish Rite membership with economic status may present another qualitative variable in the membership profile. Middle-class prosperity was as much a prerequisite as literacy.

It seemed timely and appropriate to observe the 100th anniversary of Albert Pike's birth at a moment when the Rite was experiencing considerable growth and the plans for a new House of the Temple were underway. As his birthday fell on December 29 during the Christmas holidays, the Supreme Council's celebration of the occasion was moved to the evening of January 6, 1910, at which time six speakers delivered addresses on Pike—"the Mason," "the Philosopher," "the Poet," "the Soldier and Explorer," "the Man," and "the Prophet of Masonry"—before "a large and appreciative audience" at the House of the Temple.[75] The centennial anniversary of the esteemed Grand Commander's birth was also celebrated in smaller localities by the valleys of the subordinate bodies.

On the day after the Supreme Council's observance of the Pike anniversary, Richardson consulted with eight Active Members who were present for the occasion, concerning the projected House of the Temple. Ten days later, he invited many of the leading architects to submit "sketches, designs and drawings for a new Temple."[76] Meanwhile, Treasurer General Charles E. Rosenbaum of Arkansas, who was among the eight members present for the Pike centennial, asked his friend W. H. Roberts of Washington, D.C., a prominent businessman and Scottish Rite Mason, to help in the search for an appropriate design for the temple and for a site in lieu of the one previously selected. Roberts, in response, hired an architect by the name of McAlister to prepare a design for the temple, which he did in the likeness of the Taj Mahal.

An ideal site for the building was found by Roberts on Meridian Hill, north of Florida Avenue between Fifteenth and Sixteenth Streets, one of the highest elevations in Washington. The property was owned by a wealthy socialite, Mary Newton Foote Henderson (1841–1931), wife of former U.S. senator John B. Henderson, who offered to donate the site to the Supreme Council. At the same time, she was proposing Meridian Hill also as a suitable location for the long-contemplated Lincoln Memorial. From her imposing Sixteenth Street brownstone estate, known as Henderson Castle, she virtually controlled all development of embassy construction in her neighborhood. The Hendersons had owned at one time over 300 building lots.[77] Her offer to the Scottish Rite may have been conditioned on the acceptance of McAlister's design.[78] But Richardson did not like the McAlister plan nor those of several other architects.

Upon the recommendation of John R. McLean, a Scottish Rite Mason and the owner of the *Washington Post* and the *Cincinnati Enquirer,* the Grand Commander turned to John Russell Pope (1874–1937), a young New York architect, thirty-six years old, who had designed McLean's Washington home on Eye (I) Street. Pope, who preferred classical designs in architecture, submitted a design that was based upon the Mausoleum of Halicarnassus, one of the seven wonders of the ancient world.[79]

After determining in March 1910 that various design submissions competing for the contract were unsatisfactory, Richardson recalled "that the Council had not . . . to the present time given me any specific or indeed any general description of the style of the building to be erected, and I was largely at sea, so to speak, in agreeing with the architect for a proper design . . . None of them [the proposed designs] seemed to meet the exalted ideas, that all of us had, as to what we wanted, although no one had been able to put on paper a fitting expression as to what was exactly desirable."[80]

In consultation with Elliott Woods, a Scottish Rite Mason and the architect of the U.S. Capitol, and the Grand Commander's "representative" on the House of the Temple project, Richardson enthusiastically approved Pope's basic design; and after several meetings, they signed a contract on April 16, 1910, whereby the architect was authorized to go ahead with the plans and to superintend the construction of the temple. His fee was to be 6 percent of the construction costs, which he was to share with Woods, as Richardson had requested of all the architects who had submitted designs.

Six months after the contract was signed, Grand Chancellor William Frank Pierce, who was currently the Grand Master of the Grand Lodge of California, died on October 3 at his home in San Francisco. Richardson referred to him as the "chief support of the Temple" and asked rhetorically, "Why take the most useful of our members?"[81]

Shortly after Pope signed the contract, he advised the Grand Commander that the lot on Sixteenth Street between L and M was "too small for the building then designed."[82] Richardson then tried unsuccessfully to buy adjacent property from the National Geographic Society. With the approval of Pope and Woods, among others, Richardson negotiated on May 14, 1910, the purchase of a lot at the southeast corner of Sixteenth and S Streets, NW, for $164,333.85. A year and half later in a special *Allocution* at the biennial session of 1911, he expressed his enthusiasm for the new location: "I speak from a long acquaintance with the city and its streets, when I say I consider the site one of the very best, and most appropriate, in this city, for our time."[83]

Henry White, former U.S. ambassador to France, who was then in the midst of building a Pope-designed residence adjacent to Henderson Castle, wrote to his wife in the late spring of 1911: "I saw his [Pope's] design for the Masonic Temple which is to be erected on 16th Street just below our hill. They had a lot opposite Mrs. Pullman's [1125 16th Street, later the Russian Embassy] but he told the Masons it was not nearly large enough and so they bought the large one near us. . . . His design for the Masonic Temple is simple and imposing and classical."[84] White was gladdened by Pope's design for the Scottish Rite project and the selection of the new site near his property because it would "add to the value of [their] land."[85]

Architectural historians note how "evident" it was "of the period that the Masons, while naturally desiring a fine building to house the Supreme Council, were also imbued with the spirit of the 'City Beautiful' movement of the time."[86] During this progressive era, a new plan for the city of Washington was set forth by the Senate's Park Commission in 1902. The hope to rejuvenate the majority of American cities was sweeping the country, with close attention to parks, zoos, wide boulevards, and elegant buildings. In Washington this meant the Mall would be developed in fitting magnificence from the Capitol to the banks of the Potomac, punctuated in between by the grand monuments dedicated to Washington and to Lincoln. Richardson, it should be recalled, was a member of Congress while these larger aesthetic values were being adopted through the deliberation of the McMillan Commission.

It was at this time (May 17, 1910) that the Commission on Fine Arts was created by Congress to guide the architectural future of the nation's capital. Mary Newton Foote Henderson, however Victorian and eccentric in her habits, nevertheless was a strong advocate of Washington becoming the equal in beauty of European capitals. She constantly reminded audiences that Washington was not a commercial city and that Sixteenth Street ought to become the *Champs Elysees* of Washington.[87]

The next step in the building project was to ask "eight of the very best and strongest construction companies in the United States"[88] to submit bids for the building. The lowest was that of Norcross Brothers Company of Worcester, Massachusetts, in the amount of $889,870, which was later reduced to $837,370. The contractor was the favorite builder of the renowned architect Henry Hobson Richardson. The firm also won the contract to build Henry White's house at 1624 Crescent Place for $80,000.[89]

Meanwhile, Richardson submitted to the Active Members on April 19, 1911, five resolutions granting authority to let a contract for the construction. They were adopted on May 9, and the contract was awarded the next day to Norcross Brothers Company. Three weeks later, on the 110th anniversary of the founding of the Supreme Council (May 31, 1911), the Grand Commander arranged to break ground "at nine o'clock in the morning" in the presence of F. J. Woodman, the Grand Tiler of the Supreme Council; William L. Boyden, the librarian; Sterling Kerr Jr., Deputy in the District of Columbia and the council's bookkeeper; and the Reverend William Tayloe Snyder, the Grand Chaplain; as well as several photographers and newspaper reporters.[90]

Shortly after the contract was signed, excavation for the basement and foundation began so that by the time of the biennial session the following October the work was well underway. Two days after the opening of the biennial session (October 18), in an afternoon ceremony, the cornerstone was laid appropriately in the northeast corner at the invitation of Grand Commander Richardson by Grand Master J. Claude Keiper of the Grand Lodge of the District of Columbia and other Grand Lodge officers before a large Masonic audience. The audience included several Commanderies of the Knights Templar; the Alexandria-Washington Lodge No. 22, of Alexandria, Virginia; the twenty-nine lodges and the Grand Lodge of the District of Columbia; the Camp Guard of Albert Pike Consistory No. 1, AASR, of the District of Columbia; the Grand Lodge of Maryland; and, of course, the Supreme Council.

During the laying of the cornerstone, Grand Master Keiper, Grand Commander Richardson, and other Supreme Council officers used the same trowel to spread the cement that President Washington had employed in laying the cornerstone of the U.S. Capitol. After the cornerstone was lowered into place, the consulting architect, Elliott Woods, representing John Russell Pope, the principal architect, presented the square, level, and plumb to the Grand Master for the purpose of having the appropriate Grand Lodge officers ascertain whether the cornerstone was "well-formed, true and trusty and laid according to the rules of our ancient Craft."[91]

Next corn, wine, and oil, symbolizing health, prosperity, and peace, according to the ritual of the Grand Lodge of the District of Columbia, were applied to the cornerstone, following Masonic custom. Then the Grand Master struck the cornerstone three times with the gavel that the first president of the United States had used in laying the cornerstone of the Capitol and returned the square, level, and plumb to the consulting architect, entrusting him "with the superintendence and direction of the work."[92]

After the completion of the laying of the cornerstone ceremony, the program concluded with brief addresses by Richardson; Abram Simon, rabbi of Washington Hebrew Congregation and a Mason; and Earle Wilfey, minister of the Vermont Avenue Christian Church and also a Mason; and with the singing of J. M. Neal's "The Corner-Stone" and Geibel's "March of Our Nation" by the Scottish Rite Choir of St. Louis.

• • •

The next day following the cornerstone laying at Sixteenth and S Streets, on October 19 at the biennial session, the Supreme Council adopted a resolution supporting the construction of another Masonic building, "A Memorial to George Washington the Mason," in Alexandria, Virginia, under the aegis of the George Washington Masonic National Memorial Association, one of whose charter members was the Supreme Council. The idea of a Washington Masonic monument dated back to the first quarter of the ninteenth century; but it was not until the Alexandria-Washington Lodge No. 22 called a meeting in Alexandria, Virginia, on February 22, 1910, with the approval of the Grand Master of Virginia, that the thought bore fruit with the formation of the association. Eighteen Grand Lodges were represented at this meeting. Grand Commander Richardson chaired the committee on organization, which agreed to meet the same time the following year.

At the first regular meeting on February 22, 1911, agreement was tentatively reached on a memorial temple to Washington at a cost of $500,000, later raised to several times that amount. Attracting money for this project was going to be a slow process as the Masonic membership was not initially interested. The first large contribution, in the amount of $10,000, came from the Supreme Council of the Scottish Rite, Southern Jurisdiction. Besides Richardson's support, the association enjoyed the enthusiastic aid of John H. Cowles, Sovereign Grand Inspector General and past Grand Master of Kentucky, who was elected Secretary General at the biennial session of 1911. For the first ten years of the George Washington Masonic National Memorial Association's history, Cowles was actively involved, not only as the first treasurer but also as an important individual contributor to the building fund. He selected "the site for the Temple, a lot 400 by 200 [feet] on top of Shooters Hill in Alexandria, which did not cost the Association a penny."[93]

Years later, Cowles recalled in a letter to a friend that in order to rebut the charge that the association "was a step towards the establishment of a General Grand Lodge of Symbolic Masonry in the United States, it was decided that all the regular Grand

Masonic Powers, such as Grand Chapters, Grand Councils, Grand Commanderies, and the Scottish Rite, should be on equal terms with the Grand Lodges as members of the Association."[94] The decision to bring the appendant bodies into the association on the same terms with the Grand Lodges was refuted ten years later in a surprise move that embittered Cowles.

■ ■ ■

When the Supreme Council met for the biennial session of 1911, membership in the Rite had increased by 14,693 during the previous two years. This represented a number larger than the total membership (11,946) when Richardson became Grand Commander ten years before. Total membership for the Southern Jurisdiction (Lodge of Perfection) had reached 55,588 by 1911, a gain of 35.8 percent. An important point toward conceding local autonomy, this impressive growth reflected more the efforts of the subordinate bodies than it did those of the Supreme Council.[95]

In his *Allocution* of 1911, Richardson reported that he had been taken ill in December 1910 and, at the request of Lieutenant Grand Commander Samuel E. Adams, had asked George F. Moore, the Grand Prior and editor of *The New Age,* to serve as Acting Grand Commander until he recovered. Later in the *Allocution,* Richardson spoke of "a growing evil" in American Masonry, namely, "the use of the word 'masonic,' or 'masonry,' in some form or manner, to advertise oneself, or one's business, in a commercial or merce-nary way." The Supreme Council, later in the session, declared such behavior "a Masonic Offense" and requested subordinate bodies and officers to condemn it and bring offenders to trial.[96]

Elsewhere in his *Allocution,* the Grand Commander noted with pleasure that on the previous January 24 (1911) he had issued letters temporary for the reestablishment of a consistory in Charleston, South Carolina, the see of the Mother Council, after an absence of many years. Richardson also called the council's attention to the recent estab-lishment of an "International Bureau of Masonic Affairs" in which several Masonic bodies had already become members. The Supreme Council subsequently authorized a subscription to the bureau's proposed publication and permitted the Grand Commander, after he had obtained further information about the bureau, to offer the council's cooperation.

In view of the growing tension at the time in international relations in Europe—centering on two confrontational alliance systems, the Triple Alliance (Germany, Austria-Hungary, Italy) and the Triple Entente (France, Russia, Great Britain)—and the concurrent peace movement here and abroad, Richardson devoted five pages of his *Allocution* to the subject of "International Peace and Arbitration." He urged the Supreme Council "to make a formal declaration" in support of peace and arbitration of interna-tional disputes, so that it might contribute its share, "small [as] it may be, to the great movement."[97] Two years later at the biennial session of 1913, a Committee on Peace and

Arbitration was established, which in turn endorsed Richardson's efforts in support of world peace and authorized him to continue this endeavor. This small-scale attempt at international goodwill was an indicator of American idealism, more generally represented by President Wilson and the popular song by the Scottish Rite Mason Irving Berlin, "I Didn't Raise My Son to Be a Soldier."

Another topic which the Grand Commander took up in his *Allocution* was the International Conference of the Supreme Councils that was scheduled to meet in Washington, D.C., on October 7, 1912. Seventeen Supreme Councils had already accepted invitations; but three, England, Ireland, and Scotland, declined, just as they had refused to attend the Brussels conference in 1907. Richardson could not understand their reluctance to attend as they had never provided an explanation. The Supreme Council designated him, Lieutenant Grand Commander Adams, and Grand Prior Moore as delegates to the forthcoming international conference.

In England other conclusions had been drawn about the usefulness of an international alliance within the Scottish Rite. The Supreme Council there generally kept "mum" about its hesitancy to join an international meeting. All that was allowed officially was the terse statement following: "The Supreme Council [of England] are [*sic*] always anxious to do all in their power to promote fraternal affection between the various Supreme Councils of the Universe, but they are of the opinion that such general conventions as the one proposed are more likely to hinder than promote the main object in view."[98] The reasons were never publicly spelled out, but according to one report, "no way was [the English] Supreme Council again going to risk the trauma to which it had been subjected after the first congress of Lausanne" in 1875.[99] At that particular time, the English Freemasons had to face the uncomfortable fact that not all Masonic bodies had a professing belief in God as a prerequisite for membership. This led to increasing turmoil about extending recognition to foreign councils that played by different rules. Also, the English Scottish Rite ritual had maintained a distinctively Christian and Trinitarian format which had been abandoned by Albert Pike and other ritualists.[100]

Shortly after Richardson finished his *Allocution,* William L. Boyden gave his librarian's report. He noted that since the last session, the Hailey Collection of nearly a thousand volumes on art and architecture, the gift of Daniel M. Hailey of Oklahoma, had been received. This and other collections, it should be noted, have been kept intact as independent acquisitions rather than merged with the general holdings of the library. Boyden was particularly anxious to make the Masonic collection of the material relating to Freemasonry "as complete as possible" and to make the library "the foremost library of the world in this particular class of literature."[101] Previously he had bought, among other things, "the first copy of the original edition of *Andersons Constitutions,* 1723,"[102] which is undoubtedly one of the most valuable books in the possession of the library.

Besides the reports presented and the actions taken, the Supreme Council elected John H. Cowles as Secretary General, as previously noted, together with Henry M. Teller,

Grand Chancellor, Charles E. Rosenbaum, Grand Minister of State, and John W. Morris, Treasurer General. Cowles's election, in keeping with the council's restoration of the requirement that the Secretary General must be a Sovereign Grand Inspector General, was a blow to Richardson, who opposed the change, for this meant the removal of his Acting Secretary General appointee, Sterling Kerr Jr. But the Supreme Council had become concerned about the way the office had been conducted in recent years, in particular about salary being regularly drawn in advance and the lack of routine office hours.

Cowles, whose salary was set at $4,000 ($1,000 more than what it had been), quickly set about to examine the office situation. Kerr became the Assistant Secretary General on the same day that Cowles was elected to office. The new Secretary General promptly, though not surprisingly, in light of council politics, "learned that he would receive little assistance from Grand Commander Richardson."[103] One of the first things he ascertained was that the automobile was not for general use by the members but rather was reserved for the Grand Commander. Cowles was also informed that the monthly payment of $100 to each Inspector General "should be kept strictly confidential," as wives of Active Members were not to be apprised of "such appropriation."[104] This comment is baffling, if true.

Masonry, in general, was acutely sensitive to domestic perceptions of the craft. The danger of gender social division, as potentially exceeding acceptable boundaries between the distinctive spheres of family influence, was not one of which Masonry was ignorant. On the contrary, it was very clear that the fraternity needed to be positioned in the community so as not to stand between husbands and wives in their homes. Perhaps, therefore, the confidentiality of the $100 stipend was expressed figuratively to mean that even a man's most trusted ally, his wife, for example, need not be told of the allowance.

One of the last items of business which the Supreme Council took up in executive session on the final day of the 1911 session was the adoption of a resolution appointing "an Executive Committee of Five," with the Grand Commander serving as an ex-officio member, to have full charge of the plans, building, financing, and furnishing of the House of the Temple under construction. Provision for this committee had been made in the resolution of October 23, 1909, but had not been implemented, thus leaving Richardson the complete and heavy responsibility for the project. The Executive (Building) Committee would remain in charge through the completion of the temple four years later.

The year after the biennial session of 1911 witnessed not only the International Conference of Supreme Councils in Washington, D.C., but also two historic events of both international and national significance: On April 14 through 15, 1912, six months before the meeting of the Supreme Councils, a great disaster at sea occurred with the sinking of the 882 foot, 46,000 ton, White Star liner, RMS *Titanic,* in the North Atlantic on its maiden voyage from Southhampton to New York. The news of the *Titanic*'s sinking after its collision with an iceberg was a shock to the world. "Over 1,500 people were lost in this, the greatest maritime disaster in history."[105] Months later, a hard-fought, three-way presidential campaign took place involving Governor Woodrow Wilson of New Jersey, the Democratic candidate and a non-Mason; President William Howard Taft, the Republican nominee; and Colonel Theodore Roosevelt, former president of the United States and the standard-bearer of the Progressive or Bull Moose Party.

Taft's nomination on the first ballot in the Republican Convention had led to a split with Roosevelt's supporters, who formed a third party and adopted a platform, "A Contract with the People," which called for tariff revision, tighter regulation of corporate combinations, direct election of U.S. senators, preferential primaries for presidential candidates, women's suffrage, and prohibition of child labor. The Democrats were delighted with the split in the opposition, and the liberals at their convention succeeded in nominating Wilson on a platform that pledged a virtual abolition of monopolies and a tariff for revenue only. Actually, the platforms of the two major parties were nearly identical in supporting conservation measures, banking and currency reform, and corrupt practices legislation. Although Wilson won handily in the electoral vote (Wilson, 435; Roosevelt, 88; Taft, 8), he was a minority president as he received 41.82 percent of the popular vote in the election on November 5. Also, for the first time in twenty years the Democrats won control of both the Congress and the White House.

On October 7, 1912, a little less than a month before the presidential election, the International Conference of Supreme Councils met in Washington with twenty-four members in attendance. To pave the way for this meeting, the Supreme Council met in special session beginning three days before. After the welcoming address by Inspector General Charles F. Buck of Louisiana to the visiting delegates at the conference and the responses of eight of the dignitaries, Richardson announced the appointments of George F. Moore as Lieutenant Grand Commander (Samuel Adams having died), Henry M. Teller as Grand Prior, and Charles E. Rosenbaum as Grand Chancellor. The Grand Commander then declared the international conference open, and the Supreme Council was adjourned subject to his call.

While the conference had "no historical significance in the history of the Supreme Council of the Southern Jurisdiction,"[106] the special session of the council had two noteworthy items of business: (1) a report on construction of the House of the Temple from the Executive Committee, including an estimate of $325,000 to do the interior work of the temple (the current contracts did not include this cost), an estimate of $75,000 for equipping and furnishing the building, and the architect's fees of $17,000;[107] and (2) adoption of a resolution calling for the appointment of a special committee of five active members to develop a plan for the establishment of a permanent Fund for Fraternal Assistance, similar to what Albert Pike had provided in a former statute. But, by the time of the biennial session of 1915, no plan had as yet been proposed for such a fund. The idea for wider charity was still pending, but not indefinitely.

Meanwhile, the Supreme Council met in October 1913 for what turned out to be

Richardson's last biennial session. In his *Allocution* he noted that there were nearly one and a half million Masons in the United States and more than 150,000 members of the Scottish Rite in the two American jurisdictions. He also called attention to the fact that December 24, 1914, would mark the 100th anniversary of the Treaty of Ghent, which ended the War of 1812 between the United States and Great Britain and began a century of peace between the two countries. Coming as it would on Christmas Eve 1914, and in the presence of strong Masonic feelings for peace, Richardson felt the centennial of the Treaty of Ghent should be appropriately observed "by Masons everywhere."[108]

But the outbreak of World War I intervened. At a special session in October 1914, just two months after war broke out, the Supreme Council, by resolution, instructed the Grand Commander (who was Richardson's immediate successor) "to offer his good services to the President of the United States, the Peace Commission, the Carnegie Peace Foundation, the Supreme Councils of other countries and every other agency liable to assist in bringing peace."[109] This resolution reflected the anguish and ardent desire of the Active Members of the Supreme Council to end what already appeared would be a bloodbath of unprecedented proportions. It was also representative early on in the conflict of mainstream American feelings, that it was a war to be halted by any means short of sending American forces.

Already, as Richardson had reported in his *Allocution* of 1913, the Supreme Council had sent an unspecified amount of money late in 1912 to the Supreme Councils of Greece and Turkey for relief of war victims in the First Balkan War, for which the American Southern Council had been properly and generously thanked.

Elsewhere in his *Allocution* of 1913, Richardson stated that after considerable thought he had concluded all Scottish Rite Temples should have well-equipped stages with all the necessary electrical equipment and accessories, but he added the caveat that the stage was not necessary for many of the degrees as they are "better interpreted and understood by a rendition on the floor and without the use of the stage."[110]

Before closing his final *Allocution,* Richardson called attention to the organization of "a new Masonic and Patriotic Order of Masons" at Halifax, North Carolina, on December 30, 1912, under the name of the Order of Colonial Masonic Lodges. Membership was confined to Masters and Past Masters, some fifty-five in number, of symbolic lodges in the thirteen original colonies. The purpose of the order was to unite more than ever Northern and Southern Masons and to perpetuate "the spirit of patriotism."[111] The Grand Commander was pleased to have been accorded honorary membership in this organization, which apparently no longer exists. It was, however, a talisman of future Masonic themes in the American century when patriotism became a specific fraternal virtue.

Shortly after Richardson finished reading his *Allocution,* he announced that the attorney for the estate of the late William R. Smith (a former superintendent of the National Botanical Gardens) had written to him about the possibility of transferring Smith's magnificent collection of books by and about Robert Burns, the eighteenth-century Scottish poet and unofficial Masonic poet laureate, to the Library of the Supreme Council. Burns had provided the signal phrase "the mystic tie" as an apt description of Masonry.

Meanwhile, by 1900, Kipling had supplanted Burns as the British poet most admired by English-speaking Masonic audiences. Burns, however, was once regarded as an even larger symbol in American culture than in his honored place among Masons. Mark Twain picturesquely summarized the American Civil War as a fight between Sir Walter Scott and Robert Burns. Southerners of the war generation read Scott; he celebrated the plumed cavalier who resembled the genteel planter. Northerners generally felt Burns spoke to and with them best, because "a man's a man for a' that," regardless of his race. Ironically, therefore, the Burns material looked for a home in a southern locale where he was read much less than the defender of romantic feudalism, Scott.

The Scottish Rite's central library was reportedly not the first choice for Smith's gift, since Andrew Carnegie, the wealthy benefactor of public libraries and a Scotsman by birth, was both a trustee and heir of the Smith estate. Smith and Carnegie had known each other, and Carnegie was the original destination of the Burns Collection, but he declined the bequest and, therefore, arranged its placement with the council. The Robert Burns material was delivered to the Supreme Council in 1918.

During the biennial session of 1913, Acting Lieutenant Grand Commander George F. Moore was an important figure. He was elected Lieutenant Grand Commander in his own right: As the author of the ritual for the ceremony of the Knight Commander of the Court of Honor, he presided in the East at a ceremonial of investiture of a candidate, after which he received from many in attendance their congratulations and approbation. And he was unanimously reelected editor of *The New Age* magazine, which was to be moved from New York back to Washington on or about May 1, 1914. Moore was now positioned as a key player in the coming years.

The council also agreed that the magazine should be sent free of charge after the May 1914 issue to all thirty-second degree members of the Rite in the Southern Jurisdiction. Moreover, with the return of *The New Age* to Washington, the Board of Trustees was to be replaced by a committee of five, appointed by the Grand Commander, to manage the publication.

Another significant action of the Supreme Council in this session was, upon the recommendation of the Committee on Jurisprudence and Legislation, the adoption of an amendment to the *Statutes* requiring a two-thirds majority vote to elect the Grand Commander, and for all other elected officers, a majority. The Supreme Council, understandably, wanted a new Grand Commander to have a substantial vote in his favor. This provision for a super majority is still in effect today.[112]

Pleased with the growth of the Southern Jurisdiction of the Scottish Rite and with the construction of the House of the Temple well under way, the Finance Committee recommended to the biennial session that the Secretary General be appointed the custodian of the House of the Temple and the overseer of all employees of the Supreme

Council. This recommendation was acted on favorably at the next session in 1915. In keeping with this responsibility, the Secretary General's salary was raised to $6,000 while that of the Grand Commander remained at $10,000.

James Carter notes that there were three developments of some significance stemming from the 1913 session. The Finance Committee's recommendation concerning the custodianship of the temple called for (1) "the recognition that a change in administration was imminent and the preparations [were] being made for that change; [2] the tightening of Supreme Council control over its affairs instead of allowing them to be directed by individuals without adequate organization controls." And this was also (3) "the beginning of the rise to dominance in the Supreme Council of John H. Cowles."[113] The second and third of these developments, as Carter whimsically observed, were contradictory whereas the first, which concerned *The New Age,* reflected the council's effort to tighten the operational control over the magazine. "Past history indicated the tendency of the Supreme Council to concentrate authority in one man, hence, what may have been taking place in 1911 and 1913 was a shift in authority from one man to another."[114]

It came as no surprise that less than a year after the 1913 session, Grand Commander Richardson died at his home in Murfreesboro, Tennessee, on July 24, 1914, just a few days before war broke out in Europe. "The Tall Sycamore" had not been in good health for some time. He was buried in Evergreen Cemetery at home with the usual Masonic ceremonies. During his thirteen years as Grand Commander, he had achieved three notable, long-lasting accomplishments: the founding of *The New Age,* the uniform dramatization of the degree rituals with cast, stage, and scenery; and the construction of the House of the Temple at Sixteenth and S Streets, NW, although not completed at the time of his death.

Richardson presided over a record period of growth in Scottish Rite membership and finances. His innovations clearly made a difference in the Rite's expansion, whereas other periods of growth were invariably coincidental with and affected by external circumstances, such as GIs returning in 1946 from a foreign war with intense hopes and needs for civil normalcy which Masonry offered.

Sandwiched in the Rite's history between Grand Commanders of much longer tenure, Pike and Cowles, Richardson has not received his proportionate share of homage and credit. Arguably, his impact upon the Rite—compared to other Grand Commanders —might support the case that he was the greatest among them. Put differently, if a single one or all of his major projects—a national magazine, staged degrees witnessed by large classes, and the building of a national headquarters—were erased from the record, the Scottish Rite might easily have languished and gone the way of other fraternal organizations, such as the Odd Fellows or Red Men, by mid-century. Instead, the Scottish Rite under Richardson had set the course to overtake all the fraternal competition in terms of strength, quality, and prestige.

CHAPTER VIII

Forerunner of Americanism
1915–1921

George F. Moore

Looking back on his life and fifty year career, the American pundit Walter Lippmann recalled, "It was a happy time, those last few years before the First World War." Out of Harvard in 1910, Lippmann remembered that "the air was soft, and it was easy for a young man to believe in the inevitability of progress, in the perfectibility of men, and in the sublimation of evil."[1]

It was, of course, the end of an era, the culmination of the nineteenth century that thematically stretched from the end of Napoleon's wars to the start of World War I, the years from 1815 to 1914. The British author Virginia Woolf had a startling realization that "on or about December 1910 human character changed. All human relations have shifted," she noticed, "those between masters and servants, husbands and wives, parents and children. And when human relations change there is at the same time a change in religion, conduct, politics, and literature."[2]

Change was palpable in the air of American culture, too. The fraternal world reflected exactly what was going on in the larger, changing public world on the eve of World War I. The turmoil of those years spanning the first major war between European powers since Napoleon affected the Scottish Rite, if for no more obvious reason than that in 1914, by the time the twentieth century opened, the worldview of governments and organizations everywhere was outdated. Lenin and Woodrow Wilson, for example, were really products of the nineteenth century. After all, the thought that the world could be made safe for democracy or that international communism would succeed did not for very long fit the new realities.

Similarly, American Freemasons around 1914 were being guided by nineteenth-century ideas, taken from the experience of leaders born before the Civil War, in a dramatically changed and strange world. It is no wonder, therefore, that the years from the Great War (1914–1918) to the early twenties were contentious for the Scottish Rite. Twentieth-century men were trying to find new stars with an old astronomy.

The problems of human institutions are seldom solved definitively; instead, they are often outgrown. Scottish Rite Masonry had outgrown the problems of a relatively small membership and the difficulty of maintaining uniform standards across a huge continent. But still, the Rite acted as if those old strategies, solutions, and messages applied to the new day. As a result, the once seemingly fatal alternatives to public visibility and membership growth no longer meant much and when that was realized the organization acted confused. A great deal of trial and error occurred around this time. The Scottish Rite was coming to an existential crossroads. What would be the Rite's purpose in the twentieth century? What would be its attraction? Could it appeal to men at multiple levels of sensibility? Nostalgia, anti-modernism, contemporary relevance, community service, and esoteric ritual were at issue.

Succeeding the dynamic Albert Pike was a tall order in the 1890s. However, anyone trying to understand and master the peculiar forces in the world, which were also rippling through the fraternity scene after 1914, needed to be a giant. More than likely, that key person would be less than the times required and would turn out to be short-sighted and self-serving in the longrun. Many organizations lacked imaginative genius, typifying their world and society; the churches, for instance, rejected Tolstoian pacifism to become trumpets of romantic nationalism. The Scottish Rite, for all the fits and starts of the day, turned out to be typical of American society. Because it was not exceptional in its diverse moods and proposed solutions, because the pressures against it were acute and mostly internal, this branch of Masonry is not only representative of the larger fraternal situation but presents an accurate picture of what was on the minds of men in the American middle class, jolted from a Victorian world to a world at war.

■ ■ ■

Upon the death of Richardson, Lieutenant Grand Commander George Fleming Moore became the Acting Grand Commander. One of the first things he did was to issue a summons to the Supreme Council to meet in special session on October 7, 1914, for the purpose of electing a Grand Commander. Moore and Charles E. Rosenbaum of Little Rock, Arkansas, the foremost promoter of staged degrees, were elected Grand Commander and Lieutenant Grand Commander, respectively.

The new Grand Commander was born in Talladega, Alabama, on August 9, 1848. On his father's side he was related to Meriwether Lewis of the famous Lewis and Clark

Expedition of 1804 to 1806. (Captain Clark had been the first Master of St. Louis Lodge No. III of Missouri.) As a young man Moore studied law at the University of Virginia and was, ultimately, admitted to the bar. He then practiced law at Rockford, Alabama, until 1874, when he moved to Montgomery, the state capital.

His Masonic memberships included Rockford Lodge No. 137, in which he was raised, Andrew Jackson Lodge No. 173 in Montgomery, the York Rite bodies in which he served as the presiding officer for each, and the Scottish Rite bodies of Montgomery. In 1884 he was elected a Knight Commander of the Court of Honor and an Inspector General Honorary. Four years later he was crowned an Active Member, so that by the time he was elected Grand Commander he had served for twenty-six years on the Supreme Council, having filled successively the offices of Grand Minister of State, Grand Chancellor, Grand Prior, and Lieutenant Grand Commander. Moore, it will be recalled, was the founding editor of *The New Age* magazine "and was a prolific writer in the field of Masonry and kindred subjects."[3]

During the two-day special session of 1914, Moore delivered a brief *Allocution,* although he was not required to do so. He wanted to report on his actions and decisions during his seventy-five days as Acting Grand Commander. Following his remarks, the Supreme Council added a Committee on Ritual to its list of standing committees. The council urged Moore, who had resigned as editor, to remain in charge of *The New Age* "without compensation" until the committee could find a successor.[4] And with Europe then embroiled in what became known as the Great War or World War I, the council instructed "the Grand Commander to offer his good services to the President of the United States, the Peace Commission, the Carnegie Peace Foundation, the Supreme Councils of other countries and every other agency liable to assist in bringing peace out of the present deplorable condition devastating the fair countries."[5] But within weeks after the outbreak of war, the hopes of achieving peace were transparently futile gestures; for, as Sir Edward Grey, the British Foreign Secretary, wrote prophetically at the time: "The lamps are going out all over Europe; we shall not see them lit again in our lifetime."[6]

A year after the special session, the Supreme Council convened for its regular biennial session on October 18, 1915, a memorable day in the history of the world's first council. At 10:30 A.M., a half hour after the session opened, the Grand Commander adjourned it so the Active Members and their guests could attend the dedication ceremonies at the new House of the Temple, which took place exactly four years after the laying of the cornerstone. Members of the council and their guests were taken by automobile in a line of march that included a detachment of mounted police, two bands, the Camp Guard of Albert Pike Consistory, Washington, D.C., the Camp Guard of Albert Pike Consistory, Little Rock, Arkansas, the Camp Guard of the Grand Consistory of Louisiana, and Scottish Rite Masons in columns of four. A luncheon was served in the banquet hall of the new temple. Then at 2:30 P.M. the impressive ceremony began before the front entrance of the temple with the Grand Commander, the other officers, and

Active Members occupying "the several stations and places provided for them on the grandstand."[7] For the audience, seating was provided on the broad stone terraces between the Masonically symbolical three, five, seven, and nine steps ascending in flights from the sidewalk on Sixteenth Street.

The ceremony commenced with Bishop Reginald Heber's popular processional "Holy, Holy, Holy, Lord God Almighty," which the St. Louis and Louisville Scottish Rite Choirs together with the St. Louis Scottish Rite Orchestra rendered. Further music was provided during the exercise of consecration, which included lustration by sprinkling with water, oil, wine, wheat, corn, and salt. The program culminated with a fanfare of trumpets, the unfurling of the American flag, the singing of the "Star-Spangled Banner," and the benediction by a Grand Lodge official.

The well-worn definition of Freemasonry as "a peculiar system of morality, veiled in allegory, and illustrated by symbols" explains much of the intention behind the new temple's design and detail. As one of the seven wonders of the ancient world, the mausoleum at Halikarnassos (c. 352 B.C.) was associated with the roots of Western architectural history; thus it was an important benchmark for Freemasons drawing inspiration for their symbolic system of moral lessons. Pope's plan, derived in concept from Newton and Pullman's 1862 restoration of the mausoleum, "veiled" the building's inner meaning through an "unerring sense of balanced proportional relationships between masses and details."[8] In 1921 the American architectural authority Aymar Embury proclaimed the building's superiority when he said of Pope, "Roman architects of two thousand years ago would prefer [the House of the Temple] to any of their own work."[9]

The House of the Temple reflected John Russell Pope's preference for classical styles in architecture. Its most striking feature is a Greek temple colonnade of thirty-three fluted Ionic columns, each thirty-three feet in height, surmounted by a pyramidal ziggurat roof. Pope's inspiration for the design was from numerous reconstructions by historians and archaeologists who were dependent on two surviving ancient texts that describe the mausoleum's enormous dimensions, columns, and stepped pyramidal roof supporting a quadriga. But he also ingeniously combined Greek and Egyptian motifs in exquisite harmony and subtlety.

Comprising some 88,000 square feet, the interior of the temple has four levels. The basement floor included, of course, the boiler room, storage space, and areas that would later be used for offices. In the course of digging the foundation, an underground stream was struck—perhaps Flash Run or perhaps the old river bed of the Potomac—which required the installation of sump pumps in order to keep the basement dry; without them flooding of the subbasement occurs within a few hours.

On the first floor, which is partially below grade, Pope provided for a banquet hall that would seat 400 and a kitchen, as well as several rooms that in time would be used for exhibits and office space. Museum galleries are easily accommodated in this arrangement.

The front entrance of the temple is on the third level and leads into the atrium, a large hall where the architect combined with great finesse Egyptian and Grecian forms.[10] Adjoining the atrium on the north, the offices and former living quarters of the Grand Commander are located and, on the south side, the Secretary General's office (now the office of the Executive Director) is comfortably situated. These manorial rooms together with the beautiful executive chamber, where the Supreme Council would meet in closed session, and the library constituted the main floor.

Appropriately, at the fourth level, Pope placed the majestic Temple Room, the crescendo of the composition, the principal ceremonial chamber of the structure. Included in this room were the canopied regal chair of the Grand Commander, the stations of the other officers of the Supreme Council, the seats of the Sovereign Grand Inspectors General along the sidelines, a two-manual pipe organ with pipes hidden from view, and at the center of the room the altar of imported French marble. The ceiling exultantly soars above the room's center, measuring 105 feet from the altar to the large skylight overhead. On a frieze high on the four walls of the Temple Room were inscribed in beautiful Roman letters the thoughtful words composed by George Fleming Moore, who had to be mindful of restricted letter-spacing around the perimeter: "From the outer darkness of ignorance through the shadow of our earth life winds the beautiful path of initiation unto the divine light of the holy altar."

Ten years after the dedication of the House of the Temple, Royal Cortissoz, in his comprehensive three-volume study of John Russell Pope's architecture, observed, "The Scottish Rite Temple seems to me one of the most vital buildings erected in modern times here or in Europe." He aptly called it a "masterpiece."[11]

■ ■ ■

While the dedication of the House of the Temple was the most important feature of the biennial session of 1915, Grand Commander Moore set forth several important observations in his *Allocution,* and William Boyden, the librarian, reported on two significant accomplishments. The Grand Commander felt that the rituals of the fourth through the fourteenth degrees, in particular, should be revised so as to bring them in accordance with scientific and archeological discoveries; and he proclaimed that a part of the twentieth degree, employed by the Northern Masonic Jurisdiction, had no place in the ritual of the Southern Jurisdiction. Moore's comment about the factual deficiency of the fourth through the fourteenth degrees might possibly have been directed against Masonic legends unsupported by archeological evidence, such as that of the Enochian Vault. (The story credits Enoch, at a time before Noah's flood, with saving the secrets of geometry by placing them with the Ark of the Covenant.) His difficulty with the twentieth degree may have had a similar basis because it was a historical dramatization of an event that had never occurred.[12]

Moore also thought that the *Statutes* of the Supreme Council lacked clarity and precision and thus needed revision in order to comply with the current premier status of the

Rite. It was not surprising that, with Moore's background of the bar and the bench, he was concerned with the governing laws of the Scottish Rite, which had been set down over time in many flowery phrases. Roscoe Pound, beloved dean of the Harvard Law School between 1916 and 1936 and an authority on Masonic jurisprudence, reminded his readers that the widespread "faith in the efficacy of legislative law-making is unbounded and there is no evidence of abatement of the huge annual output of our political law-making machinery." This phenomenon, Pound cautioned, "is of special significance for Masonry and is behind a similar excess of zeal for legislative law-making in too many of our jurisdictions." Pound blamed "the flood of law-making" in Masonry on "the theory of law as will." He explained, "[I]n American Masonry . . . we have all been trained in the theory that what we will collectively or in sufficient mass to make a majority is law in substance and only needs a mechanical process of receiving the legislative guinea stamp to be law in form."[13] Moore seemed to anticipate Pound's general concerns about the dangers of constantly amending the *Statutes* over the intended ends of its law.

One area of the Supreme Council's organization that was being fine-tuned legislatively was the Council of Administration, instituted by Pike as an informal advisory committee. The Supreme Council, without expanding the advisory powers, did make the Council of Administration more important and more visible. In 1917 an amendment to the *Statutes* required thirty days notice of any meeting of the Council of Administration.[14] In 1919 another official change to the Council of Administration occurred that altered the composition from elected officers of the Supreme Council to "the first nine senior members in period of membership in the Supreme Council."[15]

The revisions on face seem innocuous but actually represent a sign of tension within the Supreme Council, and perhaps eroding confidence in the performance of Grand Commander Moore. Between those two simple changes in the running of the Council of Administration, Moore had gone overseas in wartime with the Supreme Council's approval of the expenditure. The trip was not, in hindsight, viewed as necessary or wise. Moore was quietly criticized for his poor judgment and for his long absence from the office. By strengthening the Council of Administration it was hoped he might be better advised in the use of his time and in the powers of his office.

The Council of Administration had been employed, meanwhile, to adjudicate two disputes indirectly challenging Moore's authority. Moore explained that the Council of Administration "possesses and may exercise in vacation all the powers and authority of the Supreme Council, except for the election of Actives and Honorary Members."[16] The first problem brought before the Council of Administration had to do with following the protocol of issuing letters temporary to new Scottish Rite bodies forming in Colorado. Moore's prerogatives were upheld.

The second matter pitted John Henry Cowles, Secretary General, against the Executive Committee (established ad hoc to oversee the design and construction of the House of the Temple). Cowles objected to the committee's final authorization to pay the architect. Moore and the Council of Administration ruled in favor of the Executive Committee and John Russell Pope. Cowles was ordered to issue the check. In retrospect, Cowles lost the battle; Moore would eventually lose the war.

■ ■ ■

For the past fifteen years, Moore noted, the Supreme Council had paid several thousand dollars in taxes to the District of Columbia. Taxes on the new temple had been assessed "on a valuation of Five Hundred Thousand Dollars and also against some of its Personal Property by the Tax Assessor of the District."[17] In response to this assessment, Moore reported that he met with the Board of Equalization of the District of Columbia and from that discussion believed it prudent to file a printed brief arguing that the Supreme Council's property, both personal and real, should be tax exempt. By the time of the 1915 session, he had had no word from the board, the tax assessor, or any other officer in the District regarding the question.

The council's Committee on Jurisprudence and Legislation fully supported the Grand Commander on the grounds that, according to the Act of Congress setting forth exemptions, the Scottish Rite is an organization whose "purposes are, among other things, charity and universal benevolence and is embraced in the exemption contemplated by the Statute."[18] Ultimately, the question of tax exemption was resolved in the Supreme Council's favor many years later.

Meanwhile, the assessment was eventually lowered to $200,000, but the entire question may have in small measure spurred the coming philanthropic developments throughout Masonry. Charitable organizations, serving a wider public than their memberships, were entitled to tax breaks. "The major thrust in the calls for practicality in the 1920s," writes Lynn Dumenil, "was the demand that Masonry justify its existence by extending its principles beyond the walls of its temple."[19] Ambivalent as a public charitable institution in its own mind and in the view of the government, the tax question was a new "reality test" for Masonry.

The tax quandary was not the primary motivation for Masonic philanthropy, but put in the background it was serious enough to be a stimulus over time. Masonry was undergoing redefinition after 1914 as an organization that became more involved with the outside world, moving with modern times "from ritual to service."[20] The defining process, asking if Masonry was more a private club, ritualistic order, or civic organization meant that the fraternity not only had to figure out how it fit the times, but how it fit into the tax code.

In the interlude, between 1910 and 1920, Masonry nearly doubled its membership in the whole United States, growing from 1.3 million to 2.57 million, a rate that kept pace with the general population growth of the United States. In 1900 only 5 percent of all Masons were in the Scottish Rite, but by 1925 the figure rose to 17 percent.[21] The boom in popularity also meant the acquisition of valuable property in hundreds of communities and the expansion of building projects. How Masonry was to define itself would determine how the organization related to the commonweal, thereby affecting the not insignificant tax status.

• • •

As the former editor of *The New Age* magazine, Moore expressed his frustration and concern with the way the publication had been treated. He recalled that while it was published in New York City, he had spent from his salary $2,500 or $3,000 for a typesetting machine and to engage a printing plant for the handling of composition. He mentioned this simply to underscore, he said, "the interest which I took in the periodical and the work which I thought it could and would accomplish."[22] Probably Moore's greatest irritation as editor of *The New Age* was "the continual recurrence at the end of each two years" of talk to "kill" the publication.[23] He hoped that if it were to be continued, it would be placed on a secure foundation, so that an editor could work with assurance that the magazine would not close down and planned issues would not be wasted. The Supreme Council promptly responded to Moore's candid criticism and provided $50,000, or as much thereof as needed, for *The New Age*'s publication and distribution to all thirty-second degree Masons.

In another section of his *Allocution,* Moore strongly advocated—for what appears to be the first time as a major theme for a Grand Commander—official Scottish Rite support for public education,[24] noting, "We have in all the States of our great Republic a System of Public Schools designed to educate all children of all the people. I think we cannot render any greater or nobler service to the Country than to align ourselves openly and squarely in favor of the creation, the maintenance, the efficiency and the perpetuity of our Public School System. I know of no subject upon which there can be or ought to be such uniformity of opinion and action as the education of the people in *their own schools* [italics his]."[25]

Moore added that he had a suggestion to make that he did not expect the Supreme Council to act upon at that time: to underscore the importance of public education, every state should enact legislation that would give preference to public school graduates in appointments to public office, certainly a well-intentioned, though perhaps unrealistic, proposal for the support of state education.[26]

The New Age in 1914, calling itself a national magazine "devoted to literature, science, and Freemasonry," transformed its purpose subtly with an alternative motto. As of 1915 the magazine described itself as "a monthly publication devoted to Freemasonry and its relation to present day problems." Moore's position on public schools had already been tried out in the pages of the Supreme Council's official publication.

Increasingly, the magazine shifted from soft literary and fraternal set pieces to more controversial op-ed features. Before Moore's outspoken departure from neutral principles, *The New Age*, which he had managed through 1912, had started testing the new field of Masonic opinion-making. Magazine issues for 1914 editorialized about the Italian government and the Pope, state schools in New York (under a Catholic governor whom the Scottish Rite columnist admired and supported), the peace movement (to which the Scottish Rite was favorably disposed), and the war in Europe. By January 1915 the magazine—a strong indicator of Moore's agenda—featured a regular section called "Educational Notes, furnished by the U.S. Bureau of Education," an agency of the Department of the Interior.

Meanwhile, as the war in Europe entered its second year, American nervousness about involvement in a major foreign conflict was reflected in the magazine's commentary, which explored the meaning of being an American, the value of American education and American democracy. While several editorials seemed genuinely harmless, such as "The Municipal University" and "American education and democracy," a fresh sign of stridency appeared under more assertive titles, "The Jesuit party and American politics" and "America First and All the Time" (a slogan used by isolationists down through the 1930s).

It is historically significant that the "100% Americanism" program (i.e., Americanizing children and immigrants in the public schools with English-only education) that was promoted so energetically in the editorials of *The New Age* in 1915[27] appeared well before the American war effort had mobilized a spirit of intense nationalism. Four years later, these Masonic expressions of Americanism seemed Delphic as the spectacular events of the Red Scare (1919–1920) climaxed in the Palmer raids aimed at deporting alien radicals.

Scottish Rite "Americanism," however, fit somewhat uneasily with the organization's prior record of Masonic internationalism. While seeming contradictory, a pattern emerged, given that Scottish Rite membership in the Southern Jurisdiction was a reasonable demographic sampler of white, old-stock American, middle-class men. In each instance—expressions of internationalism and Americanism—there was the common thread of what Richard Hofstadter called "this Anglo-Saxon dogma,"[28] a form of yahoo ethnic pride equated to the purist American view of the nation and the world. Whether the campaign was for widening American influence abroad through fraternal channels or for restricting American identity at home, Hofstadter remembered that, carried to extremes, the Anglo-Saxonist impulses between 1912 and 1919 led to imperialism and racism. "All over the country," explained Sydney Ahlstrom, "the behavioral and linguistic norms of the Anglo-Saxon were steadily enforced" as a result of the war and its aftermath.[29] It would be hard to imagine the Scottish Rite not being affected by the powerful undertow of those war-related moods; after all, the popular cult of Anglo-Saxonism, later lampooned by H. L. Mencken as a phony superiority complex, was an outgrowth of modern nationalism and the romantic movement, both of which were intertwined with the social order and sense of place many American Masons were working out for themselves in the early twentieth century.

■ ■ ■

The day after Moore had delivered his *Allocution* (October 20, 1915), William Boyden presented his librarian's report, in which he announced the completion of the index to the *Transactions* of the Supreme Council from 1857 to 1913. This was a project of some 400 typewritten pages on which he had been working for several years and was indeed a monumental task of immeasurable value.

Another major accomplishment of the librarian of the Supreme Council was the completion of a system of "classification for Masonic literature as the result of some twenty-one years' experience with the subject," which meant that he had "reclassified our books in accordance therewith and with the most satisfactory results."[30] In response to the inadequacy of the Dewey Decimal System for classification of a voluminous Masonic literature, Boyden, who at the time of his death in 1939 was considered the dean of Masonic librarians, devised a system of Masonic classification "providing four hundred classes and subclasses. It follows the same principle as the Dewey Decimal System, but the letter M precedes all the class numbers. The Masonic scheme is divided into ten main classes,"[31] which are repeatedly subdivided seriatim. Boyden's system of Masonic classification has been used by the Library of the Supreme Council since its inauguration in 1915 and also by other Masonic libraries. The Boyden method was eventually expanded in order to serve the growing needs of large collections such as those in the Iowa Masonic Library.

During its session of 1915, the Supreme Council took significant actions which included the authorization of the Grand Commander to make final settlement of differences, claims, and counterclaims with the District of Columbia Scottish Rite bodies; the payment of $100 for a life membership in the George Washington Masonic National Memorial Association and a place on the Charter Roll of Honor; the designation of depositories for the funds of the council, including the American Security and Trust Company; the changing of the name of the Committee on Library and Buildings to the "Committee on the Library"; and the empowerment of the Grand Commander to approve the Masonic War Relief Association's appeal for funds to the local Scottish Rite bodies, if he thought it was in order. What is more, a striking feature of the budget for the biennium of 1915 through 1917, approved by the Supreme Council, was the setting of salaries for the Grand Commander and the Secretary General at $12,000 apiece, generous compensation for each officeholder when average family income in America was less than $2,500 annually. There was more here than met the eye in the equal pay allotted Moore and Cowles. In retrospect, it was one of the signs that Moore faced major difficulties within the council, insofar as the two positions were not equal in authority under the *Statutes* and would not be expected to be equal in remuneration.

Meanwhile, the Scottish Rite became a pioneer in twentieth-century Masonic charitable service. In 1910 Trevelyan W. Hugo of Duluth, Minnesota, organized an infant care clinic that continued to flourish for more than forty years. Maryland Scottish Rite Masons developed a similar program, and in San Francisco the Scottish Rite instituted a free milk distribution program.[32]

About seven weeks before the session of 1915 convened, an important event occurred in Decatur, Georgia, with the opening of the Scottish Rite Hospital for Crippled Children. Two small cottages had been converted into a twenty-bed hospital to meet the needs of the community. This was the first hospital organized by Masons in this country and was the result of the efforts of the local Scottish Rite bodies and a dedicated physician, Dr. Michael Hoke. A few years later, it served as an example for the Shriners to follow when it undertook its program of building and equipping hospitals for crippled children in various areas of the country.[33]

■ ■ ■

Between the session of 1915 and that of 1917, the war in Europe ground on with the monstrous, indecisive battles of Verdun and the Somme taking place in 1916 along the Western Front. The losses were staggering. In the battle of Verdun the French lost about 350,000 men while the Germans suffered only a little less than did the French. British losses in the battle of the Somme, in which tanks were first used by the British, were over 400,000; French losses were nearly 200,000; and German battle-related deaths were estimated between 400,000 and 500,000.

While the carnage continued on the Western Front, the Republican and Democratic National Conventions met in June in Chicago and St. Louis, respectively. The Republicans nominated for president Supreme Court Justice Charles Evans Hughes, a former governor of New York; the Democrats renominated President Woodrow Wilson. The Progressive National Convention again nominated Theodore Roosevelt for president, but he declined the nomination and backed Hughes. His defection led to the early end of the Progressive Party.

Wilson's campaign centered on his record of neutrality and preparedness, with the slogan "He kept us out of war." This slogan appealed to women's groups, especially those in the western states where they already had the vote. The opposition to the president came particularly from German-American and Irish-American elements who questioned his foreign policy. The Democrats turned this to an advantage as Hughes was slow to distance himself from the support of these groups which were at odds with American allies such as Britain and France. Nevertheless, the election on November 7 was quite close, the narrow Democratic victory in California giving Wilson the edge to win. On the Wilson coattails, both houses of Congress remained Democratic.

Five months after the election, the United States declared war on Germany on Good Friday, April 6, 1917, and thus joined Great Britain, France, and Italy, known commonly as the Allies, or as the "Associated Powers." The German renewal of unrestricted submarine warfare was undoubtedly a precipitating cause in bringing the United States into the war. Moreover, by 1917, Americans were decidedly pro-Ally (pro-democratic) and anti-German. The American entry into the war was the makeweight that assured Allied victory a year and a half later.

As a reflection of the Supreme Council's keen interest in ending the war, Grand Commander Moore, sometime late in 1916, offered President Wilson his and the council's assistance in trying to bring peace to Europe. In a letter of January 5, 1917, the president thanked Moore for the offer to help "and assured him that the offered aid would be used if and when it was possible to do so."[34]

By the time the Supreme Council met for the biennial session of 1917, units of the American Expeditionary Force (AEF) were in line on the Western Front. Unsurprisingly, Moore devoted several major parts of his *Allocution* to the American war effort. In July 1917 he attended a meeting of fraternal organizations that Herbert C. Hoover, the food administrator, had called for the purpose of consulting with community leaders on the efforts of food conservation in the United States. Moore was unanimously elected to represent the fraternal societies in Hoover's office, where he was given a desk but, because of Supreme Council business, was not able to do much. However, he was satisfied that the fraternal organizations were individually aiding the government in the efforts of food conservation; and he felt that the Supreme Council could, through its publications, lectures, and a general educational program, promote the avoidance of food waste.

On October 5, 1917, the Grand Commander met with Secretary of War Newton D. Baker for the purpose of objecting, on behalf of the Masonic fraternity, to the government's restriction in allowing only the YMCA and the Knights of Columbus to erect buildings on army cantonments. Baker judiciously revised the War Department's policy so as to permit national fraternities to sponsor service centers at posts and camps, but he enjoined them from engaging in secret meetings and initiations.

In order to provide fraternal assistance to Masons in the army and navy, Moore told the Supreme Council that it would be necessary to raise funds through voluntary contributions from the local bodies and individual Scottish Rite Masons. He noted that the Northern Masonic Jurisdiction had already appropriated $100,000 from its treasury for a war relief fund and was soliciting contributions, totaling $1 million, from their subordinate bodies. Some individual bodies of the Southern Jurisdiction made, based on his appeal, nearly $30,000 available to Moore. He was reluctant, however, to use these funds, he later reported, as he wanted to avoid waste and redundancy of effort.[35]

■　■　■

Among several matters unrelated to the war, Moore stated in his *Allocution* of 1917 that a settlement had been reached with the Washington, D.C., Scottish Rite bodies concerning the claims and counterclaims over the exchange of property that had made possible the move to Sixteenth Street by the Supreme Council. The dispute may have been exacerbated by frustrated feelings of the local members who themselves were getting an appetite for building. In October 1916, Moore had appeared before them to announce that it was "his intention to start a movement to erect a Cathedral of the Rite in [Washington] and that he would ask help from all the Valleys of the Southern Jurisdiction for that purpose."[36] The desire for a new and larger facility grew with the increasing membership in Washington itself. Moore had promised more than he could deliver to the local constituency, thereby contributing to soured relations over the 1909 land swap.

Also in his *Allocution,* Moore reported that the Council of Administration had approved the decision of the Executive Committee (overseeing the building project) allowing the temple's architect, John Russell Pope, $17,211.40 for services rendered,[37] which Secretary General Cowles had previously refused to pay. Cowles had a longstanding suspicion about the architect and contractor running up the costs. At one point the Supreme Council and the builder, Norcross Brothers, went to arbitration to settle a difference of opinion about the suitability and cost of lead gutters, the atrium ceiling, the book stacks, and bronze medallions.[38]

Cowles and Pope had earlier differences over the quality of woodwork to be installed in the suites of the Grand Commander and Secretary General. Pope was annoyed, too, by Cowles's slow action in distributing certified checks to contractors. It was not helpful, perhaps even inflammatory, that Cowles dismissed the difficulty as "the seeming muddle" which was, in his mind, caused by the architect's failure of clarity.[39] Pope's professional reputation throughout his career was that he ran a model office in terms of efficiency and attention to detail. Pope remained on excellent terms, moreover, with Charles E. Rosenbaum, chairman of the Supreme Council's Executive Committee.

In spite of Cowles's minor criticism, the Executive Committee never questioned Pope's judgment or integrity. It passed unanimously in January 1916 a resolution upwardly adjusting Pope's contract because "of the splendid quality and character of the service rendered," for Pope "was compelled to devote much additional time, labor, and intelligent thought, involving heavy and unusual expense on his part, and for which he was in no measure responsible."[40]

Cowles later questioned the authority of the Executive Committee through his challenge to Pope: "It is only fair, perhaps, to state to you that I am strongly opposed to this payment [the adjustment authorized by the Executive Committee the previous year] and I shall do my utmost to prevent the Supreme Council from paying it." Pope appealed to Rosenbaum for resolution of the dispute, saying Cowles's "attitude was anticipated." Rosenbaum hit the ball into the Grand Commander's court, insisting that Moore's intercession was the remedy of last resort before litigation. Rosenbaum made it clear, however, that the validity of the committee's other "changes or modifications of contracts" had never been questioned until "this instance" involving Cowles.[41] In the end, Pope was paid his due and the "total cost of the building enterprise, direct and indirect," was calculated in October 1917 as $1,803,339.[42] This total cost had been reported elsewhere as $160,000 less, which may not have included the indirect expenses for furnishings, interest and commissions on loans, and the Executive Committee's travel expenses.[43]

The Council of Administration, besides approving the decision of the Executive Committee, had also authorized the Grand Commander to give to the U.S. Bureau of Education and the federal government whatever help might be possible in furthering the bureau's plan "for the 'Americanization' of the hundreds of thousands of foreign born residents in our country by means of educating them in the English language through night schools and otherwise, and by means of other appropriate measures and especially through its 'America First' campaign."[44] The Supreme Council's longstanding interest in the promotion of an English-only public school system—with instruction in American history, including national customs and institutions—dates from this time during World War I.

Elsewhere in the *Allocution,* Moore reported that he had appointed on March 9, 1917, Thomas J. Shryock, the Sovereign Grand Inspector General in Maryland and the Grand Master of Masons of Maryland since 1885, as Treasurer General. Later in the session the Supreme Council elected Shryock to that office, which he did not hold for long as he died the following February.

In a section of the *Allocution* devoted to the George Washington Masonic National Memorial Association, the Grand Commander observed that the Supreme Council had thus far subscribed only $100 to the fund of the organization. At a meeting of the association in Alexandria on February 22, 1917, Moore stated he would recommend to the Supreme Council that it contribute $10,000, which it readily agreed to do at the session that fall.

Another recommendation of Moore's, to which the council gave its approval, was the need for an organist who would be responsible for the music of the thirty-third degree and the "magnificent chants" of the rituals. This is yet another aspect of incorporating theatrical trappings into the Scottish Rite degree work. Some of the largest organs built in America were for the movie palaces coming into vogue. It was a natural borrowing, therefore; the Scottish Rite now required quality organ music and accompaniment.

During this session the Executive Committee gave its final report on the House of the Temple, noting that with the exception of the two black marble representations of Egyptian figures, generically known as block statues,[45] that were to be placed at the foot of the grand stairway leading up from the atrium to the Temple Room and a few little details, the work was completed. In the final stages of its charge, the committee also proposed "that lamps of appropriate design"[46] be installed on each side of the front entrance, which was subsequently done. Meanwhile, David Edstrom, the Swedish sculptor, was commissioned to create two statues at least forty-two inches high and possibly (for more money) as high as seven feet. These were done in plaster.

Edstrom's contract, however, should it be extended, called for the use of black Swedish marble.[47] The drawings for the statues came from Otto Eggers, the architect's assistant, from a photograph Pope had shown him "of an ancient Egyptian figure which . . . would be appropriate as two flanking the main stairway in the Atrium."[48] Edstrom's work for the House of the Temple was to be the only example of his artistry in Washington. Edstrom, a Scottish Rite Mason, later executed a statue of George F. Moore for the Consistory of Dallas, Texas.[49] The matching black marble statues for the temple would not be unveiled for another ten years and not without some controversy between John H. Cowles and both the artist and architect. The project was ultimately turned over to Adolph A. Weinman, the artist responsible for the temple's exterior pair of sphinxes.

In accepting the report and discharging the Executive Committee, the Supreme Council expressed its "unanimous thanks and undying gratitude" by a rising vote, a term borrowed from British Freemasonry for a standing ovation. At the same time it recognized Moore's "masterful efforts" in providing "many appropriate mottoes of Masonic sentiment" for the House of the Temple.[50] For nearly fifty years it was believed that Moore "employed Egyptian writing symbols to his own purpose" because the symbols appeared to be "not translatable as Egyptian writing" as they were inscribed on the two statues at the base of the stairway. Moore was probably not the author of that particular motto, which was later rendered in a free translation as "Dedicated to the teaching of wisdom to those men working to make a strong nation."[51]

Realizing the importance of effective public relations to the temple, the Committee on the House of the Temple, one of the sixteen standing committees of the Supreme Council, felt that a guide should be employed during the time that the building was open to the public and requested the Finance Committee to provide funds for the position. A year later the council authorized the Committee on the House of the Temple to open the temple to the public.

It will be recalled that four years before, at the 1913 session, Moore had presided at an investiture of the rank and decoration of the Knight Commander of the Court of Honor, for which he had written the ceremony. The Committee on Ritual now recommended its adoption, which the Supreme Council promptly did.

On the last day of the 1917 session, the Committee on Fraternal Assistance and Education submitted a report, which was adopted, calling for the appointment of a committee of three to investigate the need and possibility of an agency or agencies to deal with problems of poverty and charity among indigent brethren. Moreover, the Committee on Finance submitted its budget for approval; but, surprisingly, the details, unlike previous budgets, were omitted from the published *Transactions*.

■ ■ ■

The Russian Revolution had brought about the abdication of Tsar Nicholas II; and on November 6, 1917, the Bolsheviks, headed by Vladimir Lenin, ended the rule of the provisional government under Alexander Feodorovich Kerensky. This ushered in the monolithic communist state, the Union of Soviet Socialist Republics. As Kerensky and nearly all of his cabinet were Freemasons, according to John Henry Cowles, there might have been a chance for Masonry to return to Russia. But the Bolsheviks ended that hope.[52]

Russian Freemasonry has had a complicated, tangled history, moving in and out of favor with the ruling aristocracy. The influences of English, Swedish, and German

Freemasonry were all present in eighteenth- and nineteenth-century Russia. For Russian Freemasonry, the early twentieth century marked a deviation from the worldwide Masonic mainstream.[53]

According to Boris Telepneff, writing for the Quatuor Coronati Lodge No. 2076 in London, "at the beginning of 1906, about fifteen Russians, well known for their social and political activities, mostly members of the constitutional-democratic party, joined French lodges; some became members of the Grand Orient, but the majority entered two lodges under the Supreme Council of the Ancient and Accepted Scottish Rite."[54] These Masonic affiliations, it must be carefully noted, were with irregular bodies.

The Russian government discovered the existence of these lodges in 1909, driving much of their life and work deeper underground, as they were viewed skeptically because of their potential for partisanship. As Telepneff comments, "One could hardly call those activities (around 1911) Masonic, as their chief aim was political—the abolishment of Russian aristocracy and the establishment of a democratic regime in the Empire of the Tsar."[55]

With allegiance to the Grand Orient of France, some forty Russian lodges made up a political organization in 1913 and 1914, which represented within itself two political parties—the constitutional democrats and the progressives, the latter more moderate. It was said that one of the lodges consisted entirely of members of the Duma. The division between the two parties forced ten of the lodges out of business by 1916. The remaining lodges "are credited with inspiring the first revolution in 1917 and it was said all the members of Kerensky's government belonged to them."[56]

In the decade preceding the revolution and for the period immediately following, Russian Freemasonry could be carefully delineated into three phases, none of which was compatible with American Masonic practices or experiences: the French Freemasonry of the Grand Orient (1906–1910); political Freemasonry (1910–1917); and the purging of lodges (1918–1922). The initial phase stayed within the boundaries Grand Orient operations and observances. But the second phase, involving Kerensky, "broke ties with the Grand Orient in Paris and was much more of a political confederation using the Masonic style than a true Freemasonry"[57] recognizable to the Supreme Council.

Ronald C. Moe, a political scientist at the Library of Congress, makes a distinguishing point that "many persons prominent in political Freemasonry were leaders in the February Revolution and in the Provisional Government, but there is little evidence that organized Masonry played any part in the Revolution." Moe cites the remark of one participant, Prince Vladimir Obalensky, who said that the "Revolution did not unite Russian masonry, it pulled it apart."[58]

Once Lenin and the Bolsheviks arrived, members of these political lodges left Russia, many of them becoming emigrés in France. Kerensky found asylum in the United States. It was "a sad example of a political organization usurping the name of Masonry."[59] By 1922, the Fourth Congress of the Communist International passed a resolution forbidding party members from belonging to Masonic lodges. As late as 1922, the Bolshevist police were still raiding so-called "Masonic" meetings in Moscow. Many Russian expatriates, however, actually became "orthodox" Masons in their adopted countries, thus adding to the confusion.[60]

. . .

Believing that World War I was an imperialist, capitalist conflict, the Bolsheviks published the secret treaties made by the Allies and opened peace negotiations with Germany and the other Central Powers. Negotiations led to the signing of the Treaty of Brest-Litovsk (March 3, 1918). With Russia out of the war, Germany could now concentrate on a big drive in the west.

Meanwhile, President Wilson addressed Congress on January 8, 1918, setting forth his famous Fourteen Points "as the only possible program" for peace as far as the United States was concerned. Grand Commander Moore was in complete accord with these peace proposals.

Unfortunately, the Fourteen Points, while greeted with popular cheers in America, received "an ominous silence by the Allied governments." Wilson went "public" before he had coordinated the plan with Allied officials. The president knew his plan would be rejected and so calculated that popular acclaim would put adequate pressure on European governments to make them acquiesce. The tactic backfired, leaving the Fourteen Points as a unilateral American pronouncement, not a joint declaration. The Paris Peace Conference was, consequently, in the words of Walter Lippmann, an "elusive and all-pervading chaos," a tricky balancing act resting on a decision "not to throw the unconcluded negotiations into this cyclone of distortion."[61]

As the war along the Western Front wore on during the summer of 1918, Moore became convinced that a special session of the Supreme Council was necessary. Consequently, on September 2 he called for a special session to meet in St. Louis, Missouri, at the Scottish Rite Cathedral on September 23 in order for the council to come up with a program by which it "may serve our country and humanity." By holding the special session in St. Louis, Moore thought that traveling expenses for the Active Members would be considerably less than by having it in overcrowded Washington where the cost of hotel accommodations reflected the wartime situation. In his *Allocution* the Grand Commander put forth four ways he thought the Supreme Council should proceed in order to achieve the goal of service to the nation and humankind: buy Liberty Bonds (fourth issues); engage "in distinctive work for our soldiers in France"; declare strongly that the council does not support any peace that is not in conformity with the principles that President Wilson enunciated; and promote fraternal relations between American Masons and those of the British Empire, France, Italy, and neutral European countries.[62]

In response to Moore's recommendation concerning Liberty Bonds, the Supreme Council approved the purchase of $100,000 worth of the Fourth Liberty Loan Bonds.

It also agreed at the same time to pay off the balance owed on the House of the Temple. And an appropriation of $10,000 was approved for the Educational Bureau, whose organization and responsibilities to the Rite would not be spelled out until the regular session of the following year.

Moore had eagerly wanted to go to France to investigate whether the Scottish Rite, alone or in collaboration with other American Masonic bodies, could provide a social outlet for Masons in the American Expeditionary Force (AEF) and also reestablish fraternal ties "where they have been broken (if such a course seems wise and practicable)."[63] The council approved his request to visit France or other allied countries, if he so desired, and to invite no more than two people to accompany him. It assumed the cost of the trip and appropriated $5,000.

In another action the Supreme Council authorized the Grand Commander to ascertain the possibility of purchasing property fronting on S Street, about 100 feet across and extending to an alley. If the price were reasonable, he was to buy it with the written approval of a majority of the Finance Committee. The property, some five lots, was later purchased for $60,000. By 1990 the Supreme Council owned all the land behind the House of the Temple extending to Fifteenth Street, between S Street and the alley running east and west between Fifteenth and Sixteenth Streets.

One of the most fascinating resolutions adopted by the council at the 1918 special session was one requesting and authorizing Moore "to prepare and furnish the public press with such information relative to the transactions of this session as are proper news to the American nations." That information was to be made readily available "to the daily press and the press associations."[64] This was something of a departure from Masonry's traditional shunning of publicity. Obviously, the Supreme Council wanted the American public to know about its impressive war efforts and patriotic commitments.

Six and a half weeks later the Armistice was signed (November 11), ending four years of the worst war in all history to that time. The losses in known dead were about 10 million, and the number wounded reached about 20 million. The total direct cost of the Great War was calculated at $180.5 billion, and the indirect cost, $151.6 billion.

About two and half months after the Armistice, the Peace Conference opened in Paris with seventy delegates present representing twenty-seven of the victorious nations. It culminated five months later with the signing of the Treaty of Versailles on June 28, 1919. Breaking historic precedent, President Wilson himself headed the American delegation to the conference, as he was determined to secure the adoption of a plan for a League of Nations, his Fourteen Points, which would be embodied in the peace treaty. Although Wilson realized his overriding aim of the establishment of this organization for peace, he suffered subsequent defeat of the ratification of the Treaty of Versailles by the U.S. Senate. The League of Nations was formed without the United States, and because of that void, had its effectiveness considerably diminished over the next fifteen years.

Meanwhile, about two weeks after the special session closed and only five weeks before the Armistice was signed, Moore, in company with Sam P. Cochran, Sovereign Grand Inspector General in Texas, and Dr. Hugh T. Stevenson, pastor of the Bethany Baptist Church of Washington and Grand Chaplain of the Grand Lodge of the District of Columbia, sailed for Europe. When the Armistice was proclaimed, Moore was in London recovering from influenza followed by pneumonia, which, so he reported in his *Allocution* of 1919, "came near giving me my thirty-fourth degree."[65] Upon recovery, Moore and his companions went to Paris where they established the American Masonic Headquarters at 10 Victor Emanuel III in a large, attractive, old home which was badly in need of repair. They bought furniture and had the building renovated.

Before Moore returned home in April, he asked Charles W. Connery to come to Paris, as manager of the attractive American Masonic Headquarters, which was to be open to all Masons (not just Scottish Rite members), their wives, and daughters. But the problem with the establishment of the American Masonic Headquarters was in the timing. It was established after the war had ended, and American troops were anticipating their return home. "By the end of May [1919] over 300,000 men had sailed home; thousands more were in the final stages of departing."[66] Nevertheless, Moore felt that the American Masonic Headquarters should remain as a "foothold in Europe" with the hope of becoming, if given financial and moral support, the means of bringing to the continent "the spirit of American Scottish Masonry [*sic*]."[67]

The Supreme Council thought otherwise; in one of its last actions of the biennial session of 1919, it requested the discontinuation of the American Masonic Headquarters as quickly as possible. Charles E. Rosenbaum, the Lieutenant Grand Commander and Acting Grand Commander while Moore was in Europe, regarded Moore's trip as a "fool's errand."[68] And the council's resolution regarding the closing of the American Masonic Headquarters was but one of several steps it took in challenging Moore's leadership.

To some extent, Moore's trip was judged in the same scorching light as President Wilson's efforts in Paris. For Moore, as for Wilson, what had begun as a noble crusade had ended in confusion and disillusionment. American Masonry had no business in Europe; and, as Walter Lippmann said of Wilson, in a sentiment the Supreme Council might have expressed about the Grand Commander, "Parsifal's visit . . . did not help much."[69]

■ ■ ■

During the 1919 session Moore suffered one rebuff after another at the hands of the Supreme Council. The Grand Commander wanted an appropriation for the final execution of the Egyptian block statues in marble, to replace the $1500 plaster casts rendered by David Edstrom, the distinguished Swedish sculptor. The council, out of contrariness and not aesthetic conclusions, took no action.

Moore recommended that the system of honors be carefully reconsidered, notably, the arrangement whereby each Sovereign Grand Inspector General could nominate one brother for the thirty-third degree for every hundred Perfect Elus created during the previous two years of a biennial session. The council ignored the recommendation. The ongoing tax question with the District of Columbia concerning the House of the Temple was taken from Moore, as was the preparation for publication of Pike's manuscript of the Zend-Avesta.[70]

The Supreme Council, without waiting to receive the Grand Commander's educational program, put forward one of its own and called for a special session to meet at Colorado Springs in the spring of 1920 in order to consider the course of action it should take. Moore's proposal to discuss ritual revision with the Supreme Councils of the Northern Masonic Jurisdiction and Canada was passed over. And, as a slap on the wrist, the Grand Commander was asked to amend his *Allocution,* which was something unheard of, to include "all reported bond purchases" and deaths of Inspectors General Honorary. Before adjournment the Supreme Council adopted the report of the committee on *The New Age* magazine, which criticized Moore for his failure to recognize *The New Age* "as the official organ of the Supreme Council."[71] Here the final battle line had been drawn.

In his *Allocution,* Moore reported that plans were underway for holding the Third International Conference of Supreme Councils at Lausanne, Switzerland, in 1920. At the Second International Conference, which met in Washington, D.C., in 1912, it had been agreed that the next conference would be held at Lausanne in 1917; but the war prevented that meeting. The Supreme Council approved the convening of the conference and the financing of the cost ($9,000) of sending delegates to it. Moore was unlikely to be rebuffed on such a matter as this, but over and across back channels there had been some discussion of how to stop him from attending. To ensure that Moore would not misrepresent the council, Secretary General John Henry Cowles and Grand Sword Bearer Perry Weidner were elected to join the Grand Commander as delegates to the Lausanne conference.

■　■　■

Moore also informed the council in his *Allocution* that upon learning there was no formula for inscriptions upon cornerstones by Grand Lodges, he thought the following inscription was acceptable to the Grand Lodge of the District of Columbia for the cornerstone of the House of the Temple, laid eight years before: "This corner stone was laid by the Grand Lodge F.A.A.M. of the District of Columbia, J. Claude Keiper, M.W. Grand Master, presiding and officiating, October 18, 1911."[72]

As the official, as well as titular, custodian of the temple, Cowles noted in his report that a dual pumping system had been installed to meet the water problem in the basement and a rolling ladder had been put up in the library's reading room. The steps and stone work had been pointed up and the roof had been repaired as well. Cowles "then commented that the number of repairs and their cost could be expected to increase."[73] He was right: the size and design of the House of the Temple invited regular, ongoing repair, as is generally the case for all large public buildings. No discussion ensued about a maintenance endowment.

William L. Boyden's report reflected the increasing size of the library. The Robert Burns Collection was finally transferred in the fall of 1918. Carl H. Claudy of Washington, D.C., presented to the library, about three months before the 1919 session, some 500 beautifully bound books devoted mainly to German literature and art and published mostly in German. He also sold his Goethe Collection numbering 338 volumes to the Supreme Council for $1,000, a bargain price for an excellent inventory of quality titles and rare imprints. The funds for this acquisition became available because Elliott Woods turned over his architectural consultant's fee in that amount to meet this expenditure. In March 1919 the District of Columbia Society of the Sons of the American Revolution gave to the Supreme Council their library, which consisted for the most part of the proceedings of state societies and biographical and genealogical works. Just four and a half years after the temple's dedication, the library was running astonishingly short of book space.

In addition to the acquisitions just noted, Boyden reported that the library had bought Albert Pike's celebrated poem "To the Mocking Bird," which he had handwritten, signed, and dated "December 1834." The manuscript, which was in excellent condition, was the earliest specimen of Pike's handwriting in the Supreme Council's possession.

Boyden made two important recommendations to the Supreme Council pertaining to Pike. For quite some time, he noted, he had been preparing a bibliography of Pike's published and unpublished writings, which amounted to 25,000 pages of his printed works and 36,000 pages of his manuscripts. Boyden hoped that the bibliography of 140 typewritten pages would be published. He argued that Pike was too important a literary figure, let alone Masonic innovator, to be overlooked. The council agreed to publish 500 copies at a cost of no more than $1,000. (The *Bibliography of the Writings of Albert Pike* appeared in 1921 and was significantly revised in 1957 by Ray Baker Harris.) Boyden's second recommendation called for the establishment in the temple of "The Albert Pike Memorial Room" where his memorabilia could be displayed and his manuscripts, letters, and books could be housed. Again, the Supreme Council readily accepted the librarian's proposal.

In other actions, worthy of some attention, the council agreed that bronze tablets on each side of the entrance to the atrium, pertaining respectively to the laying of the cornerstone and the dedication of the temple, should be installed and that Pike's thoughtful inscription should be cut in the panel of the main stairway's landing: "What we have done for ourselves alone, dies with us; what we have done for others and the world, remains and is immortal."[74]

Before the biennial session of 1919 closed, the Supreme Council expressed its "deepest sympathy" to President Wilson concerning his illness and added its hope for "his speedy recovery."[75] On September 25, while on a rigorous national speaking tour to arouse public support for ratification of the Treaty of Versailles and for the League of Nations embodied in it, the president had "sustained a stroke which paralyzed his left side."[76]

In another action before the session ended, the Supreme Council, wishing to honor Inspector A. L. Fitzgerald, its oldest member, on his birthday, elected him "Dean" of the council, an unofficial title that is no longer employed. In 1933 Cowles was named "Dean," which was the last time the honorific title was bestowed.

■　■　■

As the Supreme Council had resolved to have a special session in 1920 devoted to matters of education, it met on May 17 in the Broadmoor Hotel at Colorado Springs, Colorado. On the opening day Grand Commander Moore delivered his *Allocution,* for which, unfortunately, there is no record. Curiously enough, though not so astonishing since Moore had lost the confidence of key council members, it was not only unpublished in the *Transactions* of 1920 but no copy of it has ever been found in the Archives of the Supreme Council. Moreover, there is no reference to it in the committee reports. Moore had been on thin ice before, but this notable absence from the official record is evidence of how marginalized he had become.

In executive sessions Secretary General Cowles and Grand Minister of State Edward C. Day put forward proposals which underscored the Rite's "resolve to make service to our country and humanity the keynote of our labors."[77] The proposals, appearing in a resolution of Day's, which the Supreme Council adopted with only two negative votes, included a strong statement in support of free, compulsory education with instruction in English only, financed by public taxation. The proposals also called for the establishment of "a national department of public education" headed by a secretary with cabinet rank; the founding by the federal government of a national university in Washington, D.C.; the establishment of a news service for the Supreme Council, with an appropriation of $20,000; and the allowance of $100 per month to each Sovereign Grand Inspector General or Deputy for carrying into effect the purpose of this resolution. (The council also provided $60,000 to assist in the compliance of the resolution.) This decision signaled a major shift in the public life and profile of the Scottish Rite from the temple to the secular world.

Day made his case for Masonic public activism a few months before the Colorado Springs meeting in a lead commentary published in *The New Age:* "Our opportunities for service in this country are exceedingly great. We have our Lodges in every city, town, village, and hamlet of consequence. . . . In every place is a public school to be guarded; in every city a library to be established and maintained; charitable organizations to be supported, and philanthropic movements to be led or backed. . . . The Government of the United States has called upon the heads of the several Masonic Orders, as representing the greatest altruistic force in our civilization, to take and hold these plans to a successful conclusion. . . . The opportunity for which Masonry has labored for years in secret is now present."[78]

One of the dissenting votes was cast by Grand Prior Ernest B. Hussey, who promptly submitted his resignation from the Supreme Council, stating that his duty as a citizen and his obligations as a Scottish Rite Mason required him to do so. In a word, he felt the council had overstepped the immoveable boundaries of its first principles against official political expression. Through a committee of three, the council asked him to reconsider; but he refused, and so his resignation was accepted.

Meanwhile, the Smith-Towner Bill, introduced in 1919 to legislate into existence a federal Department of Education with a secretary at the cabinet level, received its "most adamant support . . . from the Southern Jurisdiction of the Scottish Rite." This was technically possible in Masonic protocol because of the Rite's "sovereignty," which meant it was "unhampered by restrictions against political activity."[79] Also in Ernest Hussey's native Pacific Northwest, the Scottish Rite was responsible for an Oregon initiative mandating compulsory attendance in public schools for children between the ages of eight and sixteen. Roman Catholic voters, to be expected, opposed the measure because the referendum was a direct slap at parochial education. At that very juncture, the Ku Klux Klan emerged to claim the Oregon school law as one of its special projects, with a campaign so intense that the gubernatorial race was overshadowed by it.[80] Hussey's caveat anticipated the guilt-by-association problem of political coalitions that would match the Rite's concerns with other action groups.

From 1920 down to the 1990s, the Supreme Council, as the policymaker for the Scottish Rite of the Southern Jurisdiction, gave unequivocal support to public education and an American school curriculum taught in English only. The national university never came to fruition, but in 1927 the Supreme Council provided an endowment of $1 million to the George Washington University, by then a nonsectarian institution, for graduate scholarships. By the 1990s, due to the perceived deterioration of American public schools, many Scottish Rite Masons were confused about the solutions and alternatives to the problem of state education. Much of the old energy for the defense of public schools was gradually rechanneled into other causes, as neutral as scholarships and language disorder clinics or as challenging as a constitutional amendment to protect the American flag from desecration.

In actions unrelated to the purpose of the special session, the council accepted with appreciation from the Supreme Council of Italy a bronze bust of Grand Commander Moore, who in 1919 was elected Honorary Grand Commander of the Italian Supreme Council. The council also instructed Moore and Cowles to purchase $500,000 worth of Fourth Liberty Loan Bonds at 4.25 percent and appropriated $10,000 for mileage and per diem expenses for the Active Members in attendance and $10,000 for an emergency fund to supplement any previous funds that might be insufficient for their intended purpose. The substantial sums of money being invested or designated for immediate spending reflected the enormous growth of membership in the Rite (nearly 200,000 members in the consistories as of 1920) and the attendant increase of income.

■　■　■

Six months after the special session at Colorado Springs, Grand Commander Moore announced that he was planning to establish a weekly newspaper under the title *Fellowship*

Forum. In a letter to the *Scottish Rite Herald* (Feb. 1921), which Carter quotes in part, Moore stated righteously that the paper "is needed; because we believe that it will be a successful commercial venture and that it will greatly aid in securing and promoting peace on earth and good will among men."[81] The Independent Publishing Company, with Moore as president and with offices in Washington, D.C., was the publisher of the *Fellowship Forum,* the first issue of which appeared on June 24, 1921. Its seemingly benign motto was "a national weekly newspaper devoted to the fraternal interpretation of the world's current events." In her well-researched study, *Freemasonry and American Culture 1880–1930,* Lynn Dumenil makes the following observation about the nature and purpose of the *Fellowship Forum:* "Dedicated to the purposes of militant Americanism, it included news of Masonry and other fraternal organizations. Within a very short time, although it continued its fraternal news, it became one of the most scurrilous KKK organs. It continually stressed the relationship between the Klan and Masonry, a policy that brought criticism from Masonic officials and authors."[82]

The newspaper over the years absorbed other publications such as the *Watsonian* (1929) and Gilbert Owen Nations's *The Protestant* (1931), finally ending its run in 1937 after Nations died. During its life it was particularly hostile to Catholicism. By the early 1930s, Gilbert Nations was the sole editor of the *Fellowship Forum,* whose mission was "to arrest and rebuke the harlotry of papal Rome." After the 1920s, fraternal news had slipped off its pages and yielded to a more radical perspective: "[S]o powerful is the Vatican grip on Hitler that his government has agreed not to enforce the sterilization law against Roman Catholic defectives. The Roman See gets what it asks in Germany under the Fascist dictator." Besides making the additional claim that Hitler was a Catholic, the now monthly paper had issued "warnings that Catholics, Communists and Jews dominate[d] the Roosevelt Administration." This culmination of harsh, highly charged opinions in the *Fellowship Forum* was an outgrowth of the Anglo-Saxon nativism that had stirred just before American involvement in World War I.[83]

In 1915 "Colonel" William J. Simmons had revived the Ku Klux Klan of Reconstruction days and had made its objectives not only anti-black but anti-foreign, anti-Catholic, and anti-Semitic. More than a few Americans, both northerners and southerners, both Masonic and non-Masonic, turned, especially after the war and the accompanying unrest and disillusionment, to the Klan and its program of Americanism entrenched in fear and hate. George Moore appeared to be one of them.

The historian Richard Hofstadter sees post-war American society around 1919 and 1920 as being wrenched between the unspent torque of Progressive values and the counterpressure of Populism's reborn impulses. "Progressivism had been founded on a mood, and with the reaction that followed the war that mood was dissipated." Hofstadter explains, "Moods are intangible, and yet the changes in America hung on mood as much as anything else."[84]

While Grand Commander Richardson had been a Progressive by temperament, his successor came out of different soil. Moore's "mood" was that of a Populist. Historically, both kinds of movements shared prejudices against the increasing ethnic mixture of American society and both recognized the practical problem of Americanization. But the indignation of the Progressives down through 1918 was "more moderate, more complex than Populist thought had been."[85] Between 1890 and 1920 the two movements were held in dynamic tension, creating a balance of reform priorities until Progressivism yielded its place after the war. Prohibition and women's suffrage mark the end of the Progressive era, but Populism hung on, turning sour and illiberal.

For a short while, politically oriented Masons had advocated a special office in Washington, D.C., to represent Masonic positions on education and immigration restriction; both concerns fell under the embryonic program of "Americanization." In a way, the Scottish Rite, Southern Jurisdiction, became that de facto Masonic clearinghouse and headquarters in Washington, a situation which Moore was prepared to exploit even experimentally with such militant Americanism platforms as the Klan's. Ironically, his successor and palace rival, John Henry Cowles, who clearly was at odds with Moore, created exactly what Moore seemed to prefer—a Masonic lobbying apparatus that was Scottish Rite based.

And yet, as Dumenil points out about Masonic political involvement, the populist and militant appeal of the Ku Klux Klan never took hold in Masonry because "Grand Masters throughout the country spoke out against the Klan-Masonry connection." Because of this internal "hostility to political activity," division in the ranks worked in favor of Masonry's long-term interests by keeping its own "political activity disorganized and sporadic."[86]

Allegiance to Americanism, however, with specific focus on public education, moved the fraternity increasingly from a moral institution to a civic forum. Moore's flirtation with a prospectively larger Scottish Rite role as an Americanist agitator was in keeping with the widening desire of many American Masons to be unified about something—in light of the disunity which had hampered Masonic war relief efforts.

Briefly, therefore, the mass and momentum of the Ku Klux Klan in 1920 absorbed some of the residual Masonic enthusiasm for Americanism and old-stock, Protestant solidarity. Any tie with the Klan was a passing fancy for a Masonic fringe, for Masonry "was less virulent in its Americanism campaign than the Ku Klux Klan."[87] In the 1920s, Masons were really no different from the average, white, middle-class American man. The biographies of Harry S. Truman, Hugo Black, and Earl Warren, among many twentieth-century luminaries, all Masons shaped by World War I and the early 1920s, bear this out. The respectable "Babbitts" of American society who joined fraternal and civic organization were all affected by the same hysteria sweeping through the country because of newsworthy phenomena such as an influenza pandemic, the Red Scare, confusion about veterans rights and benefits, and the immigration of Europe's war refugees.

Again, Hofstadter sheds light on the mood of Americans by describing the status anxiety of the proletariat: "The Klan impulse was not usually a response to direct personal relationships or face-to-face competition, but rather the result of a growing sense that . . . the country was full of naturalized citizens still intensely concerned with the politics of Europe and divided in their loyalties."[88]

• • •

Meanwhile, the country faced another quadrennial presidential election early in November, the same month in which Moore announced his plans for the *Fellowship Forum*. In their convention at Chicago early in June, the Republicans nominated for president a dark horse and a Mason, Senator Warren G. Harding of Ohio, the choice of the party bosses. Governor Calvin Coolidge of Massachusetts was selected to be his running mate. At their convention in San Francisco the Democrats nominated Governor James M. Cox of Ohio, a Mason, for president and Franklin D. Roosevelt of New York, the assistant secretary of the navy and also a Mason, for vice president.

The party platforms were similar in several respects: they both favored women's suffrage (the election of 1920 was the first time that women voted in a national election), child labor laws, tax reform, and a federal budget. Harding hedged on support of the League of Nations, saying that if elected he would work for an association of nations, "*a* league but not *the* league."[89] Democrats gave their unqualified support for ratification of the Treaty of Versailles and for the League of Nations. Harding won an overwhelming victory, receiving 61 percent of the popular vote and 404 electoral votes to 127 for Cox. The American people had voted for Harding because they were tired of the Wilson administration, and, after two terms and a world war, they simply wanted a change.

The Harding administration had been in office for more than six months when the Supreme Council convened for the biennial session of 1921. This was indeed a memorable session as the paramount events were George Moore's resignation and John Cowles's election to succeed him as Grand Commander, neither of which was a surprise. The council had not been happy with Moore's leadership for some time and, likely, could not have formed a plebiscite to support him. On November 4, 1920, Philip S. Malcolm, an Active Member, wrote to Cowles, who had become "the guiding personality in the Supreme Council after the close of the Session in 1919,"[90] that something had to be done: "Some of us out here have been corresponding about the office of Grand Commander. We think that at present our big institution has no HEAD, none of us get any reply to our letters. One member suggests that a majority call for a special session to be held in Washington next January, that the present G.C. be retired on a pension, and a new one elected. I think that we have the necessary number to call the session. What do you think about it?"[91]

Moore's involvement with the intemperate *Fellowship Forum* undoubtedly fueled the dissatisfaction. His *Allocution* reflected a sense of sadness about his resignation. He proudly noted that "all the inscriptions and emblems on the building [House of the Temple] are the work of the man who is speaking to you except the one at the head of the stairs [Pike's]."[92]

The day after the delivery of the *Allocution,* the Supreme Council accepted Moore's resignation and bestowed upon him the title of Past Grand Commander, with the same salary that he currently enjoyed as a pension for life. It was an exceptionally generous concession which may have indicated that Moore's Americanist politics could be forgiven more readily than his personal cantankerousness in dealing with individuals. The council then elected John Henry Cowles as Grand Commander, Horatio C. Plumley as Grand Prior, Trevelyan W. Hugo as Grand Chancellor, Edward C. Day as Grand Minister of State, Perry W. Weidner as Secretary General, and Melville R. Grant as Grand Almoner. As a mollifying gesture, the council invited Moore, during the remainder of the session, to preside at the consistorial sessions and at the investiture of the Knights Commander and the conferral of the thirty-third degree.[93]

Several piquant as well as important announcements appeared in the various reports that were delivered. In his last report as Secretary General, Cowles informed the Active Members that an information service had been instituted under the title Capital News Service. The committee on *The New Age* recommended increasing the size of the magazine from forty-eight pages (its then current size) to sixty-four pages, and the council readily agreed to the change. Librarian William Boyden reported that all of Pike's writings had been transferred to the Albert Pike Memorial Room. In its report the Committee on the House of the Temple dealt with what had become a perennial problem, leaks in the roof. It was ascertained that the fault was not with the roofing contractor, "but in the design of the roof itself,"[94] a problem in many other Pope buildings, too. The existing copper flashing in several places had to be changed, and a conduit had to be removed, all of which would cost about $5,500. And the Committee on Doings of Inspectors and Deputies commended in its report the Texas Scottish Rite brethren for "donating 50 percent of their entire fees for three years, and 33.33% for two years thereafter, for benevolent work in providing dormitories at state educational institutions."[95]

To strengthen the operation of the Rite throughout the Southern Jurisdiction, the Committee on Fraternal Assistance and Education recommended, as a means of enhancing the efficiency of the local Scottish Rite bodies, that the Grand Commander request uniform implementation of a standard system of organization composed of an executive committee and an executive secretary whom the Inspector General in each state would appoint. The results were to be carefully determined during the next year.

Shortly after adjournment, the Supreme Council, in response to the plan for holding the international conference at Lausanne in 1922—which had been twice postponed because of the war and its aftermath—authorized the Grand Commander, and four others whom he designated, to attend. The council was to provide $25,000 to cover the expenses of attendance.

The final action of the Supreme Council was to declare that hereafter the memorial service for Albert Pike would be held on the Sunday prior to the opening of the session, a practice which remained in effect for the rest of the century.

The biennial session of 1921 closed with the usual passing of the box of Fraternal Assistance, the formation of the chain of union,[96] and the Albert Pike memorial ceremony. As agreed upon earlier in the session, the Supreme Council was to convene again on the fourth Monday of August 1922 at Salt Lake City under a new Grand Commander.

. . .

Twenty years had elapsed from the beginning of Grand Commander Richardson's years of service to Grand Commander Moore's resignation. In its 120 years, the Supreme Council had witnessed no greater development than during these two decades bridging the nineteenth and twentieth centuries. That growth included the establishment of a monthly magazine, *The New Age;* the building of a magnificent House of the Temple and the sale of the old location and building; the expansion in membership from a little more than 10,000 to almost 200,000; the involvement in the establishment of the George Washington Masonic National Memorial Association; the avowed support of American public education; the expansion of the Library of the Supreme Council and the introduction of a Masonic system of book classification; and the support of and participation in the international conferences of the Supreme Councils.

By 1921 the Scottish Rite had weathered the difficulties of a controversial Grand Commander. It had successfully dodged the perilous Klan trap which might have hounded the Rite for the rest of the century. Perhaps Moore had done the fraternity a larger service than was realized by testing the limits of political posturing that were tolerable to a "neutral" membership organization. Also, he inadvertently but usefully demonstrated the nervous danger of code words as harmless in sound as "Americanism" or "Americanization." Out of the wrong mouths, those words sometimes have been construed as paranoid, xenophobic, nativist, anti-Catholic, or anti-Semitic. The Scottish Rite made use of potentially loaded terms as a means of expressing mainstream values. But what if the Ku Klux Klan had continued to thrive and had used double-edged, Americanist language, too?

At the end of Moore's term it was clear than Masonry was not turning back. It was less sentimental about death and immortality; it was less mindful of the symbolic majesty of the ritual. It had become part of mass society and consumer culture. Masonry's role in American history, particularly the "revolutionary brotherhood" of 1776, supplanted the past emphasis on the more sublime Masonic experience. Of a fashion, the modernization of Masonry, especially the Scottish Rite, meant that the order stressed practical (sometimes quasi-political) concerns such as the promotion of Americanism, good citizenship, and humanitarian service over the ancient Pythagorean mysteries of geometry.[97]

Moore had presided over a branch of American Freemasonry that set the tone and the agenda for the fraternity's next seventy-five years. The impulse of Americanization, even when tempered by the specificity of church-state problems in the public schools, was the cat's paw which pried open the sacred "asylum" of Masonry, bringing the light of the American Legion and similar civic clubs into the lodge room.[98]

More importantly, a study of the Moore administration reveals the process of how institutions are sometimes dragged into a new age, often reluctantly, because time and chance do not stand still. Moore's time in office, while not long, illuminates the broader scene of cultural and social change in America. For that reason, despite the brevity of Moore's service, those years turn out to be symbolic of people navigating a choppy channel between the centuries.

CHAPTER IX

Prosperity to Depression
1921–1935

John H. Cowles

慢慢慢慢慢慢慢慢.

The decade of the 1920s in America stands against parallel descriptions of other equally gray, ambiguous, but contradictory times. The 1850s and 1960s come to mind. The stereotypes of the period, popularly called the Roaring Twenties, are captured in paired opposites: bohemianism and Coolidge Republicanism; material consumption and religious sensitivity; the beautiful and the damned; the lost generation and "100% Americans"; fundamentalists and modernists; wets and dries. Division between opposites was represented in the spectacular trials of Colonel Billy Mitchell and John Scopes.

When John Henry Cowles became the thirteenth Sovereign Grand Commander of the Scottish Rite's Southern Jurisdiction, American Masonry was enjoying an expanding membership. Between 1910 and 1920 membership nearly doubled from 1.3 million to 2.57 million. In 1910 the fraternity claimed 7 percent of the native, white, adult males; ten years later, its claim had risen to 12 percent of this group.[1] There had been a corresponding growth in the Scottish Rite during this period so that at the end of 1921 the membership in the consistories of the Southern Jurisdiction totaled 192,231, an increase of more than 70,000 over the figure of 1919, which amounted to a 57 percent jump. The increase of membership reflected a growth in population, wealth, and education for the country at large. As migration to the cities rose during the first two decades of the twentieth century the Scottish Rite benefited, as it had already established its valleys in the cities, whereas the York Rite, a parallel and rival "higher degree" form of Masonry, tended to be dispersed and more concentrated in the rural areas.[2]

The motives for joining Masonry in the postwar years were essentially what they had always been, "fraternity, sociability, personal gain, and status,"[3] although the fraternity had traditionally frowned upon the latter two as reasons for joining. Added to these motives for entering the ranks of Masonry during the troublesome times after the war was "the Masons' militant embrace of 100 percent Americanism."[4]

Increased membership meant expanded administration for the various Grand Lodges. It also meant for the Supreme Council of the Scottish Rite's Southern Jurisdiction that the Grand Commander, Secretary General, Inspectors General, and Deputies had enlarged responsibilities. The growth brought with it more staff; more equipment, including a new printing press; an increase in the council's and subordinate bodies' charitable and welfare work; and the establishment of the news service and an educational program with an emphasis on Americanism. But the increase in the Scottish Rite's membership had an adverse effect: as more members were selected to receive the Supreme Council's honors, the result was, as Carter observed, that the honors (Knight Commander of the Court of Honor, thirty-third degree, and Grand Cross) were diminished.[5] This situation was corrected by placing limitations on nominations.

■   ■   ■

With the expanding membership and enlarged income of the Scottish Rite, Southern Jurisdiction, the future appeared bright for John Cowles upon becoming Sovereign Grand Commander in October 1921 at the age of fifty-eight. Born at Dripping Springs, Kentucky, in Edmonson County, on August 22, 1863, the new Grand Commander was the son of Joseph, a merchant and enthusiastic Mason, and Martha Ann Mitchell Cowles. After several moves the Cowles family finally settled in Louisville, where Joseph undertook a wholesale grocery business in which young John became a clerk. Wherever the family resided, John attended the local school, and later, Cumberland University at Lebanon, Tennessee. Because of ill health while in college, he did not receive his bachelor's degree. In time, he became a successful businessman with involvement in several enterprises, including the Globe Building and Loan Company, the Pyne Company (steel fabricators), Martin and Cowles Insurance Agency, and John H. Cowles & Company (brass founders).

At the outbreak of the Spanish-American War in 1898, Cowles, a thirty-five-year-old businessman, organized Company H of the First Kentucky Volunteer Infantry and was elected its captain (a militia practice dating to a time before the Civil War). Captain Cowles served in the Puerto Rican campaign, thence became Provost Marshal of the Mayaguez District of the island. Casualties in this short war were due more to tropical diseases and poor camp sanitation than the battlefield. After the ceasefire and surrender, American troops, because of rampant illness, were quarantined for many months before being allowed to return home. Cowles was fortunate not to have suffered from malaria, dysentery, or yellow fever.

Ten years before, Cowles had been raised in Louisville Lodge No. 400, F&AM (Free and Accepted Masons). During the war he obtained dispensation from the Grand Master of Kentucky Army Lodge No. 1, U.D. (Under Dispensation, i.e., the auspices of the Grand Master), whose jurisdiction was restricted to troops from Kentucky. Cowles was made Worshipful Master of the Lodge, which was dissolved when the regiment was mustered out in 1899.

A few years after Captain Cowles (he liked being addressed throughout his life as "captain") was raised in 1888, he joined the York Rite bodies, becoming Eminent Commander of DeMolay Commandery No. 12, KT, in Louisville in 1896. Meanwhile, he received the Scottish Rite degrees in 1890 in the Louisville bodies and the Grand Consistory of Kentucky. From 1894 to 1903, he served as Venerable Master of the Lodge of Perfection, and from 1902 to 1909, as Master of Kadosh of the Grand Consistory. In 1895 Cowles was invested with the rank and decoration of Knight Commander of the Court of Honor, and two years later the thirty-third degree was conferred upon him. As an enthusiastic Scottish Rite Mason, he was crowned a Sovereign Grand Inspector General in the Orient of Kentucky on October 23, 1909, and thus became an Active Member of the Supreme Council.

At the biennial session of 1911, he was elected Secretary General, a position which he was to occupy for the next ten years. The Supreme Council, it will be recalled, changed the *Statutes* to require that the Secretary General must be a Sovereign Grand Inspector General, which was a defeat for Grand Commander Richardson. Moreover, the council wanted to tighten up the operation of the Secretary General's office. Cowles "was the first man elected to the office of Secretary General in the Southern Jurisdiction who was experienced in business office administration."[6] Without question, he was an active and at times a forceful Secretary General who believed service to Masonry should not be on a par with governmental or corporate compensation for service. His belief was fortified by the fact that he was relatively affluent and a lifelong bachelor. The salary he earned in this job, however, was considered handsome for the time.

Cowles had served as treasurer of the George Washington Masonic National Memorial Association since 1914 and was later made chairman of its Ways and Means Committee. In his last months as Secretary General, at the meeting of the association in February 1921, Cowles experienced a distasteful coup at the hands of Louis A. Watres of Pennsylvania, the president of the association since 1918. Watres engineered the adoption of a new constitution which made the Masonic appendant bodies, including the Scottish Rite, associate members, thus reducing their active membership and their coequal status with the Grand Lodges of the United States. At the same time the Ways and Means Committee, along with some other organizational structures, was eliminated, certainly a slap in the face to Chairman Cowles. Four months later he resigned as treasurer of the association, having been the victim, together with the appendant bodies, of this effrontery. Cowles never forgot this episode,[7] which occurred while he was out of the room, although he continued support for this project to honor Washington the Mason.

As was noted earlier, Cowles, as Secretary General of the Supreme Council for ten years, had a good preparation for becoming Grand Commander in October 1921. "He was not a man of distinction at that time nor was he as well educated as many of his contemporaries. He was not wealthy, but he was considered 'well-to-do' for the times."[8] Short (five feet five inches tall) and stocky in appearance, Cowles quickly took hold of his new responsibilities. The first year, 1922, was fully scheduled for the new Grand Commander. Late in May he attended, with four other members of the Supreme Council, the International Conference of Supreme Councils in Lausanne, Switzerland, and visited Scotland, England, Germany, Belgium, and France as well. The conference voted down a proposal for the creation of "a permanent Secretariat" by five to four, one of the opposing members noting "that the objection of three delegations is sufficient to keep any deliberation out of the Acts of the Conference."[9] The delegates agreed that the next International Conference would be held in Buenos Aires in 1927 with the Supreme Council of Argentina as host.

As agreed upon at the biennial session of 1921, the Supreme Council met for an annual session, August 28 through 30, 1922, at Salt Lake City. Annual sessions in even-numbered years, alternating with the biennial sessions, continued until 1929 when Cowles recommended the return to the regular biennial sessions held in odd-numbered years and the elimination of other sessions except those specially called. Expense, time, and inconvenience, Cowles felt, did not justify the annual session.[10]

• • •

At the Salt Lake City session, the Supreme Council accepted the recommendation of the Committee on Fraternal Assistance and Education that the education work in the Southern Jurisdiction had advanced to such a degree as to necessitate "the active and continuous supervision of an executive Committee [sic]" composed of the Grand Commander, Secretary General, Treasurer General, and two other Active Members of the Supreme Council.[11] The committee, however, noted in its report that not much had been done to advance public support for compulsory education and the establishment of a national university in Washington, D.C.[12] But the Supreme Council continued to press for legislation calling for a Department of Education. "The most adamant Masonic support for the bill [to establish a Department of Education]," as Lynn Dumenil has observed, "came from the Southern Jurisdiction of the Scottish Rite. The Rite, which was unhampered by restrictions against political activity, embarked on an exhaustive campaign to arouse public sympathy for the bill. Local Scottish Rite groups were instructed to promote public school improvement and to publicize the Smith-Towner Bill," which never passed.[13]

Upon the recommendation of the Committee on Foreign Relations, the Supreme Council authorized the Grand Commander to renew recognition of the Supreme Council of Spain, which had earlier invaded the territorial jurisdictions of the two American councils, thus causing the severance of fraternal relations. He could also investigate the status of the Supreme Councils of "Czecho-Slovakia" and Poland and report the same to the Supreme Council for possible future recognition.

Responding in another action to some complaints by members concerning the organization and conduct of the Supreme Council, perhaps reflecting the expanding membership, the council by resolution stated emphatically "That any adverse criticism or complaint of the Supreme Council or any Member thereof, made by any brother except in the proper forum of the Rite, is unmasonic and violative of obligation and is hereby condemned." The Grand Commander was to report "any disloyalty or insubordination" by any recipient of the thirty-third degree within the Southern Jurisdiction or by a Knight Commander of the Court of Honor to the Supreme Council for appropriate action.[14] So long as a man was still aspiring to receive Scottish Rite honors, a natural discipline existed that ensured cooperation and allegiance. However, in order to keep those in line who had already been promoted to the highest ranks, an added measure of implicit control seemed necessary. The policy was premised on the Rite's Masonic understanding of its custodial rights to protect the sovereignty of the council and the Grand Commander. There was little room for the parliamentary idea of the "loyal opposition."

■ ■ ■

Less than ten months after the Salt Lake City session, on August 2, 1923, President Warren G. Harding died of a cerebral hemorrhage in San Francisco after a speechmaking tour of the West and Alaska. Harding had already known about the questionable activities of some of his friends in the administration, but he was not aware of the extent of the so-called scandals involving the Veterans Bureau, the Alien Property Custodian, the Teapot Dome, or the Elk Hills naval oil reserves, all of which came to light during President Coolidge's administration. Suffice to say Harding was a pathetic figure, ill-equipped to bear the responsibilities of the president of the United States.

Meanwhile, the Northern Supreme Council had elected Harding to receive the thirty-third degree, but Mrs. Harding's illness prevented him from receiving it at the annual session in Cleveland in September 1922. It was then arranged to have the degree conferred upon him the following September in New York, but his untimely death precluded it.

Two and a half months after Harding's death, the Supreme Council met in regular session at the House of the Temple. The Secretary General reported that at the end of December 1922 there were 215,697 thirty-second degree Masons in the jurisdiction (a net increase of 12.5% in one year); and the total gross receipts as of August 31, 1923, amounted to $1,869,532.82. Disbursements for 1921 through 1923 were $2,045,552.04, of which more than $696,000 were in government bonds, indicative of the Supreme Council's longstanding prudence in investment. These figures reflected the healthy status of the council at the end of Cowles's second year as Grand Commander.

In his *Allocution* of the 1923 session, Cowles announced that the bronze bust of himself, a gift of the Supreme Council of Italy to the southern Supreme Council, had arrived. On the recommendation of the Committee on the House of the Temple, still chaired by Charles E. Rosenbaum, a pedestal, costing about $700, was to be provided for the sculpture. John Russell Pope would be asked to design this special marble base.

The Grand Commander, in the course of his general remarks in the *Allocution,* interjected a thought which obviously had been bothering him, namely, the use of the word "cathedral" for Scottish Rite buildings, a term he considered "improper." It had come into use in the Southern Jurisdiction "in recent years" and "presumably from the purchase of some Church building by Scottish Rite Bodies, and remodeling it to Scottish Rite uses."[15] Cowles explained that cathedral refers to the bishop's see (or, literally, his "chair") in a diocese. The Masonic usage of the term "temple," like the appropriation of "cathedral," was never intended to connote a religious house of prayer. Rather, it was a romantic appellation to identify with the tradition of great and ancient buildings such as King Solomon's temple in Jerusalem, the imaginary backdrop of the oldest Masonic rituals.

Elsewhere in the *Allocution* the Grand Commander proposed as a part of "Our Great Work" (the name he used to refer to the Rite's philanthropic program) the building of a hospital "for the cure of our brethren who suffer from the dread malady Tuberculosis" in an environment and climate suitable for the treatment of this disease.[16] A committee of three was appointed to study the proposal and report at the next session. Ultimately it was decided that such a project was, along with others being proposed, "public in character," enjoyed general support,[17] and thus did not have a demand upon the Supreme Council's attention as did the Fund of Fraternal Assistance, which the council considered at the 1923 session to help indigent brethren of the Southern Jurisdiction as well as their widows and orphans. The Committee on Benevolence and Fraternal Assistance was asked to report on the proposal at the 1925 session.

As proposed in the session of 1923, the sum of $500,000, which would be withdrawn from the council's government bonds account, would be set aside for the Fund of Fraternal Assistance. In turn, the fund would receive the income from this sum and gifts or bequests of individual brothers or their families. But the proposal was to be jointly undertaken with local jurisdictions within the Rite and so, inadvertently, competed for attention and funds with other projects in the orients and valleys. Consequently, the Fund of Fraternal Assistance remained on "hold" for several years.

Cowles in his *Allocution* was pleased to announce that the Scottish Rite Masons in Oregon were instrumental in bringing about the adoption of a referendum in the state, by a considerable majority, requiring compulsory attendance for all children in the public schools. He also noted that the Capital News Service of the Supreme Council had been sending to newspapers in the Southern Jurisdiction information about the federal education bill, compulsory attendance in the public schools, a national university, and immigration problems, as well as material concerning Americanization.

■ ■ ■

In the early 1920s the Scottish Rite's new venture into community service became established on a permanent foundation. The care of sick children continued to be an acute problem in America long before there were government welfare agencies. Childhood diseases, before vaccination programs and before the development of antibiotics, devastated thousands of American families. Polio, or infantile paralysis, was a particularly cruel adversary of children's health.

In recognition of the dedicated humanitarian service of Dr. Michael Hoke, the Supreme Council elected him to receive the rank and decoration of Knight Commander of the Court of Honor and also "the rank and dignity of Inspector General Honorary, 33°, Honorary member of this Supreme Council, and, as a further honorarium, to receive the Thirty-third Degree at large without fee."[18] Dr. Hoke had been the surgeon-in-chief at the Scottish Rite Hospital for Crippled Children in Decatur (Atlanta), Georgia, since its establishment in 1915. Inspector Hyman W. Witcover of Georgia, who nominated him, noted that the Atlanta surgeon had served the hospital "without fee or reward" to the credit and advancement of the Rite.[19]

Inevitably, one of the most important accomplishments of the 1923 session was the Supreme Council's adoption of the revision and recodification, "section by section," of the *Statutes*.[20] At the Salt Lake City session the previous year, provision was made for a Committee of One, appointed by the Grand Commander, to do the revision and recodification. Cowles asked Edward C. Day, the Grand Minister of State, to undertake this work. Later, the Committee on Jurisprudence and Legislation reviewed Day's efforts for mechanical errors and improved clarification before the *Revised Statutes* were submitted for adoption.

On the last day of the session, the Supreme Council, in response to the devastating earthquake in Japan on September 1, 1923, resolved to contribute to the consistory in the Valley of Yokohama, Orient of Japan, $5,000, as a part of American Freemasonry's contribution to the American School of Japan, and $10,000 which the Grand Commander could use at his discretion to aid Scottish Rite Masons in Japan or to provide assistance in the relief work in accordance with the Rite's principles.

. . .

Shortly after the close of the 1923 session, Cowles received a letter of inquiry from the Reverend Orville Paul Manker, a Scottish Rite Mason from Hamlet, Indiana, regarding the Ku Klux Klan and Masonry. This was at a time when the Klan was enjoying popularity in Indiana as well as elsewhere in the Midwest and South. Manker's concern was personal and genuine: "I have been invited to become a member of the Klan but for several reasons I have refused. I wish to be informed if you and the Supreme Council feel that the Klan is thoroughly American and a proper organization for a 32nd degree Mason to belong to. I am not asking this of you to quote you or to make it public but rather that I might be correctly guided in the matter. I understand the Supreme Council is against the Klan."[21]

In his reply, the Grand Commander pointed out that the Klan was "a separate and distinct organization from Masonry and that Masonic Bodies, as such, have no connection with it whatever." He added the cautious disclaimer that Masonic bodies did not "have a right to tell anyone they [*sic*] shall or shall not join any other organization." But Cowles hedged in forthrightly condemning the Klan, his reasoning drawn from the convenience of neutral principles: "I know very little of the Ku Klux Klan. I have not attempted to ask any questions of anyone who I might think belonged to the Klan, as I believe it is none of my affair as to whether Masons, Odd Fellows, Knights of Pythias, Elks, etc., join the Klan or not. We do not approve or disapprove of many things, feeling that it is beyond the scope of our endeavors."[22]

Cowles cautioned, however, that "if a Mason should become a member of an organization that is illegal . . . then it would be proper for the Mason to either get out of the illegal organization or else be disciplined by the Masonic Bodies." Later in the same letter, Cowles told his correspondent that "unfortunately, some misguided Masons, who are members of the Klan, have [tried] evidently, and maybe some are still trying to make the masses of people believe that Freemasonry and the Klan are closely allied, or even that the Masonic Fraternity is backing the Klan. This, on the part of those Masons, is improper and does no good for the Klan, and doubtless gives out a wrong impression as regarding what Freemasonry is."[23]

A few months later Cowles again dealt with the subject of the Klan, particularly with reference to Past Grand Commander George F. Moore and the *Fellowship Forum*. In a letter to an Alabama Scottish Rite Mason, Cowles noted that the *Fellowship Forum*, which was published by the Independent Publishing Company, whose president was Moore, had "no connection" whatsoever with the Supreme Council. The Grand Commander stated that "I do not know whether Brother Moore is connected with the Klan or whether his paper is supported or endorsed in any way by the Klan. Not being a member of that institution, I have not concerned myself with it."[24]

By 1924, when Cowles discussed the possible connection between George Moore's *Fellowship Forum* and the Ku Klux Klan, the Klan had reached its high-water mark of membership and influence. Almost as quickly as the flood tide had come in, the Klan's influence suddenly receded. Although the ebb had arrived, in the November elections of that year the Klan won control of the government of Indiana, including the governor's office and a large majority in the state legislature as well as all but one of the state's congressional seats.[25]

■   ■   ■

Meanwhile, the Republican National Convention had met in Cleveland, Ohio, on June 10 and nominated President Coolidge for reelection on a platform of reduced taxes, cutback in government expenditures, limitation of armaments, and adherence to the World Court. Meeting in New York City two weeks later, the Democratic National

Convention, after a prolonged contest between William G. McAdoo (Tennessee) and Alfred E. Smith (New York), nominated on the 103rd ballot John W. Davis (West Virginia), a compromise candidate. (At that time a two-thirds majority was necessary for nomination in the Democratic National Convention.) A prominent lawyer and Mason, Davis, who had served as United States ambassador to England between 1918 and 1921, campaigned on a platform calling for a competitive tariff, disarmament, membership in the League of Nations, condemnation of the corruption of the Harding administration, and a denunciation of the Ku Klux Klan. At their convention in Cleveland on July 4, the Progressives nominated Senator Robert M. La Follette (Wisconsin), a Scottish Rite Mason, for president on a platform whose planks favored, among other things, government ownership of railroads and water powered resources, collective bargaining for labor and farmers, ratification of the child labor amendment, and limitation on judicial review. Coolidge won handily with 382 electoral votes to Davis's 136 and La Follette's 13. Moreover, the Republicans retained control of Congress.

A month and a half before the election, the Supreme Council met in annual session on September 24, 1924, in the Scottish Rite Temple at Charleston, South Carolina. The council met two days later in Shepheard's Tavern, located at the northeast corner of Broad and Church Streets, in the room where, 123 years before, it had been founded. Grand Commander Cowles made suitable comments about the importance and history of the occasion and the place. This session marked the first time that the Supreme Council had met in Charleston since 1868. Then, at the conclusion of the open session at Shepheard's Tavern, the Supreme Council recessed to make a pilgrimage to St. Michael's Church and to the grave of Frederick Dalcho, a founder and the second Grand Commander. These events demonstrated the largely ceremonial nature of this session. Later, based on Cowles's recommendations, the Supreme Council approved "a suitable headstone" for the grave of Dr. Dalcho in Charleston, as the one then in place was "badly deteriorated."[26]

In his *Allocution* for 1924 Cowles devoted a section to the Rite's educational program. He expressed deep regret that the Federal District Court of Oregon had found the Oregon School Amendment, which the Supreme Council had "fathered," unconstitutional. The amendment stated that children in Oregon must attend public elementary schools and that English must be "the language of instruction." The decision of the Federal District Court was appealed to the Supreme Court of the United States. Cowles, believing that the Supreme Council should appear in this appeal as a friend of the court, asked by letter (April 23, 1924) for a recess vote of the Active Members on obtaining legal counsel to represent the Mother Council. The recess vote promptly granted permission for legal counsel to be retained. An authority on constitutional law, Albert H. Putney, a Scottish Rite Mason and dean of the Law School in the American University, was asked to serve with the counsel for the state of Oregon.[27] The Supreme Court of the United States subsequently upheld the Federal District Court's decision.

This 1924 session also furnished an example of making haste slowly with regard to the report of the Special Committee on the Tuberculosis Sanitarium and the Committee on Benevolence and Fraternal Assistance with reference to the proposed Fund for Fraternal Assistance: there was to be a further survey of these two proposals by a special committee, which was to bring in a report at the next regular session. It might at this time appear to be late for the Scottish Rite to consider entering the medical missionary field at home. The U.S. Bureau of Public Health, however, had estimated that in 1920 the national average for life expectancy was only fifty-four years, whereas in 1901 it was slightly over forty-nine years. Another five year gain in American life expectancy would be recorded in 1933, bringing the average to fifty-nine years. While the nation's health seemed to be improving, the crippling infectious diseases, such as polio and tuberculosis, continued to ravage the public with impunity.

■　■　■

A year later at the Supreme Council's regular session, held as usual in the House of the Temple and starting on October 19, 1925, Cowles reported at the beginning of his *Allocution* that the membership numbered a little over 248,000 in the consistories and almost 290,000 in the Lodge of Perfection. The council's financial condition was sound. Moreover, the Grand Commander noted that the Scottish Rite bodies in the jurisdiction were increasing "in number and prosperity" and that new temples were being erected, in some instances resulting in heavy indebtedness.[28] To some extent this development was a sign of the times.

In the section of his *Allocution* for 1925 devoted to other Supreme Councils, Cowles reported in some detail on Italian dictator Benito Mussolini's attack on Freemasonry in his country. This resulted in the closing of some 700 lodges which were under the Grand Lodge of Italy and the Italian Supreme Council of the Scottish Rite. "No liberty-loving people," Cowles prophetically declared, "will submit forever to such, one might say, slavery."[29]

Elsewhere in the *Allocution,* the Grand Commander reported that he had requested a bronze bust of "General Pike" be "made and placed on the landing of the main stairway to the Temple Room. The sculptor, brother Ulrich S. J. Dunbar, practically donated his services, and the cost came far under the appropriation."[30] The bust was considered an excellent likeness of Pike. Dunbar had personally known the Grand Commander and had made a plaster mask of his facial features after his death. John Russell Pope, the architect of the House of the Temple, requested that his office design the pedestal for the bust without charge.

Cowles stated in the *Allocution* that the Episcopal Bishop of Washington, D.C., James Edward Freeman, a Scottish Rite member, had asked him if the Supreme Council would donate a bronze statue of George Washington, dressed as the Worshipful Master of his lodge, to the Washington National Cathedral, which was then under construction. Bishop Freeman, as a means of raising building funds, wanted to invite every Master Mason to buy a stone for ten dollars and to have the name of every contributor listed in the book of remembrance. Although Cowles was a Presbyterian, he agreed to serve as the chairman of a committee of ten or twelve Grand Masters and Past Grand Masters who would invite Masons to contribute to this effort. The Supreme Council, at this session, authorized the Grand Commander to have rendered a bronze statue of Washington the Mason. The statue would be installed in the Masonic section of the cathedral. The proposal was finally realized in October 1947 when a pure white, Vermont marble statue of Washington, standing seven feet six inches tall, was presented to the Washington Cathedral by the Supreme Council.[31]

In response to the Grand Commander's proposal that a history of the Supreme Council during the 125 years of its existence should be published, the Committee on the Library, which had advanced the idea in 1923, endorsed the proposal, and the council adopted the plan. The history was to include the biographies of all Active Members from the beginning to the present, reproduction of rare documents on file in the Library of the Supreme Council, a history of the Rite in the several jurisdictions of the Mother Council, and "a sketch of the Rite prior to the organization of our Supreme Council."[32] Cowles felt that William L. Boyden, the librarian who had been with the Supreme Council for thirty-two years, including his unsung duty as a night watchman, was well qualified to assemble the materials necessary for writing the history. The Grand Commander subsequently invited Charles S. Lobingier, a former Deputy of the Supreme Council in China and the Philippine Islands, credited with bringing the Scottish Rite to the far Pacific, to undertake the writing of it.

On the recommendation of the Committee on Jurisprudence and Legislation, the council adopted some forty-five amendments to the *Statutes*. The subject of statutory amendment was, understandably, a frequent matter of concern at various sessions. The volume of proposed changes had not decreased at all, despite the pleas of previous Grand Commanders to temper the statutory tinkering.

An idea which had been studied and restudied came up again at the 1925 session with the report of the Special Committee on altruistic matters. The proposal for aid in the treatment and eradication of tuberculosis was quietly dropped, but the committee recommended "that the Grand Commander be authorized to appoint a Special Committee to further study the subject of the establishment of the work of Fraternal Assistance and Relief, and that the present Committee be discharged."[33] The committee further recommended that if any jurisdiction wished to attempt organization in this area, it could do so with a proviso that twenty-five cents for each member of the Lodge of Perfection would be set aside to assist aged or indigent members of the Rite and widows and orphans of deceased members.

The business manager (Secretary General) of the Supreme Council's publications reported that the Scottish Rite News Bureau's circulation for October 1925 was 3,767; and *The Supreme Council, 33°, Bulletin*, whose name was changed from the *Scottish Rite Clip*

Service on April 1, 1925, had a circulation of 22,452 as of October 1925, reflecting a decrease of about 1,500.

It is interesting to note that among those elected to receive the thirty-third degree at the 1925 session was Luther Burbank of California, the renowned horticulturist and naturalist. Actually, Burbank was not coroneted until December 19, 1925. This marks the beginning of the Scottish Rite's awareness of the "advertising" value in being identified with famous and accomplished men within its ranks. The practical and useful nature of positive publicity is self-evident. But it was hardly unique to the Scottish Rite that advantage was taken of opportunities to honor and then publicize members who had attained celebrity status in American life. It was, after all, the period that introduced a revolution of advertising and public relations techniques that would remain in practice for the rest of the century. The Madison Avenue ad men were inspired indirectly by the positive results of propaganda used during World War I. Many of the original ad men were the sons of clergy, such as Bruce Barton, author of the best-selling *The Man Nobody Knows* (1925) and later a member of the U.S. Congress.

Between the close of the 1925 session and the annual session—which opened on October 25, 1926, in the Scottish Rite Cathedral at Omaha, Nebraska, in keeping with the practice of holding the annual sessions occurring in even-numbered years outside Washington, D.C.—Cowles undertook a trip around the world, which took him to the Hawaiian Islands, Japan, the Philippines, China, the Mediterranean, and Europe. In his 1926 *Allocution* he made only cursory reference to this tour of foreign Scottish Rite bodies. Nevertheless, the extensive travels of Cowles signaled a global awareness of the Southern Jurisdiction that was impossible to imagine before World War I.

Five weeks before the Omaha session, a tropical hurricane struck the east coast of Florida in the vicinity of Miami, Fort Lauderdale, and Hollywood. One thousand people were killed, and 38,000 were rendered homeless. Cowles reported in his *Allocution* that he had immediately sent $2,000 for the relief of distressed members of the fraternity in Florida. In turn, the Committee on Benevolence and Fraternal Assistance, taking its cue from Cowles, recommended an appropriation of $10,000 for the relief of Scottish Rite Masons in the affected area of Florida, which the Supreme Council promptly approved.

During this session "the Grand Commander introduced Grand Master Herbert B. Holt of New Mexico, who addressed the Supreme Council on the subject of the National Masonic Tuberculosis Sanatoria,"[34] a topic which still interested Cowles but failed to captivate the Committee on Benevolence and Fraternal Assistance. It felt that not enough information was at hand to warrant specific action. The Grand Commander was asked to investigate further and report at the next session.

Lack of information was also the reason given by the Special Committee that had been formed to investigate the subject of fraternal assistance. In its report the committee further noted that five jurisdictions—in Alabama, the Canal Zone, Kentucky, Nebraska, and northern California—had formed organizations to handle fraternal assistance, as suggested in the resolution adopted at the 1925 session, and northern California had provided "some small appropriations."[35] In the bureaucratic fashion of prolonged intensity, the resolution was to be continued in force until the next session in 1927, when the Special Committee again requested its continuation so that a report could be made, after "further study," at the 1928 session in Portland, Oregon.

. . .

The year 1927 was notable in the history of aviation, motion pictures, and the theater. On May 20, Charles A. Lindbergh, a young aviator and future Mason, flew his single-engine *Spirit of St. Louis* nonstop from Roosevelt Field, Long Island, New York, to Paris's Le Bourget airport, a distance of 3,610 miles, in thirty-three and a half hours. This was not the first trans-Atlantic crossing by air. In 1919 Alcock and Brown had flown direct from Newfoundland to Ireland. The airship *NC-4,* that same year, had made the crossing with five men aboard via the Azores. And there had been dirigible flights across the Atlantic. "The novelty of Lindbergh's flight lay only in the fact that he went all the way from New York to Paris instead of jumping off from Newfoundland, that he reached his precise objective, and that he went alone."[36]

A tremendous crowd greeted Lindbergh upon his arrival at Le Bourget. President Coolidge ordered an American cruiser to bring the young flyer and his plane home. Upon his arrival he was honored by parades in various cities, commissioned a colonel in the United States Army Air Corps, and received both the Distinguished Flying Cross and the Congressional Medal of Honor. Tall and attractive in appearance, Lindbergh was a modest, unassuming young man who fitted the role of hero that Americans so desperately wanted in an age of crime and scandal.

The following October Warner Brothers introduced in New York the first all-talking motion picture, *The Jazz Singer*, starring Al Jolson, a popular singer, actor, native of Washington, D.C., and a Mason. As a result of "talkies," the popularity of the "legitimate" theater declined, "silent" film stars whose voices were unsuitable for the new medium were eliminated, and thousands of theater musicians became unemployed.

During the Christmas holidays of 1927 *Show Boat* opened at the new Ziegfeld Theater in New York City. The theater was named for Florenz Ziegfeld, the well-known theater impresario of the Ziegfeld Follies who was also the producer of this operetta and a Scottish Rite Mason. Edna Ferber's novel *Showboat* furnished the story line for the perpetually popular operetta whose composer, Jerome Kern, and lyricist, Oscar Hammerstein II, provided such memorable songs as "Ol' Man River" and "Make Believe." A departure from the Viennese tradition, *Show Boat* was a pioneer of the American musical theater, which later saw the staging of *Oklahoma, Carousel,* and *South Pacific.*

Meanwhile, the annual session of the Supreme Council opened on October 17, 1927, at the House of the Temple. Cowles noted in his *Allocution* that the number of initiates in the Lodges of Perfection for the recent biennium was about 7,150 less than in the previous term; in the consistories the number was about 6,350 less. There was, in Cowles's opinion, no cause for alarm, "for 34,500 received the Degrees in the Lodges of Perfection and 28,000 in the Consistories, a number never dreamed of even twenty years ago."[37] Furthermore, the total membership numbered "well over 300,000." The Grand Commander, however, had some significant comments about the condition of the Rite, the problems of generating enthusiasm, and, more importantly, the falling off of interest in Masonry. In recent years thousands of men had joined the ranks of the Scottish Rite. Cowles noted, "[They] became enthused with the Rite and its possibilities of service, attended the meetings and seeing only the Degrees conferred night after night, with an occasional dinner, but no avenue of labor offered or pointed out to them, have gradually joined that large element of dues-paying members. They are not to be criticized so much as we older members [should be], who have failed to keep in touch with them to the extent of explaining our principles and policies and enlisting their services."[38]

No decade in the history of the Scottish Rite had witnessed such a sky-high growth in membership as the period from 1917 to 1927. But the Grand Commander was not hesitant to point out that "the bodies have been, in a measure, Degree mills."[39] This fact and Cowles's opinion stand in contrast to the nineteenth-century emphasis on the mystical properties of the ritual. Even though Pike's revised ritual from the 1860s was in use, Pike himself never saw the degrees staged in an auditorium and rarely in a lodge room. Instead, in Pike's day, they were typically transmitted individually in a tutorial setting, thus creating an intimacy between teacher and pupil. When the Rite discovered the advantages for a large audience to witness the degrees from theater seats, the intensity of the more studied approach had subsided. Advocates of Scottish Rite theatricality came to realize that by adding a cast of participants on the stage, more men actually learned and absorbed the ritual. Further, community bonds and impulses toward service had supplanted the "monastic" attraction of philosophical learning and allegorical interpretation.

As for Masonry in general, Cowles felt that there had been a loss of interest in Freemasonry by the membership, accompanied by indifference among the "profane" towards the fraternity. The lack of interest in Masonry among the public was largely the result of competing organizations, including a rising number of fraternal societies and clubs which "solicited" members. "Most of them are good, worthwhile institutions, altruistic of purpose and attractive to the man who desires to do some good in the world."[40]

Other causes for the difficulty of recruitment and retention of membership in Masonry at large were, in Cowles's judgment, "over-organization," "increased cost," and "over-building of temples." In time, all kinds of Masonic clubs, circles, bands, orchestras, patrols, and guards appeared, each of them requiring "dues as well as service." Cowles explained that he was not criticizing the value of these organizations but simply showing the claims "on the time and purse" of the Mason who was actively involved in several of them. The increased cost was the result of the raising of the dues and fees in many Masonic organizations because charitable activities had expanded to include building of homes for the care of the elderly and unfortunate and assisting in non-Masonic causes (of which Cowles strongly disapproved). All this was an added financial burden on the order and had a chilling effect on some of the membership, as did the heavy indebtedness as the result of mortages on new buildings, a matter which had been a cause of concern expressed by Cowles for some time.[41]

By detailing these problems, the Grand Commander was, in effect, calling for Masonry to face up to the reality of the membership question. He thought, for instance, that the Scottish Rite should build its temples so that they could be "at least partially commercialized, for no one can tell what the future holds in store."[42] The crash of the New York Stock Market, the forerunner of the Great Depression of the 1930s, was just two years ahead, but there had been an earlier foreshock of hard times nationally in the post-war years (1919-1921).

Besides the membership issue, Cowles dealt with several other matters of varying importance in his *Allocution* of 1927. He reported that he had arranged for the Indian relics, including minerals and ethnological specimens, in the museum (which was a part of the Library of the Supreme Council) to be given to the United States Museum, Smithsonian Institution, where they more properly belonged. This was not the first or last instance of the Scottish Rite contributing to the Smithsonian.

The response to his own column in *The New Age*, "Journeyings of the Grand Commander," pleased him very much. When he began writing the column, he was afraid that it would not be read or that it would not hold any interest for the membership. On the contrary, the column was well received. It was an informal, topical travel diary in which Cowles could demonstrate how hard he was working for the Rite. The feature always ended with his total mileage by train, boat, and automobile during his trip. The reports were sprinkled with human interest anecdotes which made him seem approachable.

In compliance with resolutions adopted at the 1925 session, Cowles informed the Supreme Council that he had had a large bronze tablet prepared as a memorial to former Grand Commander Richardson after conferring with several knowledgeable members and John Russell Pope. Placed on the west wall of the atrium in the House of the Temple between the columns and the north wall, the tablet read, in part, "to the memory of John Daniel Richardson, 1901–1914, Patriot, Statesman, Freemason from whose vision rose this stately House of the Temple." Richardson's own purposeful words were then quoted: "The cause of human progress is our cause, the enfranchisement of human thought our supreme wish, the freedom of human conscience our mission, and the guarantee of equal rights to all peoples everywhere the end of our contention."[43]

Other features of the House of the Temple on which Cowles had acted included the placement of attractive lighting fixtures on either side of the main entrance to the temple. He wisely deferred to Pope for their design. As for the plaster figures executed by the artist David Edstrom, the replicas of Egyptian block statues which flanked the main stairway leading from the atrium to the Temple Room, Cowles reported that after ten years it was time to install the two sculptures in black marble as originally planned. The best alternative at this time was to employ the same sculptor, Adolph A. Weinman, who had carved the sphinxes in front of the building, to complete the statuary of the building. Therefore, Weinman was placed under contract to prepare the marble figures. Later, Weinman became noted for the Spanish marble frieze of law-givers that he designed for the chamber of the U.S. Supreme Court.

A major difficulty arose in the availability of suitable materials. It was learned that Belgian black marble in the dimensions necessary was unavailable at the time: and Cowles would not accept a mottled marble that was suggested by Pope. After long negotiations, including a discussion with the Belgian Grand Commander, the preferred marble was not to be gained. Instead, Champlain black marble from Vermont was substituted, and the statues were in place by the 1929 session.[44]

In a section of the *Allocution* devoted to the rituals of the Scottish Rite, the Grand Commander opined that "of all Pike's writings and works his rituals are the most outstanding, and also his greatest legacy to our Rite. They are unequalled, unparalleled, and should be the most enduring monument to his memory and preserved just as he left them and as they are today."[45] This did not mean, however, that no word or punctuation should be changed or that the rituals should not be altered to allow for current conditions. Hasty redactions and interpolations, nevertheless, Cowles warned, must be guarded against.

Also in this section of the *Allocution* pertaining to the rituals, Cowles felt it appropriate to comment on the fourteenth degree ring. He noted that the plain flat ring as then prescribed by the Rite's *Statutes* left an ambiguity. He pondered that someone seeing it might be hesitant to inquire of the wearer. Cowles thought that the members should be "permitted to wear the ring on any finger of either hand, and that there be placed upon it some device as a means of identification,"[46] that of the Northern Masonic Jurisdiction being a satisfactory one to follow. These suggestions, added Cowles, applied also to the thirty-third degree ring.

Later in the session, the Supreme Council adopted the report of the Committee on Jurisprudence and Legislation, which had received a report of the Committee on Ritual and Ceremonial Forms concerning regulations governing the rings of these degrees. The thirty-third degree ring was to be made of triple bands of gold, no more than five-sixteenths of an inch in width, and "may be plain without any device or mark on the outside of it, or it may have on the outside of it an equilateral triangular-shaped plate with the numeral '33' on same."[47] Within the ring there was to be engraved an inscription (*Deus meumque jus,* God and my right), the name of the wearer, and the date of conferral of the degree.

In turn, the fourteenth degree ring was to be a plain gold band, not exceeding five-sixteenths of an inch in width, with "an engraved or enameled plate in the form of an equilateral triangle, and within the triangle the Hebrew letter Yod [the first letter of the

Hebrew word for Yahweh],"[48] and, like the thirty-third degree ring, was to have engraved within the appropriate inscription (*Virtus junxit mors non separabit,* virtue unites what death cannot separate), the name of the candidate, and the date of his receiving this degree.[49]

Besides its report on the fourteenth degree and thirty-third degree rings, the Committee on Jurisprudence and Legislation submitted a report, which was adopted, on the six official circular style caps that were worn at the time in the southern Supreme Council. The statement detailed the specifications for each cap—Sovereign Grand Inspector General, Sovereign Grand Commander, Inspector General Honorary, Grand Cross of the Court of Honor, Knight Commander of the Court of Honor, and Master of the Royal Secret—as to the color, material, and decorative features.[50] For example, the crown of the cap worn by the Sovereign Grand Commander was to be made of violet grosgrain silk, and the band was to be made of violet grosgrain silk of a darker shade than that of the crown and adorned in a laurel vine, a leaf and berry pattern in number twenty-six and number twenty-seven gilt bullion. On the front of the cap, the Grand Commander's Cross, the Cross of Salem with crosslets, was to be placed.[51]

In addition to the original ceremonial caps, two others were adopted some years later. A cap for men who had been continuous members of the Scottish Rite for fifty years or more was adopted in 1945 (an azure blue). Grand Commander Henry C. Clausen approved in 1981, and the Supreme Council adopted two years later, a distinctive cap for the Deputies of the council (white with a red velvet band). The milliner's design for the caps of the Southern Jurisdiction—which wags called a "bell-hop's pill box"—outlived its critics. Also, the cap always received more favorable notice for style than other Masonic headgear such as the Shriners' fez with tassel.

■ ■ ■

Without doubt, the most dramatic action of the 1927 session was the appropriation of $1 million for the establishment of "a department or school of government" at George Washington University; it was to be "a memorial to George Washington, the Mason."[52] Prior to the Supreme Council's unanimous adoption of the resolutions providing for this gift, the Grand Commander recessed the council and, in turn, invited Dr. Cloyd Heck Marvin, president of George Washington University, to speak on the need for a school of government in the university.

Cloyd Marvin, who had been dean in the University of California at Los Angeles and president of the University of Arizona, had become president of George Washington University on August 1, 1927, prior to the annual session of the Supreme Council. After Marvin spoke, the Supreme Council discussed the proposal with reference to its educational program and quickly reached agreement. A school of government in a nonsectarian university named in honor of George Washington and located in Washington, D.C., was in keeping with its concern and support of constitutional government and good citizenship. It should also be noted that Cowles and the Supreme Council were interested in a well-trained foreign service and "were particularly aroused by the fact that the only institution formally offering such training through a School of Foreign Service was a church-related institution [Georgetown University]."[53]

A little more than two months after the annual session, on December 28, 1927, the Board of Trustees of George Washington University accepted an indenture between the university and the Supreme Council, "whereby the University accepted a gift of one million dollars with the understanding that the gift would revert if at any time the institution ceased to be nonsectarian."[54] One of the results of the many conferences between Cowles and Marvin was that the grant was to be paid to the university in ten annual installments of $100,000 apiece. In recognition of the Supreme Council's particular interest in the university, as reflected in the generous gift, "The Board of Trustees at its special meeting on February 17, 1928," wrote Chairman John B. Larner, "expressed its desire that the Supreme Council be represented on the Board, as long as the gift is held by the University."[55] The Scottish Rite gift remained intact, but the Supreme Council's seat on the university's Board of Trustees was impossible to guarantee by the mid-1960s.

. . .

About two months after the adjournment of the 1927 session, Cowles was confronted with the question of whether the Supreme Council should own the building in Charleston in which it was founded in 1801. In response to a letter on this subject, Cowles replied that he could not ". . . figure out what we could do with a building in Charleston, S.C., just to hold because our Supreme Council was organized in it."[56] It had been suggested, he went on to say, that the Supreme Council should buy Albert Pike's home in Little Rock and a portion of the farm in Arkansas where Pike had lived for a while. Cowles was indeed skeptical about the desirability of such purchases. The owners of the building in Charleston had tried to sell it to the Supreme Council at a price several times more than it was worth. As it turned out, the Citizens and Southern National Bank of South Carolina purchased the building which had housed Shepheard's Tavern (where the Supreme Council was founded) as the site of its new home.

During the 1927 biennial session, the Supreme Council accepted the invitation of the Scottish Rite bodies of Portland, Oregon, to meet in that city for the next annual (even year) session on June 10, 1928. One of the more important items that Cowles took up in his *Allocution* was the history of the Supreme Council that Charles S. Lobingier had written, complete except for the last chapter pertaining to the Grand Commander's administration to date. With some disapproval, Cowles reported that a major portion of Lobingier's manuscript, which concentrated on the history of the Rite before 1801, included "those disputed points on which there is and will continue to be differences of opinions."[57]

Lobingier's original manuscript meticulously and entirely dealt with the background and formative history of the Rite prior to the establishment of the Supreme Council in

1801. Cowles realized that for Lobingier to prepare an additional manuscript covering the succeeding 130 years, in the manner of the text which had already been prepared, an additional couple of years would be required. Cowles could not wait that long.[58]

Cowles may have preferred a mere chronicling of the past over the art of history writing, which necessarily includes discernment among causes and consequences. He may have feared that a review of the work by independent professional historians would side with Lobingier. If the Grand Commander submitted the manuscript to experts, and they differed, who was to be the final judge? Rather, he concluded that the council should decide whether to publish the entire manuscript or only that portion dealing with the Supreme Council and also should determine the number of copies to be printed and the distribution of complimentary copies. The council agreed with the Grand Commander as to condensation of the history and provided for the publication of 900 clothbound copies and 100 morocco-bound copies, the latter to be distributed among the Active Members of both the Southern and Northern Jurisdictions. But the history would not be published as a history of the Supreme Council for another two years.

The volume, as published in 1931, did not list an author on the title page. Instead, Cowles had directed Lobingier, Boyden, and Hyman W. Witcover to compile historical materials, "carefully documented with references to sources," without attempting "an author's historical narrative." Ray Baker Harris judged it as "being a source book of largely unedited historical materials." A year later, however, the Supreme Council published Lobingier's already completed manuscript about the years before 1801. Of that book, Harris admiringly offered, "it is a distinguished piece of historical writing."[59]

*   *   *

Looking outside the American South and West, Cowles reminded the active membership that at the International Conference of Supreme Councils at Lausanne in 1922, the Supreme Council of Argentina had invited the next conference to be held in Buenos Aires in 1927. However, the conference had to be postponed to 1928, and again to April 30, 1929, when it moved to Paris, with the understanding that the 1934 conference would meet in Buenos Aires.

The Grand Commander closed his *Allocution* with a report of a dinner he had arranged at the House of the Temple on March 10, 1928, to honor the 11 thirty-third degree Masons who were members of Congress. The 59 senators and 317 representatives who were members of the Masonic fraternity at the time were invited to the dinner. About 200 of them attended, together with about 100 brethren from the army and navy, government, business, and the professions. Here was an instance of Cowles's ability to promote the fraternity, including the Scottish Rite, among the leadership of the nation and the city.

One of the last acts of the Supreme Council for the Portland session was to provide a suitable bronze tablet on the new bank building in Charleston, commemorating the founding of the original council. The bank had graciously extended the invitation. Accordingly, the inscription on the tablet read: "On this site stood the building in which the Supreme Council, 33°, Mother Council of the World, Ancient and Accepted Scottish Rite of Freemasonry, was founded May 31, 1801, A.D., corresponding to Sivan 19, 5561, A.M."[60]

■   ■   ■

By 1927 rapid change was presaged in American society. Ford's Model T, for instance, was discontinued. Nicola Sacco and Bartolemo Vanzetti—immigrants with radical political views whose trial for the murder of a paymaster and guard at a New England shoe factory was highly controversial—had exhausted all their defense appeals and were put to death in the electric chair at the State Prison of Massachusetts in Charlestown. The episode represented several American paradoxes entangled with attitudes about immigration, ideology, and capital punishment, issues that never left the nation in the twentieth century.

Meanwhile, the 1927 New York Yankees, behind the power of Babe Ruth (60 home-runs) and Lou Gehrig (175 RBI), won the pennant by nineteen games and swept the World Series against the Pittsburgh Pirates in four straight games. The *New York Times* described Ruth's heroics in the World Series as causing a "paroxysm of glee" in 64,000 fans. The Yankees already had the deciding game salted away, but with Ruth's charisma every at bat was suspenseful. In the seventh inning, he hit a screaming liner toward the right-field fence: "Upwards and onward, gaining speed and height with every foot, the little white ball winged with terrific speed until it dashed itself against the seat of the right field bleachers, more than a quarter of the way up the peopled slope."[61]

The country earlier in the summer was mindful of a forthcoming presidential election that was little more than a year away. Grand Commander John H. Cowles, too, was concerned about the matter of national leadership. In June he had made up his mind that a third Coolidge term was not a wise precedent. The Anti-Third Term League, a distant forerunner of the late 1980s debate over term limits for elected officials, had tried to enlist Cowles for its cause. His sympathetic response indicated that he was "strongly opposed to a third term" but that he had to maintain public neutrality, as his "position in Masonry forbids" taking sides.[62] Cowles, more than once, wrestled with the tension between his own vehement preferences and the Grand Lodges' prohibition against official Masonic stands that could be perceived as political involvement.

Nevertheless, on many public issues Cowles held strong views that were readily expressed in private channels and, at times, broke through in his official Scottish Rite communications. In the twenties, the only official Masonic activity of a political nature was in the broad realm of public education. But even these concerted efforts had the potential for divisiveness. Consequently, the drive for Masonic consensus was abandoned in order to avoid any intramural conflicts. The prevailing sensibilities of an earlier time and the codes of propriety from the eighteenth century that had disallowed opinion gathering in the lodge room were still a vivid force.[63]

Whatever worry Cowles had about a third presidential term, in the end, was pre-empted by Coolidge himself. While on an August vacation in the Black Hills of South Dakota, the president, presumably resting comfortably in his desire for the Republican nomination the next summer, announced, instead, "I do not choose to run for President in 1928." Secretary of Commerce Herbert C. Hoover, a former mining engineer, received a first ballot nomination from the Republican National Convention at Kansas City, Missouri, the summer after Coolidge's announced retirement plans.

The Democrats, meeting in Houston, Texas, nominated New York governor Alfred E. Smith on the first ballot, a remarkable achievement given the 103 ballots at the previous nominating convention. Hoover easily won the 1928 election in a landslide victory, in part because of religious prejudice against Smith, a Roman Catholic. The electoral votes of five Southern states went to Hoover; the Democratic solid South had momentarily broken ranks. Cowles, no doubt, shared the widely expressed concern about the prospect of a Roman Catholic in the White House, an issue that would be revisited by the nation in the election of John F. Kennedy in 1960. Cowles's attitude was that the Scottish Rite should feel no threat from the spiritual domain of the Catholic Church but only from its possible temporal claims and its involvement "in the political life of the nation."[64]

In response to some criticism of *The New Age* for publishing articles concerning the Roman Catholic Church, the Grand Commander declared that the spiritual domain of the Church was its own concern, that the Scottish Rite was interested "only in its temporal claims, its interference in the political life of the nation, and its discrimination against and attempt to destroy Masonry."[65] This was a subject which Cowles would return to with some regularity in the years to come. The national candidacy of the Democratic nominee Alfred E. Smith in 1928 particularly vexed Cowles because a Catholic president was "unAmerican" to one from Kentucky where few Catholics lived.

The Hoover era began with high resolve. In accepting the nomination of his party, the candidate said, "Given a chance to go forward with the policies of the last eight years we shall soon with the help of God be in sight of the day when poverty will be banished from this nation." No one could imagine the squalid shantytowns of unemployed Americans in "Hooverville" a few years later. Politicians and captains of commerce were not the only voices projecting optimism as the country approached the abyss of a stock market crash the next year. The new social sciences in the universities, too, uttered starry-eyed certainties about the eradication of barriers standing in the way of progress. Historical revisionism has necessitated a correction of the unfair image that for a long time categorized Coolidge as a president passively serving the acquisitive appetites of wealth. Rather, the national economy, contrary to the stereotype of the spendthrift twenties, prospered under Coolidge's watchfulness in some measure because he was grounded in a philosophy of thrift and debt reduction, not reckless consumption. Linking the subsequent Great Depression with Coolidge's policies and positions is, therefore, a careless generalization.[66]

Cowles, a man in his early sixties who had experienced economic depression and recovery cycles in the formative years of his life, was now in the midst of the jazzy, booming twenties. Long before the stock market crash, he called upon the words of the critic John Ruskin to sound a fire bell in the night: "A nation cannot last as a money-making mob; it cannot with impunity—it cannot with existence—go on despising literature, despising science, despising art, despising nature, despising compassion and conceding its soul to Pence."[67] Cowles might have pointedly added that the values inculcated by Freemasonry and elevated by the Scottish Rite were needed for the commonweal of the nation, in peril of being spoiled by the excesses of *nouveau riche* patterns of life.

The question of whether the country had lost its way, abandoning its Enlightenment ideals, deepened in the mind of Grand Commander Cowles. At the end of the decade his *Allocution* had the tone of a Puritan jeremiad: "But what of the spiritual and moral progress of the Nations and of ourselves? Without desiring to throw a pessimistic bomb, I am convinced that it has not kept pace with the material. Money, money, money, is the current topic of the day and night in business, in pleasure, in politics, in sports, in profession, in society, in every avenue of life's activities."[68]

In general, Masonic leaders in the 1920s did not glorify business success the way men's civic clubs such as Kiwanis and Rotary did. Cowles was, perhaps, exceptional, and more outspoken than other Masonic officials. Criticism of vulgar materialism was muted, particularly when compared to Masonic statements of the late nineteenth century, most notably those of Albert Pike.[69]

Of more immediate concern for Cowles and others was the impact upon Masonry of a post-war world, spinning like a centrifuge whose center cannot hold. The sea change in popular culture and the transformation of consumptive patterns had threatening consequences for all fraternal organizations. Freemasonry, chief among them, suffered a decline in membership, which only compounded the efforts to adjust to new circumstances, precisely on the eve of the Great Depression. The relatively good news for Masonry was that it was the last fraternal order to feel the cultural undertow and to begin a dip in membership. The last year of real growth for Freemasons was 1928 and, in the natural sequence of falling dominoes, for the Scottish Rite, 1929. Other Masonic organizations, such as Knights Templar, Royal Arch, and the Shrine, had seen membership growth becalmed by 1926.[70] By the end of the Depression, 1942, the ebb tide had turned, but not without stirring high anxiety about what to do.

■　■　■

A symptom of decline for Cowles was the growing disuse of public Masonic ceremonies. Only a handful of Masons ever seemed to be present for the Masonic burial service, and Masons were seldom seen at the laying of cornerstones of public buildings, an occasion in which they once figured prominently in all communities.[71] Cowles, in light of obvious change, wondered what was the matter with Freemasonry. An inwardly frank assessment of Masonry did not, however, yield from Cowles much corporate self-pity. He defiantly proclaimed, in answer to his question, "Nothing is the matter with *it*." He granted that something might be wrong with some individual Masons, "and their failings reflect upon the institution as a whole."[72]

With the rise of American industry and the explosive growth of cities, Masonry was able to offer "a spiritual oasis, a retreat from this world." Further, it reinforced traditional morality so that "the idea of the asylum promised harmony in a world sorely lacking it." Specifically, as Lynn Dumenil points out, Masonry "brought together men, primarily native Protestants, who shared beliefs in American social, political and religious ideals." Masonry embodied the "fusion of Protestantism and democracy which characterized American middle-class culture."[73] And yet, as the American author Willa Cather surmised in a bold hyperbole, "the world broke in two in 1922 or thereabouts."[74]

The initial appeal of Masonry, according to Cowles, may have been exhausted too soon for some. Too many men, he said, "have never gathered from its ethics and philosophy [that which] ought to benefit them; some have never become imbued with its teachings and principles; some through lassitude have become indifferent; some have never imbibed the true spirit of fraternity; some are disappointed, and some forget." Cowles admitted the problems stemmed from more than the quality of the membership; of equal importance, "the psychology of the times or age has a bearing and influence." He was wary of creating a panic mentality and finished his analysis circumspectly, "[L]ike the ocean waves that rise and fall, yet onward go, so Masonry had its days of light or progress, and its nights of darkness or retardation."[75]

Still, even in the dawn of calm common sense, Cowles was searching for some explanation of why Masonry, especially the Scottish Rite, was losing members. Perhaps it was because Masons were being hounded for donations all the time. He speculated that "there are thousands of Masons who tire of constant demands of money, and they just drop out."[76] Or, he thought, the problem was one of institutional self-esteem. Morale is a kind of self-fulfilling prophecy, so "the scare . . . we have thrown into people over the 'depression' has emphasized it and prolonged it, and the same thing has happened to Freemasonry." Masonic publications were carrying too many articles about the deficiencies of the fraternity, "giving out statements that it was going to damnation and the 'bow-wows'." Naturally, it followed that "no one wants to join a decaying institution."[77] By this line of reasoning, Cowles established a policy that nothing potentially negative should appear in *The New Age*.

Freemasonry in all its ranks was passing through a difficult time which required of it a confrontation with the reality of declining membership. The problem may have been much worse for other fraternities, but, as Cowles sharply reminded the Supreme Council in its 1931 session, there is no satisfaction or comfort in the adage "misery loves company." Revenues also decreased, but Cowles maintained that there was still cause for rejoicing. Even before the Great Depression a strategy was emerging to meet the sense and fact of membership decline. Within the Scottish Rite, modifications were beginning; while Masonry, in general, was also seeking an appropriate response. The development of a public focus and voice, sometimes in direct support of a public policy position, was one way of reinvigorating the order. This shift in emphasis dated back to the turn of the century.

Traditionally, up through the nineteenth century, the fraternity had been concerned chiefly with the private man, the individual Mason, and thereby had concentrated on religion and the personal morality of the individual Mason. By the 1920s, Masons had developed a consciousness of the external world and desired some visible part in it as Masons. The problem of low attendance at lodges, including successful lodges, revealed that a large number of the membership had come to regard Masonry "more as a symbolic than a participatory organization."[78] Innovations in Masonic programs were a response to this subtle demand within the fraternity. Over all, the organization survived as the nation entered the Depression, but Masonry suffered further membership decline.

Ultimately, "Masonry never again achieved the popularity and prestige it had enjoyed in the late nineteenth and early twentieth centuries."[79] Membership in the Scottish Rite, Southern Jurisdiction, peaked in the 1920s at 257,960 and hit a "depression low" of 154,690, a 40 percent loss. At the bottom of the Depression, in the heart of the dust bowl, the McAlester, Oklahoma, Scottish Rite bodies "lost two thirds of their membership by suspension in a single year."[80] It is no wonder, therefore, that in 1931 Cowles thought it was time, after ten years of his leadership and in the face of formidable challenges, to be thinking of a successor. As it turned out, the sixty-eight-year-old Grand Commander had twenty-one more years in office.

At a critical juncture, however, he did not hide some personal doubts about what he had accomplished: "Will anyone call to mind a kindly deed performed, or mention my name with affection for having eased the burden of a fellow-traveller or express a single regret when I have passed into eternity?"[81] Another indication of the stress that Cowles felt from his responsibilities at this time was his standing order placed through the U.S. mail for headache powders.[82]

Grand Commander Cowles and the Supreme Council stayed busy on three fronts through the next phase of the inter-war years, the early 1930s. They concentrated on the operations and policies of the Scottish Rite, including the maintenance of the House of the Temple, its library, and the general finances; they worked on select public issues outside immediate Masonic concern, such as national immigration and education goals; and they responded to pleas for assistance from the international community of Masonry.

■　■　■

In time of trouble, organizations, whether voluntary or business, react in several ways. They may consider consolidating with like organizations, or streamlining procedures, or redoubling their efforts to achieve and protect their first principles. In the case of the Scottish Rite, Southern Jurisdiction, the obvious choice was a combination of the latter two. Any possible merger or mutual recognition of two similar organizations would seem to eliminate redundancy, but the differences between the Northern and Southern Jurisdictions, though small, were deep enough to leave the status quo untouched.

The Northern Scottish Rite Jurisdiction was at the time the largest of any Supreme Council in the world.[83] To be united with its northern counterpart, without being swallowed up, the Southern Jurisdiction would have had to believe such an amalgamation was not the equivalent of Jonah volunteering to set studding sails on a whale watch. But also the southerners would have to get past an irksome difference in the use of the ritual. The main sticking point between the two bodies was and would remain the question of whether or not the Scottish Rite's Maundy Thursday ceremony was open to the public. The Northern Masonic Jurisdiction was holding an open meeting on Maundy Thursday but using the Southern Jurisdiction's script, which still called for a closed service. The issue may have been a symbolic one, as much as anything, to maintain some distinction between North and South. And yet on other matters the two Scottish Rite bodies demonstrated considerable solidarity, as, for instance, in their cooperation regarding Cerneauism.[84]

The clandestine Cerneau organization, surprisingly, was still flourishing in the late 1920s to the extent that it had the strength and will to bring a suit against the Supreme Council of the Northern Jurisdiction in the Supreme Court of the state of New York. They sought damages of $500,000. Cowles, without hesitation, allowed the records of the Bayliss case against the Grand Lodge of Louisiana to be used by the Northern Jurisdiction. Four years later the Cerneau Masonic bodies would have their suit dismissed at the level of the Appellate Court.[85]

∎ ∎ ∎

In 1931, for whatever reason, perhaps irrelevant to membership losses, Cowles felt compelled to address the question of possible recognition of Negro Masonry in the United States. The question probably was generated from pressure from abroad, as Cowles made clear the Scottish Rite position: "[Prince Hall] Masons do not ask for recognition in this country, but they do from Grand Lodges in foreign countries, and sometimes secure it." Cowles did not have to state the obvious implication of why Prince Hall Masons had not asked for American standing, but he continued the thought to an abrupt and predictable finality, "that all regular Masons throughout the world may know that regular Grand Lodges in the United States do not recognize any colored or Negro Masonry in this country."[86] That was not always the case, though the exceptions were few. The pioneering African-American comedian Bert Williams was raised in Waverly Lodge No. 597 of Edinburgh, Scotland, along with nine others from the renowned troupe called the Williams and Walker Colored Minstrels. When Williams died in 1922, his Edinburgh lodge requested that he be buried with Masonic honors, a courtesy which St. Cecile Lodge No. 568 of New York City performed.

The Scottish Rite, Southern Jurisdiction, however, was doing more than reacting against its small, large, and potential rivals of the time. The effectiveness of its own organization was also being examined at a deciding moment. Cowles expressed growing impatience over the tinkering with the *Statutes,* which seemed to obscure a larger, more pressing agenda. Too much time, he lamented, was given to changing the *Statutes* and to enlarging the scope of the Committee on Jurisprudence and Legislation.[87] One change which perhaps had increased the buzz of dubious achievement into a self-fulfilling reality of bylaw revisionism was the frequency of Supreme Council meetings. The Supreme Council, in 1921, adopted a provision for annual sessions which broke with the traditional biennial schedule. Cowles felt that such annual sessions "have not justified the expense, not to mention the time and inconvenience to those members of the Supreme Council who have additional interests that require much of them."[88] Taking its cue from the Grand Commander, the Supreme Council adopted a resolution amending the *Statutes* to abolish the regular sessions in even-numbered years. This change took place after the 1930 special session in Dallas, Texas, the last time the Supreme Council would meet in an even-numbered year. By the time of the Dallas session, Cowles, who had made a convincing case for the importance of fraternal assistance, had accomplished much of his organizational agenda, including a program he had instituted in 1925 to help struggling valleys, such as Louisville, Kentucky.[89]

Part of the Grand Commander's role in the Southern Jurisdiction was and is, naturally, to function as chief defender of the ritual. The difficulty of maintaining cordial relations with the Northern Jurisdiction, while disapproving of their looser version of the Maundy Thursday ceremony, was only one concern that Cowles carried about preserving the dignity of the ritual. Contrary to his desires, the Supreme Council in 1928 had authorized the sale of *Morals and Dogma* by Albert Pike to anyone requesting a copy.[90] While this decision was a small defeat for him, the Supreme Council would give Cowles an enormous vote of confidence when it requested him to compile rubrics, authorized interpolations and deviations from the Pike rituals. Before the 1929 session Cowles had made his position clear that no lecture should be given in the conferring of Scottish Rite degrees except those in the ritual. It would be better, Cowles insisted, to omit the entire lecture rather than risk a poor substitute.[91] For the 1931 session Cowles had prepared rubrics covering the fourth through the thirty-second degrees, which were adopted by the Supreme Council with Cowles's admonition that "if these interpolations and changes are not used, then none others are permitted, and the Pike rituals must be strictly adhered to."[92] This remains an important achievement of Cowles and the Supreme Council, preserving continuity with the Scottish Rite's founders and its prophet, Albert Pike.

Cowles set a high standard for himself and the Scottish Rite of the Southern Jurisdiction in terms of compliance with the ritual. Despite a falling membership rate in the early 1930s, Cowles boldly proclaimed that too many initiates in the Scottish Rite were unfit. He complained that during the halcyon days too many men were "expecting material benefit instead of desiring to aid in altruistic labor, and such are they who are mostly dropping out, and well it is that they are." Coupled with his valediction of good riddance was the insight that the large numbers of people initiated not only raised money but created the temptation to use the increased funds extravagantly.[93]

Meanwhile, Cowles never deviated from his position on closed Scottish Rite Maundy Thursday and Easter services. He explained that it had taken many years of discussion to bring all the Rose Croix chapters throughout the Southern Jurisdiction into conformity with the required observation of obligatory meetings, such as Maundy Thursday: "We have gone back to the original intent of those services, which was for the purpose of bringing the brethren themselves closer together." Further, whatever alternate service was still in circulation, permitting the public to attend some portion of Maundy Thursday and Easter services, was, he insisted, to be returned to the Secretary General for destruction. This practice of excluding non-Masons (and Masons below the eighteenth degree) from the services remained in force until about 1980 when Grand Commander Henry C. Clausen authorized family participation in those sections not involving the ritual of the Scottish Rite degrees, presumably the opening and closing of the Chapter of Knights Rose Croix.[94]

. . .

The moral and spiritual strength of the Scottish Rite, as reflected in the outcome ensuring the purity of the ritual's usage, was more self-evident than the brewing anxiety over the Supreme Council's financial health at the bottom of the Depression. Cowles reported in the fall of 1933 that, "considering the general situation," the financial condition of the Scottish Rite bodies was relatively good. In some cases, funds had been frozen in closed banks or "frozen in temporarily unmarketable securities or unproductive investments."

Several measures were taken by the Supreme Council to safeguard its financial stability. Mailed publications, particularly those of the Scottish Rite News Bureau, were sent as third-class matter, saving approximately $6,000 over the first-class rate. In time, the printing costs would be brought down by $10,000 annually under a new contract. Additionally, all Supreme Council salaries were reduced in order to avoid discharging any employees at the House of the Temple. Cowles and Secretary General Witcover accepted a 10 percent cut in compensation. Another indication of the Depression's impact was an added feature of *The New Age*, a "Positions Wanted" column.[95]

Cowles was a tireless promoter of the unofficial job placement service his office provided; he used all the contacts and influence at his disposal to assist a phenomenal number of unemployed men. He was also exceedingly generous with his own personal resources, rarely refusing the appeal of any family in need. Many letters soliciting assistance were received at the Supreme Council and were often acknowledged with a sizeable check from Cowles himself.

In the biennial session for 1935, the Scottish Rite per capita tax needed to be cut by more than half in order to relieve the pressure on the subordinate Scottish Rite bodies. Sixty cents for each thirty-second degree member became the adjusted assessment, instead of the previous rate of $1.25.[96] While the Supreme Council was, according to Cowles, "resting easily financially," a number of valleys were experiencing unprecedented suffering. Several Scottish Rite temples were lost to bondholders; but, because foreclosure would have obligated them to pay property taxes, bondholders often refused to take over Scottish Rite buildings.

Under the stewardship of Grand Commander Cowles and Acting Secretary General Christian F. Kleinknecht, the Supreme Council invested in U.S. government bonds and treasury notes of 1947 and 1952 at 4.5 percent. The prudence of this Depression strategy would bear favorably in the coming years. But there was, apparently, enough money still available to afford relief and assistance in "all of the Valleys."[97]

Cowles worked indefatigably during the period of national economic crisis to resolve an issue that concerned Constitutional principle and placed a financial burden on the Supreme Council. Because the Scottish Rite property was not tax exempt in the city of Washington, D.C., the Supreme Council had a hefty obligation which in the first of two equal payments in 1929 amounted to $12,808.98.[98] Cowles had both a short- and long-term plan. He worked, first of all, to get the assessment lowered, particularly inasmuch as the Supreme Council's income had "been considerably lessened, as is generally the case." There was never any question about refusing to pay the taxes, but he made it clear to the Board of Commissioners for the District of Columbia that his goal was to secure in due course the House of the Temple's tax exempt status. In both instances Cowles would succeed, first by obtaining a reduced property assessment. Then, ultimately, by a special act of Congress, the Supreme Council of the Scottish Rite, Southern Jurisdiction, became a tax exempt organization.[99]

. . .

During an uneasy period marked by sound fiscal conservatism and an overall, necessary holding pattern, the Library of the Supreme Council, nonetheless, obtained several significant acquisitions. William L. Boyden, considered the "Dean of Masonic Librarians of the world," encouraged the expansion of the Supreme Council's book and manuscript collections.[100] His stature among Masonic librarians increased the visibility of the library and, therefore, the possibilities for it to become a rich repository of valuable materials. Grand Commander Cowles seemed especially proud that the library had about a thousand volumes of Goethe's works, although nothing in them was about Freemasonry even though Goethe was a Mason for over fifty years. Cowles knew that Goethe's Lodge Amalia, at Weimar, Germany, had in its possession Masonic orations written in Goethe's hand, and he coveted this kind of material for the Supreme Council's library.[101]

What the library acquired and possessed was of the highest quality for general and scholarly purposes. A vast collection of anti-Masonic literature, including hundreds of books and pamphlets dating back to the William Morgan episode in Canandaigua, New York, and the Anti-Masonic Party activity of 1826 through 1840, had evolved over the years. Rare Masonic books of extraordinary value also came into possession of the library. James Anderson's *Constitutions of the Freemasons*, a first edition published in London in 1723, was the most noteworthy among several significant titles. The library also acquired subsequent editions of Anderson's *Constitutions of the Freemasons* from 1738, and the Pennell edition (Dublin, 1730), and also the American edition printed at Philadelphia by Benjamin Franklin in 1734—the first Masonic book published in colonial America— which had its own important place in the Supreme Council's collection.[102]

The library was able to improve its Albert Pike holdings, a particular form of compensation in view of the Supreme Council's refusal to act on the availability for purchase of Pike's old plantation home in Little Rock, Arkansas. This real estate opportunity, which may have been a tempting location for a museum, was not, in the opinion of the Grand Commander, a wise expenditure in the trough of the Depression.[103] The library received a large manuscript collection of essays by Albert Pike, which he had given to the artist Vinnie Ream. These papers, written around 1880, were presented in five large, moroccobound volumes.[104]

An unusual assortment of material that had no direct connection with Masonry came to the House of the Temple. August Burt Coolidge of Washington, D.C., turned over his collection, in excess of 300 volumes and pamphlets, dealing with Charles Dickens. Louis D. Carmen, a Scottish Rite Mason of Washington, D.C., donated his extensive store of Lincoln material that consisted of 567 volumes and 600 pamphlets, a resource that would be in constant demand as a major supplement to the holdings of the Library of Congress.[105]

One of the more novel miscellanies contributed to the House of the Temple at this time of austerity was that of Pittsburgh's Edward M. Hanauer. He had in his possession more than 12,000 Masonic chapter or mark pennies in gold, silver, aluminum, nickel, brass, bronze, and copper. Why this rare numismatic collection came to the Supreme Council of the Southern Jurisdiction and not to the Northern Masonic Jurisdiction, where Hanauer ought to have had his first loyalties, may have had nothing more to it than spatial considerations, as the House of the Temple had ample room while there was no equivalent facility in the North.

Also, Cowles may have had a longstanding friendship with Hanauer, as evidenced by a gesture of kindness made a couple of months after the repeal of the Eighteenth Amendment in 1933. Cowles placed an order with a distributor in New York for eleven cases of whiskey in behalf of Hanauer. Later, Hanauer presented the Supreme Council library with his valuable collection of 2,000 rare Masonic medals. A particularly valuable specimen was one struck in 1797 in honor of General George Washington when he was (erroneously) supposed to be General Grand Master of the United States. On one side of this medal is a bust of Washington in uniform, and around the edge on one side, "G.W.G.G.M." (George Washington General Grand Master). William L. Boyden remembered that before 1920 he had tried to purchase one of these medals at an auction in New York, but the price had been prohibitive.[106]

■ ■ ■

A form of national uplift in the midst of the Depression came as plans were being made by Congress to observe the 200th anniversary of George Washington's birth. The Supreme Council had been invited to lend its support to the special commission chaired by the president of the United States. Cowles urged ready acceptance of the invitation because Washington "was a Master Mason in the full sense of the term." Congress had set aside the days between February 22 and Thanksgiving Day, 1932, as appropriate to mark the Washington anniversary.[107]

Carefully planned to fit into the national observance of Washington's birth was the dedication of the George Washington Masonic National Memorial Temple in Alexandria, Virginia, on May 12, 1932. Cowles noted that this would be "the outstanding and most noteworthy Masonic celebration during the year," especially from the Scottish Rite point of view. On February 6, 1932, the Supreme Council sent the George Washington Masonic National Association a check for $25,000 to be used in completion of the new temple's auditorium.[108]

The successful completion of the Masonic tribute to Washington did not come without struggle, dispute, and added measures of brotherly charity. The Scottish Rite bodies of the Southern Jurisdiction had donated a total of $167,917. It was to Cowles's credit that he stood in support of the project after being humiliated in a purge which removed him from the original board and the Ways and Means Committee of the George Washington National Memorial Association.

Ironically, the man who pushed Cowles out the door, Louis A. Watres, was earlier proposed by Cowles as president of the association. Many years later, Cowles acknowledged in public, "That was one of the things that I did as a Freemason, for which I have always been sorry." Cowles was even more frank in private, explaining that he was first approached to be president of the association before Watres was considered. Of Watres, Cowles recounts, "he was the slickest politician that has ever appeared in Freemasonry of a general nature." The difficulty between the two men centered on Watres's suggestion that "unless Alexandria-Washington Lodge No. 22 would deed to the Association all of its works of art and relics," the project should be abandoned and all the money returned that had been raised by the Ways and Means Committee. [109]

More intrigue followed, however, as the association bumbled into its final stages of building. The secretary-treasurer of the association came to Cowles's office sometime in the early fall of 1931 to explain a predicament. Something in the order of $106,000 of the association's funds had been deposited with a Washington brokerage firm that had gone under. The money was earmarked for completing the auditorium. The desperate request was for the Supreme Council's help. Cowles replied that he and the Supreme Council "did not feel very kindly" as to the way he had been treated years ago, but that he would see what he could do. The council met shortly thereafter and appropriated $25,000 toward completion of the auditorium, a contribution made with Cowles's personal sense of vindication.[110]

Distinguished Americans continued to be recognized by Freemasonry as the new term "celebrity" came into vogue. Charles Lindbergh, for instance, was raised a year after his transatlantic solo flight in Keystone Lodge No. 243 of St. Louis, Missouri. Years later it was recalled to Grand Commander Cowles that "Freemasonry was lightly esteemed by him," as Lindbergh was never seen again in lodge by the St. Louis Masons.[111] The military hero and leader of the American Expeditionary Force in Europe in 1917 and 1918, General John J. Pershing, had conferred upon him the thirty-third degree in Washington, D.C., in 1930.[112] Also, Charles H. Mayo, who with his brother and father formed a surgical partnership that became the world famous Mayo Clinic, received the thirty-third degree in the fall of 1935. Delighted with such an honor, the seventy-year-old Mayo believed "the instructive work of the Degree [was] most educational."[113] Cowles conscientiously built Masonic ties with prominent leaders, not all of whom were in American public life. For example, he hosted a dinner party that honored a Mason of the Polish legation and included Freemasons of Washington's diplomatic corps in attendance.[114]

▪   ▪   ▪

Pleasant ceremonies and social occasions would at times give way to Scottish Rite involvement in the public issues of the day, such as education, immigration, and Americanization. For a number of years the Scottish Rite had supported various bills in Congress to establish a Department of Education. Cowles felt strongly that such a department was invaluable for the future of public elementary schools. Despite the strong advocacy of the Scottish Rite in various articles and speeches by Cowles, especially in testimony to the House Banking and Currency Committee in February 1933, the opposition in Congress to a new department was fierce. Cowles realized that there was little chance a bill proposing a federal Department of Education would ever make it out of committee to the House floor for a vote. The goal of a cabinet level Department of Education would finally materialize in May 1980.[115]

The Scottish Rite's lobbying and advocacy efforts in support of public education had many tangible results, in spite of not immediately attaining the larger goal of a separate cabinet post in the administration. New educational buildings were erected, consolidating, in many instances, rural, one-room schoolhouses into excellent facilities. Teacher preparation and training improved, and even children's playtime under supervision was a proud innovation supported by the Supreme Council. Scottish Rite Masons could rightly claim credit for sounding the rallying call to improve American primary and secondary education. Scottish Rite interest in education extended abroad, too. The North China Language School in Peking, China, for instance, received regular financial support up to the end of 1928, sometimes in increments as great as $5,000.[116]

Consistent with the Scottish Rite's strong position on the Oregon School Law of 1922, Cowles monitored the controversial "free-bus" bills being introduced in various state legislatures. Government aid to parochial schools in whatever form, in the mind of Cowles and most Scottish Rite Masons, remained a proposition absolutely necessary to oppose. He was disturbed by efforts in some states to "chisel in" on public school funds designated for free textbooks to all children whether they were enrolled in public or private schools. Cowles was confident "that our propaganda has been very helpful in defeating some of these measures, which were considered atrocious, or at least very hurtful, to public school education."[117]

The Scottish Rite was more than a reactionary watchdog on guard against the abuse of public school funds. Opportunities of a pro-active nature also came about. At the University of Texas an impressive Scottish Rite women's dormitory was completed in 1922 with a permanent endowment for its maintenance. While it was initially a residence for daughters, granddaughters, and nieces of Masons, the handsome, colonnaded structure in the Georgian style has been home, over the years, for thousands of students at the university.[118] Over all, because of its defense of public schools and its budding relationships with major universities, the Scottish Rite educational program, begun in the 1920s to enhance the citizenship of young people in America, had lived up to its designation of "our Great Work."

■ ■ ■

Although its influence in American education may have been a masterwork of good effect, the Scottish Rite, according to one historian, "also helped to perpetuate traditions of xenophobia and anti-Catholicism, and it contributed to the intolerant drive for conformity that characterized the 1920s."[119] Put differently, the Scottish Rite was a microcosm of the middle-class, Protestant establishment. Cowles carefully extricated himself from the appearances of political activity, such as resigning from the National Sojourners in 1935 because one of its committees "had adopted some resolutions that were political," but he was not consistently neutral.[120] His attitude toward the Roman Catholic Church and "loose" immigration laws, because he was reflecting generally acceptable Masonic opinion, did not risk running afoul of the Grand Lodges or the Supreme Council. On these issues he did not part from principles commonly held among American Masons.

For Cowles the Roman Catholic Church, well organized under the direction of American priests, bishops, and cardinals, was ultimately attempting "to destroy Masonry." Later Cowles would support the work of Christ Church Mission in Brooklyn, New York, established by Leo H. Lehmann to assist former Roman Catholic priests in their new lives. The motive for this refuge, while ostensibly benevolent, was not devoid of propagandistic purposes to embarrass the Catholic Church.[121]

Cowles also spoke out in favor of the strong immigration restrictions imposed in 1925 that cut the number of new foreign arrivals by more than half. After an even stronger quota law passed Congress in 1927, Cowles commented that such measures "while not perfect . . . are a long step forward." In 1933 only 23,000 people entered the United States, a substantial drop considering that for the years 1923 and 1924 there were 1.25 million immigrants. And yet, Cowles continued to worry about immigration and the possibility of "nullifying" the existing quotas, saying that despite such outstanding immigrants as Edward Bok, Joseph Pulitzer, and Carl Schurz, "they do not compensate for the millions of ne'er-do-wells, the insane and criminals who have flocked to our shores."[122]

Taking care of a population growing in misery from the Great Depression may explain some of the reluctance Americans had about immigration (i.e., it was all a nation could do to manage the relief of suffering within its own boundaries without inviting more trouble). This reasoning, on the other hand, will not square with the fact that opposition to a limited, but open, immigration policy coincided with American prosperity in the mid-twenties. Cowles was not unsympathetic to worldwide persecution that made the United States a desirable haven, nor was he uncritical of the American way of life. It would be a mistake to see Cowles only in the light of what Richard Hofstadter summarily called "the paranoid style" of American discourse. Rather, Cowles exhibited a poignant wisdom in challenging the public mood of depression. In 1931 he allowed that "the atmosphere seems to be charged with fear of some great cataclysm of pain and suffering, if not complete destruction." Taking the long view of history, he recalled, "Eras of prosperity and adversity, of plenty and want have followed each other since the beginning. In Egypt seven full years were followed by seven lean years; there the people wisely built granaries to store the surplus of the fat years against the deficiency of the lean. They did not waste, nor enter upon an orgy of spending, with no thought of the morrow."[123]

Cowles held Americans accountable for "so terrible a predicament" and declared boldly, "we are to blame" for the mess which he believed might "eventually prove a blessing." His assessment of national unemployment was at times unrealistic, suggesting the stereotype of lazy men loafing in parks while women provided most of the family's sustenance. The idea of a welfare state was repulsive to Cowles. He believed that "the dole marks the decay of a nation, the destruction of pride, energy, initiative, ambition." And yet by 1935 he was inclined to support Social Security as a "great advantage" to people unable to save for their future needs.[124]

■ ■ ■

The reference point of the immigration question not only served as a means of focusing on the condition of America at home but drew attention to human conditions around the world. Cowles traveled extensively as his first decade as Grand Commander came to a close. He was in Paris in April 1929 for an international conference attended by twenty-six of the thirty-four regular Supreme Councils from around the world. The previous summer he had toured Europe and had visited twenty-two of the thirty-four regular Supreme Councils, as well as the Grand Lodges of Sweden, Norway, and Denmark. A South American trip was arranged in advance of the International Conference planned for Havana, Cuba, in 1934 (which would be postponed and moved to Brussels in 1935). This was a significant Masonic pilgrimage for Cowles because so many leaders of Latin American independence, such as Bolivar, were active Masons.

The results of the Grand Commander's wide-ranging travel were strong international Masonic bonds which in time of trouble became salutary. The Supreme Council gave aid to the Dominican Republic after natural disaster and again to Cuba in the wake of the same destructive hurricane.[125] Cowles also had a first-hand look at other catastrophes in the making as the inter-war years shaped dramatic changes in European politics, particularly in Spain, Italy, and Germany.

Cowles visited Spain in 1929 and up to that time considered the trip "one of the most outstanding experiences Masonically" of his life. Apparently, he enjoyed this tour in spite of the fact that Masonic lodges had all been closed. He had been warmly welcomed, however, by at least a dozen Masons who met him at the railroad station in Madrid. The life-threatening persecution of Spanish Masons had not yet followed the lodge closings, but, as Samuel Johnson had said of another time, "intentions must be judged by acts."

Cowles noted in the same report that the conditions of Freemasonry in Italy had also deteriorated. Mussolini made "a complete and perfect job of suppressing Freemasonry in Italy." Cowles did not know about the Supreme Council of Italy or its most recent Grand Commander, but he was aware that an officer of the Grand Orient (not recognized) had been arrested and deported, without the benefit of a trial, to one of the barren islands off the Italian coast. Cowles was certain that this place of detention was where hundreds of Italian Masons had already been sent in a morbid rehearsal of what would become part of the Holocaust.[126]

The trends against Masonry in Spain and Italy not withstanding, virtually no one in Europe could have anticipated the rise and ruthlessness of Adolf Hitler in Germany. Expressed differently, the oft-quoted Portuguese proverb is a reminder of abiding historical uncertainties, as events transpire inexplicably: "God writes straight with crooked lines." Just after Christmas in 1932 Cowles made a wishful prediction that Hitler had peaked in popularity: "Hitler has announced his opposition to Freemasonry, and I think has even claimed that Freemasonry and the Jesuits are in league to hurt the country—a most absurd proposition; and yet . . . quite a number of Masons voted for him. Nevertheless, it looks at present as if his power was waning."[127]

Too bad for the world that Cowles was proved wrong. One month after the Grand Commander's hopeful assertion, on January 30, 1933, Adolf Hitler came to power in

Germany. As Chancellor, Hitler decreed that all secret societies be suppressed. At the time there were ten Grand Lodges in Germany, one of them not being generally recognized. The majority of these complied with Hitler's decree and ceased operating. General Eric Ludendorff made absurd anti-Masonic charges, published as propaganda, linking Masonry, the Jesuits, and Jews in a conspiracy "to overturn constituted authority." Together with his wife, Mathilde, Ludendorff had been publishing tracts throughout the twenties denouncing Jews and Freemasons. Despite their dubious slogans, these books, according to one historian "are nothing but a conglomeration of wild fantasies, [but] the measure of their influence cannot be underrated."[128] One of Masonry's defenders was German president Paul von Hindenburg. Hindenburg's father had been a Freemason, so he spoke confidently that the fraternity posed no threat to the German government, as "Masons were admonished at all times to be loyal to their country and to observe carefully its laws."

Grand Commander Cowles, never dreaming the destruction that Nazism and Fascism would bring upon the world, could envision the day when democratic principles and freedom of association might again prevail. His *Allocution* for 1935 prophesied the staying power of Masonry and the end of tyranny, all of which would not be realized until ten years later and after an unparalleled world war. In fact, the first free, all-German election (since March 5, 1933) would not occur until December 2, 1990. Cowles believed that

> Hitler will pass away; Mussolini will pass away; and other rulers and dictators will tread their few steps through this life and be only a memory, while Masonry will revive and continue on its good work of recognizing the principle of the Fatherhood of God and the Brotherhood of Man.
>
> Masonry and dictatorship cannot agree in principle nor exist side by side. It is noticeable when an individual grasps the power of a nation, his first act is to suppress and destroy if possible the institution which is the apostle of light, freedom, and democratic principles and one of whose mottoes is Liberty, Equality, and Fraternity.[129]

■   ■   ■

In general, the same confidence that Cowles exuded about the European situation, and Masonry within it, would also infuse his unassuming, steady sense of triumph about America's own internal adversity. His constant reiteration of the brighter morrow for Scottish Rite Freemasonry helped sustain its sense of purpose during the doldrums of the Great Depression. Some of the prosperity and expansion of the Scottish Rite in the 1920s came all too suddenly at the end of a period when "the Masonic Fraternity had worked the officers and leaders of the Bodies almost day and night, mostly in conferring Degrees, and enjoying banquets, excursions, the building of temples, and the like." Cowles's analysis was simple, but hardly simple minded: "We overdid the thing—[too many Masons] have become really tired."[130] As if invoking Ralph Waldo Emerson's dictum, "there are no straight lines," Cowles believed that "the law of balance" would endure for America, the world, and Scottish Rite Freemasonry.

CHAPTER X

Steel Helmets and Iron Curtains
1936–1952

Later Years of John H. Cowles

𐎸𐎸𐎸𐎸𐎸𐎸𐎸𐎸𐎸𐎸

America was preparing for the presidential election of 1936 after four anguishing years of unrelenting hardship, soaring unemployment, governmental experimentation, and bad weather that covered the period of Franklin Delano Roosevelt's first administration. Nothing represented the condition of the country better than the drought which began in 1932 and continued each year to the eve of the national election of 1936.

The enormous area from the Dakotas to Texas had been converted into an infinite basin of dust and dunes. Pastures and cornfields were scorched and cracked open like festered lacerations. Ranchers watched helplessly as valuable livestock toppled over from dehydration and died in a daily ritual of loss. In Oklahoma one town in 1934 recorded thirty-five consecutive days of 100 degree weather; on the thirty-sixth day the thermometer was pushed up to 117 degrees.

In cities on the lower Mississippi River, such as Memphis, people covered their faces with handkerchiefs as the sky darkened with dust to simulate nighttime conditions in the middle of the day. Cleveland, Ohio, was covered by a dust cloud 7,000 feet thick. The White House in Washington, D.C., reportedly had its furnishings covered by a fine, unmistakable yellow grit from Nebraska.

As the first stage of the New Deal was approaching an uncertain interlude, airborne dust particles from the western plains placed an orange cast over Washington. Congress in 1935 created a permanent Soil Conservation Service in the Department of Agriculture. That winter, red snow, like paprika, was dashed over New England.[1]

Through it all, Roosevelt's public face beamed assurance, cheerfulness, and drive, even if it also masked his deeper inscrutability. His supporters and critics in equal measure admired his abiding calm. Biographers uniformly endorse Justice Oliver Wendell Holmes's view that FDR had "a first class temperament." Raymond Moley, a member of the brain trust, who was also a Roosevelt speechwriter, marveled, "Not even the realization that he was playing nine-pins with the skulls and thighbones of economic orthodoxy seemed to worry him."[2] The president personified a transcendent composure that summoned the country's least well-off to patience. But Roosevelt's store of good humor was not inexhaustible, especially in personal terms.

The 1936 Democratic Convention in Philadelphia brought the incumbent to Franklin Field where he was presented. As he began his first few steps toward the stage, his polio-induced gait obvious, he stretched out his hand to Edwin Markham, a fellow Mason, the distinguished, white-bearded American poet. His momentum ahead of his center of gravity, the president lost his balance, fell, and sprawled on the ground. Deeply embarrassed, his face blanched with anger, he snarled, "Clean me up!"[3] This minor episode had a richer, implicit meaning—the country, too, had been disabled and, with incredible patience, followed a man who in similarly halting manner was trying to make a graceful recovery. By 1936, the Dust Bowl and Depression had people everywhere in a like-hearted mood, saying in unison with the president, "Clean me up."

The Supreme Council, Southern Jurisdiction, under the steadying hand of John H. Cowles, Sovereign Grand Commander since 1921, had been scraped but unbowed by the force of global economic crisis. The membership of Scottish Rite bodies in the Southern Jurisdiction had naturally fallen, and with the slippage in new members revenues also declined. Some of the Scottish Rite bodies, having erected beautiful new temples, "found it almost impossible to meet the demands of interest and maintenance." The Supreme Council, without altering the *Statutes,* had allowed the bodies the option of reducing their dues. Regulations pertaining to dues would remain suspended from 1935 through 1941, a period during which the subordinate bodies would be charged at the rate of thirty cents for each Lodge of Perfection member and ten cents for each member of the other three bodies.[4]

Generally, the financial condition of the Supreme Council was extraordinarily stable in the 1930s. The double force of declining Masonic blue lodge membership and economic disaster nationwide seemed to have little ultimate bearing on Scottish Rite Freemasonry. The only Depression-related loss of funds was from an account held in the People's State Bank of Charleston, South Carolina. Apparently an educational fund had on deposit less than $6,000 when the bank closed. As of December 1936, the Supreme Council had, over time, received only $1,705.15 in dividends from the account, including a recent windfall of $284.00. Cowles, a forthright realist, wrote off the account, assuming that the Supreme Council would "get very little more from this source."[5]

Meanwhile, Masonic membership in the United States had fallen from 3.3 million in 1930, which was then the peak of its strength, to 2.49 million in 1940. By 1950 the

American population was settling down after World War II, and an economic recovery was firmly in place. Craft membership rates returned then to the level of the late 1920s. There were 3.5 million American Masons in 1950 and just over 4 million in 1960. Another cycle of membership loss, however, had begun to show by around 1970, a time of great social tumult in America. It is significant, as an indicator of larger demographic and social changes, that the percentage of Masons making up the native, white, male, old-stock population was 12 percent in 1930. That telling statistic would never again be as high, barely holding at 9 percent during the boom years of post-war America.[6]

The only way the New Deal directly touched the Supreme Council was with the passage of the landmark Social Security Act, which went into effect January 1, 1936. Just before the U.S. Supreme Court put the brakes on many of the alphabet agencies, the New Deal, at high tide, created a national system of old-age insurance in which most employees were compelled to participate, including fraternal organizations. Only religious institutions were ruled exempt, and clergy would not be required to participate unless they chose to do so. At the age of sixty-five, workers would receive retirement annuities paid for out of taxes on their earnings and their employer's payroll. The federal government proposed to share equally with the states the care of destitute persons over sixty-five who were unable to be involved in the old-age insurance system. The Social Security Act of 1936 also provided a federal-state system of unemployment insurance, as well as federal aid to the states, in a shared arrangement, for care of dependent mothers and children, the disabled, and the blind and for public health services.

Criticism of Social Security flew from all sides. William E. Leuchtenberg, a premier scholar of the New Deal, observes that "the law was an astonishingly inept and conservative piece of legislation. In no other welfare system in the world did the state shirk all responsibility for old-age indigence and insist that funds be taken out of current earnings of workers."[7] As a mild form of regressive taxation, accumulating vast sums to build up reserves, the program had the potential to cause limitless ambiguity about eligibility and entitlement, not to mention opening loop holes. In its favor, however, the Social Security Act altered forever the public philosophy about a government's social responsibility and a citizen's basic rights. From that point the beginning of the modern welfare state can be marked, for better or for worse. The legislation was written so that it could bend without giving way to changes in political mood and could withstand the scrutiny of the courts.

The frame of mind at the Supreme Council was not initially receptive to the latest Roosevelt innovation. While Cowles had expressed qualified approbation for the concept of Social Security, his endorsement was, at best, muted and patronizing. He did not object to a forced savings plan, because he assumed that human nature, being less than thrifty, needed corporate discipline for the benefit of all. He objected, however, to having the Supreme Council and other fraternities involved in government-sponsored public welfare. After all, he reasoned, most fraternal institutions, by virtue of their organizing principles, take care of their members and serve the wider community in benevolence and relief work. Cowles lobbied the Congress for an exemption that would actually name the Scottish Rite as exempt in the bill. But to that effect, the amendments of Senators Morris Sheppard of Texas and Arthur Capper of Kansas (both Scottish Rite Masons) did not pass. Cowles next tried to obtain an administrative ruling from the commissioner of the Internal Revenue Service, a ruling which would excuse the Supreme Council and its employees from Social Security. The commissioner denied the request, and while the Supreme Council paid the tax regularly from the outset, it did so under protest. The strategy of filing payments this way was in anticipation of a possible future court decision which would reverse the commissioner's ruling. At that time, the council would have thereby established grounds for requesting a refund.[8]

A forerunner of the Social Security Act was a proposal that started in California when a physician who had been a public health officer lost his position. Dr. Francis Townsend was sixty-seven years old and had less than $100 in savings when his earned income was cut off. Alarmed by his own predicament, Townsend developed a plan for national recovery which, incidentally, made provisions for senior citizens. He realized that many elderly people, like himself, had gone to California in the 1920s from the Midwest and were facing the bleak prospect of unemployment and scarce resources. His idea spread like pollen on a flight of honeybees. Every man or woman over sixty, having retired from all gainful employment, would receive a monthly sum which they would promise to spend in the United States. It was a forced "buy American" plan. The pension would be financed by a 2 percent tax on business transactions which would be held in a "revolving" fund. The Townsendites were well organized by September 1934 and would pose some political threat to Roosevelt in 1936 if they somehow joined forces with Huey Long's "Share the Wealth" followers or Father Charles Coughlin's supporters in the National Union for Social Justice.

An assassin brought down Long on a September night in 1935, and the passage of the Social Security Act later that year combined with the specter of corruption by a Townsend official signaled the collapse of the movement. After Roosevelt's triumphant election in 1936, Father Coughlin, likening his fate to that of the persecuted Christ, announced his retirement from politics. But before the election Cowles had been keeping a watchful eye on populist crusading and fringe movements of the day. One "would probably be surprised," Cowles reported, "how many Masons there are in California who are Townsendites."[9]

Cowles recognized the danger of Masonry's potential hard brush with a controversial organization. He knew that history well, recalling the false charge in late-eighteenth-century Europe "that the Illuminati was mixed up with Freemasonry." The problem of guilt by association was rehearsed in America because "there were Masons in the Ku Klux Klan, so it was charged that the Ku Klux Klan was the militant arm of Freemasonry." Against this background—which included the rumor, from the old days in Russia, that

Freemasonry and Nihilism were in accord, the rumor leading to the suppression of Free-masonry there—Cowles had nothing to do with Townsendism.[10] His principled stance against Masonic political involvement may have reenforced his antipathy to a New Deal program (called "Raw Deal" by Coughlin) resembling the Townsend plan.

In time, Cowles found that members of the Supreme Council "regarded rather favor-ably the principles and underlying purposes of the [Social Security] legislation."[11] He indicated in 1941 that in actuality no "formal application for exemption" had ever been made. If Cowles seemed personally at odds with the Supreme Council on the matter, it was a small enough difference for him to let go of pursuing an exemption. It is hard to imagine that any employees of the Supreme Council objected to Social Security taxes being withheld and paid. At least there is no record of such complaints.

At the same time, favorable news was received from the U.S. government, a ruling that made Cowles's objections to Social Security pale in comparison. Cowles had vigorously appealed to the Internal Revenue Service for tax exempt status, and on September 9, 1940, official word was received. The Supreme Council and its subordinate bodies were exempt from federal corporate income tax under provisions of Section 101(3) of the Internal Revenue Code.[12] The importance of this official opinion cannot be overesti-mated for the shaping of the next half century of Scottish Rite Freemasonry. During the early forties, for instance, the Supreme Council possessed $4 million worth of 4.25 per-cent government bonds, then quoted at around $120. Many of the bonds had been pur-chased in the $80 to $85 range for a $100 par, which would recede to par automatically if retained until 1947. Prudent advice was given to Grand Commander Cowles, who agreed to sell them and buy 2.75 percent (1960–1965) bonds, quoted at $106. The pro-ceeds of this transaction realized a gain of over a half million dollars. The value of these latter bonds went over par and were sold yet again for another net gain of $500,000, not to mention a bonus for having bought 4.25 percent below par in the first place. A million dollar killing in the government bond market was all the sweeter in light of the Supreme Council's tax exempt status.[13]

• • •

American social historians studying the 1930s labor carefully to point out the signifi-cant increase of popular interest in sports, games, and various forms of gambling (e.g., the Irish Sweepstakes and bingo). The phenomenal growth in these activities should not be too readily dismissed as mere escapism from "real world" hardship. The middle class discovery of golf and tennis in the 1930s, for instance, provides one example of an aggres-sion release for the competitive spirit that traditional values demand, but which cannot easily be let out in the social and economic circumstances of strenuous times. It was also at this time that the Parker Brothers' board game "Monopoly" seized the American public's imagination, allowing would-be financiers to "make a killing" in a way that actual economic conditions all but obstructed.

Popular literature was another telltale mark of new patterns of interest developing in the minds and dreams of Americans. In 1936, hugely successful and diverse publications emerged in the reader's market. Margaret Mitchell's *Gone With the Wind*, with its revisionist shaping of how a way of life, so different from the 1930s, was destroyed, was the best of the historical romances written at the time. Dale Carnegie's *How to Win Friends and Influence People* was the bestseller of the era; the book, in summary, simply urged people to adjust to the existing order, to try to fit in, and to be well liked. Its "can-do" bromide needs to be taken seriously as an important cultural, perhaps spiritual, shift. *Life* magazine was founded in 1936, giving rise to the power of visual images as legitimate ways for Americans to experience the larger world. This same benchmark year found the free-verse poet Carl Sandburg going to great lengths and sentimentality to celebrate "The People, Yes." Walker Evans and James Agee began work on their extraordinary collaboration which produced the book *Let Us Now Praise Famous Men*, signaling a transformation of American consciousness.

In spite of a deep stream of pessimism in the thirties about the survival of American individualism and community loyalties, games (whether of chance or skill), books, magazines, and poetry provided a justification and means to maintain equilibrium, and to keep alive a sense of hope. One of the more fascinating literary genres to expand at this time was the detective story. The Fitzgerald and Hemingway heroes of the 1920s no longer fit the mood. Mystery writing of the 1930s had its own way of renewing the public's spirit, lifting the American standard of doing the right thing even in the worst of times. No detective was a better archetype than Sam Spade, the creation of Dashiell Hammett. In *The Maltese Falcon*, Sam "stared ahead at nothing," symbolically defining his vision of life at the moment, a reflection of Hammett's own mood of post–World War I disillusionment. And yet, fans of Sam Spade can never forget his final speech to Brigid O'Shaughnessy, the woman he loves and who offers him the prize of both her love and money. The trouble is that Brigid has killed a man, and Sam promises to turn her over to the authorities. What Sam reveals, after all things are considered, is a resolve that transcends the uncertainty of nothingness ahead. "Listen," he barks, "You'll never understand me, but I'll try once more. . . . When a man's partner is killed he's supposed to do something about it. It doesn't make any difference what you thought of him. He was your partner and you're supposed to do something. . . . I won't play the sap for you."[14]

The lines from Hammett's masterpiece can arguably be enlarged to serve as an interpretive model for understanding the general attitude of the country and, particularly, Freemasonry. Sam's sense of loyalty to a principle, when surrendering to expedience may be no better than nothingness, is in keeping with the precepts of fraternal codes. "Thus it was characteristic of the 1930s," writes Warren Susman, "for the idea of commitment to merge with some idea of culture and to produce, at least for a time, participation in some group, community, or movement." Susman insists, counterintuitively it seems, in the face of declining Masonic and Scottish Rite membership rates, that "the 1930s was *the* decade of participation and belonging."[15] Clearly, the incredible, cooperative mobilization which prepared America for war in 1941 did not arise in a vacuum. It was made possible by a sense of working together fostered in the 1930s, the fair exchange of ideas and beliefs, a sense of being intangibly unified.

It would be a grave mistake to assume automatically that Scottish Rite Freemasonry between 1936 and 1952, the later years of John Henry Cowles's commandership, was less active or was reduced to "staring ahead at nothing" because of lost ground in building and membership growth. On the contrary, the idealism of fraternal obligation, loyalty to a "partner" and doing something positive about his demise, was what Masonry instilled in the first place; and, therefore, it could not be better suited to the times. Cowles was a hard-edged realist, not an escapist nor even remotely a nihilist, in the face of seemingly immoveable challenges to the organization that he would lead through national and international "history-making" years. He looked ahead at the myriad possibilities for making a difference; he did not surrender to the despair of gazing upon empty hope. Membership and financial records, therefore, do not necessarily reflect the vitality of an organization, especially one with the "critical mass" of the Southern Jurisdiction.

Cowles kept his eye on developments within Masonry—supporting Masonic relief in various forms, lending his views to controversial Masonic issues such as the conferring of honors and the recognition of Prince Hall Masonry. He paid close attention to the deteriorating political conditions in Europe, which delivered a heavy beating on Freemasonry there. He tended to the business of running the House of the Temple, its library and museum, its ambassadorial offices. Cowles took a vital interest during this point of his Masonic career in specific public issues related to education, the separation of church and state, and the perennial demands of immigration policy.

■ ■ ■

When Grand Commander Cowles gave his *Allocution* for 1937, he turned to the sensitive matter of Masonic decline. Too many Masons, he averred, had charged the Depression "with the responsibility for ills and misfortunes which have beset the Craft." Cowles raised the point that the problems were not merely external, that perhaps too much emphasis had been placed in that regard and not enough upon "human foibles and faults" or the shortcomings of Masons. He called for a renewal of spirit and fraternal commitment as the best remedy for acute distress, reminding his brothers that "the duties of Masons cover the entire category of a righteous life: duty to God, to country, to neighbor and to self."[16]

Mindful of this prescriptive injunction, the same session scheduled time to observe the sesquicentennial of the U.S. Constitution. Cowles in the July 1937 issue of *The New Age* had recommended that all Scottish Rite valleys of the Southern Jurisdiction should select and celebrate at least one historical date connected with the Constitution, coordinating their efforts with the Grand Lodges and other Masonic bodies. As a way to inspire state and local celebrations, the Supreme Council sponsored a "Constitution Night" which featured an address by the eminent minister and Masonic scholar Joseph Fort Newton of Philadelphia. Newton was not only the author of two widely sold Masonic books, *The Builders* (1914, followed by 12 editions) and *The Men's House* (1923), but was a nationally known Protestant preacher. For years he edited the popular Harper Brothers annual volume *Best Sermons*. He held significant pulpits in London at the City Temple, in New York as a Universalist minister at the Church of Divine Paternity, and finally in Philadelphia as an Episcopal rector of the Church of St. Luke and the Epiphany. Dr. Newton spoke at the Supreme Council event on "The Covenant of Liberty." A second address was given by Sol Bloom, a member of the U.S. House of Representatives and the director general of the U.S. Constitution Sesquicentennial Commission. Congressman Bloom entitled his remarks "Masons and the Constitution." The Supreme Council made no other provision for observing the anniversary of the framing of the Constitution in 1787. Also noteworthy at this occasion was the mention of news from the French Grand Commander that Bartholdi, who had been the sculptor of the Statue of Liberty, had been a member of Lodge Alsace Lorraine and that several French patriots and notable men were members of that lodge with Bartholdi.[17]

Cowles kept before the Supreme Council another, darker aspect of Masonic heritage that required constant vigilance. Some might suggest that he was hypersensitive to the potential of anti-Masonic activity and writing, since Masonry was so institutionalized and accepted around the world. He reported that a book by Bernard Fay entitled *Freemasonry and Revolutions* had just been published in America by the Boston house of Little, Brown, but that this time the author modified to some degree his earlier anti-Masonic statements, "probably because he must have known that many of the statements he made were false and that he was actuated by prejudice." Fay, a French citizen and Roman Catholic, had been a correspondent for a Catholic newspaper before World War I, about the time he had published many views hostile to Freemasonry.[18]

Cowles made no secret of his suspicions. Roman Catholicism, to him, was a sleeping monster always threatening Masonry. Throughout the decade of the thirties, he avidly supported the Reverend Leo H. Lehman's Christ's Mission project in Brooklyn, New York, the leading organization designed to help defecting Roman Catholic priests. While the intention was to assist former priests in need of shelter and retooling, Cowles took transparent delight in showing up the Roman Catholic hierarchy who appeared to abandon its own. Cowles went on record in other ways, too, by writing Will H. Hays, president of the self-regulating Motion Picture Producers and Distributors Association. He revealed more than his recreational interests and ingrained habits of work in his complaint to the powerful "Hays Office." He said, "It has been my custom to go to the pictures about five nights a week. After an early dinner, I take in the pictures then return to my office to work. I am fast giving [movies] up however. I am tired of going to them and having Roman Catholic propaganda thrown into my face."[19]

Cowles carried his objections beyond protesting innocuous "feel-good" films such as Bing Crosby's "The Bells of St. Mary's." He carried them to the point of paying for the republication of papal encyclicals and pronunciamentos issued between 1738 and 1902 that contained various barbed assaults against Masonry. In his mind the reprints of the encyclicals were a necessary countermeasure because they offered a contrast between the sentimentally appealing Catholic crooner and official Catholic positions. He tried to show, in one way or another, the connection between a singing, loving parish priest and the ruling bishops who condemned the practice of Freemasonry as inimical to Catholicism. Leo H. Lehman edited "a magazine devoted exclusively to the field of Catholic controversy" called *The Converted Catholic*. With the endorsement of Cowles, he printed translations of seventeen papal statements treating the subject of Freemasonry and secret societies. Ironically, two of the papal condemnations are called "Allocutions," the balance of the diatribes are in the form of "Encyclicals" and "Constitutions."[20]

Still another ongoing problem for the fraternity, in the Grand Commander's mind, was the casualness in which secrets were handled by certain Masons themselves. He deplored any revelation of Masonic matters, including "anything that even borders on the esoteric of it." He was particularly incensed by Masonic scholars and writers who propounded in Masonic journals what they believed to be new interpretations. Cowles argued that "when such is done, then some other brother goes a little farther, and the tendency is to continue that trend until matters that should be spoken of only in a Masonic Lodge . . . become public property."[21]

The hard-working Cowles was indeed a bullish defender of the brotherhood's integrity, the guardian of the order's purity, but he was at times tilting at windmills, charging at straw men. The Roman Catholic Church in America has never posed much real threat to the hegemony of old-stock, establishment Protestants. Cowles made, however, an interesting point against the self-serving supposition that made the Depression or Roman Catholics the expedient culprit for Masonic membership problems. His jeremiad was a forceful call for Masonry to look inward if it would learn to renew itself. His was a summons back to ideals and duties, calling the brethren to their Masonic altars, particularly to remind them of their obligation to keep inter-fraternal matters out of the public forum.

Cowles, at this juncture, discovered an incipient danger in nagging rivalries inside and outside the fraternity. He understood that when differences were written large, they spelled out new terms of enmity for Freemasons worldwide. Masonry could now afford no enemies and, therefore, should reject the use of scapegoats to compensate for feelings of defeat in world society or the fraternal world. Not only that, but Cowles in 1937 saw this invisible enemy, intolerance, becoming a destroyer of Jews, Gypsies, Jehovah's Witnesses, disabled human beings, and even in some instances, Roman Catholics.

■ ■ ■

As a life-long bachelor, Cowles became completely absorbed in Masonic work, having ample time to make what he called extensive "journeyings" around America and the world. During more than thirty years as Grand Commander, he averaged close to 24,000 miles per year in travel, making a grand total of 708,617 miles.[22] The height of his most active period of travel came immediately before and just after World War II. While these trips had occasional aspects of glamour, he continued his "usual practice" of making many sick calls upon Scottish Rite brethren, particularly those of the thirty-third degree and Knights Commander of the Court of Honor. He included visits to the widows of deceased Active Members of the Supreme Council who happened to live in valleys that he officially toured.

In 1936, Cowles was able to represent the Supreme Council at the 200th anniversary of the Grand Lodge of Scotland, witnessing the induction of the Duke of York as Grand Master of the Grand Lodge of Scotland. The duke subsequently became King George VI.

In conjunction with his visit to Scotland, Cowles had gone on to Sweden, where he had been invited to a banquet given by King Gustaf V at the Royal Palace. Cowles was given the seat of honor, next to the king himself, and related a touching incident at the end of the sumptuous banquet. "At the finale when the fruit was served, he took a pear, cut it into halves, handed me one and he kept the other. To me," wrote Cowles, "it was the finest gesture of brotherhood that I have ever witnessed," symbolizing that "he was ready to divide half of what he had with a brother Mason." It is noteworthy that for many years the kings of Sweden had been Grand Masters of the Grand Lodge, granting Masonry a royal prestige without peer, except in Great Britain.[23]

A couple of years later, Cowles helped greet the Crown Prince of Sweden in Wilmington, Delaware. The royal visit was to celebrate the 300th anniversary of the Swedish Colony in Delaware. Cowles joined the party accompanying the Crown Prince, who was Deputy Grand Master of the Grand Lodge of Sweden, for a boat ride down the Potomac to Mount Vernon.[24]

Cowles traveled for another royal occasion on July 19, 1939, as the official representative of the Grand Lodge of Kentucky at the installation (held in London's Olympia Stadium) of the Duke of Kent as the Grand Master of the Grand Lodge of England. King George VI presided at and performed the ceremony of inducting his brother, the Duke of Kent, to the Chair in the East. In Washington, D.C., at a solidifying point in Anglo-American relations after 1941, Cowles attended a reception at the National Press Club at which the Duke of Windsor spoke. The duchess, his American wife, the former Wallis Simpson, was also present. With Senator Tom Connally, of the Senate Foreign Relations Committee, Cowles was invited to a small function at the British Embassy, to meet the Duke of Kent. But, as Cowles pointed out, it was "the rule of royalty, in traveling to other lands, that they do not appear as Masons in any Masonic capacity."[25]

The important diplomatic and military ties between the United States and Great Britain at this time were in no small way upheld, at least symbolically, through Masonic friendships. Cowles was honored in several ways by his British brothers. He was accorded the rank of Past Senior Grand Warden of the Grand Lodge of Scotland. In turn, by his recommendation and with the Mother Council's subsequent approval, the Earl of Stair, the Illustrious Sovereign Grand Commander of the Supreme Council of Scotland, became an Emeritus Member of Honor of the Supreme Council, Southern Jurisdiction. Probably of greater significance was the fact, of which Cowles was "very proud," that he was made a member of two historic English lodges in the middle of "England's finest hour." He became joined to Antiquity Lodge No. 2 and Royal Somerset House and Inverness Lodge No. 4, both in London and both part of the original four lodges forming the Grand Lodge of England in 1717.[26]

King George of Greece came to Washington, D.C., in the early forties, and because he was a Mason (a member of Wallwood Lodge No. 5143 when he lived in England in exile), Cowles attended a reception in his honor. The Greek Orthodox Church had not opposed Freemasonry and, in fact, was as badly persecuted as the Masonic fraternity during the war years. Cowles and the Supreme Council, because of prior familiarity, later responded to the distress of Greek Freemasons.[27]

After the Spanish Civil War broke out in 1936, the Grand Orient of Spain moved its offices to Brussels. Cowles immediately "took a chance on sending a New York draft for $200 to the Grand Master of the Grand Orient" at the Brussels address. The gift was soon acknowledged as having been received. The Grand Master of the Grand Orient had been detained with 200 other Freemasons as early as September 1928 for plotting against the government. Six Freemasons of Spain were hanged in October 1936 for no other reason than their fraternal membership. Cowles recognized at once that the situation of Masonry in Spain was desperate, "and should the rebels (Fascists) win, Masonry is doomed in that country." Cowles had been informed by the Secretary General of the Supreme Council of Spain, two officials of the Grand Orient, and the Spanish Ambassador himself that "horrible atrocities" had been committed in Spain against Freemasons that were "almost beyond belief, yet . . . not exaggerated." When Cowles learned on June 7, 1937, that the Spanish Ambassador was returning home for a visit, he gave him a check of $300 for "the further benefit of our Spanish brethren and asked him to deliver it to Brother M. H. Barroso, Grand Secretary General of the Supreme Council of Spain," who had moved to Valencia. The Spanish Ambassador reported that the money had gone through, but Cowles queried him about why the check had not cleared the local bank.[28]

The Franco government was unrelenting in its purge of Freemasons. "Being or having been a Mason is all the cause necessary for a brother to be put to death in Spain." Cowles had heard that "eighty Masons were garroted in one day." Spanish Masons were rounded up and sent to concentration camps, and "at one time there were six scaffolds erected in Malaga."[29] Through the Bureau de Secours in Paris, the Supreme Council rendered assistance to refugee Spanish Masons. Before the bureau was established Cowles had sent, by his own reckoning, between $1,500 and $2,000 to different Spanish Masons whom he knew in order to help save their lives and get them out of Spain. In time for the 1941 session, the Supreme Council, Southern Jurisdiction, received a letter from Mexico City, written by a Past Grand Master of the Grand Orient of Spain, thanking it for what had been done to assist the escape of Spanish Masons to other countries. "Two of the very prominent escaped Spanish Masons" were saved because their extradition, "requested by the Spanish government," was refused. Their extradition, "of course, would have meant their execution."[30]

In the early spring of 1943, travel to Europe being restricted, Cowles visited the Supreme Councils of Mexico and Central America. When he arrived in Nicaragua, he and Sovereign Grand Inspector General Frank C. Patton, the Acting Lieutenant Grand Commander who accompanied him, were taken in tow by Dr. Juan Francisco Gutierrez. Cowles learned that the strongman Anastasio Somoza, the president of Nicaragua and a Mason (about whom FDR once quipped, "he may be a bastard, but he's our bastard"), along with Grand Master Octavio Cortes, was out of Managua. However, Cowles received welcoming telegrams from both Nicaraguan leaders. The same trip brought him to the opening of the Supreme Council of Spain in the Scottish Rite Hall of Mexico City. It was an emergency convocation of active thirty-thirds, including three honorary thirty-thirds to establish its viability in exile. Cowles called it "an inspiring occasion to see the determination of these brethren to keep the light of Masonry burning" till the day "the war was over and they could return to their country and be ready to re-establish themselves and carry on." Franco, of course, remained the dictator of Spain long after World War II had concluded.[31]

Franco's hostile attitude toward Freemasonry did not cease at the end of World War II. A Mason named Strasser, who had been a leader of the fraternity in Barcelona before the rise of the Franco government, speculated in an article appearing in *Espana Nueva* (a newspaper published by the Spanish Republican government in exile) that "when Franco was a Colonel in the Army, he made application to join Spanish Freemasonry, but his petition was denied." Strasser reported in October 1947 that the Franco regime had established in Barcelona a special tribunal whose purpose was to abolish Freemasonry from Spain. Defendants in these trials were denied legal counsel. Freemasons were imprisoned on a sentencing schedule of twelve years for Entered Apprentices, thirty years for Fellowcrafts and at least thirty years or even death for Master Masons.[32]

■ ■ ■

Cowles, as an individual American citizen and not as Grand Commander, wrote a letter to Secretary of State Cordell Hull in the spring of 1937 "relative to the non-intervention policy of our Government," in which he "deplored the neutral attitude that helped Italy against Abyssinia and the rebels against the loyal government of Spain." He argued "that it did not seem fair that our country should take an isolated position which favored the wrong side of the question."[33] Cowles recognized a worldwide change in climate not only for the security of Freemasonry but for the principles of human liberty and rights.

While not advocating a specific American response, he lashed out at American isolationism: "Are we, and our country also, content to pass by on the other side, like the priest and Levite, and let the dictators without conscience, without honor, without morals, continue their careers of devastation and destruction? Have we become so soft for fear of hurting feelings of such monsters that we must remain quiescent, and even pass laws which so far have been helpful to the dictator nations and hurtful to those whom they would conquer and enslave?"[34] The enemies of Freemasonry were not imaginary bogeymen. They were legion in central Europe.

The Grand Commander of the Supreme Council, Mother Council of the World, filled a major leadership role in combating the persecution of Masons. He wrote letters; he pressured Washington officials, including the diplomatic corps, for answers; he raised hundreds of thousands of dollars and kept American Masons and, therefore to some extent, the American public informed about what was happening to people abroad. The situation around the world presented an interesting dilemma for the Supreme Council. The dilemma was reconciled, if at all, by a living paradox. On the one hand, international Masonic ties (e.g., with Spain) pulled the organization to the left, while on the other hand national commitments and attitudes pulled it to the right. The complexity of the Scottish Rite's position meant that it was neither neutral nor ideological. At times in American political history, liberalism more and more came to resemble conservatism (e.g., Franklin Roosevelt was reluctant to advocate desegregation); and sometimes conservatives (e.g., Theodore Roosevelt deployed government resources for national parks) espoused traditionally liberal solutions. The Scottish Rite leadership perhaps reflected most of all the "tough-minded" tradition of American pragmatism.

Masonry was having a difficult time throughout central Europe beginning in the mid-thirties. In Austria the danger became noticeable by 1934 when lodges were closing as a result of the *Anschluss* (the issue of union with Germany). Cowles organized a campaign to use Masonic leverage on the Austrian Hotel Managers Association since the alpine nation depended so heavily on tourism. In Romania the "Iron Guard" had charged that the fraternity was a Jewish organization and that it was "unpatriotic, unchristian and a threat to the throne"; therefore the government decided, in its own best interest, to dissolve Freemasonry. Between March and June 1939, after the fall of Czechoslovakia had produced a revolution in British foreign policy with regard to Germany, Cowles sent $500 to the Czechoslovakian Grand Commander.

Switzerland, a neutral country since 1815 and democratic since 1848, dealt with its own problem of anti-Masonic attacks with expected, though not guaranteed, judiciousness. In his 1935 *Allocution,* Cowles had mentioned Ernest Leonhardt, a Swiss agitator and publisher who had been the head of an organization called the "National Front" and was the author of several negative, defamatory articles against Masonry. These anti-Masonic writings, which would later be proven libelous in the Swiss courts, had the effect of placing 5,000 Swiss Freemasons in potential jeopardy.

The Swiss cabinet investigated the whole subject of Freemasonry and recommended to the president and Swiss legislature that the forthcoming referendum to prohibit Freemasonry, following the example of Austria and Germany, should be rejected. Barely sanguine, Cowles reported that the Swiss "legislative vote was almost unanimous not to proscribe Freemasonry and similar organizations." Further, Cowles gladly noted, "be it said to the credit of the Roman Catholics in Switzerland, who are imbued with the Swiss ideals of liberty, that they stood wholeheartedly on the side of Freemasonry." Because of the financial demands made on Swiss Masons in battling this issue, Cowles sent a contribution to assist them on behalf of the Supreme Council.[35]

Jacob Katz in his book *Jews and Freemasons in Europe, 1923–1939,* observes that "despite the open, savage incitement marking the years of Nazi rise to power, the Freemasons, like the Jews, had no inkling of the fate in store for them. Yet a few months of actual Nazi rule sufficed to show that it was bent on the total liquidation of all Masonic Lodges."[36] Germany, of course, was the central source of vicious anti-Semitic and anti-Masonic slander. The ideas linking Jews and Freemasons in a conspiracy to seize control of the world are older than Hitler's era. Interestingly, the slogan "Judeo-Masonic plot" cannot be traced to Germany until the end of World War I, though the warped connection had already been spread in France, mainly through the Dreyfus Affair (1894–1899). Dreyfus, a Jew, was made the scapegoat in a treasonable breach of French security. He was tried twice and found guilty both times. By a presidential decree he was pardoned, and on July 12, 1906, by one last appeal, the previous judgment against Dreyfus was set aside as "wrongful" and "erroneous." The next day the government decorated him and promoted him to the rank of major. But the seed of an imagined Jewish-Masonic connivance as a diabolical hybrid had been planted. The twentieth century merely nurtured it. There is strong evidence that the misanthropic label began as early as the 1870s, many years before the Dreyfus Affair.[37]

The problem of mutual guilt by association achieved added infamy when *The Protocols of the Elders of Zion* was published at the turn of the century. This brochure was purportedly a verbatim transcription of the first Zionist Congress of 1897. The "Protocols" suggested that Jewish leaders were in league with the Masonic lodges to command the world. The anti-Masonic attacks that began with propaganda derived from *The Protocols* brought forth two tortuous responses from German Freemasons—one admitting anti-Semitic prejudice, the other, more principled, upholding Masonic universalism. The Prussian lodges, representing a conservative wing of German Freemasons, were almost of the same spirit as their critics with regard to Jews. According to *Verein deutscher Freimaurer*, which may not be a fully trustworthy source for statistics, the Prussian lodges in 1928 had 57,000 members, not one of whom was a Jew. But the liberal lodges, sometimes referred to as humanistic lodges, felt acutely the competing pressures of German nationalism against harboring Jewish members, though Jewish Masons were a small minority in them.

Survival strategy proved futile for both conservative and liberal German Freemasons in the end. Hitler abhorred Freemasonry as the most moveable pawn of ambitious Jews. Masonry was, like the church, a serious rival to the new order, the new national myth and system of symbols sponsored by the Nazis. Katz summarizes the mood of Nazi society toward Freemasons in Germany as one of cynical indifference: "If the Masons expected to appease their adversaries by yielding, they were mistaken. Once the propagandists had begun to attack Jews and Freemasons in the same breath, the patriotism of the Freemasons was no longer taken for granted. While Freemasons dissociated themselves from Jews, other circles sought to dissociate themselves from Freemasons."[38] German Masons were trapped in checkmate.

In February 1930, shortly before Hitler came to power, the Scottish Rite of Freemasonry was established in Germany, but it was never recognized by the Northern or Southern Jurisdictions in the United States. Curiously, it was adamantly opposed by three Christian Grand Lodges of Germany; and, inasmuch as the Grand Lodges of Germany enjoyed amicable relations with most of the Grand Lodges of the United States, problems would have been caused by recognizing the German Supreme Council. It was also known that the three Christian Grand Lodges in Berlin tried desperately at this time to bargain with Hitler on the grounds that Hitler's program was compatible with their own regarding Jews.

Years earlier, Albert Pike was especially anxious that there be a Scottish Rite presence in Germany for the obvious reason that the Mother Council was working under the *Revised Constitutions of 1786,* which were reportedly sponsored by Frederick II (the Great) of Germany. With this connection in mind, Pike had the Lodge of Perfection ritual translated into German and printed. He also had the Rose Croix Chapter ritual translated, but it remained in manuscript form, though it is preserved in the House of the Temple archives.[39] (Frederick the Great, considered an avatar of Masonic ideals, once said he preferred speaking French, except to his horses he spoke German.)

"One of the first things that Hitler did," wrote the Grand Commander in 1943, "was to ban Freemasonry and hunt the Masons throughout the Reich." The splendid German Masonic temples were seized; some were converted into museums where Masonic regalia, books, and equipment were displayed to the public for the purpose of ridicule. Postcards and pamphlets were printed castigating Masons and showing Masonic emblems, such as the square and compasses, with the star of David superimposed over them. "Nothing was too fantastically rotten to accuse the Masons of being and doing."[40]

Nevertheless, a small group of German Masons, at the risk of their lives, resisted Hitler early on. Leopold Müffelmann, one of the two original founders of the German Supreme Council and its first Lieutenant Grand Commander, was openly fearless against Hitler. To counteract the sellout tendencies of the Christain Grand Lodges, Müffelmann started in July 1930 a tenth Grand Lodge of Germany named the Symbolic Grand

Lodge. Meanwhile, by late March 1933, after Hitler came to power, the German Supreme Council decided officially to abandon its activities. In June of that year they had named Müffelmann as Grand Commander pro tempore (*kommissarisch* Grand Commander).

On September 5, 1933, the Gestapo arrested Müffelmann, who was taken with Fritz Bensch, the Lieutenant Grand Commander, and Raoul Koner, a Supreme Council member, to the Sonnenburg concentration camp. They were set free on November 26, in large measure, according to Masonic researcher Alain Bernheim, as the result of letters written by Grand Commander Cowles. In April 1934, Müffelmann sailed for Palestine, where the Symbolic Grand Lodge had two offspring lodges. He stayed a short time there, but decided he could still be of use to Freemasons in Germany, and so returned home. He died August 29, 1934, in Germany, most likely as a consequence of his ordeal in the concentration camp.[41]

As Hitler's juggernaut moved on Paris, the pattern there remained consistent with the systematic elimination of Masonry in Germany. The Masonic temples of both the Grand Orient and the Grand Lodge, including the headquarters of the French Supreme Council, were immediately sealed following the occupation of Paris. The Germans confiscated lodge paraphernalia, furniture, banners, minute books, and records "and took them to the Petit Palais, and there two hundred laboring men worked to complete the exhibition that was being made of them." The Germans posted signs and placards with swastikas that announced the opening of the exhibit where French citizens could discover who their real enemies were. The watchwords read in part, "Come and see the satanic, ugly mimics and their disgraceful ceremonies performed by this handful of miserables who pretend to save humanity and improve mankind."[42]

After the Germans invaded the Netherlands in May 1940, they, predictably, struck at Dutch Freemasonry. General Hermannus van Tongeren, the Grand Master of the order and the Sovereign Grand Commander of the Supreme Council of the Netherlands since 1932, was one of the first arrested, on October 11, 1940, and imprisoned by the Nazis in Amsterdam for six months. He subsequently was sent to the concentration camp of Sachsenhausen in Germany, a journey that took nine days, and shortly thereafter died, on March 29, 1941. Masons were among the first on the general list of Netherlanders scheduled for deportation to concentration camps once the Nazis had taken over. All Masonic bodies were dissolved, and their funds and property, equivalent to more than $1 million, were plundered and impounded. Once again, examples of Masonic regalia were gathered up to be displayed in a Nazi scheme to eliminate the "dangers" of Freemasonry. Masons were beaten, and several committed suicide. The treasure from the libraries and archives of thirty Dutch lodges was transported to Germany, including 470 cases of books which were eventually documented in the Nuremberg trials.[43]

Yugoslavia, prior to World War II, was supportive of Freemasonry but required the lodges to register with the government and to promise that no Freemason would countenance political or revolutionary intrigue. All of that changed, of course, after the

German occupation. Black lists of the names of Masonic members were widely distributed. Many Freemasons were imprisoned, all of whom, according to Cowles, "were tortured and murdered." In one instance two university professors were executed solely for being part of the Masonic Fraternity.[44]

Not surprisingly, the German and Austrian governments banned the Scottish Rite's magazine *The New Age* from entry into those countries. Under the circumstances, the subscriptions were canceled and the amount paid was refunded.[45] Every attempt to remain in touch with European Freemasons was being made, recognizing how sensitive communications could be, given that mail was regularly examined. Cowles knew that the Grand Commander in Austria, "being a pure Aryan," was permitted to remain in his own country, though he had been "subjected to frequent questioning and restrictions." Acute outrage was expressed about the Austrian situation because, according to Cowles, "probably half of the members were Jewish, and those Jews have been terribly persecuted, being placed in concentration camps and even tortured and murdered."[46] Awareness by the American Masonic community that European Jews (and Masons) were being hunted down in a program of Nazi genocide was evident long before the presidential election of 1940.

Holocaust scholars are often very critical of American lassitude in the presence of "the final solution's" horror. Why did the Roosevelt administration turn away the cruise ship *St. Louis* full of Jewish refugees who were trying to escape Nazism? Immigration levels were actually under their prescribed quotas in many instances. Why were the rail lines leading to concentration camps not strategically bombed in 1944 and 1945? While many questions open disturbing criticism about the world's numbness to the destruction of a people, it is unfair to think absolutely nothing was being done in America to meet the specter of such human evil as Hitler's plan of race purification. Assistance was organized by American Scottish Rite Masons, though the demand to meet the appeals for help accelerated quickly to unprecedented levels of need. By the late thirties, entreaties from European Masons, "heart-rending, pitifully so," came daily to the House of the Temple. Cowles seemed to lament the U.S. immigration restrictions (which he had so vociferously supported) because the volume of applications for entry would require fifty years for all those seeking sanctuary to be taken care of under the quota law.[47]

With the prospect of friends and Masonic brothers dying all over Europe, Cowles did not sit idly waiting for the intermittent bad weather to lift. He said, "We were receiving so many requests for aid to our Masonic brothers in Europe that I suggested to Grand Commander Rene Raymond of Paris, France, that if he and other leaders of Masonry in Europe would form a Masonic Relief Society, I would endeavor to raise some money for it." Cowles was thus instrumental in forming the Bureau de Secours.[48] By 1939, the Supreme Council had contributed more than $36,000 to initiate this endeavor. Early in 1941 the Greek Grand Commander sent an urgent radiogram to Cowles signaling the dire state confronting his people, who were fighting the Italians. The Italians were soon joined by the Germans (an expense Hitler had hoped to avoid) and defeated the Greeks. Cowles got $15,000 to the Supreme Council of Greece which no doubt saved some lives.

Up to 1943, the Supreme Council had distributed $512,000 toward rescue and relief in war zones. In some instances, to get the money channeled through appropriate "Masonic sources," it was necessary to get a license from the Federal Reserve Bank to send funds to foreign countries. In the fall of 1943, the Supreme Council voted a staggering amount of money, $1 million, to assist refugees and the oppressed, regardless of whether they had Masonic connections. This magnanimity was a clear departure from earlier attempts to help only Masons.[49] Further, the Supreme Council's contributions, while mainly directed at Europe, were also applied to China in a special appropriation accomplished in a rare recess vote on February 4, 1938. Cowles received discretionary funds between $1,000 and $5,000 for relief in China in the aftermath of the Japanese invasion of Manchuria and occupation campaigns there (without a declaration of war by Japan). In addition, the Supreme Council "sent to General [Chiang] Kai Shek $5,000 in money and have bought ten chassis at $1,000 each which have been shipped to Rangoon, there to be equipped as ambulances and then used as transports over the Burma Road for medical supplies to Chung King and then delivered to General Kai Shek for the use of his Army."[50]

The suffering of Freemasons under dictatorships was hardly faceless. Cowles personally knew many of the men about whom he reported. Georges Pêtre, Belgian Grand Commander, was shot in his home by Nazi collaborators in the presence of his wife. A few weeks later, on January 20, 1943, Lieutenant Grand Commander Emile Lartigue, a general in the Belgian Army during the Great War, was also assassinated in his apartment. Eric Sasse, an alderman in Antwerp, was slain in the street. A month later, Raoul Engel, a thirty-third degree Scottish Rite Mason and past Grand Master (1928–1930), was murdered. Jules Hiernaux, who was once the Belgian Grand Master (1937–1939) and former minister for education, met a violent death on July 29, 1944. Fernand Clement, Belgian Grand Secretary General, warned Cowles "that the Germans have stolen from us all the Rituals you have furnished us with, of which we possessed a complete collection, including Secret Words." Clement feared the "manufacture [of] false Masonic identification papers," and, therefore, asked that all Supreme Councils "consider valueless all documents originating in Belgium."[51]

In one of many letters to Cowles from the Marquess of Ailsa, further devastating news was told: A German bomb fell on a London lodge, killing "the Reverend John Stafford, Minister Gretna, and companion Crawford." Apparently, "the alert had been sounded and several of the brethren who had air[raid] duties had left the meeting to attend to their posts. Unfortunately a stream of light was shown when the lights were turned on the motor cars, and this resulted in one of the raiders returning and dropping a bomb, destroying the Masonic Temple." The blast killed twenty-seven Masons, including the Master, and thirty-six more were severely injured. During the months of the

London blitz, the Supreme Council donated $50,000 to "the old Mother Grand Lodge of England, to do with as it pleased."[52]

Not long after V-E and V-J Days, which marked the end of World War II in the summer of 1945, the Supreme Council's Committee on Foreign Relations, chaired by Thomas J. Harkins, prepared an excellent summary of the effect that the Axis Powers had on Masonry during the thirties and early forties:

> It was obviously the policy of the Axis Powers to suppress Masonic Lodges and Bodies . . . and to utterly destroy not only Masonic Lodges, Bodies and Organizations, but individual Masons as well. . . . In some countries overrun by the Axis Powers it would seem that only the bare traces of the Fraternity were left. It may be said to the credit of the Masons in their states, and to the glory of Freemasonry, that there has been no voluntary surrender of the rights of the Order and no departure from its principles and ideals. It appears that wherever as much as a single spark of Masonic life was left unquenched, that spark, promptly upon the liberation of the people and the renewal of their hope for civil and religious liberty, began to glow anew, and that the few Masons who were left or who have been permitted to return have promptly engaged themselves in efforts to rebuild and re-establish the Fraternity. From practically every country where Masonry was destroyed, there have come expressions of hope and confidence that the Fraternity will rise again and be stronger than before.[53]

Later in his report, Harkins indicated that the letters, cablegrams, and radiograms received by Cowles and the Supreme Council on the subject of reorganizing and reestablishing Freemasonry in the occupied countries had been "voluminous." In response to distressed Masons and Masonic bodies in Europe and elsewhere, the Supreme Council passed a resolution that authorized Cowles to borrow up to $400,000 to provide the needed relief from the injury and loss due to war conditions. The council allowed that its U.S. government bonds or other securities would be used as collateral to borrow this money.[54] Throughout the post-war rebuilding of Europe, the Supreme Council, Southern Jurisdiction made its kindness felt. Food and financial assistance went directly to Austria, Germany, Romania, Norway, Yugoslavia, Greece, and Turkey. Many honors came to Cowles for his service to international Freemasonry. Humanitas Lodge in Vienna, Austria, made him an honorary member, and the Supreme Council of Greece elected him its Honorary Sovereign Grand Commander. Cowles, additionally, had conferred upon him "a Knight Commander, with the Red Cross, and Honorary Member of the Eleventh and Last Degree of the Norwegian Order of Freemasonry."[55]

The successful revival of Freemasonry in Norway had transparent symbolic poignancy. When the Germans occupied Norway and put Vidcun Quisling in as the puppet ruler, he established his offices in the Grand Lodge's Masonic temple, a beautiful building in Oslo. Although the exterior of the building was maintained, the interior of the temple was heavily damaged by the Quisling regime. At the end of the war, when Quisling was tried, the court proceedings were held in the Masonic temple which he had occupied and abused. The irony was not lost on Cowles, who commented, "[I]t was in one of the Grand Lodge rooms that he heard the sentence of death pronounced. It does not profit one to gloat over the end of a human being—even one condemned to death and executed. But it is the nature of man to have a feeling or thrill over this trial of condemnation for Quisling in the Temple, the interior of which he had destroyed." By the spring of 1950, the Masonic buildings and lodges in Norway had been restored. The Masonic Hall in Oslo, perhaps left in the worst condition of any Masonic property, had come back to life. In one of its special rooms, which had been totally ruined and was now occupied by its St. Andrews Lodge,[56] a plaque was installed with the inscription in Norwegian: "This room has been restored from means donated by the Supreme Council, 33°, Scottish Rite, Southern Jurisdiction, U.S.A."[57]

■ ■ ■

As the United States considered military involvement in World War II, the Supreme Council stood squarely in support of the Congress and administration in their preparation for meeting the gravest danger of the age. Months before the Japanese surprise attack on the American Pacific fleet in Pearl Harbor on December 7, 1941, the Scottish Rite Committee on Foreign Relations stated publicly its endorsement of the Congress "and of the responsible authorities of our Republic in their efforts to prepare our country adequately to meet and overcome the great danger which threatens us and our liberties, and to transform our country and the western hemisphere into an inexhaustible arsenal of democracy and unconquerable fortress of freedom."[58] Members of the Supreme Council, without dissent, seemed "certain that our country would eventually be drawn into the maelstrom of a great war." Further, many on the council "were opposed, and let it be known to the authorities, to the selling of supplies to Japan, from which, or of which, they made war matériel to be used against us."[59]

An obscure U. S. senator from Missouri rose to his feet on February 10, 1941, in the Capitol chamber to address his colleagues on the question of defense contracts. With the establishment of the Senate Special Committee to Investigate the National Defense Program, Harry S. Truman came to national prominence. The Truman Committee, as it was popularly known, sounded an alarm on "the scandalous state of military spending," especially on training-camp construction and shipbuilding. The Nye Committee (1934–1936) had earlier exposed the war profiteering of World War I. That earlier profiteering probably contributed to much of the country's isolationist feeling; and it left American defenses weak, in the mind of Senator Truman.[60]

Between February and October 1941, Grand Commander Cowles and Senator Truman carried on a spirited correspondence concerning the Scottish Rite's sponsorship of a broadcast commemorating George Washington as a Mason. More importantly, for the sake of preparing a nation for war mobilization, Truman solicited from Cowles support for a proposed Masonic-related service organization for the military and their families, a precursor to the U.S.O. Cowles was dead set against the proposition due to the projected expense of it and the fact that the Masonic Service Association was the likely coordinating body. His objection was based on a fear of a shadow national Grand Lodge undermining the proprietary interests of state Grand Lodges. Truman persisted with the counterargument and tried once more to convince Cowles to change his mind on October 11, 1941: "I still think if you would weigh the matter from every angle you could convince yourself that a proper procedure could be followed that would in no way infringe upon the authority and jurisdiction of the Grand Lodges and still enable them to cooperate and do a necessary job under present conditions. I have had much practical experience with this situation and I think that without prejudice to any one it can be worked through as a general service association."[61]

Cowles did not budge from his stance. He made sure, however, that the Supreme Council contributed "quite liberally" to the American Red Cross and the U.S.O. during the war. Moreover, the Scottish Rite bodies of the Southern Jurisdiction bought more than $1.5 million worth of war bonds between 1941 and 1943. Cowles did not think it wise for the Masonic Service Association, an "inter-Lodge association for cooperative action" developed after World War I, to compete against the Red Cross and U.S.O. Yet during World War II, the association maintained seventy-five Masonic Service Centers, including two large programs in London and Paris. The budget of the association for the years 1941 through 1946 exceeded $1.5 million.[62]

Cowles was just turning eighty in 1943, and for him to direct the Supreme Council's activity in support of the war efforts was arduous for several reasons. He had a couple of accidents that left him slightly, if temporarily, impaired. In St. Louis at the train station "some rollicking soldiers rushed along" and, as Cowles reported, ". . . without thinking one of them kicked my suit case and knocked it around in front of me and I fell over it and sprained my back and suffered intensely." Then seven months later in August, he fell down the steps at the Masonic temple in Asheville, North Carolina, and broke his left arm just above the wrist. Later, back in Washington, he tumbled down on the concrete pavement, breaking his right arm at the shoulder. "Consequently," he wrote, "I have been almost helpless. But my chauffeur has dressed and undressed me, and also he has fixed me up a little breakfast every morning and a little dinner in the evening."[63]

His problems at the House of the Temple were not limited to his own physical debilities. Government paper restrictions meant all Scottish Rite publications were reduced or consolidated. *The New Age* published eight issues a year instead of twelve. Maintenance on the House of the Temple, particularly cleaning the smoke stains on the south exterior wall, due to the adjacent building, the Chastleton, emitting exhaust from its furnaces and incinerators, was deferred. When in 1945 the work could no longer wait, the job had greatly expanded to include all of the joints of the wall and roof. One of the large columns on the outside of the building on the S Street side had cracked at the capital. Cowles indicated that "these columns carry a tremendous weight and there must have been a settling of some kind under this particular one which caused this fracture." The building was a metaphor for the man living inside it.[64]

The reduction of personnel at the House of the Temple during the war years was its own special kind of hardship, increasing the pressure and workload on Cowles. For example, Ray Baker Harris, the new librarian who replaced William L. Boyden, left for military service in the army on April 17, 1943, and did not return to the Supreme Council library until September 12, 1945. It is no wonder that under all these trying circumstances, Cowles allowed that the biennium between 1943 and 1945 was "the most difficult of any since I have been Grand Commander. We have been affected because of a lack of many things, and not the least of them is the lack of an adequate Temple force."[65]

■ ■ ■

Cowles had been in residence at the House of the Temple since 1915 when it had opened, and by the summer of 1943 he decided he wanted to be interred there, too. An act of Congress was required, similar to the right of internment granted to Washington Cathedral, which permitted President Woodrow Wilson, among others, to be entombed there. The appeal Cowles made to Congress was predicated on his fifty-five-year Masonic affiliation and the fact that half of his life was devoted to the work of the fraternity. Cowles said, "All of the interests I have had outside of my country are concentrated here, and I want to be laid away when the end comes in the surroundings where I have labored and where are the memories and happy incidents of my life." He pointed out in his petition that "there is a custom, the genesis of which is lost in antiquity, that those who were responsible for a monumental structure might have their remains rest within its walls or precincts."[66] Cowles was informed two months later that under Public Law 147 of the Seventy-eighth Congress he would be permitted "to rest for all time in the building" that represented his life work.[67]

Two crypts were designed and completed in the House of the Temple, one for Albert Pike and one for Cowles. On the 135th anniversary of Albert Pike's birth, December 29, 1944, his remains were exhumed and removed to the new crypt "set apart for him." General Pike's grandchildren, Anne Pike Smith, Mary Pike Goodman and his namesake, Albert, were present at the interment ceremony. (Surprisingly, the grandson was not a Mason, perhaps because the family had long felt antipathy to Masonry.[68]) Cowles spoke briefly of Pike's importance to the Scottish Rite, mentioning that when he died at the age of eighty-two, "his request was to be buried with Masonic ceremony in a grave unmarked by tombstone, and that wish of his was complied with." By the "gracious consent" of his descendants to accommodate Scottish Rite preferences, Pike was appropriately honored, which probably facilitated Cowles's own wish for burial, as such a precedent confirmed the propriety of the plans Cowles had quietly made for himself.[69]

No other building in Washington, except for the national monuments and the Capitol, was as imposing as the House of the Temple. The Washington Cathedral, however, was beginning to rival the Scottish Rite's own architectural masterpiece in critical esteem. In fact, the Scottish Rite was instrumental in having a statue of George Washington placed in the Cathedral's "Masonic corner." When the statue was unveiled and dedicated at the time of Washington's birthday in 1947, President and Mrs. Harry S. Truman were in attendance. The dean of Washington's fourth estate, Walter Lippmann, gave the dedicatory address before 2,000 worshippers in the Cathedral's nave, among whom was John H. Cowles, a rare churchgoer.[70]

Before World War II ended, Scottish Rite membership had nearly returned to the prior level of net annual gains. The number of initiates between 1941 and 1943 had increased to the enviable point of putting the office in arrears in printing patents. The number of new thirty-second degree Masons was 4,740 in 1941 and had almost doubled the following year.[71] Meanwhile, one very prominent American Mason presented a problem of great delicacy which had the potential for profit and could be viewed as embarrassing opportunism. Should President Franklin D. Roosevelt, a Mason, be given the thirty-third degree?

In October 1943, Grand Commander Cowles received a communication marked "personal & confidential" from his northern counterpart, Grand Commander Melvin M. Johnson. It was a sensitive matter that Johnson was raising since President Roosevelt was not uniformly admired by his brother Masons, many of whom were pro-business Republicans in the North. They may have shared the impression that the scion of one of Hyde Park's oldest families was a traitor to his class. Nevertheless, Johnson wrote, "I am . . . willing to submerge my own opinions for the good of Freemasonry. It seems to me that it is greatly to the advantage of the cause for which Freemasonry labors that [FDR] should be given the 33rd Degree."

According to a member of Congress with whom Johnson had been in contact, the president was overheard saying one day, "They gave Tom Connally [Chairman, Senate Foreign Relations Committee] the 33rd, why don't they give it to me?" Johnson was now convinced, "after a struggle . . . that this ought to be done." He said, "It seems to me that we owe it to the Rite and the Craft at large to do this thing for the President and Commander in Chief, even if we would not otherwise do it for the individual." Johnson admitted, however, that two members of the Northern Masonic Jurisdiction could not go along with the plan to confer the thirty-third degree on the president. "And I would not allow the President of the United States to be blackballed in my Supreme Council if within my power to prevent it," confided Johnson.

In view of all these good intentions and for the good of Masonry, Johnson went beyond dropping hints to a direct request: "If your Supreme Council should see fit to do the thing, and you requested a waiver of jurisdiction from me, I tell you in advance that I will grant it. This I have express authority to do under Article 403 of our Constitutions as amended in 1942, so far as divided membership is concerned."[72]

Cowles replied tersely three days later, to the effect that, were the Supreme Council of the Southern Jurisdiction to confer the thirty-third degree on Roosevelt, the Supreme Council of the Northern Masonic Jurisdiction might resent the action. If the reverse were true, Cowles related how "peeved" his Supreme Council would feel. Cowles also indicated that his letter was a certified copy of an original that along with Johnson's letters of October 3 and 8 "were lost or stolen."

There was, however, a deeper intrigue at work than missing letters, which would help to account, in part, for an abrupt decision that many Masons would come to regret, that is, not conferring the highest Masonic honor on a sitting president. Cowles, when pressed for an explanation years later, feebly rationalized "that there had never been a 33rd Degree Mason who was President. Harding had been elected to receive it, but he died before he was crowned."[73] It should be emphasized that there was abundant eagerness not to trifle away a similar good opportunity in the hurried attempt that made President Harry S. Truman a thirty-third degree Mason almost immediately after he became the commander in chief.

Johnson's inquiry had struck a raw nerve in Cowles which, as a result, denied President Roosevelt an honor he deserved. It also deepened bad feelings between the two Grand Commanders. This led to a bitter Masonic feud that did not heal easily even after the dispute was carried to "The Court of Masonic Public Opinion." It all began, apparently, in February 1942 at the Conference of Grand Masters. Johnson made some startling accusations about the Supreme Council, Southern Jurisdiction, which were subsequently published and circulated widely. In essence he said, according to the Committee on Foreign Relations, that the Supreme Council had prostituted "its dignity as to barter the honors it confers upon members of the Craft in return for influence in an effort . . . to intermeddle in and to control the action of Grand Masonic Bodies" (the committee's interpolation, not Johnson's exact words). While this, no doubt, enraged Cowles and his Supreme Council, they followed the old Masonic custom of ignoring "all such quixotic attacks." They did nothing—at first.

With underlying tensions in the near background, particularly on the question of Masonic honors, Cowles was measurably rankled by Johnson, who pressured him to confer the thirty-third degree on Roosevelt. It seemed to Cowles almost a trap that Johnson was setting. The feelings did not relax, but instead the contention escalated. Johnson's criticism was rebutted. This provoked Johnson to file a "Brief of Appeal" in which he stated, "[U]nfortunately, it has been necessary, down through the centuries of history, to have an [intramural] war to bring about unity and harmony." With one hand he extended an olive branch, but in the other he wielded knife-edge words. He questioned the Southern Supreme Council's adoption of "Mother Council of the World" as part of its title. The question Johnson raised was that of original territorial jurisdiction in the United States. The Southern Jurisdiction occupied thirty-three states, and the Northern Jurisdiction, fifteen states, though Johnson failed to mention that the Northern Jurisdiction had at this time the larger membership of the two Masonic bodies.

The answer made by the Southern Jurisdiction concerning Scottish Rite metes and bounds was that "The Census of the United States shows that at the time of the division of territory by the two Supreme Councils, the white population of the territory ceded to the Northern Supreme Council was twice as great as the white population in the territory *retained* by the Southern Supreme Council. Even to this day (1940 Census), the white population of the jurisdiction of the Northern Supreme Council is greater than the white population in that part of the United States under the jurisdiction of the Southern Supreme Council." Cowles himself wrote a detailed, nineteen-page, single-spaced, chapter-and-verse indictment of Johnson.[74] The opportunity to recognize President Roosevelt was soon moot, as he died April 12, 1945. By October of that year, President Truman was made a thirty-third degree Mason. But that achievement, too, was problematic because of the Johnson-Cowles controversy and the resulting personal differences between Masons.

When Grand Commander Johnson first criticized Cowles and the Supreme Council for giving the appearance of selling Masonic "indulgences," the Grand Master of the Grand Lodge of Missouri, Ray V. Denslow, published the Johnson diatribe in the Missouri *Proceedings*. Cowles may have been an old man, but he still played hardball. During Masonic Week in Washington, D.C., Denslow was summoned to explain his actions. Cowles's anger, already made white hot by Johnson, was further stirred by Denslow. Denslow's Grand Lodge, after all, was in the Southern Jurisdiction, and his sensitivity to Cowles could not have been so dull as to be surprised at the repercussions. Denslow failed to answer the summons and, according to Masonic law, was stripped of the degrees which the Supreme Council bestowed upon him.

However, Cowles had not heard the last of Denslow. The Past Grand Master of the Grand Lodge of Missouri was Harry S. Truman. Truman had already had disagreements with Cowles over the wartime role of a supra-Masonic clearing house for service to the military. It may be apocryphal, but a legend grew that when Truman was sworn in as president of the United States, Cowles invited him to call at his office at the House of the Temple. The perception could easily be drawn of bringing the mountain to Moses. This may be a variation on the theme of General Douglas MacArthur's alleged upstaging of President Truman at their meeting in the Pacific, which, according to Truman's recent biographer David McCullough, never happened. As the Cowles story spread, Truman was not going to let his office become subservient to any high office of the land, including that of the exalted Sovereign Grand Commander of the Southern Jurisdiction. Instead, on October 17, 1945, the Supreme Council left its chambers and called on President Truman at The White House. There the story takes another ironic turn.[75]

At the biennial session in October 1945, President Truman was elected to receive the rank and decoration of Knight Commander of the Court of Honor and the rank and dignity of the thirty-third degree honorary. Supposedly, before Truman would accept the Supreme Council's honor he let it be known through back channels that he had one contingency which had to be cleared up if the ceremony was to proceed. His long-standing friend and fellow Missourian Ray V. Denslow would have to have his degrees restored by the Supreme Council.

Denslow had appealed the decision of the special trial committee selected at the 1943 session of the Supreme Council. He was represented by counsel in the figure of Haslett P. Burke, Sovereign Grand Inspector General in Colorado. The outcome of this was face saving, in effect, trading off Denslow's apology for the committee's recommendation that the charges and report be withdrawn.[76]

Truman received the thirty-third degree in a ceremony that also included the crowning of J. C. Penney, the department store magnate.[77] Cowles was satisfied that things had worked out, but lingering annoyance pervaded his disposition at the time. Grand Commander Johnson had been invited to the biennial session as a courtesy, though he declined. Cowles stated, "However, he learned of our action [to honor Truman] and immediately made reservations for railroad and hotel and intended to come and be present at the conferring of the 33rd Degree." Cowles could not resist adding this information to his bill of complaints against Johnson, as "an example of how he [sought] publicity." Johnson was unable to attend, despite his sudden reconsideration, as his physician forbid him to travel.[78]

Cowles remained on the defensive about Truman's thirty-third degree. There had also been criticism when Douglas MacArthur became a thirty-third degree Mason. Cowles had received a number of letters and telephone calls from people who wanted to know how President Truman and General MacArthur had become thirty-third degree Masons. He insisted that "they did not receive the 33rd Degree because of their political or military successes and great accomplishments." Rather, he pointed out that they both had exemplary Masonic careers. In the case of MacArthur, who was coroneted in 1947, Cowles added, "[H]e was responsible for the new Government of Japan raising its ban against the Japanese becoming Freemasons. Since General MacArthur has been over there a number of the Japanese have joined the Masonic Fraternity."[79]

It should not be surprising that Masons were found in high places throughout the nation's capital. By 1950 eight of the nine members of the U.S. Supreme Court were Masons.[80] Secretary of Commerce Jesse Jones and General George C. Marshall—when they were made Masons-at-Sight on December 16, 1941, by Ara M. Daniels, the Grand Master for the District of Columbia—were joined in lodge by Ambassador Stanley F. Hornbeck (an authority on China whose dire warnings on Maoism, he believed, were ignored by the State Department).[81] It was not unusual for lofty government officials during this period to meet at Masonic functions around the city. It was one of the lesser social circuits in Washington that lightened the load of high responsibility. Presumably, too, if men sat in lodge together or knew of one another's Masonic connection, they were better equipped to set aside their policy differences in order to make the practical work of Washington friendlier.

Cowles was apparently present at the George Washington University commencement of May 29, 1946, when President Truman received the honorary degree of Doctor of Laws. On that same evening Margaret, his daughter, received her bachelor's degree. The university president handed her diploma to President Truman, so that he might personally give it to her.[82]

Cowles would again cross paths with President Truman, via Masonic and musical connections. The president loved classical music, playing Chopin études well into his retirement and advanced years. The Grand Commander had long admired Finland and one of its living national treasures, the renowned composer Jean Sibelius. Cowles had sent greetings to Sibelius on his eighty-third birthday and was acknowledged promptly with a note of thanks. Through J. Raymond Ylitalo in the U.S. State Department and a member of Suomi Lodge No. 1 in Finland, a book of Sibelius's Masonic music was obtained. Cowles, in turn, delivered it and presented it in person to President Truman.[83]

■   ■   ■

As World War II ended, so too ended the decline of Masonic membership in the United States. By the mid-forties there had been "a general influx of candidates into Masonry, beginning with the Blue Lodges."[84] Fraternalism was on the march, and its recovery should not be explained away as some benign extension of the Veterans of Foreign Wars or the mere show of "male bonding" emerging from common wartime experience.

Among the historical figures of the twentieth century, Adolf Hitler alone had no grave, a somber fact that most of the world would consider just. It would not be just, however, to let the dead of that war be buried in vain. Some meaning, larger than the refuge of patriotism, had to be found for the sacrifice of millions in the Allied effort to defeat evil. George Orwell, for example, once suggested that the greatest loss for Western civilization was the vanishing belief in the immortality of the soul. To some immeasurable extent, perhaps the post-war resurgence of Masonry was a check against the loss of faith that Orwell feared. And in the fifties, added to heightened Masonic interest, there was a boom in church attendance. Cowles pondered the meaning of the war in his *Allocution* for 1947, thinking along the lines of the human spirit: "Who won? None. Every nation and its citizens lost. Maybe the war did not have to come; maybe by open, fair, true diplomacy, equitable in all respects, it could have been avoided, but the war came. It may have been God's plan to bring forcibly to the people the fact there is another life beyond."[85]

Meanwhile, in practical terms, Masons returning home from war would need help in finding jobs. Cowles proposed a general Masonic employment organization for each state, because "the country need[ed] first of all jobs for the returning soldiers able to work and desiring a job." He sounded a high note of resolve in his stated belief that accomplishing this task would "prove to the world the virility, ingenuity, and humanitarianism of the

American people."[86] The G.I. Bill, with its provisions for education and mortgage loans, did exactly what Cowles had suggested; it assimilated young veterans into domestic life. The returning men, because of their formative military experience and their demand to resume productive living, shaped new contours of social relations in America. The crab-grass frontier opened; that is, the landscape outside of cities was transformed into popular suburbs.

One of the major social changes which also came as a result of the war and for which the country, including many veterans, was not prepared, was the new chapter of civil rights history for African-Americans. They served, fought, and died bravely for their country, as they had in every preceding American war. President Truman told a group of southern Democrats that he was himself from authentic Confederate stock and from a part of Missouri no different from Jim Crow society anywhere in the Deep South, but, he said, "[M]y very stomach turned over when I learned that Negro soldiers, just back from overseas, were being dumped out of army trucks in Mississippi and beaten. Whatever my inclinations as a native of Missouri might have been, as President I know this is bad. I shall fight to end evils like this."[87]

Truman achieved less in civil rights than he had wanted, but the program he proposed broke new ground as the strongest ever presented by a president. He succeeded, nonetheless, in establishing the prestigious Commission on Civil Rights; and, by Executive Order he desegregated the Armed Forces and the Federal Civil Service. His very close victory over Thomas E. Dewey in the fabled 1948 election was due in no small part to the black vote in the northern cities and the South. As president he awakened the conscience of Americans about the intolerable lack of racial equality.

In spite of the entrenched reality of racial discrimination and the predominant attitudes of white Americans everywhere in the country, Truman's capacity to change definitely made ripples. Masonry's principle of equality was now challenged in fresh ways because of the atmosphere Truman helped create. The Grand Lodge of Massachusetts in its quarterly communication of March 12, 1947, approved the idea that "informal co-operation and mutual helpfulness between the two groups when appropriate are desirable." The two groups referred to Grand Lodge Masons of Massachusetts and Prince Hall Masons. This statement set off an immediate and considerable reaction on the part of two or three Grand Lodges, including those of Texas and Florida, and also the Supreme Council of the Southern Jurisdiction, "in which Masonic relations were severed with the Grand Lodge of Massachusetts."[88]

The furor over the "Massachusetts experiment" had the intensity of a strong, silent ulcer in the belly. Cowles decried any recognition of black Freemasonry, giving ample space to the issue in his *Allocution* for 1947. Cowles, reared in a border state, resented the problem bubbling up again, since he believed "it was settled some seventy years ago." This may be a reference to the end of Reconstruction when the last Federal troops were withdrawn from South Carolina and Louisiana in April 1877. He rejected the rumor that Albert Pike had given a set of the Scottish Rite rituals to Negro Freemasonry, because in Pike's list there is no mention of it, though it seems unlikely such an offering would be documented. Prince Hall officials of the United Supreme Council, however, always assumed Pike was the source of their Scottish Rite ritual.[89]

In retrospect the Cowles argument appears almost antediluvian and is especially absurd in the presence of his strong support of persecuted Freemasons around the world, many of whom were non-white. Cowles, for instance, welcomed Filipino and Japanese men into Masonry. But he, like so many segregationists at the time, puzzled out an American exception. He stated, "[I]n this country I think every Grand Lodge prohibits bartenders and saloonkeepers from petitioning Freemasonry and, as a rule, they are mostly white men. Some of them are Christians, upright, good citizens, some of them never drink intoxicants themselves, and yet they are barred. It is the general characteristics of their business that bar them [when they otherwise seem eligible]." Cowles completed his analogy suggesting that this policy "holds good so far as Negroes are concerned, for it would be impossible to draw a line and admit some, so all of them are barred."

And if this argument, distinguishing among undesirables in an organization founded on repudiating such arbitrariness, failed, Cowles was prepared to fall back on legalism. Simply put, Prince Hall or other Negro Grand Lodges were never historically recognized by any regular American Grand Lodges.[90] This overconcern with continuity could apply easily and equally to the legitimacy of most Protestant churches that were not recognized by the mother church on parallel grounds of apostolic succession. A static representation of history falls short of meeting the present world, which will not wait or stand still. History largely reflects, instead, that people must at times change.

The Grand Lodge of Massachusetts blinked during a stare-down which rehearsed larger, painful changes coming to American society. It rescinded its earlier action on July 18, 1949, returning to the *status quo* of New England Masonry being practiced in two forms, one white, one black. The Grand Lodge of Massachusetts was, thence, accorded friendly relations with all other Masonic bodies who "de-recognized" it.[91] Cowles, born during Reconstruction, a resident of segregated Washington, D.C., said he had deliberated a long time about the problem and concluded, paradoxically, "People, races and nations get along better *together* when they are *separated.* So, as long as the Negro Masons go their way, to which no one objects, and we go our way, then both will get along harmoniously."[92]

Cowles failed to anticipate that separation as a means to promote equality was odious to many Americans, including Chief Justice Earl Warren and his Masonic brethren on the U.S. Supreme Court. The breakthrough came in a case the Court reviewed that was argued by a Prince Hall Mason, Thurgood Marshall. Brotherhood could never be fully realized without getting "along better together." That divide could be bridged only by the added strength of love, not by greater distances and higher barriers.

■ ■ ■

John Henry Cowles barely lived to see the *Plessy v. Ferguson* (1896) decision of the Supreme Court reversed by the epoch-making *Brown v. Board of Education of Topeka* on May 17, 1954, when the "separate but equal" doctrine, particularly in public elementary education, was declared unconstitutional. Before he died, however, Cowles was instrumental in building a new organization for another sacrosanct constitutional principle—the separation of church and state.

In the last years of the forties, Cowles personally contributed to a fledgling outfit with Baptist ties called Protestants and Other Americans United for the Separation of Church and State (POAU, later called "Americans United"). He could not promise future Supreme Council support to them, but was eager for the organization to succeed.[93] Under the dynamic leadership of a former midwestern law school dean, Glenn L. Archer, Protestants and Other Americans United for the Separation of Church and State became a bona fide nonprofit organization on January 29, 1948. A few contributions made possible "a modest salary" for Archer and a secretary. Archer recalls a vivid turning point on "a snowy February day of 1948," when "Sovereign Grand Commander John H. Cowles of the Scottish Rite Mason's Southern Jurisdiction handed us a check which aided us in the budgetary needs for the first year."[94]

The National Advisory Council of POAU brought together some eighty men and women, the majority of whom were religious leaders. Dr. Mary McLeod Bethune, a distinguished black educator, was one of the members. The strongest religious support came from the Baptists, historic defenders of the separation clause, who were joined in near equal measure by Methodists, Universalists and Unitarians. The Episcopalians, Presbyterians, members of the Evangelical and Reformed Church, Lutherans, Seventh-day Adventists, Disciples of Christ, Congregationalists, and Christian Scientists were also well represented as the momentum built. Through POAU strong stands were taken on borderline church-state issues such as inclusion of religious affiliation in the federal census. One of the early controversial issues involved interfaith child custody and adoption disputes; religious preference was a criterion of the law in Massachusetts, Illinois, Ohio, and Pennsylvania.[95]

Other members of POAU included Charl O. Williams, who worked with Cowles for many years; Methodist Bishop G. Bromley Oxnam; Louie D. Newton, president of the Southern Baptist Convention; John A. MacKay, president of Princeton Theological Seminary; Charles Clayton Morrison, editor of *The Christian Century;* and Edwin McNeil Poteat, president of Colgate-Rochester Divinity School. Williams served as a trustee for POAU but had been a field secretary and the president of the National Education Association (NEA). Through this connection, Cowles advised the National Education Association on the purchase of headquarters property at 1633 Massachusetts Avenue in Washington, D.C., and contributed more than a third of the cost of the real estate transaction. His $10,000 gift was perhaps the largest the NEA had received as of March 1949.[96]

A bronze tablet was presented to the Supreme Council on October 16, 1951, in recognition of Cowles's positive interest in POAU and "of his long years of untiring work to maintain the principle of separation of church and state in our country and to preserve the integrity and insure the perpetuity of our free tax-supported schools." Charl O. Williams spoke at the plaque's dedication, reminding herself and others, "[I]t has been a great thing in my life to have known and worked with a man for thirty years who has never dallied with his principles on this question [of the separation of church and state], nor hesitated to assert them on the platform, or on the printed page, cost what it may."[97]

. . .

In his ninetieth year, on the evening of February 21, 1952, Grand Commander Cowles suffered an accidental fall "by stumbling over a rumpled rug in his living quarters" in the House of the Temple. The temple had become "his cathedral and also his home for more than a quarter of a century."[98] He had few interests or pleasures outside of the fraternity. During his most active years he enjoyed travel, fine cigars, and an occasional afternoon of golf, "his only recreation." His razor-sharp memory was constantly demonstrated even in old age, perhaps no more impressively than in his ability at the end of a round of golf, or a week later, to "repeat the score not only of himself but of the other members of his foursome on each of the eighteen holes."[99]

After his accident, Cowles was taken to Mt. Alto Veterans Hospital in Washington, D.C., inasmuch as he was a veteran of the Spanish American War and still loved to be called "Captain Cowles." While Cowles was confined for six months to the hospital, two thirty-third degree Masons who happened to be physicians examined Cowles and reported on his condition and the quality of care he was receiving. After their visit, that same day, September 6, 1952, the Grand Commander resigned his office. His length and quality of service had no other rival except for that of the venerable Albert Pike.[100]

Cowles died on June 18, 1954, and the public funeral service was held on June 22 in the council chamber of the House of the Temple. He was remembered that day for his enormous capacity for work, his reserves of energy and store of wisdom, his advocacy of tax-supported free public schools, his Masonic erudition, his profound knowledge of the craft's history, the application of its fundamentals, and his personal acquaintance with leading Freemasons worldwide. He was the recipient of honorary degrees and official decorations from five foreign governments. Cowles had established in his early career in the Grand Lodge of Kentucky the Cowles Benevolent Fund and had given it in excess of $100,000. He had also started in the Supreme Council the Cowles Aid Fund, to which he had contributed more than $150,000. In life and even in death through benevolent bequests, he overlooked no Masonic duty.[101]

Fittingly, his epitaph may be drawn from the poetic conclusion of his *Allocution* of 1939, reminiscent of Pike's, beside whom he lies in shared consecration:

Lift mine eyes from earth and let me
Not forget the uses of the stars.
Forbid that I should judge others, lest
I condemn myself.
Let me feel the glamour of the world,
But walk calmly in my path. Give me
A few friends, who shall love me for what I am;
And keep ever burning before my vagrant footsteps
The kindly light of hope, and though
Age and infirmity overtake me, and I
Come not within sight of the castle of my dreams,
Teach me still to be thankful for life
And for time's golden moments, that are
Good and sweet. And may the evening twilight
Find me gentle still.[102]

John Henry Cowles, ca. 1915

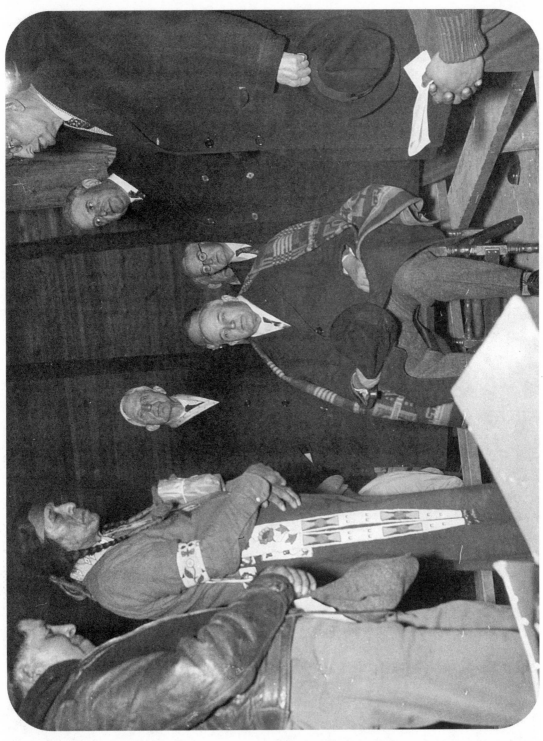

Grand Commander
John H. Cowles
being invested as
a chief in the
Shoshone Bannock
Indian tribe, Idaho,
December 1937

Grand Commander John H. Cowles, 1946,
by Harris and Ewing, Washington, D.C.

Scottish Rite Temple, Oakland, California,
view from across Lake Merritt, 1925

Scourging of Christ, Anti-Masonic
propaganda published in Germany, 1930s

*Emilio Aguinaldo and Charles S. Lobingier in Rose Croix attire
of the Scottish Rite, in the Philippines, ca. 1925. Aguinaldo was a
noted Filipino revolutionary lionized as the father of his country:
he opposed United States annexation of the Philippines and for
almost fifty years wore a black bow tie in symbolic mourning.
Lobingier established the Scottish Rite in the Philippines in 1910.*

Scottish Rite Temple of Manila, the Philippines, after Japanese occupation, 1935 to 1945

President Franklin D. Roosevelt with sons and Fiorello LaGuardia at New York's Architect Lodge 517, November 7, 1935. Courtesy of the Livingston Masonic Library, New York City.

*Dedication of flagpole given by the Franklin
Delano Roosevelt Class of 1945, Scottish Rite
Temple, Balboa, Panama Canal Zone, April 1946*

*President Harry S. Truman speaks from the East in Indiana's Beach
Grove Lodge No. 694 on his famous "whistle-stop" campaign trip,
October 15, 1948.* Courtesy of the Grand Lodge of Indiana.

Scottish Rite Library, St. Paul, Minnesota, ca. 1950. Note Egyptian motif decorating the frieze.

Grand Commander Luther A. Smith and Hurst R. Anderson, president of American University in Washington, D.C., study the foundation of the new School of International Service in 1958. The Scottish Rite contributed $20,000 toward a professorship in American studies.

President Kennedy receiving the
Eighth International Conference
of Supreme Councils: Grand
Commanders James A. Simpson
(Canada), George E. Bushnell
(NMJ), Luther A. Smith (SJ),
Renah F. Camalier, center
(Washington, D.C., Valley), and
Henry C. Clausen (background,
right, wearing dark coat and hat),
April 10, 1961. Courtesy of the
White House, National Archives,
Kennedy Library.

*Luther A. Smith being
presented the Scottish
Rite flag carried to the
moon on Apollo 11 by
Edwin "Buzz" Aldrin,
who visited the Grand
Commander on
September 16, 1969*

*Scottish Rite Masons on Capital Hill: Carl Albert,
Lloyd Bentsen, Wilbur Mills, and Bob Dole*

C. Fred Kleinknecht presents
the Grand Cross to Norman
Vincent Peale, October 1987.

William Donald Schaefer,
governor of Maryland,
in Grand Cross cap, 1987

*Burl Ives plays guitar for Supreme
Council banquet, October 1987.*

*C. Fred Kleinknecht with Senator
Sam Nunn, October 1993*

Left to right, *Senator Jesse Helms, C. Fred Kleinknecht, Burton Ravellette Jr.* (in mirror), *Senator Robert Dole, and Stephen J. Trachtenberg, October 1993*

C. Fred Kleinknecht with General Walter E. Boomer, 33°, Assistant Commandant, USMC, at Baltimore Southern Regional Conference, spring 1994

The Supreme
Council,
October 1995

Frederick the Great Medallion, minted for Supreme Council session, 1971

*Double-Headed
Eagle, painting by
Robert H. White,
1984*

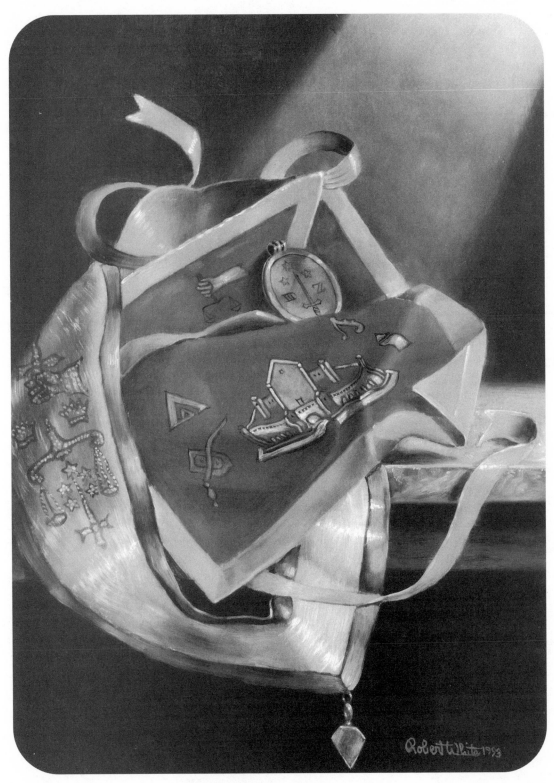

Scottish Rite regalia, 16°, apron, jewel,
and collar. Robert H. White, artist

Scottish Rite regalia, 18°, apron, jewel,
and collar. Robert H. White, artist

Rite regalia, 23°, apron, jewel,
and collar. Robert H. White, artist

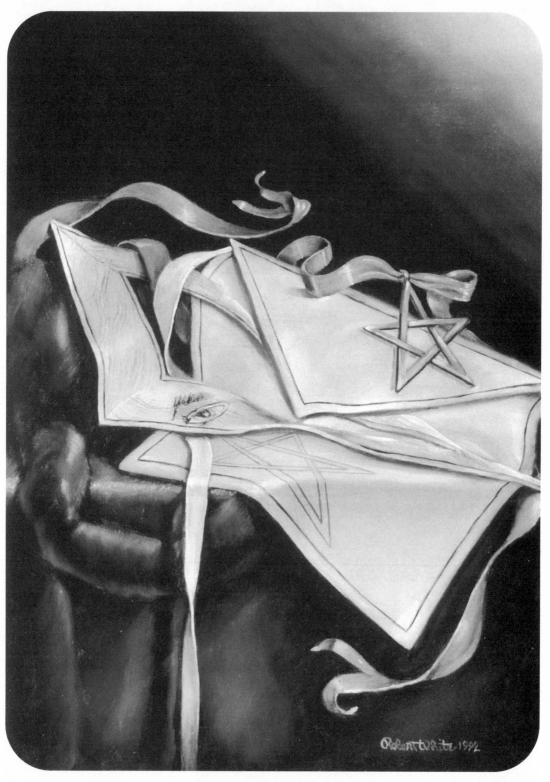

Scottish Rite regalia, 28°, apron, jewel,
and collar. Robert H. White, artist

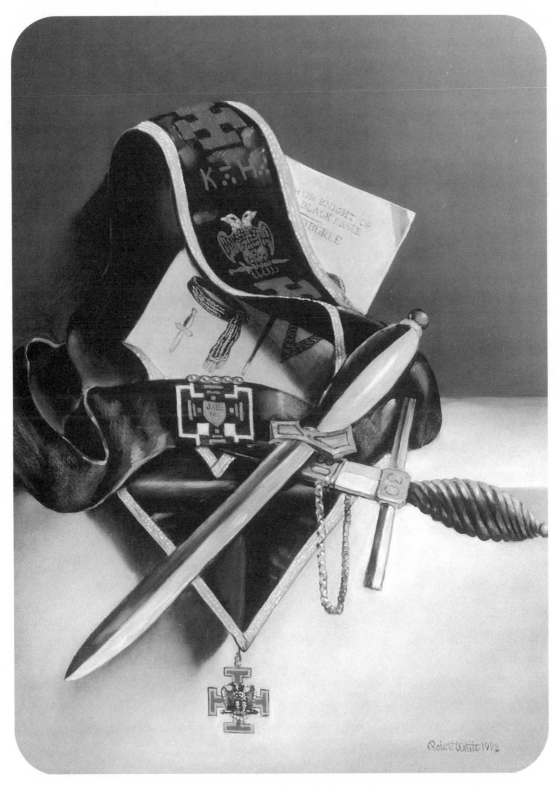

Scottish Rite regalia, 30°, apron, jewel,
and collar. Robert H. White, artist

Scottish Rite regalia, 32°, apron, jewel,
and collar. Robert H. White, artist

Scottish Rite regalia, 33°, apron, jewel,
and collar. Robert H. White, artist

House of the Temple,
Sixteenth and S Streets, NW,
Washington, D.C.

CHAPTER XI

Stretched Nerves
1950s

Harkins and Smith

🔲🔲🔲🔲🔲🔲🔲🔲🔲🔲

Discussing "the American way of life" in the 1950s as formed by a "triple melting pot" of Protestants, Catholics, and Jews, Will Herberg, writing early in the decade, insisted a "common religion" embraced "such seemingly incongruous elements as sanitary plumbing and freedom of opportunity, Coca-Cola and an intense faith in education." This "organic structure of ideas, values and beliefs," he added, constituted a faith which undergirded and transcended "all indubitable differences of region, section, culture and class."[1] Perhaps more important for American spiritual life was the additional fervor of patriotic piety that was bound up with post-war prosperity and national pride, on the one hand, and the psychological insecurity from an unprecedented cold war, on the other hand. The "under God" clause in the Pledge of Allegiance, for instance, was inserted by an act of Congress in 1954, bringing religion and Americanism together in a national credo.

The 1950s in America were shaped by many barely submerged contradictions, but even the expanding youth culture centering on rock 'n' roll music and the budding vigor of civil rights activism seemed calm when juxtaposed with succeeding decades. Rather, the smooth contours of consensus seemed to define the mood of the 1950s so that a quiet and personal religious faith was an essential element in serving and defending the American way of life. Two giant public figures, in particular, embodied the feeling of a much desired spiritual stability that Americans hoped for in their promising circumstances— Dwight D. Eisenhower and Norman Vincent Peale.

Dwight D. Eisenhower, the first former commanding general of the army elected president since Ulysses S. Grant, functioned for eight years as a lustrous symbol of generic piety and patriotic moral contentment. As George Washington had included in his inauguration address a supplication "to that Almighty Being who rules over the universe," Eisenhower began his own inaugural speech with a prayer. Managing to balance his personal family piety and his public trust of holding together a diverse society, Eisenhower provided a classic, though vague and sometimes ridiculed, justification for the new religious outlook of the times: "Our government makes no sense unless it is founded in a deeply felt religious faith—and I don't care what it is."[2] Whether or not he said those exact words, as some have questioned, the accuracy of them as a reflection of Eisenhower's generally benign religious outlook remains intact.

Eisenhower, the son of Mennonite parents, was baptized as an adult by the Presbyterian minister Edward L. R. Elson, who later served as the chaplain of the U.S. Senate. Eisenhower approximated Masonic values of spiritual universalism in his presidential rhetoric, even speaking appreciatively of the fraternity. He did not himself become a Mason as had the two previous occupants of the White House. Two of Eisenhower's brothers (Arthur, a successful Kansas City banker, and Milton, a university president), however, were Masons. Further, Eisenhower's supporter and spiritual complement Norman Vincent Peale was an ardent blue lodge and Scottish Rite Freemason until his death in 1994. If Eisenhower projected a generalized kind of civil religiosity, Peale extended his influence from mainstream Protestant practices to take in a popular therapeutic religion. Peale fed a rising public hunger for personal composure in a world dramatically altered from the end of World War II.

Peale was a phenomenon. There were other effective inspirational preachers and writers who, as Peale's contemporaries, also struck a popular chord, such as Rabbi Joshua Loth Liebman, Monsignor Fulton J. Sheen, and Anne Morrow Lindbergh. Peale, however, exceeded all the bestselling authors of the devotional genre, reaching an audience of many millions with *The Power of Positive Thinking* in 1952. His main rival in book sales that year was the newly released Revised Standard Version of the Bible.

Norman Vincent Peale (1898–1994) grew up in a Methodist parsonage in Ohio and took degrees from Ohio Wesleyan University and Boston University School of Theology. Thence, he launched successful pastorates in northern Methodist churches. In 1932 he was called to the Marble Collegiate Church on New York's Fifth Avenue, a move that required a transfer from Methodism to the Reformed Church in America, a denomination of Dutch background. In this new setting he began to test his voice as a prophet of positive thinking. His first major publishing endeavor was through a slim book, *You Can Win* (1938), which summarized the philosophy his better-known books later featured: "To win over the world a man must get hold of some power in his inward or spiritual life which will never let him down." Illustrating this fundamental outlook with anecdotes of people who had found the strength to master their circumstances and discouragements, Peale, according to his own conservative estimate, had "reached" 30 million Americans by the mid-1950s. He used every means of communication available in presenting his enthusiasm for life, including sermons and talks in crowded meeting halls and via radio, recordings, and television. The printed and broadcast word knew no greater exponent than Peale, who put into mass circulation sermons, articles, newspaper columns, booklets, and pamphlets. His own magazine, *Guideposts,* was as broadly distributed as popular Luce publications such as *Life* magazine. Peale reached the height of his influence by riding the wave of the post-war renewal of religious interest. He fit the times exactly as Eisenhower had.[3]

As minister of the Marble Collegiate Church, Peale moved into the field of mass media preaching with such blushing success that he nearly created a breach in American Protestantism because his innovative techniques of communicating on a huge scale seemed novel at best, propagandistic at worst. The eminent historian Sydney E. Ahlstrom maintained, moreover, that Peale was "as important for the religious revival of the fifties as George Whitefield had been for the Great Awakening of the eighteenth century."[4] This comparison marks Peale as one of the few seminal preachers in the American century.

During the Eisenhower years (1952–1960), Peale, along with other prominent religious leaders, set a sunny mood of confidence in "the American way." In this atmosphere, the prospects for fraternal orders everywhere to expand their memberships and programs, to bask in the sunshine of positive thinking, seemed like an endless summer. The two American Supreme Councils of Scottish Rite Freemasonry predictably aligned themselves with the favorable godly and patriotic conditions which flourished in the fifties. In the Southern Jurisdiction, two Grand Commanders, Thomas J. Harkins and Luther A. Smith, presided at a moment when American Masonry—like Eisenhower and Peale—seemed exactly matched in the fullness of time. In fact, the two Grand Commanders served in a sequence paralleling the two Eisenhower terms in office, which makes convenient the general division of the early fifties from the late fifties. In the case of Luther A. Smith, his leadership in the sixties warrants a separate chapter.

In considering the Supreme Council's tacit endorsement of "the American way of life," three areas in each historical bracket of the fifties—early and late—must naturally be explored: (1) Masonry in general, at home, and abroad; (2) institutional measures of the Supreme Council which specifically touched on its membership, publications, ritual, House of the Temple and library, foreign relations, and benevolent activity; and (3) the context of public issues in which the Grand Commanders and the Supreme Council took an interest, such as church and state matters, public education, "Americanism," civil rights, and, at the close of the decade, the possibility of a Roman Catholic president of the United States.

■ ■ ■

At the end of October 1952, Thomas J. Harkins and his wife, "Miss" Roxy (née Seevers of Oceola, Missouri), left their quarters in Washington, D.C., and returned to their home in Asheville, North Carolina, to be there for election day. Before departing, Harkins was informed by the Supreme Council of England and Wales that he had been unanimously elected an honorary member of that council, first among several similar honors he would receive the rest of the year and next. The Supreme Councils of Scotland, the Philippines, France, Canada, and the Northern Masonic Jurisdiction accorded him membership privileges, *honoris causa*.[5] Here was a man stepping in to fill the large shoes of his globe-trotting predecessor and old friend, John H. Cowles. Harkins, in contrast to Cowles, was perhaps happiest in his Blue Ridge hometown in the western piedmont of the Carolinas, for the attraction of Asheville is also explicable, perhaps subliminally, as the literary landmark in which Thomas Wolfe's American classic, *Look Homeward Angel*, was set. Cowles thrived on travel abroad, while Harkins, conversely, was a contented "small town lawyer, who in the big city of Washington was probably a little lost."[6]

Harkins came to be noted for his self-effacing manner, which his one-room log-cabin roots reflected. When he was called to assume leadership of the Supreme Council, because John H. Cowles had become enfeebled and incapacitated, Harkins, out of his sense of decency, refused to occupy the Grand Commander's office. Rather, he conducted all necessary business from more modest accommodations in the House of the Temple, an unpresumptuous, yet courtly, gesture long remembered.[7] It was not surprising, therefore, that Harkins preferred Asheville to London and Paris.

Born January 15, 1879, in Buncombe County, North Carolina, Thomas Joshua Harkins was the son of Herschel S. and Sarah Jane Jones Harkins. His ancestors were among the first settlers in western North Carolina. As a boy he was educated in the public schools of the resort town of Asheville, where the prominent George W. Vanderbilt estate, Biltmore, was also situated. Unlike Cowles, Harkins did not participate in the Spanish American War, though he was of the age to be eligible for military service. Instead, he studied law at the University of North Carolina, which he attended between 1897 and 1901.

Moving to Oklahoma after his university training, Harkins was admitted to the bar there in 1901 and began a law practice in Weatherford. Before returning to his native state in 1907, he was also engaged in the banking business. Now twenty-eight years old, he settled down in Asheville where he established his law career as a partner of the firm Harkins, Van Winkle, and Walton. Before leaving Weatherford, however, Harkins became acquainted with Freemasonry and was initiated, passed, and raised in Western Star Lodge No. 138. He demitted to Mt. Hermon Lodge No. 118, Asheville, North Carolina, in December 1911. Already in receipt of his Scottish Rite degrees, which he took in Guthrie, Oklahoma, in 1904, he later affiliated with the Asheville Scottish Rite bodies.[8]

Not long after his return to North Carolina, Harkins became active in the Republican Party, which was exceptional for someone in the Democratic "Solid South," though the Piedmont is noted for its contrarians (as there was much support for the Union in that region during the Civil War). He was a member of the Republican National Congressional Committee during an important phase of GOP history, 1912 through 1914, when the Progressives broke ranks with the Old Guard, choosing the Bull Moose as its emblem and running Theodore Roosevelt against the loyal Republican William Howard Taft and the Democrat Woodrow Wilson. Harkins attended the Republican National Convention of 1916 which nominated Charles Evans Hughes. Governor Hughes ran a close race against the incumbent, Wilson, whose victory in the popular vote was by less than 400,000 out of 18.3 million cast. The GOP of 1912 and 1916, with a few minor scene changes, provided a near duplicate script for the Republicans of 1952. Even the family name of one of the candidates, Taft, could be recycled from 1912.

In 1912, the first year in which presidential primaries really mattered, boat-rocking, young progressive Republicans supporting former president Theodore Roosevelt had shaken the party's Old Guard under the judicious William Howard Taft. That split cost them the election. The party drama of 1952, with General Dwight D. Eisenhower competing against Senator Robert A. Taft, had parallel dynamics, except that the Republicans had been out of the White House for twenty years. Eisenhower succeeded not merely because of his wartime reputation, but because he sagely out-politicked his party rival by exposing the leadership of the Taft "machine" as overweight, rumpled, cigar-smoking hacks. Only Eisenhower (or Omar Bradley) could get away with the line that he had spent his entire career leading young people, and that it was time for fresh blood to infuse the party. By comparison, coming from Generals Patton or MacArthur, whose military careers most resemble Eisenhower's, the assertion about being a youth leader would have sounded absurd.[9]

The Democrats in 1952 nominated the governor of Illinois, Adlai E. Stevenson, "whose native Corn Belt accent was heavily overlaid with the tones of Choate and Princeton." Stevenson's grandfather and namesake was a distinguished Mason. Stevenson, a brilliant orator, deplored "the increasing centralization of power over our lives in Washington" and proposed a renewed emphasis on local government, foreshadowing the themes of Barry Goldwater and Ronald Reagan. Stevenson, using a conservative voice, said, "The states are dikes which we can build more strongly against the flood water sweeping toward the District of Columbia." The difficulty for a Democratic candidate who intones the conservative song—as two sacrificial lambs of national elections both learned, Alton Parker in 1904 and John W. Davis in 1924—is that Republicans usually sing it better.[10]

Even though Eisenhower won the general election in a landslide, Stevenson drew more votes than Truman had in 1948—in fact, more votes than any previous winning candidate, except FDR. Later in the fifties, the veteran NBC news anchor Chet Huntley commented on such contests as the 1952 presidential election as demonstrating that a conservative is one who uses the clichés of the 1920s as principles, while a liberal uses the principles of the 1930s as clichés.[11]

When Thomas J. Harkins cast his vote for Eisenhower in 1952, it was *outside* the nation's capital, perhaps even an implicit vote "opposing" much of what Washington had grown to symbolize. Harkins's Masonic and professional careers, after all, developed in a pastoral milieu where principles and clichés are perhaps less interchangeable. By all accounts, Harkins was "a prince of gentlemen," who was "never a neutral" in his preferences, but did not find the public life of Washington, in which Cowles thrived from Wilson to Truman, especially appealing. While Harkins would live to near ninety, he was in 1952 a seventy-three-year-old man set in his habits, in a strange city, away from a comfortable, familiar home.[12]

In North Carolina, where from 1922 to 1926 he was special assistant to the U.S. attorney, Harkins was an esteemed public servant. He became U.S. attorney for the Western District of North Carolina in 1927, in which office he served until 1931 when he was made special assistant to the attorney general of the United States. Meanwhile, he was active in the American Bar Association, North Carolina State Bar, and served a term as president of the Buncombe County Bar Association. In 1945 Harkins received the honorary degree of Doctor of Laws from Cumberland University in Lebanon, Tennessee. Later that year Cowles had conferred upon him the honorary degree of Doctor of Letters, an occasion at which Harkins gave the address (a long oratorical tribute to Cowles!).

During this phase of his legal career, Judge Harkins also pursued a course of Masonic service. He was elected Worshipful Master of Mt. Hermon Lodge No. 118 of Asheville in 1926. On April 17, 1940, he was elected Grand Master of Masons in North Carolina. Even before attaining these high Masonic offices in North Carolina, Harkins was honored with the rank and decoration of Knight Commander of the Court of Honor in 1911, coroneted an Inspector General Honorary of the thirty-third degree in 1915, appointed Deputy of the Supreme Council in North Carolina in 1918, and crowned an Active Member of the Supreme Council on October 22, 1921.[13]

From 1921 to 1952 Harkins was regarded as "the work horse of the Supreme Council." It was felt by colleagues of the Supreme Council that "no other member of our Council contributed so much" toward the long success of Grand Commander Cowles. Harkins occupied several stations in the Supreme Council, including Lieutenant Grand Commander, before succeeding Cowles on October 6, 1952. Throughout the years of the Cowles commandership, Harkins was often "assisting in the solution of many knotty problems and giving freely of his time and rich talents to smooth the path" for Cowles.[14]

C. Fred Kleinknecht Jr. remembers Harkins as "a tall, dignified and eloquent speaker who could give a first-rate talk."[15] Years of appearing in courts, before juries and a variety of audiences, prepared Harkins for the kinds of Masonic occasions to which he easily lent dignity and presence. In his speech at Cumberland University in 1945, he praised his friend, Cowles, honoring him that day in words like those of Cassius remembering Caesar. He gently chided Cowles for his meticulous accuracy and impeccable, intimidating memory. Cowles, according to Harkins, was "always so eternally right in his facts that it [was] a source of exasperation, friendly of course, to his close associates." Harkins told the audience that, hence, this group of intimates was "always on the alert to catch him in error." After many years of "watchful waiting," Harkins announced, "I finally snared him."

Cowles begrudgingly was forced to admit that he was wrong. After some lengthy exchange of correspondence, Cowles finally wrote Harkins, "Well, I will have to admit that you are right, and that I am wrong, as you usually are." Harkins drew laughter with his story, but added that while Cowles had harrumphed to close the argument, for Harkins's part he never inquired "into its intended purport," for to do so might have confirmed his worst suspicions that Cowles was sometimes jealous and petty.

Light-hearted anecdotes, however, are revealing. First, they demonstrate the warmth between two old friends. Second, they tell one as much about the narrator as they tell about the subject of the story. Harkins, in this instance, was self-deprecating, really laughing at himself more than teasing Cowles.[16]

The speech at Cumberland University was useful, too, not only for its portrait of Cowles, but in what the speaker, Harkins, thought about himself. What Harkins admired in Cowles, he also, of necessity, must have believed to be important for himself. In several instances one could extract from the speech Harkins's own central values and character. He appreciated, for example, an independent mind "so that in the last analysis one is, and . . . must be, the architect of his own philosophy." Further, Harkins declared that "where a principle is involved, expediency and compromise have no place and are not even recognized as possibilities." He raised to the level of conviction "the inherent righteousness of human nature and limitless enthusiasm for the cause of human rights, for the dignity of the individual and the sovereignty of the peoples." Harkins lifted up to his college audience the value of hard work, long days, physical endurance, and the virtue of punctuality. To both Cowles and Harkins it was "almost a mortal sin to be late for an engagement if it [was] humanly possible to meet it."[17]

. . .

When Harkins assumed the office of Sovereign Grand Commander in 1952, the Lodge of Perfection membership, that is, the number of Scottish Rite initiates throughout the Southern Jurisdiction, had increased substantially from the previous year. With membership in excess of 400,000, Harkins's biggest concern with such rapid growth was the discrepancy between the number initiated and those who had achieved the thirty-second degree. He recommended that the Inspectors General and Deputies work out an appropriate remedy.[18] The membership statistics two years later, however, showed a similar pattern, but with higher totals. The Secretary General reported net gains in excess of 30,000 in a membership base that stood at nearly 437,000 from the 198 Lodges of Perfection. The gap between those initiated and those entering the councils of Kadosh and the consistories was appearing to close, but, most significantly, the newest Scottish Rite Masons were advancing through the degrees at a much increased rate.[19]

Meanwhile, after careful consideration, dues and fees for 1952 and 1953 remained at the Depression rate. Before the Depression, the per capita tax had been $1.25 per member in the four Scottish Rite bodies, but was reduced to $1.00, where the Committee on Finance, untroubled about revenue, given the membership growth, advised it should stay.[20] The internal business administration of the Supreme Council continued to operate smoothly, due in no small way to the continuity represented in C. F. Kleinknecht Sr., and his son, C. Fred Kleinknecht Jr. Dr. Claud F. Young, Grand Secretary General, noted the indispensability of the Kleinknecht family team—the son for his "pleasant and efficient" style and the father for "his wonderful ability and knowledge of the affairs of the Order and the management of this office."[21]

Scottish Rite policy under Harkins showed no deviation from the strict traditionalist preferences of Cowles. Harkins was adamantly opposed, for instance, to permitting any adumbration to the fourteenth degree ring. Apparently, jewelers were advertising in Masonic publications the possibility of modifying the simple ring with other symbols. Harkins also declared that the Maundy Thursday and Easter ceremonies conducted by the Rose Croix chapters could not be opened to the public and that only Rose Croix members were allowed to attend. In keeping with his firm Masonic sensibilities, Harkins, furthermore, ruled in favor of observing proficiency requirements for the third degree in blue lodge before a Scottish Rite petition could be filed. A Deputy of the Supreme Council, perhaps in a well-intentioned strategy for increasing membership, had considered taking exception to the Grand Lodge requirement. Harkins, who was largely responsible for a ten-fold expansion of Scottish Rite Masons in North Carolina (from 1,600 to 16,000), refused to take membership shortcuts.[22]

One of the signal accomplishments in the brief period of Harkins's leadership was the relaxation of tension between the Northern and Southern Jurisdictions. Members of the Committee on Visitations attended sessions of the Northern Masonic Jurisdiction in Chicago, taking delight in Dr. Melvin Johnson's warm greeting, which complimented the Southern Jurisdiction's Supreme Council by referring to it as the Mother Council of the World, a concession that would have been unnatural ten years before. The Southern Jurisdiction's Committee on Visitations in 1953 reported "that the time is appropriate for a full extension of fraternal relations between the two jurisdictions." The falling out between the American jurisdictions was, additionally, on the way to being healed when Grand Commander Johnson retired at the end of 1953. With the election of George E. Bushnell as Grand Commander of the Northern Masonic Jurisdiction, Harkins looked forward to the bright prospect of an end to the feud that had turned personal between Johnson and Cowles.[23]

Small changes came, as well, within the Supreme Council's operations, particularly in the area of publications. Harkins concluded that to sustain the quality of the *Scottish Rite News Bulletin* and, simultaneously, to save expense, the publication's format needed to be reduced. The editorial work of the *News Bulletin* and *The New Age* magazine had been carried on diligently by Elmer E. Rogers, Samuel Woodbridge, who worked under Rogers, and Norman S. Meese. Rogers had been with the Scottish Rite for more than twenty-eight years. Trained as a lawyer and having served for some years in various legal departments of government agencies and having acquired the Scottish Rite degrees in 1926, he was brought in by Grand Commander Cowles and became, in effect, Cowles's "right hand." By 1954, at the age of seventy-nine, Rogers was ready to retire. Norman Meese, sixty-five years old at the time, was appointed to replace the indefatigable Rogers.[24]

The New Age immediately had a "new look" proposed for it. The Committee on Publications, with Meese's concurrence, recommended a format change, making the magazine pocket-sized on the order of *Reader's Digest* or Norman Vincent Peale's *Guideposts*. Forty years later that modest, hallmark innovation, still in place, would make it a publication regarded as distinctive and classic.[25]

The House of the Temple, approximately forty years old, lost one of its most faithful caretakers with the death of William C. Corbett in the winter of 1953. Shortly after completion of the House of the Temple, Corbett became its superintendent. During its construction Corbett had worked as a building foreman for his stepfather, one of the project's subcontractors. Having retired shortly before his death, Corbett, according to Grand Commander Harkins, "was a mechanical genius and had the responsibility of keeping in order all of the various and sundry items of machinery, the mechanical and lighting devices, the properties and the whole premises."[26]

As the temple guard changed, fresh ideas for the building's improvement issued forth. Harkins himself proposed that an entrance be created in the rear of the House of the Temple instead of coming up the front steps, which in the opinion of Secretary General Claud F. Young was the best idea that had been expressed since the temple was built. At that time it was also suggested that the library and offices be air-conditioned and that consideration should be given to building a suitable auditorium and an extension of the library in the space east of the House of the Temple. The White House and Capitol had been air-conditioned since 1930, and in 1953, out of necessity, Washington was reported to have more air-conditioning per capita than any other city in the nation. Many federal government buildings were not able to stay cool in the "tropical" heat until 1960, and only 56 percent of the homes in metropolitan Washington were air-conditioned in 1966. At the House of the Temple the rear access and the air-conditioning system would soon materialize, but the forward thinking plans for expanding the building's capacity would wait in protracted deferment another forty years.[27]

The library, nevertheless, expanded in terms other than its physical dimensions. The capable librarian Ray Baker Harris, in his position since 1939, was joined by Inge Baum, who was transferred from the Secretary General's office around 1953. Her efficiency, intelligence, and ability to handle a large volume of routine work was noted from the start of her service in the library, where she worked lovingly for forty years. She became a certified appraiser of antiquities and rare books, performing an invaluable service throughout her career. Harris spoke enthusiastically about his ultimate successor, saying that until Mrs. Baum arrived in his department, the library had employed two assistants.

The library also grew in quality because of its important acquisitions. There are few letters which survive, for instance, from the hand of George Washington referring to his

Masonic association. Some speculate that members of the Washington family, presumably acting on what they thought was the best interest of Washington's reputation, destroyed his Masonic correspondence during the height of Anti-Masonic insurgency during the 1830s. Harris was, therefore, delighted in procuring "an original retained copy, in the handwriting of George Washington, of a letter written by him to the Editor of *The Sentimental and Masonic Magazine*, Dublin, dated in 1795."[28]

The letter from President Washington originated in Philadelphia on July 10, 1795, and acknowledged complimentary copies of an Irish Masonic publication put out by William John Jones, its proprietor. He wrote, "I have been favored with your note of the 23d Jan'y accompanied by five vols of the Sentimental & Masonic Magazine. For this mark of your obliging attention to me I entreat you to accept my best thanks. I shall, I am persuaded, find much pleasure in reading them whenever circumstances will afford me more leisure than I at present have for gratification of this sort."[29]

The library also possesses in its rare manuscript holdings another Masonic letter from Washington. Though undated and perhaps in the hand of a personal secretary during his presidency, it is signed authentically by Washington himself. This letter came as part of a gift of manuscripts from Pauline L. Mackey of Washington, D.C.; she was the great granddaughter of the celebrated Masonic authority, Albert Gallatin Mackey. In this letter to the Grand Lodge of Georgia, President Washington wrote in connection with his national tour of the South,

> I am obliged by your congratulations on my arrival in this city—and I am highly indebted to your favorable opinions. Every circumstance concurs to render my stay in Savannah agreeable, and it is cause of regret to me that it must be so short.
>
> My best wishes are offered for the welfare of the fraternity, and for your particular happiness.[30]

Yet another valuable eighteenth-century Masonic document was obtained for the library by Ray Baker Harris when he purchased a rare Benjamin Franklin imprint, "one of four known surviving copies." All four copies were in the possession of libraries, so the opportunity to find another one for sale seemed unlikely. The title of the imprint is "A Sermon Preached in Christ-Church, Philadelphia; before the Provincial Grand Master and General Communication of Free and Accepted Masons. On Tuesday the 24th of June, 1755, being the Grand Anniversary of St. John the Baptist, By William Smith, M.A. Provost of the College and Academy of Philadelphia."

William Smith was a well-known minister and Mason in colonial America. The library's copy of the sermon includes a list of prominent Masons who were present when it was delivered, including Franklin and his son. With this rare document, the Library of the Supreme Council has one of the most comprehensive collections of colonial American Masonic imprints in existence.[31]

■ ■ ■

Scottish Rite Freemasons presented a vibrant component of international relations within the fraternity. Naturally, the Supreme Council of the Southern Jurisdiction, as "the Mother Council of the World," had been criticized, at times, for referring to itself in exalted nomenclature and "had been accused of using this title to magnify its importance and power." Harkins understood the delicacy of these feelings, making it emphatically clear in his *Allocution* of 1955 that the Supreme Council did not feel superior to any other Supreme Council in the world, but, he added, "[W]e take pride in the fact that this Supreme Council was the first to be organized in the world." He carefully outlined his position, "[W]e disdain any thought that this fact entitles us to special consideration or clothes us with any special powers."[32]

Harkins promised that no inadvertent offense would occur at the international level. He was an eager participant with Luther A. Smith in the Conference of English-speaking Supreme Councils held on August 15 through 18, 1954, at the Seignory Club in the Province of Quebec, Canada. The irony of meeting in a major Francophone region seemed lost on the conferees. Harkins had been cautious about the usefulness of international conferences of Supreme Councils, expressing hesitancy at Swiss Grand Commander Paul Collet's proposal to meet. In time he agreed, however, to lend his support to such efforts, accepting the invitation to attend the International Supreme Council meeting in Havana, Cuba, in April 1956. This conference, like the United Nations General Assembly, was equipped with headphones to permit simultaneous translation of the proceedings.[33]

Harkins honored the Scottish Rite tradition of sending generous sums of money abroad for disaster relief. In February 1953 the southeast coast of England and the Netherlands were hit by storm and flood, a hardship to which the Grand Commander responded promptly. Other elements of assistance in foreign relations worth remembering include recognizing the Grand Lodge of Israel as "regular." The Grand Commander worried about Masonic conditions in China and Italy, realizing shrewdly that there was little he could personally influence in either place. About China, he indicated from a report he received that "the Chinese authorities have placed no restrictions against Masonry, but with a lack of transportation, the fact that it is unwise to be on the streets after dark, plus the fact that, as with any type of meeting where a group of people assemble, the police or soldiers are apt to come in to see what is going on, the holding of Masonic meetings has not been considered prudent."[34]

The situation in Italy since the end of World War II in 1945 was judged to be reprehensible for its disharmony. At one time the contending Masonic factions in Italy, both in the Symbolic Grand Lodges and Supreme Councils, numbered between twelve and sixteen; but by the early fifties this had been reduced to four major competing groups. Harkins summarized the four parties in conflict as systematically as one could:

> (1) The group known as the Moroli group. This group has been recognized by the Southern Supreme Council. (2) The Piazza del Gesu group. This group is presided over by Sovereign

Grand Commander Dr. Ermando Gatto, head of the School of Surgery at Rome University. (3) The Palazzo Giustiniani group. The group has been recognized by the Northern Supreme Council. (4) The Labriolo group. I believe that neither the Piazza del Gesu group nor the Labriolo group has been recognized by any regular Supreme Council.[35]

The complexity of the Italian Masons was no more clear or closer to resolution forty years after Harkins's fretful observation. While he was indifferent to working for the accomplishment of some reconciliation, he believed the best policy was to leave the Italian Masons alone as "they seem to resent efforts or help from the outside."[36]

. . .

Benevolent activities within Scottish Rite orients engendered steadfast heedfulness throughout the Southern Jurisdiction. The Scottish Rite dormitory for women, established back in 1922, at the University of Texas in Austin was able to accommodate 340 residents on a seven-acre tract that was wooded and landscaped. Also the Texas Scottish Rite Hospital for Crippled Children had operated in Dallas for almost thirty years. In an average year, the hospital admitted, treated, and rehabilitated about 550 children, most of whom, in the early fifties, were still polio patients. The older Scottish Rite Hospital for children in Decatur, Georgia, also flourished. In St. Louis, the Scottish Rite Endowment, Philanthropic, and Educational Foundation, run by the local Missouri bodies from total assets of nearly a quarter million dollars, supported the important work of deaf education, buying equipment for the Gallaudet School for the Deaf and providing scholarships at the Central Institute for the Deaf.[37]

Taking its cue from these varied, worthwhile local charitable programs, the Supreme Council unanimously adopted a resolution in 1953 to establish the Scottish Rite Foundation for benevolent and educational purposes. By 1955 the Scottish Rite Foundation was incorporated in the state of Maryland, with the initial gift of $50,000 coming from the Supreme Council, although it had appropriated $100,000 at the time of the resolution. Five trustees were elected to direct the new foundation, the president being Grand Commander Harkins. Luther A. Smith was vice president, Claud F. Young, secretary, and William E. Schooley, treasurer. Robert V. Smith of the Washington law firm Ristig and Smith gave legal advice and service in connection with the foundation. This was perhaps the greatest achievement of the Harkins administration.[38]

All over America the Scottish Rite received acclaim for its community service. The Scottish Rite Hospital for Crippled Children in Decatur, Georgia, celebrated its fortieth anniversary in 1955. Scottish Rite Masons in Tacoma, Washington, operated a successful DeMolay Boys' Camp.[39] Probably the foremost innovation of Scottish Rite charity in this era originated in Colorado, where the bodies organized to begin work on treating aphasia among children. The Supreme Council's interest in childhood learning dysfunctions, particularly aphasia, began sometime around 1953 when Grand Commander Harkins appointed a special committee, of which Henry C. Clausen served as chairman, to consider possible directions for the Scottish Rite Foundation to aim its energy. At the 1955 biennium, the Colorado project was presented in a compelling narration displaying color photographs of the work being conducted with brain-injured children.

Aphasia, as the Supreme Council learned, typically is caused by an injury to areas of the brain that control and govern speech and process ideas. Among several possible causes of aphasia are shock, oxygen deficiency at birth, brain fever, or the improper use of drugs or instruments at the time of birth.[40] The development of this program over the next forty years would parallel other major Masonic charities, such as the internationally famed Shriners' Crippled Children Hospitals and Burns Institutes. By 1994 there would be 112 Children's Language Disorders Centers nationwide, a monumental feat started in the Harkins era.

■ ■ ■

Diverse public issues of the day caught the attention of the Supreme Council in assorted ways, both obliquely and directly. Wanting to avoid divisiveness, but not sacrifice conviction, Harkins found no objections to discussions in Scottish Rite bodies regarding freedom of conscience and religion, despite the traditional Masonic prohibition against political or religious debate. He offered a middle ground in the hopes that members could "discuss dispassionately in Lodge . . . the ideals set forth in the Constitution of the United States with its amendments." If Harkins seemed naive on such a possibility, since the U.S. Supreme Court itself rarely reached perfect consensus on the ideals of the Constitution, he tried to err on the side of positive intentions.

One change which reflected the tenor of the times, particularly tied to the aftermath of the McCarthy anti-communist purge hearings on Capitol Hill, was the inclusion of two paragraphs to the Scottish Rite petition for the twenty-nine higher degrees of Masonry. The Supreme Council announced as its fundamental principles "the inculcation of patriotism, respect for law and order and undying loyalty to the Constitution of the United States; the entire separation of Church and State and opposition to every attempt to appropriate public monies—federal, state or local—directly or indirectly, for the support of sectarian or private institutions." The petitioner was asked to endorse these statements and to indicate if he had "ever held or expressed opinions contrary to the foregoing or been affiliated with any organization which has." A similar "loyalty" addendum was already incorporated in the standard U.S. Civil Service (171) personnel application.

At the invitation of President Eisenhower, Harkins attended the White House Conference on Education that was planned to consider the needs of American public schools. Out of the conference came a landmark rededication to meet higher standards for educating the post-war "baby boom" generation. The Supreme Council, however, with Harkins assenting, consistently opposed federal funds for education, a position that fell out of step with national policy development. It was not always clear what motivated such passionate objection to federal assistance in education—concern over money possibly being distributed to aid church-related schools, latent Jeffersonian purity, the wish to avoid too much centralized government, which nationalizing education symbolized, or strong "states' rights" preferences for deciding sensitive matters such as curriculum and desegregation. Urban Catholics, by the way, also opposed federal aid, as they did not want to compete with public schools infused with riches.

The Supreme Council's Committee on Education went so far as to say critically, "[I]t is difficult for one outside the [teaching] profession to understand all the solicitude evidenced about teachers' compensation." What, one may later wonder, was so difficult about understanding the economic relationship between quality and salary? The committee thought the growing encouragement of teachers to earn Master's degrees by offering economic incentives, such as pay raises, was unnecessary when most teachers who were "employed in country school districts" were present in the classroom "only for the short time that usually elapses until marriage beckons."[41] From this statement, it would appear that the committee was not especially conversant about the operation and increased demands of American public education. Although the committee reflected at some level "the national distaste for intellect" (the memorable and biting words of Richard Hofstadter), the fact is that once federal aid began, the disparity in teacher salaries, given the amount of training and certification required, remained an issue down to the 1990s.

$$\bullet \quad \bullet \quad \bullet$$

On October 21, 1955, Sovereign Grand Commander Thomas J. Harkins announced, due to the marked deterioration of his vision, his immediate resignation from office. The physicians with whom he consulted could not offer the promise of any effective remedy. In view of competent medical advice and in the interest of the Supreme Council's welfare, he thought it best to step aside.[42] He was so visually impaired that C. Fred Kleinknecht Jr. recalled one morning being seated at his desk as the Grand Commander breezed by. Kleinknecht was greeted with the friendly salutation, "Good morning, Mrs. Bell."[43]

The brief tenure of Harkins as Grand Commander is best viewed as a symbolic bridge within an organization that, from all appearances, also reflected very accurately the larger social transitions of America. His short time at the top of the Southern Jurisdiction spanned the divide between the era shaped by the Depression, ending with a world war, and the era of an acute post-war appetite for stability. The early fifties converged policy and mood simultaneously as a global defensive strategy of "war" without the heat of battle and the close-to-home liberating penchant for an affordable convertible coupe with streamlined chrome accents and recessed bumpers.

Harkins's self-effacing personality may be marked down as part of a summary of accomplishments as Grand Commander. He did not have the confidently embellished ego of John Henry Cowles and, therefore, was a calming influence during the period that began as a new epoch of Freemasonry, the fifties. Several tangible achievements, however, place Harkins more prominently in Scottish Rite history. He oversaw a rapid increase in membership, deciding to hold the traditional line on standards and fees. He encouraged better relations with the Northern Masonic Jurisdiction, putting aside the nagging differences that had built up for more than a quarter century. Harkins was partly responsible for the fresh reformatting of *The New Age* magazine into the popular pocketbook size that would remain unchanged for more than forty years. Modifications to the House of the Temple, such as a back entrance with an elevator and air-conditioning, were proposals coming directly from the Grand Commander. But perhaps foremost of his attainments while in office was the establishment of the Scottish Rite Foundation and the beginning of the first national programs for the treatment of children with learning and language disabilities, particularly children who suffered from aphasia.

Before Thomas J. Harkins died thirteen years later in Asheville, North Carolina, on November 22, 1968, he witnessed with appreciation most of his successor's accomplishments, which his own brief commandership had indeed helped to foster. Given his failing eyes, the poetic tribute paid by the Supreme Council at the end of his life seemed a choice image, "Passing out of the shadows into a purer light, / Stepping behind the curtain, getting a clearer sight."[44]

• • •

All was calm in America during the summer of 1955. The national recession of the previous year was disappearing; the economic woes of 1957 were not yet on the horizon; Elvis Presley's first hit song, "Heartbreak Hotel," was a year off. Elections were not on the fall calendar, so political campaigns were dormant. The career of Senator Joseph McCarthy, whose televised hearings investigating alleged subversion in the U.S. Army had riveted the country only a year earlier, was ending in dissipation. Congress had adjourned until the fall. The president, just back from a successful summit conference in Europe, planned a fishing trip in Colorado.

At dawn on a September morning in the Rocky Mountains the president, rising with the sun, fixed himself a hearty breakfast of griddle cakes, fried mush, sausage, and bacon. Then after a couple of hours at his desk, Eisenhower played a round of golf at Denver's Cherry Hill Country Club. After a hasty hamburger, trimmed with raw onions, he then played another nine holes. As he finished the twenty-sixth hole of the day, he felt the slight discomfort of what he thought to be indigestion. Returning to his mother-in-law's house, he sat in front of an easel, painting from a pallet of oils, had a leisurely evening, and went to bed at ten o'clock. Around 2:30 the next morning, the First Lady, realizing he seemed unusually agitated in his sleep, summoned the president's personal physician who diagnosed at once a coronary infarction.

The president was a lucky man and so was the nation. Historians wonder about this moment, asking, hypothetically, What if the heart attack occurred a few months earlier, when China and the United States seemed intensely belligerent with each other, or a year later when the world witnessed the Hungarian revolt and the Suez crisis? Paul A.

Carter reflected on the charmed timing of events: "If the U.S. presidency *had* to be interrupted in the fifties, fortune picked the right moment."[45]

In the fall of 1955, Luther A. Smith, Sovereign Grand Inspector General in Mississippi since 1937, was elected Sovereign Grand Commander to succeed Thomas J. Harkins. Only four years younger than Harkins, Smith would lead the Supreme Council, Southern Jurisdiction, through the remaining years of the decade and through all of the sixties. Born in Alpharetta, Georgia, on September 20, 1883, Smith was the son of a Methodist minister, which meant that the family moved every few years to a new parsonage, following his father's appointments. He was educated in the public schools of Georgia and attended Young Harris College for a year (1900–1901). In June 1904, he received a Ph.B. degree from Emory College, then in Oxford, Georgia. Five years later he earned the LL.B. degree from Vanderbilt University in Nashville, Tennessee.

For nearly a half century he practiced law in Hattiesburg, Mississippi, where he raised three children with his wife, Lorraine McInnis, a native of Hattiesburg. They would become grandparents nine times. Smith's law practice culminated in 1953 when he was appointed by the state governor as a judge of the Court of Chancery for the Tenth District of Mississippi. He was elected to that office without opposition in 1954 for a four year term, but resigned in October 1955 when elected Sovereign Grand Commander.

His life in Hattiesburg touched not only the legal community but banking and civic interests, too. He organized the Trust Department of the Hattiesburg Bank and Trust Company in 1918, and later founded the First Building and Loan Association of Hattiesburg. For a time he served as president of the Morgan Plan Bank Association of Hattiesburg. Smith was a charter member of the Kiwanis Club in his community, which also elected him chairman of the school board. Smith also served on the Board of Trustees of the State Teachers College (now Mississippi Southern College).

Smith was a deeply devoted Mason. He was raised in Inoccopola Lodge No. 310, Toccopola, Mississippi, in 1907. Smith's career touched nearly every possible Masonic affiliation. He received the thirty-second degree from the Meridian, Mississippi, consistory in 1920, was honored with the rank and decoration of Knight Commander of the Court of Honor in 1923, and was coroneted with the thirty-third degree in 1929.[46] Within several years of his election as Sovereign Grand Commander, Smith was designated an honorary member of the Supreme Councils of Brazil, Greece, France, Belgium, Colombia, Cuba, the Philippines, and Germany.[47]

Shortly after Smith became Grand Commander, he received a request from *Life* magazine to do an article on Freemasonry. He generally thought the proposed feature to be a good idea and offered *Life* his cooperation. Smith explained "that while Freemasonry did not seek publicity . . . the right of magazines and other periodicals to publish articles about it if they saw fit to do so" should be recognized and even used to possible advantage. Smith promised to furnish *Life* with "the facilities of our Library for doing research on Freemasonry if they proposed to do a dignified, scholarly, and worthwhile article."

The feature story appeared in the issue of October 8, 1956, and while Smith noted several minor errors, he was pleased that it was "generally creditable" to Freemasonry.[48]

In terms of "in-house" journalism, Norman S. Meese, Smith's principal aide in publishing *The New Age,* the Scottish Rite magazine printed without interruption since being brought into existence in June 1904, announced a long-planned new layout. Beginning in January 1956, the magazine was changed to the approximate size of five inches by seven inches, making it comparable to the popular, general-circulation, pocket-sized magazines, such as *T.V. Guide, Reader's Digest,* and *Guideposts.* Also the *Scottish Rite News Bulletin* was, at last, discontinued in August 1956 to hold down overall expenses and avoid redundancy, as all newsworthy items appeared monthly in *The New Age* anyway.[49]

Smith was eager to ensure that attractive, readable Scottish Rite publications circulate broadly. He stated his purposes in a familiar refrain: "We Masons should be more aggressive in proclaiming the ideals and teachings of our Fraternity . . . One of our faults is that many of us seem to be too self-satisfied and too complacent."[50] Smith proposed two remedies for what he perceived to be a major problem—that an up-to-date history of the Supreme Council be undertaken and that a Masonic news center be established.

By the spring of 1956, Smith had commissioned Ray Baker Harris, whom he thought to be most highly qualified, given his familiarity with the records, his competency as a writer, and his publishing experience, to prepare a history of the council. Harris's work yielded almost immediately the excellent volume *Eleven Men of Charleston* (1958). Based on Smith's recommendation, the Supreme Council appropriated $20,000 for the new history in 1957.[51]

The idea for organizing a Masonic news center, meanwhile, began to take hold, and plans for it were delineated by the Grand Commander. It was Smith's vision that a new Masonic organization, supported by all other Masonic bodies, should become the chief vehicle of disseminating information related to Masonry through newspapers, ads, radio, and television. Smith hosted the leaders of various Masonic groups in his office one Sunday afternoon in February 1959, achieving a consensus about the need for such a news agency. It would require substantial financial support and a suitable manager. Richard Amberg, a thirty-third degree Scottish Rite Mason and publisher of the *St. Louis Globe Democrat,* immediately endorsed the proposal. Unfortunately, after several trial balloons and much lip-service enthusiasm, Smith let go of the idea for lack of genuine commitment.[52]

The New Age remained the chief conduit of Scottish Rite communications. The Supreme Council in 1959 devoted an entire session to *The New Age,* exchanging thoughts on how to increase interest in the publication. Of note was the fact that the subscription rate of $1.50 per year, set in 1904, was unchanged right up to the session of 1959. One proposed change recommended that, if possible, the word "copyright" be taken out of the publication so that use of any portion of *The New Age* for other types of distribution would be encouraged, not embargoed. In July 1958 a staff change also transpired. With the retirement of Samuel Woodbridge, a vacancy occurred that allowed Grand Commander Smith to appoint forty-two-year-old Aemil Pouler, a member of St. John's Lodge No. 11 of the District of Columbia, to assist Norman S. Meese.

Meese recommended Pouler, a naturalized American citizen born in Istanbul, Turkey, because of his linguistic skills and publishing experience. Additionally, he had received his Scottish Rite degrees in Charleston, South Carolina. Academically, Pouler had degrees in theology and philosophy from Turkey, but he had moved to the United States soon thereafter to try the American way of life. Pouler labored diligently behind the scenes at the House of the Temple for a period of nearly thirty years, closing with his retirement in 1987. His son Christopher, ten years old at the time Pouler was brought on board, would later join the staff himself in managing multifarious elements of publishing the monthly journal.[53]

■ ■ ■

For nearly two months during the spring of 1958, Grand Commander Smith toured the Far East in behalf of the Supreme Council, a trip that included stops in Japan, Okinawa, Taiwan, Hong Kong, the Philippines, Guam, and Hawaii. The principal purpose of the trip, Smith advised the council, "was to revive our personal association with our brethren in the Orient and to thereby encourage them" in their progress. In Japan, the Grand Commander and Mrs. Smith enjoyed visiting "the beautiful estate and lovely home of Brother Ichiro Hatoyama, former Prime Minister of Japan and one of its first public officials to be initiated into Freemasonry."[54]

In Tokyo, Smith attended the anniversary banquet on April 26, 1958, to commemorate the seventy-fifth anniversary of the Scottish Rite bodies in Japan. Overall, Smith observed that the Japanese were "inclined to be conservative and cautious about joining organizations, and Freemasonry, having been a forbidden institution for them until the past twelve or fifteen years," will be slow, but sure to catch on. His presence, no doubt, helped to resolve differences between the Philippine and Japanese Grand Lodges, which, perhaps because he was there representing the prestige of American Masonry, occasioned official mutual recognition by both Grand Lodges.[55]

In Taiwan, he visited Chiang Kai-shek "and found him to be in good physical condition and full of hope and courage as to the future success of his great ambition to return to the mainland of his country." He and Mrs. Smith met with Madame Chiang Kai-shek at her home, where she was presented a $1,000 check to help the Huahsing Children's Home, an orphanage in Taipei.[56]

Because of the long itinerary of his Far Eastern trip and his many visitations to orients and valleys in the Southern Jurisdiction, the Grand Commander was unable to attend meetings with his European and South American counterparts who were sponsoring hemispheric conferences for the Supreme Councils. Further, Smith's heavy involvement in the late fifties with educational programs, including "Americanism" in the public schools, the whole nature of public education as it interfaced with the federal government, the expansion of the George Washington University Fellowships, and other university associations, precluded additional travel and international contact.[57]

. . .

Throughout much of the first half of the twentieth century, with the spreading impact of immigrant populations such as the Irish and Italians, American Protestants held a deep-seated bias against "Rome." Anti–Roman Catholic agitation was one expression of old-line Protestant frustration in an America which was becoming so religiously plural as to be recognized generally as "a triple melting pot" or a "salad bowl" of mixed, fresh ingredients. It did not help matters, of course, that a papal condemnation of Freemasonry in 1884, known as the encyclical *Humanum Genus*, was still a symbolic reference point in the tension between American Catholics and Protestants. In this document Pope Leo XIII claimed that "Masonry generates bad fruits mixed with great bitterness" and that "inebriated by its prosperous success, Masonry is insolent, and seems to have no more limits to its pertinacity" against the Church and civil governments. The Pope declared that "those who love the Catholic faith and their own salvation must be sure that they cannot give their names for any reason to the Masonic sect without sin."[58]

Scathingly hostile language from *Humanum Genus,* more than seventy years old, lost little of its bite, especially when European Freemasons were persecuted and killed in the Nazi Holocaust in a vivid expression of anti-Masonry, and more particularly, at a time when post-war American Protestant sensitivities were highly acute. A shift from a Protestant to a post-Protestant era in America, reasoned Winthrop Hudson, "is not to be explained solely in numerical terms." Before the breath-taking change which Pope John XXIII introduced with the Council of Vatican II, such hostile documents as *Humanum Genus* served Protestant purposes as polemical lightning rods. The worst Protestant assumptions spilled over into national politics by 1958 while the nation began contemplating, for the second time in American history, a Roman Catholic presidential candidate. The counterintuitive reality, however, expressed in the U.S. Census Bureau's study in 1958, was that two-thirds of all Americans claimed a Protestant identity, whereas only one fourth of the population thought of itself as Roman Catholic. And yet, the general perception about the actual balance of influence seemed to favor the view that Rome had some conspiratorial design on America, just as Protestant cultural hegemony appeared to suffer erosion.[59]

To further complicate matters the fifties brought to pass a new flurry of Supreme Court decisions around issues of church and state. Judicial activity in this First Amendment area exploded in the following decades, so that the establishment clause in the Bill of Rights, which lay virtually dormant for its first 150 years, became a regular source of litigation. These issues were all the more confusing in the late fifties as they were reviewed by many courts for the first time. Layers of meaning were being stripped from the surface of public interfaith associations. It may have been "one nation under God" by 1954, and Congress might open legislative sessions with prayers from its government paid chaplain, and the U.S. Supreme Court might allow its crier to begin each day proclaiming "God save the United States and this Honorable Court," but other signals being sent—for instance, religious expression in the public schools—suggested inconsistency. This highly charged atmosphere naturally invited the participation of Grand Commander Smith. But it is significant that even among Supreme Court Justices, some of whom were Masons (e.g., William O. Douglas, Hugo Black, and Potter Stewart), consensus about the propriety of the government's relation to religion was seldom achieved.

Prescriptive support of Protestants and Other Americans United for the Separation of Church and State (POAU) continued without question from the Scottish Rite.[60] Smith was also aggressive in defending Masonry from the residual effects of the bugbear treatise *Humanum Genus*. He endorsed the theory of Paul Blanshard that there existed a "Catholic plan for America." Smith made no secret of his antipathy to Catholicism, believing almost obsessively that Rome had infiltrated stealthily the American government: "Things in our government might have been quite different if 50 years ago the Masons of this Country had awakened to the necessity of seeing to it that the Government was supplied with eligible officials from among those who are dedicated to American principles of freedom, separation of church and state, etc. We have let the Roman Catholics fill up the vacancies from their School of Government at Georgetown University. However, we are mixing it with them now [through support of George Washington University], but we got into that field of endeavor pretty late."[61]

Smith's strong emotions were even expressed to a former Catholic priest who had been, in Smith's mind, "incarcerated by the Roman Catholic Church" but was now "released to breathe the fresh air of freedom, and to enjoy the thrill of participating in and contributing to the American way of life."[62]

Smith, to his credit, tried to be consistently principled, even though his conclusions about American Catholics now seem myopic, impractical, and undesirable. The Masonic ranks in America were joined, in time, by many devout Roman Catholics who silently defied the order of their church, just as many Catholics conspicuously practiced artificial birth control against the Pope's will. In any case, as he was wary of "Catholic designs" on power, Smith fervently opposed federal aid of any kind to Protestant institutions, seeing it as breaching the wall of separation. He criticized harshly the Methodist Church, for instance, which voiced no objection to Emory University, a Methodist institution in Atlanta, Georgia, "for accepting public property and funds in aid of their sectarian operations." He also demurred against a Methodist hospital in Oak Ridge, Tennessee, for receiving from the federal government land and a building valued at $4 million. It is notable that Smith was a birthright Methodist himself and an Emory alumnus.[63]

One programmatic response to the restless mood of social transition which America of the late 1950s experienced was Smith's plan for an "Americanism" and education initiative sponsored by the Scottish Rite. Smith approached Virgil M. Rogers, dean of the School of Education at Syracuse University, on the matter, in the hopes of recruiting him to lead the project. Rogers declined the job offer but supported the idea, suggesting that such a program was needed to "promote broader understanding and deeper appreciation of the American heritage which the Founding Fathers vouchsafed to the nation's citizens through the Constitution and the Bill of Rights." Rogers also cautioned the Grand Commander with a wise word of warning: "One of the biggest problems in the inception of any such plan will be the need to avoid scrupulously the stigma attached to the many groups which have used the banner of *Americanism* to promote their own selfish aims. Every school administrator in the country has experienced some pressure at the hands of some of these, if only in the form of unsolicited periodicals delivered to him in the mails. Educators in the public schools are therefore on their guard against those who shout 'Americanism!' and 'Freedom!' and 'Founding Fathers!' and have learned to look carefully behind and under the slogans to discover what a given group is really after."[64]

With this admonition in mind, Smith's program was endorsed by the Supreme Council's Committee on Education and made ready for implementation. Not only was suitable literature to be developed and distributed but also the Americanism program planned to award annual scholarships "for the best theses or dissertations on Americanism and public schools by graduate students working for doctorate degrees in the field of education." The program, additionally, intended to sponsor and support an annual national observance of Public School Week.[65]

Smith aimed high with his Americanism program. He wanted the Scottish Rite to become an integral part of the national debate generated by Rudolf Flesch's bestselling critique of public education, *Why Johnny Can't Read* (1955). He solicited advice from the highest academic circles, hoping in his wide conversations to enlist a suitable director for the new education program. Smith learned that when Dwight D. Eisenhower was president of Columbia University, a citizenship project had been established under the supervision of William S. Vincent. Smith had Vincent come down to Washington two or three times to discuss the gaps in American civics and history instruction.

William R. Odell, a Stanford University professor of education and former superintendent of schools in Oakland, California, had initially accepted an employment offer tendered by Smith to fill the position of director of education of the Supreme Council. After a week of second thoughts, Odell informed Henry C. Clausen, Sovereign Grand Inspector General in California, that he had decided against taking the position. Finally, William E. Givens, who was also a former Oakland superintendent of schools, was appointed by the Grand Commander in March 1958 to be director of education. In little time, Givens produced and got to press *Our Public Schools*, "the Supreme Council's first major publication in support of the Sovereign Grand Commander's Program of Americanism."[66]

While Smith extended the Supreme Council's resources to the cause of public schools, he also maintained its selective support of higher education. In addition to the fellowships at the George Washington University, which increased from twenty-five awards in 1957 to fifty-two in 1959, Smith saw to it that Baylor University also was provided with a $10,000 donation to establish a new program named the J. M. Dawson Studies in Church and State, through which required courses for all Baylor students were to be developed. In similar manner, the American University in Washington, D.C., opened its fledgling School of International Service in September 1958 with the help of a $20,000 Scottish Rite contribution. Colonel William E. Schooley, General Treasurer of the Supreme Council, as a result of this financial support, became a trustee of the American University.[67]

Despite the vital commitment to higher education, Smith stood foursquare against the National Defense Education Act of 1958. Smith conducted a large correspondence with members of Congress, especially those with Masonic ties, submitting a brief that was predicated upon a supposed conflict over the separation of church and state. Congressman Robert C. Byrd of West Virginia, the future Senate majority leader and a devoted Scottish Rite Mason, wrote Smith an explanation that the bill provided scholarship assistance to individuals, not institutions, and, therefore, posed no such Constitutional problem as the Grand Commander had assumed.[68] The bill's ultimate success was largely determined by the way it was named. So long as the word "defense" was linked with the legislation, its opponents were at a seeming disadvantage, for who could find fault with an endeavor wrapped in the cloak of national security while there was the present danger of the Cold War?

Although Grand Commander Smith was on the losing side of congressional legislation, he remained undaunted. He could point proudly, after all, to the list of some 900 Scottish Rite Masons in the Southern Jurisdiction who were serving on public school boards of education or on boards of trustees of colleges and universities. Scottish Rite influence was even clearer when the Supreme Council was invited to the White House Conference on Children and Youth, held in the early spring of 1960.

■ ■ ■

Much of Smith's experience in the late fifties forecast the agenda for the second and remaining portion of his time in office, albeit a period radically at odds with "the American way of life," as the sixties turned up the volume on debate and conflict in every corner of American society. Before turning next to that difficult time, it is wise to remember that in the swirl of large, sometimes complicated public issues, in the strain of routine institutional responsibilities offset by the testing of traditions, dwell individual leaders with their values firmly and necessarily centered in personal faith. Luther A. Smith's even temper is explained, perhaps only in part, by what he earnestly volunteered in 1958 when proclaiming publicly his personal dependence on prayer as a source of strength in the clamor of working, thinking, and living in a time of strained nerves: "To me prayer is not a matter of asking God for favors but is the means by which I consciously feel His Presence in my life. He is the Spirit, the Power, and the Explanation of the Universe. . . . I open wide the windows of my soul and the Divine Light flows quietly in and I humbly thank God for the resulting confidence and courage that is mine. . . . When I fail or refuse to open the windows there is a definite loss and damage to my power of mind and efficiency; but when by voluntary act I open the window I guess that is prayer, and it is efficacious. God is always ready to come in when the way is open."[69]

CHAPTER XII

The Moon Above, Perplexity Below
1959–1969

Luther A. Smith

Before summer arrived in 1960, while both the Democrats and Republicans anticipated their nominating conventions, American national prestige smarted from some of its worst embarrassments since the Soviet Union launched the satellite *Sputnik* in 1957. In the fiery, testy diplomatic atmosphere centering on the future of Berlin as a Cold War flashpoint, Soviet Premier Nikita Khrushchev raised the temperature in January by boasting that he had the nuclear missiles capable of obliterating any country "off the face of the earth." Knowledgeable Americans perceived otherwise, or at least believed that the United States still preserved its strategic advantage in the nuclear arms race, but Khrushchev's bullying rhetoric aroused masses of the less informed.

Meanwhile, in May, just before a scheduled NATO–Warsaw Pact Summit Conference in Paris, the Russians shot down an American *U-2* high-altitude spy plane loaded with sophisticated cameras focused on Soviet military installations 1,200 miles inside the Soviet borders. To the bewilderment of the Eisenhower administration, the captured American pilot, Francis Gary Powers, was paraded in front of the world like a trophy. The Paris Summit proceeded, nevertheless, but the president had to endure Khrushchev's acrid censure about the spy flights. With his back up, Eisenhower refused to apologize, but left Paris feeling intensely dejected.

In June 1960, as the president prepared to embark for Japan, anti-American riots in Tokyo forced his counterpart and host to rescind the invitation indefinitely. Communist pressure, moreover, grew in the Middle East and Africa; the military situation was degenerating in Southeast Asia; and Fidel Castro, who met and informally debated Vice President Richard Nixon in the United States a year earlier, was advancing the Cuban Revolution into the Soviet orbit at full speed. Somewhat glum and morose, Americans generally came to the realization in the spring of 1960 that the positive thinking of the 1950s was, at certain unplumbed levels, yielding to a new temper, new time, and new players on the stage.[1]

The fifties were over.

■　■　■

In February 1960, seventy-six-year-old Sovereign Grand Commander Luther A. Smith stumbled over a rolled up carpet in the lobby of the Hotel Twenty-four Hundred in Washington, D.C., where he and his wife, Lorraine, had their apartment. The accident caused a shoulder dislocation, possibly a fracture, and other injuries. He was confined to the hospital and his apartment for two weeks. He remained unbowed and unbroken; a less determined person might have glimpsed defeat in such a traumatic setback. Smith, however, was a fighter.

The Grand Commander did not know it then, but more than his shoulder was dislocated, for so, too, were the times in which he now rededicated himself to defend his principles. Most men his age were setting down their burdens, pulling back from the pressure and contention of active careers to enjoy the quiescence of retirement. Soon after mending, Smith changed residences, moving from the Hotel Twenty-four Hundred to the Rittenhouse, a handsome new building overlooking the woods of Rock Creek Park, at 6101 Sixteenth Street, NW, just a few blocks south of the famous Walter Reed Army Medical Center. By all indications, the Smiths planned to stay in Washington on some permanent basis.[1]

Smith's chief preoccupation and main focus was the presidential election of 1960, not his sore shoulder. As a lifelong Mississippi Democrat, he had been deeply troubled by the prospect of a northern, Roman Catholic candidate running on his party's ticket. He aired some tenacious opinions through his private correspondence, and he also ventured to express them as the Grand Commander, using all the Scottish Rite communications available to his high office. While this involvement in seemingly partisan electoral politics was without precedent in the Supreme Council, and arguably un-Masonic, it is probably to Smith's credit that a passion for involvement still burned so hot—because it shows him to be part of his era, not living as an old man in the memories of the past. Emotions, of course, were stirred everywhere in America as the sixties began to form. Smith and his administration were, therefore, points of reference of larger shifts, struggles, and dislocations in American society.

The election of 1960 became a turning point in American political history, not unlike the landmark election of 1860. It attracted the highest voter turnout since 1908 (64%), and signaled the emergence of a charming, youthful, and witty leader who was later compared to the mythical heir of King Arthur's castle and mantle, the prince of romantic Camelot.

John Fitzgerald Kennedy seems seldom remembered for tangible contributions, but more as an extraordinary symbol of promise that hinted at great triumph tragically deferred. He was, however, a resourceful and superb politician who only gave hint of that talent when he came within a few votes of winning the nomination for vice president at the 1956 Democratic Convention. Until then he was regarded as something of a Washington matinee idol; he was the author of the Pulitzer Prize–winning book *Profiles in Courage,* a war hero, and twice blessed by being the son of a millionaire and the husband of a beautiful former debutante. In sum, it was generally thought that he dabbled in politics but did not take it seriously.

Senator Hubert Horatio Humphrey, a liberal Democrat from Minnesota, by contrast, compiled a legislative record in the fifties that next to Kennedy's was the difference between lightning and a lightning bug. Kennedy was discreetly silent on the whole subject of McCarthyism, and as late as 1957, he sided with the South on some peripheral issues pertaining to the civil rights bill passed that year. But in 1957 Kennedy began touring the nation, charming audiences, making friends, setting the stage for his run at the presidency. Smith saw it all coming before anything was officially announced. For him, and for many others at the time, the thought of a Roman Catholic in the White House was abhorrent.

By the fall of 1958, before Kennedy's massive reelection to the Senate, Smith registered his concern, but kept his counsel "personal and confidential." Writing to the governor of Mississippi, J. P. Colman, he expressed his grave doubts about "the apparent growth of sentiment favorable to nominating Senator John Kennedy as Democratic candidate for president. To me this would be the supreme insult. In the first place he is a man of very mediocre ability. I have been in Washington now for three years and I know what the judgment of public men is when they speak privately about him. His greatest asset seems to be that he is the son of a multi-millionaire Roman Catholic layman and the Catholic hierarchy has decided that he should be president, and if money and high pressure methods can achieve that goal, it will be done and if that should happen the [Catholic] hierarchy will run the presidency, because it is a known fact that he checks with his bishop on all major issues."[2]

Smith continued in the same vein, stressing that the Catholic Church ordered the integration of its schools in the South despite the objections of southern bishops. The *Brown v. the Board of Education* decision of the U.S. Supreme Court was, of course, already four years old, so that the parochial schools, though not required to do so, were complying with the spirit of the Constitution. Smith's overall assessment of Senator Kennedy as an indifferent legislator in the 1950s, however, was the mainstream view and has remained acceptable to historians. His hyperbolic suspicions of the Catholic hierarchy, while often common (and unspoken) throughout Protestant America at mid-century, distorted the perceived Catholic power base. There was nothing to fear, for the aggregate total of Protestants in America well exceeded the number of Catholics.

Smith was right, though, to assume that the issue of a candidate's religion mattered. There has not been, in fact, a serious presidential contender who was Catholic or Jewish from the election of 1960 to the mid-1990s on the grounds that the faith of a non-Protestant made him unelectable. Ironically, the one exception since 1960 was the election of the Southern Baptist Jimmy Carter in 1976. *Church and State* magazine correctly surmised that with Carter in the field "more religious and church-state related issues than any since 1960" were raised.[3] The trouble with Carter's faith was that it mattered to him unambiguously and deeply—a different problem than affiliation.

When John F. Kennedy received the Democratic nomination for the presidency, Grand Commander Smith, not surprisingly, "was greatly disappointed," blaming the results on "the most meticulous and cold blooded manner" of national machine politics. Smith astutely observed the hard and rough edges of high politics when he wrote, "[Kennedy] and his cohorts admittedly had been working at the job for four years and as President Truman said, he really had the Convention rigged in his behalf. It was very significant that the big Democratic city bosses and the Catholic Governors and Mayors all got on the bandwagon and in due time, as it has been planned, put him over."[4]

The stressed alliance between northern urban Democrats and southern rural Democrats (and black voters) was clearly demonstrated in Smith's assessment. And yet, what Smith failed to understand was that Kennedy's nomination was barely welcomed by the northern liberals, officially organized as Americans for Democratic Action (ADA). Only hostility for the Texan Lyndon Johnson, Kennedy's running mate, was greater than for Kennedy himself as the ADA issued a deliberately tepid endorsement after the convention.[5]

Smith had other reasons for opposing Kennedy's candidacy, having little to do with his noncontroversial congressional record or winsome, captivating style that some critics might have found too coolly detached. With a Kennedy presidency Smith automatically assumed that Vatican agents would be put in positions of power and influence in the government. On that hypothesis, he bluntly stated, "It poses a tremendous threat, and I am sure that we Masons will do our duty and exert to the utmost our influence against accomplishment of such a tragic result."[6]

Smith's views were already widely known by election day. In contemplating the likelihood that Senator Kennedy might secure the Democratic nomination through the primary process and win the general election, Smith published three conspicuous articles in *The New Age*. The titles indicate the vinegar with which they were penned: "An Atrocity Within Our Republic?" "Catholicism—Religion—the Presidency—Common Sense," and "The Ultimate in Catholic Arrogance." Although Smith had reservations about the Republican alternative, Richard Nixon, he adopted the view related to him by Nixon's Scottish Rite supporter, Congressman Otto E. Passman of Louisiana, who told him, "It is more important that Kennedy be defeated than it is to elect Nixon."[7] Smith himself went beyond considering "the lesser of two evils," using much stronger terms to describe the vehemence of his position. "We must," he said, "for the sake of our country and for the sake of the principles of our Freemasonry, do all in our power to defeat this menace."[8]

He was touching on a question that even the Democratic candidate and many American Catholic bishops conceded was appropriate. The inflammatory rhetoric, reminiscent of McCarthy's "red menace," was toned down, however, for the editorial Smith prepared for the November 1960 issue of *The New Age*. Boundaries of Masonic propriety, nevertheless, were crossed as Smith calmly put forward his argument:

> *The New Age* has pursued the policy in the presidential election campaign that the Supreme Council and many other nonpolitical organizations have followed—that of trying to point out to its readers and members some important and very pertinent facts regarding one of the great issues involved in it by reason of the fact that one of the candidates is a life-long and loyal member of the Roman Catholic Church. This candidate himself and his church have, during the past few years kept this fact before the people. However, when responsible citizens began to make serious inquiries about the implications involved in this candidate's relationship to the Roman Catholic Church, whose headquarters are in the Vatican in Rome and which is ruled over by the Pope, an Ecclesiastical and temporal aristocrat, there was a loud chorus of denunciation with bitter charges of intolerance and bigotry against any and all who dare question the eligibility of the candidate to fill the office of President. . . . Neither *The New Age* nor the Supreme Council engages in partisan politics. Their business is to teach and expound the truth and to uphold the great landmarks of the American Heritage of Freedom. . . . Our thanks and appreciation go to the thousands who have encouraged us with their plaudits for what we did for the better enlightenment and understanding of the question: "Why would it be unwise to elect a Roman Catholic President of the United States?"[9]

Al Smith, the Democratic nominee for president in 1928, was defeated handily by Herbert Hoover, not so much because Smith was Catholic, though religion was a factor, but probably because of other issues, such as his stand against prohibition. Al Smith did his best to avoid any serious discussion of Roman Catholicism, not only on grounds of political prudence but also out of his own lack of interest in Catholic doctrine. When confronted with the question of papal infallibility quoted to him from a nineteenth-century papal encyclical, Smith is reported to have responded with genuine befuddlement, "What the hell is an enkiklikal?"

Unlike Al Smith, who was reluctant to explain his faith, John F. Kennedy brought up the "religious issue" often. His forthright discussion of religion in the West Virginia primary of May 1960 disarmed his critics to the extent that in some improbable inversion of packaging candidates, a vote for Hubert Humphrey became a vote for intolerance and bigotry. Despite the absurdity of pinning such a label on Humphrey, Kennedy later spoke directly to his detractors in Texas, which went far to neutralize the impact of religion. In Houston Kennedy said in earnest,

I believe in an America where the separation of church and state is absolute—where no Catholic prelate would tell the President (should he be a Catholic) how to act and no Protestant minister would tell his parishioners for whom to vote. . . . I ask you . . . to judge me on the basis of fourteen years in Congress—on my declared stands against an ambassador to the Vatican, against unconstitutional aid to parochial schools, and against any boycott of public schools (which I attended myself). . . . I do not speak for my church on public matters—and the church does not speak for me. . . . But if this election is decided on the basis that 40,000,000 Americans lost their chance of being President on the day they were baptized, then it is the whole nation that will be the loser in the eyes of Catholics and non-Catholics around the world, in the eyes of history, and in the eyes of our own people.[10]

Smith's mind continued unchanged. After Kennedy's speech he wrote to a friend in Texas: "[A]lthough I have been a Democrat all of my life, I shall certainly not vote for the Democratic nominee this year for President. In my judgment it would be one of the most disastrous things that could happen to our Republic . . . [and] our American way of life. . . . [A] Catholic has a dual allegiance, and his allegiance to his church is, according to the Catholic teachings, permanent above all other allegiances."[11]

His views, in retrospect, may sound inflexible and cranky, but the issue drew the interest of many thoughtful, fair-minded people across the land, too. The Episcopal Bishop of California, James A. Pike, who had once been a law professor, gave the matter extensive treatment in his book *A Roman Catholic in the White House*. Pike politely said, "when it comes to the crucial question of the highest office in the nation, some of us can be reasonably concerned as to whether it is really possible for a Roman Catholic—when all the chips are down—to hold such genial views." Bishop Pike suggested the need to assess the "various types of informal ecclesiastical pressures" to which a Roman Catholic president would be subjected. In the end, Pike came "back to the basic question of trust. . . . A Roman Catholic for President? *It depends.* The asking of the question is not bigotry. It is the exercise of responsible citizenship."[12]

Smith's editorials in *The New Age*, had they taken the reserved tone of Bishop Pike's discourse, might have passed as a tough but impartial line of questions. Smith found himself, not surprisingly, at odds with a number of Scottish Rite Masons, including his counterpart in the Northern Masonic Jurisdiction, George E. Bushnell. Bushnell reminded members of his jurisdiction that even tangential political involvement by Masonic officials was exceedingly dangerous to Masonic unity and strength. He clearly had Smith in mind when he warned against any "formal action or attempt to exercise pressure or influence for or against any particular legislative project or proposal . . . to procure the election or appointment of governmental officials, whether executive, legislative or judicial."[13]

Smith received many hard-hitting letters of protest from within his own jurisdiction. One Masonic correspondent began by saying that the October (1960) article by the Grand Commander "was one that I feel that Freemasonry can do without." He explained:

"I've been a 32° Mason for many years and never have I felt or have been taught by any of the teachings of Masonry to hold any animosity toward the Catholic religion. . . . The continuation of such bigotry toward our fellow men and fellow Americans is going to do nothing but split America and our way of life. In my mind it is a sin to degrade another man's religion even though we may not see eye to eye on some of the policies they believe in."[14]

In another blistering letter the writer minced no words in expressing his view, telling the Grand Commander, "[Y]ou suggest through vicious subtleties, that as a good Mason, [one should] vote for Nixon. You talk of Catholic prejudice, what about Masonic prejudice? . . . These pamphlets that you have mailed out are just another form of smear tactics, and dirty politics, and are on a par with the dirty, low, below-the-belt type of politics such as was used by Nixon, when he campaigned against Helen Gahagan Douglas."[15] Still another distraught Mason from Texas viewed the Grand Commander's message as "a clever and insidious way of campaigning for the Republican party."[16]

From traditionally conservative Montana came an admonishing missive from a group of Masons: "We want to lodge a protest, that you have no authority nor right to enter into politics in behalf of the Lodge because there are many thousands of true Masons who are Democrats and have equal rights with you and your kind of politicians. . . . If you want to persist in your campaigning, you should resign your office and do just that."[17]

Smith did not, of course, resign as a result of the fire he drew. But he did not apologize, either. In defending his position he said, "[A]ll that I have done has been simply to remind our members of a few fundamental facts . . . as to the disasters that have befallen the liberties of the people of those nations that have fallen under domination of the Papal authority and his hierarchy." He did not in this instance enumerate specific examples of modern tyrannical "papal" states, but concluded doggedly, "I therefore have no apology to make for anything I have said or done because it has been not for any personal aggrandizement of my own . . . but to be a humble servant of the things I have held dearest in this life."[18]

His irritation with former president Harry S. Truman, who endorsed the Kennedy-Johnson ticket, was, doubtlessly, palpable. Even six weeks after the election, Smith's repugnance had not cooled to conciliation. He addressed condescending remarks to a Scottish Rite Mason in California: "Since it appears from our records that you are a 32° Scottish Rite Mason, I am surprised that you apparently know very little, if anything about the fundamental principles of the Roman Catholic outfit. If you did, you would know that it is not content to be just a church and a religion, but it is a political machine for power in every country where it can find a foothold. In those countries where it has become the dominant element in the population it has its religion declared to be the religion of the state and prohibits, if it can, all other religions and denies freedom of worship. Such countries as Spain, Portugal, Italy and Colombia are fine examples of what its purposes are."[19]

Smith was also challenged for his unreconstructed views in one important way. In February 1961 he was visited in his office at the House of the Temple by Grand Commander George E. Bushnell and Lieutenant Grand Commander George Newbury of the Northern Masonic Jurisdiction regarding his position toward Roman Catholics. Smith wrote in his notes that they met for two and a half hours, his visitors trying to persuade him to make a retraction or, at least, offer some modification of his more controversial statements. About the meeting Smith reported that little was accomplished "except an agreement to maintain friendly relations in spite of fundamental differences in our procedure in supplementing Scottish Rite teachings." It was a forthright discussion that probably staved off a reopening of old wounds, though policy differences stayed on the table.

Bushnell and Newbury pleaded with Smith to be more discreet because *The New Age* was widely read throughout the Northern Masonic Jurisdiction; they said that "[Smith's] attacks on Roman Catholicism disturbs the friendly relations they have with that church and that many Masons up there don't like [Smith's] attitude—are leaving the fraternity or becoming apathetic." Smith admitted that "they were rather bitter" about the Southern Jurisdiction's policies and publications. He, nevertheless, rejected the Northern Jurisdiction's cautious strategy:

> They seem to think they must take a *soft* attitude toward Roman Catholicism and give many personal instances where George Newbury has cooperated with them to accomplish local purpose for the good of the community.—He is on the Board of [a] Catholic College and makes speeches to "Christians and Jews" Goodwill Meetings. They think they're making progress toward getting individual Roman Catholics to repudiate the Hierarchy and Pope when they take "medieval" and "dark ages" actions. I told them that so long as the Pope and the Hierarchy are Bosses of the Show, all reform efforts will fail. . . . they are *afraid* of the Church even to the extent that they will not openly give *approval* to our public school program. [They said,] "It would be construed as an indirect attack on parochial schools."[20]

The election of 1960 was one of the closest in American history, being decided by a margin of about 100,000 votes out of more than 64 million cast in the popular vote. Why it was so close has been something of a mystery, especially since the Democrats performed impressively that year in congressional elections. According to historian Allen J. Matusow, "[T]he most important issue in the campaign was not the Cold War, economic growth, civil rights or social welfare. It was Kennedy's Catholic religion, which stirred fears among strongly Protestant voters of a popish plot."[21] It was calculated that the religious issue hurt Kennedy the most in the South, where, according to one highly respected analysis, Protestant defectors cost Kennedy around 17 percent of the normal Democratic vote. Grand Commander Smith, a staunch southerner, consequently, typified the salient characteristics of the election. He spoke for millions of American voters.

In spite of the large number of Protestant voters whom Kennedy lost nationwide, the extra Catholic votes he gained in northern swing states compensated just enough for the setbacks elsewhere to be discounted. The religious issue most clearly beat Kennedy in only two southern states—Tennessee and Oklahoma. In sum, Kennedy's Catholicism damaged him in the popular vote, but actually helped him win his majority in the electoral college.[22]

The New Age maintained silence on the results of the election for the next three issues. Then in March 1961, the Grand Commander's Message communicated a sober, measured, and dignified response, which even quoted John F. Kennedy favorably, if purposefully, to make an oblique point about the dangers of a growing welfare state. Smith placated himself with some principled common sense when he wrote:

> Political campaigns often tend to magnify the importance to the country of individual candidates, but "We, the People," know when elected they are merely our representatives who rely upon us to produce the wealth that feeds and clothes all citizens, manages the commerce and pays the taxes that run the government, educational institutions, and pays for the defense of the country. Presidents and Congressman, Senators and Governors come and go —are good or bad according to whether they enlarge or limit the liberties of the people— but "We, the People," stay on and "keep the store. . . ." This sentiment is very strongly supported by John F. Kennedy, now President . . . as follows: "The scarlet thread running through the thoughts and actions of all people all over the world is the delegation of great problems to the all-absorbing leviathan—the State. Every time that we try to lift a problem to the Government, to the same extent we are sacrificing the liberties of the people."[23]

Within Masonry Smith also extended a hand to repair and strengthen relations between the Northern and Southern Supreme Councils. The Grand Commander reported to the Supreme Council in October 1961 that he and Grand Commander George Bushnell had had a full and frank exchange of views "without acrimony or hard feelings." Their differences were not just between two individual Masons, Smith explained, but had grown out of certain fundamental and longstanding variances about what the scope of legitimate Masonic activity and involvement should be. Though Smith did not say it, essentially the dispute centered around the fact that the Northern Supreme Council did not approve of the position taken by the Southern Supreme Council with regard to Catholicism, involvement in national public education policy, and the issue of separation of church and state. But because of the forbearance and tempering in each man's personality, Smith and Bushnell discovered enough common ground to be resolved as partners, despite disagreement, in kindred Masonic principles. They became Grand Commanders about the same time and actually became fond of each other, so that when Bushnell died suddenly in September 1965, Smith lost not a rival but a friend.[24]

Smith recognized immediately that with the election of John F. Kennedy a new stage was marked in American religious and social history. Sydney Ahlstrom dramatized the change by taking the long view through the lens of Anglo-American continuities: "A Great Puritan Epoch can be seen as beginning in 1558 with the death of Mary Tudor, the last monarch to rule over an officially Roman Catholic England, and as ending in 1960 with the election of John Fitzgerald Kennedy, the first Roman Catholic President of the United States." To underline the point, Ahlstrom bluntly announced that "the age of the WASP, the age of the melting pot, drew to a close."[25] Thus, a momentous decade commenced, often identified as a watershed in American history. And for Scottish Rite Freemasons the new times brought a mixture of excellent opportunities (for growth and national service) and the facing up to a chain of national calamities.

■ ■ ■

The strength of the Scottish Rite in the Southern Jurisdiction during the 1960s resembled no other time in Masonic history. Exuberant national economic growth and dramatic increases in American living standards combined to swell a tide that lifted many boats, especially organizations that in their own manner consciously celebrated the American way of life. From 1950 to 1970, by bursts and retreats, the United States's GNP grew at an average annual rate of 3.9 percent, regarded by many economists as perhaps the best performance in the nation's history. This distinctive affluence of the fifties and sixties, giving Americans more leisure time and greater discretionary income, assisted the expansion of the Scottish Rite proportionately.

In the period from 1956 to 1968, based on membership figures in the Lodges of Perfection, the Scottish Rite in the Southern Jurisdiction grew overall by 22 percent. Given that Masonry does not solicit prospective members to petition for initiation, that in fact its "recruiting methods" are indeed a counterintuitive marketing strategy, this growth is extraordinary. By 1961 R. Lee Lockwood, chairman of the Committee on the State of the Order, announced that the Rite's membership was then "at an all-time high." The remarkable aspect of the good news was that this was at a time when some of the Grand Lodges were actually showing a drop in membership. The Grand Commander in 1961 also elaborated that the Southern Supreme Council, which included 205 valleys, led all other Masonic bodies in membership. Furthermore, Smith reported, "[O]nly a very small number have any mortgage debt and none is experiencing any financial embarrassment. Large numbers have substantial surpluses and sound investments."[26]

MEMBERSHIP FOR LODGES OF PERFECTION [27]

Year	Members
1956	464,380
1958	485,728
1960	503,761
1962	518,185
1964	532,425
1966	548,226
1968	563,017

Adding nearly 100,000 new members during the commandership of Luther A. Smith stands as probably the most notable accomplishment at mid-century for the Supreme Council. Also under Smith the ownership of all Scottish Rite properties by the Supreme Council was clarified. Drawing from the resolutions of the executive sessions and the

Supreme Council sessions of 1961 and 1965, Grand Commander Henry C. Clausen in 1979 reminded his audience, "The Supreme Council, which is a District of Columbia Corporation, is the ultimate, actual, or beneficial owner of all properties of all the Subordinate Valleys."[28]

Of lesser importance, but pertaining to the challenge of maintaining standards of an organization while it is being infused with fresh blood, were questions about practices and procedures. It is not surprising that goading irritants were present as part of natural growing pains in the fraternity. Smith was asked, for instance, about eliminating the Scottish Rite designation and courtesy "Illustrious," as it sounded too immodest for most Americans. One of the Inspectors General Honorary encouraged Smith to issue a decree to the effect that since "Illustrious" is not a title (as its usage is along the lines of "the Honorable" and "the Reverend") it should be discarded from the parlance of the Southern Jurisdiction. Wasn't it overstating it, wondered various brethren, when mutual regard supplies such affectation? Was it not the masquerade of gilding the lily? Smith demurred, refusing to issue such a decree, conceding the point that the present *Statutes* did not include "Illustrious" as part of any Masonic titles. But since it had been in use for a good many years among members of the Supreme Council, not only in the Southern Jurisdiction but in many others, too, Smith thought it best to leave well enough alone. Besides, he reasoned, "Too much emphasis on simplicity may also be a form of vanity, when a person gets into the habit of mind of congratulating himself on how great is his simplicity."[29]

With the enlargement of the valleys in the early 1960s, Smith was pleased, noting, "[T]he observation of Maundy Thursday and Easter Sunday is widespread, even . . . where there are no Chapters of Rose Croix. This is a healthy sign of progress." Regrettably, Smith also worried about the efficacy of these annual rites, particularly "the small percentage of our Rose Croix Brethren who appreciate the obligatory nature of these ceremonies. As far as may be determined from reports, it would be hazardous to fix the percentage of faithful observance above the 10 percent level." Smith thought the problem was only in part due to the competition with Holy Week church services, assigning most of the blame on some failure of Rose Croix Masons to make "due allowance for these apparent conflicts." He did not entertain the possibility of other equally valid reasons, such as the ritual itself no longer connecting as well with the participants as it had in the past, which might explain the drop in Maundy Thursday attendance while membership was booming.[30]

Without identifying which one of the large consistories in the Southern Jurisdiction he had in mind, Smith told of how he, at one stage in the growth period, had to defuse some problematic insurgency born of internal discontent. Apparently, "a group of malcontented members sought to control the election of officers, and secretly organized a club without the authority of the Inspector General or any other officer." Although it would seem difficult to prove, Smith accepted the threatened Inspector General's contention that the club's "main purpose was to disseminate propaganda against certain officers in the Scottish Rite Bodies and to urge the members of the club to aid in supplanting them with others of their choice." When asked by the Inspector General what to do, Smith told him to set the election aside and to announce there would be no election. He also advised him to go ahead and appoint and install the necessary officers so that the work of the Scottish Rite bodies in question could continue. Meanwhile, the principal members involved in the alleged cabal sent a petition to Smith with a large number of signatures, but Smith turned it aside, standing firmly by the Sovereign Grand Inspector General.[31]

· · ·

The House of the Temple during this time was maintained and preserved in its accustomed luster. Fire and water within and crime and riot without, however, tested the building's ability to absorb disruption in the late fifties and through the sixties. At two o'clock in the morning, January 19, 1956, a fire started in the council chamber on the second floor of the House of the Temple. Draperies on the north window or a cushion on one of the long benches caught fire; most likely the former came into contact with a nearby light globe. The fire probably accelerated when embers fell down on the bench, thus adding fuel. Cigarette smoking by a guide or a custodian probably was not involved in the fire's origin, according to an insurance inspector.

Fortunately, a tenant in the nearby Somerset House apartment, who observed the fire, reported it to the fire department, while someone else notified C. Fred Kleinknecht Jr. and Claud F. Young. Both officials rushed to the scene immediately. Grand Commander Smith was in Tampa, Florida. The fire was soon extinguished, but the resulting damage was considerable. The walls were scorched all the way up to the ceiling, smoke damage was pervasive and the glass and bronze figures in the north windows were distorted and broken from the heat. Restoration was, luckily, possible and was completed after several months.[32]

Also, as safety conditions in general were being reconsidered, the neighborhood surrounding the House of the Temple showed signs of deterioration. The Grand Commander, mindful of building security, had installed an electronic protection system (by American District Telegraph Company) throughout the temple, thus eliminating the necessity of two night watchmen and a laborer. The alarm served as a protection against fire as well as trespassing and burglary.[33]

Keeping a dry basement along any S Street property in northwest Washington, D.C., is a chronic difficulty because of a deep subterranean creek which flows beneath the street as a minor tributary of the Potomac watershed. Claud F. Young noted that a constant stream about two inches in diameter ran through the House of the Temple's basement around the clock. The stream, he admitted, had "been running continuously since the foundation was laid." An ingenious but short-lived solution was devised so that with a special plumbing system this water could "be diverted and pumped directly on to [the] grounds," and this enabled the custodians "to maintain a much more beautiful lawn without the cost of city water."[34]

To compensate for outgrown space, the Supreme Council expanded modestly its physical operations when it acquired from Joseph Gawler's Sons Funeral Home the garage at the rear of the House of the Temple in the spring of 1969. Because of rampant neighborhood vandalism, which included the desecration of local churches, it was decided that it was cheaper to brick up the windows of the two-story garage, which resembled many of the old livery stables found behind townhouses throughout the historic sections of Washington. With a new asphalt roof on the garage, it was rendered fit for service.[35]

The Supreme Council's library and Scottish Rite publications continued in the sixties to warrant the Grand Commander's attention. The library, a steadfast member of the American Library Association (ALA) for many years, maintained high professional standards as prescribed by the ALA in developing its holdings of rare Masonic books, manuscripts, and prints. The *Washington Post* in a Sunday feature article in 1961 noted the importance to the city of the Robert Burns Collection at the House of the Temple. The collection was assembled by William R. Smith, long-time director of the National Botanical Gardens. When Smith died, Andrew Carnegie, the Pittsburgh industrialist, a trustee of Smith's estate, decided that since the much-beloved Scottish national poet was a Freemason, his work should have a permanent home in the Supreme Council's national headquarters. The terms of the gift meant that the collection would always be open to the public without charge. Among three thousand items, the Burns material contained a rare manuscript of unpublished verse.[36]

As Ray Baker Harris once pointed out, the library was "unique in that from its establishment in 1878 it has embodied the characteristics of three different kinds of Libraries: Public, Reference, and Archival." Ever since the days of Albert Pike, the library was open to the public, and books have been loaned under the usual public library regulations without hindrance.[37]

Grand Commander Smith himself offered the reference capacities of the library to the international community of Scottish Rite Masons. Realizing that requests by researchers from around the world flow through the library daily, Smith asked, in turn, for specific reciprocal privileges whenever necessary. In one instance he communicated with Grand Commander Erich Schalscha of Germany in behalf of James D. Carter, who was working then on the early history of the Scottish Rite. Carter needed to verify the Masonic affiliations and activities of Frederick II of Prussia, with particular regard to his approval of the *Grand Constitutions of 1786* of the Scottish Rite. Smith sought access for Carter to the archives of Germany. With the death on April 22, 1963, of Ray Baker Harris, who had served as librarian since 1939, Grand Commander Smith appointed Carter as librarian-historian, thereby continuing the level of competency required in that temple station.[38]

James D. Carter came to Washington from Texas, where he was a member of the Waco Scottish Rite bodies and a former editor of the *Texas Grand Lodge Magazine*. Carter held B.S. and M.A. degrees from North Texas State University (at Denton) and a Ph.D. from the University of Texas. Carter was commissioned to complete the official history of the Supreme Council, begun by Harris.[39] Harris had performed yeoman service in his research and writing on the Rite; he was an authority on Masonic imprints and a superb stylist as an author. Drawing from materials in the archives and library, Harris traced the origin of cornerstone customs from ancient times, extending down into American history. The resulting publication, *The Laying of Cornerstones,* a fifty-five-page booklet, included a chronology of Masonic cornerstones laid in Washington, D.C., over a period of nearly 200 years.[40]

The History of the Supreme Council (beginnings to 1860, volume 1), on which Harris had devoted six years of preparation and Carter required two years to finish, was published and distributed in 1964. The book was well received, though three small questions arose over possible historical errors, which were described and explained by Carter through the Grand Commander's *Allocution* (1965). Carter addressed matters in the *The History of the Supreme Council* concerning "the statement that five Lodges formed the Grand Lodge in London in 1717; the summary of the introduction of Masonry into South Carolina; and the identification of a picture said to be that of Grand Commander Moses Holbrook. The first was a typographical error that escaped the proof-readers; the second cannot be demonstrated to be materially incorrect because the records of the period have been almost totally destroyed; and it cannot now be determined upon what evidence Brother Harris made his identification of the picture in 1957."[41]

Carter brought out the second volume of *The History of the Supreme Council* (1861–1891) just before the retirement of Grand Commander Smith in 1969. He projected a four-volume work (though three were actually completed). About volume two, Carter reported that it had been positively reviewed in several Masonic publications. He also noted, "[S]ome objection has been raised to the detail included in the book, but when readers are told that it was intended to present all available information of any historical interest to make a compendium of facts in chronological order, they have agreed that the objective has been achieved."[42] In other words, Carter's history was not intended to be so much a thematic narrative as a work of chronicling.

In his dual role as librarian-historian, Carter purchased a set of Hogarth prints dated 1747 and entitled "Industry and Idleness." He planned and directed a short film and published a colorful brochure supplement based on the Hogarth prints, under the auspices of the education program.[43] Perhaps of greater historical value to the library and museum was the discovery of a medallion-sized silhouette portrait thought to be of Colonel John Mitchell, first Grand Commander. Shortly after taking over for Harris, Carter met John H. Crowe, a Scottish Rite Mason whose ancestor was Grand Commander Mitchell. Crowe located "a badly damaged miniature portrait on ivory of his ancestor among family possessions." The family granted permission to the Scottish Rite to photograph the cameo-sized image of Mitchell. From a photographic enlargement, Allyn Cox, a Mason and one of the most acclaimed portrait painters in America, produced a portrait which was added to the museum.[44]

During the sixties, the Supreme Council's channels of publicity were numerous. *The New Age*, as a monthly magazine, reached over a half million homes as of 1963. By 1965, the Committee on Education and Americanism reported a distribution level of 4 million copies for its publications, including *The Road to Freedom* and *Our Public Schools*. An address entitled "The Faith of Free Men," given by famed FBI Director J. Edgar Hoover after he was elected to receive the Grand Cross Court of Honor, had been published as a press run of nearly 400,000 copies. Through the Americanism program, the Hoover pamphlets mostly went to schools and civic organizations.[45]

Scottish Rite film production began earnestly in the mid-sixties, thus making broad use of current communications technology. Using source material almost exclusively from the library, the film "In the Hearts of Men" dealt with famous Americans who were Masons. The internationally renowned news commentator Lowell Thomas, a Master Mason, was enlisted as the film's narrator. Richard Amberg, a Mason with many years of experience in print media, was responsible for overseeing the production of this film which was twenty-nine minutes in length as a sixteen-millimeter, black-and-white presentation. After two years of availability, all 500 original copies of the film had been sold by 1967.

Based on this success, immediate plans were directed by Smith to sponsor a second film, "Summer of Decision," centering on "the ideals and hopes of American civilization."[46] That cinematic sequel depicted a young man in a high-school classroom discussing American values with the teacher and other students. It was filmed in color, intended for Masonic and general audiences, but never had the success of its predecessor; sales were half of the feature work "In the Hearts of Men."

. . .

The quality of Scottish Rite programs, facilities, benevolences, and publications rested on the attainment, in no minor way, of stable financial management. Sound investments in stocks and government bonds, generous bequests, and an expanding membership base contributed to the flourishing health of the Rite. The Scottish Rite Foundation, for example, while it was barely a few years old, received $141,600 from several sources in 1959. It also received a deed from William B. Massey, Sovereign Grand Inspector General in Missouri, for one-half undivided interest in a tract of nearly 370 acres consisting of lead and dolomite deposits. The foundation bought the remaining half of the land for $50,000, on the supposition that it would be worth several million dollars in time.[47]

The budget, of course, expanded considerably in the sixties, but was already impressively demonstrating solvency at the beginning of the decade. The total operations per biennium of the Supreme Council climbed over the $2 million mark by 1965. For the fiscal years 1960 and 1961, the budget reflected enormous optimism for sustained financial health:[48]

Classification	Expenditure (for 2 years)
Americanism and Education	$100,000
Charitable Activities	50,000
Contingent	36,500
Deputies Allowance	24,000
Entertainment	26,000
Foreign, Domestic, Fraternal Relief	12,000
House of the Temple (improvements)	135,000
International SR Conference (1961)	44,000
Library, Supplies & History	20,000
Morals and Dogma	70,000
The New Age (printing)	509,000
Office Supplies	8,500
Paraphernalia and Jewels	6,500
Patents	20,000
Printing (Transactions, Rituals)	40,000
Propagation of the Rite	200,000
Salaries	440,000
SR Foundation (maintaining)	1,000
Session (including mileage)	55,000
Social Security Tax	15,000
Transportation and Communication	23,000
Travel (GC, GS, etc.)	19,000
Total	$1,854,500

Grand Commander Smith reported in 1965 that the Supreme Council was spending annually about $100,000 on charitable activities. He mentioned with deepening interest that $5,000 was given to the California Scottish Rite Institute for Childhood Aphasia located at Stanford University Medical Center. As a relatively new program of Scottish Rite benevolence, Smith explained that "the extraordinary service" rendered at Stanford was "in the field of diagnosis and experimental research on the nature of the problems associated with brain injury, particularly in cases where failure to have earlier treatment has complicated the trouble." In random order, Smith also mentioned the Supreme Council's regular contributions to DeMolay ($10,000), Doane College ($5,000), Baylor University ($10,000), New Orleans Baptist Theological Seminary ($10,000), College of the Pacific in California ($10,000), School of the Ozarks in Missouri ($5,000), and Protestants and Other Americans United for the Separation of Church and State ($40,000). For earthquake damage in Alaska and flood relief in Colorado and California the Supreme Council gave $12,500.[49] Significantly, the president of George Washington University, Cloyd H. Marvin, a thirty-third degree Scottish Rite Mason, acknowledged that about one-third of the operating budget of the School of Government came from the Scottish Rite Endowment.[50]

. . .

External relations of the Scottish Rite—with universities, foreign Masonic bodies, and alternate Masonic structures, such as Prince Hall Masons—were vigorously supervised by Smith. The impetus of past Grand Commanders continued, and so Smith, while not developing new policies, enforced what had seemed to work well in the past.

The Scottish Rite's mission to promote a strict separation of church and state was fruitful for both itself and its beneficiaries in the academic community. This combination promoted the First Amendment generally, funded research and scholarship, trained future American leaders in international business and diplomacy in a "neutral" (i.e., non-Catholic) environment, and kindled added prestige for the Scottish Rite in view of its being associated with higher education at a time when it was a national priority. From 1959 through 1961, the Scottish Rite Foundation gave $20,000 to the American University in Washington, D.C., for the continuation of its support for the School of International Service.

The aid to American University was based on an agreement, reached between the Scottish Rite Foundation and the university, to reserve a place in their curriculum, in freshman and sophomore required courses, for inclusion of the Rite's Americanism program. Also, the Scottish Rite gift allowed American University to invite Ralph H. Gabriel, a distinguished American historian at Yale University, to be the key advisor at a meeting aimed at the development of these essential courses. Eventually, at the spring commencement of 1963, Grand Commander Smith was awarded an honorary degree of Doctor of Laws from the American University, which cited him for his "religious and spiritual idealism which shines through your success as a lawyer, judge and banker in the state of Mississippi, and your service to the fraternal order which has been a part of your life."[51]

During the biennium of 1961, the Scottish Rite Foundation donated $10,000 to Baylor University in support of an innovative program, the J. M. Dawson Studies in Church and State. One of the Scottish Rite's publications in its education program, entitled "Church and State," was primarily a result of research and editorial work done at Baylor. When the Baylor program was ten years old in 1967, the Scottish Rite was acknowledged as a chief contributor, having given a total of $50,000 up to that point. By the spring of 1968, the "program" was sufficiently strong and promising enough to be elevated within the university to the status of a "Research Center."[52]

For the level and the length of commitment to George Washington University exercised by the Scottish Rite for more than thirty years, Luther A. Smith received the honorary degree of Doctor of Laws at the June commencement ceremonies in 1961.[53] From 1927 to 1960, the Supreme Council had given George Washington University about $2 million. Smith once noted, however, that before this official relationship was cemented, a prior generation of Scottish Rite Masons, independent of the Supreme Council, had contributed "about a quarter of a million dollars to this cause."[54]

Beginning in 1965, the Scottish Rite Foundation appropriated $5,000 to the School of Law at Vanderbilt University "for such purposes, and upon such terms and conditions as may be agreeable to the School of Law and Judge Luther Andrew Smith." This resulted in the Judge Luther A. Smith Scottish Rite Scholarships at the Vanderbilt Law School. For the fall of 1966, five full tuition scholarships were awarded from a fund that was then valued at $125,300.[55]

■　■　■

Grand Commander Smith could hardly compete against the extraordinary length of overseas travel conducted by John H. Cowles, but he managed foreign relations skillfully, especially in the face of several challenges. He and Grand Commander Bushnell (Northern Masonic Jurisdiction) received gold medals in 1961 from Italian Masons in appreciation of their efforts to bring about unification in a Masonically fractious Italy. Part of the problem which Smith and Bushnell also sought to ameliorate involved questions of property with the Italian government. Specifically, Smith maintained that "the Government [of Italy] owed the Fraternity some equitable adjustment and compensation for the injustices it had suffered under the Mussolini dictatorship." In the end, the Italian Masons came together, "assured of a respectable and adequate national home from which to operate and carry on their work upon reasonable terms."[56]

One of Smith's primary concerns about Masonry abroad was the amount of suffering and political persecution endured by some European brethren. Smith organized in 1957 the delivery of CARE packages, mostly consisting of clothing, to Yugoslavian Masons, their widows, and dependents. The Supreme Council found there was no point in sending money to them as they could not buy things they needed due to a lack of availability. An outpouring of return correspondence, letters of sincere gratitude which Smith found profoundly touching, was set aside for public perusal. He commented, "[O]f all the acts of charity and donations to benevolences that this Supreme Council has ever made, I do not think that anything we have done along this line has been exceeded by these gifts of mercy to the distressed and very deserving Yugoslav brethren." Smith communicated frequently with the former Grand Commander of Yugoslavia, who before World War II was a prominent lawyer and leading citizen, but as of 1961 was having a difficult time.[57]

Congressman Otto E. Passman, an avid Scottish Rite Mason, asked Smith, during the summer of 1959, what he knew about the political conditions in Spain as they related to Freemasons. Long after the end of Nazism in Germany and Austria and the fall of Fascism in Italy, Franco lingered in power in Spain. Smith's reply to Passman was a thoroughly itemized bill of lament about the treatment of Freemasons in Spain, going all the way back to Torquemada's Inquisition. He said plainly, "[T]hat Freemasonry has survived there at all over the centuries is that man's yearning for Freedom and Justice can never be totally suppressed." Smith made the point that Spain's policy had been historically consistent, in that when Spain controlled the Philippines, Freemasonry had been "just as viciously persecuted" as it was in Spain. He insisted that Franco's policy was "actually a pogrom against Freemasonry" which originated in the Franco Concordat with the Vatican. This Concordat, widely publicized, placed the Franco regime "on record as promising to suppress any form of proselytizing which [was] not for the exclusive benefit of the Roman Catholic faith." Further, Smith iterated that Franco had "privately requested other governments not to send officials to Spain who [were] Freemasons."[58]

The memory of World War II was, of course, freshly vivid in the minds of the survivors, especially in Europe and Asia. A stream of horror stories relating to the premeditated and systematic persecution and elimination of Jews, Freemasons, Gypsies, homosexuals, and the mentally retarded continued. This overshadowed the hoped-for decency of the fifties and sixties. Even fifty years after V-E and V-J Days, which marked the end of the war and the Holocaust, memories and newly retrieved documents continued to surface. The Dutch Sovereign Grand Commander, Marius ten Cate, addressed the Supreme Council in 1959 with a personal and powerfully gripping description of what the Nazis did to Dutch Masons. In a rapid staccato, made all the more urgent by broken syntax, as if one could not humanly dwell long on such atrocity, he reported:

> Men taken from their beds all of a sudden at night, brutal body mutilation of the most aweful [sic] type, castration, imprisonment, execution, medical experimentation, mental and physical threats, that in my country are still as fresh in mind as they have been real, just recently. The [German] occupational forces had complete lists of our Masonic Members, intruded suddenly in our homes and lives, searched our houses, deported Freemasons, of whom many were executed, often after endless physical injury; they required our stated communication reports, destroyed all Masonic properties, Lodge buildings, Temples, sacred possessions. They displayed in the most ridiculous way exhibitions and dishonest expositions of ritualistic objects and books. It is no wonder, therefore, that fear had grown deeply in my country-people for the devilish work of dictatorial power both in politics and in religion. In this moment I will not forget the martyrdom of my predecessor as Sovereign Grand Commander, Brother van Tongeren, a most honorable man, who suddenly was imprisoned and found his death in the Concentration Camp Sachsenhausen.[59]

The prospects for Masonry in the Western Hemisphere were sometimes no different from recent European experience, as Smith realized in considering Fidel Castro's Cuban Revolution. In light of the April 1961 debacle known as the Bay of Pigs, by which the United States through the CIA had directed 1,400 commandos in a failed invasion of Cuba, many Masons escaped from the island and took refuge in Miami, Florida. As of 1961, Castro had not specifically outlawed Masonry, but he merely occupied the Masonic temple in Havana making it impossible for Freemasons to operate unencumbered. Meanwhile, the Grand Lodge of Cuba-in-exile was recognized by the Grand Lodge of Florida. Cuban Masonic refugees were given ample relief funds, including money sent by Smith in behalf of the Supreme Council.[60]

Smith involved himself personally in the liberation of the former Grand Secretary General of Romania, Nubar Bohceli. Bohceli's exodus to the free world, made complete by his expression of "unbounded gratitude" for Smith's help, was recounted by him in his address to the Supreme Council: "Only recently I was released from one of their prisons where I was held captive for more than 10 years. My crime was that I was Grand Secretary General of the Supreme Council of Romania. During the period of my imprisonment I learned what tortures the human mind can conceive—and what the human spirit can endure. The lash, the bludgeon, and chains were part of my everyday life for a decade."[61]

Near the end of Smith's commandership, the Supreme Council severed relations with the Supreme Councils of Spain-in-exile, Germany, and Peru. The case of Germany caused Smith the most distress because its Supreme Council had ceased to believe in the existence of God, and accordingly showed no respect for "the Volume of the Sacred Law as part of the required furniture and symbols of regular lodges."[62]

The trend of scientific humanism in Continental Masonic lodges, however, was not new. It was an extension of deeply rooted tendencies, "a streak of freethinking or deism" which "turns up at moments in the history of Continental freemasonry right into, and especially during the 1790s."[63] The Germans were actually following their own tradition and interpretation of Masonry which, not surprisingly, had offended the English Masons of the Victorian period over the same issue of theism. And yet, secular religiosity was not born apart from the earliest Masonic sources known. It was found, too, in Anglo-American Masonry right from the beginning of the speculative phase. Rather, Christian piety was introduced in trans-Atlantic Masonry with the rise and spread of evangelical impulses more commonly experienced in America and the British Isles than in the European continent.

Smith's last trip across the Atlantic as Grand Commander, at the age of eighty, was principally to attend the second meeting of the English-speaking Supreme Councils of North America and the British Isles. His wife, Lorraine, accompanied him, insisting that she would only go by passenger ship, not by plane. They left for England on May 22, 1964, joined by the Grand Commanders of Canada and the Northern Masonic Jurisdiction. It was the last tour the Smiths ever made. The meeting was scheduled to begin June 1 in London and last several days. Unfortunately, on May 31, while the North American delegation visited Eton College Chapel, Mrs. Smith fell, fracturing her hip. She was taken to the Royal Masons Hospital in London where she underwent surgery "by London's leading orthopedic surgeon." Smith, once his wife was safely in a reasonable state of recovery, went on to attend during the following week the Ninth Conference of the Grand Commanders of Europe in Brussels. On July 1 the Smiths arrived in New York where they were met by C. Fred Kleinknecht Jr., then assistant to the Grand Secretary General, who had come up from Washington with Frank Simpkins, the Grand Commander's chauffeur, to bring the travelers home.[64]

■ ■ ■

The unshielded Achilles heel of American society—so often expressed by the Constitutional crises of the nineteenth century (sometimes disguised as economic issues), brutally cut open by the Civil War, left festering by base hatred, sometimes legally codified—remained assailable throughout the twentieth century. Racial equality was far from being achieved even after President Truman desegregated the armed forces and, because it was a federal city, the District of Columbia. Truman's fellow thirty-third degree Scottish Rite Mason, Chief Justice Earl Warren, whom President Eisenhower had appointed, wrote the opinion of the Supreme Court's unanimous decision that "in the field of public education the doctrine of 'separate but equal' has no place. Separate educational facilities are inherently unequal." Such public facilities, Warren argued, produced in black children "a feeling of inferiority . . . that may affect their hearts and minds in a way unlikely ever to be undone." Since the ruling in the landmark case of *Brown v. Board of Education of Topeka* (1954) did not require immediate compliance, a vague timetable encouraged southern states to resist and, consequently, caused various forms of agitation and protest for the cause of equality to be organized. This governmental complacency was a major moral failure of President Eisenhower's leadership according to his biographer Stephen E. Ambrose.[65]

The entire tenure of Luther A. Smith as Grand Commander was staged against this tense national background presenting a contrast of American (and Masonic) ideals of freedom, equality, and justice against the terrible reality of racism. How could Americans, for instance, as exemplars of democratic principles, boast to the world that the "American way of life" was superior to other ways, so long as racial divides existed? It was, perhaps not unexpectedly, an awkward, uncomfortable time of acute change. Nothing that occurred in American society at large, then, especially matters of race, exempted Masonry from feeling the exigencies of the moment. While no official Masonic response to the civil rights movement could be overtly stated, as American Masonic tradition prohibited the fraternity from being a political agent of change, there were varieties of individual stands which represented the times, particularly in the South, where Scottish Rite Masonry was so strong.

Grand Commander Smith, while a fierce advocate of freedom and liberty in defending the human rights of Masons who were persecuted abroad, drew a different line in his assumptions about black citizens in American society. It is fair-minded to recall that as he entered his advanced age he was a product of his time, of the deep South at the height of segregation. Smith's thinking was ingrained with theories and attitudes on race still drawn from plantation days in Mississippi. He had, like so many white southerners of his generation, known only one possibility for dealing with two populations. As one would expect, consequently, a substantial body of correspondence exists regarding Smith's opposition to civil rights legislation, beginning with his antagonism toward the repeal of the Connally Reservation in 1960. Smith, for instance, encouraged Senator

James O. Eastland to "go to the mat with those fanatics who would crucify the South again on a cross of 'Civil Rights' Legislation."[66]

Smith applauded the ostensibly "gradualist" approach to desegregation suggested by J. Edgar Hoover in a public address before 400 distinguished Masons and their wives. Hoover spoke for many Americans when he said, "I am greatly concerned that certain racial leaders are doing the civil rights movement a great disservice by suggesting that citizens need only obey the laws with which they agree. Such an attitude breeds disrespect for the law and even civil disorder and rioting. The citizen has no latitude as to what laws he must obey. If he feels a law is wrong and unjust, he has recourse to established constitutional procedures to have it changed through his legally elected representatives."[67] Hoover's generalizations failed to mention the citizen's cherished right of free speech which, so long as it is in the form of nonviolent protest and incites no mobs to riot, was to be protected under the full power of the federal government. Hoover's remarks ignored the unlawful, brutal attacks of white vigilantes against other whites and blacks trying peaceably to register voters in the South. Also, by Hoover's reasoning, any analogous resistance to offensive, unfair laws in totalitarian countries should be discouraged, especially if "constitutional procedures" are on the books. In other words, Masons in the Nazi period or those living behind the Iron Curtain should disregard their first principles out of respect for the letter of the law.

Smith's position on African-American Masonry or African-Americans in mainline regular Grand Lodges was sealed, though he kept his views largely hidden behind the ruse of technicalities. His personal preferences were clear, nonetheless, no matter how much he supported the Bill of Rights and the Fourteenth and Fifteenth Amendments. Once in 1960 a polite inquiry which solicited clarification was addressed to *The New Age*. The writer began,

> I am an American soldier, Negro, Master Mason (Blue Lodge). I have a question that I feel you may be able to answer for me. Is it a doctrine of White Masons that there are no Negro Masons? Do all whites feel the same about us in Masonry as one man serving with me in the Army? I indeed do hope not. A Negro soldier asked my First Sergeant if he knew of anyone that could recommend him (that is, if he couldn't) for candidacy in Freemasonry. He further asked if there was a Lodge around here, and if so, maybe he would find someone that he knew from the U.S. [Army] that knew him and could recommend him, but he was confronted with this answer: "As far as I am concerned, there are *no* Negro Masons."[68]

Norman Meese, as editor, promptly replied with what has been the longstanding platform plank. The exchange was not published in *The New Age*.

> Your inquiry will be answered to your satisfaction, I think, if you will consider the fact that Freemasonry in the United States is governed by Grand Lodges, and that each Grand Lodge has exclusive jurisdiction within its own geographical area, and that as each Grand Lodge was organized it became recognized by other Grand Lodges as the *regular* Grand Lodge for its jurisdiction. Furthermore, that all these Grand Lodges in

the United States were organized by white Masons, therefore, all the *regular* Grand Lodges in the United States are composed of white Masons.

When the negros [*sic*] began to organize Masonry and to establish Grand Lodges they could not be recognized because other Grand Lodges had already been organized. This would be true whether organized by white men or negros.[69]

The form of Meese's argument is syllogistic; that is, if only the first and oldest Grand Lodges can be *regular,* and if by historical circumstances they were organized by white men, then, if Grand Lodges are organized by black men they must be irregular.[70] In time, however, the Southern Jurisdiction admitted black members, though very few by the 1990s. Further, there was never any statutory prohibition against doing so, as there had been in some Grand Lodge bylaws.[71]

Smith used the same form of argument when asked to comment on Grand Commander Bushnell's mild interest in pursuing informal relations with Prince Hall Masons:

> The Southern Jurisdiction, however, has given no official notice of any Prince Hall history. Our Supreme Council settled that issue in some Resolutions which were adopted, October 22, 1947, as shown by the attached Extract from our records. The pertinent fact is that no regular Grand Lodge in this country, or in Great Britain, has accorded the Prince Hall Grand Lodge any recognition. So far as we are concerned, there the matter rests. We have no communications, visitations, discussions, or conferences with any of these irregular or clandestine groups, and we do not appreciably concern ourselves with their history. That seems to be the point at which Judge Bushnell got himself and his Supreme Council into controversy.[72]

While Smith and Bushnell played an active role in trying to reconcile the complicated Italian Masonic situation, with comparable issues of recognition, regularity, and clandestine practices, the nearly parallel concerns in the United States with regard to Prince Hall Masonry were treated not by similar efforts of mediation but by uniformly ignoring the matter, blind to the potential opportunity.

Masonry is certainly not alone in struggling with the complicated and sensitive history of race in America. A popular, though painfully embarrassing adage at the time of the sixties' civil rights movement stated that the most segregated hour in America was eleven o'clock on Sunday mornings—when whites and blacks, reading the same Bible, worshipping through the same faith, attended separate churches. Perhaps, likewise, to some intangible degree, African-American lodges, like the black churches, have served their communities in similarly potent ways. But the issue and its agonizing history will not disappear so long as it remains a vulnerable spot in many Masonic organizations.

Some southern Scottish Rite Masons, nevertheless, were energetic advocates of civil rights legislation, clearly the most important domestic issue of the sixties. Congressman Brooks Hays, a thirty-third degree Mason in the Southern Jurisdiction, representing Little Rock in the Fifth District of Arkansas since the early forties, sacrificed his legislative and political career when he took a courageous stand against Governor Orval E. Faubus, who had opposed a local plan for gradual school desegregation. The Eisenhower administration in 1957 federalized the Arkansas National Guard and sent paratroopers to Little Rock in order to protect black children attempting to enroll at formerly all-white schools. Hays, a popular, seven-term incumbent and a charming raconteur of parables and stories, lost his reelection in 1958 because of his position on racial equality. He was at the time an active Baptist layman and president of the Southern Baptist Convention, the largest (mostly white) Protestant denomination in America. Hays spent most of his remaining career in Washington, where he was in constant demand as a churchman and civic speaker. When Brooks Hays died in 1981, he was given a statesman's funeral in Little Rock, honored at home, at last, for his vision and integrity.

■   ■   ■

Grand Commander Smith was an eighty-five-year-old man in 1968, a year in modern American history that was unarguably cataclysmic. After the assassinations of civil rights leader Martin Luther King Jr. and presidential candidate Robert F. Kennedy, the firestorm of urban riots (particularly in the nation's capital), ongoing disturbances on college campuses, the turmoil of the Chicago Democratic National Convention, the recent escalation of the increasingly unpopular Vietnam War, the My Lai massacre, the demoralized Great Society social welfare program, and the political demise of Lyndon Johnson, the country could not take much more. And perhaps neither could an octogenarian at the House of the Temple who had weathered a tumultuous period in the city of Washington and the South. Smith was, nevertheless, ending his term of leadership with several grace notes. He was, for example, the recipient of the Freedoms Foundation Principal Award for 1968, mainly for his oversight of *The New Age* magazine.

Then in the summer of 1968 he entered the hospital for surgery for an undisclosed problem and, remarkably, was able to resume his regular routine at the office by the first of October. Old age had taken its toll, however, and Smith wisely finished out the year, resigning his long-held position just before the Supreme Council session of 1969.[73]

The Supreme Council had planned for the inevitable end of Smith's active Masonic career at least two years before his retirement from office. Creating the office of Deputy Grand Commander in 1967, which permitted the executive duties of the Grand Commander to continue if he were absent or specifically requested a temporary transfer of responsibilities to the Deputy as needed, meant that the machinery for a smooth transition of leadership was in place.[74]

Henry C. Clausen, Sovereign Grand Inspector General in California, Smith's eventual successor as Grand Commander, was the first to hold the office of Deputy Grand Commander. Many years later Clausen revealed some additional background concerning the predicament which needed to be addressed as it became evident Smith was slowing down: "[T]he Supreme Council had a delicate problem regarding advancement. The Council wanted me in line to become the next Grand Commander." The natural line of succession pointed to the Lieutenant Grand Commander, in this instance, Joshua K.

Shepherd. Normally, the Lieutenant Grand Commander was regarded as an understudy to the Sovereign Grand Commander.

Clausen learned that Shepherd "was one of those who wanted [him] to succeed Smith but [Clausen] also detected he did not wish to step down to take a lower station than Lt. Grand Commander [i.e., vacating that office for Clausen to be positioned correctly in the proper order of promotion]." Establishing a new office of Deputy Grand Commander, similar to the California Grand Lodge which Clausen knew intimately, seemed to make everyone happy. Clausen may have had some serious reluctance about coming to Washington, but by becoming Deputy Grand Commander in 1967 a *fait accompli* was in hand. He reflected on his circumstances twenty years later, "[H]aving committed myself that far I could not very well refuse the office of Grand Commander when it was tendered, although I had many other interests and a lively law practice and lived in what was paradise compared to Washington where I had served during World War II."[75]

Smith outlived his wife by two years. He died February 9, 1975, at the age of ninety-one, remembered as a man "possessed [of] a strong and luminous mind, virile enthusiasm, a magnetic, dynamic yet pleasing personality. Accomplished in the fields of law and finance, his foremost achievement came in his fourteen years as Grand Commander," staying the course, preserving traditions, through a stressful time in American society.[76]

Smith, growing up one generation removed from the Civil War and Reconstruction, in a time of steamers and rural stage coaches, lived long enough to see literally a new age begin. As a boy, he knew, undoubtedly, ex-slaves and their masters, a world from long ago. But as an old man he had already gone far into the future, especially when he met a brother Mason who had flown to the moon and back.

The sixties are frustratingly difficult to describe or even to imagine, but those years are probably best remembered for certain human accomplishments larger than any or all of the problems and divisions facing a world-wise American society. In an experimental day, mixed with uncertain measures of failure and success, the U.S. space program served as an epochal counterpoint to American social conditions.

Scottish Rite Masons, like so many earlier pioneers with Masonic roots, were also found among the top astronauts that NASA recruited and trained in its heyday. From Leroy Gordon Cooper, a thirty-third degree Mason and an early astronaut who traveled many miles in space to prepare the way for those first human steps beyond the reach of earth, came sentiments offered on behalf of his thirty-third degree class in 1963, subtly associating symbols of initiation with his own experience of space flight. "I am sure," said Major Cooper, "that all of us recall when we made our first step in Masonry by entering with three distinct knocks on a door and how step by step as we advanced we were given more and more light."[77] In other words, what Cooper learned in Masonry, including his Scottish Rite "journey," helped him keep things in perspective as, step by step, outer space was probed and charted and more and more light was added as the farther reaches darkened.

The astronaut Walter M. Schirra, a thirty-third degree Mason, was the final dinner speaker at the session which essentially served as Smith's farewell, again uniting themes of ending a life's work with dignity while advancing a new day in the Scottish Rite's wide domain of influence.[78] Fittingly, and in the spirit of a new age, one of Smith's final official duties as Grand Commander was to receive back from Colonel Edwin (Buzz) E. Aldrin, also a thirty-third degree Mason, the Scottish Rite flag, made by librarian Inge Baum, "emblazoned in color with the Scottish Rite Double-headed Eagle, the Blue Lodge Emblem and Sovereign Grand Commander's insignia," which was carried on the Apollo II mission to the moon.[79] On July 20, 1969, Aldrin was the second man to walk on the moon, only a few steps and some minutes behind Neil A. Armstrong. Thus, the Smith era closed with a vivid application of Masonic symbols, *ad astra per aspera* (to the stars through difficulties).

CHAPTER XIII

When the Waves Went High
1969–1985

Henry C. Clausen

A fiery soul, which working out its way,
Fretted the pygmy-body to decay:
And o'er-informed the tenement of clay.
A daring pilot in extremity;
Pleased with the danger, when the waves went high
He sought the storms . . .

John Dryden, "Absalom and Achitophel"

A little past five in the morning on April 18, 1906, an enormous seismic shock wrenched San Francisco from sleep. Since before the turn of the century the city had aspired to transform the raw energy of its pioneering forebears into a solid and splendid form, the "Eden of the West." It was a dream already beyond mere exploration, for San Francisco seemed destined to be a city beautiful, of nature and art, health and heritage, reaching for an urban elegance to supersede its provincial roughness. Now the city lay in ruins, still burning from fires fed by ruptured gas lines three days after the earthquake's mighty tremor.

Louis and Lena Clausen had become part of the new city, too, welcoming the arrival of a baby boy there, less than a year before the disaster heaved the city out of its dream. On the morning the earthquake struck, nine-month-old Henry Christian Clausen (born June 30, 1905) was asleep on a Murphy (fold-away) bed. When the whole house began to shake and pitch, the bed unlatched from the floor and snapped itself back against the wall to which it was hinged. Thus, the baby was held "securely against the strongest interior support while the exterior of the house crumbled away." When the quake subsided, the young parents got to the bed, pulled it down, and felt blessed to find that their son was alive.

Henry C. Clausen, near the end of his life, near the end of the century, surmised, "I was born to survive calamitous events."[1] His life and career, while sometimes touching the edges of battle and often entering the center of controversy, was only in part about survival, for that would diminish his achievements to a form of chance or accident. Rather, he was a productive agent of repair and rebuilding in both concrete and intangible terms. His record of national service during World War II while a "civilian" officer in the Judge Advocate General's Corps demonstrates clearly his ability to fix big things. Clausen was dispatched by Secretary of War Henry L. Stimson to investigate the root causes of Pearl Harbor. He was charged, in effect, to repair the damage from the shockingly inaccurate Army Pearl Harbor Board, whose reports "were based on tainted or perjured testimony."[2] Clausen's report, which provided a finely detailed chronology of events, helped measurably to rebuild the reputation of the military's integrity at a time when rumors of conspiracy and intrigue began to gain dangerous momentum.

Meanwhile, within days after the San Francisco earthquake, Daniel Hudson Burnham, renowned architect and city planner, arrived post haste from France, confident that the demolished city could be rebuilt. He announced, "San Francisco of the future will be the most beautiful city of the continent, with the possible exception of Washington."[3] For Henry C. Clausen these two cities, so very different in all respects of mood and purpose yet linked by common symmetries born of aesthetic design, were centers of his life and work. He had much more of himself invested in San Francisco, naturally, but his preferences were twice overridden—first to serve at the Pentagon during the early forties and, then, twenty-five years later to assume the leadership of the Supreme Council, Southern Jurisdiction.

Clausen was educated in a San Francisco invigorated by a quickened purpose, to regenerate California heroism and enterprise. Many saw apocalyptic symbolism in the destruction of the city. Notorious for vice and corruption, San Francisco had passed through an ordeal of the refiner's fire. Hubert Howe Bancroft, a pioneering historian and publisher, believed "the cleansing effect of fire" had rescued the city from sinful idleness and brought back a sense of spiritual mission. To become America's new "City on a Hill," recalling John Winthrop's seventeenth-century Puritan Boston, infused urgency into the rebuilding process.

San Francisco, however, was mostly impatient, lacking Puritan restraint in its hurry to put up a facade of grandeur. Unbelievably, downtown San Francisco was rebuilt within three and a half years. By 1911 hardly a trace of destruction could be seen. Architectural critics questioned the rush to completion without giving ample time for deeper themes and contexts to mature into substantive plans. The reviews of the rebuilt city were not usually favorable, for the new city (except for fire-proof construction in commercial buildings) replicated "the worst features of the old: gridiron streets crowded with flimsy wooden units packed side by side in treeless monotony." An aura of temporariness mostly struck the critics, as if another horseman of the apocalypse were expected to visit soon.[4]

Henry C. Clausen, however, loved San Francisco. He owed his life to the reborn city, and his personal history runs closely parallel to its development in the twentieth century. When his father died prematurely, young Henry, barely in high school, assumed much of the bread-winning responsibilities to support his mother and sisters. Taking his law degree in night courses from the University of San Francisco, a private Catholic and Jesuit institution, in 1927 and continuing his studies in the University of California at San Francisco, Clausen was already established in the legal profession when he married Virginia Palmer in 1935. He was then thirty years old and had recently served as the chief counsel for Joseph B. Strauss, the engineer who had the main construction responsibilities for the Golden Gate Bridge.

For Clausen's generation of San Franciscans, nothing better represented the phoenix quality of the city, rising from the ashes, than the majestic bridge across the bay. Perhaps by being intimately connected with the completion of the bridge, Clausen's identity with California was forever fixed. (As Sovereign Grand Commander, he maintained a residence at the staid Wardman Park in Washington, but actually seldom left San Francisco, where he lived about half the year) For him and his wife, their personal hopes were also placed in the birth of four children, Henry Christian (Jr.), Florian, Donald, and Karen. Donald eventually became an artist and rendered his father's portrait, later placed in the House of the Temple.

Regarded many years later as "one of the giants of modern American Freemasonry," Clausen entered the fraternity in Ingleside Lodge No. 630, San Francisco, the same year he was married, 1935. Within five years he passed through the chairs to become his lodge's Worshipful Master in 1940. The following year began his association with the Scottish Rite in the Valley of San Francisco.

During the war years, Clausen, like so many Americans in uniform, suspended his Masonic activity. In 1942 and 1943 the army sent him to the University of Michigan "to learn the Judge Advocate General's law and procedure." One of his Michigan classmates was Carl Albert, the future Speaker of the House of Representatives, upon whom Clausen conferred the thirty-third degree in 1971.[5] He served in the army at the rank of major (later lieutenant colonel), living in Washington and performing his duty, but able occasionally to enjoy the local golfing opportunities.

Then in 1944 he was assigned by Secretary of War Stimson to reinvestigate the possibility of American foreknowledge prior to the Japanese attack on Pearl Harbor, December 7, 1941. The Japanese naval codes had been broken by American cryptographers sometime before "the day that will live in infamy," raising the suspicion that Pearl Harbor could have been prevented but served ulterior motives to galvanize American public opinion to go to war. In preparing his exhaustive report for Stimson, which found no basis for the darker accusations of dissembling on the part of President Roosevelt or the Joint Chiefs of Staff (that is, that high officials did not intentionally withhold tactical information from the navy, which otherwise would have meant that Pearl Harbor was "allowed" to happen for political purposes), Clausen had to travel 55,000 miles.

He conducted nearly 100 interviews all around the world, including visits with ranking generals, admirals, and civilian officials. While Clausen maintained that "most definitely, there was no reason why the Japanese attack should have been a surprise," he concluded it was absurd to assume any complicity on the part of President Roosevelt or General George C. Marshall. Rather, the problem was in communications, so that "the proximate cause or guilt for the disaster at Pearl Harbor was an unworkable system of military intelligence, including the fact that the Navy withheld from the Army vital intelligence information that called for Army action."[6] Not only did he successfully refute insidious conspiracy theories, but he recommended "that there be a complete integration of Army and Navy intelligence agencies in order to avoid the pitfalls of divided responsibilities which experience has made so abundantly apparent." Clausen's judgment about unified military intelligence made him one of the first advocates for what later became the National Security Agency.[7]

When Clausen returned to civilian life, he became a law associate of Judge George E. Crothers and Francis V. Keesling; this partnership lasted twenty years (1947–1967). Clausen also resumed his active Masonic career. In 1947 he was invested with the rank and decoration of Knight Commander of the Court of Honor. Before being elected Grand Master of the Grand Lodge of California in 1954, he also became Inspector General Honorary and Deputy of the Supreme Council in California. The next year he was appointed Sovereign Grand Inspector General.

By the sixties he was a prominent figure in the deliberations of the Scottish Rite. Among the offices he held as an Active Member of the Supreme Council were Grand Master of Ceremonies (1961), Grand Orator (1963), Grand Minister of State (1965), and Deputy Grand Commander (1967). In addition to his Masonic duties, Clausen had a visible civic life, too. A leader in San Francisco's YMCA and Junior Chamber of Commerce and in local and state bar associations, Clausen was also a member of the prestigious Bohemian Club, founded in 1872 by the city's leading lights. The early bohemians included Mark Twain, Bret Harte, Ambrose Bierce, Henry George, and John Muir.[8] Clausen enjoyed, too, his memberships in the Commonwealth Club and the San Francisco Golf Club. (While living in Washington as Grand Commander he held memberships in the Metropolitan, Columbia, and Burning Tree Clubs).

At the executive session on October 23, 1969, Grand Commander Luther A. Smith installed Clausen, then Deputy Grand Commander and Sovereign Grand Inspector General in California, as Sovereign Grand Commander of the Supreme Council. At the same time Smith installed the other officers elected for the ensuing two years: R. Lee Lockwood, Deputy Grand Commander; Joshua K. Shepherd, Lieutenant Grand Commander; Dee A. Strickland, Grand Prior; Marshall S. Reynolds, Grand Chancellor; Charles P.

Rosenberger, Grand Minister of State; C. Fred Kleinknecht Jr., Grand Secretary General; Charles E. Webber, Grand Treasurer General; and Joseph W. Seacrest, Grand Almoner.

Clausen wasted no time in taking charge. On that same day he presided at a senatorial session and the thirty-third degree conferral.[9] He was the first Grand Commander whose personal roots were struck on the Pacific coast. Like many westerners, he was fiercely independent in his ideas, sometimes to the point of iron-clad predilections. Having lived through the rebuilding of San Francisco early in the century and having endured the pressures of a war-time investigation fraught with the potential disrepute of the highest office in the land, Clausen was unafraid to confront the necessity of change, if it was purposeful and rational. He assumed at once an aggressive style of leadership—modifying staff configurations, increasing the volume of publications, refining internal policy, streamlining ritual, developing regional Scottish Rite workshops, and broadening Scottish Rite community relations.

■ ■ ■

In his first address as Grand Commander at the closing banquet in 1969, Clausen proposed that regional Scottish Rite workshops be instituted at once. He stated that tremendous benefits from a similar idea had been derived when he was Inspector General for the California valleys and that, in his mind, the workshop model could be applied "with even greater benefits to the Supreme Council on a jurisdictional-wide basis."[10] He divided the Southern Jurisdiction into six areas for regional meetings, which were to be informal and without any official business to be decided. "The purpose was to get better acquainted, to exchange ideas, to improve our leadership and administrative techniques, to furnish guidance, to make for more efficient and effective functioning, and to bring our Supreme Council Headquarters' staff close to our valleys." It was a landmark project, which to a latter day may seem obviously necessary, but when initiated had the air of an exciting experiment. The results were "gratifying beyond measure" as Clausen sought "to strengthen and modernize the Rite."[11]

The agenda for these first regional workshops undergirded the existing means and habits of discussing specific issues. The Grand Commander, for instance, could report on Supreme Council legislation of recent sessions and review tax and insurance problems for fraternal organizations. After a Friday night dinner, Saturday was devoted to a variety of seminars on membership maintenance and expansion, *The New Age* magazine, the George Washington University Fellowships, and charitable programs to help children with learning and language disabilities.[12]

Another important innovation which Clausen introduced immediately was the establishment of the Archives of the Supreme Council. He enlisted Aemil Pouler to assemble, organize, file, and index records and documents that had been gathered and haphazardly stored over the years. The project was an enormous undertaking—ultimately concluding with a card index of 400,000 entries. Clausen, realizing that the council lacked any archival system whatsoever, also hired Aemil Pouler's son Chris, who assisted his father in the work. By 1971 the indexing of the *Transactions of the Supreme Council* from 1857 to 1890 and from 1955 to 1969 had been completed. Also, because the council had no proper space for historical records, five rooms in the House of the Temple were made over in order to store documents in a climate-controlled environment in acid-free folders and boxes placed in fireproof cabinets and shelves.[13]

Clausen made some other changes in staffing during his first two years. He appointed Robert B. Watts, a highly esteemed Scottish Rite Mason, lawyer, writer, and Episcopal minister, as director of education, with the charge to reorganize the previous volumes published in the Americanism program, rewriting them so that they included up-dated illustrations and statistics. The new series of booklets were published under the general title "Dynamics of Freedom." Watts, without seminary matriculation, had studied for the ministry and was ordained a priest of the Episcopal Church. He served for some years as assistant rector of St. James-by-the-Sea Episcopal Church at La Jolla, California.[14]

The Grand Commander, acutely conscious of history's importance to an organization, was eager to have finished the multivolume history project begun by Ray Baker Harris and continued, after Harris's death, by James D. Carter. When the new administration commenced, Carter was wearing several hats at once—historian, librarian, curator, and scholarship director. Clausen separated "the work in the Library and Museum . . . from that of the Historian." Carter, as a result of reorganization, was relieved of his responsibilities in the library and museum, being directed by Clausen to concentrate his attention on research and writing.

As of August 1970, Inge Baum managed single-handedly the library and museum as assistant librarian. Clausen had the highest regard for Mrs. Baum, whom he publicly commended "for her dedication to her work and the cheerful and willing assistance she render[ed] to all who [sought] her aid." In 1980, she received the title "Librarian," and she served faithfully in that capacity, earning the plaudits of many readers and visiting scholars, until her retirement in September 1993.[15]

Clausen's annoyance with the Grand Historian was partly mitigated when he saw that in mid-1972 volume three of *The History of the Supreme Council* was finally published in a pressrun of 3,000 clothbound copies, at a cost of $23,850. The production of this volume covering the years 1891 through 1921 seemed to Clausen unnecessarily prolonged, so he put Carter on notice that he was eager that the planned fourth volume not hit any snags. Carter had indicated he would need at least two years to complete a first draft of the next installment. This schedule probably did not sit well with the Grand Commander, who was himself a quick study and fast pen.[16]

Carter left Washington in the early summer of 1972 to reside in Dallas, Texas, a move that Clausen had strongly urged. Carter accepted a two-fold assignment—to complete the final volume covering 1921 through 1951 and, "acting for the Supreme Council" and specifically for Clausen, to "be [Clausen's] eyes and ears, and make recommendations with reference to the Texas situation" (a matter relating to the possible misuse of funds at the Scottish Rite Hospital). Soon after Clausen had given his orders, Carter had filed a report. Clausen fired back a stern admonition, telling Carter, "[O]mit your opinion and interpretations." Clausen, irritably concerned about the legal difficulties in Texas, not to mention the potential for adverse publicity, warned Carter, "[R]efrain from expressing to *anyone* your opinions and interpretations. That is most important." Carter was also required to submit a weekly written summary of his activities; and Clausen insisted that he himself review chapters in the history as they were freshly drafted.[17]

Clausen routinely pressed Carter for a completion date for the history. They agreed that June 1974 was a reasonable target. Revisions, editorial preparation, and selection of illustrations seemed all that was left to finish the job and turn it over to the printers. And yet, somehow the arrangement between author and publisher at this penultimate stage deteriorated. Carter had raised the question with Clausen about obtaining the copyright of the forthcoming publication for himself, thereby retaining royalty rights, too, or perhaps the opportunity to sell the copyright back to the Supreme Council. But that prospect had been addressed definitively at the session of 1971. With regard to material in *The New Age*, the histories, and all other publications, it was ruled that since those individual authors are either members volunteering their work or already paid staff, they forfeit their proprietary interests in their creativity. The ownership question had a simple answer: "It belongs to the Supreme Council." The fourth volume in question was never published. Carter was last listed as Grand Historian in *The New Age* in November 1974.[18]

Generally, Clausen inherited a dedicated and competent staff. One of its strengths was in its combined longevity and continuity. Christian Frederick Kleinknecht Sr., known as Chris, was completing a half-century of service to the Scottish Rite when Clausen arrived in Washington. And, of course, his son, C. Fred Kleinknecht Jr., who succeeded Clausen as Grand Commander in 1985, had already been on board for nearly twenty years.

Chris Kleinknecht, who embodied the deepest kind of staff loyalty, left Evansville, Indiana, on March 25, 1919, for Washington, D.C. He was taking a position that he had seen advertised in the *Washington Post* as clerk-bookkeeper for the Supreme Council. Twice he held the position of Acting Grand Secretary General, first in 1934 and 1935 and then for the years between 1940 and 1952.

The last fourteen years of his career as a Masonic executive were in the office of the Assistant Grand Secretary General, working closely with his son, the future Grand Commander. Kleinknecht established a system of membership record-keeping which was regarded as his greatest contribution, a real masterpiece of organization. John H. Cowles, who, before he was elected Grand Commander, had served briefly as Grand Secretary General, said on one occasion, "Chris was a much better Secretary General than I ever was." At the age of eighty, in 1969, Kleinknecht was selected for the Grand Cross Court of Honor. During his fifty-year career, Chris Kleinknecht developed an avocation of collecting philosophical aphorisms. Having amassed around twenty-seven manuscript volumes of quotations, he distilled the best of them into a useful set of books, *Gems of Thought Encyclopedia.*[19]

Before Clausen himself retired in 1985, Robert W. Cox stepped down as superintendent of the House of the Temple due to poor health. Marion Russell Stogsdill in May 1983 assumed the duties of overseeing the building's maintenance and improvement. Stogsdill was recognized early on as "a superior craftsman [who] has a natural affinity for exactness and detail." Major building repairs were planned and executed by Stogsdill down through the 1980s and early 1990s.[20]

While Grand Commander Luther A. Smith realized the futility of extending deferred maintenance any longer and began to revitalize the physical condition of the House of the Temple, it was Clausen who had the vision "to spike it up."[21] Mechanically, the building was asthmatic. It needed a new heating and air-conditioning system by the mid-1970s. The existing system for heat was sixty years old and had become inefficient. It took great amounts of fuel to make steam for the entire building. The House of the Temple was, therefore, fitted in 1977 with "a solar-heat pump system that included 21 modular collectors on the roof . . . that cannot be seen from the street." Some of the lower level rooms were reconditioned with paint and carpeting at this time, too. And by 1983 a new Schantz pipe organ was built for the Temple Room. Overall, an intensive six-year period of renewal, which "had become absolutely necessary," restored and refurbished many areas of the House of the Temple to their "former usefulness." This set the stage for advancing the temple beyond mere function to new levels of beautiful form in the years following Clausen's era.[22]

In terms of administration and management, Clausen was no less attentive to policy matters than he was to the physical condition and functioning of the headquarters building. Using the Supreme Council's committee structure, he guided the organization through several liability issues. One of the main fiduciary concerns was any possibility of conflict of interest on the part of Scottish Rite officials. The Supreme Council, therefore, adopted a resolution that was applicable to all officers and trustees of Scottish Rite related corporations, so that a possible conflict of interest on the part of any official (e.g., investments, construction contracts, or professional services) must be disclosed and "the minutes of the meeting shall reflect on such disclosure and the abstention from voting."[23]

Clausen exercised a strictness not only in financial decisions (he once objected to putting Scottish Rite money in a money market fund of government securities because it was a "type of uninsured mutual fund"[24]) and policy refinement; he took an avid interest in the details of running every Supreme Council program. In the case of the library and museum, for instance, he directed an inventory of the library's general collection, evaluating rare and significant works to place them "in a locked limited-access area" and discarding extraneous "book club clutter." It pleased him that after ten years as Grand Commander the use of the library (borrowing of books and reader services) had increased by 25 percent. Clausen proudly, perhaps immodestly, claimed that "a significant portion of this enlarged readership can be attributed to the use of the writings of your Grand Commander."[25]

Albert Pike referred to the beginnings of the library in the humblest terms, recalling that "in the autumn of 1878 the Supreme Council, except for its own publication[s], was not the owner of a single book."[26] Two years later over 1,000 volumes had been accumulated and a catalog was produced. A century after Pike's recollection about the library's incipience, it contained over 175,000 volumes. The Maurice H. Thatcher Collection, including approximately 800 books, many of which were autographed by the authors, and 100 cubic feet of manuscripts and personal papers, went into the library around 1971. A good deal of the Thatcher Collection is devoted to the building of the Panama Canal, where Thatcher served as the American governor.[27]

The California Scottish Rite bodies lent their support to the library in a significant way, too. They presented the library with a Renaissance dictionary, *Vocabularium Rerum*, that was in its original leather binding, printed in 1495. This five-hundred-year-old book, one of only three copies known to exist, was by far the oldest book in the library. The library, meanwhile, continued to keep alert for rare antiquities pertaining to Masonry. Herbert Orr's 1798 edition of *A History of Free Masonry; and the Duties Incumbent on the Craft* was successfully procured once it was made available. By far, however, the most novel item that entered the library or museum in Clausen's time was the gift by an anonymous donor of "a double-barrel, muzzle-loading shotgun in its original wooden case, formerly belonging to Albert Pike."[28]

．　．　．

Clausen possessed "the habit of command." He left a distinctive mark on the morale and organizational aspects of the Rite by keeping a firm finger on the most minute particulars and an eye on new trends, such as workshops and procedures for modernization. He had his greatest impact, undoubtedly, in reshaping some of the deep contours of Scottish Rite ritual and practices. Also of important note is the prolific amount of literature which flowed from the Grand Commander's office. As early as 1969 he chaired a special committee on *Morals and Dogma* that reported a need to supplement Pike's classic treatise. Out of this committee discussion grew the development and publication of *Clausen's Commentaries on Morals and Dogma*. In his retirement years Clausen, speaking of his book, reflected, "[I]t became my *magnum opus*, a more modern means of telling our candidates the story and lessons of the Scottish Rite in a manner which could be more easily received and digested than the scholarly prior compilations of Pike."[29]

By 1974 each new candidate, upon receiving the thirty-second degree, was usually given a copy of *Clausen's Commentaries*, replacing, in some instances, the traditional gift copy of Pike's original 1871 *Morals and Dogma*. Clausen noted, "[A] famous lawyer once told his young associates to be sure their legal codes were 'well thumbed.' I, similarly, would be most happy if our workers and members will use my efforts frequently, the better to understand, prepare and present the great teachings of our Scottish Rite."[30] First published in 1974 with an astoundingly large pressrun of 100,000, *Clausen's Commentaries* within ten years reached a distribution level exceeding 450,000 copies, including its translation into French, Italian, German, Spanish, Chinese, Japanese, and Portuguese. By Clausen's own satisfied reckoning, it was "the most popular book in Masonic history."[31]

Clausen's Commentaries kept to the stylistic formula that simplicity is equivalent to elegance. In defining the purpose of the Scottish Rite, the author averred an unadulterated credo, summarizing the overall mission as one "To seek that which is [of] most worth in the world; To exalt the dignity of every person, the human side of our daily activities and the maximum service to humanity; To aid mankind's search in God's Universe for identity, for development, and for destiny; And thereby achieve better men in a better world; happier men in a happier world, and wiser men in a wiser world." He concluded the book with an apt, interrogating word—forcing each reader to assess his life against the Rite's overarching goal, which has not been to teach any specific doctrine but rather to help each member to discover something of life, his life, the life beyond this life—"What must you do to assure the possibility there is a creative, eternal continuance of your life? In short, will your life serve a cosmic purpose?"[32]

Before his retirement as Grand Commander, Clausen was the author of at least nine books and over thirty pamphlets. It was "a steady outpouring of addresses, booklets, Grand Commander's messages, and other literary productions"[34] which ranked Clausen next to the inimitable Albert Pike in the sheer volume of publications he authored. He tried his hand at improving the quality of particular aspects of the ritual, too. The installation ceremony for Scottish Rite officers was prepared by Clausen with the significant alteration of allowing the public to attend. The opportunity for families and friends to be present for installations proved widely popular.[34]

Similarly, Clausen decided to open the Maundy Thursday and Easter morning ceremonies to friends and relatives of the Scottish Rite members. He noted, "Of course the esoteric and ritualistic portions of our work must be conducted prior to the 'open' portion [of the exercises]." In every instance of showing more openness, Clausen gained a favorable response. There was also an increasing tendency at this time to conduct the investiture of Knight Commander of the Court of Honor in open ceremony. The Committee on Rituals and Ceremonial Forms reported that "the Valleys seem universally to approve the modified open public services and increasing numbers express their intention to adopt them."[35]

At issue for several years, however, was the length of reunions in the valleys. The three-day reunions, with "the exemplification of all the degrees," was considered the norm. In rare instances some valleys extended their reunions to four days or more, and at least one valley annually held two six-day reunions. While the practice of multiple-day reunions was a desirable goal, it was not always practical. A new reality pointed to a trend of consolidating degree work that, in some places, found instant appeal and easy success by organizing an abridged one-day reunion. The growing custom of compressing the degree work into a single long day was "almost always the most popular and . . . may be justified on the basis that for one reason or another candidates [found] it impossible to spend greater length of time," which the older, preferred practices required.[36]

Rituals and ceremonies continued to be an area of potential reconsideration. Edward J. Franta, a thirty-third degree Mason from North Dakota, and Frank H. Davison, a thirty-third degree Mason from Idaho, whose home districts both fell within the Southern Jurisdiction, registered their objection to the phrase in the fourteenth degree obligation: ". . . and in the Lodge, if I know that any absent brother would, if present, vote against a candidate, I will myself vote in the negative, if otherwise I cannot have the election postponed until such brother shall have opportunity to be present." Their complaint was made on "the grounds that it violates the basic principle of absolute secrecy of the Masonic ballot."[37] Perhaps because this hypothetical situation seldom, if ever, arose, no alternative wording was ever worked out. Consequently, despite the eagle-eye attention to consistency and precision, by which Clausen became famous in Masonic circles, the wording remains unchanged.

Clausen issued a proclamation early in his term of office requiring all candidates for Scottish Rite degrees to witness, at least one time, a DeMolay degree. While the idea was to establish a solid link between two Masonic organizations, it was an order observed more in the breach than the practice. Milton E. Ammann, who was director of Masonic relations for the Order of DeMolay, called to Clausen's attention the apparent gap in implementing the coordination of such a practice in the valleys. Clausen's response stated that his directive was "sufficiently reduced to writing" in *The New Age* and that he was confident his wishes would be carried out "without further instruction."[38] For Clausen, the supreme realist on most matters, this was a rare case of catching him in the framework of hope triumphing over experience. Beyond their commitments to attend and learn Scottish Rite degree work, most men were simply too busy in all but exceptional cases to add DeMolay meetings to the calendar.

By the mid-1970s the Scottish Rite message was not only being effectively communicated through degree work, ritual, and ceremonies, but through the regular monthly magazine, *The New Age*. As of October 1975, the circulation stood at 640,000 and was continuing to grow. These were all-time peak levels which, before Clausen's departure, began to sag noticeably as Scottish Rite membership fell back to earlier averages. Clausen seized every opportunity he could to get the printed word into the hands of more and more people. His critics might have tagged him with the charge of verbosity or of never having an unpublished thought. His writings, however, circulated in remarkably high volume. Over 40,000 copies of bound editions of *Dynamics of Freedom* were sent to DeMolay chapters. For the national bicentennial in 1976, Clausen prepared the short but effective work *Masons Who Helped Shape Our Nation*, which had an immediate distribution of 19,000 copies. Another 11,000 copies were sold soon thereafter.[39]

In March 1979 he brought out *Authentics of Fundamental Law for Scottish Rite Freemasonry*, which was one of his books most in keeping with his training, qualifications, and experience as an attorney. This treatise was intended to "set the record straight and to prove without doubt the historical accuracy and genesis of our fundamental Scottish Rite organizational document, the *1786 Grand Constitutions. . . .*" Clausen went on to describe his research and writing as using "care and clarity" to stress the fact that "Frederick the Great personally sanctioned and signed the original document." The book included in the appendix Albert Pike's English translation from Latin of the *Grand Constitutions* and "a complete photocopy of the Mother Jurisdiction's confirming *Manifesto of 1802*." Clausen presented the traditional view of constitutional authorship before more convincing contrary interpretations were available to him.[40]

After Clausen wrote *Practice and Procedures for the Scottish Rite* (1983), "to assure uniformity and coordination consistent with high quality formal observances," an abiding interest characteristic of his legal mind, he entered a new phase of writing. Clausen was approaching his late seventies when he began to depart from prior book topics covering historical themes, public policy, and procedural matters of the Scottish Rite. He next turned to practical spiritual concerns.

Some might view these last efforts at Masonic book publishing as fitting the "self-help" genre which became popular in America through the 1980s. Norman Vincent Peale, of course, had spawned the expansive market for mass-audience literature which was devotional and uplifting. Clausen wrote *Beyond the Ordinary, Toward a Better, Wiser, and Happier World* (1983) to encourage people "when self-doubt riddles confidence and determination." His *Emergence of the Mystical* (1980) and *Your Amazing Mystic Powers* (1985) are also works devoted to self-mastery through "inherent powers," so that "when our mental energies are concentrated, great accomplishments automatically occur."[41]

Clausen's efforts in this popular literary genre represented a deviation from most postwar Masonic publishing strategies that had concentrated on standard pointers such as running a lodge meeting, producing a newsletter, serving patriotic causes, or, with a little more sophistication, understanding the ritual. Clausen's entries constituted a shift that was aimed at what the historian and social critic Christopher Lasch called our "therapeutic culture." Lasch explained that "the achievement of selfhood" is the difficult acknowledgement "of the tension between our unlimited aspirations and our limited understanding."[42] Lasch identified the explosion of success manuals in the 1970s as a reflection of the deepening concern over psychic survival in American culture. The human potential movement, the medical and psychiatric literature on "coping," and the generic usefulness of meditation adopted by many non-church groups provided warnings accompanied by remedies for "psychic numbing" and "emotional anesthesia." Clausen's ambiguous entries were an outgrowth and imitation of the surrounding field.

The development of the New Age phenomena, beginning around 1972 when the ex-Harvard psychologist Richard Alpert repackaged himself as Baba Ram Dass, was formless enough to engulf almost any author's practical guide for self-improvement through "transcendent awareness" or "holistic healing." But the amorphous term "New Age" is not very useful in the end because its protean qualities fail to differentiate among enthusiasms as diverse as those by the Masonic writer Henry Clausen, the Church of Scientology founder L. Ron Hubbard (author of *Dianetics: The Modern Science of Mental Health*, 1950), and the Reformed Church in America pastor Robert Schuller, whose "possibility thinking" was concretized in the glass colossus called the "Crystal Cathedral," built in 1980.

A better way to correlate Clausen's pensive foray into the self-affirmation movement is to view it as part of what the American historian Sydney Ahlstrom called "harmonialism." By that term Ahlstrom traced into the nineteenth century a tradition of shifting forms based on the premise that present worldly experience corresponds with higher truths in other realms of being, which is the end purpose of humanity's search for ultimate meaning. The accomplishment of this truth is essentially intellectual, though the benefits can be visionary, healing, and psychologically comforting.

Ahlstrom found "harmonial" currents in the teachings of Freemasons, Swedenborgians, Mormons, Theosophists, Rosicrucians, Christian Scientists, and those in the Unity School of Christianity and other New Thought groups. He included Norman Vincent Peale, Anne Morrow Lindbergh, and the Trappist monk Thomas Merton as standing in continuity with harmonial spiritual expressions.[43] And yet, Clausen does not base his confidence-building advice solely on the "transformative tools" of Freemasonry. Rather, he mouthed much of the shared common sense found in Schuller's ideas that possibilities are inherent in each individual, which have been stifled by inadequate knowledge and negative thoughts.

In the books he produced about unrealized mental and emotional abundance, Clausen did not promote the specific therapeutic benefits of practicing Masonry by itself. Instead he attempted to integrate Masonry, albeit unsystematically, with some of the harmonial alternatives that were already enjoying success in American culture by moving away from ritual esoterica understood by a few into a closer alignment with "positive" thinkers. Put into different terms, Clausen tried to widen his influence beyond fraternal boundaries. He endeavored to expand his views, hoping to cross over and reach an audience of non-Masonic readers. In that attempt his reach exceeded his grasp. The field was crowded with people who attracted greater notice.

■　■　■

Clausen's tenth anniversary as Grand Commander came in 1979. After sighing one well-deserved exhalation of "Whew!" he took stock of his achievements during that time, mentioning "workshops, membership gains, new ongoing programs, expanded services, modern charities, secure financing, new Bodies, Temple constructions, adherence to rituals and advocacy of the moral, spiritual and patriotic overtones, executive, administrative and evangelistic improvements."[44] What he did not mention was the slightly deteriorated general condition of American Freemasonry at the end of the seventies; it had suffered sizeable membership erosion among other lesser setbacks. With that additional background, Clausen's accomplishments seem all the more impressive. The Soutern Jurisdiction, like any garden with roses, had a few thorns needing to be plucked. But overall, Clausen had performed well in his first decade as Grand Commander. He also might have mentioned his key role in cementing fraternal bonds between the Supreme Council and prominent American Freemasons who were public or elected officials in the nation's capital.

In American history, as of the conclusion of Clausen's era in 1985, there had been fourteen U.S. presidents and nineteen vice presidents who were Masons. Military, business, and labor leaders, scientists, judges, and artists have also been dually represented in the highest ranks of Masonry and the professions. President Gerald R. Ford, a thirty-third degree Mason in the Northern Masonic Jurisdiction, invited Grand Commander Clausen to the White House in the fall of 1974 to discuss issues bearing on the separation of church and state. It was the kind of meeting that mostly illustrates the importance of fraternal associations and friendships which sometimes extend from the pinnacles of elected office to prominent constituents.[45] Clausen's White House visit was a courtesy, honorable and posing no conflict of interest to the president; that Clausen's voice was a determining factor in Ford's moderate policies seems very unlikely.

There is, of course, no way of assessing what political benefits, if any, accrue from Masonry's representation in national leadership, or whether, on the other side of the street, the politically famous enhance Masonry's social status. It probably helps some candidates to make public their Masonic ties, but not always. Masonry and American political history have been paired at times either inseparably or at odds. The American electorate is historically mercurial about a candidate's fraternal membership or social affiliations. Because Henry Clay in 1832 refused on principle to "renounce or denounce" his Masonic membership in his Lexington, Kentucky, lodge in order to gain votes (i.e., pandering to those viewing fraternal membership either as a favorable asset or as an objectionable liability), his prospects for succeeding as a presidential candidate were greatly diminished, though Anti-Masonry alone did not defeat Clay. Andrew Jackson's popularity was Clay's main obstacle. However, Clay did not believe an election should be decided on the basis of a candidate's private relationships.[46]

It is extremely doubtful that any form of favoritism or conflict of interest could ever be shown where executives of Masonry have had personal contact with elected or politically appointed officials. Simply put, it runs against the Masonic code of honor to capitalize on potentially profitable connections that originate through a mutual devotion to the lodge. Masonry's fundamental belief in the equality of men, regardless of their life's station, is a built-in guard against it becoming a vehicle of political influence. Every man becomes a Mason in the same way, carrying no sign of wealth or social importance into the Lodge.

The oft-told story of President Truman visiting lodges while still occupying the White House, and sitting on the sidelines like any other Mason, is an example of Masonry's propriety that insists no individual is ever regarded as greater than the brotherhood. Truman attended lodge in one instance while his White House gardener presided as the Worshipful Master. At best, therefore, the benefit to the Order of having men in powerful positions has been moral, never material. It may elevate the prestige of the fraternity, but neither Masonry nor individual members can find the precedent or the possibility to exploit fraternal relationships for purposes other than the intrinsic promotion of Masonic ideals. While hard to document, business or professional relationships formed between brothers ideally originated in circumstances external to Masonry and not for the sole reason of a common lodge association, though fraternal bonds did none of them any harm.

Speaker of the House of Representatives Carl Albert wrote Clausen that he felt "doubly honored" by serving as the thirty-third degree class candidate and the class spokesman at the Supreme Council session of October 1971.[47] At the next session in 1973, North Carolina senator Samuel J. Ervin, a thirty-third degree Mason, was elected to receive the Grand Cross Court of Honor.[48] Ervin, though claiming to be a humble "country lawyer," was a leading Constitutional authority in Congress. At the time of his Scottish Rite investiture he was chairman of the Senate Select Committee on Campaign Practices. It was Ervin's nationally televised committee hearings that revealed, through the testimony of Nixon White House aides, particularly that of John Dean, the extent of a presidential cover-up over the break-in at the Democratic National Committee's headquarters at the Watergate apartment-office complex on June 17, 1972. The committee also learned that a secret tape-recording system was operating at the White House, authorized by President Nixon himself, and that conversations about Watergate had been preserved. Ervin's brilliant and even-tempered role in the drama brought him national celebrity that was based on affection and respect.

Senator Lloyd M. Bentsen, a thirty-third degree Mason from Texas, was the speaker, representing the class of new Inspectors General Honorary, at the coronation banquet in 1973.[49] Bentsen's later career in the Senate culminated with the chairmanship of the Senate Committee on Finance. In 1993 he became President William J. Clinton's secretary of the treasury.

A Capitol Hill "personality" for several decades, House Sergeant-at-Arms William M. "Fish Bait" Miller, a thirty-third degree Mason, was appointed more than once by Grand Commander Clausen as Grand Tyler of the Supreme Council. Miller was on hand for many council ceremonies. In 1977 Senator Robert C. Byrd, a thirty-third degree Mason from West Virginia who was later the Senate Majority Leader, and Representative John J. Rhodes, a thirty-third degree Mason from Arizona who was later the House Minority Leader, were together elected Grand Crosses of the Court of Honor.[50]

In an unusual sequence of events connecting the rise and fall of political power with Masonic recognition, Wilbur D. Mills, a thirty-third degree Mason, became a controversial figure during Clausen's administration and was potentially an embarrassment to the Supreme Council. Mills, a senior member of Congress from Arkansas, was elected to receive the Grand Cross Court of Honor in 1971. He was then the much feared chairman of the potent House Ways and Means Committee. Mills was considered a cunning player in the allocation of congressional favors as a means of getting votes for the enacting of legislation. For a politician of the stature that Mills had achieved by the early seventies, Machiavelli proposes that "it is far safer to be feared than loved." Congressman Mills, though intimidating and greatly feared, was not immune to power's corruption. Not by his enemies, however, but by his own self-destructive behavior Mills fell from office. After several notorious public episodes of heavy drinking, one of which ended in the company of the burlesque dancer Fannie Foxe, with whom he fell into the Tidal Basin of the Potomac River late one night, Mills was forced out of power. His Masonic honors were stripped from him almost immediately. Mills worked hard over the next few years to rehabilitate his reputation, acknowledging his personal problems with alcohol and accepting the blame for the harm he had caused himself, his family, his constituents, and the Congress. By unanimous action in a special executive session of the Supreme Council in 1981, Mills had restored the Grand Cross Court of Honor.[51]

■ ■ ■

Freemasonry in America during the national tumult of the late sixties and seventies was battered from the outside and hardened from the inside along with all other "establishment" institutions—churches, schools, universities, political parties, and the American family. The social chaos of 1969, following the presidential election, touched every organization in America for the next twenty years. President Richard M. Nixon appeared on television on April 30, 1970, to announce that the United States had launched an "incursion" into Cambodia, a neutral country bordering war-torn Vietnam. Nixon had campaigned on the promise of ending the war quickly through a secret plan. Anti-war protest exploded on campuses that had not been known for any particular activism. On May 4, 1970, Ohio National Guard units, exhausted from peace-keeping duties in riot-prone inner cities, fired into a crowd of fleeing students at Kent State University, killing four young people. Less than two weeks later, police and state troopers armed with automatic weapons strafed a women's dormitory at Jackson State University, a historically black college in Mississippi. Two students were killed, nine were wounded. No evidence was ever found to substantiate the police claims that they were fired upon first; the police neither lobbed in tear gas nor fired warning shots.

The Nixon presidency inherited a public mood of distress and suspicion. Frustrated by its inability to reverse the anger and fear rampant in America, the Nixon administration itself became edgy and distrustful of even small degrees of normal opposition.

Despite a landslide victory in 1972, the die was already cast for the Nixon presidency, because the atmosphere in the country and in the White House had spiraled downward beyond immediate revocation. When a petty burglary, which turned out to be authorized by high officials in government, was interrupted, causing the arrest of five men, the White House panicked. Incriminating documents were destroyed, and the FBI was discouraged from its investigation on the pretext that national security might somehow be compromised. As the plot unfolded and a cover-up became apparent through congressional hearings and the U.S. District Court proceedings, the Nixon presidency, during the next two years of its second term, unravelled, ending with Nixon's resignation and the controversial postscript of his preemptive pardon by President Gerald R. Ford. The Watergate scandal did more than merely inspire remedies and restrictions about the use of executive power; it infected public morale at every level. Suddenly, it seemed, scandalous behavior was at the top of every kind of organization in America. The disturbing perception of universal chicanery dominated the headlines for the rest of the decade.

Unfortunately, Scottish Rite Freemasonry was not exempt from its own share of this peculiar and alarming national trend, which was uncovering all manner of graft. Early in 1972 Grand Commander Clausen learned that "a scandal of major proportions concerning the Valley of Dallas, the Orient of Texas and related corporations"[52] had surfaced. At a time when blue lodges nationally were in a period of declension, the news of a scandal was embarrassing and damaging. Clausen was eager for the criminal investigations to proceed while he conducted his own inquiry through the auditing services of Arthur Andersen and Company and in the rigorous course of Masonic tribunals.

It was a straightforward case of embezzlement, whereby Paul Prasifka, secretary of the Endowment Division of the Texas Scottish Rite Hospital, had written checks to himself "from the revolving funds of the Dallas Lodge in the amount of $29,300." Also involved in the misappropriation of funds was Prasifka's father-in-law, a former Dallas Crime Commission president, John McKee. The audit revealed that there were unsupported, undocumented disbursements made to McKee on his instructions in 1971 totaling $49,058. The Andersen audit mentioned that McKee subsequently reimbursed the Dallas bodies $11,834 of the original sum, which included repayment relating to two automobiles. But, in addition, another expenditure of $7,702 was made in January 1972 without supporting documentation.[53]

Clausen, meanwhile, dispatched James D. Carter to keep tabs on the developments in Dallas, as Carter had already been directed by Clausen to move from Washington to Texas in order to complete the final volume of the Supreme Council's history. Clausen raised specific questions about the accounting practices in Dallas: "Was there a devious cover-up of the revolving fund to which Grant and Company or other accountants were a party so that the Inspector General was misled? Did the accounts as furnished fail to disclose information to the Inspector that our Statutes or policies or regulations required to be furnished? What accountants failed to keep an account of the revolving fund and what were their excuses for doing so?"[54] Carter reported that McKee's expenses were "authorized" from as long ago as May 1955 and, from that point on, were usually covered routinely by the Lodge of Perfection at each December meeting through a "blanket resolution ratifying all acts of the Executive Committee for the year."[55]

The Texas Scottish Rite Hospital and Scottish Rite Foundation, according to Arthur Andersen and Company, also used some of their funds in a questionable way. Hospital monies were deployed in several instances relating to the foundation or to Sovereign Grand Inspector General Lee Lockwood. The hospital paid $3,055 for furniture in Lockwood's office in Waco and, in addition, had provided a secretary for Lockwood since March 1966 at an annual salary of $8,000. Further, the Scottish Rite Foundation of Texas paid Lockwood $5,400 annually for supplemental secretarial services; this latter payment was discontinued in 1971. Andersen reported incidents of other improvident financial activity when "in 1971 hospital funds were loaned" to individuals or local businesses related to Masonic executives; the loans totaled at least $517,000. The Andersen audit strongly recommended that financial transactions between Masons and "entities which they own or control" be avoided where a transparent question of conflict of interest could be raised. "For example, between $250,000 and $300,000 in certificates of deposit were in institutions associated or controlled by [Lee] Lockwood." The report suggested "that such deposits be put in unrelated institutions."[56]

Criminal prosecutions, meanwhile, resulted from the district attorney's investigation. Paul Prasifka pleaded guilty to four counts of embezzlement and one for theft. He was sentenced to ten years of probation, and ordered to repay $24,500 to the Scottish Rite. John McKee was given a seven-year probated sentence for embezzling $3,802.[57] Masonic trials also concluded with expulsions, while civil actions were filed for damages.

James D. Carter offered a sobering reflection, writing to the Grand Commander, "[A]s a Masonic historian I can assure you that the corruption which broke out in Dallas in 1971 is not unusual nor is it restricted to Subordinate Bodies." He went on to say that "irregularities in the operation of the Dallas Bodies were of long standing and unknown to the present Inspector General and Grand Commander. They began as early as 1904 when an Executive Committee was formed and began to usurp the authority, powers, functions and duties of the Bodies and their officers, and even that of the Inspector General who was, at that time Assistant Secretary General of the Supreme Council." During the Depression, for instance, the business of the Inspector General of Texas went bankrupt after he had spent his personal fortune trying to rescue it. Until his death he used funds from the "revolving account" for his personal needs. Carter was, in the end, reassured that the criminal activity in Texas was not as extensive as his earlier reports had indicated, since only two Masons were indicted by the grand jury and subsequently received guilty verdicts.[58]

His report was never publicized, as Clausen firmly and eagerly wished to minimize the ill effect of scandal. Without needlessly dwelling on it, Clausen assumed that significant lessons were drawn from the Texas situation and, along with so many positive achievements, were also left for the posterity of Scottish Rite bodies nationwide.

■　■　■

Membership in the Southern Jurisdiction between 1970 and 1980 increased dramatically, leaving high-water marks like a river upon its banks after a flood's crest. The increase in the Scottish Rite, Southern Jurisdiction, was an enormous boon to morale because all other Masonic organizations during the seventies were undergoing significant downturns. Volunteer societies and mainline Protestant churches also suffered heavy membership erosion in those years. The Grand Lodges of America were uniformly losing ground each year, as young men of the Vietnam era, often disenchanted with traditional public structures, turned away from supporting fraternal organizations and community associations which had been filled with their fathers and grandfathers. Young people, in general, were reluctant to make commitments that had been a matter of duty for prior generations. By the late seventies, their era was often and popularly cited as the "Me-generation"; many recently college-educated members of that generation began hearing themselves referred to derisively in the broadcast and print media as YUPPIES (an acronym standing for "young urban professionals"). Thus, the ties were loosened all across America. Even the institution of marriage was reshaped as many young couples cohabited for trial periods of living together. Masonry's overall loss, therefore, was not exceptional. It had enough critical mass, however, to retrench without being threatened with elimination. But a number of fraternal organizations by the eighties were struggling to survive, such as the Redmen, the Odd Fellows, the Moose, and the Elks.

In an odd disparity, however, while blue lodge membership decreased by about 10 percent during the seventies, Scottish Rite membership in the Southern Jurisdiction over the same period rose by more than 12 percent. Membership in the Grand Lodges, U.S.A., for the first half of the decade showed no precipitous drop, but clearly showed a discernible downward trend.[59]

MEMBERSHIP IN THE GRAND LODGES, U.S.A.

Year	Numerical Decrease	Percent Decrease
1971	53,991	1.44
1972	58,065	1.57
1973	53,721	1.47
1974	55,256	1.53
1975	53,333	1.50
1976	45,347	1.31
Total	319,713	8.82

Comparing Scottish Rite membership increases to blue lodge decreases during the same period probably bears no cause-and-effect relationship; it was a lag factor that would eventually catch up with the Rite. Against blue lodge retrenchment, Scottish Rite membership success was a false positive, especially so because the only way to join the Scottish Rite was through the gate of craft Masonry. Blue lodge trends, therefore, were reliable predictors of what happened in time to the Scottish Rite. The blue lodge was a great contracting reservoir of nearly 4 million members, but even with its striking rates of attrition, it still provided the Scottish Rite a relatively large and excellent source of fresh members for ten years beyond the dip in overall Masonic membership.

SCOTTISH RITE MEMBERSHIP, SOUTHERN JURISDICTION[60]

Years Ending 12/31	Lodges of Perfection
1970	581,025
1972	601,495
1974	625,690
1976	647,657
1978	658,587
1980	659,468
1982	654,009
1984	641,785

By 1982, when a slight drop in Scottish Rite membership first appeared, the fifty U.S. Grand Lodges reported a loss of 66,380 out of a total membership of 3,121,746, a 2 percent loss for one year. Ten years after the first signs of Scottish Rite slippage, the Southern Jurisdiction had just under 500,000 members, which still made it a sizeable force. But all the trends had caught up to the same reality, though not as rapidly nor at the same overall rate. The Scottish Rite, fortuitously, bought recovery time by its growth during the Clausen years.

The York Rite, however, did not fare as well. The reasons the York Rite was shrinking faster than the Scottish Rite were perhaps several. First, the York Rite was Christian only, so its appeal had one built-in restriction. Secondly, it was closely associated with the life of the local blue lodge, meeting in the lodge hall, whereas Scottish Rite properties were generally independent of the blue lodge patterns of activity. When the blue lodge fared well, so did the York Rite. Thirdly, as American culture drifted away from formality in etiquette and attire, the York Rite simply had too much plumage. Along the same lines, according to Masonic scholar Brent Morris, prestige and status might have also been a marked factor of difference between the Scottish Rite and York Rite. Morris points out that "from a purely marketing point of view, being a 32° Mason sounds more important than being a Knight Templar." Still another reason was that those Masons interested in the Shrine might have found that the Scottish Rite avenue required less time.[61]

Among the explanations of why the Scottish Rite in the Southern Jurisdiction prospered, some were more plausible than others. The regional workshops, no doubt, helped to generate suggestions and facilitate the exchange ideas of what worked and what flopped in membership recruitment.[62] Everett Houser, however, made a well-meaning, though misplaced, stab at an explanation in theorizing to Grand Commander Clausen that the increase of membership in the Valley of Long Beach, California, was mainly due to Clausen's "improved rituals." While flattering to the Grand Commander, it was a questionable attribution.[63]

Clausen was wise to recognize that the fortunes of Scottish Rite Freemasonry were tied ultimately to the success of the blue lodges. In 1981 he established a committee of the Supreme Council on Masonic Relations and Masonic Membership Erosion. William E. Eccleston, an Active Member of the Supreme Council and Past Grand Master in the District of Columbia, was appointed chairman of the committee. Clausen communicated his intentions for the committee in crisp, clear terms—Masonry's image needed improving. Publicizing Masonry's historic fight for freedom; making its facilities clean and attractive; cultivating former DeMolays, of whom 50 percent already went on to become Masons; adjusting fees for younger candidates who were under the age of thirty-one; and circulating the pamphlet "To a Non-Mason: You Must Seek Masonic Membership!" were all positive suggestions that did some good and did no harm against a tide of change in American society that, in the last analysis, was outside anyone's control to alter seriously.

. . .

External relations of the Supreme Council under Grand Commander Clausen's leadership were steady, but often delicate. He attended many international conferences, touring Europe extensively in the fall of 1978. From Athens, Greece, during that long European trip he went on to Tehran, Iran, where the twenty-eighth conference of the European Sovereign Grand Commanders was supposed to meet; but because of civil hostilities culminating in the overthrow of the Shah of Iran by radical Islamic forces led by the Ayatollah Khomeni, the conference was cut short. His experience in foreign relations climaxed decisively when he served as host for the Thirteenth International Conference of Supreme Councils in Washington, D.C., in late May 1985. Twenty-six Supreme Councils from all over the world sent delegations. One of Clausen's most noteworthy contributions in the field of international Masonry, however, came in 1973 when he decided to restore fraternal relations with the Supreme Council of Germany and the Supreme Council of Peru. Luther A. Smith had suspended relations with Germany in a decree dated December 27, 1967. The disagreement over the Scottish Rite creedal prerequisite of an individual's belief in God was put to rest so that Clausen could enjoy the benefits of foreign communication without controversy. It was this gesture which made his travels so fruitful and the 1985 conference in Washington so helpful. Clausen was presented the Cross of Merit by the German Supreme Council which was the first time that a Masonic medal was given to a Freemason outside of Germany.[64]

The Supreme Council's external concerns on the home front continued to be challenged occasionally on the issue of race in America. Clausen, like his three immediate predecessors who served as Grand Commander, heard frequently from Masons around the country who were troubled by the racial divide in America, which one might suppose Masonry could help transcend and, therefore, heal. From a navy captain came a pointed but polite inquiry representative of many fellow Mason's views:

> As a career military man I have possessed a frustration since becoming a Mason. Through the guidance of my parents and military teachings, I speak squarely when I say I have no racial prejudices. After 21 months in Vietnam and serving with pride with Americans of all colors and religions, this frustration becomes more pronounced as I observe the attitudes of Americans in the continental U.S., many of whom are Masons.
>
> The frustration is this. In the 18 years I have been a 3rd degree Mason I have observed Masonic rings and pins on many Black Americans, yet I have never seen one in our Lodges. I am told that all Negro Lodges are clandestent [sic], of many racial heritages. Thus my questions to the Council are: Is the Masonic order a fraternity of segregationists? Are Negro Americans permitted to join the Masonic fraternity? If not now, is there consideration being given to open the doors?[65]

Clausen's reply was brief, but most importantly, said nothing new. He fell back on the position lined out by all other Grand Commanders of the Southern Jurisdiction: "Freemasonry must maintain our time-tested standards and laws of regularity. Thus, regardless of misconceptions as to the reason, we do not recognize clandestine Masons. Regularity is the test." Clausen perhaps helped his argument by adding that "the charities of our regular Masonic organizations aggregate gifts of many millions of dollars each year without regard to race, color or creed."[66]

After an article of Clausen's appeared in *The New Age*, entitled "This Changing World and Masonry," one sensitive correspondent wrote that "in this changing world, there is room for change in Masonry, too. . . . I refer to the exclusion of black persons from being raised in our Lodges." The writer, a thirty-second degree Mason from Tucson, Arizona, brought into the issue a new quandary: "As a white Mason, who has grandchildren with colored blood in their veins—I would certainly have a hard time justifying to them, should they ever be interested in joining the order, the fact that they would be barred from associating with their Grandfather and his brothers."[67]

Clausen was unwilling to press for any modification of the technically consistent policy of "the sovereign right of a private organization not to accept any persons, regardless of race, color, creed, or culture, who [it] feel[s] might provoke local or jurisdiction-wide dissension and disharmony." In a letter marked personal and confidential to Charles W. Parkhurst, a thirty-third degree Deputy in Puerto Rico, Clausen argued, "[W]e must also realize that this is a two-way street and that obvious alternatives are available to persons we do not accept. For example, they may join other organizations which, in turn, could bar us as members." He did not cite a specific example where that had actually happened but merely invoked the argument of authority based on the decisions of Cowles, Harkins, and Smith: "We are bound to follow that confirmed policy."[68] The Supreme Council under the leadership of Clausen's successor as Sovereign Grand Commander, C. Fred Kleinknecht, would begin to ease that "confirmed policy" by developing a warm rapport with Prince Hall Scottish Rite Masonry. Some shared public ceremonies, such as the 1993 reenactment of the Masonic cornerstone laying at the U. S. Capitol (1793), included representatives of Prince Hall Masonry along with the Grand Lodges of Maryland, Virginia, the District of Columbia, and the Supreme Council, Southern Jurisdiction.

The Southern Jurisdiction's longstanding support of American public schools, vis-à-vis the separation of church and state, was sorely tested by both judicial and legislative activity in the seventies. It was irksome to the Committee on Education and Americanism that Senators Henry Jackson of Washington, Bob Dole of Kansas, Lloyd Bentsen of Texas, and Barry Goldwater of Arizona, all of whom were thirty-third degree Masons, voted for the Packwood-Moynihan Bill of 1978, otherwise called the Tuition Tax Credit Act. Parents who sent their children to parochial or private schools instead of local public schools were entitled to a tax credit in lieu of their share of benefits in public, tuition-free education, according to a majority of U.S. senators. This position ran counter to the historic Scottish Rite belief in nonsectarian public schools as representing egalitarian goals and the best vehicle of citizenship training. In 1979 the Supreme Council received an assessment of American education, from within its own ranks, that reflected the view of many citizens: "Our problem is compounded by a steady deterioration of the public schools. Demands on them have increased. They are called upon not only to handle education, but also to solve social problems which have little or nothing to do with the educational process. Bussing of students to promote racial integration is an example. Discipline has become a serious problem. Teacher morale is declining. In a political campaign in Washington state, an argument for state aid to private schools was that public schools are not doing the job of teaching."[69]

Between 1966 and 1978, twelve states held referenda which dealt with various plans for "parochiaid." In every case the measures were defeated at the polls. But by 1978 the mood began to swing another way, particularly as confidence in American public education declined. Timely alternatives were emerging out of local experiences; more and more voters were demanding a choice in how their children were to be educated. The strategy for supporters of direct government aid to parochial or private education was forced to shift also as a result of U.S. Supreme Court decisions such as *Committee for Public Education and Religious Liberty v. Nyquist* (1973).

A divided court struck down three New York programs—direct grants to private schools for "maintenance and repair" of facilities and equipment, a tuition reimbursement plan for parents of low-income status with children in private schools, and tax deductions for parents who did not meet the test for tuition reimbursement. As University of Virginia law professor A. E. Dick Howard points out, *Nyquist* did not succeed for the proponents of direct or indirect public support of parochial education, but it did mark a substantial change. The Supreme Court had always been nearly unanimous in previous cases that struck down federal aid to parochial education. The *Nyquist* case brought about a more divided Court, three justices dissenting in whole or in part. As the seventies progressed, the Court relaxed the barrier somewhat on private schools receiving state funds.[70] The Scottish Rite found itself in puzzlement about what to do, beyond helping to support financially the Americans United for the Separation of Church and State. But the old tide had gone out.

John D. Blankinship, Sovereign Grand Inspector General in Washington, lamented that "in 1983, [Justice] Powell completed his switch by joining Justices Burger, White, Rehnquist, and O'Connor in upholding a Minnesota statute which gave parents a tax deduction for tuition paid to grade schools and high schools." Blankinship forecasted additional breaches in the wall of separation based on Justice Rehnquist's remark "that some of the landmark decisions of the Supreme Court in the field of church/state relationships are open to reconsideration. These include cases on government aid to sectarian schools, prayers in public schools, released time and similar matters."[71]

One of the Scottish Rite's firmest stands in the public arena was in need of renewal for other reasons, too. Not only were state and federal courts and legislatures thinking twice about absolute separation of church and state, particularly with regard to public schools, but so, too, was the executive branch of the federal government. The Reagan administration, responding partly to its fundamentalist Christian support, expressed dissatisfaction with court rulings which strictly kept religious influence out of public schools or public money out of religious schools. Reagan's second secretary of education, William J. Bennett, publicly stated the possibility of trying to "nullify" the court rulings prohibiting public school districts from providing private and parochial schools with teachers to supplement their curriculum. The attorney general, Edwin A. Meese III, expressed disagreement with the Court. According to John D. Blankinship, the Department of Justice fought to delay implementation of those court rulings. Further, President Reagan advocated legislation to provide credits against federal income tax for tuition payments, a de facto subsidy of private and parochial schools, since public schools do not charge tuition.[72]

In some respects the fires of earlier inspiration, fueled by the disputed religion clause of the First Amendment, which burned so fervently and brightly for the Scottish Rite under Grand Commander Cowles as a galvanizing force, were by the seventies too hot and unpredictable to put out, and too widespread to fight systematically. The Supreme Council's strong backing of the separation of church and state, which corroboratively meant unflinching dedication to the principles of public education accessible to all Americans, had not changed under Clausen. The intensity around a single principle, however, was increasingly more difficult to sustain for groups such as the Scottish Rite, in light of the complexity of the situation: the perception of the declining quality in public schools, making the desire for alternatives more understandable; the rightward political shift of the nation with the election of Ronald Reagan in 1980, which many Scottish Rite Masons certainly welcomed; and the linkage of troubled family paradigms

LODGE OF THE DOUBLE-HEADED EAGLE

— 342 —

with the "failure" of the schools, thus creating the sense of crisis in American values, from table manners to reverence for life. Put differently, the Reagan coalition formed of traditional American conservatism (historically embracing free enterprise and individual choice and responsibility)—which still included moderate Republicans such as George Bush, and southern and Sun Belt whites, and was composed largely of evangelical and fundamentalist Protestants—constituted a confusing package of positions.

Old patriotic values and symbols, cherished by American Masons, were somehow slipped alongside newer demands for church moral authority to infuse itself into state power, while simultaneously keeping the state "off the backs" of individuals. As a consequence, the early activism of Grand Commanders and the Supreme Council immediately before and after World War II could not be duplicated in a politically altered setting that was highly complex in its new, crisscrossed alignments. No one could have predicted that southern white (fundamentalist) Protestants and conservative Roman Catholics, two groups traditionally at odds theologically, would find themselves agreeing in the seventies and eighties on so many social issues, such as parochial school aid, abortion, and the role of women. Clausen remained attentive, but to do more in the theater of public issues than simply reminding Masons of their shared ideals and heritage would have been tilting at windmills or, worse, creating a house divided.

The Scottish Rite maintained, meanwhile, other avenues of support in the field of education besides its promotion of the American public school system. Grants to educational institutions and scholarship aid continued to be an important means of touching the lives of young Americans pursuing their dreams of building successful careers. Grand Commander Clausen estimated in 1985 that the Supreme Council's college and university scholarships, when combined with various awards made by many of the orients, exceeded in their totality $1.25 million annually.

Participating in higher education, therefore, continued to be an emphasized priority for the Grand Commander. In March 1970 Clausen was elected to the Board of Trustees of the George Washington University, making him the third consecutive Grand Commander to be elected to the university's board. The relationship with George Washington University began comfortably for Clausen, who in 1975 presented the devoted Scottish Rite member Renah F. Camalier with the honorary degree of Doctor of Public Service.[73]

Sometime before Camalier received his well-deserved recognition by the George Washington University, the first breezes of criticism about the university's Scottish Rite Fellowship program began to blow from within the Southern Jurisdiction's ranks. Many of the students completing their work at the university, according to the grousers, were going into business and not into government for which the fellowship program had been designed. By 1977 Dr. Phillip D. Grub had been designated by Clausen to be the director of the Scottish Rite Fellowship program at the George Washington University. That same year Clausen proudly reported that there were forty Scottish Rite Fellows, all of whom were Master's degree candidates at George Washington, eighteen of them in the

School of Public and International Affairs and twenty-two in the School of Government and Business Administration.[74]

After 1980, however, Clausen, for reasons that are only partly understood as a degree of personal animus toward the university, made threats about withdrawing support from the George Washington program. Near the end of his commandership he actually carried them out, suspending the Scottish Rite's presence at George Washington. In the spring of 1980, Grub, who was also a professor of public administration at George Washington, wrote an article for *The New Age* entitled "Scottish Rite Fellows Are Tomorrow's Leaders." His title as given was "Director, Scottish Rite Fellowship Program, The George Washington University, Office of the President." It may have been that final designation of Grub's position, "Office of the President," which most rankled Clausen. From that point forward, the two men fell out, the university was accused of deception, and the continuity of a successful program was in jeopardy.

By early 1983 Clausen ordered, "[T]he George Washington project [would] be suspended, except for scholarships then pending, unless and until my complaints as set forth in my letters to [university president Lloyd H. Elliott] are resolved to my satisfaction." Clausen's apparent objection was that the university was using Scottish Rite Fellowships to help students prepare for careers in other fields besides foreign service. Grub responded to the decree by contacting the Active Members and Deputies of the Supreme Council, "without consulting [Clausen]," to inform them of Clausen's artless use of power. Grub's memo infuriated Clausen, who wrote immediately to Lloyd Elliott, a thirty-third degree Mason, "[Grub's] transparent attempt to by-pass myself as Grand Commander . . . also intercepts the negotiations between us, on our level." Clausen was referring to his request of Elliott that he "produce figures showing [his] 'track record' on recruits for the Foreign Service in comparison with other universities." He told Elliott, "If George Washington cannot or will not carry out the original intent, or if the State Department recruitment is nationwide, then many of our Orients have universities with programs in the desired field the equal, if not superior, to George Washington." Clausen also complained that George Washington University had not fittingly recognized the Scottish Rite by naming a building or hall for it. His letter also awkwardly raised the touchy question of honorary degrees.[75] In spite of some relevance, such as Clausen's valid concern about university accountability to its donors, he mostly seemed out of touch and vindictively overreacting.

Cooler heads, in time prevailed, and were first made manifest by President Elliott's measured and gracious rebuttal. Elliott responded to all three areas of Clausen's diatribe. With regard to Elliott's understanding of the original purpose of the Scottish Rite Scholarship Program, he wrote: "I find nothing in the records of the University which differs in substance from the outline you gave going back to President Marvin's report to the Supreme Council in 1931. The School of Government at George Washington University was indeed established with the help of the Scottish Rite grant to prepare students 'for either foreign or domestic service under our government.' When President Marvin reported that 30% of the then student body of the School of Government was preparing for foreign service he was referring, of course, to the field of international diplomacy."[76]

Later in his letter Elliott dealt with the supposed lack of recognition by pointing out that in the main lobby of the Hall of Government, which was constructed in 1937, there was a bronze plaque that recorded the role of the Scottish Rite in establishing the School of Government. Elliott went on to specify that the two schools which grew out of the original School of Government—the School of Government and Business Administration and the School of Public and International Affairs—had a combined operating budget for 1982 through 1983 of about $8 million. Income from the Scottish Rite endowment, he indicated, was running approximately $170,000 annually.

Lastly, in taking up the question of honorary degrees, which Clausen indecorously mentioned in his letter, Elliott deftly reminded Clausen that during his term as an active trustee Clausen was aware of the procedures for nominating people for an honorary degree: "[A]ny nominations from you would be given the more careful consideration and would indeed be welcomed."[77] Fortunately, Clausen's displeasure with the George Washington University program did not extend beyond his term as Grand Commander. The historic ties between the Scottish Rite and this major research university were restored to full levels of mutual trust soon after Grand Commander Kleinknecht was elected.

■ ■ ■

Henry C. Clausen served as Grand Commander for sixteen years, ending October 1985. He lived in contented retirement another seven years, dying in his hometown of San Francisco on December 4, 1992, at the age of eighty-seven. In 1986, soon after Clausen's return to private life, the Supreme Council received from California Scottish Rite Masons a bronze bust of Clausen, which was placed prominently in the House of the Temple in Washington, D.C.[78]

One of his lasting legacies—among several, such as the innovation of national work-shops, the promotion of membership growth and services, the revision of rituals, and an assortment of publishing ventures—was his commitment to Scottish Rite clinics for children with learning and language disorders. In his final *Allocution,* therefore, the last official word of his distinguished Masonic career, he said, "[T]he afflicted remain the forgotten children and all we seek to do is to start . . . projects." These projects were dedicated to the improvement of young lives.[79] This sympathetic reference, sewn by one whose own childhood began with the survival of "calamitous events," became the golden thread which lengthened into a major theme of Scottish Rite service for the next ten years and beyond.

CHAPTER XIV

Continuity and Opportunity
1985 and Forward

C. Fred Kleinknecht

By the 1980s two buzzwords—*heritage* and *glasnost*—one common, the other foreign, enjoyed popular currency in American culture. They are fraternal twins, joined by the same moment, born of similar inducements, but not looking exactly alike; they share, nevertheless, the same linguistic lifespan. References to heritage, taking the more familiar term first, are readily traceable to the 1930s. At the time when the major historic preservation project at Colonial Williamsburg was first contemplated during the Great Depression, the word *heritage* began its popular coinage, but really sunk permanent roots after World War II.

American Heritage magazine, preeminent carrier of the word and the ideas of tradition and memory which the word nurtured, made its debut in 1947. The demand for heritage seemed natural following unmuzzled warfare and the uncertainty of the Cold War. The appeal of a structured, permanent past, offering a nostalgic sense of comfort and belonging at a moment when discontinuity seemed most threatening, is understandable.

The concept of heritage, guarding and saving old structures and protecting sacred, inherited values, while sometimes serving as an antidote to painful historical realities such as economic depression and war, became manifest throughout American society during the second half of the twentieth century. Many public institutions and events carried the name *heritage* in their identity, especially in the 1980s. State parks, preservation societies, a political think-tank and foundation, a religious theme park, government commissions, regional historical associations, buildings, annual festivals, and dinners—all carried *heritage* in their names. One outstanding example of the word's widespread usage, signaling an important cultural trend, was the opening of the Museum of Our National Heritage in Lexington, Massachusetts, on April 20, 1975, by the Scottish Rite of Freemasonry, Northern Masonic Jurisdiction. The phenomenon of the heritage movement symbolized the vague human desire for reassuring continuity and illuminated the complex ways Americans understand their past.[1]

Similarly, the 1980s can also be represented by a Russian word, which became a household term in America, too. *Glasnost* means openness. One of the most popular foreign dignitaries to visit the Western world in this era was Soviet premier Mikhail Gorbachev, who first appeared on the global stage in March 1985, after the death of his predecessor and mentor, Yuri Andropov. By early 1987, Gorbachev expressed his wish to expand the thinking in his country not only about its complicated past but also about its future. He started programmatically by proposing a fresh openness about history, startling a world audience with his speech in February 1987 in which he said, "[T]here should be no blank pages in history or literature. Otherwise it is not history or literature, but artificial constructions."[2] This was an extraordinary declaration of openness from the leader of a society enthralled for seventy years by the tyrannical party line limiting contrary thought and public expression.

The word *glasnost* was readily adopted worldwide, even as Gorbachev made the stunning admission that Stalin had been guilty of "enormous and unforgivable crimes." Once he demonstrated open-mindedness about the past, Gorbachev coupled the lessons of history with the aspirations of the Russian people for political, social, and economic reforms. *Glasnost* created opportunity (what Gorbachev called *perestroika*). When the Berlin Wall came down in 1989, the end of an age, really the end of the twentieth century (a 75-year "century" bracketed by 1914 and 1989), was marked. Opportunity became a dominant theme globally as the 1990s unfolded, while the need for continuity remained ever strong as new and old ideas converged, sometimes in dissonance.

What is true from a broad, bird's-eye perspective holds particular relevance for testing out the same generalities in local circumstances and in smaller entities during the corresponding time frame. The spacious background formed by the catchwords *heritage* and *glasnost,* suggestive of large movements, actually is helpful in locating institutional attitudes and the qualities of mind that leaders bring out in relating to their institutions. The Scottish Rite of Freemasonry, Southern Jurisdiction, for instance, had to find ways to express its sense of continuity with the past and simultaneously create additional opportunity for itself as it stayed part of, not removed from, the world it occupied at the close of the American Century. These dual themes are as present in Masonic life as they are in the larger world; they helped fashion what may be regarded, in time, as a major transitional decade, 1985 to 1995, for the Scottish Rite.

Under the leadership of C. Fred Kleinknecht, opportunities for new programs, connections, and experiments were offered. It is very likely that in several instances, particularly in the area of finance and fund-raising, crucial moments would have slipped by the Scottish Rite, had Kleinknecht not been open, in the first place, to fresh ideas and possibilities. And yet, his openness did not permit him an exemption from being revisited by historic controversy as old as Freemasonry itself. No other Grand Commander in the twentieth century had to withstand the blistering anti-Masonic snipes of the American religious right and the annoying protests of radical libertarianism that Kleinknecht faced. In this way, and others, he understood the Masonic heritage and the importance of the Scottish Rite's continuity with it and protection of it.

This chapter concentrates on how the interplay of the new and the old, the frontiers of possibility and the boundaries of memory, are featured in the mature phase of Kleinknecht's long Masonic career. For the sake of consistency with previous chapters, the foregoing discussion is presented topically. Broad areas considered here include a biographical sketch of the Grand Commander, Scottish Rite philanthropy, public life, external relations, organization, membership, ritual, and communications. The next chapter necessarily, because of the topic's widening scope in the late 1980s and '90s, will treat the problem of anti-Masonic attacks and the measures put in place by Grand Commander Kleinknecht and the Scottish Rite.

But each of the sections which form this present chapter demonstrate a general pattern of intertwining themes, particularly how beloved traditions overlap and compare with the foreground of transforming opportunities. Take, for example, the House of the Temple. Major historic preservation efforts on and around the building have been conducted since 1985. There is no more recognized symbol of Masonic heritage in America than the Supreme Council headquarters in Washington, D.C. Noticeably significant changes, however, have occurred in remodeling the facility and increasing its public and fraternal visibility. In this and other endeavors, Kleinknecht has not allowed the Rite to stand still. In his own way and style, he has perpetuated a strong heritage while embracing a spirit of *glasnost*, each of the two complementary traits (a social trend writ small) speaking to and with the times from within a vital Masonic organization.

■ ■ ■

A birthright Washingtonian, Christian Frederick Kleinknecht Jr. was born on St. Valentine's Day, 1924, the second and middle child in a second generation German-American family. Kleinknecht's paternal grandfather, Gottlieb F. Kleinknecht, was born in Württemberg, Germany, on November 7, 1850, and reared there before immigrating to America on the day he turned thirty, joining the late-nineteenth-century wave of western and northern Europeans in search of a better land. Gottlieb's wife, Regina, one year younger, embarked with him to America. They settled with many other German-speaking families in Evansville, Indiana, and lived there until death came, first to Regina in 1928, then to Gottlieb in 1931.

On Kleinknecht's mother's side (the Barr family), both grandparents were born in Missouri in the early 1850s and lived out their days together through the middle of 1940 in Stecker, Oklahoma.[3] John Thomas and Nancy Jane Barr died five months apart. Fred Kleinknecht's parents, "Chris" and Nell May (née Barr), arrived in Washington a year before President Woodrow Wilson left the White House in 1920. Hard working, middle class, and disciplined, they saw to it that their three sons, Kenneth, Fred, and Robert, had the benefit of what was considered, then, the finest public school education in America. Fred played first base on the Calvin Coolidge High School varsity baseball team and, around this time, began to notice across the alley, behind the Kleinknecht home on Piney Branch Road in northwest Washington, that the Kamms had a teenaged daughter. His budding "good neighbor" policy would, however, undergo the interruption of time and war. A romance kindled despite the intervening years.

As Fred Kleinknecht completed his secondary education in the District of Columbia school system, America was preparing for war in two theaters, Europe and the Pacific. Though Benjamin Franklin University in Washington, D.C., had already enrolled him, Kleinknecht joined millions of young Americans in uniform as the nation mobilized and fought the war against Germany, Austria, Italy, and Japan. He entered the U.S. Navy and, with training at Bainbridge, Maryland, and Jacksonville, Florida, he earned the rank of aviation machinist mate, first class, and was stationed at the Great Lakes Naval Training Base in Illinois. Remaining proud of his navy enlistment rank, those war-time memories kept him modest, and deeply patriotic, as he advanced in the high offices of Scottish Rite Freemasonry.[4]

Upon returning to Washington, D.C., after the war, he worked briefly for the Major League Washington Baseball Club, the parent organization of the perennial American League "welcome mat," the Washington Senators. While he loved sports, savoring the hours at Griffith Stadium on Seventh Street in Washington, the prospects of a settled life with a professional team in those years were usually temporary. Yet, for several seasons, he operated the concession stand behind home plate, selling a Coke and a hot dog for a quarter.

In 1948 his life forever changed. That summer his mother died at the age of fifty-six, a loss which left his father a widower for more than twenty years. Next, he went to work at the Supreme Council, where his father had been on the administrative staff since 1919. At the same time, he was seriously courting Gene Elizabeth Kamm, the girl across the alley, whom he married on January 21, 1949. He was not yet twenty-five years old. The two events—his secure employment and his marriage—not only had direct correlation with each other, but also typified the experience of millions of returning veterans. Over time, Fred and Gene Kleinknecht contributed four children to the postwar baby boom— Gene Ellen, Henry, Scott, and Joan.[5]

Kleinknecht's first job at the Supreme Council was in the Grand Secretary's office, performing clerical and bookkeeping tasks.[6] Later, he became the building superintendent, but only after he qualified for an engineer's license from the District of Columbia. The license required a high level of competency in running low-pressure steam boilers. As so many men of that day took advantage of the G.I. Bill in order to enter college, so, too, did Kleinknecht, who graduated from Benjamin Franklin University in 1954, at the age of thirty.

Also after World War II, Kleinknecht was initiated into Silver Spring Lodge No. 215 in Silver Spring, Maryland, on October 17, 1949, was raised on December 19, 1949, and entered the Scottish Rite in the new year, 1950. Silver Spring, where he and his wife made their home, was a sprawling metropolitan community on the city line. Kleinknecht, from his Silver Spring base, appropriately made his home Scottish Rite valley in Baltimore, Maryland, where he also affiliated with the Shrine, enjoying fellowship at the renowned Boumi Temple.

In 1955, Kleinknecht was invested with the rank and decoration of the Knight Commander of the Court of Honor; he was one of the youngest Scottish Rite Masons ever selected for that signal recognition. Four years later, in 1959 at the biennial session, he was one of 337 Knight Commanders of the Court of Honor elected as Inspector General Honorary of the thirty-third degree.[7] At this time, Kleinknecht's Masonic involvements were extensive and included the York Rite, too.

Before being appointed assistant to Grand Commander Luther A. Smith in 1966, the affable and enthusiastic Kleinknecht (who had been affectionately nicknamed "Freddie" by Smith) had already served eighteen years as an assistant in the office of the Grand Secretary General. He possessed superb working knowledge of Supreme Council operations, which was rare for someone only forty-two years old in an organization with a tableau of many second-career, long experienced, retired executives.

One major alteration Kleinknecht introduced was in the Supreme Council's accounting system, which had always been a single entry process. One consulting firm had bid $10,000 to change the council's accounting practices. Kleinknecht, with the help of an independent CPA who was married to a member of the staff, initiated a double-entry system for $650, a system which, he boasted later, "was sometimes easier to comprehend than the later computer records."[8]

When Grand Secretary General Claud F. Young resigned on December 31, 1966, due to failing health, Grand Commander Smith, himself very near retirement, appointed the relatively youthful Fred Kleinknecht as Acting Grand Secretary General; this was the highest office ever held by his father, Chris Kleinknecht. In a move that allowed Kleinknecht eligibility and mobility in the organization, Grand Commander Smith next appointed Kleinknecht as Sovereign Grand Inspector General at Large during the 1967 session. This now opened the possibility for the temporary title "Acting" to be removed, something that Grand Commander Cowles was too stubborn to do for the senior Kleinknecht. For the next eighteen years, Fred Kleinknecht held the office of Grand Secretary General, loyally supporting the work of Grand Commanders Smith and Clausen. Of the six Grand Commanders in the first eighty-five years of the twentieth century, Kleinknecht had served under four, and became himself the seventh in 1985.[9] Neither Albert Pike nor John H. Cowles, as the longest serving leaders in Scottish Rite history, could claim a comparable advantage of continuity with their predecessors.

Henry C. Clausen gave sixteen years of leadership, longer than any Grand Commander, save Pike and Cowles, but he decided to step aside to allow an orderly transition in 1985. At a special executive session on October 18, 1985, C. Fred Kleinknecht, sixty-one years old, was elected Sovereign Grand Commander. Clausen, while he was Grand Commander, had split his time between offices on the east and west coasts. But Kleinknecht was not only the Scottish Rite's "man in Washington," he was *from* Washington with wide contacts built up over a lifetime. One of his strengths, which was to be open-minded about the Scottish Rite's image and work, appeared manifest immediately as he assumed his new office. He donned an activist's style of leadership; he was a "can-do," one-man energy field, radiating the desire to invigorate the Rite.[10]

Early on, Kleinknecht made it clear both to the staff that he was developing under him and to the Supreme Council with whom he worked, "Whatever we do, we must be first class." Kleinknecht's vision from 1985 forward was to promote Scottish Rite interests and activities tastefully but aggressively.[11] Adopting President Jimmy Carter's rhetorical question, the title of a campaign memoir and mantra, "Why not the best?" Kleinknecht emphasized quality with dynamic activity.

The criticism he occasionally experienced along the way, however, usually materialized in the atmosphere of barbershop hindsight, when the full results of one's time in the chair are analyzed through off-setting mirrors, one of which is held up to the back of the customer's head. Rather, faultfinding was absent publicly during official Scottish Rite sessions. Occasional concerns were expressed to the Grand Commander about style, not substance, which in itself is remarkable, since no one would dare have approached any of Kleinknecht's predecessors this way. His openness, however, invited all forms of commentary.

Kleinknecht's executive decisions were sometimes more instinctive than deliberative, sometimes more like an intuitive flash than an exact weighing out of options. His speedy methods of getting tangible things accomplished, sometimes running yellow lights in the process, were based on his consistent refusal to settle for less if "the more excellent way" of results appeared to him as obvious. Kleinknecht's push to make changes sometimes abided by the Washington pragmatism of it being easier to ask for forgiveness than for permission.

About his trademark habit of starting something with a dogged, single-minded focus and not resting until it was completed, Kleinknecht once reflected that this has meant some decisions in his office were rushed. The Grand Commander's goals were usually indisputable through his first ten years and rarely, if ever, questioned, especially the expansion of children's programs and raising money. His leadership style sometimes meant bypassing a long checklist of potentially useful, though distant, advisers. He tended to be more selective in seeking advice, even though, arguably, a slower-forming consensus may have strengthened the Grand Commander's position. At the same time, rapid, resolute, and centralized responses, especially appropriate in public relations and in the urgencies of foreign Masonic recognition, might just as easily have been obstructed by any process other than the one Kleinknecht employed at the time. A judicious observer remarked that Kleinknecht's decisiveness "cause[d] things to get done," which was commendable, but one sometimes "shouldn't be too quick to pull the trigger."[12]

Kleinknecht brought to the job of Grand Commander a storehouse of Masonic understanding drawn from years of administrative adroitness and from his presence in the privy councils where major decisions were made over several decades. He also brought an entrepreneurial spirit, readily countering the temptation to say, "Well, we've never done it this way before." Kleinknecht's friendly manner has been a major asset in winning people to his point, especially if it could help advance the Scottish Rite. He has had a ready capacity for friendship, taking to heart Dr. Johnson's sage advice to James Boswell: "If a man does not make new acquaintances as he advances through life, he will soon find himself left alone. A man, sir, should keep his friendships in a constant repair." His ability to relate equally to all persons never deviated from place to place.[13] His natural instincts about people, understanding especially the value of the personal touch, served as the signature of his many accomplishments.

W. Gene Sizemore, as Grand Executive Director of the Supreme Council, whose prior career experience in the U.S. Navy included a tour as defense attaché at the American Embassy in Moscow under Ambassador Thomas J. Watson Jr., once commented that "Fred is the most generous man" with whom he had ever worked.[14] By the same token, Sizemore, a retired rear admiral, ex–fighter pilot, and former executive director of the Navy League, brought added prestige and an aviator's calm to the Scottish Rite's operations and plans. Kleinknecht quickly recognized Sizemore's many talents and learned to count on his advice frequently. Together, they became an effective combination, like battery mates, such as the famed St. Louis Cardinals' Tim McCarver and Bob Gibson.

Kleinknecht keeps on his desk a double-sided paper weight with engraved brass plates on each face of the object, reminding him and visitors of his guiding outlook. On one side is the sentence, "You can accomplish much if you don't care who gets the credit." On the reverse side, a related, but profounder aphorism is conveyed, "The true measure of a man is how he treats someone who can do him absolutely no good."

■ ■ ■

A chief focal point of activity for American Scottish Rite Masons since before the 1980s has been its philanthropic programs, particularly for the Southern Jurisdiction, in its specialized area of children's language-learning difficulties. Between 1985 and 1995, the number of Scottish Rite sponsored clinics, centers, and programs increased dramatically from 35 to 112. Along with this charitable community presence came significant fund-raising milestones. The Masonic Service Association estimated that at the close of the 1980s the total annual value of American Masonic philanthropies exceeded $360 million. By the middle of 1991, the figure was recalibrated at $525 million per year. The Shriners Hospitals and Burns Institutes as of 1990 were operating on nearly $228 million annually. Specifically, Scottish Rite philanthropies for that same year were generating combined donor budgets of approximately $62 million. The Supreme Council of the Southern Jurisdiction accounted for $16 million, or 26 percent of the Scottish Rite's annual distribution of public charity. Still, the largest portion of Scottish Rite public philanthropy occurred locally in Dallas, Texas, and Atlanta, Georgia, at the special hospitals for children.[15]

Masonic retirement homes and orphanages were the first fraternally organized institutional forms of relief in America, dating to the antebellum period of the nineteenth century. As early as 1841 an attempt was made in Missouri, a relatively new state, to sponsor a Masonic college, which modestly succeeded until 1857, the year the country experienced a serious economic recession, further antagonizing the North and the South into political belligerence. While Masonic charity in the nineteenth century typically favored members or families of the fraternity, later developing life and unemployment insurance and other forms of mutual aid, the emphasis was clearly more public oriented in the twentieth century. Beginning in 1920 with the planning of the Shriners Hospital for Crippled Children in Shreveport, Louisiana, followed by thirteen additional hospitals before 1930, Masons extended helping hands equally to all families, without regard to the question of their fraternal connections. Masons, particularly the Shriners, adopted the credo that one becomes a bigger person when stooping to help a child.[16]

Around the time the Shriners opened their first hospitals, Scottish Rite Masons in Dallas, Texas, and Atlanta, Georgia, opened public hospitals for children, primarily devoted to orthopedics, and, in Dallas, urgent and acute care. By 1995, their success was self-evident, as the Scottish Rite Hospital in Dallas managed assets of $750 million. Using figures compiled from the Masonic Service Association of the United States, S. Brent Morris estimates that in 1990 58 percent of Masonic charitable dollars went to the general American public; that is, the largest portion of an annual half billion dollars went to people without any Masonic attachment whatsoever.[17] Put differently, it works out to $812,000 per day that the public received from Masonic philanthropies. Morris raises the cogent point, moreover, about the impossibility of assessing the value placed on volunteer hours given to hospitals and clinics. The Veterans Administration hospitals alone are supported by a half million hours of Masonic volunteer time every year. Meanwhile, the Scottish Rite inclined toward a new Masonic pattern of concentrating on only one focused human need for the long term.

In early 1952, a Colorado Scottish Rite Mason, William G. Schweigert, serving as Almoner of the Rocky Mountain Consistory, received an unusual plea for help from a social worker. Apparently, a four year old boy was receiving speech therapy at Children's

Hospital in Denver, but the mother, a single parent, was about to discontinue the treatments because of their relatively high cost. The mother was recently widowed, but was working hard for a monthly salary of $265. With two young children to support, feed, and clothe, she simply could not afford the speech therapy for her son.

Schweigert checked out the story with the hospital's speech therapy director, who verified all the circumstances. After that, he committed Scottish Rite funds to cover one month of treatments for the boy. Meanwhile, he visited this relatively unknown corner of the hospital, receiving a demonstration of this fledgling department's work with young children who were diagnosed with vague, often unnamed, language disorders. Hearing a recording of the boy in question, made when the youngster first came to the hospital and could sound only unintelligible tones, Schweigert was pleasantly impressed that the boy had learned to pronounce some words. Recalling that transforming moment, Schweigert testified later, "It seemed almost beyond my comprehension that most of the children who once were considered feeble-minded, imbecilic, idiotic or fatuous were educable and that they might have the chance of developing towards a normal, or near normal life, if some dedicated organization could enter this new field of service."[18]

By February 1953, acting on the enthusiasm of Schweigert and the initiative of a Colorado Sovereign Grand Inspector General, Judge Haslett P. Burke, the Colorado Scottish Rite Foundation was formed. That year 14 children received treatment due to the new foundation's principled commitment to change lives. The idea spread to California and, over time, it became a nationally recognized program, receiving commendations from the White House, state governors, and regional medical associations. Upwards of 10,000 children a year, as of 1995, visited Scottish Rite clinics and centers to receive special care for disorders that inhibit the learning of communication and comprehension in the critical early childhood years.

The general nature of language disorders, such as aphasia and dyslexia, so often misunderstood or mislabeled as mental retardation, was given clear exposition in layman's terms by Kleinknecht in his *Allocution* for 1987:

> The youngsters suffering from these conditions are normal or even superior in intellect. Research has yet to discover the cause of these language disorders, but some breakdown in neural communication exists, and there is a gap between what the child visually senses and mentally understands. He or she can see the line of letters printed on the page, for instance, but assembling them into a meaningful word is impossible. Similarly, though a child may know very well what he or she wishes to say, the means of communication fail. Frustrated, the child too often regresses into isolation and hostility. If left unaided, he or she will slip out of the mainstream class in school and be relegated to ever lower and lower educational tracks. In fact, the child is not "slow" or in any way retarded. What he or she needs is the expert care and loving concern [of the Scottish Rite] Language Disorders Program.[19]

The Supreme Council's special interest in childhood learning problems began within the year of the Colorado aphasia program's founding. Henry C. Clausen chaired a special committee appointed by Grand Commander Thomas J. Harkins in 1953, devoted to exploring prospective areas of service. A consensus had been forming among the Active Members and Deputies of the Supreme Council that the time was right for "a new, productive channel for Scottish Rite philanthropy." By the time Clausen became Grand Commander in 1969, his commitment to the cause had sufficiently deepened so that he urged pilot programs throughout the United States, including Alabama, Florida, Georgia, Kansas, Mississippi, North Carolina, Tennessee, Texas, Virginia, Oklahoma, Nebraska, and Oregon.[20]

A promising model of partnership between the Scottish Rite Orient of California and Stanford University Medical Center materialized in the 1950s, lasting happily until 1972. Stanford, worth noting, had strong Masonic ties dating to its original Board of Trustees in 1885 and to the university's benefactor, Leland Stanford, the railroad tycoon, who was also elected to the U.S. Senate in 1885. Strikingly, many Stanford professors were members of the fraternity until the 1960s changed all notions of faculty relationships with perceived establishment organizations, other than the academy itself.[21]

In the meantime, as occasionally happens between long-term donors and recipients, disaffection surfaced and deepened, whereby a university policy came into conflict with Scottish Rite preferences in the directorship of the clinic. In this case, Jon Eisenson, director of the Scottish Rite Institute for Childhood Aphasia at Stanford University Medical Center, was at the time listed on the faculty roster as emeritus professor in the School of Medicine. The university, however, had an ironbound policy restricting the active status of its faculty and staff to those under sixty-five years of age. Under the rules, Eisenson could no longer provide leadership to the Scottish Rite program at Stanford.

Clausen, never bashful and living much of the year nearby, fervently supported Eisenson, arguing that Stanford should consider making an exception in his case. By interjecting his view and being rebuffed, Clausen asserted to Stanford officials that Scottish Rite support of the speech and language program was at stake, unless some allowance was made. Clayton Rich, dean of the Stanford University Medical School, did not accede to Clausen's pressure tactics, responding instead in diplomatic terms, "[W]e very definitely plan to continue the program in language and speech therapy, including the treatment of aphasia . . . irrespective of whether or not the very generous support that has been provided over the years by the Scottish Rite can be continued."[22]

Having his bluff called, Clausen believed the relationship with Stanford had soured, had gone beyond repairing the breach or splitting the differences and, therefore, it would not remain productive under the strained conditions. In his view, Stanford had unnecessarily subordinated Scottish Rite involvement. He informed Eisenson a few months later, with no apparent regret, "[Y]ou may assume as termination of our support at Stanford [ensues], we shall transfer this to San Francisco State [University] on the same terms."[23] When the move subsequently occurred, it was timed, ironically, with Eisenson's actual retirement, which had precipitated the falling out in the first place. Apparently, the issue in the Stanford controversy was not only Eisenson's right to work, but mostly Clausen's unyielding stand that he should be granted greater voice in a program involving the Scottish Rite's funds and reputation.

The lesson learned from this minor episode at Stanford for future Scottish Rite partnerships in the language-learning mission field was simply to avoid direct involvement in clinical management and operations whenever possible. Fragile programs do not long survive contention. Instead, drawing from collective experience, the Scottish Rite discovered how to excel in two important ways—in local fund-raising and in placing regional centers in strategic sites.

■ ■ ■

The growth of the language disorder programs was steady, increasing to thirty-five operations nationwide by 1985. Many of the orients established their own charitable foundations to support these projects. One of Clausen's final acts in office was to assemble a high-powered subcommittee to plan the development of large assets for the council's Scottish Rite Foundation. Members of this select group of financiers included Grand Treasurer Andrew Benedict, Joseph L. Albritton (Washington, D.C., banking and broadcast mogul), James D. Berry, Henry A. Bubb, and Emmett G. Solomon. It was recommended by them that any fund-raising at the jurisdictional level be carried out so as not to take away from funds that otherwise would go to the orients and valleys. What money was received by the promotion of the council's foundation would, in turn, be available as seed money for orients and valleys to use for starting or remodeling language disorder clinics for children. While the committee never kindled into wakeful action, Clausen's foresight prepared the ground for the remarkably rapid growth of the Scottish Rite Foundation and philanthropies under Kleinknecht.[24]

The foundation's central thrust of philanthropic activity continued smoothly as a major support mechanism for all childhood language-treatment centers within the Southern Jurisdiction. In order to meet the growing costs of functioning properly and the demand to open new centers, Kleinknecht became an effective and purposeful innovator in raising money. In August 1986, by recommendation of the Finance Committee and in consultation with business advisors, such as Washington, D.C., valley secretary Martin D. Carlin, the Supreme Council introduced an affinity credit-card program as a means of generating substantial income for the Rite's language disorder programs. The agreement with Maryland Bank of North America (MBNA) allowed the Scottish Rite name, logo, or image to appear on individual VISA cards which would be offered to the entire membership. The incentive for subscribing to a new credit card was the royalty feature offered by the bank, so that every purchase made with the Scottish Rite VISA card returned a portion to the foundation. Gradually, 42,000 Scottish Rite credit cards were issued, having been approved by the bank's application process. This made it possible to distribute $433,000 in 1987.[25]

The credit card program, for an interval of about two years, was moved to First Virginia Bank in the hope of a higher rate of returns in the throes of a national recession. The switch caused some confusion among the original card-holders, most of whom stayed with MBNA. The experiment with another sponsoring bank proved unsatisfactory, but due to Kleinknecht's persistence, as well as his willingness to cut losses and the effective negotiating skills of Executive Director W. Gene Sizemore, the initial terms with Maryland Bank of North America were restored, providing immediately a $100,000 bonus and projecting an annual income in 1995 approaching previous levels.[26]

Kleinknecht instituted three other significant fund-raising arrangements, breaking new ground for an organization governed by staid financial inclinations. When Kleinknecht began, the resources for implementing any kind of modest growth strategy were severely hampered by lack of large endowments. The House of the Temple, for instance, while always imposing and monumental, was also an old building. The Supreme Council committee charged with overseeing and sustaining the House of the Temple realized that "this obligation is all the more important since, as each year passes, this great building increases in architectural significance."[27]

Kleinknecht seized on the committee's assessment as a critical priority. With rapid dispatch, he took charge of an ambitious remodeling program. As a result, the House of the Temple Historic Preservation Foundation was established in 1990, allowing tax-deductible contributions to be collected which were specially designated for major building improvements, including infrastructure and decor.

The Grand Commander assigned the executive staff to develop ways to support the new building-preservation foundation he created. Through the publication of an attractive annual calendar featuring the architectural studies of prize-winning photographer Maxwell MacKenzie, the historic preservation foundation received in its first several years about $1 million per year. Guided by its chief business representative, Earl Ihle, a Scottish Rite Mason, the Baltimore publishing firm Barton-Cotton, Incorporated, artfully planned the layout and produced a consistently useful and colorful fifteen-month calendar. In five years, the House of the Temple Historic Preservation Foundation was worth about $6 million.[28]

A second innovation, also a royalties-based program, offered Scottish Rite members a supplemental cancer-insurance policy through an established, licensed underwriter. Enough participants were enrolled to produce yearly income for the Scottish Rite Foundation of close to $230,000 during the early 1990s.[29] The credit card, calendar, and cancer insurance programs, as fund-raising instruments, had become popular throughout the wider American nonprofit sector, too, as the Scottish Rite got on board with universities, museums, and medical foundations. What was a novelty in traditional Scottish Rite circles was already customary in other public organizations that had likewise required imaginative solutions to the problem of decreasing operating and capital assets.

In early 1991, Kleinknecht took another bold step forward in financial development by appointing a retired, broadly experienced businessman, Thomas M. Boles, to chair the new Committee for Scottish Rite–Masonic Children's Programs. Boles was asked to design opportunities for deferred giving and estate planning which would help an individual's tax position while ultimately benefiting the Scottish Rite Foundation.[30] Through the financial acumen of Boles, the Scottish Rite developed by April 1992 a Pooled Income Fund, requiring a minimum $5,000 deposit, and a program for charitable remainder trusts, unitrusts, and gift annuities. By the next year Boles was named director of development and was based in LaHabra, California. Working in tandem with Kleinknecht, Boles counseled donors in planning and executing irrevocable trusts that in total had amounted to nearly $17 million in market value by December 1995.[31] Funds, real estate, or securities held in a living trust do not become an organization's property until the person (or couple) executing the trust has died. During that person's remaining years of life, however, the trust provides a regular flow of income with significant tax advantages (mostly through minimizing or circumventing capital-gains taxes) not allowed before the trust was created.

The ultimate beneficiaries of Kleinknecht's progressive fund-raising techniques continued to be children. As new opportunities were created by having national funds available for local language-disorder programs, the expansion of childhood language-disorder clinics over ten years was breathtaking. Kleinknecht also saw beyond the need for money. He enlisted the talents of his old friend and fishing companion, the Academy Award–winning actor Ernest Borgnine, in producing an animated video film, "On the Wings of Words." Borgnine, a devoted Scottish Rite Mason, gave his name, voice, and reputation to the endeavor the Grand Commander was leading. The film enjoyed nearly instant success.

By 1995, over 75 new centers opened, bringing the total to 112. At the same time, independent of these efforts but inspired by them, the Northern Masonic Jurisdiction began two programs modeled on the Southern Jurisdiction's procedures. Thereafter, northern Grand Commander Robert O. Ralston, urged by Kleinknecht, redoubled his jurisdiction's commitment by announcing plans to open at least 6 additional clinics by the year 2000, but projecting a goal of 15 as the next achievable plateau. The Northern Masonic Jurisdiction planned differently from its southern counterpart, in that it would operate from one central foundation, whereas the Southern Jurisdiction contained forty-six separate, local foundations in addition to the two nationally based foundations under the auspices of the Supreme Council.

One example of national recognition which was bestowed upon the Scottish Rite's mission in behalf of children came in Washington, D.C., when the local Center for Childhood Language Disorders was opened. Present for the dedication ceremonies on June 23, 1989, First Lady Barbara Bush, whose special interest in literacy attracted her to the Scottish Rite project, spoke of her delight in touring the $3 million facility. Endorsing the center's motto, "unlocking the barriers to the mind," Mrs. Bush told the large audience that "George would approve" and later told Kleinknecht that the program was "definitely one of George's 1,000 Points of Light." She finished her tribute by naming the center "another gem in Masonry's crown of achievements for American children."[32]

Tommie L. Robinson Jr., director for the Scottish Rite Center for Childhood Language Disorders, Hearing, and Speech, a part of Children's National Medical Center of Washington, D.C., explained in 1995 that the hospital's program in hearing and speech had existed for thirty years, but with the community partnership solidified by Scottish Rite support, new opportunities had opened quickly. Robinson, a graduate of the University of Mississippi, who earned his Ph.D. at Howard University with a specialty in the problem of stuttering, came to the clinic in 1992. At the Scottish Rite Center in the nation's capital, 300 appointments per month became the average after six years in the new facility, meaning that fifty children were being regularly treated during any given week, more than half of whom were nonpaying or often were Medicaid patients. Consequently, the local Scottish Rite Valley of Washington paid the entire diagnositic and treatment expenses for 27 percent of all patients coming to the clinic because there was no third-party payment, insurance, or Medicaid allowance. Robinson commented that "without Scottish Rite support, the clinic would be operating in the red."[33]

Robinson's program placed emphasis on diagnosing language delay, since, if treated by the time a child is three or four years old, the likelihood of that child becoming dyslexic is considerably diminished. The demand on the center rose significantly in a brief period for several reasons, according to Robinson. Maternal drug abuse and lack of services in the public schools contributed in part to the higher patient load, but so too had the training of health care professionals and teachers who were better equipped for identifying problems in children. Parenthetically, Robinson pointed out, children in Washington from financially stable or prosperous homes also come to the center when necessary, because its reputation for quality is so widespread. Over time, the waiting list was gradually reduced from an average of 100 children needing attention of some kind to less than 50 children whose first appointment would be scheduled within eight weeks of initial contact with the center. The exemplary Washington center typifies other Scottish Rite programs; it is served by a well-trained, bilingual staff in properly equipped therapy rooms with bright, inviting, soothing, and cheerful settings.[34]

■   ■   ■

Kleinknecht's first term in office coincided with the lengthy national celebration of the U.S. Constitution on its 200th anniversary of being written and ratified. In 1986, the Scottish Rite, through a cooperative effort between the Southern and Northern Jurisdictions, began a five-year program to observe the Constitution's bicentennial; this included the sponsorship of public ceremonies and a variety of film and publication projects.

The goal, as Kleinknecht proposed in his first *Allocution,* was to engender a "new appreciation of the Constitution" in all Americans and to "reaffirm Freemasonry's support of constitutional values." The Scottish Rite's bicentennial program was inaugurated in Philadelphia's Independence Hall where W. Gene Sizemore served as master of ceremonies. Later, a special ceremony was held on November 17, 1986, in the former Supreme Court Chambers located in the U.S. Capitol in Washington, D.C.[35] Of enormous assistance in coordinating the Scottish Rite's patriotic agenda was former Iowa Congressman Fred W. Schwengel, devoted Scottish Rite Mason and founder of the U.S. Capitol Historical Society. Schwengel diligently insisted on Masonry's presence at commemorative cornerstone-laying reenactments, such as at the White House and the Capitol—not that there was any opposition to it, just benign ignorance among some planners who were unaware of Masonry's historic role in the nation's early traditions.

The Scottish Rite's leadership in contributing to American patriotic celebrations honoring the early federal period was felt not only in public programs, events, and parades, but also in publications. *Let's Celebrate America,* a children's illustrated guide to national holidays, had wide distribution (over 30,000 copies) in elementary schools from 1987 and after. The book's popularity among young readers between ages six and nine gained for it the respect of elementary school teachers nationwide. Of similar usefulness in promoting themes of patriotism was the June 1989 issue of the Scottish Rite's monthly journal, *The New Age,* which dealt with the American flag. This issue's success required running an additional 227,000 offprints in order to meet the demand from schools and civic groups. It brought Kleinknecht and the magazine's staff the prestigious recognition of the Freedoms Foundation of Valley Forge, Pennsylvania.[36]

In the 1790s cornerstones were originally placed in defining the federal city's District of Columbia boundaries and, of course, in erecting the executive mansion and the U.S. Capitol. In all instances, dating back 200 years, Freemasons conducted the ceremonial dedication of a structure's most important building block, its cornerstone. The contemporary artist John Melius, a former Smithsonian consultant, was commissioned in 1993 by the Supreme Council to paint, with as much historical accuracy as available sources could document and support, the scene of President George Washington in a Master's apron, wearing the Master's jewel, laying the cornerstone of the U.S. Capitol in a Masonic ceremony. Melius's oil on canvas painting, on permanent display in the Banquet Hall at the House of the Temple, shows Washington with the Master's gavel, tapping a limestone ashlar held in a tripod block and tackle, assisted by bearers of corn, oil, and wine, in what public historians believe is verisimilitude. During these years of Masonic participation in national anniversaries, George White, the architect of the U.S. Capitol since 1972, became enamored of Masonic tradition and was made a Mason-at-sight, later extending his ties to the Scottish Rite, too.[37]

Other Washington dignitaries who maintained a cordial relationship with the Scottish Rite at this time, as they were members in their home states, included Senators Robert Dole, Jesse Helms, Alan K. Simpson, Sam Nunn, J. Bennett Johnston, and Conrad Burns. Fourteen senators and thirty-four members of the House of Representatives were Masons as of April 1995, according to the Masonic Service Association.

President Ronald Reagan on February 11, 1988, at the White House was presented a special certificate by Grand Commander Kleinknecht, conferring on him the title of Honorary Scottish Rite Mason. While Reagan may have embodied Masonic ideals, he was not, however, a member of the craft. Other Masonic leaders were also present at the unprecedented occasion, which Reagan later recalled as a signal honor because it included him among "the ranks of the sixteen former Presidents in their association with Free-masonry."[38] President George Bush on October 13, 1992, less than a month before the closely contested election determining the return or repeal of his incumbency, also received Kleinknecht and other Masonic leaders in White House ceremonies, which this time marked the cornerstone bicentennial there.[39]

In 1992 Governor William J. Clinton of Arkansas, a Past Master Councilor of an Arkansas DeMolay chapter, was elected president of the United States, but with scarce mention during the campaign of his youthful Masonic connection in Hope, Arkansas. Instead, Clinton's participation as an adolescent in Boys' Nation, an American Legion program, was the centerpiece of conveying to the electorate his formative experiences. As a curious indicator of the times, it illustrates an adverse foreshadowing of Masonic social and cultural status in American society at century's end.

While demanding public lives limited the commitment of many Masons holding political office, electoral advantages of membership had probably been neutralized by the 1980s. In fact, the winds had shifted in many election districts so that Masonic membership was sometimes perceived as less than a political asset and more as a poten-tial liability. In any event, politicians in other times who were inclined to emphasize fraternal involvement were, even then, often termed "buttonhole Masons."

Pressure over the years from women's political advocacy groups, troubled by the appearance of insensitivity in all-male organizations (such as clubs, fraternities, and even Little League Baseball) to the needs of women, particularly in new-begotten career roles, meant that by the late 1980s men running for public office had to demonstrate special awareness for the concerns of women constituents. This meant that men often distanced themselves from male-only structures.

Men in all vocations learned, sometimes painfully, that women were historically and routinely excluded from equal access to American public institutions and opportunities. Membership in a Masonic lodge did not always square with the acceptable perceptions a candidate needed to establish and maintain in the face of a diverse electorate. Country club memberships, similarly, became out-of-bounds for public careers in Washington, as they represented in popular imagination mostly white, masculine privilege. Moreover, the perception of Masonry by some conservative evangelicals and fundamentalists was also increasingly problematic. For them, Masonic ritual was often considered religiously taboo.

However, Senator Alan K. Simpson, among other veterans of elective office, did not capitulate his strong support of Masonry when he observed, during a Scottish Rite ses-sion in the Southern Jurisdiction, that if the fraternity could get people interested in the lodge and its work, "then, we will be able to share Masonry for what it is, a festival of life, learning, and love." Perhaps with the enemies of Masonry in mind, Simpson quoted his mother as having instilled in him the saying that "hatred corrodes the container it is carried in."[40] Masonry, nevertheless, received its share of stripes in the early 1990s as a convenient fall guy for angry controversialists pressing extreme political and religious ideologies.

Freemasonry by the late '80s may have become suspect for some Americans on the grounds of perceived male chauvinism. Also, conservative Christians, distrusting the deep tradition of an adamant theological neutrality, often criticized Masonry for its inherent lack of Christian theological orthodoxy (what Christian fundamentalists pejoratively labeled "Masonic universalism"). Some Masons thought they were merely misunderstood by conservative Christians and that dialogue could repair the misinterpretation. Rather, the Christian fundamentalists understood exactly that Freemasonry was broadminded about religious diversity and not specifically Christian; and they didn't like it. Additionally, and vaguely, Masonry suffered the indifference of some wider form of middle-class self-possession or embarrassment among the children of the World War II generation who rejected time-honored community institutions. This was a time of membership decline for many community organizations, including Jaycees, Rotary, and Kiwanis. In other significant ways, however, Masonry fit the times perfectly.

■   ■   ■

Questions were raised in some quarters of American society about Masonry's purpose and usefulness. It proved difficult to make the negative commentary penetrate very deeply or project adversely on the public mood for the simple offsetting reason of highly visible Masonic charity and benevolence. Occasionally, Masonry endured various forms of ridicule, perhaps to be satirized as an all-male bastion of formalized "bonding," or, at other times, being lampooned for the necessity of the ritual's private nature. Popular television shows from long ago, such as "The Honeymooners" in the 1950s, "The Flintstones" in the 1960s, and "Happy Days," in the 1970s, each of which enjoyed revival in the 1990s, had spoofed lodge meetings. A 1990s prime-time animated television hit, "The Simpsons," also had its fun at the expense of Masonic traditions. But worse were the occasional serious expressions through the popular media, including comic books published by a subsidiary of the corporate giant Time-Warner, leveling the wildest charges against Masonry, insisting that it functioned as a conspiratorial mafia. Meanwhile, despite the burlesque quality of the aspersions, no questions were ever posed by critics about Masonry's sincere patriotic fervor. The historian Michael Kammen remarks that "by the mid-1980s orthodox Americanism was very much in vogue once again, prompted by President Reagan's rhetoric."[41]

It would be misleading to assume, therefore, that Freemasonry was out of step with the climate in America that had recovered traditional expressions of patriotism. Because Masonry had always embraced patriotic customs, though perhaps not corresponding completely with the exuberant displays of the American Legion and the Veterans of Foreign Wars, it was not necessary for the fraternity to pass through a period of post-Vietnam patriotic recovery. In this regard, the country had caught up with the Masons, who had kept the fires of Americanism banked throughout a period of patriotic dormancy—a "bad dream" low point between 1967 and 1975.

The turning point for the country—mindful of its 1979 and 1980 humiliation when Americans in diplomatic service were held hostage in Iran by the revolutionary Ayatollah Khomeni—probably arrived during the 1980 Winter Olympic Games held in Lake Placid, New York. When the underdog U.S. hockey team defeated its better-trained Soviet opponent for the gold medal, pent-up feelings of American national pride were suddenly unleashed as the U.S. team's goalie skated a victory lap, draping the American flag around his shoulders like a much-beloved "security" blanket. Once again, the stars and stripes had cachet in American popular culture, and Masonry, particularly the Scottish Rite, was correctly positioned to encourage the rediscovered pleasure of old-fashioned flag-waving. Kleinknecht typified this fresh outpouring of patriotic expression when he wrote in 1988, "[T]he American flag is no mere cloth of three colors, however they may be interpreted. It is the very fiber of our national being."[42]

Although average Americans yearned for national pride and simple values of decency —which President Ronald Reagan brilliantly supported in his use of patriotic themes and touching stories—some confusion about the meaning of American national symbols persisted throughout the 1980s. What actually occurred in the 1980s will seem, in time, more complicated than merely plotting the upturned coordinates on the graph of national symbols measuring American self-confidence. Still, there was the aggravating problem of ambiguity about patriotism whenever the sacred symbols of one person's American pride turned into the means of expressing another person's sarcastic despair. Consequently, Americans became more attuned to code words and euphemisms. Even the name "patriot" carried a double meaning of being a loyal American and a very conservative activist or voter. In other words, interest groups that successfully captured the image of the flag, as if owning it in the first place, had the potential occasion to dictate the terms of what being an American meant. In Christian circles, a similar struggle over the cross and Bible transpired. And this risked, of course, the intense possibility of creating, perhaps without premeditation, social division.

The American flag was not immune to contentious debate at this time, even though it was assumed by Masons to be the most neutral and least controversial symbol in American usage. Inextricably, this was not the case, as nuances also flew at full staff. The flag, for Masons, supposedly transcended differences among people, which is why the Pledge of Allegiance (regarded universally as an apolitical credo) was always recited in lodge meetings. But Old Glory was also at this time being manipulated to very partisan purposes in public discourse.

The frustration found in trying to prevent the flag from becoming a politically or religiously partisan insignia greatly complicated matters on all sides. The sensitivities were so hair triggered that the middle ground of Masonry was placed in the line of crossfire. The American flag indeed became a "hot button" in the 1980s and '90s. In some quarters of American politics the flag served as a patriotic litmus test. In other places the flag was respected but not worshipped as the most important symbol of American democracy. In those instances and places the Constitution was held up as the most sacred American "object." Contention infected much of the American scene while festive and diverting bicentennial anniversaries were being observed. This meant, ironically, that patriotic observances, intended for the uniting of all Americans, were sometimes tinged with feelings of anticlimax.

Strong sentiments of national patriotism were carried into the Statue of Liberty Centennial in 1986, particularly by Masons, who properly claimed the sculptor, Frederic Auguste Bartholdi, as one of their own. Masons in North America contributed $2 million to the restoration of Bartholdi's world-famous masterpiece of public art.[43] In the first week of June 1989, when Chinese students rallied in support of democratic reform in Beijing's Tianamen Square, having been captivated by the spreading mood of *glasnost*, they chose as their cause's symbol the Statue of Liberty. American symbols were not only an inspiration in China but remained powerful in the U.S. national election of 1988, when candidates, in addition to greeting auto workers at plant gates, made speeches at flag factories.

Meanwhile, the U.S. Supreme Court in 1989 *(Texas v. Johnson)* and 1990 *(United States v. Eichmann)* ruled five to four in both cases to uphold the rights of protesters, no matter how offensive their acts were to the public, to burn the American flag as protected free speech under the First Amendment. This ruling set off a fiery populist outrage, so that by 1994 the American Legion, with the official endorsement of several Masonic bodies, such as the Supreme Councils of the Northern and Southern Jurisdictions, sponsored a national petition drive toward a Constitutional amendment which granted the states power to make laws prohibiting the desecration of the American flag.

Kleinknecht, long before there was a national bandwagon to follow, boldly attacked the Supreme Court rulings. In light of the high court's endorsement of flag burning as protected symbolic speech, he said, "[N]ow it was the Supreme Court, an institution created by our Founding Fathers as the cornerstone of American justice, that was, in effect, burning the American flag by declaring Constitutional this act of desecration."[44]

The grassroots effort to counterbalance the Supreme Court decisions was organized by August 1994 under the auspices of the Citizens Flag Alliance, Incorporated, a nonpartisan, national interest group which claimed at year's end a membership of eighty-three organizations, "representing 26 million people." W. Gene Sizemore, executive director of the Southern Jurisdiction's Supreme Council, became a founding member of the Citizens Flag Alliance's Board of Directors. Among the diverse nonprofit operations in the alliance, united organizationally with Scottish Rite Masons, less than half were veterans groups; also included were the African-American Women's Clergy Association, the Italian Sons and Daughters of America, the Laborers' International Union of North America, the Polish Roman Catholic Union of North America, and the U.S. Pan-Asian American Chamber of Commerce. The Citizens Flag Alliance was featured prominently in several articles and notices in the *Scottish Rite Journal* and the Northern Masonic Jurisdiction's magazine, *The Northern Light.*[45]

The tangle of conflicting interpretations of the Constitution and American patriotic symbols was probably unavoidable, despite Masonic assumptions which consistently maintained that a position of high, neutral ground was possible (at least in a lodge) between the Preamble's declaration of "domestic tranquility" and the proffered right to redress grievances against the government. Masonry became part of a complex debate mixed with a modicum of pragmatic reasoning and much emotion.

Reaching back more than fifty years in American jurisprudence, the view from the bench suggested leaving well enough alone with the Constitution. The U.S. Supreme Court in 1943 heard the case of *West Virginia State Board of Education v. Barnette,* which was brought when the children of a Jehovah's Witness family, refusing to salute the flag in their public school, were expelled for their nonconformity. Writing the majority opinion, Justice Robert H. Jackson, a devoted Scottish Rite Mason (NMJ), argued that "the very purpose of the Bill of Rights was to withdraw certain subjects from the vicissitudes of political controversy, to place them beyond the reach of majorities." Jackson explained further, "If there is any fixed star in our constitutional constellation, it is that no official, high or petty, can prescribe what shall be orthodox politics, nationalism, religion, or other matters of opinion—or force citizens to confess by word or act their faith therein."[46]

The U.S. House of Representatives on June 28, 1995, before the traditional Fourth of July recess, nevertheless, approved a Constitutional amendment, by a vote of 312 to 120, that consigned to the states power to create legislation against the desecration of the American flag. A similar bill had failed in Congress only five years before the amendment proposal was finally adopted in the lower chamber. A two-thirds majority vote in the Senate would be required before the states could vote on the amendment's ratification. Forty-nine state legislatures, however, had already adopted peremptory resolutions making it a crime to desecrate Old Glory. In late 1995, the bill failed in the Senate by a small margin. After the Senate vote, the *New York Times* noted on the front page that members of Congress "exhorted on the House floor with passion that typified this culturally divisive debate."[47]

The tradition of American patriotism in the Scottish Rite, addressed in the degree work too, has at some uncredited level served to influence the much larger phenomenon of democratic culture that has experienced incidental spasms of ups and downs with respect to national icons. While there is danger in being associated too closely with tidal movements more acutely tuned to what is in and what is out, the Scottish Rite successfully shunned, for the most part, problematic connections that would be so present-minded and faddish that the Rite would seem one day to have foolishly betted on the wrong horse. Kleinknecht, as a prominent Masonic representative, maintained that the flag amendment was a uniting force across partisan lines, especially in the face of a Congress that seemed "hopelessly divided on how to conduct the nation's business." Instead, the amendment, he reasoned, "is budget neutral and gives back to Americans something they treasure, something an overwhelming majority of Americans can agree on."[48]

"The history of American patriotism," according to one credible observer, has been "a curiously neglected subject" for professional historians.[49] The Scottish Rite, however, made no historically noteworthy deviations during the period under review, neither adding Americanist energy nor downplaying prior patriotic enthusiasms. Devotion to the American flag, for Scottish Rite Masons, served only to stimulate their continuous, steady, public verification of deep national loyalty during some of the controversies of red, white, and blue posturing. The American flag was not, however, exclusively so central that it pushed off-stage other important fraternal symbols or correspondent efforts representing the Rite's foremost interest of fellowship and humanitarian service.

■ ■ ■

The Kleinknecht period of leadership was not, of course, wholly consumed by defending the fraternity's raison d'être. Nor were Scottish Rite efforts at this point serving exclusively as public countermeasures in order to promote neo-Americanism aggressively. Many positive steps were also taken to improve the Rite itself, innovations which had timeless, intrinsic goals in mind and had little to do with the expenditure of resources and time focused on outside distractions or agitation. Kleinknecht, for example, oversaw numerous creative projects, such as new publications. In many of these projects he was guided by the indefatigable John W. Boettjer, managing editor of the *Scottish Rite Journal* since 1989.

Taking early retirement from a college teaching career to join the Supreme Council staff, Boettjer's editorial judgment and fertile imagination became indispensable. His remarkable productivity was recognized in 1993 when he was presented Scottish Rite's rare honor, the Grand Cross. Part of Kleinknecht's knack for leadership was his ability to assess and use talent. Here was an occasion, therefore, of the Grand Commander's principled insistence that hiring good people is the keystone in the arch. He used all of Boettjer's strengths to the advantage of the Scottish Rite.

Boettjer was not, however, a newcomer to the Scottish Rite. Prior to 1989, he had enjoyed a twenty-two-year part-time contractual relationship as a principal consultant to the former *The New Age* magazine. Boettjer's various publishing innovations, including in-house layout, graphics design, and desktop typesetting, meant that a new genre of books and pamphlets could be prepared from a central place.

Before Boettjer's arrival in Washington, D.C., Rex R. Hutchens, at Kleinknecht's urging, wrote *A Bridge to Light*, an illustrated work interpreting Scottish Rite degrees, published in 1987 and instantly acclaimed as helping to revitalize interest in the quality of the ritual's presentation. Hutchens's successful treatment of the Scottish Rite degrees was designed as a complementary gloss and was based on a descriptive, not prescriptive, scheme of the degree work. The book, because of its ability to summarize and explain meanings, was later translated into German, Italian, Portuguese, and Romanian.

A Bridge to Light, with all its popularity within the Scottish Rite, signaled a dual shift in the formulation and presentation of ritual. On the one hand, the book served to reinforce and conserve the centrality of ritual in the Scottish Rite. But it also, on the other hand, opened up discussion about the ritual's relevance, its problems, such as length and language, and its interpretation. Was a largely nineteenth-century romantic form of theater, with its melodrama and ghostlike actors, capable of holding the interest of men entering the twenty-first century? Had the moral lessons and lectures become too complex, too abstruse? Were the numerous degrees intelligible, particularly when presented in rapid-fire reunions of two or three days? Furthermore, how much of a liability had certain Scottish Rite symbols become, not only because there were many in use (e.g., crosses, geometric forms, and Hebrew letters), which inhibited a simple means of ready identification, but also because they were possibly moribund or easily used against Masonry?

In preparing a permanent display at the House of the Temple of Robert H. White's series of oil paintings representing all Scottish Rite degrees, close attention was given to the composition of each picture. Each one of the still-life depictions showing the full complement of Scottish Rite regalia (consisting expressly of an individual degree's special apron, collar, and jewel) benefited from careful research and scrupulous review. Certain changes were recommended and approved by Jess W. Gern, chairman of the Ritual and Ceremonial Forms Committee, with the consent of other committee members, to reduce the risk of public misunderstanding. The ninth and tenth degrees, in particular, had previously used the gruesome image, appearing on a white lambskin apron, of a severed head or heads, dripping blood, as the chief means to communicate "the just punishment of those who degrade and brutalize the human soul, by hiding from it the light of knowledge." A more general rendering is that Masonry's light can drive out the darkness of human ignorance. In the case of the tenth degree, the heads impaled on spikes "represent ignorance, tyranny, and fanaticism."[50]

The vividly decapitated heads now seemed an ill-suited ornamental form and potentially offensive to a benevolent fraternity's image and, thus, were officially removed. It was felt generally, though, that by retaining the ceremonial daggers in the regalia of these two degrees, the ritual's proper solemnity was not endangered. But the issue of where to draw the line in making revisions stayed close by the Rite into the 1990s. After all, the dagger may still inadvertently intensify the silly notion of Masonry serving "cloak and dagger" purposes. Kleinknecht was especially mindful of public perceptions of Masonry, often shaped by Masonic images in jewelry and even, more generically, on license plates. "Freemasonry . . . has a material culture corresponding to its spiritual aspiration," which is why, in the Grand Commander's view, special care and periodic modification were warranted in the display of Masonic insignia on ceremonial regalia.[51]

The text of the ritual itself warranted similar internal scrutiny. By 1991 the Ritual and Ceremonial Forms Committee planned an exhaustive survey of the valleys. Their inquiry began by asking whether adherence to the Pike-based ritual was "as needful as many of us think." One underlying presupposition in the exercise of garnering opinions was the necessity of uniformity throughout the jurisdiction. Quality of presentation also required greater even-handedness in scripts. The results of the survey reflected the depth of concern and tension around the issue of ritual modification: "In regard to the question [about] emphasis on the Pike degrees, 78 [valleys] would like them modernized and tightened while 74 preferred no change."[52]

The apparent division in the Southern Jurisdiction over ritual not only indicated the wisdom of going slow in carrying out change but it meant, additionally, that the question of prospective unity with the Northern Masonic Jurisdiction, operating independently of a Pike-based ritual system, was further complicated. By contrast, the Northern Masonic Jurisdiction regularly revised and rewrote its rituals, while the Southern Jurisdiction had changed almost nothing since Pike. If uniform ritual were a requirement of union or merger, then wide gaps remained unbridged between the two Scottish Rite jurisdictions in the United States.

A long-range plan, nevertheless, was proposed in light of the questionnaire, beginning with the rudiments of a common outline "of the totality of the Degrees" that would be used by all Inspectors General and Deputies. Further, the direction was signaled that any "attempted revision of the Degrees begin with the obligatory Degrees [4°, 14°, 18°, 30°, and 32°]." It was also recommended that expert ritualists, such as Rex R. Hutchens and James T. Tresner, be engaged formally to draft the revisions of all degrees.[53] Hutchens was subsequently appointed the project's chief consultant.

Kleinknecht, after ten years as Grand Commander, reiterated much of this trend toward ritual revision in an address to the Supreme Council during a midterm informal meeting of 1995. It was his goal that "a universalized Ritual and pattern of ceremonies for all Supreme Councils in the world" be ultimately adopted and put into timely use.[54]

■ ■ ■

Whatever meaning anthropologists and developmental psychologists specializing in adult stages of maturing or in gender specific activity may find in fraternal ritual at the end of the twentieth century, it is clear that ritual is important to the participants. Scottish Rite philanthropy and support for patriotism, while increasingly present on the American Masonic agenda, had not displaced ritual from its deep roots of necessity. Men drawn into the adult phenomenon of fraternal experience still craved the symmetry, structure, and beautiful language of higher-degree lodges. Determining the explanation for why some men of the late twentieth century desired the apparent stimulation that ritual offered cannot be easily ascertained.

Social theories of association, broad undercurrents of anti-modernism, or such invisible cultural factors as the amorphous malaise of "cognitive dissonance" (which translates from social-science jargon into the sense of being a misplaced person) do not go far enough to explain the reborn appeal of formal ritual. The experience still spoke to a wide variety of men, but probably not in one voice. For some it was the appeal of the stage, for others it was the mystery of a subliminal language, and for others it was perhaps a relaxing escape from the pressures and realities of the "profane" world.

Some cultural historians are, perhaps, drawn to the subject of ritual because of what it may say about issues of class and gender identity. Those are extrinsic questions, beyond the scope of this study. It is helpful, however, when historians recognize that ritual, far from being dismissed as the single defining aspect of a primitive tribalism, is not moot in a modern context. Mark C. Carnes, correcting set notions of older American historians (who had disparaged serious consideration of fraternal orders, believing they were composed mostly of jolly "joiners," the majority of whom cared little or nothing about ceremony), proposes that for all its arcane and esoteric manner, the world of fraternal ritual must be revisited on its own terms. He says, "[I]t is more likely . . . that current members have rearranged the symbols and motifs of Freemasonry and conferred upon them new and different meanings."[55]

It may be that as American society became less structured, more informal—school children were often heard addressing their teachers with first name familiarity—a ritual restored some equilibrium, especially for males who had been repositioned in family and social structures. As formal rituals were disappearing from the public world, they became more important for the fraternal world as an intangible law of compensation.

The Scottish Rite ritual, as is true of the blue lodge ritual, also transported both initiates and ritualists to a world that was a long time removed from the current daily round. Further, it would be misleading to accentuate secrecy overmuch as the central, generic, appealing force in the rituals conducted by Masonry. Secrecy has a role, if only to create a mild forbiddenness or to distance ritual from the "real" world. But given the reality that most Scottish Rite Masons do not bother to learn, nor are they required to learn, the grips and passwords of the higher degrees, secrecy is not the basis for defense of the ritual, as either a purist or a revisionist. Rather, the serious interest in ritual at the end of the twentieth century may be viewed as part of an elementary fact of life that J. M. Barrie explored in his Peter Pan and the "lost boys."

Like the disappearing world of radio drama in a video culture, ritual allows one to revisit something of the play-world in a child's imaginary life, which according to Bruno Bettelheim is where all the great moral lessons are derived.[56] If Carnes is right, then "by mid-century few Americans took fraternal ritual seriously," but by the end of the century the interest in participating in a dramatic degree ceremony, at least within the fraternal world, including college Greek letter fraternities, returned almost full circle.[57] The Masonic ritual was not, therefore, rapidly dismissed as passé. Instead, it became important again to fraternalists and, outside fraternities, to scholars intrigued by the phenomenon.

Another scholar, American theater historian C. Lance Brockman, offers fresh insight when noting a possible correlation between membership growth periods and "the integration of theatrical techniques" in Scottish Rite degree work. Brockman views the change in Scottish Rite initiation practices from the lodge room to the stage, "from a participatory to presentational space," and the spectacular growth after 1920 as more than coincidental. Rather, "the incorporation of scenery, lighting, and visual effects that rivaled turn-of-the-century opera houses pushed this fraternity [Scottish Rite] in a new direction. This created for both members and initiates a highly charged and romantic experience that represents for many . . . a form of amateur or community drama."[58]

Brockman avoids the temptation of a hasty conclusion, for he does not go so far as to claim a direct cause-and-effect relationship between good theater and more members. Yet it seems he is mostly right in positing that the improved staging of Scottish Rite ritual, while not bearing immediately on new member recruitment, facilitated processing and assimilating new members through mass communication. The order at the end of the nineteenth century could not grow until it modified the ritual, from each initiate individually experiencing the degree in the lodge room to an audience (or class) all together witnessing the degree from theater seats. Thus, the Scottish Rite, which became America's "premier fraternity in this century," in Brockman's opinion, was best positioned to receive a flood of new members.[59]

■ ■ ■

Kleinknecht also visualized the importance of Masonic studies, launching a major renovation of the Supreme Council's library in 1994 and fostering the phenomenal expansion of the Scottish Rite Research Society. The research society, the brainchild of S. Brent Morris, the only American member of the elite British research lodge Quatuor Coronati, No. 2076, in London, was proposed in order to allow a forum for serious Scottish Rite dilettantes and researchers to present or publish in-depth papers. The Grand Commander, issuing letters temporary, appointed Warren D. Lichty as the first president, Forrest D. Haggard as vice president, Reynold J. Matthews as treasurer, Plez A. Transou as secretary, and S. Brent Morris as editor of publications. Chartered under Nebraska's laws of incorporation, the Scottish Rite Research Society was open to all Masons throughout the world, without regard to Scottish Rite affiliation.[60]

Beginning with fifty-four charter members as of July 1991, Kleinknecht decided that the Scottish Rite Research Society needed to be properly marketed. Adjusting membership fees and offering incentives to join meant that by 1994 the organization had over 2,000 members, many of whom were coming to Washington for an annual conference on Scottish Rite history, historic textual issues pertaining to source documents, and collections management in local orients and valleys. The Society began publishing a regular newsletter, *The Plumbline,* and a scholarly journal, *Heredom,* which served immediately as an important outlet for fraternalist talent and learned abstracts to be exhibited. The society claimed 5,300 members by December 1996, a benchmark of growth due mainly to Kleinknecht's aggressive marketing campaign.

The House of the Temple was also a center of attention, as Kleinknecht made its excellent repair and appearance a high priority. The executive chamber and the Pike, Thatcher, Finance, Burns, and International Rooms were remodeled exquisitely to echo the Grand Commander's words: "[W]hatever we do must be first class." Mechanically, the building was similarly brought up to topnotch standards with a resealed roof, modernized, zoned heating and cooling systems, and improved wiring and plumbing.[61]

Kleinknecht reached out to the neighborhood, perhaps concretely for the first time since Albert Pike made the Supreme Council's library open to the general public. More than 60 of the temple's neighbors tended garden plots behind the building in an otherwise vacant lot. Moreover, in October 1990 the House of the Temple served as a host for a neighborhood house tour benefiting the DuPont Circle Citizens Association. Over 1,200 people came through the House of the Temple, being received by docents giving tours, which ended with an afternoon tea and, later, a candlelight evening reception.[62]

In 1991 Kleinknecht expressed a long-held dream that an annex be built behind the House of the Temple. All the land extending from the alley on the south side of the building to the parallel boundary of S Street, being enclosed where each thoroughfare is bordered perpendicularly by Fifteenth Street, had been acquired after years of careful negotiations. He envisioned a 50,000-square-foot structure of limestone, matching the color and texture of the House of the Temple. Estimating that the proposed building would cost well in excess of $10 million, Kleinknecht emphasized the need principally for library and museum space, but also for a public auditorium.[63]

Close to home the Grand Commander revived an alliance with the Scottish Rite's Washington neighbor, the George Washington University. Through the leadership of the university's president, Stephen Joel Trachtenberg, who like his immediate predecessors was a Scottish Rite Mason, and with Kleinknecht's resolve, an educational partnership was rekindled. One of the largest endowed scholarship funds at the university bears the Scottish Rite name. This scholarship fund in 1995 was valued at around $5 million; twenty undergraduate scholarships of $10,000 each and ten graduate fellowships of $10,000 each have been awarded annually beginning in 1990. Eligibility for the scholarship funds was open equally to men and women, so long as the candidate's father, grandfather, or uncle is or was a Scottish Rite Mason.[64]

Mindful of the world picture, too, the ripple effect of *glasnost* caught up with the modern history of Masonry abroad during Kleinknecht's watch. When the Berlin Wall came down in 1989, Freemasonry caught fire again in Europe, with embers glowing even in Russia and Ukraine. Kleinknecht's Masonic experience and international contacts provided much needed guidance and vision in countries where Masonry had been absent for sixty-five years or longer. He will be remembered, predicts Sam E. Hilburn, Sovereign Grand Inspector General in Texas, as "the Grand Commander who helped revitalize

Masonry in Europe."[65] Kleinknecht helped bring to pass the reconstituting of Supreme Councils in Portugal, Romania, and Poland. The Czech Republic, Yugoslavia, Hungary, Russia, and half of Germany began in the 1990s to recover their Masonic heritages. Colombia also made an impressive return, as its new Supreme Council came to Washington, D.C., in 1994 for special ceremonies of installation. Kleinknecht was especially eager to encourage the growth of Masonry in Africa and Asia, in post-colonial nations such as the Ivory Coast, believing that "as the world becomes smaller, Masonry will help measurably to hold it together."[66]

■ ■ ■

In the summer of 1994 a Louis Harris poll was commissioned by the Imperial Order of the Shrine, which, because of its own membership prerequisites, depends absolutely on the feeder organizations of the Scottish Rite and York Rite of Freemasonry. The average age of a Shriner in 1994 was sixty-two, and the average annual loss of membership since 1990 was 28,000. Using 1979 as a baseline for the Shrine's highest level of membership, which peaked at 942,000, the decline of 32 percent in fifteen years was alarming. North American membership in the Shrine as of late 1994 stood at 634,000. Since the fate of the Shrine was tied to the fortunes of the Scottish Rite, the results of the national poll of 1994 were telling for both Masonic bodies. The news announced that "men are not likely to join any organization that resembles the Shrine," because men between thirty-five and fifty-five years old "lead busy lives with little excess time."[67]

Even more revealing information about the membership challenge in the 1990s can be gleaned from the select sampling of the Southern Jurisdiction's second largest orient. After Texas, California has the highest number of Scottish Rite Masons in the jurisdiction. Out of 44,114 members only 4,584 were born after 1945, covering the years of the famous American population bulge, the baby boom. Allowing for a 10 percent correction because the membership records of two valleys did not report birth years of their members, the number of Scottish Rite Masons in California under age fifty in 1995 stood at approximately 5,071.

Put more dramatically, in 1995 the number of California Scottish Rite Masons born after 1945 made up only 11 percent of the entire orient. At the same time, about 16 percent of the Valley of Washington, D.C., a possible geographic and cultural counterpoint to California, were born after 1945.[68] If, in the best light, a range of between 10 and 20 percent of all present Scottish Rite Masons will form the core of membership in the early decades of the twenty-first century, then the failure to attract larger numbers from the post–World War II generation leads to several foregone conclusions.

First, there will probably be a return to early-twentieth-century membership levels and totals, perhaps making the Scottish Rite in fresh ways more selective, if these future membership rolls can attract, as do the elite colleges and universities, a high proportion of bright, capable men. Consolidations of orients and valleys are conceivable as minimal, critical mass is reformulated. Financial assets may, inevitably, be redistributed, so that debt burdens are minimized as Scottish Rite property becomes ever more expensive to maintain. "Downsizing" in corporate America became a byword after 1992 and a theme in many of the country's leading nonprofit institutions.

Second, the news points to a further cultural marginalization of Masonry in American society, which is not altogether a bad thing, if, like the wandering tribes of ancient Israel, you need time to restore old covenants and find a distinctive identity. Third, the predictable attrition may make the case for attempting creative solutions, such as resourceful and unexampled marketing. Historic Masonry has also included androgynous degrees for men and women which some have suggested might possibly serve as a "fringe" solution to be revived if membership needs drastically shift, though in the mid-1990s it seemed most unlikely. Moreover, going "co-ed" in the 1980s did not check the membership erosion of many U.S. Rotary Clubs, which some viewed as a credible indicator for Masonry.

The uneasy fraternal environment in the 1990s reflected not only the rapid decline of old-fashioned American male institutions, such as clubs and lodges, but perhaps the end of an era in American middle-class culture. The older doctrine of spheres, granting men a place of enshrined individualism (that is, a night out at lodge) while offering women a place of submerged or attached social identity (which is symbolized by the dated joke of women earning the coveted "M-r-s." degree), was forever fading. Babbit had, at last, caught up to the "last Puritan" who was supposedly dominant until the time before the defining year, 1914.

Like the Yankee Brahmins, the men in the marriages of Lucy and Ricky Riccardo, Ralph and Alice Kramden, or Ward and June Cleaver were models that fell out of favor. Their sons in the 1990s are free agents searching for clarified roles and meanings of manhood and have less anxiety about sharing power with women and minorities. These are the men not joining Masonry, and one social historian hints that because of a potential for criticism and ridicule of those belonging to single-gender organizations, a general sign of "great harm" to men may have been transmitted inadvertently. Instead, "the unfettered man on the make" is not enjoying his cherished individualism within healthy structures but is experiencing an increasing "personal isolation."[69]

The Scottish Rite, of course, was in the middle of a larger chain reaction. Its membership losses from 1979 to 1994 were the results of falling blue lodge initiations over a long period from the peak year of 1959 (4.1 million), and, in turn, were the cause of the Shrine membership slide. But behind all this "bleeding" were larger social trends that cannot be undone or avoided, but which, nevertheless, require some effort to staunch. One obvious though hard to coordinate strategy was to admit that all of Freemasonry was plagued with a common problem. The Shrine, for example, in its national Imperial Session of July 1993, considered eliminating the Scottish Rite or York Rite requirement for membership in the Shrine, thus allowing all Master Masons to join. The proposal was roundly defeated (71% to 29%), but it pointed up the desperation, the need to experiment tactically in trying to correct the regression. A greater realization emerged from the debate, however, which pointed to redefining Masonic unity.[70]

While the condition and development of blue lodge, Scottish Rite, and Shrine memberships were intimately interconnected, the Scottish Rite had probably the strongest profile in Freemasonry. Its peak membership year, when compared to blue lodge statistics, was delayed by twenty years, coming in 1979. Scottish Rite membership in the Southern Jurisdiction was last under 500,000 in 1959, rising and holding, then gradually declining until 1993, when again it dipped below a half million. The rate of the slide, however, from 1984 sharply accelerated and began to look like a free fall that might return the numbers to Depression-era figures by the year 2001, the bicentennial of the Supreme Council of the Scottish Rite, Southern Jurisdiction.

MEMBERSHIP IN THE SCOTTISH RITE, SOUTHERN JURISDICTION[71]

Year	Lodge of Perfection Members
1979	660,928
1980	659,468
1981	656,081
1982	654,009
1983	648,201
1984	641,785
1985	632,718
1986	621,069
1987	608,248
1988	592,731
1989	575,747
1990	552,081
1991	532,466
1992	513,589
1993	495,478
1994	480,230

In ten years, between 1984 and 1994, the Scottish Rite lost 161,555 members, or 25 percent of its membership, mostly to the Grim Reaper, not because of an exodus of the discontented. To look for a similar period of membership crisis, one must turn to the decade of the 1930s. Membership had leveled to an all-time high in 1928 at just over 300,000. By 1941, the point of American mobilization for war and the end of the Great Depression, the Scottish Rite had fallen to 175,131, or 41.8 percent of its previous peak membership.

Seen in this perspective, and knowing the Scottish Rite rebounded in annual growth for over thirty years between 1947 and 1979, the membership dip of the 1990s may seem troubling, but not catastrophic. There is, however, one telling difference in the comparison between the two twentieth-century eras of serious membership reduction. The cause of the decline in the number of Scottish Rite Masons during the 1930s was transparently economic. Further, the average age while that prior period of decline ensued was probably much younger than the over-sixty average age for the majority of members in the 1990s. Birth year statistics were not consistently recorded until the late 1980s, making calculable comparisons hard to document.

The diagnosis of the problem in the 1990s is far less clear because social and cultural factors are harder to detect than economic ones. Routine analysis showed that the cost of becoming a Scottish Rite Mason had little bearing on why the precipitous loss occurred. Rather, the culprits were vague, subtle, deeply nuanced. For one thing, expansive television programming, increasingly frequent travel opportunity, the growth of professional or trade associations, and even the heightened culture of spectator sports could all be identified in various permutations as Goliath competitors against a night at lodge, when conceived in terms of entertainment and social benefits.

One thing that was decided among many Grand Lodges, the Shrine, and the Scottish Rite was that if "image" had become a problem which detracted potential candidates from petitioning to become members, then an overhaul was necessary. This was easier said than done. A Masonic Renewal Task Force in 1987 pinpointed the issue of time and commitment as being the biggest factor in a man's decision to join or not join a fraternal organization. Family activities and community involvement had a much higher priority among those surveyed. If the issue were solely a matter of repackaging Masonry to show the male public how worthwhile time spent in the fraternity could be, then the solution was fairly apparent. But a second survey in 1989 showed that despite losses of membership and declining interest, Masons themselves were content with Masonry in general. The translation of this one finding was also apparent. Change would be met with stiff resistance from within.[72]

The Masonic Renewal Committee of North America was established to improve public awareness and suggest methods of membership "recruitment." Kleinknecht and John D. Blankinship were prominent in their support for progressive ideas to be given a try. Grand Lodges, for instance, prepared bumper stickers with the logo of the square and compasses, followed by the message, "Ask One to Be One." A New Jersey campaign in 1992 similarly yielded about 1,000 new blue lodge members by stressing Masonry's positive history, its diversity of members, and its numerous civic and philanthropic efforts.[73]

Within the Masonic fraternity, a consensus about unity began evolving, at least philosophically, which spoke to the necessity of tighter knit cooperation among the branches of Freemasonry. Discussions were opened on two fronts in the early 1990s, pointing toward eventual Masonic fraternal unity and, consequently, a harmonious public image.

First, there was the realization by some Masons, who were thinking hard about the membership problem, that a remedy was needed in the near term with regard to the recognition of the Prince Hall branch of Masonry composed of African-Americans. Second, while there was no desire from any corner of Masonry for reorganizing the

American Grand Lodge system into one Grand Lodge of the United States, Kleinknecht recognized the many potential advantages of unified jurisdictions for the Scottish Rite which could be brought into a single Supreme Council of the United States. While both areas of discussion warrant separate treatment below, neither had advanced far beyond the hypothetical preliminaries by 1995. Each, however, was becoming a priority of Masonic reform, so that a sense of inevitability was present in the widespread reexamination of how the fraternity could succeed in its purposes.

A longstanding criticism of Freemasonry, that it discriminated racially, needed to be addressed. Some recognized this issue as the most assailable weak point of the order. Others went further to insist it was a time bomb with a fuse already burning. Not only was this potentially damaging "image" of Masonic racism keeping out prospective members but it was drawing down the reputation of Masonry like a silent acid dissolving the polished finish of fine metal craft. The squirming question of race in the minds of many Masons had to be confronted, or it might become lethal, despite the wonderful public charity that had helped preserve the good image of Masons practicing their ideals. For many, the convenient silence on black and white Masonry in America had been a form of complicity by avoidance for too long.

Prince Hall Masonry began in 1775 when fifteen black Bostonians, including one named Prince Hall, were raised as Master Masons. These Masons constituted the original African Lodge, and from them a petition for a warrant was sent to the Grand Lodge of England. The warrant was granted on September 29, 1784.[74] Although the Grand Lodge of England for years listed in its register of lodges African Lodge No. 459, that recognition slipped between the chairs around 1813 when the two rival Grand Lodges in England (handily known as "Moderns" and "Antients") came together in forming the United Grand Lodge of England. After the union, many lodges in the former British colonies (particularly the older group named the Moderns) lost contact with England and were, subsequently, removed from the rolls. About fifty American lodges were expunged from the official roster, including African Lodge.

In 1827, the Grand Lodge of Massachusetts officially opposed recognizing African Lodge, which opened the way for black Masons to announce the creation of an independent Grand Lodge. In the 1840s several new lodges warranted by the original African Lodge adopted the name of Prince Hall to honor the first master of the original black lodge. At least two attempts to arrange reciprocity between blue lodge and Prince Hall Masons were initiated and failed, once in 1897 by the Grand Lodge of Washington and again by the Grand Lodge of Massachusetts in 1947. In each instance, the pressure of an ultimatum from other American Grand Lodges, who were prepared to sever Masonic relations over the recognition of the legitimacy of Prince Hall Masonry, was so negative that good intentions were quickly reversed in order to preserve general harmony. It is surprising that Masonry, unlike most American institutions and organizations, including private clubs, seemed to bypass the era of civil-rights, class-action suits, and affirmative-action programming.

Then in the 1980s the mood and the strategy began to shift. The United Grand Lodge of England, perhaps fearing the potentially damaging impact on relations with many American Grand Lodges, initially refused to accept a petition in 1988 for recognition of the Prince Hall Grand Lodge of Massachusetts. The door, however, was left ajar for reconsideration and deeper discussions in 1991, which led to the United Grand Lodge of England accepting Prince Hall Masonry as legitimate in 1994. During this time, in 1989, the Grand Lodge of Connecticut took action to accord Prince Hall Masons visitation privileges.[75]

The momentum quickly gained speed and mass. By mid-1995, eleven American and three Canadian Grand Lodges joined England in reaching out to Prince Hall Masonry in a spirit of unity. These developments, naturally, placed the issue on the doorstep of Scottish Rite Masonry. The Northern Masonic Jurisdiction, composed of fifteen states that generally shared a less complex history on the issue of race than that found in southern states, had opened negotiations with the Prince Hall Northern Jurisdiction of the Scottish Rite. The broad agreement between the two parallel Scottish Rite organizations in the North allowed each to retain its sovereignty and remain autonomous within its respective jurisdiction. Further, visitation courtesies in the Northern Jurisdiction would be extended within those states in which the Grand Lodges had already reached an agreement allowing mutual recognition.

For the most part, the first phase in the lengthy process of recognition of Prince Hall Masonry's legitimacy created few tensions. Perhaps the situation warrants comparison with ecumenical discussions that have occurred between predominantly white Christian denominations and those church groups that are mostly black. Here is one parallel issue that has had its fraternal equivalency: can a minister licensed and ordained by one denomination conduct the sacramental offices and ordinances in another?

The situation in Idaho and Oregon (both in the Southern Jurisdiction), however, was one exception which complicated matters unnecessarily, in part because Prince Hall Masons in Idaho derived their charter from Prince Hall Masons in Oregon. When the Grand Lodge of Idaho recognized Prince Hall Masons (implicitly in Oregon, too, because of the chartering history), the neighboring Grand Lodge of Oregon instantly cut off relations, prohibiting Oregon Masons from attending any lodge whose jurisdiction had favorable communications with Prince Hall Masons in Idaho.[76] It was not a hopeless impasse, merely a frustrating one that would likely repeat itself in other places as the idea of recognition spread.

Taking a cue from the Northern Masonic Jurisdiction, Kleinknecht appointed a subcommittee of the Supreme Council to discuss the possibility of reaching fresh accord with Prince Hall Masonry in its equivalent Southern Jurisdiction. Members of the committee included William R. Miller as chairman, H. Wallace Reid, Robert L. Goldsmith, and Ronald A. Seale. Grand Commander Kleinknecht realized that the position of the Scottish Rite in the Southern Jurisdiction was almost utterly dependent on the actions and expediency of the Grand Lodges within the jurisdiction. To move any faster than the dilatory pace of individual Grand Lodges might jeopardize the whole fragile prospect.

One sticking point which needed exploration and resolution by the Grand Lodges themselves was what to do when there was more than one Prince Hall body claiming to be the Grand Lodge in a state, such as in South Carolina. But even with this awkwardness in mind, Kleinknecht declared in mid-winter 1995, "[T]he time is right for us to have conversation among ourselves because, if we do not discuss [Prince Hall], many who are inside or outside the Order will assume the worst about us."[77]

Another form which the unity question took came specifically in the Scottish Rite when Kleinknecht suggested in 1992 to his counterpart in the Northern Masonic Jurisdiction, Francis G. Paul, that a Joint Scottish Rite Committee on Unity begin meeting several times a year. Immediately, the Joint Committee on Unity went to work based on a consensus that "there are many more similarities than dissimilarities between the Northern and Southern Jurisdictions; that there are several advantages to unifying the two Jurisdictions." Robert O. Ralston, successor to Francis G. Paul as Sovereign Grand Commander for the Northern Masonic Jurisdiction, became an enthusiastic partner with Kleinknecht in pursuing a "cooperative approach that [would] address common goals." The Joint Committee on Unity, as if to reassure more cautionary observers of the process, reported in June 1993 that "unification, at the present time, is not a realistic possibility."

Rather, the committee outlined many overlapping areas that could serve as cross-jurisdictional avenues of mutual benefit, such as handling the recognition of foreign jurisdictions, dealing with membership decline by using similar initiatives, collecting and processing data, and developing a universalized ritual. The most delicate and critical component of the unity deliberations was not in linking administrative operations at various levels, but remained the question of whose ritual held the greatest appeal as a source for fresh coherence.

■ ■ ■

With all the dangers and possibilities for Freemasonry to face in the waning years of the twentieth century, Fred Kleinknecht, after half a century in Masonic service and leadership, had seen his share of triumphs, gaffes, and novelties. He was witness to all the foibles of the lodge room, the missed words of the ritual, and the lapses in protocol. But also, more importantly, by that same quickening memory, he was able to associate all the years of going in and out of lodge with the discovery of that more sublime experience which makes and keeps friends. In terms of continuity with Masonry and the Scottish Rite, no other Grand Commander, not even Pike or Cowles, had deeper-laid foundations from which to build or more vexing problems with which to contend. He did not squander his advantage in accrued Masonic experience, from which he tried to project forward his dreams for the fraternity.

Continuity, however, has a partner in openness, or perhaps it is best put as a larger capacity for the highest things. The combined witness of popular words such as *heritage* and *glasnost,* in circulation at the same time, suggests an apparent linkage. Thus, Kleinknecht embodied both attributes found in these two popular terms.

One of Masonry's most accomplished twentieth-century essayists, the noted American clergyman Joseph Fort Newton, who had served Baptist, Universalist, and Episcopal churches, discussed the secret of Masonry in the question When is a man a Mason? He answered, "When he can look out over the rivers, the hills, and the far horizon with a profound sense of his own littleness in the vast scheme of things, and yet have faith, hope and courage."

Newton expanded his reply to add that a man is a Mason "when he has learned how to give himself, to forgive others, and to live with thanksgiving." He commented further, "Such a man has found the only real secret of Masonry, and the one which it is trying to give all the world."[78] Newton was playing on a well-worn theme, perhaps first introduced by Benjamin Franklin's 1730 assertion about gentleman Masons: "Their Grand Secret is, That they have no Secret at all."[79]

C. Fred Kleinknecht, a loyal respecter of on-going Masonic traditions, nevertheless made "the only real secret" open knowledge to all his enemies and friends. Kleinknecht's sense of proportion in the scheme of things, his identification with common values and tastes, and, especially, his self-knowledge, never overestimating his abilities or under-rating his limitations, have made him a symbolic personality of his era and of American Masonry on the threshold of change.

CHAPTER XV

The Scottish Rite and the American Right
1990s

Religious Prejudice as a Source of Anti-Masonry

The Scottish Rite, despite its probable eighteenth-century French origins and accent, arguably made in the nineteenth and twentieth centuries the most distinctively *American* contribution to worldwide Freemasonry of any Masonic organization in the United States. Generally, Masonry practiced in a local (blue) lodge or in the York Rite form were not notably American innovations as they are readily traceable to either European-derived customs and ideas or Enlightenment influences. The Shriners of North America, a uniquely American phenomenon and the most publicly recognizable American Masonic organization (due to their hats and hospitals), were never as expansive globally as the Scottish Rite.[1]

The Scottish Rite is especially prominent in American Freemasonry, claiming about 40 percent of all Masons. It is predictable that when Masonry was criticized in the United States during the 1990s, the Scottish Rite was invariably singled out for attack or, at least, a disproportionate share of negative judgment. This has been true of most anti-Masonic attacks in the late twentieth century. Significantly, the anti-Masonic emphasis which targeted "higher-degree" Masonry had roots in the notorious Morgan Affair of 1826 to 1840.[2] In 1990 William T. Still, writing about "an ancient plan for world conquest," claimed intemperately that the Scottish Rite was "the most powerful Masonic Order in the world . . . and [was] the path usually chosen by those who seek worldly power, position, and wealth out of Masonry."[3]

By the late 1980s or sooner, the shared perception in the public mind and among diverse faultfinders was that local lodge activities were marginal, but that the relatively strong, purposefully organized Scottish Rite Masons could still be taken seriously. Because the Scottish Rite bodies typically operate from their own public buildings and maintain a quiet profile and dignified image, they acquired a reputation as Masonry's brain trust. Over the years, members were sometimes pejoratively named "Masonic Jesuits," perhaps meant also as a grudging compliment. Consequently, in the early 1990s, the Scottish Rite was at the center of three freshly ignited attacks against American Freemasonry.

The principal antagonists—Lyndon LaRouche, a right-wing libertarian; the reconstituted Southern Baptist Convention of the late 1980s, under fundamentalist control; and Pat Robertson, a broadcast evangelist of the Christian right—challenged the Scottish Rite on seemingly different issues. The LaRouche organization attempted to link the Scottish Rite to the Ku Klux Klan. The Southern Baptist Convention, meeting annually, drew sharp lines trying to decide a pesky question about heretical or blasphemous incompatibility among those sharing both Masonic and Baptist identities. Finally, Pat Robertson reintroduced his large following to xenophobic scapegoating by proposing that many of America's difficulties were caused by a monstrous, underground, global conspiracy led, in his mind, by Scottish Rite Freemasonry.

At a glance, the three anti-Masonic forces seemed to share nothing but a common target, all lined up with different aims. The two variations of a grand conspiracy—the LaRouche and the Robertson versions—mixed up differently the ingredients of the composite bogeyman, though in each case the constant in the recipe was the Scottish Rite. In the case of the militant Southern Baptists, the emphasis was on deviation from acceptable Christian doctrine. And yet, with a harder look, all three forms of criticism, instead of being significantly dissimilar from each other, are more analogous than unrelated. They drew energy from a common cultural heritage with deep, sometimes buried roots in the American past.

In a time of widespread susceptibility to feelings of personal insecurity—financial uncertainty, erosion of middle-class consumptive power, fear of crime, political disenchantment, and acutely shifting demographics—being a mainstream American was subject to second thought and redefinition. Sometimes in America's national history, being an American has meant exercising a prerogative of calling others "un-American," "unpatriotic," or, when going for a sucker-punch knockout, employing the loaded term "unchristian."

To understand that the Scottish Rite's external controversies of the early 1990s were not necessarily three separate, unconnected events but the parts of a larger phenomenon, it is helpful to survey the broader outcroppings of anti-Masonry in the American past. Each of the 1990s episodes of protest against Freemasonry has its historical forerunner and counterpart. All three challenges were outgrowths of a single thematic entanglement in American history, perhaps identified too sweepingly by Richard Hofstadter as "the paranoid style of American politics." LaRouche, the fundamentalist Southern Baptists, and Robertson, too, expressed the urgency of their concern sometimes in equivalent terms of being chased by demons and phantoms, sinister forces working against their sense of personal righteousness.

Perhaps there has been an immoderate degree of academic hauteur and ridicule, disdaining conservative Christians or conservative libertarians for looking over their shoulders, even if they irrationally imagined someone wearing a Masonic apron was following them, holding for them the ominous potential of transforming personal fears into apocalyptic realities. The labeling of these expressions as merely paranoia, however, is dismissive and unfair. Ironically, the counteroffensive use of such explanatory clichés as "nutty irrationality" becomes its own form of demonization. A wiser strategy is to examine the complaints with care and in the context of American history.

Each of the three movements discharging fire upon the Scottish Rite merits separate discussion, but one must not lose sight of what all three represent together—the complexity of religious prejudice.[4] While the Scottish Rite is clearly not a religious institution, it encourages, without prescribing, personal practices of piety among its members. Because of its favorable disposition toward private worship on the basis of an individual's own faith, the Scottish Rite has often been mistaken for a religion, making for an identity problem which is a recurrent difficulty. And while the LaRouche group has no religious affiliation, its ideology is as rigorously doctrinaire and orthodox as any fundamentalist creed or systematic theology in the Christian right. At the heart of it all, the Scottish Rite's opponents typified a range of religious prejudices extending from tempered philosophical counterpoints to vicious bigotry provoking threats and the potential for physical harm.

■ ■ ■

Major scholarly interpretations of American religious prejudice, nativism, anti-Semitism, and anti-Masonry in the early 1990s drew upon analyses developed during the 1950s and early 1960s which tended to lump most American countersubversion into a broad category of "extremists" stirred by "status anxiety." As a historian studying the American right, Leo P. Ribuffo points out that older studies of the Christian and political right "underestimated conspiratorial and xenophobic attitudes within the cultural mainstream, slighted economic origins of ethnic conflict, too neatly divided villains from victims, and missed continuities between psychological normality and abnormality."[5]

Viewing anti-Masonry as a form of American religious prejudice with links to past anti-Semitism and nativism probably serves better as an interpretive model than the older diagnostic terms of resentment towards Masons based on their perceived privileges. Hostility manifested against Masonry often has been inspired by religious beliefs or expressed in religious language. It is not surprising, therefore, that overlapping vocabularies occur in anti-Masonic and anti-Semitic episodes in American history.

More recently, some scholars have provided a remodeled framework for expanded definitions of religion or, more specifically, the broadened representations of sui generis religion wherever dimensions of time, space, story, and ritual are present. The activities at a football game, for example, might qualify as a form of "religious" experience because a broad interpretation can identify in a sporting event ritual acts and gestures, the human reality of time running out, forms of congregational chanting, and even the antiphonal characteristics of alternating offense and defense. Certainly, a religious impulse is present in the transformation of athletes into half-gods despite its challenge to the Decalogue's first admonition against idolatry. More particularly, the attributes of fraternal associations began to be conceived as part of a phenomenon named "civil religion" by Robert Bellah. Masonic organizations are clearly not churches, yet they have "important rituals, ethical codes, and stands on public issues that are distinctly religious in flavor."[6]

The existence of "non-church" religion in America shifted from the close scrutiny of academic speculation and argument in 1975 to a new level of popular acceptance by the 1990s, not unrelated to the increased interest in "New Age" practices or even to what Canadian novelist Robertson Davies lamented was the transference of psychotherapy to a priesthood.[7] Employing the broadest scope for defining religion, therefore, casts a view of piety and morality that must include Freemasonry. It also includes Boy Scouts and Girl Scouts who follow a regular ritual encouraging all members in their duty to God and country.

The religio-moral character of Masonry has long been acknowledged by scholars.[8] But these claims became better focused later in viewing fraternal associations as a form of institutionalized civil religion. The idea of civil religion as proposed by Robert Bellah in 1975 is centered on the undiscriminating belief of one nation under God, undergirded by a common set of moral understandings, expressed in public ceremonies and national holidays which hold equivalent values and functions on a religious calendar of seasons. Hence, the evidence is strong that "Freemasonry, the oldest, largest, and most prestigious of American fraternal associations, is an organization dedicated to the maintenance and propagation of civil religion."[9]

While Freemasonry adamantly and officially distanced itself from any kind of doctrinal conceit, maintaining neutral principles concerning religion, it is not difficult to see how in the 1990s a fraternal association whose meetings began with a generic invocation and closed with a similar sounding benediction was perceived from the outside to be demarcated entirely by vague religious concepts. Through the early 1990s, Roman Catholic theologians, for instance, never deviating from century-old assumptions of their predecessors in the church, still abhorred the possibility that Masons were "receiving instructions on the nature of God within the barricaded secrecy of a rival teaching body having no divine commission to exercise such a function."[10] This far-flung impression, shared among conservative Christians—both Protestant and Catholic—formed a prerequisite condition, naturally, for Masonry to become a theological straw man and then, consequently, a victim of energetic antagonism shaped mainly by religious prejudice. According to constructs of social-psychology, "Freemasonry certainly has the cultic, creedal, behavioral, and organizational characteristics of organized religion, yet its central focus appears to be the maintenance and propagation of civil religion."[11]

Perhaps, therefore, it is the anti-particularism of Masonic civil religion which attracted the animosity of the religious right in the 1980s. After all, the particular goal of the religious right was to re-Christianize the American nation, and clearly the civil religion of Masonry was far less vague and far more tangible than the invisible anti-Christ named "secular humanism."

Other reasons for this echo of religious prejudice reverberating through late-twentieth-century anti-Masonry originate in an older central theme of late-eighteenth-century ideology—that hidden foreign conspiracies threatened American freedom. The fear of the insidious Trojan horse became a constant presence as religious and ethnic pluralities evolved in American society. American sensitivity about unwelcome religious competition from newly arrived groups or even from secular forces threatening religious participation was longstanding before the late twentieth century. Of particular note, the two decades following the American Revolution were probably the least pious in U.S. history.

The early national eclipse in traditional church membership (1775–1815) also coincided with a period of Masonry's first major rise in popularity.[12] In the 1790s and early 1800s, the increase of Masonic lodges surpassed the growth rate of the established churches. Between 1780 and 1800 fifty new Masonic lodges were created in Massachusetts. "Everywhere the same expansion took place."[13] Some ministers gazing out from their pulpits, concerned about defending the faith from an eroding rear-guard viewpoint, began to notice rivals in the religious marketplace. Freemasonry in many communities, for instance, represented "an Enlightenment suspicious of traditional Christianity," while it also offered an alternative in "ritual, mystery, and congregativeness without the enthusiasm and sectarian bigotry of organized religion."[14]

Meanwhile, not only were many Americans unchurched in the early national period (rates of church affiliation may have been as low as 20%), but an influential minority experimented with "rational" religion. Enlightenment deists, for example, whose intellectual contribution to the American Revolution had plainly competed with Protestant ministers, represented a wide range of tolerance and belief. The big three colonial churches—Congregational, Presbyterian, and Episcopal—adjusted and repositioned themselves for a less ascendant role in American religion in a post-revolutionary society, but not without strong reactions and efforts to tighten the grip on their past moral power and dominance.[15] At the same time, the fraternity became increasingly identified with an enlightened middle way, as a link between nonbiblical rationalism and Christianity's practices of piety, "the most powerful, and the most troubling, elements of the fraternity's new, post-Revolutionary identity," which began to provoke objections. The trouble came first during the years after the American Revolution when "a wide spectrum of religious thought moved toward the enlightened ideals represented in Freemasonry."[16] And "for thousands of Americans," Masonry provided the "major means by which they participated directly in the Enlightenment."[17]

The authority of the clergy and the churches seemingly diminished as the "contagion of liberty" spread. Similar challenges or lack of deference occurred when a debtor class sought financial liberty from the authority of creditors. The delicate coalition that had developed earlier among evangelical, enlightened, and unchurched revolutionaries in the 1770s strained the boundaries of its scanty common ground by the late 1790s. While most clergy favored separation of church and state, though many fought to retain state support of the churches because voluntary contributions declined, they never doubted that the United States must remain a Christian nation. Dissenting or nonconforming Christians, such as German pietists and Quakers in the mid-Atlantic states or Freewill Baptists and Universalists in rural New England, were sufficiently isolated geographically to pose no vital threat to the broad evangelical alliance beginning to take on "a new form of establishment."

In response to a perceived slipping away from religion, a second Great Awakening was organized nationally from the Yale campus; this mirrored the positive results of the religious revival of the 1740s. Down to the Civil War, the Second Awakening energized an entire generation for social, political, and religious activism. This strand of evangelical Protestantism was a leading engine of democratic reform, positioned at the core of all the important issues of the day—slavery, tariffs, and the West.[18] But there was also another response to the apparent decline of religious power in the early national period which manifested itself in the form of the scapegoat.

As early as 1798, the militant Federalist Jedediah Morse (Samuel F. B. Morse's father), a New England Congregationalist divine, saw the demise of Christian values and church life as the result of a nefarious plot. Both Morse and Timothy Dwight (principal sponsor of the Second Awakening, president of Yale, and grandson of Jonathan Edwards) created a sensation when they warned the public in printed sermons and tracts about the followers of a radical German professor, Adam Weishaupt, lurking in their midst. They sounded alarms of a "secret plan" to destroy American "liberty and religion" which would lead the nation into a condition of atheistic anarchy. According to Morse, whose primary source was a 1797 work by the Scottish academic John Robison,[19] the French Revolution resulted from the plot of an international Enlightenment fraternity (the Bavarian Society of the Illuminati) that had infiltrated European Masonic lodges. He nimbly adapted these charges to fit widening American circumstances of social anxiety.

Firing a salvo of jeremiads censuring Americans for their Christian infidelity was nothing new, but Morse and Dwight turned the apocalyptic rhetoric on the Masonic movement, too. Using a religious idiom, Dwight named Masonry the Antichrist or the Beast of Revelation. He implored that the "sins of these enemies of Christ, and Christians," invited comparison with "the malice and atheism of the Dragon, the cruelty and rapacity of the Beast, and the fraud and deceit of the false Prophet."[20] Early anti-Masonry was only in part a means of working off a swollen spleen against aristocracy and privilege. Rather, the reactionary force of it was largely religious in motivation and character because much of its momentum was powered by the belief that Masonry was "an engine of Satan." More than being anti-republican in the minds of its early national opponents, Masonry was anti-Christian.

With the imminent collapse of New England religious and communal hegemony, and the distress caused by political and economic shifts in the region, it is not surprising that Morse's use of the "Illuminati scare" was recognized by many at the time as a desperate attempt to reclaim a fading significance for his brand of Calvinism. Morse miscalculated, however, when he claimed to have in his possession a list of Virginia Illuminati who were prepared to sponsor terrorism led by black slaves who had escaped from Santo Domingo.[21]

Taking aim at American Masons, particularly the Virginia associates of George Washington, not only egregiously missed the mark but antagonized old-line Protestants, deists, and democrats, which ultimately brought Morse permanent discredit. And yet, the dynamics of the Illuminati scare surfaced again in the 1830s with the rise of the Anti-Masonic party, a strong reaction tied to Morse's earlier assumptions of Masonic cronyism. Poignantly, as late as 1868, Congressman Thaddeus Stevens, an Anti-Mason turned radical Republican, feared that the "invisible powers" of Masonry might save Andrew Johnson from impeachment.

■　■　■

Between 1880 and 1930, nearly 27 million immigrants were admitted to the United States, most of them Catholics and Jews from eastern and southern Europe. This major transmigration from the Old World dredged up residual fears and created new ones, drawing from built-in American nervousness about foreign ideas and the discontented people carrying those ideas. Josiah Strong, a social Darwinist who as general secretary of the Evangelical Alliance wrote the influential book *Our Country* (1886), worried about Catholics who might escape the moral grip of their Church and turn to political radicalism in the United States. By the 1890s there were widespread restrictions against Jews in American patrician circles, keeping them out of deluxe hotels, clubs, and private schools. Boycotts against Jewish businesses, riots over hiring Jewish factory workers, and housing prohibitions to ensure the Anglo-Saxon purity of neighborhoods were commonplace by 1900.[22] Nativism and anti-Semitism, different forms of religious prejudice, wrapped themselves in league against Jews. Immigrant Catholics up to the 1920s suffered from similar institutional and invisible bigotry, though without the racial component of anti-Semitism.

By the 1920s, Henry Ford's newspaper, the *Dearborn Independent*, published a series of articles collectively gathered under the title *The International Jew*, spreading the notion that Jews menaced the United States. Ford, who was a thirty-third degree Scottish Rite

Mason (NMJ), placed Jews in the middle of a conspiracy theory as wild as Jedediah Morse's denunciation of the Illuminati. Ford may have joined and embraced the Freemasons, who strongly opposed religious intolerance, but his publication derived its vilification of Jews from *The Protocols of the Learned Elders of Zion,* ostensibly the records of Jewish collaborators but actually a fabrication concocted by Russian anti-Semites.

The complexity of religious prejudice is evident when, later, patterns of scapegoating converged so that anti-Semitic versions of the Illuminati conspiracy were promoted as a seamless narrative linking Jews and Freemasons. Henry Ford, a staunch Freemason in his public life, was raised in a lodge whose degree team that particular night in 1894 was composed of men in overalls, because they all worked at the nearby Edison plant. And yet, in an odd irony, the Mason Ford gave assistance to later anti-Masonry because of the historic cross-over ties to anti-Semitism. In the 1930s, for instance, Father Charles Coughlin, the Reverend Gerald B. Winrod, and the Reverend Gerald L. K. Smith became the nation's loudest voices on the far right, politically and religiously, blaming national problems on an international Jewish conspiracy transmitted through Illuminati channels.

After World War II, boosters of the American melting pot trumpeted the evidence of subsiding religious prejudice, nativism, and anti-Semitism. Masonic lodges were crowded with new members, too. Winrod and Smith were off-stage in obscurity; Coughlin was muzzled by his bishop. While McCarthyism shifted the national focus to the potential of a Communist conspiracy in high places of government authority or in major institutions of cultural influence, only the fledgling John Birch Society, an extremist political organization, kept alive the Illuminati-Jewish conspiracy theory.

■ ■ ■

Conspiracists remained relatively dormant throughout the 1960s and '70s. The only visible ripple of new obsessions with confederacy in American popular culture was the growing genre of books and magazines devoted to doubting the official findings and conclusions of the Warren Commission on the assassination of President Kennedy. The Watergate scandal of the early 1970s, no doubt, began to confirm some people's suspicions of government corruptibility, secrecy, and duplicity. Then, in the 1980s the old "culprits" of collusion began to be mentioned again.

Fringe leaders, such as the Black Muslims' Louis Farrakhan, publicly employed hate speech based on their predilections of a secret worldwide plan. In 1984 Minister Farrakhan, leader of the Nation of Islam, denounced Judaism as "gutter religion." His organization published a venomous book, *The Secret Relationship Between Blacks and Jews,* purporting it to be scholarly. In 1995 through the national media, Farrakhan referred to Jews as "bloodsuckers."

Farrakhan's nearly three hour lecture at the Million Man March on the Mall of Washington, D.C., in October 1995 employed not-so-veiled tinges of anti-Masonry, too, while studiously avoiding his usual anti-Semitic inferences. He said about the occasion,

"[H]ere we stand in the capital of America, and the layout of this great city . . . is all placed and based in secret Masonic ritual, and at the core of the secret of that ritual is the black man."[23] Farrakhan believes that Masons are serious adepts of Islam who were betrayed by white supremacy and Jews.[24] Paradoxically, he cut Masonry both ways: he favors some Masonic practices and legends when they are "black," linking lodge history to the precedents of Africa; he opposes Masonry when it is "white" because he believes this was one cause of corruption that gave Masonry a role in the "stolen legacy" that robbed Africa of its cultural importance in the West.[25] His anti-Masonry, therefore, is an anomaly, for it is based considerably on color and race. On religious grounds, however, Masonry for him is a potential vehicle for his Black Muslim program that repudiates Western Christianity.[26]

Against a two-hundred-year background, complicated by implausible links, illusory coincidences, the supposition of backroom subplots, and the complex motives of differing personalities, the anti-Masonry of the 1990s can be neither divorced from the history of organized suspicion in America nor separated from the broad patterns of American religious prejudice. Clearly, the phenomenon of the 1990s pursued religious objectives. Gary H. Kah, anti-Mason and conspiracy theorist, author of two 1990s books, *En Route to Global Occupation* and *Demonic Roots of Globalism*, admitted in a national radio interview with sympathetic talk-show host Bo Gritz that his conclusions were premised on his central interest in "the spiritual motivation underlying this move toward one world government [advocated by American Masons]." As a conservative Christian opposed to ecumenism, Kah also claimed that "if you study the World Council of Churches you will find that it is predominantly Masonic."[27]

The recurrent revival, in slightly altered iterations, of the Illuminati myth, combined with the deadly thesis of *The Protocols of the Learned Elders of Zion*, touches more than the chords of populism, isolationism, and paranoid styles of anti-intellectualism. It also strikes at the paradoxical core of American national sensibilities which require not only the ideals of an open society but the instincts of closed, settled minds. At stake, in the minds of many conspiracy propagators, is the survival of America as a Christian nation, or even the future of Christianity itself. With this in view, the attacks upon American Scottish Rite Masons in the 1990s were enmeshed with strong religious ideologies.

▪ ▪ ▪

Other public controversies put the fraternity on the defensive, rather than on the fence. In October 1992, a proposal to remove the eleven-foot Albert Pike bronze statue was submitted to the city council of the District of Columbia. The Pike Monument was erected in 1901 in the Judiciary Square area of Washington, D.C., as authorized by an act of Congress passed in 1898.

Protesters had picketed weekly at the statue for the purpose of expressing their anger over the presence of a monument to a Confederate general in the nation's capital. In fact, the Pike statue is the only Civil War monument in Washington which honors a Confederate veteran. Further, the protesters contended that Pike was stoutly linked to the founding of the Ku Klux Klan. Contradicting the demonstrators' claim, Walter Lee Brown, Pike's biographer, maintained that there was "no direct evidence of this" and the sources cited by the protesters were "secondary and unreliable." Brown said that if he knew Pike were a Klansman, he would say so without hesitation.[28]

The chief spokesman for the protesters was initially James Bevel, a former running mate of the perennial, right-wing libertarian presidential candidate Lyndon LaRouche. LaRouche had become a puzzling figure. He began his organization as a kind of schismatic Marxist effort, but moved on to seeing Platonism as the key to all good, and then progressed to his libertarian economic and political theories. There are connections among the phases of his philosophical development, but there are no straight lines.

Bevel had organized demonstrations at the Pike Monument during the summer of 1992, distributing fliers which named Pike "the chief strategist of Klan terrorism and murder." The protest literature was published and officially distributed by Lyndon LaRouche's organization headquartered in Leesburg, Virginia, and known as the Schiller Society, named not for the German poet-philosopher but for LaRouche's wife. The protests became increasingly passionate and inflammatory when on at least one occasion the small group draped the statue in a Klan costume. On other occasions, police presence was required to prevent the statue's defacement.

Anton Chaitkin, head of the Schiller Society, and James Bevel were subsequently arrested by the U.S. Park Police for the misdemeanor of climbing on a U.S. statue. Both defendants were convicted of the crime as charged, but when they "refused to accept the judge's offer to remain on bond pending appeal, by giving their personal recognizance, they were led off to jail to start serving their sentence of one week."[29]

Charles S. Iversen, a seasoned Washington attorney and Scottish Rite spokesman, as its Sovereign Grand Inspector General for the District of Columbia, was present when the case of *United States v. Bevel and Chaitkin* was heard in the U.S. District Court. One of Chaitkin's many outbursts in court declaimed, "Pike is on trial here," at once revealing the defendants' agenda, which was to broaden the scope of the court's interest, to include their notions of a master plan. Judge Royce C. Lamberth replied that he had only two defendants before him, neither one of them named Pike. After a brief recess at midday, the judge returned for the afternoon court session and announced that the two attorneys for the defendants had been excused from further participation in the trial. Apparently, both attorneys visited the judge in his chambers during the lunch break, and while there, they were excused from the case. While no reasons were given by the judge, it is not unreasonable to imagine that the two clients of the defense lawyers were belligerent, possibly uncooperative with their counsel, or preferred other legal representation.

Chaitkin and Bevel had hoped for a show trial, to carry their propaganda program against Pike and the Scottish Rite to greater notice. At one point, Chaitkin went into a derogatory tirade against the Scottish Rite and "its Satanism." His vilification of the Scottish Rite was derived from sources based on the well-known hoax of Leo Taxil.[30] At another moment during the trial, Chaitkin suggested that the Scottish Rite operates "over 90 hospitals," implying that it does so in order to give its members the opportunity to abuse children in "Satanic ritual."[31]

While the hyperbole of religious prejudice was a starting point of the LaRouche attack, their tactics did not stay on point, but tried to exploit the canard of a Masonic conspiracy led by the Scottish Rite. In the United States, however, a large number of fraternal associations had become "a widely accepted part of the social terrain" and were not regarded with the suspicion one might expect to be focused on groups converging symbolically on esoteric passwords and grips. As early as 1906, the pioneer sociologist Georg Simmel argued that most American fraternal associations, particularly Masons, no longer made secrecy an important aspect of their existence. Even their ritual secrets were known to many.[32]

Prior to the trial, the defendants Chaitkin and Bevel entered a motion that Judge Lamberth recuse himself because of his affiliation as a youth with the Albert Pike Chapter of DeMolay in Texas. The judge denied the motion on the grounds that he was a DeMolay between the ages of fourteen and eighteen, therefore was under age, and had not pursued Masonic membership after becoming eligible at age twenty-one.[33]

Next, the defendants submitted "a motion for discovery" to determine what inroads had been made by the Scottish Rite into the various agencies of the government involved with their arrests and prosecution. Again, the defense motion was denied by Judge Lamberth, while all motions by the U.S. attorney to quash subpoenas were granted. Many of Chaitkin's recorded statements in court, anyway, gave reasons for the motion for discovery. He insisted throughout various digressions that the U.S. Park Service (and its constabulary), the U.S. District Court (including Judge Lamberth and the U.S. attorney), the English Duke of Kent, and the Italian Mafia were all controlled by the Scottish Rite. Then he proposed that "the Scottish Rite of Freemasonry and their allies, their brothers, including the ADL [Anti-Defamation League of B'nai B'rith]" could be identified obviously as "the people who created the Ku Klux Klan [and] run the Ku Klux Klan today."[34]

After Lamberth announced the guilty verdict, he allowed the defendants to speak before being sentenced. James Bevel had said very little during the proceedings and remained quiet to the end. Chaitkin responded, however, in fiery tones, which the judge ignored. Chaitkin at first hesitated to announce their plans to appeal "this disgusting decision," but then, in refusing the judge's stay of execution, he said they would go to a higher court, telling Lamberth, "You are going to have to take the consequences for having taken an act on behalf of the Ku Klux Klan."[35]

All this time, Lyndon LaRouche was sitting in a federal penitentiary for felony fraud. He was not removed, however, from the events centering on his disciples, Bevel and Chaitkin. In a statement made from prison on March 21, 1993, entitled "Albert Pike and Satanism: From the Civil War to C. Fred Kleinknecht," he said:

After the Civil War, with the execution of Lincoln by circles which were associated with the treasonous Southern Jurisdiction of the Scottish Rite and with its B'nai B'rith offshoot —which was the treasonous and racist section of a very small minority of American Judaism at the time—a more agreeable President, at least from the traitors' standpoint, Andrew Johnson, became President. As a result of a number of developments leading into the election of such atrocities as Confederate sympathizers Teddy Roosevelt . . . and the Confederate who became Woodrow Wilson, who, among other things, incidentally, co-sponsored the founding or re-founding of the Ku Klux Klan in 1915 . . . To this date, the internal history of the United States . . . has been based on a takeover of more and more of the institutions of the United States *by the circles associated with the leadership of the Southern Jurisdiction of the Scottish Rite of Freemasonry* [italics are by LaRouche]. These are the racists, these are the accomplices of those who ignited two world wars in this century.[36]

LaRouche aimed his disjointed attack at the Grand Commander specifically, in charging, "Kleinknecht and company have adopted the provably treasonous, satanic degenerate Pike as their own. . . . [and] in the meantime, the major visible public campaign of the Southern Jurisdiction of the Scottish Rite, since the 1940s, has been to serve the cause of Satan exactly as General Pike advocated, by attempting to destroy Christianity in the United States." LaRouche's diatribe then went beyond decency, having already discharged credibility in his preceding statements, when he also wrote, "[T]hese people behind the KKK, the Scottish Rite Masons and their friends, are *now* [emphasis LaRouche's] organizing the killing in Bosnia and Croatia."[37]

■ ■ ■

The court of public opinion is mercurial and oft-times disappointing. LaRouche, through the Bevel-Chaitkin trial, once again had his day in court and lost. The Pike statue remained standing. His verbal browbeating, however, penetrated the filter of the mainstream media which, undoubtedly, disturbed the increasingly pliant public image of Freemasonry. The picketing of the Pike statue by "disciples of imprisoned fringe politician Lyndon LaRouche"[38] was reported in the *Washington Post* regularly. The freely publicized, unchallenged message of the LaRouche protesters had, if only in the least possible way, a subliminal negative effect on the reputation of Pike's defenders. The *Washington Post* coverage remained mostly a local story based on rumor, played as a pipe "blown by surmises, jealousies, conjectures."[39]

Meanwhile, Grand Commander Kleinknecht requested Charles S. Iversen to prepare a position paper "as our official reply to criticisms of Pike or his statue."[40] Kleinknecht's bold decision to respond in a direct way put on notice more reserved members of the Rite who preferred abstention and anti-Masonic critics within American society—that a new day had arrived in which Masons would not stay above the fray.

The resulting sixteen-page document, "Should the Statue of Albert Pike Be Removed?" examined all of the developments and allegations in the controversy. Iversen focused mainly on tracing the rumor and charge that Albert Pike was the "Chief Justice of the

Invisible Empire" while serving as the Sovereign Grand Commander of the Scottish Rite. This claim was first made in 1982 by Joseph A. Walkes Jr., a Prince Hall Mason, in the *Phylaxis* magazine. For Walkes, Pike represented a paternal figure for "the sons of darkness" who "hide behind Masonic aprons, as their forefathers hid behind sheets of shame," referring in the latter mention to the Klan trademark. The same article was reprinted ten years later in the spring 1992 edition of *New Quarterly,* a journal of Prince Hall Scottish Rite Freemasonry.[41] Walkes, several years earlier, in preparing a one volume history of Prince Hall Freemasonry, had shown a more tempered view of Pike, through whom, Walkes had maintained, the United Supreme Council, Ancient and Accepted Scottish Rite, Prince Hall Affiliate, had received Pike's personal copies of Scottish Rite rituals and his famous commentary, *Morals and Dogma.* Walkes had written, "It is hard to reconcile Pike's actions and words, but his conduct is clearly one of those curious contradictions so often found in race relations in America. An older generation of Prince Hall Masons assert Pike had all the prejudices of his slave-holding caste. He was violently opposed to the recognition or absorption of colored Masons. But, they say, he was perfectly willing that the Prince Hall Craft function as an independent fraternity. With this explanation it is possible to partly reconcile the utterances and deeds of this great Masonic scholar."[42]

It was not long thereafter, in the summer of 1992, as mentioned previously, that the leaflets had first appeared in Washington, D.C., demanding the immediate removal of the Albert Pike statue. The message of the original Walkes magazine commentary had been appropriated and exploited in the leaflets, without the explication of Walkes's more dispassionate historical writing. The LaRouche position, half of which was stolen verbatim from the fraudulent Leo Taxil, was essentially that "Pike was a Satan-worshipping racist, who wrote the terrorist propaganda for the Klan night-riders."[43] LaRouche, who had a long record as a conspiracy theorist, spreading the worst false assumptions about American Freemasonry, apparently saw a fresh opportunity to gain publicity.

Using race relations as a wedge, implicit religious prejudice against Jews as leverage, and a larger-than-life statue as a convenient whipping boy, LaRouche was able to insert himself for almost a year into the public arena. Besides, LaRouche imagined that American Masons would probably abide by the longstanding fraternal protocol of not responding to critics. LaRouche was taking advantage of both Masonic etiquette and protracted racial sensitivities, particularly in a city whose minority population was the majority. It was a publicity campaign worthy of Machiavelli's advice: employ the usefulness of the Caesarian strategy of "divide and conquer" through the corollary term "injured friends make the bitterest of foes."

The controversy spread nationally. City councils of Austin, Texas, and Buffalo, New York, passed legislation recommending that the federal government remove the statue based on the unproved claim tying Pike to the Klan. Joseph A. Walkes seemed appalled, especially after being bombarded by interview requests from radio talk shows and newspaper reporters. He issued an apology for somehow triggering a quarrel he never intended, a quarrel which had all the prospects of sending healthy interfraternal Masonic relations back to Albert Pike's lost world of slavery and Jim Crow. Walkes issued his defense of the Pike statue in the *Phylaxis* magazine: "It is the sowing of discord among the brethren that lies heavy in my heart. My love for Freemasonry outweighs all other considerations, [so] I would rather see the statue remain in place than harm the gentle Craft. I have labored for more than twenty years to bring American Freemasonry together and to have each other respect the two systems, Caucasian and Prince Hall. If the removal of the statue would in any way harm Freemasonry, then I say let it stay in place."[44]

Howard L. Woods, Grand Master of Prince Hall Masons in Arkansas, issued a similarly strong public statement repudiating the LaRouche position: "As a Prince Hall Mason, an African American, and supposedly a free-thinker, I can see a higher power than the mortal mind of Albert Pike guiding his pen as he wrote such beautiful works, not only on Freemasonry, but life itself. One cannot write beautiful words of life without an occasional helping hand from someone 'bigger than you and I.' Let the statue stand, even if it is proven Albert Pike did write the ritual for the Ku Klux Klan; more ignoble deeds have been done by others without sacrafice [*sic*] of their historic heroism."[45]

Iversen went to the heart of the matter in the Scottish Rite's official position paper in opening a discussion of "Pike's alleged connection with the Klan." Iversen insisted that rumors had been converted "into truths by mere repetition," but that no primary source materials—such as Pike's voluminous correspondence, journals, and published essays; the papers of Nathan Bedford Forrest, the first Grand Imperial Wizard of the Klan; or Klan documents—connect Pike with the Klan. Iversen neither dodged nor sanitized Pike's complicated views on race, which were typical of his time and milieu.

Pike's opinion on the subject of race relations appears at least once in his writings, wherein he stated that he believed the Prince Hall organization of Freemasonry was legitimate, or in Masonic parlance, "regular," but that he would not want a black man as a member of his fraternity and would resign if one became a member. Also, while he worked as a newspaper editor of the *Memphis Appeal* around 1867, Pike wrote at least one editorial in which he spoke in grotesquely unflattering terms about blacks. In *Morals and Dogma*, written around this same time, he allowed approvingly that "one race, superior in intellect, avails itself of the strong muscles of another that is inferior," leaving no doubt about what he had in mind.[46] During Reconstruction, when federal forces occupied military districts in the South, he voiced opposition to freedmen's suffrage, a passionately debated subject at that time. These statements, however, according to the official Scottish Rite position, while rightfully abhorred by all American public institutions in the last half of the twentieth century, "do not mean that he was affiliated with the Klan."[47]

While proving a negative is a logical impossibility in rational disputation, it was just that problem which the LaRouche position created for the Scottish Rite in 1993. Iversen, however, succeeded, insofar as calm reason and exposition could ever go, in countering LaRouche's sophistry:

If such a record [of Pike's participation in the Klan] existed, as it most likely would have to, it would not have been excised, since throughout Pike's life and for a considerable period after his death, denial of and, therefore, deletion of KKK information from records was not necessary. For instance, Hugo Black (1886–1971), one of the most liberal United States Supreme Court Justices, felt no need to edit the record of his Klan participation. Similarly, there are no records to prove that Pike *was* a member, much less a founder or officer of the Klan. If you were accused of having been a member, could you disprove it? All you could do is deny your membership and show the improbability of such membership. Pike today cannot deny it, having died 102 years ago. We can, however, show some historical facts which tend to prove the improbability of his membership.[48]

Despite the careful delineation in the position paper, which examined charges and evidence pointing to the unlikeliness of Pike's Klan involvement, it was not enough. Reputation is fragile, "oft got without merit, and lost without deserving,"[49] and Pike's reputation, even while alive, was hardly static. But the issue in 1993 rippled beyond the statue itself. Gary Scott, regional historian for the U.S. Park Service, whose office has oversight of all federal statues in Washington, D.C., commented in a briefing statement, "If Pike is condemned and demands are made for the removal of his statue because he *may* have been a member of the Ku Klux Klan, then the Park Service may be asked to condemn and remove the statues of George Washington, Thomas Jefferson, and many other Americans who owned slaves."[50]

Additionally, Shelby Foote, a nationally recognized author on the Civil War and Southern history, was interviewed by the Associated Press on the symbolic issues involved in the matter of the Pike statue. Foote remarked, "Some man called and told me he was trying to take the statue down because it was offensive to any decent person. I told him, 'I am a decent person and I don't want it taken down.' I don't know if Pike was a member of the Ku Klux Klan, but I don't believe in judging a man 100 years after his death."[51]

In one instance, however, the LaRouche cannonading on the Pike statue scored a public relations hit when the *Washington Post* published an interpretive story by its reporter Michael Farquhar. His article, "Pike's Pique: Why This Statue Is a Bust," did not appear in either the news or editorial pages of the paper, but rather in the section of breezy journalism called "Style." Farquhar took the LaRouche bait "and so did some research," none of which consulted credible biographies or primary sources or involved the obvious journalistic standard of interviewing knowledgeable scholars. The writer flippantly contended, "We wish to report here that Albert Pike's only failings were that he was a blustering blowhard, a feeble poet, a laughable hypocrite, a shameless jingoist, a notoriously insubordinate military officer, and yes, a bigot with genocidal inclinations."[52]

Farquhar's post mortem, ad hominem hatchet, while entertaining to readers needing a little sensationalist spice, did not hold up too well under the scrutiny of Scottish Rite spokesman John W. Boettjer, managing editor of the *Scottish Rite Journal*. In a letter to the editor, published ten days after Farquhar's sophomoric taunt (his article ended with the words, "Albert Pike, come on down"), Boettjer pointed out to the *Washington Post*'s readership all the obvious research Farquhar had neglected. In the end, Boettjer surmised, "[T]here is not a jot of reliable proof that Albert Pike was ever a member, much less an officer, of the Klan."[53]

Scottish Rite efforts alone, notwithstanding Boettjer's defense in the press, and no matter how dignified and rational otherwise, would not have been enough to preserve the Pike Monument. Rather, Grand Commander Kleinknecht recollected two years later, "the United States Park Service, and Prince Hall Masons, too, demonstrated courage in holding the high ground during a moment charged with 'political correctness.'"[54]

• • •

Around the time of the LaRouche-Pike statue controversy, a direct attack on Freemasonry was made within the fractious Southern Baptist Convention, the largest single Protestant denomination in America. During the 1980s, the Southern Baptist Convention had become increasingly rancorous, finally being dominated by its well-organized fundamentalist constituents. The longstanding diversity within the Southern Baptist Convention, binding moderates such as Presidents Jimmy Carter and Bill Clinton and Vice President Albert Gore, conservatives such as Senator Jesse Helms (also a 33° Scottish Rite Mason), and fundamentalists such as W. A. Criswell, Adrian Rogers, and Pat Robertson together in a shared history, culture, and fellowship, seemed irreparably broken by the late 1980s. The new leadership insisted more and more on fundamentalist Christian doctrine. The fundamentalist credo included an inerrant Bible, a rejection of theological and secular modernism (i.e., no accommodation to "worldliness"), and strict millenarian teachings. The latter article of faith is probably the most critical, but least understood, component of fundamentalist doctrine.

• • •

American and British millenarianism grew from common nineteenth-century sources and impulses and is most commonly expressed as "dispensational premillennialism"; it divides all history into distinct eras, or dispensations. The final dispensation would be the "millennium," or the thousand year reign of Christ on earth, concluding with the final judgment. Scholars of American evangelical religion, such as Mark Noll and Grant Wacker, recommend to other specialists and interested students a modified course correction in their usual assumptions, because "secularized academics and journalists . . . can scarcely imagine, let alone appreciate, the breadth of popular apocalypticism in contemporary America." Wacker contends that "premillennialism proves to be one of the most resilient and widely held belief systems that has ever gripped the American imagination."[55] The fervor of millennial speculation may cause skeptics to dismiss the importance of these beliefs as being overestimated. Historian Garry Wills cautions that "the millennial approach of the year 2000 will teach" the doubters how deeply these ideas reside in America.[56] It is notable, for instance, that by 1990 the largest-selling work of nonfiction in American history, after the Bible, was *The Late Great Planet Earth* (1970) by Hal Lindsey, the modern patriarch of premillennialism. The book, in print over twenty years, has sold an astronomical 28 million copies.

Against this scenery of "end times" urgency, a contentious mood infused the Southern Baptist Convention around a variety of issues, including theological litmus tests for faculty at Baptist-related educational institutions and the doctrinal compatibility of Freemasonry with Christianity. Baptist layman James L. Holly and Baptist pastor Charles Z. Burchett first proposed a general resolution to the annual Southern Baptist Convention meeting in 1985 that condemned Freemasonry. The resolution, "Free-masonry Not Compatible with Baptist Faith . . . ," was referred to the Home Mission Board for future consideration, but the board refused to take up the matter on the grounds "that Freemasonry [did] not fall within the scope of assigned responsibility of the Home Mission Board."

Holly and Burchett remained undissuaded. Instead, by methodically redoubling their campaign, they successfully brought to the floor of the annual meeting in 1991 a resolution, similar to their original proposal, denouncing Freemasonry. This time they had gained enough support to place their cause on the new Baptist agenda. Their contention was a rehash of old anti-Masonic propaganda, taking the position that Freemasonry espoused a heretical theological doctrine, which was, of course, a red herring, since Freemasonry never has had in any of its history a systematic or programmatic theology of any sort.

What Freemasonry developed as hazy religious thought had as its only goal a moral order for human affairs, not divine intervention or a soteriological outcome. Transcend-ing the Abrahamic faiths of Judaism, Christianity, and Islam, the Masonic designation for God was ascribed the title Grand Architect of the Universe, a term first used by the Apostolic Father Clement of Rome and later employed by the Protestant theologian John Calvin.[57] This indeterminate ascription acknowledges leastwise a detached deistic God who is found at the top of the ladder of Masonic wisdom. From God emanates a rational order for the universe, most especially a discernible moral system of laws for human society. Eighteenth-century positions on natural law, common sense, and moral responsibility began with premises mirrored in Freemasonry's applied philosophy. This blending of Masonic intellectual sources was at the root of premillenialist animosity which objected to human agency in the shaping of cosmic outcomes. Common sense and the common man, no matter how celebrated in public corners such as Freemasonry, would be pointless in the end time.

Further, the attack of Holly and Burchett extended beyond intellectual grounds, when they disparagingly stigmatized Freemasonry as "an occultic organization" and "a practi-tioner of the black arts" springing "from the pits of hell and the father of lies, Lucifer."[58]

The Home Mission Board could no longer defer review and comment, especially being surrounded and transversed by recent battle lines drawn in Southern Baptist publishing houses, seminaries, universities, and local congregations. Pressure had built up in all areas of Southern Baptist life, education, and communal expressions of piety, spilling over to challenge the propriety of Masonic organizations being supported by faithful church members.

Within the Home Mission Board, and among its senior professional staff, Gary Leazer, as director of the Department of Interfaith Witness, was asked to organize and write an official report on Freemasonry. Leazer conscientiously set out to prepare a balanced study that would take fair measure of both sides in the dispute. The report aimed for a June 1993 deadline in time for the Southern Baptist Convention's annual meeting in Houston, Texas. Leazer had not sought the assignment to produce *A Study of Freemasonry*, but carried it out scrupulously.

When the report was submitted to the Home Mission Board, on its way to the floor of the convention, Leazer found himself holding an iron rod in a lightening storm. His draft report was significantly altered, so that his critique of Holly and others was watered down to pabulum and the anti-Masonic tone was noticeably turned up. His original recommendation, for instance, beginning with the modifying words "In light of the fact that many tenets and teachings of Freemasonry are compatible with Christianity and Southern Baptist doctrine . . . ," deviated considerably from the revised exposition. The Home Mission Board, for instance, changed "are compatible" to "are not compatible."

Leazer later saw, in retrospect, the constant pressure from callers "to get me fired if I didn't label Masonry a Satanic cult." When he protested the high-handed way his study was being massaged, requesting his name be removed from the study if his original meaning was going to be reversed, Leazer's career was in jeopardy. After being reprimanded for corresponding with a Southern Baptist churchman who happened to be a Mason, Leazer was asked to take a demotion, being told, next, to work at home instead of at his office. Several months after the June 1993 annual meeting of the convention, Leazer, who identifies himself as a conservative evangelical, was forced to resign. He had been a member of the staff for more than a decade. During the period he was engaged in the research and writing of the official study of the Home Mission Board, Leazer noted, "the Masons did not try to influence me but were open to me, providing access to their libraries and answering my questions."[59]

In the February 1993 issue of the *Scottish Rite Journal*, Grand Commander Kleinknecht announced that "Masonry's history of turning the other cheek . . . has only encouraged more criticism," and that he was "breaking the silence." As editor in chief of the *Scottish Rite Journal*, Kleinknecht designated the magazine's February edition a "Special Issue on Freemasonry and Religion." The magazine was devoted entirely to informing the public about Masonry's intrinsic purposes, expressed in simple objectives of making "good men better," moral goals which were meant to "complement, not contradict, sound religious beliefs."[60] This special issue included essays from several Christian clergyman, perhaps Norman Vincent Peale being the most recognizable from a list including Bishop Carl J. Sanders, Thomas Sherrard Roy, William M. Suttles, and James M. Dunn.

Probably the most compelling testimony about the spiritual and moral efficacy of Freemasonry issued from eminent Baptist contributors who readily insisted that Masonic membership did not imperil church membership. William R. White, president emeritus of Baylor University, a historically Baptist institution, explained, in the face of misconceptions, that "Masonry is neither a church nor a substitute for a church. . . . It in no sense has a system of theology. It is set against bigotry and intolerance." Masonry, advised White, "does not purpose to be either a synthesis of all beliefs or a world religion." Rather, "the churches and Masonic Bodies should be cordial allies. . . . Masonry is not to permit the Mason to replace the church, but to reinforce it."[61]

Herbert H. Reynolds, White's successor as president of Baylor University and a fellow Baptist, not only endorsed White's view but added forcefully that more than Masonry was at stake in the Southern Baptist deliberations: "In my judgment, the reason that the foes of Freemasonry would like to see its influence destroyed or diminished lies in their knowledge that Masons have always been staunch supporters of individual religious liberty for every human being and that we take an exceedingly dim view of demagogues, like some of those in the Southern Baptist Convention today, who would like to turn America into a church state run by their particular brand of religionists."[62]

The *Scottish Rite Journal* also published a classic apologia of Freemasonry from the former Grand Master of the Grand Lodge of Massachusetts, Thomas Sherrard Roy, forty years an active Baptist minister in New England, who once gave an address that clearly articulated important distinctions between "the religious factor in Freemasonry" and the misleading supposition that Freemasonry is a religion:

> We have none of the marks of a religion. We have no creed, and no confession of faith in a doctrinal statement. We have no theology. We have no ritual of worship. . . . Our purpose is not that of a religion. We are not primarily interested in the redemption of man. We seek no converts. We solicit no new members. We raise no money for religious purposes. . . . We are condemned because we say that a man may be obligated on the Scripture of his own religion, and that we thus place all religions on an equality. But Freemasonry does not assert and does not teach that one religion is as good as another. We do not say that all religions are equal because we admit men of all religions. We refuse to apply a theological test to a candidate. We apply a religious test only. We ask a man if he believes in God, and that is a religious test only. If we asked him if he believed in Christ, or Buddha, or Allah, that would be a theological test involving a particular interpretation of God. Belief in God is faith; belief about God is theology. We are interested in faith only, not theology.[63]

Kleinknecht not only permitted the "silence" to be broken in the face of many adversaries by publishing the expanded issue of the *Scottish Rite Journal*, he also furnished buttressing behind a newly formed Masonic Information Center, set up within the Masonic Service Association in Silver Spring, Maryland. Through the center, 5,000 copies of the *Scottish Rite Journal's* special issue were mailed to Southern Baptist leaders and over 30,000 copies were delivered to every blue lodge in America. In May 1993, a second special issue of the *Scottish Rite Journal* continued the theme of "Freemasonry and Religion," featuring

President Harry S. Truman prominently on the magazine's cover. Truman was a Southern Baptist and a high-profile Scottish Rite Mason.

By now, the final draft of the Home Mission Board's report had been published, ready for consideration by the full body of the Southern Baptist Convention in June. The report, from the Scottish Rite's perspective, was generally balanced, recommending, in the end, "that consistent with our denomination's deep convictions . . . membership in a Masonic order [is] a matter of personal conscience." While falling back on the first principle of individual autonomy, characteristic of Baptist tradition, the report did not find Masonry faultless. In particular, the Masonic vocabulary, especially the ambiguous usage of "light" and "worshipful," remained problematic, as did the comprehensive term "furniture" of the lodge. Among various items designated as "furniture," the Bible is typically included. Pietistical concerns in the latter instance arose in the suspicion that the Bible was being denigrated, as if serving as a doorstop or footrest. Rather, it was not clear enough to the Home Mission Board that a Masonic lodge cannot be assembled without the "essential equipment," which is what "furniture" means in an antiquarian Masonic vernacular. One patient response attempted to clarify the matter simply by explaining that "in Masonry, the square is a symbol of the world, while the compasses are symbols of spirituality. They rest upon the Bible because the truths it contains are the foundation and underpinning of both the world and of spirituality."[64]

At the June 1993 meeting of the convention, the report on Freemasonry was presented for acceptance or rejection. To be expected, the board's report was severely criticized by diehard opponents of Freemasonry who spurned the findings as being too conciliatory. Larry L. Lewis, president of the Home Mission Board, went on record to say that the end product, costing $111,000 (more than any other project ever funded by the board), was an "accurate, fair report and recommendation that I believe most Baptists would want to live with. I don't think most Baptists want us to condemn Freemasonry." The proceedings and debate were combative, but the convention, by a show of ballots, voted overwhelmingly to endorse the Home Mission Board's conclusion that Masonic membership was a matter of an individual's own scrupulousness and responsibility. The dissenting votes amounted to no more than 20 percent of the final tally.[65]

The difficult events of the Southern Baptist Convention formed the acme of public controversy for the Kleinknecht years of the Scottish Rite between 1990 and 1995. Sam E. Hilburn, Grand Treasurer General and Sovereign Grand Inspector General in Texas, called the episode "the greatest challenge" since he had joined the Supreme Council: "The attack by fundamentalist groups on Freemasonry, [especially where] the Scottish Rite and Albert Pike have been the main target . . . was serious, making us realize that we have a job to do in communicating to the average public what Masonry is all about." Hilburn took the long view when he also cautioned, "[T]he problem is chronic and it will return." He gave special credit to the Scottish Rite for taking a necessary stand when it really counted, arguing that the Scottish Rite's peculiar form of hierarchy and its continuity of leadership (in contrast to the Grand Lodge system and York Rite where the turnover is constitutionally frequent) enabled Kleinknecht to respond rapidly and consistently. The successful outcome of the 1993 Home Mission Board investigation, in Hilburn's mind, was tied directly to the unique structure of Scottish Rite governance, investing the Grand Commander with large discretionary powers. Other Masonic bodies were not as well positioned or prepared to meet the early 1990s barrage of anti-Masonic attacks.[66]

· · ·

Ralph Waldo Emerson loved to recite an old Arabic proverb that has Masonic application: "He who has a thousand friends has not a friend to spare, And he who has one enemy will meet him everywhere."[67] At no other time in the history of American Freemasonry, with the possible exception of the 1830s during the rise and fall of the Anti-Masonic Party,[68] did the fraternity have "not a friend to spare." If one enemy is too much, the Kleinknecht years of the Scottish Rite were compounded by militant opposition not only from the extreme political right and a fringe within a major Christian denomination, but also from the politicized religious right, too. Perhaps an even greater challenge, and representing a more formidable enemy than the annoying Lyndon LaRouche or James L. Holly, was the assault of some highly visible Christian fundamentalists against Freemasonry.

Pat Robertson, the Christian broadcaster and 1988 Republican primary candidate, advanced surprisingly beyond his previous eschatological speculations and anti-Jewish pronouncements when, in 1991, he published a fevered opus in paranoia, *The New World Order*. The book appeared on the *New York Times* bestseller list, which indicated that Robertson put into circulation at least 344,000 cloth copies, along with 134,000 editions in paperback. "Robertson's philosophy, in this light," concluded a 1994 Anti-Defamation League study, "is not merely troubling—it's a national issue." That philosophy was riddled with xenophobia, conspiracy theories, anti-Jewish bigotry, and anti-Masonic innuendo.[69]

By the mid-1990s, the shifting winds of discourse in American society left much in dispute about whose values would prevail in politics and religion. Labels of left, right, and center, liberal, conservative, and moderate became blurry and were even less applicable or useful in trying to understand the times. What was not left undetermined, however, was the growing sense of meanness that had infected American public life. The rhetoric in all places was served with greater heat and less light, plenty of lightning and added measures of superfluous thunder.

The growing political power of the American religious right contributed to the reborn sense of Masonry being politically taboo for some public officials in the 1980s and '90s. The conservative televangelist Pat Robertson wrote in 1991 that "Jimmy Carter and George Bush . . . are in reality unknowingly and unwittingly carrying out the mission and mouthing the phrases of a tightly knit cabal whose goal is nothing less than a new order for the human race under the domination of Lucifer and his followers." Robertson pointed his finger at Freemasons, Jews, and international or central bankers as being joined in the devil's tripartite conspiracy.[70] *The New World Order* is a title drawn from the speeches of President Bush during the months when the Soviet Union and its partner satellite countries politically disintegrated. Bush's idiom was, of course, taken from the Latin slogan on the back of the U.S. dollar bill, *Novus Ordo Seclorum* (a new order for the ages), reflecting the popular ideology of the American Revolution.

Robertson's work is an unfriendly polemic detailing many of his anti-Masonic views. The book contributed to a high-strung election climate, representing a revived strand of religious prejudice and nativist anxiety. His message was a symptom of certain voter attitudes, and to some measurable extent he was a shaper of the public agenda in the early '90s. In a Gallup poll conducted in December 1994, 18 percent of the adult public said they thought of themselves as members of the religious right, more women than men, more Republicans than Democrats and, counterintuitively, proportionately more blacks than whites.[71] If there were already a reluctance among many local candidates to become Masons or publicize their prior Masonic connections, then the Robertson spectacle and the religious right phenomenon somehow accentuated it.

■　■　■

The leading personality of the religious right in the early 1990s was, unarguably, Marion Gordon "Pat" Robertson, whose international operations, centered in the Christian Broadcasting Network, were valued at more than $1 billion. Robertson had popularized the figurative tropes of warfare in describing "a spiritual battle" against "Satanic forces." He tapped into deepening post–Cold War anxieties, felt on both the left and the right, that American schools, families, and communities were decaying. But the hysteria of his "spiritual warfare" rhetoric seemed, nevertheless, out of the ordinary since it emanated from a son of the genteel, patrician culture of Virginia, the society of Robertson's upbringing.

He was a Phi Beta Kappa graduate of Washington and Lee University, a former Marine officer, and recipient of a law degree from Yale University. Furthermore, Robertson was the son of a Virginia statesman, Absalom Willis Robertson, who served seven terms as a conservative Democrat in the U.S. House of Representatives (1932–1946) and nearly four terms in the U.S. Senate (1946–1966). More importantly perhaps, in looking at the mainstream sources which helped to launch Robertson's religio-political trajectory, he also came from a Masonic family. Pat Robertson's father was a Freemason, Past Master of Buena Vista Lodge No. 186 of Virginia and Past District Deputy Grand Master.[72]

Premillennialist beliefs and filial identity with his father's conventional public career placed him awkwardly in the national political arena. At some level his situation invited comparison to William Jennings Bryan (1860-1925), a prominent American evangelical who ran unsuccessfully for the presidency three times. One glaring difference between them was Bryan's strong Masonic affiliation. And yet, the combination of fundamentalist beliefs and family tradition carried Robertson into an unprecedented role for an American evangelist around 1985. He fared better in the 1988 Republican state primaries than many party officials expected, beating Senator Robert Dole in Iowa and Minnesota caucuses and prompting the successful candidate, George Bush, a mainline moderate before 1980, to realign his position on the issues accordingly.

Robertson tried to put together a comprehensive statement integrating his view of history, his political philosophy, and his public vision. *The New World Order* came out a year before the presidential election which retired George Bush from office. It was unlike anything else Robertson had produced, both in its sales and its content.

One of the first serious critiques of *The New World Order*[73] appeared in the February 1993 *Scottish Rite Journal* under a review article entitled "The Sound and the Fury," written by S. Brent Morris. Morris did not dwell on all aspects of Robertson's conspiracy speculations, which included the wild notion that Lincoln's assassin, John Wilkes Booth, was hired by "European bankers" (Robertson's disturbing euphemism for Jews). Rather, Morris examined the errors Robertson perpetuates about Masonry, including, in particular, the demonstrably bogus quotation from A. C. de la Rive (translated by Edith Starr Miller, known as Lady Queenborough, author of *Occult Theocrasy*, 1933), who had maliciously attributed to Albert Pike the absurd claim that Lucifer and Adonai were equivalent.[74] Meanwhile, Grand Commander Kleinknecht had earlier appealed to Robertson's sense of fairness in a conciliatory letter, pointing out the erroneous source of his charges against Pike and the Scottish Rite.[75] Other than Morris and, through private channels, Kleinknecht, there seemed to be few other challenges to Robertson's polemical bestseller until the winter of 1995.

Then, after a major transition occurred in the House and Senate majorities through the mid-term congressional elections of 1994, in which Robertson's political organization, the Christian Coalition, had no small part, the evangelist's published views were revisited by the national media. Michael Lind, former writer for the conservative journal *Commentary* and former staff member of *National Review*, challenged the American conservative intelligentsia to reconsider Robertson's place in their movement based on his book, *The New World Order*. William F. Buckley, Midge Decter, William J. Bennett, and Irving Kristol had all, Lind claimed, given Robertson a free pass on his anti-Jewish and anti-Masonic conspiracy assertions. In fact, they had, according to Lind, camouflaged "the bizarre interpretations of Biblical prophecy and world history" of the religious right to promote the objectives of political success at the polls. It was as if they had adopted a solidarity slogan—"no enemies on the right"—without drawing distinctions among intermingling conservative political and religious philosophies or pondering the implications of their unified coalition.[76] Lind warned that mainstream conservative opinion makers gave implicit approval of Robertson's social thought by ignoring his highly questionable beliefs and theories of history.[77]

Abraham Foxman, national director of the Anti-Defamation League, pleaded with

Robertson (who like many fundamentalists was a pro-Israel supporter) to clarify his views presented in the widely distributed book under question. Robertson responded publicly that he never intended to sound anti-Semitic in using the term "European bankers," but was only expressing concern about the right of Americans to determine their own destiny in foreign policy. *New York Times* columnist Frank Rich twice within a single week on his paper's op-ed page contradicted Robertson's disavowal of these well-recognized, inflammatory code words as being notably unctuous and insupportable.[78]

Robertson, throughout all the focused attention brought by at least two *New York Times* writers, was never challenged to "repudiate his gross anti-Masonic propaganda" until the paper published a letter to the editor sent by me (as a staff member of the Scottish Rite headquarters in Washington, D.C.). The letter proposed that Robertson show a similar spirit of goodwill to Masons, as that offered to the American Jewish community, on the grounds that conspiracy theories have gotten people hurt or killed in the past: "As Jews and Freemasons have been inseparably linked by . . . Robertson in *The New World Order* as co-conspirators in 'the grand design' to eliminate private property, national governments and traditional Judeo-Christian theism, thence creating a world government controlled by 'adepts' and 'illuminated,' he has not gone far enough to explain his meaning. Whom does Mr. Robertson have in mind when he speaks about 'the world designs of a well-known but secret fraternal order'? In other times and places this kind of speech has been deadly."[79]

The closest Robertson came to addressing these concerns was in his editorial submission to the *Wall Street Journal* a month later. He again reiterated his prior attempts at palliation in the interest of promoting harmonious Jewish-Christian relations, but never mentioned any similar willingness to make peace with Freemasonry. Instead, he dismissed all other criticism, except that which he had already admitted was plausible in his mind with regard to the embarrassing usage of "European bankers." He claimed, without a whit of rebuttal in the face of being challenged in print, to have "embraced no conspiracy theories."[80]

In an unpublished letter to the *Wall Street Journal*, I (as a spokesman for the Scottish Rite) called into question Robertson's "reply to his critics." Among several indiscretions committed by Robertson, the Scottish Rite response pointed out that a conspiracy theory by the evangelist was put plainly in view by him with even a casual reading of *The New World Order*.

> Rather, in chapter 8 Robertson features such dire subheadings as Dark Secrets (170), A Subversive Agenda (173), The Grand Design (176), The Masonic Connection (178), and The Missing Link (181). A casual reader will not mistake Robertson's meaning when he writes, ". . . in Frankfurt, Jews for the first time were admitted to the order of Freemasonry. If indeed members of the Rothschild family or their close associates were polluted by the occultism of Weishaupt's Illuminated Freemasonry [the Bavarian Illuminati], we may have discovered the link between the occult and the world of high finance" (181). How does

Robertson square his insistence that Freemasonry moves "along parallel tracks with world communism and world finance," which he calls a "very frightening vision" (185), with his latest claim of harboring no conspiracy theories of history?[81]

The particular relevance of Robertson to the Scottish Rite was also taken up in the same dispatch, hoping to expose Robertson's grip on the neck of an imaginary bogeyman.

When Robertson claims that recent American presidents "are in reality unknowingly and unwittingly carrying out the mission and mouthing the phrases of a tightly knit cabal . . ."(37), what is he doing, if not embracing a conspiracy theory? He cannot hide from his own published record behind slippery semantics distinguishing "cabal" from "conspiracy." Robertson perpetuates his suspicions of intrigue throughout his book, devoting much of his attention to the "missing link" between "Europe's most powerful bankers" and Freemasonry. By suggesting that Scottish Rite Freemasons, specifically, "are ready to learn that Satan is the good god waiting to liberate mankind" and that they are obligated to "strike back at . . . the government, organized religion, and private property" (185), Robertson impugns the decency of a long-standing American public organization.[82]

Reviving the poisonous humbug of secret master planning was an odious affront to American Freemasons whose public lives have been a constant circumstance of observable record. Normally, *The New World Order* could have been disregarded as mostly banal daffiness, except for the fact that Robertson had influenced American politics for over a decade and commanded a major movement dedicated to the reconstruction of American moral life. James Buchanan, who lost his congressional seat in Alabama in 1980, acknowledged that he was among the first defeated by the religious right, observing, "They beat my brains out with Christian love."[83] Robertson was widely quoted throughout the 1980s when he said that his brand of Christianity "had enough votes to run the country." Masonry, especially the targeted Scottish Rite, had to take him seriously.

. . .

In a 1995 visit to Pat Robertson's Regent University at Virginia Beach, Virginia, Harvard professor Harvey Cox, an observer of contemporary American theology, noted an eschatological position different from the one he had expected to find. Most believers of pre-millennialist doctrine responded to conditions of a fallen world with a sense of the inevitable return of Christ, which made political activism pointless in their minds. But Cox declared that Robertson "now subscribes to a postmillennial eschatology in which Christians—at least the ones who share his views—are called upon to try to assume positions of power wherever they can in order to build a more righteous and God-fearing society."[84]

Not without contention among Robertson's Regent faculty, one upshot of this eschatological shift, according to Cox, is a new school of "Dominion theology." Dominion theologians interpret the Genesis creation story ("Be fruitful and multiply . . . have dominion over . . . everything that moveth upon the earth," Genesis 1:28) to mean that believers are permitted to have "dominion" over all the world's major institutions. Robertson's political theology in *The New World Order* not only attacks religious enemies but prescribes its own order of "kingdom" institutions run by qualified Christians. The inference of Harvey Cox's discovery raises the embarrassing question of whether or not Robertson has his own new order to take over the world.

Christian America, the Christian Coalition's tabloid newspaper, which Robertson publishes, regularly advertised his own book, *The New World Order,* and the works of noted conspiracist Texe Marrs. Publicity in the coalition's newspaper for Marrs's *Dark Majesty* invites readers to "imagine a *secret society* of grotesque rituals, with candidates lying naked in a coffin as hooded figures, carrying candles, chanting strange epithets and magical formulae . . . A secret society that includes in its ranks three U.S. Senators, the overseer of one of the world's greatest banking fortunes, *and the president of the United States of America* [emphasis in text]."[85] Why was the Robertson organization serving up such sensationalism if not to exploit the indefinite feelings among premillennialist believers of being left out or done in by the American system? The enemy for Robertson was a spiritual one, not a mere political rival.

For many on the religious right, political tolerance and religious pluralism, very traditional Masonic and American values, had been infused with menacing connotations amid the growing and beleaguered feeling that modern life was a horror show. Bitter dissatisfaction with the variety of American religious and political expressions led, more and more, to oversimplified speech of fear and suspicion and a proposed solution of nationally uniform belief. Robertson was tapping into the complicated emotions that many citizens had about a multicultural America, a diversity sometimes promoted officially by "affirmative action" policies, goals, and measures.

Diversity and tolerance, constitutional principles, albeit imperfectly demonstrated in late-twentieth-century America, were blamed for the ills of society. Ethnic and religious diversity, and the social tolerance giving birth to it, were culprits in this assessment of what ails America. If this line of argumentation were accepted, the consequences would include, in the end, a host of innocent bystanders becoming targets of hate. The results were not surprising, wrote Abraham Foxman, who exhorted in 1994 that when the blare of grievance and scapegoating supersedes valid debate about the country's social ills and remedies, "the fragile structures of consensus are bulldozed by sectarian, absolutist declarations."[86]

. . .

Bickering within many American institutions, whether the Congress of the United States, universities, corporations, nonprofit organizations, or religious associations, became highly personal and often uncivil. Sometimes the object was not to persuade one's counterpart on an issue by making a reasoned argument, embodying the American tradition of agreeing to disagree, so much as it was to destroy him personally. Invective and innuendo were often employed to bypass the means of achieving polite consensus. Remarking on the growing lack of courtesy among disagreeing parties, the Anti-Defamation League (ADL) correctly identified one source of new shrillness as the religious right. It stated officially, "[T]he religious right, in its attempt to unite its sectarian religious witness with the force of law, strives to supersede the most democratic form of discourse: the argument. The movement's disdain for consensus instead assumes the superiority of coercion to persuasion." In the next breath, the ADL worried out loud that the religious right's tendency to reject a shared life with others of different outlooks is facilely transformed into "feelings of besiegement—reflected in phony histories and fevered rhetoric," all of which, in turn, "easily slides into paranoia and scapegoating."[87]

Within the LaRouche, Southern Baptist, and Robertson episodes, a common note sounded which portrayed Masonry as an ungodly Satanic cult. The revival of old brick-bats was a remarkably curious switch, especially since Masonic Americanism, values, and occasional public positions (e.g., supporting the separation of church and state, English as the official language of public schools, or a constitutional ban on flag desecration) are at the locus of a traditionally conservative social agenda.

In an independent scholarly study of the Scottish Rite's monthly journal (then *The New Age*) between 1964 and 1974 by sociologists Pamela M. Jollicoeur and Louis L. Knowles, the "ideological" material of the publication was tracked in order to indicate an explicit identification with traditional American conservatism. The importance of a belief in God, for example, a linchpin of conservative thinking, was mentioned in the Scottish Rite magazine in nearly half (46.5%) of all the articles reviewed over a ten-year period.[88]

In those ten years, 482 articles (60% of the total) covered general topics not necessarily related to Masonry, such as the defense of freedom, threats to the American way of life, value of the American way of life, religion, civil religion, personal conduct, and civil morality. Like myriad Christian fundamentalists of the 1980s, many of the Scottish Rite's magazine articles in the 1970s, building up to the 1976 American bicentennial, stated a tacit belief in the divine origins of America's founding documents, such as the Magna Carta, Mayflower Compact, Declaration of Independence, and Constitution. Jollicoeur and Knowles concluded, "[T]he result of the close identification of Divine Providence with the American Revolution is [for Scottish Rite Masons] a strong sense of the ultimate significance of the American experiment."[89]

In addition, like the fundamentalist lament in general, Masonry viewed through the lens of a major Scottish Rite publication seemed to make the case for a return to fixed forms of American devotion from which the country had deviated. Masonry's solution to changing American society called for conservative remedies instead of liberal demands for new structures to fit altered conditions. Again, Jollicoeur and Knowles noted that "the conservative nature of Masonic prophecy is illustrated by the fact that 102 of the 149 articles focusing on the American way of life are defensive in nature and concerned with internal and external threats to the constitutional order." The authors added that "the most serious challenges to the American way of life are Communism, creeping Federal control of the nation, and civil disobedience," according to Masonry. Between 1972 and 1974, the Watergate scandal that forced the resignation of Republican president Richard M. Nixon never received a single mention in *The New Age,* as it was not considered at the time, in generally conservative quarters, a major threat to the American republic.

How, then, did Scottish Rite Freemasonry find itself at odds with radical conservative movements of the far right when its long, published record espoused fundamentally similar messages? Several possibilities might be formulated as an explanation, none of which is satisfactory without the nonrational psychological component of hate and prejudice. First, it could be sheer ignorance about Freemasonry that would have its broad, social conservative nature overlooked by radical conservatives or countersubversives. Secondly, the Scottish Rite's long tradition of supporting public education, particularly the strong principle of keeping religious preference or practice out of the classroom, may have driven a wedge between it and Christian fundamentalists. The restoration of prayer in the American public schools became a tall banner flown by the religious right. And yet, the difference on a single constitutional issue, and perhaps no other, except similar issues about the propriety of governmental religious expression, seems not to be a likely source of the scorching attack against Masonry from the Christian right.

Finally, there may exist other religious grounds on which the Christian right's hostility to Masonry is derived. As argued by followers of Robert Bellah's interpretive matrix, Freemasonry was a chief exponent of American civil religion. It stands to reason that within the increasingly popular conservative "law and order" group, certain rivalries emerged over time about the "ownership" of American symbols. It should not go unnoticed that some of the largest, oversized American flags flown in front of public buildings in the 1980s and '90s were hoisted on the flagstaffs of Christian fundamentalist churches. Jealousies of the Masonic biographical heritage and the prominence of Masonic symbols (e.g., cornerstones and details of the nation's Great Seal) identified with American institutions, perhaps in some indefinable way, provoked the attacks aimed at destroying the legitimacy of an older civil religion. Masonry may have inadvertently obstructed those ends by not valorizing patriotism with sword-of-the-lord Christian piety.

To supplant civil religion with Christian religion and also to push aside Masonry (devoted to a transcendent, universalistic set of values identified with God but not with sectarian religion) in favor of a Christianized state meant that attempts to defeat Masonry were based on religion. The compatibility of Masonry with the conservative social agenda of the late twentieth century, without the Christian national chauvinism, places its interpretation of civil religion directly in the path of certain conservative philosophies trucking religious partisanship, too. Hence, the Christian right, like Bolsheviks purging Trotskyists, had to find ways to clear the stage of similar sounding actors.

Ironically, if it were not for their rigid theological opinions and religious particu-
larism, many Christian fundamentalists predictably would find themselves at home in
the Masonic community where familiar, old-fashioned, made-in-America values received
honor. Instead, a peculiar religious prejudice prohibited many Christian conservatives
from acknowledging the positive influence of Masonry in American civil life. Anti-
Masonry in America, accordingly, entered a novel phase which introduced an additional
virulent strain of *civil* religious prejudice, while also using old aspersions that viewed the
brotherhood as contaminated by the germs of the Antichrist and Satan. From those
incipient feelings, words formed and names stuck.

Epilogue

The straight lines of history appear rarely, perhaps as often as baseball's triple crown or as infrequently as Halley's Comet. Instead, the crooked grains of the past bend toward the present, usually bulging into the future by rounded curves like those encircling a dark knot in a pine board. Some philosophers of history insist on the grand theme of returning cycles; they believe starting points and destinations share a similarity approaching sameness. Consequently, history's potential circularity remains a popular form of understanding the arching sweep of the past.

Surprisingly (and that is the attraction), history is not simply a turning wheel with compass points fixed and known in advance. History indeed has its circles, but it also has its diagonals and chords. This is apparent in the ever-ancient and ever-new question Where have we been? which does not yield all in a tightly drawn loop. It is, in fact, a far more problematic question than Where are we going?

From the past a historian can extrapolate a few tendencies, underline noticeable trends, examine causes and outcomes, but these variables do not help predict next year's weather. Rather than a sense of inevitability about the cyclical lessons of history and their bearing on what happens next, a trustworthy and memorable coincidence occasionally offers the interlude that lets us have history both ways—as nothing new under the sun and as a direct beam of light.

. . .

In preparing this history by the zigs and zags of group biography and with an eye on contemporary events and moods, there emerged one remarkably straight line of continuity which suggests that even a period of two centuries is as a quickly passed watch in the night. Well within the fence line of Scottish Rite history were men who shared an experience and heard words that for seven or eight generations had a sameness. That is to be expected, but something else momentarily sets the Scottish Rite apart from other American social institutions that have cycled through time and happenstance. It also suggests an alternative pattern of unity.

Between the American Revolution and the end of the twentieth century stand only two men, known to each other, who were connected through a common association with the Scottish Rite, Southern Jurisdiction.[1] C. Fred Kleinknecht, elected Grand Commander in 1985, was hired to work at the Supreme Council by John Henry Cowles in the 1940s; as a young man, Cowles met Albert Pike, once having passed an afternoon with him in the older man's library. Going back another sixty years or so, Albert Pike, as a fifteen year old boy, shook hands with Lafayette sometime in 1824.[2]

Lafayette was, of course, instrumental in the success of George Washington's army, playing crucial roles at Brandywine and Yorktown. Later, Lafayette was on hand during the French Revolution and the Napoleonic era. Lafayette, besides his esteemed military and political reputation, also carried Scottish Rite honors at the end of his life as a thirty-third degree Mason, a designation conferred upon him in all probability by Cerneau sympathizers in New York.

Thus, Kleinknecht was, by the time of his term as Grand Commander, only two hand-shakes removed from the point of the Supreme Council's founding. Between the 1790s and 1990s in America, when viewed through the experience of only three Grand Commanders, the bridge shortens, the lines straighten. A line this straight suggests proximity to people and events that at first seem deceptively distant. The past is closer than we think.

Also, it is a line that establishes a sense of institutional longevity and strength. And because such a straight route is a rapid means to return in time, the days between 1801 and 2001 are not impossible to number. Along the way, however, certain days appear as fragile moments. None were perhaps as delicate as the first day. And none may be as near to the present day as the early days when linked by the pulled mystic of acquaintanceship.

■ ■ ■

When the Scottish Rite of Freemasonry formed its first Supreme Council in 1801, Napoleon Bonaparte had just defeated the Austrians in Italy, instituted breath-taking reforms in the French legal system, and accomplished tranquillity with the Roman Catholic Church by the Concordat of 1801. It makes little sense for these fraternal, military, and political events to be listed together as if they were a strand of pearls all of uniform size. If they are related in any way, the tangents are seemingly oblique.

It is curious, nevertheless, why a particularly embellished philosophical extension of the Masonic order, with ritual origins in France and later associations (though in name only) with Scotland, would be officially constituted in the United States, in Charleston, South Carolina. Why not in France? In a word, Napoleon is a key piece to the enigma.

Napoleon was not a Freemason, but his four brothers, a stepson, and a nephew were active in the fraternity. His first wife, Josephine, belonged to the Rite of Adoption. Jean Jacques Cambaceres, Napoleon's right-hand advisor, played a prominent part in both Freemasonry and post-revolutionary politics, which were sometimes indistinguishable from each other. Napoleon was not, therefore, indisposed to Freemasonry. By most yard-sticks, he used its prestige and influence to further his own ends without being involved with the fraternity himself.

French lodges, for instance, presented places and occasions noted for the rabid venera-tion of Napoleon; his series of military triumphs inspired instantaneous Masonic gather-ings and patriotic speech-making. French Masonic sycophancy made it naturally tenable for the Grand Orient to appoint many Napoleonic officials to high Masonic offices.

Despite the variety of favorable circumstances for the Supreme Council's birth to occur in France, too many prior entanglements and rivalries remained unknotted. To achieve a needed consensus about the direction of French Masonic innovations such as the higher degrees in the Rite of Perfection (i.e., the Scottish Rite's direct French forerunner), only the validity of Napoleon's will and intervention might have made a difference.

Chaos in French Freemasonry, like a thicket arising from unimproved grounds, continued throughout Napoleon's time; it had grown uncontrollably from a time long before the weeding out process of the Revolution of 1789.[3] The opportunity to turn around the many inconsistencies in French Masonic practices after the Republic was formed quickly evaporated. Brotherly turmoil and a quagmire of intrigue within French society pulled Masonry into complicated partisanship.

Had French Freemasonry been a more stable institution, not tying its fortunes so patently to the fickle destiny of Napoleon, whose interest in the fraternity was exploitative at best, the chances for codifying a uniquely Gallic Masonic system of degrees under a central authority might have been stronger. Napoleon was too big a distraction, too large and too seductive a personality, not to have impacted the fraternity even by acts of indifference and omission.

■ ■ ■

The French failure at fraternal unification and ritual consolidation is ironic in light of Napoleon's success in overhauling the courts, streamlining procedures of law, and returning the judicial system to Latin antecedents. He put to rest, at least officially, the tensions between the Catholic Church and French secular culture. In an atmosphere of Napoleonic treaty-making interspersed by military conflict, no agreement was ever successfully negotiated by public powers with fraternal associations or by Masonic officials.

The warring between the Grand Lodge and Grand Orient, therefore, continued without a truce. Their quarreling differences, often based on rural-urban contention, ran deep and invariably along class lines, sometimes dividing bourgeois men (typically, Grand Orient) from men born into the aristocracy (more likely, Grand Lodge). This tension resembled the original class division between the Antients (middle class) and the Moderns (elites) in Anglo-American Freemasonry. The other difference between them was that an "Orient" was run by a council whose Grand Master was appointed, not elected. Ironically, in Napoleonic society, French Freemasonry revealed that the aristocrats had some democratic tendencies and the bourgeois (perhaps imitating aristocratic attitudes) developed oligarchical habits.

Acrimony was endemic to French Freemasonry because it was living at the intersection of two colliding mental worlds. The first and older position embraced privilege and inherited status. The second and newer one argued on democratic grounds that men (generally not women), who were all endowed equally with the capacity of reason, ought to be judged by their merits. The fault lines of the Enlightenment, which still project into the twentieth century, were easily exposed within the French Masonic lodges; they were caused by the tectonic energies of democratic ideology rubbing against the social reality of inequality.

One prospective bridge across the divide was the early French version of "Scottish" Masonry, especially popular in the 1780s and 1790s because it took degrees clearly invented for the aristocracy and made them available to bourgeois men who coveted the status and the merit-based recognition that the degrees expressed. Since these "Scottish" degrees and ceremonies in France were probably Jacobite in their origin or, according to Margaret C. Jacob, at least baroque and Catholic in their first nature (which made them appealing to men long accustomed to Catholic rituals), the increasing number of men in the bourgeoisie who traveled by this Scottish route felt themselves closer to achieving the leveling ideals of the fraternity.[4]

When the traditionally elite Grand Lodge attempted to impose centralization, order, and control over the higher grades of Masonry, it met a strong counterforce from other quarters. The resistance wanted to translate the lessons of the higher degrees into reforms of the lofty hierarchical structure of French lodges. As would be expected, hostility and distrust resulted.

By 1801, it was clear that Napoleon had inherited an old and festering situation. It was a running dispute that had stayed alive for a quarter century and had put stratified classes at odds within the Masonic lodges. It was a problem so thorny that it was beyond his interest, ability, or scope to repair. From the Masonic perspective, the vacuum created by the impasse was filled elsewhere. Just as with certain geometric proofs as legendary as Euclid, sometimes one has to venture outside the perimeters of a given figure to achieve a solution. The consequences of Napoleon's indifference toward Freemasonry and Masonic intractability in France made it necessary for the French system to find other soil in which to root its experimental cuttings.

Loose and unregulated practices and uncontrolled numbers of patents issued over many signatures, without a central bureau to register them and validate them, meant the French system of higher degree Masonry was in jeopardy of allowing disorder and dissolution to triumph. Bypassing France, as it turned out, provided the best chance for the turmoil around Scottish Masonry to be resolved.

The isolation of the French West Indies, particularly in Jamaica and Haiti, had given the uniquely French form of the craft a salvific moment. There it had forty years to achieve control of its fluid ritual material without the vicious provocations of competing lodge groups, and from that firm base it had a golden chance to establish itself at a place that was receptive to things French and things Masonic. Charleston, South Carolina, was not an arbitrary choice for Masons of the Napoleonic era to organize the first Supreme Council.

Charleston was long experienced in harboring French exiles. Huguenots and their descendants had been present for more than a century when the Supreme Council was formed in 1801. Ten years before that, the slave revolt in Haiti caused another wave of French refugees to enter Charleston. Out of their number, many of the new arrivals were Roman Catholic. Equally significant, colonial Charleston had been hospitable to

Jews, giving that Atlantic port a worldly eclecticism that had defining power for the Scottish Rite, too.

For the early history of the Supreme Council, the French connection is transparent from the evidence. There were over forty members in the Charleston Lodge of Perfection in 1801, nearly half of them with French surnames, having been born in France or in French colonies. A few years after the Supreme Council began, de Grasse-Tilly, one of the original eleven founders, returned to Paris with a definite agenda. There in 1804 he set up a Supreme Council of the Ancient and Accepted Scottish Rite in France, the year Napoleon crowned himself Emperor.

Before Napoleon abdicated in 1814, de Grasse-Tilly was forced by Masonic rivals in France to clarify what he was up to. He explained that his Supreme Council was one *for America in France.* He tacitly admitted by his choice of unctuous words that the future of the Scottish Rite was not in France where it was conceived, but in America where it was transplanted. Meanwhile, Napoleon's exile to Elba in 1814 had sealed the claim of American precedence for regulating the French-inspired higher degrees of Scottish Freemasonry.

■ ■ ■

Napoleon endures as the major reference point for Western history during the entire nineteenth century. No less is true of a fledgling Masonic order in South Carolina with Latin values of the high Renaissance at its core, the same values Napoleon promoted.

When Leo Tolstoy began his monumental *War and Peace* on the eve of the American Civil War, Napoleon was his preoccupation. Within the compelling epoch story of *War and Peace,* which features five hundred characters, Tolstoy slips past the specific plot to pose on occasion the broadest questions a historian can ask. What made Napoleon act the way he did? What causes historic events? What is the relationship between power and freedom? Does it lead to inevitability?

Napoleon haunts the Scottish Rite, too, if only in the background during the opening years of the Supreme Council. Without the shadow of his presence, there might have been different outcomes in French Freemasonry; and without the almost spectral phenomenon of Napoleon, what transpired in the first decade of the 1800s at Charleston would undoubtedly have been different or even unnecessary.

In some way the problem of making sense of the Scottish Rite in America from its beginning down to the end of its second century starts with Napoleon, as is the case for Tolstoy, also. And the answers to the philosophical questions that arouse interest about the past, after the long-ago events are chronicled, are somehow where Tolstoy indicates they always are to be found—in the details and personalities. And even then, the answers are elusive and incomplete. What does all this mean? asks Tolstoy in his Second Epilogue.

The general themes of causation and unplanned consequences, the contradictions between forms of power and expressions of independent thought, and the struggle between personal will and group fogyism are all present in the history of the Supreme Council in America's Southern Jurisdiction. There have been hundreds, later thousands, of characters in the story. But generalizations, while tempting at the point where the story either ends or ends with the promise "to be continued," must be avoided.

For every generalization, there is some multiplier of exceptions to be found. The Supreme Council has not been all of one thing, but a composite of many attributes often reflecting the qualities of the day in some unusual or typical way, just as contemporary Napoleonic allurements of grandeur are around the edges of its founding.

When all the anecdotes, descriptions of social milieu, and personal vignettes have fashioned the story of the Supreme Council in America's Southern Jurisdiction, the details fold into at least five shared themes that are linked to each other. In each era of its history the Scottish Rite faced up to or was confronted by at least one of several specific motifs: fraternity, ritual, membership, charity, and public life. For any one of these topics ample room has been left for more scholarship to enter the field. All five historic themes converge at the end of two hundred years, and their convergence and meanings surely speak to the Scottish Rite's potentially resonant posterity.

■ ■ ■

The concept of fraternity, for example, fits in with numerous recent studies on manhood and masculinity. The question of how men defined themselves as brothers transcends the Scottish Rite, of course, but therein are nuances not found in ordinary men's groups.

The discipline of the brotherhood, for instance, has called for individual acts of decency and placed moral deviancy out of bounds. Masonic jurisprudence as a regulator of men's behavior is a kind of constitutional microcosm. Betrayal of the order was an unpardonable transgression. Masonic duty in 1801 and for the next two hundred years, explains Margaret Jacob, resembles both civic and domestic obligations to which a member must conform. In the Southern Jurisdiction of the Scottish Rite, the protocol of honors, the probationary wait between Knight Commander of the Court of Honor (red cap) and the thirty-third degree (white cap), is a subtle instance of discipline (some refer to it as fealty) that has kept the boat from rocking. The very concept of fraternity, Jacob emphasizes, "is a living creed that bridges the space between the public and the private."[5]

The uneasy gender environment of the late twentieth century established grounds for the idea of manhood having a history. Since the gender theme matters in social and historical analysis, fraternity can hardly be overlooked as silly and incongruous. How the Scottish Rite as a more "intellectual brotherhood" supported or altered constructs of masculinity is a research question of fascinating proportions.

When Roscoe Pound once remarked that Freemasonry was tied figuratively to the "development of societies out of the primitive men's house," he gave not only a title to a popular Masonic book by Joseph Fort Newton but also an invitation to consider fraternal ritual from the perspective of an anthropologist. He extends his premise to the ends that "in this same men's house are the germs of civilization."[6] Scholarly interest in primitive male rites of passage ought now to bring wider scrutiny upon the barely explored reasons why Masonic ritual has been so meaningful to so many men.

What the Scottish Rite ritual experience has meant to candidates and performers has yet to be treated adequately. Few men perhaps have written down what they thought about the degrees in emotional or spiritual terms. But there are clues, and historians would be wise never to underestimate the emotional undertow of Masonic rituals and the intensity of brotherly devotion they could often embolden.

Occasionally references to an individual's own initiation ceremony are found in the admission of it being the "moment of transformation." James Tresner speaks of it personally as "literally, an overwhelming moment." For him, there is a certainty that "there will never be a more important moment in my life until I make that even more glorious transformation which is death."[7]

Tresner's statement compared to Tolstoy's older description of a similar moment suggests a thematic constancy as equally relevant to early-nineteenth-century Masons as to men of the late twentieth century. As Pierre in *War and Peace* entered the lodge room for his initiation: "He experienced a variety of the most complex sensations. He felt afraid of what would happen to him and still more afraid of showing his fear. He felt curious to know what was going to happen to him; but most of all, he felt joyful that the moment had come when he would at last start on that path of regeneration and on the actively virtuous life of which he had been dreaming."[8]

Nancy F. Cott views this sort of male experience as a "repetition-compulsion ritual, in which the individual is made more isolated, more alone, more vulnerable than ever, and after experiencing the depth of isolation is reincorporated into the male group."[9] With repetition, the anxiety of being isolated subsides and the bliss of belonging takes over. Cott's thesis is provocative, but needs greater consideration and testing.

Membership in the Scottish Rite also has rich topical relevancy. Conferences of professional American historians have been dominated in the 1990s by the trinity of concerns centered on "race, class, and gender." Scottish Rite membership trends, particularly with accessible records at the Supreme Council, incorporate all three modes of current interest in American social history.

Comparing personal backgrounds and internal status perceptions through the fraternal lens has major implications for demographic, economic, and social issues of the American past. On other important matters, analyzing the composition of membership could be very telling. There have been, for instance, predominantly white and entirely black Supreme Councils in America. Getting at the historical division of race by fresh approaches could be highly instructive for many reasons bearing on future questions. Some writer ought to be wondering what differences and similarities are to be found between black men and white men in America who have been in lodge settings. Did the Scottish Rite, specifically, serve as a more particular demarcation of class and educational status in the black community than in the white?

One of the familiar roles men have filled within their families and societies has been that of the "good provider." What does that say about the phenomenal rise of Masonic philanthropy in the twentieth century when examining both the size of funds (an aggregate easily ranking Masonic charities in America's top 100 nonprofit foundations) and the commitment to voluntarism? Interestingly, as Scottish Rite membership has contracted in the last quarter century, its charitable endeavors have expanded. There is another story here that is still evolving.

Finally, the Scottish Rite has had periodic public visibility and a life lived in open view, sometimes welcomed and initiated by the Supreme Council. More recently, it seems, a disproportionate amount of the attention has been distracting and undesirable (see chapter 15). Responding to the "public relations spin" will continue to challenge old organizations such as Masonry. There is a temptation to withdraw into more guarded, private boundaries, to ignore the nit-picking and become an increasingly separate club. In the confusing difficulty of the recent past, however, fresh opportunity may yet appear for maturer fraternities to match another generation's needs.

■ ■ ■

In his posthumously published lamentation entitled *The Revolt of the Elites and the Betrayal of Democracy* (1995), Christopher Lasch has much to say about the dangers of elitism found in the wealthy professional classes of America, the decline of public culture, and the importance of common sense which increasingly is in a state of absence. He points out that as the world becomes smaller because of technology and travel advantages, "the unification of the market goes hand in hand with the fragmentation of culture."[10]

American society is troubled, pronounces Lasch, because it has left behind the value of pride in craftsmanship and forgotten civic lessons of self-restraint, earned respect, and mitigated expectations. He emphasizes that the decline of civility, decency, and participatory democracy "may be directly related to the disappearance of third places."[11] For most people there is home and there is the workplace, but no other informal meeting places exist in which to enter the crucible of civic life.

The political scientist Robert Putnam takes stock of the fact that voluntary organizations as different as the PTA, American Legion, League of Women Voters, and the Masonic lodges are losing membership in exact correlation with a substantial decline in U.S. political participation. He puts it colorfully, "[T]he most whimsically and discomfiting bit of evidence of social disengagement in contemporary America . . . is that more Americans are bowling than ever before, but bowling in organized leagues has plummeted in the last decade or so."[12]

When Lasch worries about "the democratic malaise," he is coldly unsentimental, even humorless compared to his kindred spirit Putnam. It is a mood that travels without the baggage of nostalgia as he proposes a solution or, at least, a recovered first principle: "Civic life requires settings in which people meet as equals, without regard to race, class, or national origins."[13]

If Lasch's critique is correct, it seems obvious that his recommended corrective measure points to established "third" places such as Freemasonry. As befitting its public history, the fraternity has cohered both as a sphere of influence and along an independent axis. As a result, sometimes by straight lines, more often by loops and curves, flexible historical forces stay in play for a while longer.

The Scottish Rite comes to a moment after two centuries that is much like its beginning. In 1801, experimentation with democracy was highly animated in the West and its possibilities clearly differentiated between America and France. Those differences affected the history of the Rite in more than one way. The Americanization of French high-grade Masonry and the accompanying rapid democratization of American society now come forward together from a point of previous interplay between them.

Democracy is once again an experimental polity, but not noticeably in America (or France). Democracy is fighting for survival in Russia and may one day have a chance, too, in China. But democracy in America also must put up a fight, for it has been abandoned by too many talented, well-educated people for the fleshpots of Dow Jones and the alien gods of satellite TV.

Distinctive kinds of revolutionary experience once produced contrasting results. In France the elites never fully accepted the leveling of society. In America they did. But America has recently seen its best and brightest imitating the values of Napoleonic elites.

American society, therefore, will perhaps enter 2001 looking very much like French society of 1801 with widening discrepancies between privilege and duty. It is not an imitated Napoleonic imperialism that will be troubling, but a cultural and economic Bonapartism. If, however, there is to be a recovery of earlier American democratic principles of public participation, then the worst kind of elitism—that which bowls alone—ought to be consigned to Elba.

Meanwhile, the Scottish Rite of Freemasonry sits on an uncertain landscape that it must not retreat from. There it is possible to imagine a new alternative taking shape, perhaps brought to pass one day by a counter-revolt against an overindulged and overwrought modern order. Too many people at the conclusion of the twentieth century assume they are all on their own in life. They ponder in isolation over what can be trusted, where the sources of courage can be found, and how the future can be faced.

Such a counter-revolt in the "hearts of men" would attempt to bring "loving brothers" together across class, race, and nation to participate in the democracy of civilized conversation, shared loyalties, and deepening emotions. The Scottish Rite, all things considered, ought to be relevant in such a changing time, for it was born of both a living antiquarianism and a life-giving revolution.

Notes

CHAPTER I
The Scottish Rite's Prehistory
The Genesis and Genius of Freemasonry

1. The most indispensable treatment of colonial Freemasonry in America is Steven C. Bullock, *Revolutionary Brotherhood: Freemasonry and the Transformation of the American Social Order, 1730–1840* (Chapel Hill: University of North Carolina Press, 1996).

2. David Stevenson, *The Origins of Freemasonry: Scotland's Century, 1590–1710* (Cambridge: Cambridge University Press, 1988), 5. For a different and, in the minds of many professional historians, fanciful interpretation as to the origins of Freemasonry, see John J. Robinson, *Born in Blood: The Lost Secrets of Freemasonry* (New York: M. Evans & Co., 1989) xix, 376.

3. Stevenson, 5–6.

4. Geddes MacGregor, *Dictionary of Religion and Philosophy* (New York: Paragon House, 1989), 261–62.

5. Margaret C. Jacob, *The Radical Enlightenment: Pantheists, Freemasons, and Republicans* (London: George Allen & Unwin, 1981), 109–37. Cf., Margaret C. Jacob, *Living the Enlightenment: Freemasons and Politics in Eighteenth-Century Europe* (New York: Oxford University Press, 1991).

6. Stevenson, *The Origins of Freemasonry,* 13–18; and by the same author, *The First Freemasons: Scotland's Early Lodges and Their Members* (Aberdeen: Aberdeen University Press, 1988), 8–9.

7. "All the evidence suggests that accepted Masonry emerged in England and spread from there to Scotland," says John Hamill in his *The History of English Freemasonry* (London: Lewis Masonic Books, 1994), 31.

8. Bullock, 10.

9. Jacob, *The Radical Enlightenment,* 115.

10. Ibid., 115.

11. E. L. Hawkins's article in James Hastings, ed., *Encyclopedia of Religion and Ethics* (New York: Charles Scribner's Sons, 1914), 118–20; Hamill, 34–38; Stevenson, *The First Freemasons,* 58; and Stevenson, *The Origins of Freemasonry,* 197.

12. Hamill, 39.

13. Bullock, 13.

14. Ibid., 14.

15. Albert G. Mackey, *Encyclopedia of Freemasonry,* revised and enlarged by Robert I. Clegg (Richmond, Va.: Macoy Publishing and Masonic Supply Co., 1946), 1: 260.

16. Ibid.; Roscoe Pound contributed this definition to *Dictionary of Religion and Ethics* (New York: Macmillan Co., 1921).

17. From Dr. James Anderson, "The New Book of Constitutions" (1738) as quoted in Joseph Fort Newton, *The Builders: A Story and Study of Freemasonry* (Richmond, Va.: Macoy Publishing and Masonic Supply Co., 1951), 169–70.

18. How Hermetic lore fits pre-Enlightenment Masonry is sometimes confusing. It is generally the case that certain esoteric strings came to have Enlightenment resonances by 1700. Hermeticism represented, in this transitional context, the belief promulgated by Isaac Newton among others that the ancients had possessed secret wisdom of immense, even occult, power. It may be surprising that a major symbol of modern scientific confidence, Newton's *Principia,* insisted that all of its originality had been known first by ancient societies. By comparison, Newton's attempt to decipher the hidden wisdom of alchemy and biblical dreams was similar to the discovery interests of lodge members. The relevance of Hermeticism to Masonic craft wisdom was the conviction that it was a modern entry point into ancient mysteries and knowledge. The name Hermes is connected with two "keepers" of ancient wisdom: the Graeco-Roman messenger god, the "god of going between" divine

knowledge and human ignorance; and the Egyptian magus, Hermes Trismegistus (meaning three times great Hermes) who was, if he actually existed as one man or was a name for a school producing an encyclopedia, the font of secret wisdom. It is important to distinguish Hermeticism, a form of Renaissance learning, from popular magic, which "the fraternity clearly scorned." With the Renaissance recovery of ancient texts (e.g., represented in the pre-Reformation Christian humanism of Erasmus), the Platonic tradition that encouraged mystical impulses was often added to continuities of alchemy and spiritual magic. This amorphous conglomeration traveled under the name of Hermes Trismegistus, an encyclopedic symposium belonging to the fifth century, supposedly authored by an Egyptian savant with an advanced understanding of Christian philosophy. The insights of the *Hermetica* were dismissed by later Christian theologians as "redemptive gnosis" which placed humanity "in a position to rise above [its] earthly form of existence, to become divine." Hans Leitzmann, *A History of the Early Church* (New York: Charles Scribner's Sons, 1950), 3:48–49. While Masonry was part of a magical "pursuit seeking to recover the ancients' religious understanding," it "only partially participated in this tradition" of the Newtonian era. See Bullock, 18–20.

19. John C. Brooke, *The Refiner's Fire: the Making of Mormon Cosmology, 1644–1844* (Cambridge: Cambridge University Press, 1994), 94–95. Brooke's interpretation relies on Margaret C. Jacob, who is strongly partial to the Enlightenment strand (vis à vis the hermetic roots) of Masonic intellectual sources.

20. Ibid., 95.

21. While Desaguliers was educated at Oxford, Newton's connections were with Cambridge. Oxford was less open to the new science, making Desaguliers's inclinations somewhat unusual.

22. Brooke, 95. John Hamill explains why the Templar connection is implausible: "A long-standing, though now discarded, theory saw Freemasonry as the direct descendant of the medieval Knights Templars. . . . [Supposedly] they gathered at the mysterious Mount Heredom (or Heredon) near Kilwinning and, fearful of further persecution, transformed themselves into Freemasons, turning the supposed secrets of the Templars into those of Freemasonry. Unfortunately for supporters of this theory the mysterious Mount Heredom (which was to become a central feature of many additional degrees invented in eighteenth-century France) did not exist. Nor were the Templars persecuted in Scotland. Indeed they formed a part of Scottish religious and political life up to the Reformation," in Hamill, 25–26.

23. Henry Sadler, *Masonic Facts and Fictions Comprising a New Theory of the Origin of the 'Antient' Grand Lodge* (1887; reprint, Wellingborough, Northamptonshire: Aquarian Press, 1985).

24. Conrad Hahn, Ch. I, "Freemasonry Comes to Our Shores," in *Colonial Freemasonry*, ed. Lewis Wes Cook (*Transactions of the Missouri Lodge of Research* 30 [1973–74]), 9.

25. Bullock, 97–102.

26. Gordon S. Wood, *The Radicalism of the American Revolution* (New York: Alfred A. Knopf, 1992), 223.

27. Bullock, 86.

28. Ibid., 5.

29. Bullock identifies Franklin as Grand Master; cf., Bullock, 47. It is also noteworthy that Franklin as a "Modern" was by 1790 "simply the wrong sort of Freemason for the Philadelphia brothers" who were "Antients." As a consequence, there was no Masonic participation at Franklin's funeral; cf., Bullock, 85.

30. On the significance of American military lodges see Bullock, 121–28.

31. Allen E. Roberts, *Freemasonry in American History* (Richmond, Va.: Macoy Publishing and Masonic Supply Co., 1985), 157.

32. See J. Hugo Tatsch, *Freemasonry in the Thirteen Colonies* (New York: Macoy, 1933); see also Bullock, 106, 110–19.

33. Mark C. Carnes, *Secret Ritual and Manhood in Victorian America* (New Haven: Yale University Press, 1989), 23.

34. Ibid.

35. As quoted in Robert A. Rutland, *James Madison, the Founding Father* (New York: Macmillan, 1987), 31.

36. Henry Wilson Coil, *Coil's Masonic Encyclopedia* (New York: Macoy Publishing, 1961), 159.

37. Ibid., 529.

38. Robert F. Gould's account, not always reliable, suggests a relationship between the Rite and French Jesuits: "In 1754, the Chevalier de Bouneville [*sic*] established a Chapter of twenty-five Degrees, of what were known as the High Degrees in the college of Jesuits at Clermont, Paris. This college was the asylum of the

adherents of the Stuart cause, most of whom were Scotsmen. One of the Degrees was that known as Scottish Master, hence the origin of the name Scottish Rite . . . . In [1758 the degrees] were revived in Paris under the authority of the Council of Emperors of East and West. In consequence of internal warfare in this organization, caused, it is said, by the Jesuits, who endeavored to sow dissension with the view of suppressing the Order, a new organization was formed which was called the Council of Knights of the East, which practised what was known as the Rite of Perfection, the name by which the Clermont Degrees were originally known." Robert F. Gould, *History of Freemasonry*, ed. Dudley Wright, revised edition, (New York: Charles Scribner's Sons, 1936), 4:296–97. Without credible evidence, Gould's theory only has the ring of possibility, and not what later historians are willing to concede as a probability.

39.   Charles S. Lobingier, *The Ancient and Accepted Scottish Rite of Freemasonry* (Washington, D.C.: The Supreme Council, S.J., 1932), 53. *Le Parfait Maçon, ou les Veritables Secrets de quatre Grades d'Apprentis, Compagnons, Maîtres Ordinaires et Ecossais de la Franche-Maconniere* is in the Library of the Supreme Council, Southern Jursidiction. N.B.: With no printed date of publication, page 6 of the pamphlet mentions the date of 1739 which may challenge Gould's commonly accepted date of 1744. And yet, according to Henry Carr, ed., *The Early French Exposures* (London: Quatuor Coronati Lodge, 1971), 162, there is ample bibliographic evidence (e.g., Wolfsteig) to support the 1744 dating; additionally Carr offers the 1739 date in the text as a reference to the death of the anonymous author's sister-in-law. Carr gives a complete English translation of the document, *Le Parfait Maçon.* Cf., Carr, 197.

40.   Coil, 256; cf., Lobingier (1932), 62.

41.   The ritual source material of the Scottish Rite and its earliest renderings are not rooted on particularly firm grounds of authorship. A. C. F. Jackson has strongly argued that Etienne (Stephen) Morin invented the twenty-five degree system, which means that during this formative time the name "Rite of Perfection" is misleading. Instead, it is believed that Morin added degrees "atop" a pre-existing Rite of Perfection (which consisted of 1°–14°) to create a twenty-five degree rite. If Jackson is right, then the immediate predecessor of the Scottish Rite is more accurately designated "Morin's Rite," a term proposed in the case made by Jackson. See, A. C. F. Jackson, *Rose Croix: A History of the Ancient and Accepted Rite for England and Wales,* 2nd ed. (London: Lewis Masonic Books, 1987). Jackson makes his argument particularly compelling in the evidence introduced in A. C. F. Jackson, "The Authorship of the 1762 Constitutions of the Ancient and Accepted Rite," *Ars Quatuor Coronati* 97 (1984): 176–91. He proposes that Morin likely forged and backdated the "Constitutions and Regulations of 1762."

42.   A number of scholars have suspected the Secret Constitutions of 1761 to be a post-1801 forgery, a companion piece to the improbably dated "Constitutions and Regulations of 1762." The assumption is that the documents were created to help bolster the Scottish Rite's claims to antiquity. Samuel H. Baynard Jr. and Albert Pike published these texts. When Pike brought them out in *Grand Constitutions and Regulations of 1762, Statutes and Regulations of Perfection, Vera Instituta Secreta et Fundamentia Ordinia of 1786* (New York: Masonic Publishing Co., 1872), he also included a 33° text which he joined to the manuscript. Nevertheless, Pike apparently doubted the validity of the Secret Constitutions of 1761 when he judiciously opined, "As to their authenticity, and when and where they were made, I leave every one to judge for himself. If I have an opinion on these questions, I do not care to express it," from *Grand Constitutions,* 303. I am grateful to Arturo deHoyos for pointing out to me these unresolved textual issues.

43.   Alain Bernheim, "Notes on Early Masonry in Bordeaux (1732–1769)," *Ars Quatuor Coronati* 101 (Oct. 1989): 92–97.

44.   Coil, 601.

45.   Harold Van Buren Voorhis, *The Story of the Scottish Rite* (Richmond, Va.: Macoy Publishing and Masonic Supply Co., 1980), 3; Bernheim, 119 n. 12.

46.   Ibid., 608; *Constitutions and Regulations of 1762 . . . and 1786 Including the Statutes of 1859, 1866, 1870, and 1872 of the Supreme Council,* compiled by Albert Pike (New York: Masonic Publishing Co., 1872), 5.

47.   Voorhis, 5. Albert G. Mackey reported that "an authentic copy" of Morin's letters patent of August 27, 1761, issued from Paris by the Council of the Emperors of the East and West was "now lying before me" from the Archives of the Supreme Council "at Charleston." Mackey quotes the petition in the patent that Morin "was about to sail for America, and was desirous to be able to work regularly for the advantage and increase of the royal art in all its perfection." Albert G. Mackey, *History of Freemasonry in South Carolina* (1861; reprint, Charleston: Grand Lodge of South Carolina, 1861), 519–20. See also Frederick W. Seal-Coon, "The Island of Jamaica and Masonic Influence," *Ars Quatuor Coronati* 104 (1991): 174–76. The latter reference draws on

Frederick W. Seal-Coon, "An Historical Account of Jamaican Freemasonry" (xeroxed ms, 1976), the Supreme Council, Southern Jurisdiction, Archives (hereafter referred to as TSC), 2–281.

48. Morin is something of a mystery. He has been identified at various times as a Jew, sometimes as a Huguenot, and most recently a Catholic. Part of the myth has even questioned whether Morin was his real name. See Alain Bernheim, "Questions About Albany," *Heredom* 4 (1995): 139–40. Bernheim notes, "Morin attested on March 27, 1762, that he was Catholic, from Cahors . . . , and forty-five years old (accordingly, he was born about 1717)." See also *Ars Quatuor Coronati* 105 (1992): 255. About Morin's religious identity, it was not uncommon to attest membership in a predominant religious group for the sake of political expediency and the ability to travel. The most surprising claim is that Morin's Masonic records were in the Archives of the Grand Lodge of Ukraine; cf., N. Choumitzky, "Etienne Morin," a biographical note (April 3, 1928, in French), TSC, Vlt. bx. 58. Stephen Morin's Rite of Perfection patent of August 27, 1761, authorizing him to carry the Rite to America has been reproduced frequently, but according to a later edition of Gould's *History of Freemasonry*, "the fact must be borne in mind that the original has never been produced." Robert F. Gould, *History of Freemasonry*, ed. Dudley Wright (New York: Charles Scribner's Sons, 1936), 4:297.

49. Presumably, Morin placed in Francken's hands the Ritual of the Rite of Perfection. This document is named "the Francken Ritual" of 1767; the (1783) original is in the Archives of the Supreme Council, NMJ.

50. The Minute Book of the Albany (New York) Lodge of Perfection, 1767–1774, was reproduced in photo-facsimile in its entirety from the original manuscript; cf. *Proceedings of New York Council of Deliberation* (1906), 28–132. The original Minute Book and *Constitution of the Ineffable* are in the Archives of the Supreme Council, NMJ (verified by Catherine Swanson, Archivist, August 7, 1996); see Newbury and Williams, *A History of the Supreme Council, NMJ* (Lexington, Mass.: The Supreme Council, NMJ, 1987), 43; see also Alain Bernheim, "Questions About Albany," 141, 171 n. 19. The documents may be viewed in Samuel Baynard, *Scottish Rite Freemasonry, NMJ* (Boston, Mass.: The Supreme Council, 33°,NMJ, 1938), 1:49–52. Also see Julius F. Sachse, *Ancient Documents Relating to the . . . Scottish Rite* (Philadelphia, Penn.: Grand Lodge of Pennsylvania, 1915), 5–10. One of the oldest known surviving Scottish Rite documents in America is a patent issued to Ossonde Verriere, a planter of San Domingo, signed by Stephen Morin, October 26, 1764. The certificate is in the possession of the Archives of the Grand Lodge of Pennsylvania. See note 53.

51. Kent Walgren, "An Historical Sketch of Pre-1851 Louisiana Scottish Rite Masonry," *Heredom* 4 (1995): 190.

52. Ray Baker Harris and James D. Carter, *History of The Supreme Council, 33° (Mother Council of the World), Ancient and Accepted Scottish Rite of Freemasonry, Southern Jurisdiction, U.S.A., 1801–1861* (Washington, D.C.: The Supreme Council, S.J., 1964), 13.

53. Ibid., 13–14; Lobingier (1932), 147; John R. Platt Jr., Librarian and Curator, Grand Lodge of Pennsylvania, letter, July 20, 1990, to WLF, Sr. The oldest Scottish Rite document in the Pennsylvania Grand Lodge Archives, as indicated in note 50, is a certificate issued to Ossonde Verriere, a planter of San Domingo, that Etienne (Stephen) Morin signed. It is dated October 26, 1764; cf., Sachse, 11ff.

54. Harris and Carter, 14.

55. Lobingier (1932), 150.

56. To understand the varying points of view on this subject see Pike, "A Historical Inquiry," in *Grand Constitutions*, 125–205; Henry C. Clausen, *Authentics of Fundamental Law for Scottish Rite Freemasonry* (Washington, D.C.: The Supreme Council, 33°, Ancient and Accepted Scottish Rite of Freemasonry, Mother Jurisdiction of the World, 1979), 1–16; Robert B. Folger, *The Ancient and Accepted Scottish Rite in Thirty-three Degrees* (New York: published by the author, 1881), 64–75; Voorhis, 11–16; R. S. Lindsay, *The Scottish Rite for Scotland* (Edinburgh: published for the Supreme Council for Scotland by W. & R. Chambers, Ltd., 1958), 43–57; Jean-Pierre Lassalle, "From the Constitutions and Regulations of 1762 to the Grand Constitutions of 1786," *Celebration du Bicentenaire des Grandes Constitutions de 1786* (Supreme Conseil pour la France, 12 decembre 1986), 43–76.

57. Lobingier (1932), 105.

58. Pike, *Grand Constitutions*, 235.

59. Ibid., 227.

60. Ibid., 229.

61. Ibid.

62. Ibid., 237.

63. Ibid., 237, 239.

64. Ibid., 239.

65. Ibid., 241, 243.

66. Ibid., 243, 245; James D. Carter to Henry C. Clausen, memorandum, March 13, 1970, TSC, B-2005. It has been widely, perhaps erroneously, assumed that the source from which Dalcho was working must have been something older or requiring translation. This has been called into question recently (contra Clausen) since the English-language version of Dalcho's text of the *Constitutions of 1786,* the earliest known copy, in his own hand, was appended to the ca. 1801 ritual of the thirty-third degree; cf., Harris and Carter, 92, 337–46. Nothing is older than Dalcho's "primitive" *Grand Constitutions of 1786,* including Latin and French renditions. Latin was a decorative after-thought, for it shows a fully developed structure, long before organizing principles seemed to exist in the early stages around 1801. It was Albert Pike who thought the Latin Constitutions (first published in 1834) were the original form; cf., Pike, *Grand Constitutions,* 125ff, 279–83. The Dalcho version of the *Constitutions of 1786,* only rediscovered in the 1930s, follows more closely the French, not the Latin version. This is because the French copy (1804) was probably derived from Dalcho, not the other way around. Also, the Latin rendering, made to appear more "ancient," cannot be the oldest because it is much too elaborate and ordered for an early version. The so-called Dalcho *Constitutions of 1786* is a manuscript in the Archives of the Supreme Council, NMJ, Lexington, Massachusetts. This material is not to be confused with the copy De La Motta gave to Gourgas. It is also useful to note that taking liberties with the appearances of historic founding documents, such as falsifying authorship and dates, was not a peculiar phenomenon of Freemasonry. Forgeries in the history of Christianity, such as the Donation of Constantine or the Pseudo-Isidorian Decretals, have been commonplace (and tolerated in the story even after exposure). The larger point about these simultaneous, spurious, and influential governing documents was a subtle difference of intention between giving support to an organization and deceiving people for gain. In the instance at hand, the institution's initial survival was the overriding concern.

67. Pike, *Grand Constitutions,* 245.

68. Ibid., 253.

69. Ibid., 249; James D. Carter to Henry C. Clausen, memorandum, June 1, 1970, TSC, B-2005.

70. Although the Latin Constitutions describe the degrees of the "Ancient and Accepted Scottish Rite" by name, the *1802 Manifesto,* contrarily, presents a primitive structure of the Rite as evidenced by omitting certain degrees, while lumping together others (see facsimile in Harris and Carter, 324). Just as in the current assumptions of biblical scholarship, when comparing texts based on the internal evidence present, the one that is clearly less ordered and less elaborate is usually the older among them. This discrepancy suggests that the *1802 Manifesto* predates the Latin Constitutions (allegedly) of 1786. I am grateful to Arturo deHoyos for pointing out these textual problems.

71. *Transactions of The Supreme Council, 33° (Mother Council of the World), Ancient and Accepted Scottish Rite of Freemasonry, Southern Jurisdiction, U.S.A.* (Washington, D.C.: The Supreme Council, S.J., 1924), 25.

72. James D. Carter to Orville Ray Abbott, letter December 1, 1970, TSC, B-2005.

73. N.B.: perhaps of coincidence or oblique connection, there apparently existed a "Scot's Masters Lodge" which met in London, at the Devil's Tavern at Temple Bar in 1733; similarly, records of a meeting in 1735 at the Bear Inn Lodge mention that the Master and Wardens were made "Scots Masters." See A. C. F. Jackson, *Rose Croix.*

74. Harris and Carter, 323.

75. Ibid., 27, 29.

76. Jones Point is presently a public park, south of Old Town in Alexandria, Virginia.

77. Claude H. Harris Jr., "Foundation Stones of Our Nation's Capital," *Scottish Rite Journal* 98 (October 1990): 30–31.

78. Ray Baker Harris, *The Laying of Cornerstones: Freemasonry's Part in Preserving the Practice of One of the World's Most Ancient Customs* (Washington, D.C.: Supreme Council, 33°, Ancient & Accepted Scottish Rite, 1961), 25.; see also S. Brent Morris, *Cornerstones of Freedom: A Masonic Tradition* (Washington, D.C.: Supreme Council, 1993), 32–33.

79. Morris, 30. For the most recent exposition on the potential locations of the original U.S. Capitol cornerstone, see Morris, 58. Also consult Jackson H. Polk, *The Cornerstone of Democracy* (Silver Spring, Md.: Capstone Productions, 1993), videotape.

80. Harris and Carter, 9.

81. Ibid., 17.

82. Ibid., 95.

83. Ibid., 96–97. Henry Wilson Coil makes the interesting observation that any date between May 25 and 31 might well have been the birthdate of the Supreme Council. May 31 may have been chosen arbitrarily, and possibly it was selected as it was the anniversary of Frederick the Great's accession to the Prussian throne, and he was the alleged author of the *Grand Constitutions of 1786.* "The fact that Dr. Dalcho was the son of a Prussian military officer lends credence to this supposition." Coil, 604.

84. Harris and Carter, 97.

85. Ibid., in the *Manifesto of 1802,* 96.

86. Dumas Malone, *Jefferson the President: First Term, 1801–1805,* vol. 4 of *Jefferson and His Time* (Boston: Little, Brown and Company, 1970), xxiii.

CHAPTER II
First Light, 1801–1826
Mitchell, Dalcho, and Auld

1. *The Facts of Scottish Rite* (Boston: The Supreme Council, 33°, Ancient and Accepted Scottish Rite, NMJ, n.d.), 3. See also George A. Newbury and Louis L. Williams, *A History of The Supreme Council, 33° of the Ancient Accepted Scottish Rite of Freemasonry for the Northern Masonic Jurisdiction of the United States of America* (Lexington, Mass.: Supreme Council, AASR, NMJ, 1987), 26–27, 232.

2. Rex R. Hutchens, "Magister Interior: The Inward Master," unpublished manuscript, 1990, 5; and Rex R. Hutchens to William L. Fox Sr., letter, Oct. 13, 1990, both in possession of author. Also see, Newbury and Williams, 28–30.

3. John Hamill, *The History of English Freemasonry* (London: Lewis Masonic Books, 1994), 24–25. See also, Margaret C. Jacob, *Living the Enlightenment: Freemasonry and Politics in Eighteenth-Century Europe* (New York: Oxford University Press, 1991), 25.

4. Arnold Whitaker Oxford, 33°, *The Origin and Progress of the Ancient and Accepted (Scottish) Rite for England, Wales, The Dominions and Dependencies of the British Crown* (London: Oxford University Press, 1933), 7.

5. The Dalcho Register is in the Supreme Council Archives of the Northern Masonic Jurisdiction.

6. Ray Baker Harris, *Eleven Gentlemen of Charleston: Founders of The Supreme Council, Mother Council of the World Ancient and Accepted Scottish Rite of Freemasonry* (Washington, D.C.: The Supreme Council 33°, Southern Jurisdiction, 1959), 50. *Eleven Gentlemen of Charleston* is an excellent though brief biographical study of the eleven founders of the Supreme Council and was subsequently incorporated as chapter 2 in Ray Baker Harris and James D. Carter, *History of The Supreme Council, 33° (Mother Council of the World), Ancient and Accepted Scottish Rite of Freemasonry, Southern Jurisdiction, U.S.A., 1801–1861* (Washington, D.C.: The Supreme Council, 1964). The reference above is also found in Harris and Carter, 47–48.

7. Harris and Carter, 49–50.

8. Ibid., 51–56.

9. Ibid., 57.

10. Ibid., 60.

11. Ibid.

12. Ibid., 62.

13. Ibid., 68.

14. Ibid., 70.

15. *Manifesto of 1802,* "Circular throughout the Two Hemispheres," in Harris and Carter, 323.

16. Harris and Carter, 79.

17. Ray Baker Harris to Luther A. Smith, letter, June 26, 1959, the Supreme Council, Southern Jurisdiction, Archives (hereafter referred to as TSC), 4–1200.30.

18. Harris and Carter, 319.

19. Ibid.

20. James D. Richardson, *The Ancient and Accepted Scottish Rite: Centennial Address October 23, 1901* (1901; reprint, Washington, D.C.: Supreme Council, 33°, S.J., 1958), 8.

21. Harris and Carter, 324. "Ecossais" in the original printed document is rendered as "Ecossois."

22. Harris and Carter, 107.

23. James D. Carter, *History of The Supreme Council, 33° (Mother Council of the World), Ancient and Accepted Scottish Rite of Freemasonry, Southern Jurisdiction, U.S.A., 1861–1891* (Washington, D.C.: The Supreme Council, 33°, S.J., 1967), 359. Carter's chronology (November 12, 1763) is rendered differently in Kent Walgren, "An Historical Sketch of Pre-1851 Louisiana Scottish Rite Masonry," *Heredom* 4 (1995): 190, 198 nn. 5, 6. Walgren proposes April 12, 1764, as the opening of the Lodge of Perfection in New Orleans. He gets no argument in his claim, "in U.S. Scottish Rite Masonry, priority goes to New Orleans, not Albany," which is not at odds with Carter's point. Walgren, however, submits that a petition of an Ecossais warrant from Masons in New Orleans was signed April 12, 1756, and was granted a year later, April 17, 1757. The gap between 1757 and 1764 is due to the Seven Years War involving the world's major powers, Britain, France, and Spain.

24. Harris and Carter, 108.

25. "The French Constitutions of 1786," *(Grand Constitutions of 1786),* as published in 1832 by the Supreme Council for France, in Albert Pike, *Grand Constitutions and Regulations of 1762, Statutes and Regulations of Perfection, Vera Instituta Secreta et Fundamenta Ordinis of 1786* (New York: Masonic Publishing Co., 1872), 295.

26. Newbury and Williams, 92, 94.

27. The earliest known version of the *Grand Constitutions of 1786* appears in Dalcho's own hand. Cf. note 62 in chapter 1 of this book.

28. Charles S. Lobingier, *The Supreme Council, 33°, Mother Council of the World, Ancient and Accepted Scottish Rite of Freemasonry, Southern Jurisdiction, U.S.A.* (Washington, D.C.: The Supreme Council, S.J., 1931), 63. This work is commonly referred to as the "Lobingier History" after Charles S. Lobingier, who undertook much of the research and prepared a detailed manuscript that was extensively revised by the Supreme Council.

29. Ibid., 68.

30. Harris and Carter, 109; Newbury and Williams, 83. Cerneau's original patent and facsimile copies of it are in the Supreme Council (SJ) Archives in Washington, D.C.

31. Harris and Carter, 124.

32. Newbury and Williams, 89.

33. Ibid.

34. Cf. Arturo deHoyos, "The Union of 1867," a Scottish Rite Research Society lecture given October 10, 1995, in *Heredom* 4 (1995).

35. Steven C. Bullock, *Revolutionary Brotherhood: Freemasonry and the Transformation of the American Social Order, 1730–1840* (Chapel Hill: University of North Carolina Press, 1996), 223.

36. Bullock, 111.

37. Ibid., 138.

38. The term "Mother" in an all-male organization of "brothers" is suggestive of Victorian domesticity and sentimentality. Perhaps it is tied obliquely to the Romantic recovery of medieval expressions (e.g., the cult of "motherhood" surrounding the Mater Dei name for Mary). Nationalisms, too, for the sake of family-state unity, often exploited parental links with a people's past to foster affection for one's own country. Hence, Mother Russia stands juxtaposed to the Fatherland of Germany. Masonry's familial nomenclature embraced "motherhood" for other reasons, according to Mark Carnes. He comments, "fraternal scholars and authors of rituals often described the order as 'mother' and initiation as a form of rebirth." See Mark C. Carnes, *Secret Rituals and Manhood in Victorian America* (New Haven: Yale University Press, 1989), 119–22.

39. Harris and Carter, 101, 132–33, 216.

40. Ibid., 135.

41. Ibid., 41.

42. Ibid., 135.

43. Thomas Jefferson to John Holmes, letter, April 22, 1820, in *Thomas Jefferson Writings*, The Library of America (New York: Literary Classics of the United States, 1984), 1434.

44. Harris and Carter, 135.

45. DeHoyos, "The Union of 1867." A year after Dalcho's departure, Joseph M'Cosh, one of "The Eleven," described the incident: ". . . the Grand Commander having withdrawn from the Council during the present disturbances, from the nature of his vocation, and having desired no voice either directly or indirectly in the transactions which might ensue, desired not to be consulted in any respect about the business," in Lobingier, 125. See also, Joseph M'Cosh, *Documents upon Sublime Free-Masonry in the United States of America* (n.d.; reprint, Charleston, S.C.: Charles C. Sebring? 1823), 100.

46. Harris and Carter, 138.

47. Ibid., 151.

48. *Charleston Courier*, March 1825, quoted in Harris and Carter, 158.

49. In a letter that rushed to a historical assessment about Lafayette and the Cerneau Scottish Rite degrees, John H. Cowles, who was Grand Commander of the Supreme Council, S.J., from 1921 to 1952, wrote: "Of course, we knew that Lafayette was hoodwinked into taking the Scottish Rite degrees by the Cerneau outfit in New York. We know this to our sorrow. Several years ago we were offered the Scottish Rite patent of Lafayette for a considerable price. Fortunately, however, we found that it was from this Cerneau outfit, and refused to buy it." John H. Cowles to Charles A. Brockway, letter, October 25, 1933, TSC, 4–1000.27. The value of the document is not only intrinsic because of its Lafayette connection, but, unbeknownst to Cowles, is worth much more in dollar-value *because* of the rare nature of the "irregular" Cerneau material. Additionally, in spite of what Ray Baker Harris wrote (Harris and Carter, 158–59) concerning Lafayette's "second thoughts about the 'honor' he had accepted in New York" from the Cerneauists, there is recent evidence that the Marquis was neither naive nor embarrassed about his "tainted" Cerneau 33°. A Lafayette letter published in Robert B. Folger, *The Ancient and Accepted Scottish Rite*, 2d ed., vol. 1 (New York: self-published, 1881), 179, 219–20, was authenticated by Claude Gagne, Archivist of the Supreme Council of France. The letter suggests that Lafayette died a proud, unreconstructed Cerneauist. Cf. Michael R. Poll, *The Elimination of the French Influence in Louisiana Masonry* (Lafayette, La.: self-published, 1996), 7.

50. John Quincy Adams was not an Anti-Mason up to the presidential election of 1828, but after his bitter, personal defeat to Andrew Jackson he began to lament the decline of civic virtue, associating cronyism and excesssive patronage with Masonry. Five years after the dissappearance of William Morgan, Adams declared himself an Anti-Mason. In a long letter in the possession of the Supreme Council, S.J., Adams explained that the final straw of impatience with Freemasonry for him was the attempt to exploit his father's name. He wrote: "The Letter from my father to the Grand Lodge of Massachusetts which Wm Sheppard has thought proper to introduce into his address was a *complimentary* answer to a friendly and patriotic address of the Grand Lodge to him. In it he expressly states that he had never been *initiated* in their order . . . . All that my father knew of Masonry in 1798 was that it was *favourable to the support of civil authority;* and this he *inferred* from the characters of intimate friends of his, and excellent men who had been members of the Society. The inference was surely natural; but he had never seen the civil authority in conflict with Masonry itself. To speak of the Masonic institution as favourable to the support of civil authority at this day and in this Country would be a mockery . . . . The use of my father's name for the purposes to which Wm Sheppard would now apply it is an injury to his Memory." John Quincy Adams to Stephen Bates, Boston, letter, August 22, 1831, ms in Library of the Supreme Council, S.J., vertical file.

51. Cf. Robert V. Remini, *Henry Clay: Statesman for the Union* (New York: Norton, 1993), 258.

CHAPTER III

Keepers of the Flame, 1826–1858
Holbrook, McDonald, and Honour

1. Some speculation has remained that the lodge minutes recording Morgan's name would have been deliberately purged or burned. While it is true no evidence of Morgan's regular membership has surfaced, there is a counterpoint view that such records would not have been purposely destroyed because they would have

contained the membership information of innocent others who were made Masons on that occasion. In fact, instead of destroying records, Morgan's signature on the Royal Arch By-laws that he endorsed May 31, 1825, was later smeared so that other names would not be effaced from the record. Another theory of Morgan's membership has it that he perhaps displayed a forged Canadian patent to his employer, a Mr. Warren who, believing Morgan was legitimate, took him as a visitor to Wells Lodge No. 282. Thus, possibly under fraudulent credentials, according to some Masonic legends, Morgan launched his Masonic "career." Cf. Rob Morris, *William Morgan; or Political Anti-Masonry, its Rise, Growth and Decadence* (New York: Robert Macoy, 1883), 81–2.

2. William Preston Vaughn, *The Antimasonic Party in the United States 1826–1843* (Lexington: University Press of Kentucky, 1983), 1–3. Miller and Morgan anticipated huge returns—a million dollars, according to Lucinda Morgan's sworn statement, September 22, 1826, which is in Morris, 271. The nineteenth-century Masonic bibliophile Enoch T. Carson penciled a gloss into his personal copy of Morris's book: "The same & very much more had been published by Wm Carlisle in an infidel weekly, 2 penny in London in 1825—A further *exposé* was included in 24 numbers—Total cost, 4 shillings. What the publishers of the Illustrations [were] is beyond doubt—it proves what fools!" Carson meant Richard Carlile, not William. Cf. Richard Carlile, *The Republican*, vol. 7 (London: n.p., 1825), later published as the *Manual of Freemasonry* (London: Reeves & Turner, c. 1845).

3. Vaughn, 5.

4. Ibid.

5. Ibid., 7.

6. Ibid., 12.

7. Steven C. Bullock, *Revolutionary Brotherhood: Freemasonry and the Transformation of the American Social Order, 1730–1840* (Chapel Hill: University of North Carolina Press, 1996), 80–82.

8. Dorothy Ann Lipson, *Freemasonry in Federalist Connecticut* (Princeton: Princeton University Press, 1977), 329.

9. Ibid., 330.

10. Ibid., 336.

11. Ibid., 338.

12. Bullock, 280–81, 296.

13. Bullock, 313–14.

14. Whitney R. Cross, *The Burned-over District: the Social and Intellectual History of Enthusiastic Religion in Western New York, 1800–1850* (Ithaca, N.Y.: Cornell University Press, 1950), 4.

15. See John L. Brooke, *The Refiner's Fire: The Making of Mormon Cosmology, 1644–1844* (Cambridge: Cambridge University Press, 1994), 3–4, 143–46, 168–71.

16. Lynn Dumenil, *Freemasonry and American Culture, 1880–1930* (Princeton: Princeton University Press, 1984), 5.

17. Bullock, 297–98.

18. Vaughn, 170.

19. Moses Holbrook, Charleston, South Carolina, to J. J. J. Gourgas, New York City, New York, letter, March 6, 1830, the Supreme Council, Southern Jurisdiction, Archives (hereafter referred to as TSC), 4-vlt-6. Nine months later Holbrook wrote again to Gourgas about Masonry continuing at "a low ebb," stemming "more from the want of cash and a cordial unanimity among the Brotherhood than from the *paltry exertion of Antimasonry* (emphasis added)." Moses Holbrook, to J. J. J. Gourgas, letter, January 1, 1831, TSC, 4-vlt-6.

20. Since 1984, when the Grand Lodge of Utah opened its doors to allow Mormon membership in the fraternity, friendlier relations with the Church of Jesus Christ of Latter-day Saints have developed. With the increase of Mormon membership in the lodges of Utah, the Church has desisted from its censure of Masonry.

21. Bullock, 318.

22. The Holbrook Register is presently in the Archives of the Supreme Council, S.J., in Washington, D.C.

23. In 1970 James D. Carter, who was then librarian and historian of the Supreme Council, S.J., stated that "no one knows when 'Mother Supreme Council' was first used in reference to this Supreme Council or why it was adopted instead of 'Father Supreme Council.'" He added that the reference became common "throughout the Scottish Rite world and was used on the Grand Commander's flag in deference to this usage." James D. Carter to Orville Roy Abbott, letter, December 1, 1970, TSC, B-2000.

24.   *Balustre* literally means in French a "hand-rail." The term's usage, therefore, has to do with setting boundaries or guidelines.

25.   Ray Baker Harris and James D. Carter, *History of The Supreme Council, 33° (Mother Council of the World), Ancient and Accepted Scottish Rite of Freemasonry, Southern Jurisdiction, U.S.A., 1801–1861* (Washington, D.C.: The Supreme Council, S.J., 1964), 174.

26.   Ibid., 177.

27.   James D. Richardson, *The Ancient and Accepted Scottish Rite*, Centennial Adress, October 23, 1901, pamphlet reprint, (Washington, D.C.: The Supreme Council, 1958), 24.

28.   Charles S. Lobingier, *The Supreme Council, 33°, Mother Council of the World, Ancient and Accepted Scottish Rite of Freemasonry, Southern Jurisdiction, U.S.A.* (Washington, D.C.: The Supreme Council, S.J., 1931), 71–78.

29.   George A. Newbury and Louis L. Williams, *A History of the Supreme Council, 33°, of the Ancient Accepted Scottish Rite of Freemasonry for the Northern Masonic Jurisdiction of the United States of America* (Lexington, Mass.: Supreme Council, AASR, NMJ, 1987), 170.

30.   Harris and Carter, 194.

31.   This correspondence, of which there is a record, included forty-five letters that Gourgas wrote to Holbrook and thirty that Holbrook addressed to Gourgas between 1826 and 1832: Newbury and Williams, 98. Cf. Samuel H. Baynard, *History of the Supreme Council . . . Scottish Rite Freemasonry . . . Northern Masonic Jurisdiction,* 2 vols. (Boston: The Supreme Council, NMJ, 1938).

32.   Ibid., 141.

33.   Harris and Carter, 216.

34.   In honor of John James Joseph Gourgas who "may be considered the real founder of the Scottish Rite in the Northern Masonic Jurisdiction, as well as its 'Conservator' during the dark days Masonry suffered following the 'Morgan Affairs in 1826,'" the "Gourgas Medal for Distinguished Service" was established in 1938 for the purpose of honoring any Scottish Rite Mason, regardless of jurisdiction, for "notably distinguished service in the cause of Freemasonry, humanity or country." Senator, later President, Harry S. Truman was the first recipient of the Medal. Newbury and Williams, 223, 225.

35.   William L. Boyden, comp., *Chronology, 1801–1859, of The Supreme Council of the Ancient and Accepted Scottish Rite of Freemasonry of the Southern Jurisdiction of the United States of America* (Washington, D.C., The Supreme Council, SJ, November 1939), 39–40.

36.   Charles E. Rosenberg, *The Cholera Years: the United States in 1832, 1849, and 1866* (Chicago: University of Chicago Press, 1962), 37.

37.   Bullock, 311–12. "Masonry still continues at a low ebb with us" due to Anti-Masonic fever, wrote Holbrook to Gourgas, his counterpart in the North. Holbrook to Gourgas, January 1 and February 20, 1831, letters, TSC, 4-vlt-6. See Boyden, *Chronology* (1939), 38–39.

38.   Harris and Carter, 221.

39.   Ibid.

40.   "Baltimore Convention, 1843," *The Short Talk Bulletin of The Masonic Service Association of the United States* 14, no. 1 (January 1936): 6.

41.   Mark C. Carnes, *Secret Ritual and Manhood in Victorian America* (New Haven: Yale University Press, 1989), 28.

42.   Reynold J. Matthews, interview with William L. Fox Sr., March 26, 1991, Washington, D.C.

43.   Carnes, 25.

44.   Harris and Carter, 223.

45.   George Fleming Moore, "The Souvenir of the Celebration of the Centennial Anniversary of the Establishment of The Supreme Council of the Thirty-third Degree of the Ancient and Accepted Scottish Rite of Freemasonry for the Southern Jurisdiction of the United States of America," pamphlet (Washington, D.C.: The Supreme Council, 1901), 22.

46.   Harris and Carter, 228.

47.   Ibid., 230–31. According to Coil, Clavel was a pseudonym for a French Masonic writer by the name of F. T. Begue whom the Grand Orient of France disciplined for publishing *Histoire Pittoresque* without its

permission and for later publishing a Masonic journal bearing the title *Grand Orient*, for which he was expelled. Henry Wilson Coil, *Coil's Masonic Encyclopedia* (New York: Macoy Publishing, 1961), 130.

48. Harris and Carter, 233.

49. Ibid., 236.

50. Lobingier, 68–79.

51. C. C. Goen, *Broken Churches, Broken Nation: Denominational Schisms and the Coming of the American Civil War* (Macon, Ga.: Mercer University Press, 1985), 63.

52. Samuel Eliot Morison, *The Oxford History of the American People* (New York: Oxford University Press, 1965), 568.

53. Harris and Carter, 241.

54. Ibid., 244.

55. Albert Pike, "Beauties of Cerneauism," no. 6, 7, quoted in Harris and Carter, 244.

56. *Transactions of The Supreme Council, 33° (Mother Council of the World), Ancient and Accepted Scottish Rite of Freemasonry, Southern Jurisdiction, U.S.A.* (Washington, D.C.: The Supreme Council, S.J., 1878), 20.

57. Harris and Carter, 249.

58. Ibid., 246.

59. Ibid., 255.

60. Walter Lee Brown, "Albert Pike, 1809–1891" (Ph.D. diss., University of Texas, 1955), 4: 737.

61. Ibid.

62. Harris and Carter, 257.

63. Ibid., 261.

CHAPTER IV
Exodus from Charleston, 1859–1870
Albert Pike

1. Albert Pike to Albert G. Mackey, January 5, 1859, Pike Correspondence, 1859, the Supreme Council, Southern Jurisdiction, Archives (hereafter referred to as TSC); Ray Baker Harris and James D. Carter, *History of The Supreme Council, 33° (Mother Council of the World), Ancient and Accepted Scottish Rite of Freemasonry, Southern Jurisdiction, U.S.A., 1801–1861* (Washington, D.C.: The Supreme Council, S.J., 1964), 265; William L. Boyden, comp., *Chronology, 1801–1859, of The Supreme Council of the Ancient and Accepted Scottish Rite of Freemasonry of the Southern Jurisdiction of the United States of America* (Washington, D.C., The Supreme Council, 33°, S.J., 1938), 60.

2. *Harvard University Quinquennial Catalogue of the Officers and Graduates, 1636–1930* (Cambridge, Mass.: Harvard University, 1930), 1169.

3. "Albert Pike," obituary, *New York Times*, April 3, 1891. The obituary notice indicated "when he was sixteen years old he entered Harvard, graduating in 1829." Another erroneous mention of this occurred in the *Masonic Standard*, October 26, 1901. In a report on the unveiling of the Pike Monument in Washington, D.C., reference is made to a time "during his college days at Harvard." In fact, Pike never spent a day on the campus, except perhaps as a visitor.

4. Albert Pike to William H. Tillinghast, letter, March 17, 1890, Harvard University Archives (HUG) 300. Pike's reference to "a diploma of A.B." may be mistaken. He may have meant the honorary A.M. degree which he received in 1859.

5. The practice of paying for one's university *degree* as prescribed by a scheduled program, and regardless of accelerated progress to finish the degree requirements sooner than allowed, is still a Harvard policy. There is no economic incentive to complete a degree any sooner than the suggested timetable of the university.

6. Harris Elwood Starr, "Albert Pike," in *Dictionary of American Biography*, vol. 7 (New York: Charles Scribners, 1934), 593.

7. Mark C. Carnes, *Secret Ritual and Manhood in Victorian America* (New Haven, Conn.: Yale University Press, 1989), 135. Preexisting tension between Pike and his employer was admitted by him many years later, so

his firing was not entirely arbitrary. He had asked for an assistant and in his persistence set himself up for the pretext of his dismissal. Fiddle-playing on a Sunday before dusk was not his real "crime." Rather, his independent opinions kept him from fitting in. Cf Albert Pike, "School Teaching," in *Essays to Vinnie,* vol. 5, essay 26 (Washington, D.C.: Supreme Council Archives, ca. 1880).

8.   Robert Lipscomb Duncan, *Reluctant General: The Life and Times of Albert Pike* (New York: E.P. Dutton, 1961), 14.

9.   Pike's obituary in the *New York Times* (April 3, 1890) portrayed him at this stage of life as more of a conquistador than a peacemaker. It was reported that "he explored the headwaters of the Brazos and Red Rivers, fighting his way against Indians, with four companions, from thence to Fort Smith, Arkansas." Pike as an "Indian-fighter" misrepresents his positive experience, record, and attitude in dealing with Indians. In fact, before reaching Fort Smith, Pike sold his rifle to the Choctaws for twelve pounds of meat. See Albert Pike, "Narrative of a Journey in the Prairie," in David J. Weber, ed., *Prose Sketches and Poems of Albert Pike Written in the Western Country* (College Station: Texas A & M Press, 1987), 76–77.

10.   James W. Collins, Sovereign Grand Inspector General in Utah, "A Memorial Address Honoring Albert Pike," *Transactions of The Supreme Council, 33° (Mother Council of the World), Ancient and Accepted Scottish Rite of Freemasonry, Southern Jurisdiction, U.S.A.* (hereafter referred to as *Transactions*) (Washington, D.C.: The Supreme Council, S.J., 1951), 9.

11.   Starr, 595.

12.   Walter Lee Brown, Professor Emeritus of History, University of Arkansas, Fayetteville, Arkansas, interview by telephone with William L. Fox Sr. (hereafter referred to as WLF Sr.), September 28, 1988.

13.   Luther A. Smith, Sovereign Grand Commander, "The Battle of Pea Ridge and General Albert Pike's Connection With It," address to the Civil War Round Table of the District of Columbia, March 8, 1960, 1–2, Smith Correspondence 1959–1961, TSC, 4-1200.50.

14.   *Little Rock Banner*, December 18, 1849, quoted in Walter Lee Brown, "Albert Pike, 1809–1891," (Ph.D. diss., University of Texas, 1955), 250.

15.   Ibid., 253.

16.   William L. Boyden, "The Masonic Record of Albert Pike," *The New Age Magazine* 28, no. 1 (January 1920): 34–37.

17.   Albert Pike, "Of Rowing Against the Stream," in *Essays to Vinnie,* vol. 3, essay 13.

18.   Abraham Lincoln, "Eulogy on Henry Clay at Springfield, Illinois," July 6, 1852, in *Speeches and Writings, 1832–1858,* vol. 1, (New York: Viking, The Library of America, 1989), 259–72.

19.   Brown, "Albert Pike, 1809–1891," 449.

20.   Dumas Malone and Basil Rauch, *Crisis of the Union, 1841–1877* (New York: Appleton-Century-Crofts, 1960), 72.

21.   Brown, "Albert Pike, 1809–1891," 449–50.

22.   Ibid., 450.

23.   *Little Rock Democrat*, April 1, 1856, quoted in Brown, "Albert Pike, 1809–1891," 484.

24.   An excellent discussion of Pike's evolving political views is found in Walter L. Brown, "Rowing against the Stream: The Course of Albert Pike from National Whig to Secessionist," *Arkansas Historical Quarterly* 39 (fall 1980): 230–46.

25.   Brown, "Albert Pike, 1809–1891," 494.

26.   Ibid., 495, 497.

27.   Lincoln quoted in David Herbert Donald, *Lincoln* (New York: Simon and Schuster, 1995), 181.

28.   The weaknesses of the so-called "conditional emancipationists" whose position was dubbed "conditional termination" of slavery are discussed in William W. Freehling, *The Road to Disunion,* vol. 1, *Secessionists at Bay, 1776–1854* (New York: Oxford University Press, 1990), 119ff.

29.   Brown, "Albert Pike, 1809–1891," 412, 418.

30.   By the time of his election as Sovereign Grand Commander, he reported to Mackey that the 18th, 30th, 31st and 32nd degrees were completed and ready for inspection—"also the funeral ceremony, ceremonies of Baptism, or Reception of a Louveteau, of adoption of a child of the Lodge; and also the Inauguration and Installation ceremonies for each of the five appendant bodies of the Scottish Rite." He also had revised the 33rd degree. Albert Pike to Albert Mackey, letter, January 5, 1859, Pike Correspondence, TSC.

31. Harris and Carter, 265.

32. Ibid., 267.

33. Ibid., 267.

34. Ibid., 269.

35. Ibid., 268.

36. John Henry Cowles to Elbert H. Bede, Portland, Oregon, letter, March 23, 1944, Cowles Correspondence, TSC, 4-1000.65. Only two Grand Consistories remained at the time of Cowles's letter, namely those in Kentucky and Louisiana. There are none today in the Southern Jurisdiction.

37. Harris and Carter, 277.

38. Ibid., 269. Despite the later contention of Grand Commander John H. Cowles, that "the name adopted by the Grand Constitutions was 'Ancient and Accepted Scottish Rite of Freemasonry,'" this name did not appear in that document. John H. Cowles to Cyril T. Stevens, San Lorenzo, California, letter, January 16, 1950, Cowles Correspondence, TSC, 4-1000.96.

39. Harris and Carter, 368.

40. *Transactions* (1865), 348.

41. Harris and Carter, 270. The ceremonies of baptism, adoption, and reception of a louveteau were presumably rarely conducted and are not performed today.

42. Quoted in Robert D. Richardson, *Emerson: The Mind on Fire* (Berkeley: University of California Press, 1995), 545.

43. *The Annals of America*, vol. 9, *1858–1865* (Chicago: Encyclopedia Britannica, 1968), 33.

44. Harris and Carter, 281.

45. *Statutes of the Supreme Council of the Thirty-third Degree, Ancient and Accepted Scottish Rite of Freemasonry, S.J., U.S.A.* (Oct. 1989), 11.

46. Former Grand Commander Henry C. Clausen gave a historical explanation of the word "allocution" in his *Allocution* of 1971 to the Supreme Council: "In olden times an allocution was an address by a general to his soldiers. It then became an address of a church leader to his clergy. In law it is the formal inquiry of a judge to the defendant as to whether he has any cause to show why sentence should not be pronounced." *Transactions* (1971), 23.

47. *Transactions* (1860), 86.

48. Ibid., 87.

49. Ibid.

50. Harris and Carter, 283.

51. Ibid., 281.

52. *Transactions* (1861), 196.

53. Henry Steele Commager, ed., *Documents of American History* (New York: Appleton-Century-Crofts, 1949), 376.

54. *Transactions* (1861), 196.

55. Baptist and Methodist divisions over slavery occurred in the 1840s; the Presbyterians, being divided already by Old School and New School doctrines, split over the slavery question in 1861 just as the war broke out.

56. C. C. Goen, *Broken Churches, Broken Nations* (Macon, Ga.: Mercer University Press, 1985), 67, 190.

57. *Transactions* (1861), 230.

58. Ibid., 246.

59. Ibid., 202.

60. Ibid., 245.

61. Ibid., 246.

62. Brown, "Albert Pike, 1809–1891," 539.

63. Ibid., 545.

64. W. Craig Gaines, *The Confederate Cherokees: John Drew's Regiment of Mounted Rifles* (Baton Rouge: Louisiana State University Press, 1989), 26.

65. Ibid., 4.

66. Brown, "Albert Pike, 1809–1891," 592–93.

67. William L. Shea and Earl J. Hess, *Pea Ridge: Civil War Campaign in the West* (Chapel Hill: University of North Carolina Press, 1992), 58.

68. Walter L. Brown, "Pea Ridge: Gettysburg of the West," *Arkansas Historical Quarterly* 15 (1956): 5. See also Michael A. Botelho, "Albert Pike and the Confederate Indians," *Heredom* (Transactions of the Scottish Rite Research Society) 3 (1993): 41–56.

69. Gaines, 85.

70. Shea and Hess, 143–44, 313. The authors comment that Pike was "an inept amateur soldier who could not even control his two Indian regiments." They go on to rate Pike's generalship as "hopelessly ineffectual."

71. Walter L. Brown, "Pea Ridge," 15–16.

72. William T. Sherman as quoted in Shea and Hess, 317.

73. Brown, "Albert Pike, 1809–1891," 657.

74. Carnes, 136.

75. New York *Daily Tribune*, March 21, 1862, as quoted by Walter L. Brown, in "Albert Pike and the Pea Ridge Atrocities," *Arkansas Historical Quarterly* 38, no. 4 (1979): 350–51.

76. Brown, "Albert Pike, 1809–1891," 667.

77. Ibid., 667–68.

78. Ibid., 716. In a footnote in his biography of Pike, Walter Lee Brown notes that, despite efforts to the contrary, he "has found no evidence to substantiate" assertions that Albert Pike wrote *Morals and Dogma of the Ancient and Accepted Scottish Rite of Freemasonry* (Washington, D.C.: The Supreme Council of the Thirty-third Degree, S.J., 1966), his renowned work, while living on the Little Missouri.

79. Brown, "Albert Pike, 1809–1891," 742.

80. Ibid., 751.

81. *Transactions* (May 1868), 8. Reynold J. Matthews, Grand Archivist of the Supreme Council, S.J., aptly described *Morals and Dogma* as "a comparative and historical review of the ancient mysteries related to Freemasonry." Reynold J. Matthews, interview with WLF Sr., July 23, 1991.

82. Carnes, 137–38.

83. *Transactions* (1870), 158.

84. Charles S. Lobingier, *The Supreme Council, 33°, Mother Council of the World Ancient and Accepted Scottish Rite of Freemasonry, Southern Jurisdiction, U.S.A.* (Washington, D.C.: The Supreme Council, S.J., 1931), 340.

85. Pike, *Morals and Dogma*, iii. In 1909, T. W. Hugo of Duluth, Minnesota, published *Digest of Morals and Dogma* (Duluth, Minn.: Duluth Consistory, 1909) with a detailed index of the book's contents. Some of Pike's intellectual sources and derivations can be readily traced in the works of Godfrey Higgins, Eliphas Levi, J. G. R. Forlong, and others.

86. On the "Unity Concept," see Rex R. Hutchens, *Pillars of Wisdom: The Writings of Albert Pike* (Washington, D.C.: The Supreme Council, SJ, 1995), 39–44.

87. Richardson, 569.

88. Hutchens, 44.

89. Carnes, 135.

90. See Thomas L. Livermore, *Numbers and Losses in the Civil War in America: 1861–65*, Civil War Centennial Series (Bloomington: Indiana University Press, 1957). Colonel Livermore's book was first published some ninety years ago.

91. Henry Seidel Canby, introduction to *John Brown's Body*, by Stephen Vincent Benet (New York: Rinehart & Co., 1928), ix.

92. John F. Brobst, as quoted by Reid Mitchell, *Civil War Soldiers* (New York: Viking, 1988), 199.

93. James D. Carter, *History of The Supreme Council, 33° (Mother Council of the World) Ancient and Accepted Scottish Rite of Freemasonry, Southern Jurisdiction, U.S.A., 1861–1891* (Washington, D.C.: The Supreme Council, 33°, S.J., 1967), 5.

94. Brown, "Albert Pike, 1809–1891," 756.

95. Ibid., 757.

96. Ibid., 758.

97. *Transactions* (1865), 257.

98. Ibid., 258.

99. Ibid., 262.

100. Duncan, 265.

101. Brown, "Albert Pike, 1809–1891," 763.

102. *Transactions* (1866), 444. In 1867 the Scottish Rite degrees were conferred upon President Andrew Johnson at the White House.

103. Brown, "Albert Pike, 1809–1891," 764; Duncan, 266.

104. Brown, "Albert Pike, 1809–1891," 765.

105. *Transactions* (1866), 418.

106. Ibid.

107. Ibid., 448.

108. Ibid., 451.

109. Arturo deHoyos, "The Union of 1867," Scottish Rite Research Society Lecture, October 10, 1995, *Heredom* 4 (1995): 7–46.

110. J. Carter, *History,* 21.

111. Albert Pike presented a copy of his 1868 rituals to Josiah H. Drummond in 1870 "with permission to use" as deemed appropriate by the recipient, Archives, NMJ; see also, Arturo deHoyos, *op. cit.*

112. *Transactions* (1866), 455.

113. Jack Hurst, *Nathan Bedford Forrest: A Biography* (New York: Alfred A. Knopf, 1993), 325.

114. Ibid., 344.

115. Brown, "Albert Pike, 1809–1891," 783. There is no question, however, that during Reconstruction Pike had acid views about black suffrage. He was violently opposed to blacks being given the franchise, but he made his case by a distinction with a difference, hard to comprehend and accept in the late twentieth century. He opposed black voting not because the emancipated slaves were black, but because he felt they were not prepared. See *Morals and Dogma*, 154; also, Jim Tresner, author of *Albert Pike: The Man Beyond the Monument* (New York: M. Evans, 1995), an informal collection of biographical anecdotes and musings, carefully explains: "Often in *Morals and Dogma* [Pike] makes the point that a people has to become fit to be free and fit for the franchise. His speeches as well as his letter to the people of the Northern States suggests that he thought, in time, Blacks would both be free and able to participate in government. It is also true he thought it would take a long time. Democracy was a sacred thing to Pike . . . . He believed that a people evolved slowly toward it . . . . I really do not think that, to Pike, 'not yet,' was really a way of saying 'never.' [Because] of our own late twentieth century perspective, it is so easy to assume that Pike's statements are excessively racist or exclusively pointed at Blacks. By the standards of our time, they would be. In the context of his own time, I think they were not." Jim Tresner to William L. Fox, letter, May 20, 1996.

116. Susan Lawrence Davis, *Authentic History: Ku Klux Klan, 1865–1877* (New York: American Library Service, 1924), 276.

117. Walter Lee Brown, Fayetteville, Arkansas, interview by telephone with WLF Sr., June 1991.

118. Duncan, 268.

119. See Allen W. Trelease, *White Terror: The Ku Klux Klan and Southern Reconstruction* (New York: Harper and Row, 1971); David M. Chalmers, *Hooded Americanism: The History of the Ku Klux Klan*, 3rd ed. (Durham, N. C.: Duke University Press, 1981), makes no mention of Pike. See also, Wyn Craig Wade, *The Fiery Cross: The KKK in America* (New York: Simon and Schuster, 1987), 58 n. 459. Wade relies on the hearsay of Susan Lawrence Davis when he says Pike was among prominent state leaders whose initial association with the Klan "was usually in name only and nowhere lasted longer than 1869." He cites no primary sources for even this sweeping assumption. Stanley F. Horn, in *Invisible Empire: The Story of the Ku Klux Klan, 1866–1871* (Cos Cob, Conn.: John E. Edwards, 1969), depends also on the untrustworthy secondary source of Davis for his statement that Pike was Chief Justice of the Ku Klux Klan, an office, according to Walter L. Brown, that is never mentioned in the Klan constitution. Further, Steven C. Bullock, in *Revolutionary Brotherhood: Freemasonry and the Transformation of the American Social Order, 1730–1840* (Chapel Hill: University of North Carolina Press, 1996), 404 n. 17, disperses, without adequate questioning, the speculation that "Albert Pike also seems to have been a Klan leader."

Bullock's citation is an article by William M. Stuart, "The Anti-Masonic Phase of Johnson's Impeachment," *American Lodge of Research Transactions,* 2 (January 6, 1936–May 28, 1936): 152. Stuart's claim, however, is drawn from another secondary source, a 1933 article in the *American Legion Monthly* magazine, which circles back to the unsubstantiated assertions of Davis. The most sure-footed scholar, therefore, needs to tread carefully over this slippery ground.

120.   Trelease, 20. The author cites Albert Pike as one of the potential mystery leaders in the Klan's founding. His reasoning, however, is entirely circumstantial and inferential. He writes,"General Pike, editor of the *Memphis Appeal,* has been identified as the Klan's attorney general and as a collaborator in drawing up its ritual. The [Klan] Prescript makes no provision for this office . . . Pike may well have affiliated with the Klan, however. He was intrigued by secret societies and rituals, was a leading student and interpreter of Freemasonry, and sympathized with the Klan's stated objectives." Trelease is here on the thin ice of a syllogism formed on the misleading evidence of guilt by Masonic association.

121.   Charles Reagan Wilson, *Baptized in Blood: The Religion of the Lost Cause, 1865–1920* (Athens: University of Georgia Press, 1980), 112.

122.   Carnes, 137.

123.   Wilson, 100.

124.   Carnes, 174. He shares the view of Horn, in *Invisible Empire: The Story of the Ku Klux Klan,* that the KKK ritual was derived from college Greek letter fraternities. Alternatively, Albert C. Stevens, in *Cyclopedia of Fraternities* (New York: E. B. Treat and Co., 1907), suggests the KKK ritual was borrowed from the Sons of Malta. An authority on the history and "genealogy" of Masonic ritual, Arturo deHoyos, who has examined the Ku Klux Klan ritual, maintains that there is no comparison between the two, as the latter is "juvenile" and the work of "inexperienced amateurs."Arturo deHoyos, interview with William L.Fox, February 16, 1996.

125.   Hurst, 302.

126.   Ibid., 303–4. Hurst may be correct in his assumptions about the incipient connection between the Democratic Club and the Klan's first public appearance in Memphis. Not long after the Club assembled, fifty Klan night-riders appeared in Memphis for the first time. According to one witness (Lee Meriwether), the identity of the Memphis Klan organizers—Nathan Bedford Forrest, Matthew C. Gallaway (an editor), and Minor Meriwether—was never well dissembled. A man of Pike's prominence in Memphis public life could not easily hide from notice were he also a part of something other than Democratic politics.

127.   *Transactions* (1868), 8.

128.   Ibid.

129.   Ibid., 15.

130.   Henry Wilson Coil, *Coil's Masonic Encyclopedia* (New York: Macoy Publishing, 1961), 547–50. The spurious nature of the Oriental Rite of Memphis is characterized by Coil as "the last, the largest, and most pretentious product of the Masonic degree and rite fabricators."

131.   Ibid.

132.   S. Brent Morris, e-mail interview with William L. Fox, January 1, 1996.

133.   Ibid., 12.

134.   J. Carter, *History,* 22.

135.   *Transactions* (1868), 69, 73.

136.   Ibid., 90.

137.   See appendix II in J. Carter, *History,* 421–27.

138.   Brown, "Albert Pike, 1809–1891," 838.

139.   Cf. James J. Marples, "125th Anniversary of the KCCH," *Scottish Rite Journal* 104 (June 1995): 29–30.

140.   Brown, "Albert Pike, 1809–1891," 788. There were some all black Democratic Clubs forming at this time which is probably what provoked Pike's warning. From the view of political pragmatism, Pike felt it was a waste of time to court the black vote because it would only weaken the Democratic party to imitate the Republican voting strategy.

141.   Ibid., 789.

142.   J. Carter, *History,* 44.

143.   Dumas Malone and Basil Rauch, *The New Nation, 1815–1917,* vol. 2, *1841–1877* (New York: Appleton-Century-Crofts, 1960), 264.

144. James D. Richardson, Sovereign Grand Commander, 1901–1914, *The Ancient and Accepted Scottish Rite: Centennial Address*, October 23, 1901 (reprinted by the Supreme Council, 33°, Washington, D.C., 1958), 26.

145. Pike, *Morals and Dogma*, 238.

CHAPTER V
The Washingtonian Pike, 1870–1891

1. James D. Carter, *History of The Supreme Council, 33° (Mother Council of the World), Ancient and Accepted Scottish Rite of Freemasonry, Southern Jurisdiction, U.S.A., 1861–1891* (Washington, D.C.: The Supreme Council, S.J., 1967), 39.

2. Ibid., 45.

3. Ibid., 47.

4. *Official Bulletin* 1, no. 3, as cited in Carter, 49.

5. Circular letter as cited in Carter, 106.

6. Carter, 49.

7. Ibid., 50.

8. Ibid., 61.

9. Charles S. Lobingier, *The Supreme Council, 33°, Mother Council of the World Ancient and Accepted Scottish Rite of Freemasonry, Southern Jurisdiction, U.S.A.* (Washington, D.C.: The Supreme Council, S.J., 1931), 734–35.

10. Walter Lee Brown, "Albert Pike, 1809–1891," (Ph.D. diss., University of Texas, 1955), 829.

11. Stephen W. Stathis and Leed Roderick, "Mallet, Chisel, and Curls," *American Heritage* 27, no. 2 (February 1976): 45–47, 94–96.

12. Brown, 364.

13. Thurman Wilkins in *Notable American Women, 1607–1950: A Biographical Dictionary*, vol. 3 (Cambridge, Mass.: The Belknap Press of Harvard University Press, 1971), 122.

14. Paul Richard, "The Sculptor Who Knew Lincoln," news feature, *Washington Post*, February 24, 1990.

15. Brown, 833.

16. Vinnie Ream file, the Supreme Council Library, Washington, D.C.

17. "X.Y.Z.," "A Protege of the Scottish Rite," *The New Age* 22 (January 1915): 15.

18. Richard, "The Sculptor Who Knew Lincoln."

19. Brown, 833.

20. Vinnie Ream died November 20, 1914, of kidney disease. She was buried in Arlington National Cemetery. Her grave is marked by a bronze replica of her idealization of "Sappho," the Greek lyric poet much admired by Pike.

21. Carter, 66.

22. Brown, 841. The false legend of Pike's omniscient linguistic skills was perpetuated in his obituary (*New York Times*, April 3, 1891) in which it was reported that "notwithstanding his great age, the General devoted his time to the study of Sanskrit, of which he translated seventeen volumes since 1875." He was an accomplished dilettante and devotee, but much of his study was second-hand, dependent on specialists.

23. Robert D. Richardson Jr., *Emerson: The Mind on Fire* (Berkeley: University of California, 1995), 114–15.

24. *Transactions of The Supreme Council, 33° (Mother Council of the World), Ancient and Accepted Scottish Rite of Freemasonry, Southern Jurisdiction, U.S.A.* (hereafter referred to as *Transactions*) (Washington, D.C.: The Supreme Council, S.J., 1872), 53–54.

25. Ibid., 38–39.

26. Carter, 77.

27. Ibid., 83.

28. *Transactions* (1874), 64.

29. Ibid., 4.

30. Ibid., 5.

31. Carter, 117.

32. *Transactions* (1876), 42.

33. Ibid., 28–29. Pike's 1876 criticism of the Northern Jurisdiction's eighteenth degree Rose Croix ritual is aimed at Enoch T. Carson's 1870 revision of the ritual. Whereas earlier Northern Jurisdiction Rose Croix rituals were superficially Christian (as were those degrees taken by the three Jewish founders, de la Motta, Levy, and Lieben), the Carson "emendation" added the Apostle's Creed, the Ascension of Christ, and several select texts of Paul that would make a Jewish candidate feel particularly uncomfortable. A sample of these quotations would include, "The Cross, unto the Jew a stumbling block," "The Son of God who died and was raised again," and "The only name given . . . whereby ye can be saved." According to Arturo deHoyos, the degree of the Northern Jurisdiction to which Pike objected remained "virtually unaltered from 1870 to 1942, when a new revision infused a more tolerant spirit" into the work. Arturo deHoyos to William L. Fox (hereafter referred to as WLF), letter, May 10, 1996.

34. *Transactions* (1876), 28.

35. Carter, 120–21.

36. *Transactions* (1876), 38. Arturo deHoyos makes an important clarifying point in reaction to Pike's statement deeming York Rite (so-called "Webb-form") Craft ritual as "adulterated early in the present century." Pike's assumptions are historically misguided, as deHoyos explains: "Contrary to Pike's belief, the Webb-form rituals commonly used throughout the United States are as old as those of the Scottish and French Rites *(Rit Ecossais* and *Rit Francais)*, and older than those of England (which resulted from the union of "Antients" and "Moderns" in 1813). The American rituals have much more in common with older Scottish and Irish workings, and with the exposures of the 1760s, because our ritual was planted and took root prior to the influential philosophical speculations beginning to sweep Europe about this time." Arturo deHoyos to WLF, letter, May 10, 1996.

37. Lobingier, 572–73.

38. Ibid., 574–75.

39. *Transactions* (1876), 19, 58–59, 83; Lobingier, 907, 910.

40. Lobingier, 911.

41. Ibid., 72.

42. Samuel Eliot Morison, Henry Steele Commager, and William E. Leuchtenberg, *The Growth of the American Republic* (New York: Oxford University Press, 1969), 1:817.

43. *Transactions* (1878), 8, 134–35.

44. Albert Pike to Frederick Webber, letter, November 25, 1877, quoted in Carter, 136.

45. Ibid, 137.

46. Albert Pike to Frederick Webber, letter, January 17, 1878, quoted in Carter, 139.

47. Ibid.

48. Ibid., 140.

49. *Transactions* (1878), 20, 66.

50. *Transactions* (1880), appendix, 5.

51. *D.C. Libraries* 13, no. 1 (October 1, 1941): 1. (Official Publication of the District of Columbia Library Association).

52. For the Masonic collection of the Library of the Supreme Council, William L. Boyden, who was librarian for forty-six years, devised a special cataloguing system using the well-known Dewey Decimal System as a base. In May 1883, Grand Commander Pike announced that Thomas H. Caswell (SGIG in California) had given a mineral collection to the Library of the Supreme Council that was valued at $5,000. This collection was housed in the library until June 1927, when the council presented it to the U.S. National Museum (later renamed as the Smithsonian Museum of Natural History).

53. *Official Bulletin* 4, as cited in Carter, 87–88.

54. Carter, 180.

55. Ibid., 93.

56. *Transactions* (1878), 68.

57. Ibid., (1880), 18.

58. Carter, 209.

59. *Transactions* (1880), 35.

60. Confidential Allocution, 1880, Pike Correspondence, the Supreme Council, Southern Jurisdiction, Archives, 4-vlt-10.

61. Carter, 200.

62. Ibid., 202.

63. Brown, 854.

64. Ibid.

65. Carter, 259.

66. Ibid., 217.

67. Albert Pike to James C. Batchelor, letter, August 20, 1882, as quoted in Carter, 246.

68. *Transactions* (1882), appendix, 7.

69. Dumas Malone and Basil Rauch, *The New Nation 1815–1917* (New York: Appleton-Century-Crofts, 1960), 125.

70. Oscar Handlin, *The Uprooted* (Boston: Little, Brown and Company, 1952), 33–34. See also, John Higham, *Send These to Me: Immigrants in Urban America* (Baltimore, Md.: The Johns Hopkins University Press, 1984).

71. Carter, 265.

72. Ibid., 268.

73. Ibid., 276.

74. Ibid., 279.

75. Ibid.

76. Mark C. Carnes, *Secret Ritual and Manhood in Victorian America* (New Haven: Yale University Press, 1989), 81.

77. There were exceptions, of course, as Vinnie Ream received from Albert Pike Masonically derived degrees. Pike's excursion into adoptive Masonry included Apprentice, Companion, Mistress, Perfect Mistress, Elect, Ecossaise, and Sublime Ecossaise. He conferred upon Vinnie an "Eighth" degree, too, in which he named her "Syrene Directress of the work." According to Arturo deHoyos, a Scottish Rite specialist on the history of ritual, the degrees Pike conferred on Vinnie Ream came from the French Adoptive Rite, intended for women. Pike published his own text of the first four degrees in the book *The Masonry of Adoption* (1866). DeHoyos explains that the term "Co-Masonry" in the late twentieth century refers specifically to the order *Le Droit Humain*, or International Co-Masonry, an organization which confers degrees that resemble those offered by the United Grand Lodge of England, from Arturo deHoyos to WLF, letter, May 10, 1996.

78. Pope Leo XIII and Albert Pike, *The Letter "Humanum Genus" of The Pope, Leo XIII Against Freemasonry and the Spirit Of The Age, April 20, 1884 and The Reply of Albert Pike, 33°, Sovereign Grand Commander of the Ancient and Accepted Scottish Rite of Freemasonry, Southern Jurisdiction to The Letter "Humanum Genus" of Pope XIII* (Washington, D.C.: The Supreme Council, 33°, 1962), 7.

79. Ibid., 13.

80. Jaroslav Pelikan, *The Riddle of Roman Catholicism* (New York and Nashville: Abingdon Press, 1959), 88, 97–98. Pelikan explains the Catholic perspective on the twin realms, church and state, as the justification for parochial schools: "Interestingly, education [in traditional Catholic doctrine] does not qualify as . . . an area of legitimate concern to both the state and the church. Authority over education belongs to parents and to the church by divine right. When the state educates, it is not doing so on the basis of any inherent right, but is merely taking the place of the parents." Supported by arguments of natural law, education belongs to the realm of the church and parents; "abdication by either or both is a neglect of divinely established duty."

81. *Transactions* (1884), 57–58.

82. Ibid., 70–71.

83. It is one of many ironies of Christian history that the pontificate of Pius IX marks the end of the papacy's geopolitical power, which had actually reached the highwater mark in the thirteenth century under Innocent III and had been slowly receding over the next 600 years, yet Pius IX was declared supreme and infallible.

84. Among the errors to be rejected were some of the following: "15. That each person is free to adopt and follow that religion which seems best to the light of reason. . . . 18. That Protestantism is simply a different form of the same Christian religion, and that it is possible to please God in it as well as in the Catholic church. . . . 47. That the good order of civil society requires that public schools, open to children of all classes . . . be free of

all authority on the part of the church . . . . 55. That the church ought to be separate from the state, and the state from the church." From Justo Gonzalez, *The Story of Christianity*, vol. 2, (San Francisco: Harper Collins, 1975), 297–98.

85.   One of the most vivid scenes in world literature depicting the tension of revolutionary Italy and the anxiety of the Roman Catholic Church occurs in Lampedusa's masterpiece, *The Leopard*. Father Pirrone, a Jesuit, confronted the prince, "and even became acid again." He said, "Briefly, then, you nobles will come to an agreement with the Liberals, and yes, even with the Masons, at our expense, at the expense of the Church." The prince let the priest rant until he "was breathing hard . . . having lost control of himself again." Then the prince, sometimes called "the leopard" by his people, calmly responded. "We're not blind, my dear Father, we're just human beings. We live in a changing reality to which we try to adapt ourselves like seaweed bending under the pressure of water. The Holy Church has been granted an explicit promise of immortality; we, as a social class, have not. . . . Solace is implicit in [the Church's] desperation. Don't you think that if now or in the future [the Church] could save herself by sacrificing us She wouldn't do so?" Prince of Lampedusa, *The Leopard,* Everyman's Library ed. (New York: Alfred A. Knopf, 1991), 48–49.

86.   Gonzalez, 300.

87.   Peter W. Williams, *American Religions: Tradition and Culture* (New York: Macmillan Publishing Company, 1990), 283.

88.   Justin D. Fulton as quoted in Robert T. Handy, *Undermined Establishment: Church-State Relations in America, 1880–1920* (Princeton, NJ: Princeton University Press, 1991) 42.

89.   Leo XIII and Pike, *The Letter . . . and The Reply,* 13, 26.

90.   Ibid., 5.

91.   Ibid., 5, 24.

92.   Ibid., 28.

93.   Charles Coppens, S.J., "Is Freemasonry Anti-Christian?" *American Ecclesiastical Review* 21, no. 6 (December 1899): 573. Coppens is even more sympathetic to Pike (though not to Masonry) in his subsequent discussion entitled "Albert Pike's Response" in *American Ecclesiastical Review* 22, no. 2 (February 1900): 124–36. He thinks that Pike in 1884 was too far past his prime to give a vigorous defense of Freemasonry. Coppens views Pike as essentially a pious man, but allows, "I do not maintain that Freemasons in the United States have anything to do with the worship of Satan or Luciferianism, even in their most secret meetings of the highest degrees" (135).

94.   *Transactions* (1884), 93, 95.

95.   Carter, 299.

96.   Ibid., 298.

97.   Ibid., 301.

98.   Ibid., 302.

99.   Ibid., 301.

100.   *Transactions* (1886), 36.

101.   Ibid., 10.

102.   Ibid.

103.   Carter, 327.

104.   "Albert Pike," obituary, *New York Times*, April 3, 1891.

105.   *Transactions* (1886), appendix, 9.

106.   Carter, 327.

107.   Ibid., 337.

108.   Ibid.

109.   Ibid., 232.

110.   Ibid., 238, from reproduction of *The Book of Infamy*'s title page.

111.   Ibid., 355.

112.   Ibid., 356.

113.   *Transactions* (1888), appendix, 4, 5.

114.   Ibid., appendix, 22.

115. Ibid., appendix, 23.

116. Carter, 351.

117. Ibid., 365.

118. *Transactions* (1890), appendix, 3.

119. Ibid., appendix, 29.

120. Ibid., appendix, 30.

121. Ibid. On the recommendation of the Committee on Finance at the 1890 session, the Supreme Council approved the printing of 1,000 copies of Pike's "Words Spoken of the Dead."

122. *Transactions* (1890), 47–48.

123. Ibid., 39.

124. Carter, 375.

125. Duane E. Anderson, interview with WLF, March 16, 1996, St. Louis, Missouri. T. W. Hugo (1848–1923) may have become acquainted with Pike first through Odd Fellows. Hugo founded in 1910 the Infant Welfare Bureau in Duluth, Minnesota, which was run under Scottish Rite auspices until 1957.

126. Brown, 867.

127. Ibid.

128. Henry Wilson Coil, *Coil's Masonic Encyclopedia* (New York: Macoy Publishing, 1961), 474.

129. Carnes, 135.

130. Carnes, 139.

CHAPTER VI

A Fragile Interim, 1891–1900

Batchelor, Tucker, and Caswell

1. "Albert Pike," obituary, *New York Times*, April 3, 1891.

2. James D. Carter, *History of The Supreme Council, 33° (Mother Council of the World), Ancient and Accepted Scottish Rite of Freemasonry, Southern Jurisdiction, U.S.A., 1891–1921* (Washington, D.C.: The Supreme Council, S.J., 1971), 6.

3. *Transactions of The Supreme Council, 33° (Mother Council of the World), Ancient and Accepted Scottish Rite of Freemasonry, Southern Jurisdiction, U.S.A.* (hereafter referred to as *Transactions*) (Washington, D.C.: The Supreme Council, S.J., 1892), appendix, 6.

4. Ibid., appendix, 10.

5. Ibid.

6. Carter, 46–47.

7. This per capita reduction was repeated 100 years later in 1992.

8. *Transactions* (1892), 110–11.

9. Carter, 49.

10. Thomas A. Bailey, *Presidential Greatness: The Image and the Man from George Washington to the Present* (New York: Appleton-Century, 1966), 249.

11. Thomas H. Caswell, "In Memoriam, Philip Crosby Tucker, 33°," in *Transactions* (1895), appendix, 328.

12. *Transactions* (1893), "Allocution," 21.

13. *Transactions* (1893), 108, 109.

14. Carter, 68.

15. Minutes, Council of Administration, June 25, 1894, cited in Carter, 71.

16. Ibid.

17. *Transactions* (1885), 7.

18. Kevin Starr, *Americans and the California Dream, 1850–1915* (New York: Oxford University Press, 1973), 52.

19. Charles S. Lobingier, *The Supreme Council, 33°, Mother Council of the World, Ancient and Accepted Scottish Rite of Freemasonry, Southern Jurisdiction, U.S.A.* (Washington, D.C.: The Supreme Council, S.J., 1931), 300.

20. Starr, 55–56.

21. *Transactions* (1895), 15–17.

22. Carter, 75.

23. *Transactions* (1895), 13.

24. Ibid., 50.

25. Carter, 90.

26. *Transactions* (1895), 20.

27. Ibid., 59–60.

28. Ibid., 116.

29. Carter, 87.

30. Thomas A. Bailey, *The American Pageant: A History of the Republic* (Boston: D.C. Heath and Co., 1956), 599.

31. *Transactions* (1897), 21.

32. Carter, 108.

33. Ibid., 108; *Transactions* (1897), 14–15.

34. T. Jackson Lears, *No Place of Grace: Anti-Modernism and the Transformation of American Culture, 1880–1920* (New York: Pantheon, 1981), 194.

35. Albert Pike, *Morals and Dogma* (Washington, D.C.: The Supreme Council, S.J., 1871), 106.

36. William D. Moore, "From Lodge Room to Theatre: Meeting Spaces of the Scottish Rite," Susan C. Jones, editor, *Theatre of the Fraternity: Staging the Ritual Space of the Scottish Rite of Freemasonry, 1896–1929* (Minneapolis: Frederick R. Weisman Art Museum, University of Minnesota, 1996), 49–50.

37. Lears, 91, 101.

38. Ibid., 193.

39. Ibid., 16.

40. Reynold J. Matthews, interview with William L. Fox Sr., February 6, 1992.

41. Carter, 92.

42. Ibid., 93.

43. *Transactions* (1897), 30–33, 59.

44. Ibid., 46.

45. "The Pike Monument: Handsome Memorial Unveiled Last Wednesday at Washington, D.C.," *Masonic Standard*, newspaper, October 26, 1901.

46. Carter, 108.

47. *Transactions* (1897), 73.

48. Carter, 106–7.

49. Bailey, 627.

50. Carter, 196.

51. *Transactions* (1899), 263.

52. Ibid.

53. Ibid., 274.

54. Ibid., 258.

55. Ibid., 331.

56. Ibid., 281–82.

57. Carter, 119.

58. *Transactions* (1899), 416.

59. Carter, 131.

60. Starr, 158.

61. Richard Hofstadter, *The Progressive Historians: Turner, Beard, and Parrington* (Chicago: The University of Chicago Press, 1968), 155.

62. Peter W. Williams, *America's Religions: Traditions and Cultures* (New York: Macmillan Publishing Company, 1990) 231.

CHAPTER VII

New Century, New Age, New Temple, 1900–1914
James D. Richardson

1.   Mark Sullivan, *Our Times 1900–1925*, vol. 1, *The Turn of the Century* (1926; reprint, New York: Charles Scribner's Sons, 1971), 12 (page citations are to the reprint edition).

2.   James D. Carter, *History of The Supreme Council, 33° (Mother Council of the World), Ancient and Accepted Scottish Rite of Freemasonry, Southern Jurisdiction, U.S.A., 1891–1921* (Washington, D.C.: The Supreme Council, S.J., 1971), 140.

3.   Charles S. Lobingier, *The Supreme Council, 33°, Mother Council of the World, Ancient and Accepted Scottish Rite of Freemasonry, Southern Jurisdiction, U.S.A.* (Washington, D.C.: The Supreme Council, S.J., 1931), 544.

4.   *Transactions of The Supreme Council, 33° (Mother Council of the World), Ancient and Accepted Scottish Rite of Freemasonry, Southern Jurisdiction, U.S.A.* (hereafter referred to as *Transactions*) (Washington, D.C.: The Supreme Council, S.J., 1901), 35–36.

5.   Ibid., 66–67.

6.   Ibid., 41.

7.   Carter, 146.

8.   *Transactions* (1901), 106.

9.   Ibid., 46.

10.   Ibid., 55.

11.   In 1977 the Albert Pike statue was moved to the south side of Fourth Street and Indiana Avenue, NW, and was rededicated.

12.   *Transactions* (1901), 138.

13.   Ibid., 139.

14.   Ibid., 193.

15.   Ibid., 208–9.

16.   Ibid., 222; Richardson's remarks are only a slight paraphrase of a statement by Albert Pike: "Masonry propagates no creed except its own most simple and Sublime One; that universal religion, taught by Nature and by Reason. Its Lodges are neither Jewish, Moslem, nor Christian Temples. It reiterates the precepts of morality of all religions. It venerates the character and commends the teachings of the great and good of all ages and countries. It extracts the good and not the evil, the truth, and not the error, from all creeds; and acknowledges that there is much which is good and true in all." Cf. Albert Pike, *Morals and Dogma* (Washington, D.C.: The Supreme Council, S.J., 1871), 718.

17.   *Transactions* (1901), 222–23. The Scottish Rite Creed was amended in recent years by John W. Boettjer, the managing editor of the *Scottish Rite Journal*, with the approval of the journal's editorial board and the Supreme Council, to read as follows: "Human progress is our cause, liberty of thought our supreme wish, freedom of conscience our mission, and the guarantee of equal rights to all people everywhere our ultimate goal." From the *Scottish Rite Journal* 98, no. 1 (Janauary 1990): 17–18.

18.   Ray Baker Harris, Washington, D.C., to Luther A. Smith, Sovereign Grand Commander, letter, July 30, 1958, Smith Correspondence 1957–1959, the Supreme Council Archives, S.J., 4-1200.30. Shortly after this correspondence, Richardson's *The Ancient and Accepted Scottish Rite, Centennial Address,* October 23, 1901, was reprinted by the Supreme Council with a foreword by Grand Commander Smith.

19.   Theodore Roosevelt, "The President's Speech," from Souvenir of the Luncheon Given . . . in Little Rock, Arkansas, October 1902, pamphlet (Little Rock, Ark.: AASR, Orient of Arkansas, 1902).

20.   Carter, 167.

21.   Ibid.

22.   *Transactions* (1903), 71.

23.   C. Lance Brockman, "Catalyst for Change: Intersection of the Theater and the Scottish Rite," *Heredom* 3 (1994), 121. Of added interest, Pike ordered that appropriate music be selected for all the Scottish Rite degrees and oversaw its publication in several large volumes.

24.   Brockman, 126.

25. See Lawrence J. Hill, "Beyond the Scenery: Effects Used to Enhance Scottish Rite Ceremony," *Heredom* 3 (1994): 147–58.

26. Ibid., 407.

27. Carter, 179.

28. *Transactions* (1903), 42.

29. Ibid., 43.

30. Ibid., 125.

31. Carter, 196.

32. *Transactions* (1903), 55, 146.

33. Ibid., 56.

34. Ibid., 147.

35. Ibid., 57.

36. *The New Age* 10, no. 4 (April 1909): 351.

37. Carter, 200–202.

38. Ibid., 229.

39. Ibid.

40. Harry E. Echols Jr., U.S. Dept. of Labor, Washington, D.C., telephone interview with William L. Fox Sr., April 14, 1992.

41. Richard B. Morris, ed., *Encyclopedia of American History* (New York: Harper & Brothers Publishers, 1953), 268.

42. Carter, 207.

43. *Transactions* (1905), 38.

44. Ibid., 28.

45. *Transactions* (1907), 108.

46. *Transactions* (1905), 132.

47. Carter, 223.

48. See William Lloyd Fox, "Harvey Wiley" (Ph.D. diss., George Washington University, 1960).

49. Ibid., 257.

50. *Transactions* (1907), 144.

51. Ibid., 47.

52. Ibid., 121.

53. Ibid., 122.

54. Carter, 256.

55. Ibid., 259.

56. Ibid., 263.

57. *Transactions* (1911), 62.

58. George F. Moore, "Recent Cerneauism," *The New Age* 8, no. 4 (April 1908): 354.

59. Ibid., 358.

60. *The New Age* 10, no. 3 (March 1909): 279.

61. Carter, 274.

62. Ibid., 275.

63. *Transactions* (1909), 68.

64. Carter, 269.

65. Ingeborg R. Baum, librarian of the Supreme Council, Washington, D.C., to William L. Fox Sr., memorandum, December 7, 1989.

66. Carter, 290.

67. *Transactions* (1909), 186.

68. Ibid., 183.

69. *Transactions* (1911), Special Allocution, 115.

70. Ibid., 116.

71. Carter, 296.

72. Ibid., 331.

73. Ibid.

74. Ibid., 175.

75. Ibid., 300.

76. Ibid., 301.

77. Sue A. Kohler and Jeffrey R. Carson, *Sixteenth Street Architecture*, vol. 1, (Washington, D.C.: The U.S. Commission of Fine Arts, 1978), 344–47.

78. Hugh Y. Bernard, "The Architectural Career of John Russell Pope," *The New Age* 96, no. 8 (August 1988): 15.

79. John Russell Pope was a celebrated architect of his day whose architectural accomplishments in Washington, D.C., included DAR Constitution Hall, National City Christian Church, American Pharmaceutical Institute, National Archives, National Gallery of Art (west building), and Jefferson Memorial. For a proposed plan of Gothic design for the House of the Temple, see William D. Moore, "A Gothic House of the Temple," *Scottish Rite Journal* 100, no. 10 (October 1992): 42–50.

80. *Transactions* (1911), 121.

81. Carter, 305.

82. *Transactions* (1911), 122.

83. Ibid.

84. Henry White to Mrs. White, letter, June 14, 1910, Henry White Collection, Manuscripts Division, Library of Congress.

85. Ibid.

86. Kohler and Carson, 283.

87. Ibid., 345.

88. *Transactions* (1911), 123.

89. Kohler and Carson, 351.

90. *Transactions* (1911), 124. See Kohler and Carson, 285. A building permit was issued in July 1910 with a cost estimate of $1.1 million.

91. *Transactions* (1911), 195.

92. Ibid., 196.

93. John H. Cowles, Sovereign Grand Commander, Washington, D.C., to Arthur S. Crites, Bakersfield, California, letter, February 27, 1946, Cowles Correspondence, the Supreme Council Archives, S.J., 4-1000.73.

94. Ibid.

95. Carter, 330.

96. *Transactions* (1911), 64, 161.

97. Ibid., 95–96.

98. As quoted in John Mandleberg, *Ancient and Accepted: A Chronicle of the Proceedings 1845–1945 of the Supreme Council Established in England in 1845* (London: The Supreme Council of England and Wales, 1995) 734–35.

99. Ibid., 740.

100. Ibid., 307.

101. *Transactions* (1911), 108.

102. Carter, 282.

103. Ibid., 333.

104. Ibid.

105. Walter Lord, *The Night Lives On* (New York: William Morrow and Co., 1896), 12.

106. Carter, 348.

107. The records of the Executive Committee are in a bound volume nearly six inches in thickness in the Supreme Council Archives, S.J., under the title *Records of the Executive Committee, The Supreme Council, 33°, Ancient and Accepted Scottish Rite of Freemasonry, Southern Jurisdiction of the United States of America.* They cover the period from February 28, 1912, to October 12, 1917, relating to the erection and equipment of the House of the Temple, Sixteenth and S Streets, NW, Washington, D.C.

108. *Transactions* (1913), 49.

109. *Transactions* (1914), Special Session, 18.

110. *Transactions* (1913), 94.

111. Ibid., 98.

112. Article VI, Section 21, *Statutes of The Supreme Council, 33°, Ancient and Accepted Scottish Rite*, Southern Jurisdiction, U.S.A.

113. Carter, 381.

114. Ibid.

CHAPTER VIII

Forerunner of Americanism, 1915–1921

George F. Moore

1. Walter Lippmann, in Ronald Steel, *Walter Lippmann and the American Century* (Boston: Little, Brown, 1980), 45.

2. Virginia Woolf, in William L. Fox, *Willard L. Sperry: The Quandaries of a Liberal Protestant Mind, 1914–1939* (New York: Peter Lang Publishing, 1991), 38.

3. Charles S. Lobingier, *The Supreme Council, 33°, Mother Council of the World Ancient and Accepted Scottish Rite of Freemasonry, Southern Jurisdiction, U.S.A.* (Washington, D.C.: The Supreme Council, S.J., 1931), 544.

4. *Transactions of The Supreme Council, 33° (Mother Council of the World), Ancient and Accepted Scottish Rite of Freemasonry, Southern Jurisdiction, U.S.A.* (hereafter referred to as *Transactions*) (Washington, D.C.: The Supreme Council, S.J., 1914), 16.

5. Ibid., 18.

6. Edward Grey of Fallodon, *Twenty-five Years,* vol. 2 (London: Hodder & Stoughton, 1925), chap. 18.

7. *Transactions* (1915), 40.

8. Pamela Scott and Antoinette J. Lee, *Buildings of the District of Columbia* (New York: Oxford University Press, 1993), 306.

9. Aymar Embury, as quoted in Scott and Lee, 306.

10. William L. Fox, "How the Sphinx Came to Washington: Egyptian Themes in the House of the Temple," *Scottish Rite Journal* 104 (May 1996): 19–27.

11. William Lloyd Fox Sr., "A Temple for All Time," *Scottish Rite Journal* 100 (October 1992): 8–9. John Russell Pope was awarded in 1917 the Gold Medal of Honor by the Architectural League of New York for designing the finest building in America over a five year period, the interlude during which time the judging for the medal is conducted.

12. I am grateful to Arturo deHoyos for his insights on Moore and the Southern Jurisdiction's ritual. Mr. deHoyos submits a summary of the twentieth degree, any part of which may have been objectionable to Moore, which is drawn from "Historical Notes" (at the Supreme Council, 33°, NMJ, Lexington, Mass.) of the Northern Masonic Jurisdiction's 1951 version of the degree, a ritual used from 1896 to 1922. That degree was based on "a colorful drama commemorating the 25th anniversary of the Masonic career of Frederick II of Prussia. Historical characters were used in the cast but there was no basis for the action. The drama records a visit of Frederick, his entourage and distinguished guests, to a Lodge meeting—on August 14, 1763. In an exchange of Masonic reminiscences, a dramatic story was told of a spy who had gained entrance to a Masonic Lodge with a patent which was, in fact, a map of the fortress." Arturo deHoyos to William L. Fox, e-mail, May 23, 1996. Moore, a historical literalist, questioned the liberties taken with the evidence upon which the degrees were presumed to be based.

13. Roscoe Pound, *Masonic Addresses and Writings* (Richmond, Va.: Macoy Publishing, 1953), 379–80.

14. *Transactions* (1917), 206.

15. *Transactions* (1919), 227, 243.

16. *Transactions* (1917), 39.

17. *Transactions* (1915), 99.

18. Ibid., 223–24.

19. Lynn Dumenil, *Freemasonry and American Culture, 1880–1930* (Princeton, N.J.: Princeton University Press, 1984), 170.

20. Dumenil, 148–84.

21. Dumenil, 150, 275.

22. *Transactions* (1915), 112.

23. Ibid., 119.

24. Albert Pike, sixteen years before he became Grand Commander, took immoveable editorial stands in *The Arkansas Advocate* (1843) calling for state-supported education. Later, in Albert Pike's *Morals and Dogma* (Washington, D.C.: The Supreme Council, S.J., 1871) on pages 44 and 173, he continued his advocacy of public education in the pithy argument: "Equality has an organ;—gratuitous and obligatory instruction. We must begin with the right to the alphabet. The primary school *obligatory* upon all; the higher school *offered* to all. Such is the law. From the same school for all springs equal society."

25. *Transactions* (1915), 146.

26. This theme was carried forward into an unsigned editorial in *The New Age* entitled "The Question of Sectarian Schools," in which the author stated that "there can be no objection to sectarian schools *provided* [italics original] they are open at all times to the inspection of government officers" to make sure students "are not being taught to be traitors to the Government." The comment continues, "And no one should be eligible for public office of any kind who is not a product of the public schools." *The New Age* 25 (March 1917): 115. While the piece was unsigned, the views, if not their exact expression, clearly belonged to Moore.

27. "America First and All the Time," *The New Age* 23 (December 1915): 259.

28. Richard Hofstadter, *Social Darwinism in American Thought* (1944; reprint, Boston: Beacon Press, 1992), 172 (in reprint).

29. Sydney E. Ahlstrom, *A Religious History of the American People* (New Haven: Yale University Press, 1972), 856.

30. *Transactions* (1915), 167–68.

31. Ray Baker Harris, preface to *Classification of the Literature of Freemasonry and Related Societies,* by William L. Boyden (1915; reprint, Washington, D.C.: The Supreme Council, 33°, Ancient and Accepted Scottish Rite of Freemasonry, S.J., 1959), 4 (in reprint).

32. Dumenil, 175.

33. Fred Van Deventer, *Parade to Glory: The Story of the Shriners and Their Hospitals for Crippled Children* (New York: William Morrow and Co., 1959), 182–83; "Scottish Rite Hospitals for Crippled Children," *The New Age* 66 (June 1958): 336.

34. James D. Carter, *History of The Supreme Council, 33° (Mother Council of the World), Ancient and Accepted Scottish Rite of Freemasonry, Southern Jurisdiction, U.S.A., 1891–1921* (Washington, D.C.: The Supreme Council, S.J., 1971), 446.

35. *Transactions* (1918), Special Session, 11.

36. Ralph A. Gauker, *History of the Scottish Rite Bodies in the District of Columbia,* centennial ed. (Washington, D.C.: Mithras Lodge of Perfection, 1970), 505.

37. Pope's commission (originally slightly less than the recommended 6 percent of the American Institute of Architects contract; reduced in order to give consulting architect Elliott Woods a portion) worked out to be less than the commission paid to the sculptor, Adolph A. Weinman, who executed the two limestone sphinxes for $17,600. Elliott Woods to John Russell Pope, letter, September 16, 1912, the Supreme Council, Southern Jurisdiction, Archives (hereafter referred to as TSC), 2-250.2.

38. Norcross Brothers vs. the Supreme Council, Report of the Board of Arbitration, May 23, 1916, TSC, 2-250.1.

39. John Russell Pope to C. E. Rosenbaum, letter, May 7, 1914, TSC, 250.2; John Russell Pope to C. E. Rosenbaum, letter, May 23, 1914, TSC, 250.2.

40. Minutes, Executive Committee, Ninth Session, January 6 and 7, 1916, Records of the Executive Committee, Erection of House of Temple, 1911–1917, page 78, TSC, 2-250.2.

41. John H. Cowles to John Russell Pope, letter, February 2, 1917; John Russell Pope to Charles E. Rosenbaum, letter, February 3, 1917; Charles E. Rosenbaum to George F. Moore, letter, February 6, 1917, all in TSC, 250.2.

42. From Report of the Executive Committee, October 1917, TSC, 250.2.

43. *Transactions* (1917), 145–46.

44. Ibid., 45.

45. Cf. Fox, "How the Sphinx Came to Washington." The identity of the two statues is uncertain, but they have been frequently named as Isis and Nephthys or as scribes. Egyptologists do not rule out that such specific representations may have been indicated in the tombs of the pharaohs. But it is just as likely that the figures could represent humanity as any of the gods, or a three-dimensional form of the Egyptian hieroglyph Ma'at, the Egyptian idea of truth and order. Technically, therefore, the statues are nameless and as works of art are properly referred to as "block statues."

46. *Transactions* (1917), 145.

47. Contract, Supreme Council and David Edstrom, July 26, 1918, TSC, 2-250.

48. Otto Eggers to Ray Baker Harris, letter, September 8, 1958, TSC, 250.1. Eggers would later become the senior principal partner in Eggers and Higgins in New York.

49. *The New Age* 27 (January 1919): 2.

50. Ibid., 193.

51. Ray Baker Harris to Otto Eggers, letter, September 2, 1958, TSC, 250.1; *Transactions* (1963), 157.

52. *Transactions* (1947), 175.

53. It has been variously reported, without substantiation, that Nicholas II was a "mason" in the Martinist Rite. According to Arturo deHoyos, "Martinism is a type of Illuminist philosophy, organized as a fraternity with four degrees. It was the brain-child of the French philosopher Louis Claude de Saint-Martin (1743–1803), who is believed to have been initiated into a similar tradition by the Rosicrucian adept, Martinez de Pasqually. . . . At one time Martinism required Masonic membership, but this has lapsed." He continues on another point that in his opinion the "real" Russian Masonic tradition, "as described by Tolstoy, *War and Peace* (Book 5, chapters 3–4) is, in fact, a version of the Swedish Rite." Arturo deHoyos to William L. Fox, e-mail, May 24, 1996.

54. Boris Telepneff, *Ars Quatuor Coronati, Transactions of Quatuor Coronati Lodge* 35 (1922): 291.

55. Boris Telepneff, "An Outline of the History of Russian Freemasonry," reprinted from the pamphlet *The Freemason* (London: 1928, pamphlet), 35 (copy in TSC).

56. Henry Wilson Coil, *Coil's Masonic Encyclopedia* (New York: Macoy Publishing, 1961), 588.

57. Nathan Smith, "Political Freemasonry in Russia, 1906–1918: A Discussion of Sources," *The Russian Review* 44 (April 1985): 158. Masonic impulses in late czarist and early revolutionary Russia are important to the interpretation of George Katkov's history, *Russia 1917: the February Revolution* (New York: Harper and Row, 1967).

58. Ronald C. Moe, "The Princess Yusupov: A Great Russian Family" (book ms.), from chapter entitled "Fighting for Russia," n. 11.

59. Telepneff, 291.

60. C. N. Batham, "Russian Freemasonry, 1731–1979," pt. 3, *Scottish Rite Journal* 99 (July 1991): 16–17.

61. Walter Lippmann, in Steel, 136, 152.

62. *Transactions* (1918), Special Session, 9, 17.

63. Ibid., 19.

64. Ibid., 42–43.

65. *Transactions* (1919), 64.

66. Frank E. Vandiver, *Black Jack: The Life and Times of John J. Pershing*, vol. 2 (College Station and London: Texas A&M University Press, 1977), 1016.

67. *Transactions* (1919), 69.

68. Carter, 491.

69. Walter Lippmann, in Steel, 156.

70. In 1874 Pike had assembled a manuscript of over 2,000 pages which concentrated his interest on Indo-Aryan theosophy. These sacred writings from ancient Persia, attributed to Zoroaster, were discovered by Pike in modern translations, probably French, from which he created an English text. The terms Zend and Avesta refer to language groups; the language of the Avesta, for instance, is sometimes called Old Bactrian and formed, along with Old Persian, the Iranian family of Indo-European languages. Pike was fascinated by the linguistic bridges between civilizations, even though he was far removed from actually knowing more than

general concepts of obscure Avestan. His study confirmed for him the universality of human religious experience, which he always maintained was fundamental to Masonic principles of religious liberty.

71.   Ibid., 525; *Transactions* (1919), 247.

72.   *Transactions* (1919), 126.

73.   Carter, 508.

74.   *Transactions* (1919), 239.

75.   Ibid., 245.

76.   Edwin A. Weinstein, *Woodrow Wilson: A Medical and Psychological Biography* (Princeton: Princeton University Press, 1981), 353.

77.   *Transactions* (1920), 11.

78.   Edward C. Day, "Masonry—Its Opportunity and Its Obligation," *The New Age* 26 (November/December 1918): 485–86.

79.   Dumenil, 141.

80.   Ibid., 143.

81.   Carter, 543–44.

82.   Dumenil, 259–60.

83.   *Fellowship Forum* 13, no.2 (August 1933); *Fellowship Forum* 13, no. 8 (February 1934); *Fellowship Forum* 14, no. 3 (September 1934); see New York Public Library, microform serials, *ZAN-H118.

84.   Richard Hofstadter, *The Age of Reform* (New York: Alfred A. Knopf, 1955), 280.

85.   Ibid., 133.

86.   Dumenil, 129–30.

87.   Ibid., 147.

88.   Hofstadter, *The Age of Reform,* 292.

89.   Thomas A. Bailey, *The American Pageant: A History of the Republic* (Boston: D.C. Heath and Co., 1956), 762.

90.   Carter, 537.

91.   Ibid.

92.   *Transactions* (1921), 41.

93.   After George Moore resigned, he took with him all of his correspondence files and other papers, together with his books. Thus the Archives of the Supreme Council have none of Moore's papers. Luther A. Smith to James C. Jones, former Secretary of the Scottish Rite Bodies, Dallas, Texas, letter, August 13, 1958, Smith Correspondence, TSC, 4-1200.29. Ray Baker Harris noted in his correspondence with Otto Eggers (*op.cit.*) that Moore's papers were never found after his death.

94.   *Transactions* (1921), 146.

95.   Ibid., 158.

96.   The "chain of union," sometimes referred to as "mystic chain," is probably derived from the Royal Arch degree. A circle is formed with participants facing the center, each crossing arms to take the hand of persons on the right and left.

97.   Dumenil, 161–62.

98.   Ibid., 219.

CHAPTER IX

Prosperity to Depression, 1921–1935
John H. Cowles

1.   Lynn Dumenil, *Freemasonry and American Culture, 1880–1930* (Princeton, N.J.: Princeton University Press, 1984), 150.

2.   S. Brent Morris, "Trends Affecting American Freemasonry: A Commentary on Declines in Fraternalism in General, and in the York Rite in Particular" (paper presented to the Maryland Masonic Research Society. Centreville, Md., February 6, 1982), 6.

3. Dumenil, 151.

4. Ibid., 153.

5. James D. Carter, *History of The Supreme Council, 33° (Mother Council of the World), Ancient and Accepted Scottish Rite of Freemasonry, Southern Jurisdiction, U.S.A., 1891–1921* (Washington, D.C.: The Supreme Council, S.J., 1971), 564.

6. Ibid., 332.

7. John H. Cowles to Arthur S. Crites, letter, February 27, 1946, the Supreme Council, Southern Jurisdiction, Archives (hereafter referred to as TSC), 4-1000.73.

8. J. Carter, 573.

9. *Transactions of The Supreme Council, 33° (Mother Council of the World), Ancient and Accepted Scottish Rite of Freemasonry, Southern Jurisdiction, U.S.A.* (hereafter referred to as *Transactions*) (Washington, D.C.: The Supreme Council, S.J., 1922), 34.

10. *Transactions* (1929), 84.

11. *Transactions* (1922), 64.

12. Ibid., 63.

13. Dumenil, 141.

14. *Transactions* (1922), 69.

15. *Transactions* (1923), 99.

16. Ibid., 106–7.

17. *Transactions* (1925), 206.

18. *Transactions* (1923), 223.

19. Ibid.

20. Ibid., 239.

21. Orville Paul Manker to John H. Cowles, letter, October 30, 1923, TSC, 4-1000.5.

22. John H. Cowles to Orville P. Manker, letter, November 6, 1923, TSC, 4-1000.5.

23. Ibid.

24. John H. Cowles to Marvin L. Calhoun, letter, February 6, 1924, TSC, 4-1000.4.

25. Richard K. Tucker, *The Dragon and the Cross: The Rise and Fall of the Ku Klux Klan in Middle America* (Hamden, Conn.: Archon Books, 1991), 101, 126, 155.

26. Shepheard's Tavern at Broad and Church Streets in Charleston, South Carolina, had been in existence since the 1730s. The original building, having withstood disastrous fires and several earthquakes, was demolished in July 1928 to make room for the Citizens and Southern National Bank. Remnants of Shepheard's Tavern, such as mantels, cornices, chair rails, windows, doors, and paneling, were in the possession of the Charleston City Museum until 1995, when the material was sold at auction. See information in *Guides for Historic Charleston* (Charleston, S.C.: City of Charleston, 1975), 92–95. In early 1997, H. Wallace Reid, Grand Minister of State and Sovereign Grand Inspector General in South Carolina, with the assistance of Scottish Rite colleagues Richard A. Wooden and Tommie Epting and the staff of City Museum of Charleston, located the private owner of Shepheard's Tavern's interior, which included the paneling of the room designated for the lodge.

27. *Transactions* (1924), 21–22.

28. *Transactions* (1925), 54.

29. Ibid., 92.

30. Ibid., 121.

31. "Statue of Washington in Cathedral," *The New Age* 73 (February 1965): 42–44.

32. *Transactions* (1925), 226.

33. Ibid., 207.

34. *Transactions* (1926), 34.

35. Ibid., 48.

36. Frederick Lewis Allen, *Only Yesterday* (New York: Bantam Books, 1957), 156. This book, an informal history of the 1920s in the United States, was first published by Harpers Brothers in 1931 and underwent numerous printings before Bantam Books began to publish it in 1946.

37. *Transactions* (1927), 71.

38. Ibid.

39. Ibid.

40. Ibid., 72.

41. Ibid.

42. Ibid., 73.

43. Ibid., 83.

44. *Transactions* (1925), 124–25; *Transactions* (1927), 84; *Transactions* (1929),86–87.

45. *Transactions* (1929), 85.

46. Ibid., 87–88.

47. Ibid., 234.

48. Henry Andrew Francken, *Manuscript Rituals and Regulations,* typescript, 1783, TSC. Francken made several manuscript copies of Morin's Rite, 1771, 1783, and 1786; of these the best copy is the 1783 version in the possession of the Supreme Council, N.M.J. The fourteenth degree ring was a very old design. The ring is mentioned in the 1783 Francken manuscript and probably can be found in the 1771 edition or earlier. It is worn by Scottish Rite Masons of the Northern Masonic Jurisdiction, too.

49. The 1783 Francken manuscript specified, for the fourteenth degree, "a gold ring for every cand[ida]te with this inscription in it. Virtue unites, what death cannot separate," Francken, 143. According to Arturo deHoyos, the earliest ritual giving the Latin phrase *virtus junxit, mors non separabit* (which was also used inside the ring) is that which Albert Mackey gave to Albert Pike, from an edition supposedly dated 1803. The Northern Masonic Jurisdiction used the English motto as late as 1850. DeHoyos points out that a clumsy Latin rendering, *mors non disjungat quid virtus conjungat,* appears in Enoch T. Carter, *Monitor of the Ancient and Accepted Rite* (Cincinnati, Ohio: Applegate & Co., 1858), 63. Arturo deHoyos to William L. Fox, e-mail, June 25, 1996.

50. The black cap is for the thirty-second degree; red cap for Knight Commander of the Court of Honor; white cap for thirty-third degree; white cap with blue band for Grand Cross; white cap with red band for Deputy; violet caps with different embroidery and shading for Sovereign Grand Inspector General and Grand Commander. The Northern Masonic Jurisdiction adopted a different system of caps to distinguish rank and office among its members. Though the black cap is worn by Masters of the Royal Secret in the North, a yellow cap with a cross is used for officers in a chapter of Rose Croix, and a red cap with a gold, double-headed eagle indicates the Masonic Service Award. One other distinguishing feature of the Northern Jurisdiction is the triangular apron. Interestingly, the Cerneauists may also have worn caps.

51. For detailed specifications and descriptions of the caps, see the special pages between 236 and 237 in the *Transactions* (1927).

52. *Transactions* (1927), 241, 243.

53. Elmer Louis Kayser, *Bricks Without Straw: The Evolution of George Washington University* (New York: Appleton-Century-Crofts, 1970), 259.

54. Ibid., 260.

55. *Transactions* (1928), 21. Later in this history, the Supreme Council's endowment of George Washington's School of Government will be discussed further, particularly its program and admissions.

56. Frank C. Jones to John H. Cowles, letter, December 29, 1927 and John H. Cowles to Frank C. Jones, letter, January 3, 1928, TSC, 4-1000.6.

57. *Transactions* (1928), 23.

58. Ray Baker Harris and James D. Carter, *History of The Supreme Council, 33° (Mother Council of the World), Ancient and Accepted Scottish Rite of Freemasonry, Southern Jurisdiction, U.S.A., 1801–1861* (Washington, D.C.: The Supreme Council, S.J., 1964), 2.

59. Ibid., 2–3.

60. *Transactions* (1929), 88.

61. *New York Times* (October 1927) as quoted in Warren I. Susman, *Culture as History: The Transformation of American Society in the Twentieth Century* (New York: Pantheon Books, 1984), 142–43.

62. John H. Cowles to Anti-Third Term League, New York, New York, letter, June 22, 1927, TSC, 4-1000.1.

63. Dumenil, 130.

64. *Transactions* (1927), 76.

65. Ibid., 76.

66. Paul A. Carter, *The Twenties* (New York: Thomas Y. Crowell Company, 1968), 34–40.

67. John Ruskin, as quoted by John H. Cowles (hereafter referred to as JHC) in *Transactions* (1925), 60.

68. *Transactions* (1929), 49.

69. Dumenil, 82.

70. Morris, "Trends Affecting American Freemasonry," 2–3.

71. *Transactions* (1929), 66–67.

72. Ibid., 56.

73. Dumenil, 109.

74. Willa Cather as quoted in Susman, 105.

75. *Transactions* (1929), 56–57.

76. Ibid., 58.

77. JHC to William C. Bond, letter, April 30, 1931, TSC, 4-1000.14. It was also reported that the circulation of *The New Age* had decreased between 1929 and 1931, *Transactions* (1931), 190.

78. Dumenil, 131, 202.

79. Ibid., 218.

80. C. F. Kleinknecht, "Fifty Years of Service," pamphlet (Washington, D.C.: The Supreme Council, S.J., March 25, 1969), 3. During the Depression, Christian F. Kleinknecht did some moonlighting, supplementing his modest salary at the House of the Temple in order to support his family. He obtained a brokerage license and over the years saved the Supreme Council thousands of dollars by donating his commissions on work he did for the council.

81. *Transactions* (1931), 169.

82. JHC to Starks and Company, Midway, Kentucky, September 3, 1930, TSC, 4. 1000.19.

83. *Transactions* (1931), 116.

84. Norris G. Abbott, Sovereign Grand Inspector General in Rhode Island, N.M.J., Providence, Rhode Island, to JHC, March 7, 1928, TSC, 4-1000.18.

85. *Transactions* (1929), 106; *Transactions* (1933), 63.

86. *Transactions* (1931), 84.

87. *Transactions* (1929), 83.

88. Ibid., 84.

89. Ibid., 65; cf., *Transactions* (1927), 89–90.

90. JHC to Reynold E. Blight, letter, December 6, 1928, TSC, 4-1000.14.

91. JHC to Harry E. Gantz, letter, July 24, 1929, TSC, 4-1000.15.

92. *Transactions* (1931), 267.

93. *Transactions* (1933), 58.

94. JHC to Arthur W. Riggs, letter, December 5, 1933, TSC, 4-1000.37; see also, *Transactions* (1935), 27.

95. *Transactions* (1935), 165; *Transactions* (1933), 56–57, 139, 190–91.

96. JHC to Joseph Seinsheimer, letter, November 19, 1935, TSC, 4-1000.37.

97. *Transactions* (1935), 25–26.

98. JHC to William P. Richards, Assessor, Washington, D.C., letter September 26, 1929, TSC, 4-1000.25.

99. JHC to Luther H. Reichelderfer, President, Board of Commissioners, District of Columbia, letter, December 4, 1931, TSC, 4-1000.25.

100. *Transactions* (1935), 215.

101. JHC to C. M. Goethe, Paris, France, letter, June 29, 1929, TSC, 4-1000.25.

102. *Transactions* (1929), 181; *Transactions* (1933), 142.

103. JHC to Otto A. Reisinger, letter, March 31, 1932, TSC, 4-1000.25.

104. *Transactions* (1931), 218.

105. *Transactions* (1931), 220. The Coolidge Collection of Dickens was removed from the library about 1952; its disposition is unknown.

106. *Transactions* (1929), 183; see also, JHC to F. C. Linde Co., Inc., New York City, letter, February 12, 1934, TSC, 4-1000.29; *Transactions* (1937), 181.

107. *Transactions* (1930), 25–27.

108. *Transactions* (1931), 112, 215; *Transactions* (1933), 132.

109. *Transactions* (1947), 81; JHC to Walter L. Stockwell, letter, February 19, 1948, TSC, 4-1000.87.

110. *Transactions* (1947), 83–84.

111. Arthur Mather to JHC, letter, May 19, 1941, TSC, 4-1000.52.

112. JHC to Senator Henry J. Allen, letter, December 21, 1929, TSC, 4-1000.14; *Transactions* (1931), 79, 101.

113. Charles H. Mayo, M.D., Rochester, Minnesota, to JHC, November 4, 1935, TSC, 4-1000.35.

114. *Transactions* (1933), 104.

115. *Transactions* (1929), 69; *Transactions* (1933), 201; *Transactions* (1935), 31; cf., JHC to Congressman J. J. Mansfield, letter, January 16, 1925, TSC, 4-1000.5. Cowles tried to dissuade Mansfield from his opposition to the Sterling-Reed Bill to establish a Department of Education and a funding program for public schools.

116. *Transactions* (1931), 90, 91, 93; JHC to W. B. Pettis, Peking, China, letter, November 26, 1928, TSC, 4-1000.14.

117. *Transactions* (1935), 32.

118. Pamela Archer, "Scottish Rite Dormitory," *The New Age* 97 (June 1989): 53–57.

119. Dumenil, 141.

120. JHC to Col. R. L. Queiaser, National Sojourners, August 30, 1935, letter, TSC, 4-1000.30. Later, however, Cowles encouraged and applauded the work of National Sojourners, especially during World War II.

121. *Transactions* (1927), 76; the Reverend Leo H. Lehmann, D.D., Christ Church Mission, to JHC, letter, September 7, 1933, TSC, 4-1000.24.

122. *Transactions* (1925), 62, 122; *Transactions* (1929), 55; *Transactions* (1935), 30–31.

123. *Transactions* (1931), 72–73.

124. *Transactions* (1935), 39.

125. *Transactions* (1931), 134; *Transactions* (1933), 39.

126. *Transactions* (1929), 149, 129.

127. JHC to W. W. Carpenter, letter, December 28, 1932, TSC, 4-1000.22 The support Hitler received from some Masons at the beginning was probably tied to commonly held anti-Communist sympathies as much as anything else, though the Christian lodges likely would not have stood against restrictions imposed on Jews.

128. *Transactions* (1935), 110; Jacob Katz, *Jews and Freemasons in Europe, 1723–1939* (Cambridge, Mass.: Harvard University Press 1970) 188.

129. *Transactions* (1935), 110.

130. *Transactions* (1933), 44.

CHAPTER X

Steel Helmets and Iron Curtains, 1936–1952

Later Years of John H. Cowles

1. William E. Leuchtenberg, *Franklin Roosevelt and the New Deal, 1932–1940* (New York: Harper and Row, 1963), 172.

2. Raymond Moley, *After Seven Years* (1939) as quoted in Leuchtenberg, 168.

3. Ibid., 169.

4. *Transactions of The Supreme Council, 33° (Mother Council of the World), Ancient and Accepted Scottish Rite of Freemasonry, Southern Jurisdiction, U.S.A.* (hereafter referred to as *Transactions*) (Washington, D.C.: The Supreme Council, S.J., 1939), 28; *Transactions* (1941), 51.

5. *Transactions* (1937), 41.

6. Lynn Dumenil, *Freemasonry and American Culture, 1880–1930* (Princeton, N.J.: Princeton University Press, 1984), 225. The membership figures for Scottish Rite Masons in the Southern Jurisdiction reflect exactly the national trend for blue lodge membership. In 1930 the Southern Jurisdiction had an all-time high of 253,898; by 1935 the dip was noticeable, 177,763, nearly a 30 percent decrease; and by 1940 the Scottish Rite hit bottom (in terms of 20th-century figures, starting after 1920), listing 156,844 members. The losses in the 1930s were considerably less in the Northern Jurisdiction; cf., Bobby J. Demott, *Freemasonry in American Culture and Society* (Lanham, Md.: University Press of America, 1986), 46.

7. Leuchtenberg, 132.

8. *Transactions* (1939), 38.

9. John H. Cowles (hereafter referred to as JHC) to General Amos A. Fries, President, National Sojourners, Washington, D.C., letter, October 13, 1936, the Supreme Council, Southern Jurisdiction, Archives (hereafter referred to as TSC), 4-1000.34.

10. Ibid.

11. *Transactions* (1939), 37–39; *Transactions* (1941), 38–40.

12. T. Mooney, Deputy Commissioner, Office of the Commissioner of Internal Revenue, to JHC, letter, September 9, 1940, in *Transactions* (1941), 165–68.

13. Christian F. Kleinknecht, "Fifty Years of Service," pamphlet (Washington, D.C.: The Supreme Council, S.J., March 25, 1969), 3–4.

14. Dashiell Hammett, *The Maltese Falcon* (1930; reprint, New York: Dell, 1966), 188–89 (page citations are from reprint edition).

15. Warren I. Susman, *Culture as History: The Transformation of American Society in the Twentieth Century* (New York: Pantheon Books, 1984), 172.

16. *Transactions* (1937), 61–62.

17. Ibid., 58, 96, 161.

18. Ibid., 96.

19. JHC to Will H. Hays, letter, September 22, 1937, TSC, 4-1000.4. There is no record in the same file of how Hays responded, if he did at all.

20. Leo H. Lehman to JHC, letter, February 4, 1941; and JHC to Leo H. Lehman, letter February 7, 1941, TSC, 4-1000.48, file C (2).

21. John H. Cowles, "Revelations," *The New Age* 45(August 1937): 452.

22. *Transactions* (1951), 233–34; cf., *Transactions* (1943), 40: 35,000 miles traveled between 1941 and 1943, of which 27,000 miles were by rail, 4,500 miles by automobile, and 3,100 mile by airplane.

23. *Transactions* (1937), 30

24. *Transactions* (1937), 119, 125; *Transactions* (1939), 96.

25. *Transactions* (1939),47; *Transactions* (1943), 101.

26. *Transactions* (1943) 127, 244; *Transactions* (1945), 81. Cowles "contributed personally to several of the Masonic charities in England" as it was, to him, his duty to do so because of his memberships in British Lodges. He also contributed to the aid of Ethiopia through British sources. See *Transactions* (1941), 106–7.

27. *Transactions* (1943), 106–7.

28. *Transactions* (1937), 41, 121–22.

29. *Transactions* (1939), 95; *Transactions* (1941), 131.

30. *Transactions* (1939), 95; *Transactions* (1941), 134–35.

31. *Transactions* (1943), 47, 129. Cowles later stated that Anastasio Somoza had "a great record as President," adding that Somoza had actually vetoed a measure that would have guaranteed his reelection—"an example of patriotism worthy of following." Cowles may have been deliberately window-dressing Somoza's qualifications, for it was well know that Somoza, though a Mason, was one of the worst Central American dictators. See *Transactions* (1945), 64.

32. *Transactions* (1949), 122–23; cf., *Transactions* (1947), 178.

33. *Transactions* (1937),124.

34. *Transactions* (1939), 54.

35. *Transactions* (1937), 70, 117, 127–28; *Transactions* (1939), 77.

36. Jacob Katz, *Jews and Freemasons in Europe, 1723–1939* (Cambridge, Mass.: Harvard University Press, 1970), 192. See also, Ronald Modras, *The Catholic Church and Antisemitism in Poland, 1933–1939,* Series in Jewish Studies (Buffalo, N.Y.: Harwood Academic Publishers, 1994), which deals with "the myth of a Masonic Jewish alliance to subvert Christianity as it spread to Poland."

37. Katz, 162–64.

38. Ibid., 191.

39. *Transactions* (1937), 98. Dr. Otto Arenemann, Deputy Grand Master of the Grand Lodge in Hamburg, wrote Cowles on April 25, 1948, that in 1930 the Supreme Council of Germany had been authorized and brought

into being under the joint auspices of the Supreme Councils of the Netherlands and Switzerland. Then when Hitler assumed control, it, along with all other Masonic bodies, had to cease. Cowles seemed surprised and held doubts about the legality of the Supreme Council in Germany; cf., *Transactions* (1949), 105–6. Supposedly, the Supreme Council of Germany had Dr. Johannes Bing as its first Grand Commander, but as soon as there was opposition in the thirties Bing dropped out. He was followed by Leopold Müffelmann, who then moved the Supreme Council to Palestine; *Transactions* (1951), 98–100.

40. *Transactions* (1943), 146.

41. Alain Bernheim, Gottmadingen, Germany, to William L. Fox Jr., e-mail, March 5, 1997. Bernheim points out that Müffelmann, Koner, and Bensch were arrested solely because they were Masons. None of them were Jewish. Their bravery stands out in light of later developments whereby the newly accessible Nazi Party membership records held in the Bundesarchiv Aussenstelle Berlin-Zehlendorf list names of men who after World War II became involved with the Scottish Rite in Germany. Although the correspondence of John H. Cowles with German Masons from 1932 to 1947 cannot be found (memo to file by Aemil Pouler, November 17, 1982. Leo Müffelmann folder, TSC, 2-108.3), the later German perspective gave Cowles credit for helping Müffelmann, Koner, and Bensch: "Their release was the result of an initiative of Grand Commander Cowles." Jurgen Fitzenreiter, Grand Secretary General, Supreme Council of Germany, to C. Fred Kleinknecht Jr., letter, May 7, 1982, TSC, 2-108.3. See *Transactions* (1931), 142–45; *Transactions* (1935), 108–11; "Müffelmann Dead," *The New Age* 43 (February 1935): 122. According to Alain Bernheim, Leo Müffelmann kept a diary in 1934 and was writing it when he died. The Müffelmann Diary surfaced many years after World War II, and from Bernheim's typescript and translation there is strong evidence that Cowles was instrumental in getting members of the German Supreme Council released from a German concentration camp. During an interrogation in early February 1934 by Bandow, a Gestapo official, Cowles's name came up. "Then Bandow asked who, in fact, was Cowles. Whether he played a part in Freemasonry. A letter was said to have come to the Fuhrer from a government outside Germany, including questions about persecution of Freemasonry in Germany, in which information was requested about the imprisonment of Dr. Müffelmann, Bensch, and Dr. Koner in a concentration camp. From the declarations of Bandow we could only draw the conclusion that the letter to Hitler came from Cowles." Alain Bernheim to William L. Fox Jr., e-mail, March 13, 1997. See Alain Bernheim, "German Free-masonry and its Attitudes Toward the Nazi Regime," *The Philalethes* 60, no. 1 (February 1997): 18–22.

42. *Transactions* (1943), 104.

43. Ibid., 115; cf., Henry Wilson Coil, *Coil's Masonic Encyclopedia* (New York: Macoy Publishing, 1961), 61. Cowles reported from a newspaper dispatch in Switzerland that Seyss-Inquart, Reich's commissioner in Holland, not only closed the Masonic lodges, "but confiscated their funds, amounting approximately to $795,000 and also Masonic jewels, from which the gems were removed and the metal and the jewels sold"; *Transactions* (1941), 120–21. See also, "Freemasonry and the Nurnberg Trials: A Study in Nazi Persecution," *Transactions of the Missouri Lodge of Research* 16 (1959): pt. 2, 11. Of further note, Hermannus van Tongeren's family became active in the Dutch resistance.

44. *Transactions* (1943), 140.

45. Business Manager of *The New Age* to The American News Company, unsigned letter, September 3, 1938, TSC, 4-1000.40.

46. *Transactions* (1939), 64; *Transactions* (1941), 77.

47. *Transactions* (1939), 47–48.

48. JHC to American Security & Trust Co., Washington, D.C., letter, May 13, 1941, TSC, 4-1000.47.

49. *Transactions* (1939), 47–48; *Transactions* (1941), 112, 208; *Transactions* (1943), 49.

50. *Transactions* (1939), 114–15; JHC to Mrs. Carl A. Bloesing, letter, May 23, 1941, TSC, 4-1000.47.

51. *Transactions* (1945), 56–57.

52. *Transactions* (1941), 61, 130.

53. *Transactions* (1945), 222–23.

54. Ibid., 235.

55. *Transactions* (1947), 104, 142, 165; *Transactions* (1951), 78, 102, 117, 128.

56. The Swedish Rite (practiced in the Masonic Hall in Oslo) is divided into three bodies of degrees: St. John's Lodge, first through third degrees; St. Andrew's Lodge, fourth through sixth degrees; and the Chapter, seventh through twelfth degrees. This designation is somewhat parallel to a Lodge of Perfection or Council of

Kadosh in the American Scottish Rite. Cf., Sverre Dag Mogstad, *Frimurei Mysterier Fellesskap Personlighets-dannelse* (Oslo: Universitets Forlaget, 1994), 40.

57. *Transactions* (1947), 163–64; *Transactions* (1951), 110.

58. *Transactions* (1941), 247.

59. *Transactions* (1943), 17–18.

60. David McCullough, *Truman* (New York: Simon & Schuster, 1992), 257–58.

61. Harry S. Truman to JHC, letter, October 11, 1941, TSC, 4-1000.56.

62. *Transactions* (1943), 22–23, 220–21. The Supreme Council's contribution to the American Red Cross and U.S.O. in 1943 was $10,000 each; *Transactions* (1945),30; cf., JHC to Richard Priest Dietzman, letter, January 18, 1943, TSC, 4-1000.59.

63. JHC to W. D. Barnard, letter, December 28, 1943, TSC, 4-1000.65.

64. *Transactions* (1943), 30; *Transactions* (1945), 44; JHC to H. J. Nelson, letter, April 11, 1945, TSC, N.4-1000.69; *Transactions* (1941), 170; *Transactions* (1945), 33, 131–32.

65. *Transactions* (1945), 34, 115.

66. JHC to Senator Pat McCarran, Chairman, Committee on the District of Columbia, letter, June 5, 1943, TSC, 4-1000.62.

67. Gertrude M. McNally, Secretary-Treasurer, National Federation of Federal Employees, to JHC, letter, August 9, 1943, TSC, 4-1000.62.

68. Of Pike's ten children only three survived him. During his Arkansas years he was not especially close to them because he was away much of the time riding the circuit in his law practice. It was also a depressed home environment made sad by the loss of so many children and a mentally ill wife. Pike was perhaps closest to his daughter Isadore who died in 1869 at the age of 27. After that, there just was not much of a family line to which Pike could hand down his enthusiasm for the fraternity.

69. *Transactions* (1945), 20–21, 24; JHC to Albert Pike, letter, December 12, 1944; and Albert Pike to JHC, December 27, 1944, TSC, 4-1000.70.

70. *Transactions* (1941), 48; *Transactions* (1947), 76; *Washington Post* (February 24, 1947). Cowles earlier in the year admitted he had been dragged to a service at the Washington Cathedral by visiting English Masons, saying, "it has been some time since I attended a church in Washington. Still I am not a heathen, but I have to do so much preaching myself that I am not particularly interested in hearing others." *Transactions* (1947), 138.

71. *Transactions* (1943), 25, 157.

72. Melvin M. Johnson to JHC, letter, October 3, 1943, "Personal & confidential," TSC, 4-vlt-3.

73. JHC to T. E. Doss, Grand Secretary, Grand Lodge of Tennessee, letter, September 2, 1948, TSC, 4-1000.81.

74. *Transactions* (1945), 224–27, 231; cf., John H. Cowles, "Melvin M. Johnson, Past Grand Master of Massachusetts and S.G.C. of The Supreme Council for the Northern Masonic Jurisdiction," July 16, 1946, 19 pages, TSC, 4-vlt-3.

75. *Transactions* (1945), 174.

76. Ibid., 216–19.

77. JHC to Henry P. Barrett, letter, October 22, 1945; and JHC to Judge Bryne E. Bigger, letter, October 23, 1945, TSC, 4-1000.65.

78. Cowles, "Melvin Johnson," 17.

79. *Transactions* (1947), 57, 256; *Transactions* (1951), 43–45, 57–59.

80. L. P. Blakemore to JHC, letter, January 30, 1950, TSC, 4-1000.94.

81. W. B. Pettis (California College in China), Berkeley, California, to JHC, letter, October 17, 1944, TSC, 4-1000.70.

82. *Transactions* (1947), 71. Cowles resigned from the George Washington University Board of Trustees on November 22, 1949, in order to reduce his commitments. *Transactions* (1951), 74.

83. *Transactions* (1949), 103–4; *Transactions* (1951), 97.

84. *Transactions* (1947), 296.

85. Ibid., 26.

86. *Transactions* (1945), 38–39, 205.

87. Harry S. Truman, as quoted by David McCullough, *op. cit.*, 588.

88. *Transactions* (1949), 65–66.

89. It is highly probable that Pike gave a set of rituals to his Prince Hall counterpart. In a 1945 letter from the United Supreme Council's Grand Commander, Willard W. Allen, detailing the presumed source of the Prince Hall ritual, some light is shed: "Ill. Thornton A. Jackson was Sovereign Grand Commander of our Jurisdiction from September 14, 1887 until his death on October 18, 1904. Much of this time he was engaged in business in the City of Washington and came to know General Albert Pike intimately and was his personal friend. He frequently went to General Pike with his Masonic problems. On one occasion he mentioned to General Pike how seriously handicapped his organizations were for lack of adequate rituals. Thereupon General Pike gave him a complete set of Scottish Rite rituals. It has been generally stated and assumed that some or all of these books were autographed." See Willard W. Allen to George W. Crawford, letter, January 16, 1945, Archives, Philadelphia, Pennsylvania, Cathedral, United Supreme Council (PHA). Photocopy of original in possession of author. In a careful analysis, comparing philological precision in the PHA *Book of the Scottish Rite* with Albert Pike's *Magnum Opus,* Arturo deHoyos has concluded that a majority of the PHA material is either derived from or is essentially the same as Pike's ritual. Cf. Arturo deHoyos, "On the Origins of the PHA Scottish Rite Rituals," (unpublished paper, August 1996), 10 pages.

90. A statement credited to Albert Pike and written by him on September 13, 1875, to the Grand Secretary of Ohio, turns Cowles's suppositions upside down: "Prince Hall was as regular a lodge as any Lodge created by a competent authority; and had a perfect right (as other Lodges in Europe did) to establish other Lodges, making itself a mother Lodge. That's the way the Berlin Lodges, Three Globes and Royal York became Grand Lodges." From Albert C. Stevens, ed., *Cyclopedia of Fraternities* (New York: E.B. Treat and Co., 1907), 73.

91. *Transactions* (1947), 86–92.

92. *Transactions* (1949), 35, 63–77; JHC to T. E. Doss, letter, March 7, 1949, TSC, 4-1000.81; *Transactions* (1951), 69–70.

93. JHC to Charl Ormond Williams, letter, March 7, 1949, TSC, 4-1000.88; *Transactions* (1951), 69–70.

94. Glenn L. Archer and Albert J. Menendez, *The Dream Lives On: The Story of Glenn L. Archer and Americans United* (Washington, D.C., and New York: Robert B. Luce, Inc., 1982), 69.

95. Ibid., 73–74, 137.

96. Charl Ormond Williams (NEA) to JHC, letter, March 1, 1949, TSC, 4-1000.88.

97. *Transactions* (1951), 183–87.

98. *Transactions* (1953), 32; *Transactions* (1955), 106.

99. *Transactions* (1941), 80; *Transactions* (1947), 309.

100. *Transactions* (1952–1953), 4–5.

101. *Transactions* (1955), 22–23.

102. *Transactions* (1939), 101.

CHAPTER XI

Stretched Nerves, 1950s

Harkins and Smith

1. Will Herberg, *Protestant, Catholic, Jew* (Garden City, N.Y.: Doubleday & Co., 1955), 88–90.

2. Ibid., 97.

3. Sydney E. Ahlstrom, *A Religious History of the American People* (New Haven and London: Yale University Press, 1972), 1033.

4. Ibid., 956.

5. *Transactions of The Supreme Council, 33° (Mother Council of the World), Ancient and Accepted Scottish Rite of Freemasonry, Southern Jurisdiction, U.S.A.* (hereafter referred to as *Transactions*) (Washington, D.C.: The Supreme Council, S.J., 1953), 42, 107.

6. C. Fred Kleinknecht Jr. (hereafter referred to as CFK), interview with William L. Fox Jr. (hereafter referred to as WLF Jr.), May 31, 1994.

7. *Transactions* (1969), 266.

8. Ibid., 322–23.

9.   Paul A. Carter, *Another Part of the Fifties* (New York: Columbia University Press, 1983), 6–9.

10. Ibid., 9, 14.

11. Ibid., 15.

12. *Transactions* (1969), 265–66.

13. Ibid., 323–24.

14. Ibid., 267.

15. CFK, interview with WLF Jr., May 31, 1994.

16. "Address by Thomas J. Harkins, 33rd Degree, Sovereign Grand Inspector General in North Carolina," *The New Age* 60 (November 1952): 649.

17. Ibid., 646–48.

18. *Transactions* (1953), 99–100.

19. *Transactions* (1955), 113.

20. *Transactions* (1952 and 1953), 220.

21. *Transactions* (1953), 130.

22. *Transactions* (1955), 36, 201.

23. *Transactions* (1952 and 1953), 199; *Transactions* (1955), 59.

24. *Transactions* (1953), 105.

25. *Transactions* (1955), 235.

26. *Transactions* (1953), 36–37.

27. *Transactions* (1953), 127; *Transactions* (1952 and 1953), 203–4; air-conditioning data in the *Washington Post,* June 16, 1994.

28. *Transactions* (1953), 172.

29. Transcribed by WLF Jr. from original in the Supreme Council, Southern Jurisdiction, Archives (hereafter referred to as TSC).

30. Cf. *Transactions* (1957), 309; transcribed by WLF Jr. from the original in TSC. Curiously, knowledge of the existence of these two George Washington letters had been forgotten since the fifties, or perhaps since Roy Baker Harris's death in 1963. Miraculously, they survived in a subbasement room not only lacking security and proper archival climate control but which had suffered water and mildew damage. Prompted by my inquiry and then, after some staff surprise, by my insistence that such documents presumably were stored at the House of the Temple, they were located. Consulting an appraiser on the value of these documents revealed each letter was probably worth around $26,000 as of 1994.

31. *Transactions* (1955), 133.

32. Ibid., 57–58.

33. Ibid., 39, 89.

34. Ibid., 60, 69, 101.

35. Ibid., 72–73.

36. Thomas J. Harkins to Rev. Robert W. Anthony, letter, July 28, 1954, TSC, 4-1100.11.

37. *Transactions* (1953), 178–79.

38. *Transactions* (1955), 33–34, 203–4, 246–7.

39. Ibid., 223, 226.

40. *Transactions* (1952 and 1953), 176; *Transactions* (1979), 27; *Transactions* (1955), 140.

41. *Transactions* (1955), 57; *Transactions* (1953), 182; *Transactions* (1955), 233–34.

42. "Grand Commander Harkins Retires" (two page statement), issued by Luther A. Smith, TSC, 4-1200.40; *Transactions* (1955), 241.

43. CFK, interview with WLF Jr., May 31, 1994.

44. *Transactions* (1968), 320.

45. P. Carter, 46–47.

46. Smith biographical background from Smith Correspondence, 1957–1959, TSC, 4-1200.24.

47. *Transactions* (1957), 77, 79, 83, 89, 92; *Transactions* (1959), 128.

48. *Transactions* (1957), 71–72.

49. Ibid., 30–31, 249–50; CFK, interview with William L. Fox Sr., June 27, 1989.

50. Luther A. Smith (hereafter referred to as LAS) to T. R. Brecto, letter, February 15, 1960, TSC, 4-1200.48.

51. *Transactions* (1957), 32; *Transactions* (1959), 38–40, 309.

52. LAS to C. H. Goethe, letter, November 4, 1958, TSC, 4-1200,27; LAS, rough draft: memo ref. Masonic News Center Report, TSC, 4-1200.32; Minutes of conference meeting of Masonic leaders, Washington, D.C., 3 P.M., February 22, 1959, TSC, 4-1200.32; *Transactions* (1959), 66; LAS to Homer Chamberlain, letter, March 9, 1961, TSC, 4-1200.50.

53. *Transactions* (1959), 36, 259, 284–85; Norman S. Meese to LAS, memorandum, June 6, 1958, TSC, 4-1200.35.

54. *Transactions* (1959), 122, 131–32, 138.

55. Ibid., 143, 145–47, 282.

56. Ibid., 151–52; see also "People to People," October Activities Report, Office of Private Cooperation, United States Information Agency, Washington, D.C., November 5, 1958 (copy in TSC, 4-1200.35).

57. Ibid., 81.

58. *Humanum Genus,* April 7, 1884, papal encyclical of Leo XIII, from the appendix in John J. Robinson, *Born in Blood: The Lost Secrets of Freemasonry* (New York: M. Evans & Co., 1989), 349, 356, 358.

59. Winthrop Hudson, *American Protestantism* (Chicago: University of Chicago Press, 1961), 130–34.

60. *Transactions* (1957), 69–70; *Transactions* (1959), 76, 79.

61. LAS to Charles E. Sampson, Mayor, Greenwood, Mississippi, letter, February 28, 1958, TSC, 4-1200.37; cf. Paul Blanshard to LAS, letter, August 29, 1958, TSC, 4-1200.21.

62. LAS to Emmett McLoughlin, letter, January 4, 1961, TSC, 4-1200.60.

63. *Transactions* (1959), 73–74.

64. Virgil M. Rogers, Dean, School of Education, Syracuse University, to LAS, letter, April 22, 1957, TSC, 4-1200.36.

65. *Transactions* (1957), 281.

66. *Transactions* (1957), 43–49; William R. Odell, Stanford University, to Henry C. Clausen, letter, November 11, 1957, TSC, 4-1200.34; *Transactions* (1959), 50–51.

67. *Transactions* (1959), 32, 56, 63–64, 69.

68. Robert C. Byrd to LAS, letter, July 30, 1958, re: National Defense Education Act of 1958, TSC, 4-1200.24.

69. LAS to L. M. Brings, T. S. Denison (Publishing) Co., letter, April 4, 1958, TSC, 4-1200.21.

CHAPTER XII

The Moon Above, Perplexity Below, 1959–1969

Luther A. Smith

1. *Transactions of The Supreme Council, 33° (Mother Council of the World), Ancient and Accepted Scottish Rite of Freemasonry, Southern Jurisdiction, U.S.A.* (hereafter referred to as *Transactions*) (Washington, D.C.: The Supreme Council, S.J., 1961), 122; Luther A. Smith (hereafter referred to as LAS) to Clarence C. Buchanan, letter, March 10, 1960, the Supreme Council, Southern Jurisdiction, Archives (hereafter referred to as TSC), 4-1200.48; LAS to Richard H. Amberg, letter, February 29, 1960, TSC, 4-1200.46.

2. LAS to Governor J. P. Colman, Jackson, Mississippi, letter, October 21, 1958, TSC, 4-1200.23.

3. "The 1976 Elections," *Church and State* 29 (December 1976): 4.

4. LAS to Ernest N. Clark, letter, July 26, 1960, TSC, 4-1200.23.

5. Allen J. Matusow, *The Unraveling of America: A History of Liberalism in the 1960s* (New York: Harper & Row, 1984), 16–17.

6. LAS to Ernest N. Clark, letter, July 26, 1960, TSC, 4-1200.23.

7. LAS to Henry W. Coil, letter, April 30, 1960, TSC, 4-1200.51.

8. LAS to C. N. Hanna, letter, September 19, 1960, TSC, 4-1200.55.

9. Luther A. Smith, "The Grand Commander's Message," *The New Age* 68 (November 1960): 3–4.

10. *New York Times,* September 13, 1960, 22.

11. LAS to Lester Haile, letter, October 18, 1960, TSC, 4-1200.55.

12. James A. Pike, *A Roman Catholic in the White House* (Garden City, N.Y.: Doubleday & Co., 1960), 130–33.

13. George E. Bushnell, Allocution, Northern Masonic Jurisdiction, *Newsletter* 19, no. 2 (November 1960): 2.

14. R. E. Driscoll to *The New Age,* letter, October 6, 1960, TSC, 4-1200.52.

15. M. Frisberg to LAS, letter, October 27, 1960, TSC, 4-1200.53.

16. Leo D. Branstetter to *The New Age,* letter, October 29, 1960, TSC, 4-1200.48.

17. E. H. Trandum to LAS, letter, November 3, 1960, TSC, 1200.69.

18. LAS to E. H. Trandum, letter, November 17, 1960, TSC, 4-1200.69.

19. LAS to Phillip Corrin, letter, December 28, 1960, TSC, 4-1200.51. Smith's implicit analogy, comparing the United States to Iberian and Latin American experience, however, fails to note the critically different determinants among countries, such as racial and ethnic diversity, geography, democratic origins, and the influence of the British Enlightenment. America, simply, began from different premises and was one of the unlikeliest places to be a pawn of a foreign power. Smith carried his impassioned first principles to a state of overreaction.

20. LAS, memorandum regarding conference held February 24, 1961, with Grand Commander George E. Bushnell, NMJ, and Lieutenant Grand Commander George Newbury, NMJ, TSC, 4-1200.51.

21. Matusow, 27.

22. Ibid., 28.

23. Luther A. Smith, *The New Age* 69 (March 1961): 4–5; Smith quoted Kennedy from remarks he made in 1950, and while it might have been the case that he was employing some self-serving name-dropping in the editorial, he was also making a gesture of burying the hatchet.

24. *Transactions* (1961), 68; *Transactions* (1965), 109–10.

25. Sydney E. Ahlstrom, *A Religious History of the American People* (New Haven: Yale University Press, 1972), 1079.

26. *Transactions* (1961), 24–25, 290.

27. *Transactions* (1957), 234; (1959), 232; (1961), 237; (1963), 28; (1965), 32; (1967), 193; (1969), 186. Lodges of Perfection statistics generally showed the lowest net gain over this period when compared with chapters of Rose Croix, councils of Kadosh, and consistories. As of the 1967 session there were 26 Active Members, 17 Deputies, 4 Grand Crosses, 10 Emeriti Members of Honor, 3,135 thirty-third degree Inspectors General, and 7,628 Knights Commander of the Court of Honor.

28. *Transactions* (1979), 55.

29. *Transactions* (1959), 46.

30. *Transactions* (1965), 304–5.

31. Ibid., 37.

32. LAS to Active Members and Deputies of the Supreme Council, memo, February 15, 1956, TSC, 4-1200.

33. *Transactions* (1957), 28–29.

34. *Transactions* (1963), 159. Apparently, the ph factor in the water was not suitable for growing grass. Also of note, without the two sump pumps running continuously to fill a ten-foot-deep cistern, the basement of the House of the Temple would easily flood. A power outage, for instance, of not more than five hours will leave a foot of water in the basement, according to Russell Stogsdill, temple superintendent (as told to William L. Fox Jr., July 15, 1994).

35. *Transactions* (1969), 204.

36. *Washington Post,* Potomac (Sunday Magazine), October 15, 1961, 14.

37. *Transactions* (1961), 253.

38. *Transactions* (1963), 93, 256.

39. Ibid., 45.

40. *Transactions* (1961), 33, 256. For the best discussion of cornerstone customs see the superb book by S. Brent Morris, *Cornerstones of Freedom: A Masonic Tradition* (Washington, D.C.: The Supreme Council, S.J., 1993).

41. *Transactions* (1965), 64–66; James D. Carter to Henry C. Clausen, letter, March 3, 1972, TSC, B-200.5.

42. *Transactions* (1969), 108–9.

43. Ibid., 112–13.

44. *Transactions* (1965), 71.

45. *Transactions* (1963), 162; *Transactions* (1965), 275; *Transactions* (1967), 271.

46. *Transactions* (1965), 63, 68; *Transactions* (1967), 50; *Transactions* (1969), 93–94.

47. *Transactions* (1959), 295.

48. The Supreme Council, "Status of Budget Allotment," as of June 30, 1961, Luther A. Smith papers, TSC.

49. *Transactions* (1965), 82–83; the dollar amounts, unless otherwise stated, are biennial totals. Also of particular irony is the Scottish Rite support of a Southern Baptist seminary in New Orleans, because twenty-five years later a marginal but energetic faction of the Southern Baptist Convention became one of the leading sources of Anti-Masonry in the United States. Traditionally, the strong views on the separation of church and state shared by the Scottish Rite, Southern Jurisdiction and Southern Baptists have formed a united front between them. By the 1990s, fissures were created when from within Southern Baptist ranks fundamentalist misunderstandings and distortions about Masonry as a "religion" were spread. In June 1993, the Southern Baptist Convention officially adopted a policy that neither condemned nor endorsed the fraternity, leaving one's Masonic affiliation a matter of personal conscience for each individual Baptist.

50. Cloyd H. Marvin, "The Scottish Rite Fellowships and Their Significance," *The New Age* 65 (October 1957): 587.

51. *Transactions* (1961), 54, 262–69; *Transactions* (1963), 128–29.

52. *Transactions* (1961), 55–56; *Transactions* (1967), 76; *Transactions* (1969), 121.

53. *Transactions* (1961), 128.

54. *Transactions* (1965), 77. In 1966 the School of Government, for several reasons, including providing greater specialization and closer cooperation with various departments and bureaus of the federal government, was divided into two schools: the School of Public and International Affairs and the School of Government and Business Administration. Among modern presidents of George Washington University who have been Scottish Rite Masons are Cloyd H. Marvin, Lloyd Elliott, and Stephen Joel Trachtenberg. The founders of George Washington University, including the early leader, Luther Rice, were also Masons. Cf. Elmer Louis Kayser, *Bricks Without Straw: The Evolution of George Washington University* (New York: Appleton-Century-Crofts, Educational Division, 1970), 243, 259–61.

55. *Transactions* (1965), 270; *Transactions* (1967), 50.

56. *Transactions* (1961), 146; *Transactions* (1959), 101; *Transactions* (1961), 65, 99–101, 130–33, 138, 175.

57. *Transactions* (1957), 108; *Transactions* (1959), 118; *Transactions* (1961), 118.

58. LAS to Congressman Otto E. Passman, letter, September 10, 1959, TSC, 4-1200.35.

59. *Transactions* (1959), 229.

60. *Transactions* (1961), 84.

61. *Transactions* (1963), 106–7.

62. *Transactions* (1969), 148–49; LAS to all Regular Supreme Councils, 33°, of the World, memo, December 27, 1967, TSC, B-2013.

63. Margaret C. Jacob, *Living the Enlightenment: Freemasonry and Politics in Eighteenth-Century Europe* (New York: Oxford University Press, 1991), 94.

64. *Transactions* (1965) 112, 125, 160, 163–64.

65. Stephen E. Ambrose, *Eisenhower: Soldier and President* (New York: Touchstone, 1991), 542–43.

66. LAS to Sen. James O. Eastland, letter, March 29, 1960, TSC, 4-1200.53.

67. *Transactions* (1965), 207, 212.

68. T. F. McLean, U.S. Army, to the Editor, *The New Age*, letter, March 11, 1960, TSC, 4-1200.60.

69. Norman S. Meese, Editor, *The New Age*, to T. F. McLean, letter, March 21, 1960, TSC, 4-1200.60.

70. Put differently, the logic Meese represents, if transferred to ecclesiastical polity, would raise the possibility that since the Methodist-Episcopal Church was organized by white men and women, the African Methodist-Episcopal (AME) Church, organized by former slaves, was not eligible for membership in any council of churches because there can be only one church body calling itself Methodist-Episcopal.

71. Cf. *Ancient and Accepted Scottish Rite of Freemasonry, the constitutions and regulations of 1762 . . . with the statutes of 1859, 1866, 1868, 1870, and 1872, of the Supreme Council of the 33d degree for the Southern Jurisdiction of the United States,* compiled by Albert Pike (New York: Masonic Publishing Company, 1872; new edition, J. J. Little & Co., 1904). Revisions of the *Statutes* occurred in 1878, 1884, 1897, 1905, and 1929. In no instance was a restrictive racial qualification for membership ever inserted. But also there was never any challenge to the existing reality of racial homogeneity which might have otherwise necessitated a statutory prohibition against black membership in the Scottish Rite. The dual fact that the Grand Lodges often had official restrictive policies and that the Grand Lodges served as gatekeepers to the Scottish Rite meant that even though blacks could join the Scottish Rite they had no means to qualify Masonically.

72. LAS to Edward R. Cusick, letter, March 13, 1962, TSC, 4-1200.78.

73. *Transactions* (1969), 3, 175, 180–81.

74. *Transactions* (1967), 4.

75. Henry C. Clausen, San Francisco, California, to William L. Fox Sr., letter, September 14, 1989.

76. *Transactions* (1975), 86, 158–59, 217–19.

77. *Transactions* (1963), 273–74.

78. *Transactions* (1969), 284.

79. Edwin E. Aldrin Jr., NASA, Houston, Texas, to LAS, letter, September 16, 1969, TSC, 4-1200.47.

CHAPTER XIII

When the Waves Went High, 1969–1985
Henry C. Clausen

1. Henry C. Clausen and Bruce Lee, *Pearl Harbor Final Judgment* (New York: Crown Publishing, Inc., 1992), 21.

2. Ibid., 4. For a complete summary of Clausen's professional and Masonic careers, see Henry C. Clausen, *Clausen's Commentaries on Morals and Dogma,* 2d ed. (Washington, D.C.: The Supreme Council, S.J., 1981), 213–16.

3. Kevin Starr, *Americans and the California Dream: 1850–1915* (New York: Oxford University Press, 1973), 293.

4. Ibid., 293–95.

5. Henry C. Clausen (hereafter referred to as HCC) to the Honorable Carl Albert, Speaker of the House of Representatives, letter, January 12, 1971, the Supreme Council, Southern Jurisdiction, Archives (hereafter referred to as TSC), 8-2000.

6. Clausen and Lee, 90, 300.

7. Ibid., 293.

8. Starr, 246.

9. *Transactions of The Supreme Council, 33° (Mother Council of the World), Ancient and Accepted Scottish Rite of Freemasonry, Southern Jurisdiction, U.S.A.* (hereafter referred to as *Transactions*) (Washington, D.C.: The Supreme Council, S.J., 1969), 279–80.

10. HCC to William L. Fox Sr. (hereafter referred to as WLF Sr.), letter, October 18, 1988.

11. *Transactions* (1973), 23–24; *Transactions* (1983), 21.

12. *Transactions* (1975), 22.

13. HCC to WLF Sr., letter, October 18, 1988; *Transactions* (1971), 41–42. The card index was not originally placed in a computer data bank; this was an equally daunting but necessary project. With the appointment of the multi-talented Reynold J. Matthews as Grand Archivist in 1988, the monumental task of computer indexing was begun.

14. *Transactions* (1971), 33–34; *Transactions* (1983), 113.

15. Inge Baum to HCC, Memorandum Library Report, March 30, 1971, Clausen Correspondence, 1969–1978, TSC, B-200.2; *Transactions* (1971), 37; HCC to James D. Carter, letter, April 13, 1971, Clausen Correspondence, 1969–1978, TSC, B-200.5; *Transactions* (1975), 178; *Transactions* (1981), 119.

16. James D. Carter to HCC, letter, March 3, 1972, TSC, B-200.5; Neyenesch Printers, Inc., San Diego, California, statement, August 31, 1972, TSC, B-200.5.

17. HCC to James D. Carter, letter, May 25, 1972, TSC, B-200.5; HCC to James D. Carter, letter, July 26, 1972, TSC, B-200.5; HCC to James D. Carter, letter, August 17, 1972, TSC, B-200.5.

18. *Transactions* (1973), 41; HCC to James D. Carter, letter (not sent), February 4, 1974, Clausen Correspondence, 1969–1978, TSC, B-2005; James D. Carter to HCC, weekly report, February 11–18, 1974, TSC, B-200.5; *Transactions* (1971), 177. Despite their falling out, when Carter suffered a heart attack on November 2, 1976, Clausen sent his wishes for a speedy recovery. He went on to say: "It seems a long time 'fought, bled and died' together in our joint efforts here and I'm deeply appreciative of the many things you did to help me." HCC to James D. Carter, letter, December 14, 1976, TSC, B-200.5.

19. *Transactions* (1971), 204.

20. *Transactions* (1983), 207.

21. C. Fred Kleinknecht Jr., interview with WLF Sr., February 14, 1989.

22. *Transactions* (1977), 27, 116, 119; *Transactions* (1983), 208; *Transactions* (1981), 218–20.

23. *Transactions* (1975), 170, 204.

24. *Transactions* (1983), 67.

25. *Transactions* (1979), 40.

26. Albert Pike, as quoted in *Transactions* (1981), 206.

27. *Transactions* (1971), 43; *Transactions* (1985), 44.

28. *Transactions* (1979), 43; *Transactions* (1985), 44.

29. HCC to WLF Sr., letter, October 18, 1988.

30. *Transactions* (1975), 47.

31. *Transactions* (1981), 53; *Transactions* (1985), 46.

32. Clausen, *Commentaries*, 1, 212.

33. *Scottish Rite Journal* 101 (March 1993): 25.

34. *Transactions* (1973), 184–85; *Transactions* (1975), 193.

35. *Transactions* (1983), 68, 221–22.

36. *Transactions* (1979), 217; *Transactions* (1983), 220.

37. *Transactions* (1971), 216.

38. Milton E. Ammann to HCC, letter, March 1, 1972, TSC, 8-2000.

39. *Transactions* (1975), 31, 120; *Transactions* (1977), 44, 47–49.

40. *Transactions* (1979), 50, 225; *Transactions* (1981), 57. Cf. A. C. F. Jackson, "The Authorship of the 1762 Constitutions of the Ancient and Accepted Rite," *Ars Quatuor Coronati* 97 (1985): 176–91.

41. *Transactions* (1983), 54–56; *Transactions* (1985), 52.

42. Christopher Lasch, *The Minimal Self* (New York: W. W. Norton, 1984), 20.

43. Sydney Ahlstrom, *A Religious History of the American People* (New Haven: Yale University Press, 1972), 1019–36; Peter W. Williams, *America's Religions: Traditions and Cultures* (New York: Macmillan, 1990), 309–19.

44. *Transactions* (1979), 103.

45. *Transactions* (1975), 2, 95, 99.

46. Robert V. Remini, *Henry Clay: Statesman for the Union* (New York: W.W. Norton & Company, 1991), 410.

47. Carl B. Albert to HCC, letter, October 27, 1971, TSC, 8-2000.

48. *Transactions* (1973), 2.

49. Ibid., 226.

50. *Transactions* (1977), 3, 49.

51. *Transactions* (1971), 3; *Transactions* (1979), 109; *Transactions* (1981), 2.

52. *Transactions* (1973), 48–49.

53. Donald R. Wurtz, Arthur Andersen and Company, to HCC, letter, July 5, 1973, TSC, 8-2000.

54. HCC to James D. Carter, letter, October 4, 1972, TSC, B-200.5.

55. James D. Carter to HCC, letter, November 9, 1972, TSC, B-200.5.

56. Donald R. Wurtz, Arthur Andersen and Company, to HCC, letter, August 8, 1972, TSC, 8-2000.

57. *Dallas Morning News,* December 21, 1972.

58. James D. Carter to HCC, letter, March 29, 1973, TSC, B-2005.

59. *Transactions* (1977), 22.

60. *Transactions* (1971), 25, 156–57; *Transactions* (1973), 25, 131; *Transactions* (1975), 23, 103; *Transactions* (1977), 98; *Transactions* (1979), 25, 169; *Transactions* (1981), 27, 125–26; *Transactions,* (1983), 18, 238–39; *Transactions* (1985), 94.

61. S. Brent Morris, "Trends Affecting American Freemasonry: A Commentary on Declines in Fraternalism in General, and in the York Rite in Particular" (paper presented to the Maryland Research Society, February 6, 1982).

62. *Transactions* (1975), 172.

63. *Transactions* (1985), 19–20.

64. *Transactions* (1979), 71; *Transactions* (1985), 59; *Transactions* (1973), 47; *Transactions* (1983), 199.

65. Captain J. C. Henderson, U.S.N., to the Supreme Council, letter, December 15, 1970, Clausen Correspondence, 1969–1978, TSC.

66. HCC to Captain J. C. Henderson, U.S.N., letter, January 13, 1971, Clausen Correspondence, 1969–1978, TSC.

67. George A. Bender to Lt. General Willard Pearson, V Corps, USAR EUR, letter, July 7, 1972, Clausen Correspondence, 1969–1978, TSC.

68. HCC to Charles W. Parkhurst, letter, June 29, 1970, TSC, B-200.5.

69. *Transactions* (1979), 210–11.

70. A. E. Dick Howard, "Up Against the Wall: The Uneasy Separation of Church and State," in John F. Wilson and Donald L. Drakeman, eds., *Church and State in American History* (Boston: Beacon Press, 1987), 292–95.

71. *Transactions* (1983), 200–202.

72. *Transactions* (1985), 181–82.

73. *Transactions* (1985), 41; *Transactions* (1971), 93; *Transactions* (1975), 96.

74. *Transactions* (1973), 203; *Transactions* (1977) 21, 30–31.

75. HCC to Lloyd H. Elliott, President, George Washington University, January 27, 1983, letter, Clausen Correspondence, 1969–1978, TSC.

76. Lloyd H. Elliott to HCC, August 17, 1982, letter, Clausen Correspondence, 1969–1978, TSC.

77. Ibid.

78. The bronze likeness of Clausen was subsequently returned to California, where it could be appropriately displayed for the benefit of West Coast Scottish Rite Masons.

79. *Transactions* (1985), 23, 150–51.

CHAPTER XIV
Continuity and Opportunity, 1985 and Forward
C. Fred Kleinknecht

1. Michael Kammen, *Mystic Chords of Memory: The Transformation of Tradition in America* (New York: Alfred A. Knopf, 1991), 621.

2. Ibid., 698.

3. Christian F. Kleinknecht Sr., *The Kleinknecht Gems of Thought Encyclopedia,* vol. 3 (Washington, D.C.: The Roberts Publishing Company, 1954), 7–10.

4. C. Fred Kleinknecht (hereafter referred to as CFK), interview with William L. Fox Jr. (hereafter referred to as WLF Jr.), April 3, 1995.

5. Ibid.; *Who's Who in America,* 45th ed., vol. 1 (Providence, N.J.: Marquis Who's Who, 1989).

6. CFK was hired by Grand Commander John H. Cowles who was opposed, at first, to the proposition, because one Kleinknecht was already on the staff. Changing his mind, Cowles saw no disadvantageous conflict and, in the end, took full credit for "his good idea." It is more than likely that Chris Kleinknecht had planted

the seed for his son's first job to materialize at the Supreme Council. Nevertheless, Cowles was firmly in command on all hiring decisions regardless of the one making recommendations. CFK to William L. Fox Sr. (hereafter referred to as WLF Sr.), interview, February 14, 1989.

7. *Transactions of The Supreme Council, 33° (Mother Council of the World), Ancient and Accepted Scottish Rite of Freemasonry, Southern Jurisdiction, U.S.A.* (hereafter referred to as *Transactions*) (Washington, D.C.: The Supreme Council, S.J., 1959), 213.

8. CFK, interview with WLF Jr., April 3, 1995.

9. *Transactions* (1967), 6, 60, 67.

10. *Transactions* (1985), 2, 3.

11. CFK, interview with WLF Jr., January 22, 1995.

12. CFK, interview with WLF Jr., April 3, 1995; Robert L. Goldsmith, letter to WLF Jr., March 31, 1995.

13. Kleinknecht in the 1990s became a favorite among the caddie corps at Burning Tree. As has been said often enough, a golf course is a revealer of human character, perhaps more than the office. Kleinknecht showed traits of generosity not only in his official capacity but informally, too, when during rounds of golf he frequently helped out a caddie financially, in one instance so that the man could pay his lodge dues in a Prince Hall affiliate. CFK, interview with WLF Jr., February 15, 1995.

14. Admiral W. Gene Sizemore, interview with WLF, Jr., April 4, 1995.

15. S. Brent Morris, *Masonic Philanthropies: A Tradition of Caring* (Lexington, Mass., and Washington, D.C.: The Supreme Councils, 33°, N.M.J. and S.J., 1991), xiii, 18–20.

16. Rules for being admitted to a Shriners hospital are simple: a child must be under eighteen years old; the child's condition, in the opinion of the medical team, must be such that it can be substantially helped or cured at the hospital; treatment will be offered free of charge if it is determined that another facility of equal capacity would place a financial burden on the family; and the hospitals have absolutely no admitting restrictions which give any preference based on race, religion, or Masonic relationship.

17. Morris, 16–17.

18. William G. Schweigert, as quoted by Dwight A. Hamilton, in "For a Child's Sake," *Scottish Rite Journal* 104 (April 1995): 29.

19. *Transactions* (1987), 41.

20. *Transactions* (1981), 30–31.

21. Paul J. Rich, *Stanford Patriarchs* (Cambridge, England, and San Francisco, Calif.: Enneit Press, 1993), i–ii; cf., Paul J. Rich, *Stanford Symbolism and Stanford Freemasons* (Cambridge, England, and San Francisco, Calif.: Enneit Press, 1994).

22. Jon Eisenson to Henry C. Clausen, letter, June 19, 1972, the Supreme Council, Southern Jurisdiction, Archives (hereafter referred to as TSC), B-2010; Clayton Rich to Henry C. Clausen, letter, August 23, 1972, TSC, B-2010.

23. Henry C. Clausen to Jon Eisenson, letter, December 19, 1972, TSC, B-2010.

24. *Transactions* (1983), 205, 206; *Transactions* (1985), 28.

25. *Transactions* (1987), 38; CFK, interview with WLF Sr., February 14, 1989.

26. C. Fred Kleinknecht, "The Tenth Step: The Progress of a Decade," report to Active Members and Deputies, informal meeting, March 20, 1995, Grand Commander files, TSC.

27. *Transactions* (1991), 180.

28. Kleinknecht, "The Tenth Step."

29. Ibid.

30. *Transactions* (1991), 39.

31. "Cash and Securities Comparison between 1989 and 1995," prepared by the Grand Executive Director of the Finance Committee, January 1996.

32. *Transactions* (1989), 34, 36–38.

33. Tommie L. Robinson Jr., interview, with WLF Jr., June 15, 1995.

34. Annual Report, 1993–1994, of the Scottish Rite Center for Childhood Language Disorders, Washington, D.C., July 1, 1994.

35. *Transactions* (1987), 31.

36. *Transactions* (1987), 53; *Transactions* (1989), 22.

37. S. Brent Morris, *Cornerstones of Freedom: A Masonic Tradition* (Washington, D.C.: The Supreme Council, S.J., 1993), 54–58, 62–67.

38. *Transactions* (1989), 62.

39. Ibid., 38–41.

40. Alan K. Simpson, as quoted in *Transactions* (1989), 127–28.

41. Kammen, 652.

42. C. Fred Kleinknecht, "Our Flag," *The New Age* 96 (June 1988): 2.

43. Morris, 115–19.

44. C. Fred Kleinknecht, "Flag Burning and True Freedom," *The New Age* 97 (September 1989): 3.

45. Senator Larry Craig, "Only an Amendment Can Protect Our Flag," *Scottish Rite Journal* 104, no. 5 (May 1995): 24–25, 33.; memo, "Member Organizations," from Citizens Flag Alliance, Inc., December 19, 1994, Grand Executive Director's files, TSC.

46. Justice Robert H. Jackson, *West Virginia State Board of Education v. Barnette,* 1943; cf., Nat Hentoff, "How to Desecrate the Flag," editorial, *Washington Post,* June 26, 1995.

47. "House Easily Passes Amendment to Ban Desecration of Flag," news article, *New York Times,* June 29, 1995.

48. C. Fred Kleinknecht, "Protecting Our Flag," *Scottish Rite Journal* 104 (June 1995): 3.

49. Ibid., 5.

50. Rex R. Hutchens, *A Bridge to Light* (Washington, D.C.: The Supreme Council, S.J., 1988), 55, 63. The fifteenth degree regalia was also revised for similar reasons of taste. The broad white sash, fringed with gold, was adorned with embroidered body parts. These details were eliminated as of 1993. All such revisions, however, are part of an on-going, evolutionary precedent. Masonic symbols and rituals have repeatedly undergone such modifications as those occurring in the 1990s.

51. C. Fred Kleinknecht, "Masonry's Material Culture," *Scottish Rite Journal* 100 (September 1992): 4.

52. *Transactions* (1991), 232; *Transactions* (1993), 230.

53. *Transactions* (1993), 231.

54. Kleinknecht, "The Tenth Step."

55. Mark C. Carnes, *Secret Rituals and Manhood in Victorian America* (New Haven: Yale University Press, 1989), 156.

56. Bruno Bettelheim, *The Uses of Enchantment: The Meaning and Importance of Fairy Tales* (New York: Alfred A. Knopf, 1976).

57. Carnes, 156.

58. C. Lance Brockman, "Catalyst for Change: Intersection of the Theater and the Scottish Rite," *Heredom* 3 (1994): 133.

59. Ibid., 121.

60. S. Brent Morris to John D. Blankinship, letter, January 30, 1989; S. Brent Morris, "A Preliminary Concept for a Research Lodge of Perfection," memo, 1989; S. Brent Morris to Scottish Rite Research Society officers and founders, memo, July 1, 1991, all from Grand Commander's files, TSC; *Transactions* (1991), 21.

61. *Transactions* (1989), 39; *Transactions* (1991), 37–39.

62. *Transactions* (1991), 39.

63. *Transactions* (1991), 42–43.

64. *Transactions* (1991), 32; cf., Reynold J. Matthews, "The George Washington University: A New Era of Partnership with the Scottish Rite," *Scottish Rite Journal* 98 (March 1990): 13–18.

65. Sam E. Hilburn to WLF Jr., letter, April 5, 1995.

66. Kleinknecht, "The Tenth Step." Cf. Allocution in *Transactions* (1993), 11–13.

67. "Graying Temples: Uncertainty Reigns on the Shriners' Parade as Membership Flags," *Wall Street Journal,* front page, February 9, 1995.

68. Membership data and statistics are from the official records of the Supreme Council prepared by Delmarva Associates. The Valley of Los Angeles with 4,474 members and the Valley of Palm Springs with about 400 members did not report birth years. Extrapolating from the overall totals and making conservative correc-

tions, however, gives a fairly accurate picture of between 10 percent and 12 percent. In Washington, D.C., there were 3,510 Scottish Rite Masons on the register for 1995; that total includes an aggregate of 588 born after 1945.

69. E. Anthony Rotundo, *American Manhood: Transformations in Masculinity from the Revolution to the Modern Era* (New York: Basic Books, 1993), 292. See Pat Conroy's novel *The Prince of Tides* (New York: Bantam, 1987) for a description of the displaced man.

70. *Transactions* (1993), 16–17.

71. *Transactions* (1993), 355–57; Lodge of Perfection Membership Gain and Loss Report, AASR, S.J., U.S.A., December 31, 1994, Grand Executive Director's files, TSC.

72. CFK to Active Members and Deputies, letter, June 28, 1991, Grand Commander's files, TSC.

73. "Freemasons Begin to Lift the Veil of Arcana: A Society With Medieval Roots Seeks to Recruit Members and Dispel Rumors," news article, *New York Times,* June 6, 1993.

74. Arthur Diamond, *Prince Hall* (Philadelphia: Chelsea House, 1992).

75. William R. Miller, "Prince Hall," *Scottish Rite Journal* 104 (February 1995): 20–22.

76. *Transactions* (1993), 151.

77. Kleinknecht, "The Tenth Step."

78. Joseph Fort Newton, *The Builders: A Story and Study of Freemasonry* (Richmond, Va.: Macoy Publishing, 1951), 288–89.

79. Steven C. Bullock, *Revolutionary Brotherhood: Freemasonry and the Transformation of the American Social Order, 1730–1840* (Chapel Hill: University of North Carolina Press, 1996), 53.

CHAPTER XV

The Scottish Rite and the American Right, 1990s
Religious Prejudice as a Source of Anti-Masonry

1. The inspiration for the founding of the Ancient Arabic Order of the Nobles of the Mystic Shrine occurred in 1867 while Billy Florence, an American actor, was visiting in Marseilles, France. There he was invited by a Middle Eastern diplomat to attend a musical comedy that concluded the performance by "initiating" the audience into a secret society. Combining his organizing talents with those of Walter M. Fleming, an American physician, Florence developed the first draft of the Shrine ritual in 1870. So, while the "playground for Masons" is as American as the Boston Red Sox, its Arabic theme first came to mind from an American in France. It would be, nevertheless, overreaching to claim that both the Scottish Rite and the Shrine share French origins.

2. Steven C. Bullock, *Revolutionary Brotherhood: Freemasonry and the Transformation of the American Social Order, 1730–1840* (Chapel Hill: University of North Carolina Press, 1996), 277–80, 313.

3. William T. Still, *New World Order: The Ancient Plan of Secret Societies* (Lafayette, La.: Huntington House Publishers, 1990), 109.

4. Leo P. Ribuffo, "The Complexity of Religious Prejudice," in *Right, Center, Left: Essays in American History* (New Brunswick, N.J.: Rutgers University Press, 1992), 26.

5. Ribuffo, 66.

6. Pamela M. Jollicoeur and Louis L. Knowles, "Fraternal Associations and Civil Religion," *Review of Religious Research* 20, no. 1 (fall 1978): 4.

7. Cf. Charles C. Lemert, "Defining Non-Church Religion," *Review of Religious Research* 16, no. 3 (spring 1975): 186–97.

8. Noel P. Gist, "Secret Societies: A Cultural Study of Fraternalism in the United States," *University of Missouri Studies* 15 (1940): 9–176.

9. Jollicoeur and Knowles, 4.

10. Hubert S. Box, *The Nature of Freemasonry,* as cited by William J. Whalen in "The Pastoral Problem of Masonic Membership" (a background report prepared for the U.S. Bishops Committee for Pastoral Research and Practices, March 20, 1985), *Origins NC Documentary Service* 15, no. 6 (June 27, 1985), 84–91. Cardinal Bernard Law of Boston, chairman of the bishop's committee, said, "The report should be seen in the context of the 1973 and 1983 decrees of the Congregation for the Doctrine of the Faith dealing with ex-communication

and incompatibility." According to the Whalen report, the chief objection of Roman Catholicism to Free-masonry is its naturalism (i.e., assigning to human nature, agency, and reason sufficiency for knowing God), its relativism (i.e., that faith systems other than Christianity are valid), and its rival set of symbols (i.e., the com-patibility of the Grand Architect of the Universe and the triune God). Whalen summarizes the official Catholic position with a rhetorical dichotomy: "Perhaps a religious naturalism is better than no religious belief at all, but for the professing Christian it represents a retreat from the Gospel." Whalen also says that Catholic theological opposition to Masonry is based on the use of ritual oaths. In general, the negative tone of the Whalen report, while conceding American Masonry some benefit of the doubt, is much less contentious than tracts of the Christian right. See also, Robert I. Bradley, *The Masonic Movement and the Fatima Message,* Queen of Apostles Series, vol. 10 (Wilmington, N.J.: World Apostulate of Fatima, AMI Press, 1990).

11. Whalen, "The Pastoral Problem," 14.

12. Roger Finke and Rodney Stark, *The Churching of America, 1776– 1990: Winners and Losers in Our Religious Economy* (New Brunswick, N.J.: Rutgers University Press, 1992), 15–16, 54–56.

13. Gordon S. Wood, *The Radicalism of the American Revolution* (New York: Alfred A. Knopf, 1991), 223.

14. Ibid., 223.

15. Jon Butler contends that historians "by-pass other religious issues and traditions that influenced revo-lutionary political discourse, exaggerate religion's general importance to the Revolution, and slight the difficulties that the Revolution posed for the American churches." Butler points out that "as Americans turned from war making to nation making, clergymen turned to deism to explain their postrevolutionary failures and crises. . . . The eagerness to uncover deism produced two major campaigns of religious paranoia." The first antideist campaign focused on the scare of the Bavarian Illuminati, the second one denounced Thomas Jefferson as he ran for presi-dent in 1800. Jon Butler, *Awash in a Sea of Faith* (Cambridge, Ma.: Harvard University Press, 1990), 196, 218–19.

16. Bullock, 164. Also, Henry F. May offers that by the 1780s "there is evidence . . . that some of the orthodox were already worried about deism, infidelity, and general religious decline." In Virginia, "with the Revolution and disestablishment [the church's], weaknesses were exposed and it went into a period of almost fatal decline. It was at this point that a considerable part of the top class turned toward deism." Henry F. May, *The Enlightenment in America* (New York: Oxford University Press, 1976), 122, 72.

17. Wood, 223.

18. Cf. Nathan O. Hatch, *The Democratization of American Christianity* (New York: Oxford University Press, 1991).

19. John Robison, *Proofs of a Conspiracy Against All the Religions and Governments of Europe, Carried On in the Secret Meetings of Free Masons, Illuminati, and Reading Societies, Collected from Good Authorities* (Philadelphia: T. Dobson, 1797). Morse had also read the work of the exiled Catholic priest Abbe Augustin de Barruel, *Memoirs of Jacobinism* (Hartford, Conn.: Hudson and Goodwin, 1799), in English, and (London: Ph. Le Boussonnier and Co., 1797), in French. Both of these works are believed by most historians to be based on spurious evidence if not demonstrably untrue. And yet, both tapped into a fear that the social structures pre-serving middle-class stability in countries resembling England and Germany and undergirding personal secu-rity were under serious threat. Neither one had anything to say about Jewish involvement in events of the day. Robison's *Proofs of a Conspiracy* was reprinted by the John Birch Society in 1967, an edition that Pat Robertson cites in his 1991 bestseller *The New World Order.* Robison is also a source for William T. Still's *New World Order: The Ancient Plan of Secret Societies* (Lafayette, La.: Huntington House Publishers, 1990).

20. Timothy Dwight, cited in Robert Fuller, *Naming the Antichrist: the History of an American Obsession* (New York: Oxford University Press, 1995), 86.

21. White fears about a black uprising were exploited in many modern recastings of the American Illuminati theory. Cf. Ephraim Radner, "New World Order, Old World Anti-Semitism," *The Christian Century* 112, no. 26 (September 13–20, 1995): 847.

22. Ribuffo, 48.

23. Louis Farrakhan, "Excerpts from Farrakhan Talk," *New York Times*, October 17, 1995.

24. Charles Paul Freund, "From Satan to the Sphinx: The Masonic Mysteries of D.C.'s Map," op-ed article, *Washington Post*, November 5, 1995.

25. It is important to remember that Louis Farrakhan's mother was a sometime follower of Marcus Garvey and that his father came from Jamaica, Garvey's birthplace. In the 1920s, Garvey popularized the idea that the

Greeks (i.e., Western philosophy) plagiarized their ideas from Africans, namely Egyptians. This became a full-fledged interpretation in the 1954 book by George G. M. James, *Stolen Legacy* (New York: Philosophical Library, 1954). The James book, however, makes its case on fanciful Masonic literature instead of standard scholarly works on the history of religion. In particular, the Scottish Rite Mason Charles H. Vail, who wrote *The Ancient Mysteries and Modern Masonry* (1909; reprint, Chesapeake, N.Y.: ECA Associates, 1991), is cited as an authority on Egyptian origins of many Western institutions. Here, apparently, is the source and foundation of premises assumed true by Farrakhan, which are also shared by Afrocentrist writers. These views are controversial in the academic community: "Since these premises . . . are demonstrably false, James's work has virtually no historical value. But the book is interesting nonetheless, as an example of how and why mythic or propagandistic 'histories' come to be written." See Mary Lefkowitz, *Not Out of Africa: How Afrocentrism Became an Excuse to Teach Myth as History* (New York: Basic Books, 1996), 10, 94.

26. Farrakhan's religious thought has an analogue in gnosticism. Farrakhan's faith "is an apocalyptic faith that sees two antagonistic forces on the verge of a cosmic showdown, with a chosen sector of humanity bearing witness to the coming victory of the good force." This is not peculiar at all in ancient Jewish or Christian traditions. Farrakhan merely turns the symbols around to make whiteness the badge of the devil. Since gnosticism plays on human nature's "profound wish to read the inmost secret of the universe and to join the ultimate cosmic battle," Farrakhan's warring message has intrinsic appeal. According to some of his apologists, his sometimes disjointed narrative of good and evil is all part of his larger "anti-Satanism." Whom or what he names "satanic" is the source of much conflict all around. One consequence of this (gnostic) belief is that some blacks see it as a way to "become part of a reality larger than America itself." See Garry Wills, "A Tale of Three Leaders," *New York Review of Books*, September 19, 1996, 64, 66.

27. Gary H. Kah, interview, on the Bo Gritz national radio show, "Freedom's Call," May 3, 1995, cassette tape in the Supreme Council, Southern Jurisdiction, Archives (hereafter referred to as TSC). About the World Council of Churches, Kah elaborates, "[I]t is pushing for the unity of all Protestant denominations together with the Catholic Church in having one world [which is] a false unity trying to hoard Christians into a one world system."

28. Walter Lee Brown, in "Statue of Confederate General Linked to Ku Klux Klan Draws Protesters," *Huntsville (Tennessee) Times,* November 30, 1992.

29. Charles S. Iversen to C. Fred Kleinknecht, letter, April 26, 1993, TSC. Cf. *U.S. v. James Bevel and Anton Chaitkin*, Criminal No. 93-0093 and 93-0094, U.S. District Court for the District of Columbia, transcripts, April 19, 1993, court record, vol. I, 27. See also, "Judge Convicts Two Protesters," *Washington Post*, April 26, 1993, sec. 5C.

30. The Leo Taxil hoax, which began around 1886, concerned fabricated passages attributed to Albert Pike, such as "*Oui, Lucifer est Dieu, et malheureusement Adonai l'est aussi.* [Yes, Lucifer is God, and unfortunately, so too, is Adonai.]" Thus, with this bogus quotation a long string of Anti-Masons have convinced themselves that Freemasonry is a Luciferian conspiracy. Leo Taxil, whose real name was Gabriel Antoine Jagand-Pages, was turning out simultaneously anti-Catholic and anti-Masonic tracts. Sometimes, under different pseudonyms, he cynically played one off the other for a profit. Jagand-Pages was also publishing pornography. Other fraudulent channels of the Taxil-Satanism canard were Abel Clarin de la Rive (*La Femme et L'Enfant dans la Franc-Maconnerie Universelle*, 1894) and Lady Queenborough, Edith Starr Miller (*Occult Theocrasy,* 2 vols.[1933; reprint, Hawthorne, Calif.: Christian Book Club of America, 1980]). Both were duped in their dependence upon Taxil, which de la Rive later regretted and recanted (*Freemasonry Unmasked* [*La Franc-Maconnerie Demasquee,* novelle serie no. 38, April 1897], 4, 77–79). Taxil had dramatically confessed his elaborate deception in 1897 at a Roman Catholic Congress filled with bishops, episcopal delegates, the press, and hundreds of spectators. See Leo Taxil, "a la Salle de la Societe de Geographie, a Paris" in "Douze ans sous la Banniere de l'Eglise: La Fumisterie du Palledisme," *La Froundeur* (a weekly Paris newspaper), no. 13, April, 25, 1897. Many Catholic officials who had used Taxil's material for the purposes of anti-Masonic propaganda and who had written in support of Leo XIII's *Humanum Genus* (1884) were chagrined. Taxil apparently wanted to shame the Roman Catholic Church by exposing its credulity in regard to Freemasonry. Often when two "victims" discover a common enemy, they put aside their own differences and unite. Such was not the case in the aftermath of the Taxil scam. See Henry Wilson Coil, *Coil's Masonic Encyclopedia* (New York: Macoy Publishing, 1961), 649. Also see Arturo deHoyos and S. Brent Morris, *Is It True What They Say About Freemasonry: The Methods of Anti-Masons* (Silver Spring, Md.: Masonic Service Association of the United States, 1994), 6–25.

31. U.S. District Court for the District of Columbia, transcripts, April 19, 1993, court records. Iversen sagely remarked in his April 26, 1993, letter to Kleinknecht, "Years ago I had a client whom I would not represent in court. He filed a suit and then fed a lot of irrelevant material into the records. Afterwards, he wrote a book and incorporated much of the material in the book as the official record in the case of————, in the United States District Court. It made it sound like official facts determined by the court, whereas it was only a repetition of his fantasizing statements."

32. George Simmel, "The Sociology of Secrecy and Secret Societies," *American Journal of Sociology* 11 (January 1906): 441–98. Cf. Jollicoeur and Knowles, 5–6.

33. Transcript, *U.S. v. James Bevel and Anton Chaitkin,* Criminal Nos. 93–94, court records, vol. 1, 64–67.

34. Ibid., vol. 2, 106–10.

35. Ibid., vol. 2, 121.

36. Lyndon LaRouche, "Albert Pike and Satanism: From the Civil War to C. Fred Kleinknecht," *The New Federalist* 7 (April 1993): 3–4.

37. Ibid., 6–7. LaRouche's references to Satan and Albert Pike continue to propagate the Taxil hoax of the 1880s and 1890s. Cf. note 22.

38. Michael Farquhar, "Pike's Pique: Why the Statue Is a Bust," *Washington Post,* March 14, 1993, sec. 1F. Cf. Anton Chaitkin, "It's a Monument to Terrorism," Letters to the Editor, *Washington Post,* April 4, 1993. Chaitkin called the Pike statue "a national monument to terrorism."

39. "Rumor is a pipe . . . Blown by surmises, jealousies, conjectures." from Shakespeare, opening lines of *Henry IV,* Part II.

40. C. Fred Kleinknecht to All Active Members, Deputies, Personal Representatives and Secretaries, memorandum, February 1, 1993, Grand Commander's files, 1992–1993, TSC.

41. Charles S. Iversen, "Should the Statue of Albert Pike Be Removed?" position paper of the Supreme Council, Grand Commander's Office, February 1, 1993, 2–3.

42. Joseph A. Walkes Jr., *Black Square and Compass: 200 Years of Prince Hall Freemasonry* (Richmond, Va.: Macoy Publishing, 1979), 141–42.

43. Iversen, 2.

44. Joseph A. Walkes, press release, January 9, 1993, attachments in Iversen.

45. Howard L. Woods, January 12, 1993, attachment in Iversen.

46. Albert Pike, *Morals and Dogma* (Washington, D.C.: The Supreme Council, S.J., 1871), 829; Pike today is a living contradiction, but he was somehow consistent for his time. On the one hand he applauded Masonry for its ideas of human liberation and equality, but then he wrote in his Masonic primer, *Morals and Dogma* (304), a horrendously racist insult, "the ape is but a dumb Australian [i.e., Aborigine]."

47. Iversen, 5.

48. Ibid., 6.

49. Shakespeare, *Othello* (II: iii, 270).

50. Gary Scott, National Park Service, Department of Interior, National Capital Region, Office of Professional Services, "Briefing Statement, The Albert Pike Statue," March 11, 1993, Grand Commander's files, TSC; cf. Gary Scott, "Attack on the Albert Pike Statue, Washington, D.C.," *The Philalethes* 46 (August 1993): 93–94. Scott, as a member of the college fraternity Kappa Alpha and a Scottish Rite Mason, was accused by Anton Chaitkin of the Schiller Society of acting improperly in his official government position in the Pike matter. All of Scott's superiors in the U.S. Department of Interior supported his professionalism.

51. Shelby Foote as quoted in "Statue of Confederate General Linked to Ku Klux Klan Draws Protesters," *Huntsville (Tennessee) Times,* November 30, 1992.

52. Michael Farquhar, *op. cit.*

53. John W. Boettjer, "No Proof of Klan Membership," *Washington Post,* letter to the editor, March 24, 1993.

54. C. Fred Kleinknecht, "The Tenth Step: The Progress of a Decade," report to Active Members and Deputies, informal meeting, March 20, 1995, Grand Commander's files, TSC.

55. Grant Wacker, as quoted in Ibid., 151. Two seminal studies in American fundamentalism are Ernest R. Sandeen, *The Roots of Fundamentalism: British and American Millenarianism, 1800–1930* (Chicago: University of Chicago Press, 1970; reprint, Grand Rapids, Mich.: Baker Book House, 1978) and George M. Marsden,

Fundamentalism and American Culture (New York: Oxford University Press, 1980). While premillennialists believe the end times are imminent and Jesus Christ is returning to rule soon, there appears in other evangelical circles the theological argument which works out the second coming on a different schedule, called "postmillennialism." In the latter instance, it is posed that history's conclusion and the second coming will follow, rather than precede the millennium. Liberal evangelical reform movements, including nineteenth-century abolitionism and twentieth-century civil rights activism, draw energy from postmillennial conceptions, believing that God's elect will rule the earth during a period of a thousand years. Some maintain that this "trial" period has already begun, meaning there is no time to waste in improving, reforming, and perfecting human society as necessary preparation for the Kingdom of God. American utopian movements, usually very small, have been steeped in perfectionist ideals. Meanwhile, a liberal Baptist, such as Jesse Jackson, represents postmillennial rhetoric. Cf. William L. Fox, "Jesse Jackson's Kingdom of God Theology," *The Christian Century* 105, no. 15 (May 4, 1988): 446–47.

56.   Wills, "A Tale of Three Leaders," 66.

57.   Clement (ca. 96 CE) wrote, "[U]pon all of these the great Architect and Lord of the universe has enjoined peace and harmony, for the good of all alike." First Epistle of Clement to the Corinthians, chapter 20 in *Early Christian Writings: the Apostolic Fathers*, Maxwell Staniforth translator (London: Penguin Books, 1987), 32. John Calvin used the same metaphor in his *Commentary upon the Book of Psalms* (1557) and his best-known exposition, the *Institutes of the Christian Religion* (1536). His exegesis of Psalm 19 argues, "As soon as we acknowledge God to be the supreme Architect, who has erected the beauteous fabric of the universe, our minds must necessarily be ravished with wonder at his infinite goodness, wisdom and power." See *Commentary upon the Book of Psalms*, bk. 1 (Grand Rapids, Mich.: Wm. B. Eerdmans, 1949), 309. Also see *Institutes of the Christian Religion* (Grand Rapids, Michigan: Wm. B. Eerdmans, 1953), 141. Plausibly, according to Wallace McLeod, the term was easily absorbed into the Masonic *Constitutions of 1723* because the author, James Anderson, a Presbyterian divine from Aberdeen, Scotland, would have been intimately familiar with Calvin's works. Wallace McLeod, *The Grand Design* (Des Moines, Iowa: Iowa Research Lodge No. 2, 1991), 108.

58.   James L. Holly, *The Southern Baptist Convention and Freemasonry*, vol. 1 (Beaumont, Tex.: Mission and Ministry to Men, Inc., 1992), 1, 5, 35. Besides denouncing Masonry because it "is pledged to . . . and works for the glory and honor of a foreign god" (iv), Holly uses typical conspiracy language, too. He concludes, "[T]he occultic, secret society of Freemasonry with its offering of Eastern Star, Rainbow Girls and Demolay [*sic*] are among the successors of Kabala. They are condemned by the Word of God" (50). The term "cabal," implying the presence of a conspiracy, is derived from the medieval Jewish mystical work called the Kabala. Holly's "Lucifer" rhetoric in volume 1 came directly from Leo Taxil's long exposed hoax. Later, he admitted he had used this fraudulent source, but offered only a mild retraction. See *The Southern Baptist Convention and Freemasonry*, vol. 3 (Beaumont, Tex.: Mission and Ministry to Men, Inc., 1994), 130. Also see Gary Leazer, *Fundamentalism and Freemasonry: the Southern Baptist Investigation of the Fraternal Order* (New York: M. Evans, 1995), 160–5.

59.   Gary Leazer, *Fundamentalism and Freemasonry: The Southern Baptist Investigation of the Fraternal Order* (New York: M. Evans Company, 1995), 99–102, 110–11.

60.   C. Fred Kleinknecht, "Breaking the Silence," *Scottish Rite Journal* 101, no. 2 (February 1993): 3–5.

61.   William R. White, "A Religious Quality, But Not a Religion," *Scottish Rite Journal* 101, no. 2 (February 1993): 65.

62.   Herbert H. Reynolds, "Straight Talk," *Scottish Rite Journal* 101, no. 2 (February 1993): 64.

63.   Thomas Sherrard Roy, "An Answer to Anti-Masonic Religious Propaganda," *Scottish Rite Journal* 101, no. 2 (February 1993): 71–72. Roy continued his apologia in behalf of Freemasonry: "[W]e can claim to be a tolerant group. We believe that there should be some place where men can meet without having to assert or defend the peculiarities of their doctrines. There should be some place where men can meet and know that their right to worship God in their own way is respected completely; a place where a man learns that the only respect he can claim for his beliefs is the respect he accords to the beliefs of others. There should be some place where men can face the realities of life and know that the only barriers that separate men are those of ill-will and enmity. Freemasonry is that place."

64.   T. Max Tatum and Jim Tresner, "A Masonic Response to the Report on Freemasonry by the Home Mission Board, SBC," *Scottish Rite Journal* 101, no. 5 (May 1993): 46–49.

65.   Larry L. Lewis, President, Home Mission Board, cited in "Baptist Vote Vitalizes Masonry," *Scottish Rite Journal* 101 (August 1993): 36.

66. Sam E. Hilburn to William L. Fox Jr., letter, April 5, 1995.

67. Ralph Waldo Emerson, "Considerations by the Way," *The Conduct of Life* (New York: Harcourt Brace, 1951). Emerson cites Ali ibn-Abi-Talib (602–661) as the original source of the saying. Ali ibn-Abi-Talib is significant in Muslim history as the son-in-law of Muhammed and as the fourth caliph. He was sometimes called the Lion of God and was assassinated by the Unmayads, rivals from Muhammed's own tribe.

68. For the political history see William Preston Vaughn, *The Anti-Masonic Party in the United States, 1826–1843* (Lexington: University of Kentucky Press, 1983); for focused discussion of religious sources of anti-Masonry see Paul Goodman, *Towards a Christian Republic: Antimasonry and the Great Transition in New England, 1826–1836* (New York: Oxford University Press, 1988); for treatment of the social history of anti-Masonry see Steven Bullock, *Revolutionary Brotherhood*.

69. David Cantor, *The Religious Right: The Assault on Tolerance and Pluralism in America* (New York: Anti-Defamation League, 1994), 25.

70. Pat Robertson, *The New World Order* (Dallas, Tex.: Word Publishing, 1991), 9, 37, 67–71, 176–185.

71. "Who Belongs to the Religious Right?" *The Christian Century* 112, no. 14 (April 26, 1995): 451–52.

72. Absalom Willis Robertson, Pat Robertson's father, detailed his Masonic affiliation in a letter to Ray Baker Harris, librarian of the Supreme Council:

> Replying to your letter of the 8th, will say that I was made a Master Mason in Buena Vista Lodge No. 186 and later served as master of that Lodge and also as District Deputy Grand Master. While living in Buena Vista I joined the Rockbridge Royal Arch Chapter No. 44, expecting at that time to take the necessary work for membership in the Shrine, but unfortunately never got beyond the Royal Arch. I left Buena Vista in the summer of 1917 for Army service and upon my discharge from the Army in the summer of 1919 I moved my residence to Lexington. Being unable to keep up with my Lodge work I took a demit from the Buena Vista Lodge and since then have held no active membership in any other Lodge, although I have continued my membership in the Rockbridge Royal Arch Chapter No. 44. Technically, therefore, I am not now a member of a Blue Lodge but am a member, I assume, of the Masonic Fraternity.
>
> Fraternally yours,
> A. Willis Robertson

From A. Willis Robertson to Ray Baker Harris, letter, March 10, 1941, vertical files, TSC.

73. Robertson's book received no mention in the standard library reference *Book Review Digest* (New York: H. W. Wilson, 1993).

74. S. Brent Morris, "The Sound and the Fury," *Scottish Rite Journal* 101 (February 1993): 91–92; cf. Arturo deHoyos and S. Brent Morris, *Is It True What They Say About Freemasonry?* (Silver Spring, Md.: Masonic Service Association of the United States, 1994).

75. C. Fred Kleinknecht to Pat Robertson, letter, May 12, 1992, TSC. Kleinknecht advised Robertson that indeed some writings about the fraternity by Masons have occasionally offended him over the years, but, he said, "Freemasonry has no *Imprimatur*; everyone, Mason or not, is free to write about it what they will." He did not object to Robertson criticizing the fraternity. His difference with Robertson was based on the specific use of a long-discredited document. He continues, after detailing the elaborate hoax of Leo Taxil, "If we must disagree let us base our disagreement upon truth. It appears that your opinion of Freemasonry has been, at least in part, based upon false information drawn from a dubious source." Robertson neither acknowledged nor responded to Kleinknecht's letter.

76. A. M. Rosenthal, *New York Times*, column, May 9, 1995.

77. Michael Lind, "Rev. Robertson's Grand International Conspiracy Theory," *New York Review of Books*, February 2, 1995, 21–22.

78. Gustav Niebuhr, "Pat Robertson Says He Intended No Anti-Semitism in Book He Wrote Four Years Ago," news article, *New York Times*, March 4, 1995; Pat Robertson, "Our Foreign Policy Should Put U.S. First," letters to the editor, *New York Times*, March 5, 1995; Frank Rich, "Bait and Switch," column, *New York Times*, March 2, 1995; Frank Rich, "The Jew World Order," column, *New York Times*, March 9, 1995.

79. William L. Fox, "Attack on Freemasons," letters to the editor, *New York Times*, March 15, 1995.

80. Pat Robertson, "A Reply to My Critics," op-ed piece, *Wall Street Journal*, April 12, 1995.

81. William L. Fox to the editor, *Wall Street Journal*, unpublished letter, April 14, 1995.

82. Ibid.

83. James Buchanan, as quoted in Cantor, 63.

84. Harvey Cox, "The Warring Visions of the Religious Right," *Atlantic Monthly* 276 (November 1995): 66.

85. Texe Marrs, as quoted in Cantor, 43. Marrs probably has in mind the Skull and Bones fraternal society at Yale.

86. Abraham Foxman in Cantor, iv.

87. Cantor, 145.

88. Jollicoeur and Knowles, 12.

89. Ibid., 10–13.

EPILOGUE

1. I am grateful that Rex Hutchens pointed this out to me.

2. "I shook hands with Lafayette when he went through New England; and I expected to see President Monroe when he came to New England, but something happened that night, no one knew what," remembered Albert Pike in *Autobiography of General Albert Pike: From Stenographic Notes Furnished By Himself* (Washington, D.C.: The Supreme Council, S.J., 1886), 71.

3. See Margaret C. Jacob, *Living the Enlightenment: Freemasonry and Politics in Eighteenth-Century Europe* (New York: Oxford University Press, 1991), 212–14. According to a popular though disputed legend, a Scottish Rite apron of the eighteenth degree (Rose Croix) in the possession of the Supreme Council of England and Wales was "said to have been taken from [Napoleon's] carriage after the Battle of Waterloo." There is no corroborative proof that Napoleon was a Mason or in the Rite of Perfection. John Mandleberg, *Ancient and Accepted: A Chronicle of the Proceedings 1845–1945 of the Supreme Council Established in England in 1845* (London: The Supreme Council for England and Wales, 1995), 332, 572, and illustration no. 39.

4. Jacob, 208–9.

5. Ibid., 166.

6. Roscoe Pound, "A Twentieth Century Masonic Philosophy," *Masonic Addresses and Writings* (Richmond, Va.: Macoy Publishing, 1953), 99.

7. James Tresner to William L. Fox, letter, September 20, 1996.

8. Leo Tolstoy, *War and Peace,* vol. 51 of Great Books of the Western World, trans. Louise and Aylmer Maude (Chicago: Encyclopedia Britannica Publishing, Inc., 1952), bk. 5, chap. 3, 199.

9. Nancy F. Cott, "On Men's History and Women's History," in Mark C. Carnes and Clyde Griffin, ed., *Meanings of Manhood: Constructions of Masculinity in Victorian America* (Chicago: University of Chicago Press, 1990), 210–11.

10. Christopher Lasch, *The Revolt of the Elites and the Betrayal of Democracy* (New York: W. W. Norton, 1995), 93.

11. Ibid., 123.

12. Robert D. Putnam, "Bowling Alone: America's Declining Social Capital," *Journal of Democracy* 6 (January 1995): 65–78.

13. Lasch, 117.

Bibliographical Essay

The simultaneous problem and advantage of source materials in Masonic history is the overwhelming abundance of treasure. Even in the hidden history of ritual development there is a wealth of useful documents easily obtainable. In terms of the Scottish Rite's higher Masonic degrees, for instance, the officially sanctioned publication of Rex R. Hutchens's *A Bridge to Light* (Washington, D.C.: The Supreme Council, S.J., 1988) leaves no doubt about the nature and aim of the ritual presented in the Southern Jurisdiction. And yet, the difficulty with such a thick paper trail of sources is putting the pieces together coherently in thematic and contextual terms.

The purpose of this brief note is to point out where this coherence has been recently accomplished in an exemplary manner. Were it not for painstaking, scholarly forerunners in the field of Masonic studies, the task before new researchers would be as daunting as Holmes's definition of the common law, which he described as chaos without an index. In the case of many Masonic archives, by the way, indexing remains scanty, which means the scholarly frontier has not yet been closed despite the exploration of others who have gone before.

Secondly, this note serves as a pocket guide to less accessible primary sources pertaining to the Scottish Rite in America. What is not intended for this note, however, is a full-dress bibliography. It is apparent that a Masonic bibliography is developing into a major necessity and there are currently efforts to do this with real care. The independent bibliographer Kent Walgren, for instance, has done much to advance this specialty in rare books and imprints of Scottish Rite titles. A portion of his work has been presented for the Scottish Rite Research Society as "A Bibliography of Pre-1851 American Scottish Rite Imprints (non-Louisiana)" in *Heredom* 3 (1994): 55–119. Walgren has also prepared "A Bibliography of Pre-1851 Louisiana Scottish Rite Imprints," published in *Heredom* 4 (1995): 207–39.

Because of the nature of this book, references which readers may wish to consult are conveniently mapped in the notes section. This is done not only to avoid redundancy, but to admit the difficulty of a comprehensive bibliography. Bibliographies are often uselessly too brief or, equally troubling, too dense and crowded with ephemera. There is plenty of work in this arena; historians and bibliographers need not get in the way of each other. For my purposes, the path to the sources is easily broken and traceable by the book's citations.

A generation ago there were only a few Ph.D.'s awarded to specialists in the history of American Freemasonry. James D. Carter, who later brought forward *History of The Supreme Council, 33° (Mother Council of the World), Ancient and Accepted Scottish Rite of Freemasonry, Southern Jurisdiction, U.S.A.,* to the year 1921, extending the efforts of his predecessors Charles S. Lobingier and Ray Baker Harris, began his professional career with "Freemasonry in Texas: Background, History and Influence to 1846" (Ph.D. diss., University of Texas, 1954). Walter L. Brown wrote "Albert Pike, 1809–1891" (Ph.D. diss., University of Texas, 1955), which even in manuscript form remained the definitive treatment on the most vivid Scottish Rite Grand Commander of the nineteenth century. Fortunately, Brown's biography of Albert Pike will reach a wider audience with its revision and publication as *A Life of Albert Pike* (Fayetteville: University of Arkansas Press, in press).

Meanwhile, during the era of Carter's and Brown's training, many more doctoral students delved into the fascinating American Anti-Masonic movement of 1826 through 1843. The dissertations produced generally bypassed the intrinsically worthwhile study of the fraternity on its own grounds and gave scholarly preference to its adversaries.

Then, beginning in the late 1970s, the winds of interest shifted and all of a sudden a new generation of graduate students discovered the relatively untapped possibilities found in Masonic records. Interpreting Masonic experience and thought as representative of significant themes in American social and cultural history yielded exceptionally fruitful scholarship. Fraternal undercurrents in the American Revolution, class structures in Federalist society, ideological and emotional needs of Victorian men, group identities in America before and just after World War I, and distinctive architectural forms and decorative design of Masonic halls after the Civil War were proving to be excellent research topics because of rich repositories and the availability of primary Masonic sources.

The subsequent books about Masonry that have resulted from Ph.D. dissertations suggest a strong trend that begins in natural curiosity about the fraternity and ends with the major benefit of dramatically elevating the terms of scholarship about lodge life. Steven C. Bullock, Mark C. Carnes, Mary Ann Clawson, Lynn Dumenil, and Dorothy Ann Lipson represented in the 1980s the exacting standards of doctoral research that could be transformed into important books that were ultimately published by university presses. This is a significant breakthrough in Masonic historiography. As a result, other dissertations ought to be forthcoming in an increasingly significant field that has expanded into American material culture studies. Furniture, jewelry, costumes, coins, murals, stamps, and postcards all have a story waiting for a teller.

Other recent works by historians that focus on the roots and outcroppings of the fraternity include seminal studies by Margaret C. Jacob, David Stevenson, and Kathleen S. Kutolowski. Each author deserves the attention of anyone hoping to be serious about Masonry in its varieties of historical contexts in European and American society. Though demanding for even well-informed readers, the following present new depths of interpretation and important background to the Scottish Rite in general: Margaret C. Jacob, *The Radical Enlightenment: Pantheists, Freemasons, and Republicans* (London: George Allen & Unwin, 1981) and her *Living the Enlightenment: Freemasons and Politics in Eighteenth-Century Europe* (New York: Oxford University Press, 1991); David Stevenson, *The First Freemasons: Scotland's Early Lodges and Their Members* (Aberdeen: Aberdeen University Press, 1988) and his *The Origins of Freemasonry: Scotland's Century, 1590–1710* (Cambridge: Cambridge University Press, 1988); and Kathleen S. Kutolowski, "Anti-Masonry Reexamined: Social Bases of the Grass-Roots Party," *Journal of American History* 71, no. 2 (1984): 269–93, and her "Freemasonry and the Community in the Early Republic: the Case for Anti-Masonic Anxieties," *American Quarterly* 34, no. 5 (1982): 453–61.

Within the English Masonic establishment the writings of John Hamill serve in combination as an excellent primer for understanding the fraternity's beginnings, traditions, and structures. Hamill's *The History of English Freemasonry* (London: Lewis Masonic Books, 1994) complements his *World Freemasonry: An Illustrated History* (London: Harper Collins, 1992). To a list of titles building up a reader's competence in managing the complexities of early Masonic history, especially in America, I add one that does not have Masonry as its primary focus. In it, nevertheless, the fraternity is a major supporting actor of another group's intriguing story. I refer to John C. Brooke, *The Refiner's Fire: the Making of Mormon Cosmology, 1644–1844* (Cambridge: Cambridge University Press, 1994).

There are, of course, many standard histories produced by Masons themselves, such as Albert G. Mackey, Robert Freke Gould (revised by Dudley Wright), J. Hugo Tratsch, Samuel H. Baynard, Robert B. Folger, Ray Baker Harris, George A. Newbury, Louis L. Williams, and Henry Wilson Coil. The Transactions of various Lodges of Research (the American, Texas, Missouri, and Iowa) are often rewarding as are local lodge, Grand Lodge, and Scottish Rite commemorative histories. Since 1866 the Quatuor Coronati Lodge, No. 2076, in London has published annual Transactions, journal length serials of particular excellence under the familiar title *Ars Quatuor Coronati* (AQC). A recent scholarly journal produced by Masons themselves, but whose pages have been served well by non-Masonic authors as well, is *Heredom,* published by the Scottish Rite Research Society. There is no higher scholarly standard in American Freemasonry than that found in *Heredom* under the editorship of S. Brent Morris. In fact, considering the Masonic literature since 1960, the most complete discussion of buried aspects and missing vignettes of Scottish Rite history appear there.

It is perhaps to be expected, too, that so little in the academic literature deals specifically with Scottish Rite Freemasonry. One notable exception is an analysis prepared by Pamela Jolicoeur and Louis L. Knowles in "Fraternal Associations and Civil Religion: Scottish Rite Freemasonry," *Review of Religious Research* 20, no. 1 (Fall 1978): 3–22. It is an article that examines through the Southern Jurisdiction's *The New Age* magazine the public values of Scottish Rite Masons over a recent decade; it suggests a model for a larger work that could support the ambitions of a substantial monograph.

Specific attention to the Scottish Rite has, at this point in a survey of available sources and scholarship, the appearance of Peer Gynt's onion. Peer was that Ibsen hero who, after many adventures in foreign lands, realized there was no true self, for he was like an onion after all the layers had been peeled away. Once the important secondary literature has been swept into the pot, there is not much left about the Scottish Rite alone. Therefore, like getting at the essence of the onion, the kernel of what can be known about the Scottish Rite remains as primary documents and archival manuscripts at the Supreme Councils.

The two principal centers of original sources are in Washington, D.C., and Lexington, Massachusetts. In the collections of both Supreme Councils there are mother lodes of ritual manuscripts, inter-fraternal correspondence, and private papers. The Northern Masonic Jurisdiction, for example, has a pristine 1783 edition of Henry Francken's manuscript ritual. The Southern Jurisdiction has the actual patent of that Masonic rogue Joseph Cerneau as well as Albert Pike's handwritten ruminations on Eastern religions. For researchers, however, both collections lack full-scale catalogues with descriptions and guides, though they are in better shape than many archives that an experienced scholar will have seen.

What remains to be tapped for future studies are the records housed in local Scottish Rite temples. In Gutherie, Oklahoma, for instance, a previously unknown speech by Albert Pike surfaced in 1996. In Little Rock, Arkansas, unusual photographs have been discovered. These places and others like them have provided valuable material in the study directed by C. Lance Brockman on the intersection of the American theater and the fraternity. His project is best summarized in the exhibit catalogue, Susan C. Jones, editor, *Theatre of the Fraternity: Staging the Ritual Space of the Scottish Rite of Freemasonry, 1896–1929* (Minneapolis, Minn.: Frederick R. Weisman Art Museum of the University of Minnesota, 1996).

In conducting interviews with many Scottish Rite officials, one of them allowed a bibliographic grace note. H. Wallace Reid offered a tantalizing possibility. He maintained that during his years of collecting Masonic artifacts, rare books, and jewelry, principally in South Carolina, he came to believe as true the rumor circulating for more than a generation that a leather trunk exists and purportedly contains Rite of Perfection and Supreme Council documents from the early years in Charleston. According to Reid, the leather trunk was removed from Charleston, perhaps in the 1870s, and taken to the South Carolina state capital of Columbia, where he conjectures it has safely rested anonymously in an old house attic. In time, whether from fresh sources or existing ones, we may yet learn more about the Ancient and Accepted Scottish Rite.

Index

Compiled by Susan Carroll

abolition movement, 66–67
Accepted Masons: origins of, 3–4, 5–8, 421n7
Adams, John, 13, 428n50
Adams, John Quincy, 37–38, 428n50
Adams, Samuel Emery, 128, 138, 144, 164, 165, 167
African Americans, 225, 243, 264–65, 266, 313–16, 339–41, 376–79, 393–94, 417–18, 435n115, 436n140, 457n89, n90, 462n70, n71, 468n25, 469n26, 470n46. *See also* Prince Hall Masons
African Lodge, 377. *See also* Prince Hall Masons
Ahlstrom, Sydney E., 179, 271, 301–2, 331
Albany, N.Y., 16, 20, 44–45, 424n50
Albert, Carl, 321, 333
Albert Pike Memorial Temple, Little Rock, Ark., 146
Albert Pike Monument, 134–35, 138, 144–45, 389–96, 431n3, 443n11, 470n38
alcoholic beverages: use at Masonic meetings, 11, 47, 148
Aldrin, Col. Edwin (Buzz) E., 318
Alexander, Abraham, Sr., 26, 27
Alexandria, Va., 10, 21, 163–64
Alexandria-Washington Lodge No. 22, 163–64
Allen, Willard W., 457n89
Amberg, Richard, 285, 307
Ambrose, Stephen E., 313
"America First" campaign, 184
American flag: desecration of, 364–67
American Indians, 71–73, 77, 82, 432n9, 434n70
American Legion, 365
American Library Association, 305
American Masonic Headquarters, Paris, France, 189
American Party, 62, 63
American Red Cross, 257, 456n62
American Revolution, 9, 10, 34
American Union Lodge, 10–11
American University, D.C., 290, 309
Americanism, 269
 and *Fellowship Forum*, 194
 and Ku Klux Klan, 194–96, 198
 and Luther Smith, 287, 288–90, 307, 309
 Masonic precursors of, 179
 and Masons, 194–96, 197, 198, 202, 363–67
Americans for Democratic Action, 296
Americans United for the Separation of Church and State, 266–67, 288, 308–9, 342
Ammann, Milton E., 329
Ancient and Accepted Scottish Rite: origin of name, 18, 45, 65, 425n70, 433n38
Ancient Free and Accepted Masons (A F & A M), 9
Anderson, James, 229, 471n57

Andersons Constitutions (1703), 165
anti-Catholicism, 109
 and John H. Cowles, 232–33, 244–45
 and 1960 presidential campaign, 221, 287, 288, 294–302
 and Luther Smith, 288
Anti-Defamation League, 401, 404, 407
Antients, 8–9, 33–34
Anti-Masonic Movement, 42–43, 47, 77, 475–76
Anti-Masonic Party, 11, 42, 43, 229
anti-Masonry:
 among Catholics, 10, 16, 106–10, 287–88, 384–85, 467n10, 469n30
 in Cuba, 311
 directed at higher degrees, 41–42, 381, 400–401, 404
 in the eighteenth century, 40–41
 in Europe, 234–35, 247–56, 287, 310–11, 312, 455n39, n41, n43
 failure as a political movement, 41, 42
 linking Jews and Masons, 250–52, 387–89, 404–5
 literature, 229, 250
 in the nineteenth century, 428n50, 429n19, 430n37, 469n30
 in the North, 39–43
 in the Philippines, 310–11
 and religious prejudice, 383
 and the religious right, 363, 381, 397–406, 407, 467n10, 471n58
 resulting from the Morgan incident, 40, 42, 381
 and Pat Robertson, 401–7
 roots of, 382–83, 385, 386–87
 as a social movement, 41, 42–43
 in the South, 43
 in television programs, 363–64
 in the twentieth century, 362–64, 381, 383–409
 among women, 40, 362–63
 writings, 249–50
anti-Semitism, 383, 387–89, 393, 401, 402, 403–4, 455n36
aphasia: treatment of, 280–81, 283, 308, 355–57
Archer, Glenn L., 266
Arkansas, 52, 61, 62, 64, 71–73, 75, 81–82, 315–16
armed forces:
 as a "Masonic Jurisdiction," 125, 146, 152
 Masonic Service Centers for, 257
 and Masonry in World War I, 181–82, 188
 and Masonry in World War II, 256–57
 in the Spanish-American War, 202–3
Arnold, Benedict, 10
Arthur Anderson and Company, 335–36
Ashmole, Elias, 5
"Associators, The," 35

astronauts, 317–18
atheism, 110
Atwood, Edward W., 114
Auld, Grand Commander Isaac, 27, 29, 34, 36–38
Austin, Tex., 197, 232, 280
Austria, 249, 253, 255
Authentics of Fundamental Law for Scottish Rite Freemasonry (Clausen), 330

Bacot, Thomas W., 34
Baker, Newton D., 182
Baltimore, Md., 20, 89
Baltimore Convention of May 1843, 47
Bancroft, Hubert Howe, 320
Barrie, J. M., 370
Bartholdi, Frederic Auguste, 365
Barthomieu, Bertrand, 15
Barton-Cotton, Incorporated, 358
Batchelor, Grand Commander James C., 66, 101, 117, 118, 121–22, 124
Baum, Inge, 277, 318, 324
Bavarian Society of the Illuminati, 386, 387–88, 389, 405, 468n15, n21
Bayliss, Major W., 156–57, 225
Baylor University, 290, 308–9, 399
Begue, F. T., 430n47
Belcher, Jonathan, 10
Belgium, 110, 147–48, 254
Bellah, Robert, 384, 408
Benedict, Andrew, 357
Bennett, William J., 342
Bentsen, Lloyd M., 333, 341
Berlin, Irving, 165
Bernheim, Alain, 252
Bettelheim, Bruno, 370
Bevel, James, 390–91, 392
Bibliography of the Writings of Albert Pike, 191
Bideaud, Antoine, 30–31, 33
black Americans. *See* African Americans
Blaine, James G., 111
Blankinship, John D., 342, 376
Blanshard, Paul, 288
Bloom, Sol, 244
blue Masonry. *See* symbolic lodges
Boettjer, John W., 367–68, 395–96, 443n17
Bohceli, Nubar, 312
Boles, Thomas M., 358–59
Bolsheviks, 185–87
Bonaparte, Napoleon, 412–13, 414, 415, 473n3
Bonneville, Chevalier de, 14, 422n38
Book of Infamy, The, 114
Borgnine, Ernest, 359
Boston, Mass., 10, 44
Boswell, John, Laird of Auchinleck, Scotland, 5
Bowen, Maj. Thomas Bartholomew, 26–27
Boyden, William L., 128–29, 152, 162, 165, 175, 180, 191, 197, 211, 219, 228–30, 438n52

Brazil, 33
Bridge to Light, A (Hutchens), 367–68, 475
Brockman, C. Lance, 147, 371
Brooke, John C., 7
Brown, Walter Lee, 54, 62–63, 79, 81, 82, 93, 390, 434n78, 435n119, 475–76
Browne, John Mills, 126–27
Brussels, Belgium, International Conference of Supreme Councils of Scottish Rite Freemasonry, 154, 165
Bryan, William Jennings, 130–31, 142, 156, 402–3
Bullock, Steven C., 4, 6, 9, 41–42, 43
Burbank, Luther, 212
Burchett, Charles Z., 397
Bureau de Secours, Paris, France, 253–54
Burke, Haslett P., 262, 355
Burns, Robert, 168–69
Bush, Barbara, 359–60
Bush, George, 359–60, 362, 401–2, 403
Bushnell, Grand Commander George E., Northern Jurisdiction, 276, 298, 300, 301, 310, 315
Butler, Jon, 468n15
Byrd, Robert C., 290, 333

California, 101–2, 127, 134, 152–53, 180, 323, 327, 373
California Scottish Rite Institute for Childhood Aphasia, 308
Camalier, Renah F., 343
Canada, 98, 272, 279, 312–13
Canandaigua, N.Y., 39
Canby, Henry Seidel, 77
Capital News Service, 197, 206
Capper, Arthur, 240
caps (Masonic), 158, 217
Carlin, Martin D., 357
Carmen, Louis D., 229
Carnes, Mark C., 76, 370, 427n38
Carson, Enoch T., 429n2, 438n33
Carter, James D., 20, 77, 89, 91, 95, 112, 135, 146–47, 150, 159, 170, 193–94, 202, 305–7, 324–25, 335–36, 427n23, 429n23, 463n18, 475–76
Carter, Jimmy, 296, 352, 401–2
Carter, Paul A., 283–84
Castro, Fidel, 294, 311
Caswell, Grand Commander Thomas Hubbard, 101, 116, 121, 125, 126, 127–28, 129, 131, 133–34, 135–36, 137, 138–39, 142, 438n52
Cate, Marius ten, 311
Cather, Willa, 223
Central Institute for the Deaf, 280
ceremonial visits to Washington's grave, 68–69
ceremonies:
    adoption, 66, 83, 93, 432n30, 433n41, 439n77
    baptism, 66, 83, 432n30, 433n41
    cornerstone-laying, 20–21, 50–51, 162–63, 222, 361–62
    dedicatory, 145, 174
    differences between Northern and Southern Jurisdictions, 225, 226, 227, 276, 303, 328
    Easter, 227, 276, 328

funeral, 66, 83, 118, 126, 139, 222, 432n30
    initiation, 3–4, 147, 417, 427n38
    installation of officers, 66, 152, 328, 432n30
    investiture of rank of Knight Commander, 169, 185
    as key to ancient wisdom, 6
    Lodge of Sorrow, 83
    Lodges of Perfection, 66, 83
    Maundy Thursday, 225, 226, 227, 276, 303, 328
    opened to public, 225, 226, 227, 276, 303, 328
    personal meaning of, 416–17
    reception of a louveteau, 66, 83, 432n30, 433n41
    Rose Croix, 66, 227, 276, 303
    used by the public, 222
    used to promote morals, 7
Cerneau, Joseph, 31, 32–33, 45
Cerneauists, 112, 114–15, 128, 428n49, 451n50
    in Charleston, S.C., 35, 36, 37, 52
    in Louisiana, 156–57
    and *The New Age*, 156–57
    in New York, 32–33, 37, 45, 80, 84, 225
Chaitkin, Anton, 390–91, 392, 470n38, n50
Chamberlin, Austin Beverly, 149, 155
Chapter of Clermont, 14
charity:
    duties of, 7, 214–15
    expenditures on, 308–9
    relief for Cuban Masonic refugees, 311
    relief for persecuted Masons in Europe, 253–56, 310–11
    and Supreme Council, 151, 280–81, 313, 418
    See also fraternal assistance; philanthropy; philanthropy, Scottish Rite
Charleston, S.C., 21–22, 37, 45, 46, 209, 218, 219–20, 414–15, 450n26
    disaster relief aid to, 113
    Grand Council of Princes of Jerusalem established, 17, 20
    Masonic divisions, 33–34, 52
    Scottish Rite membership, 34–35, 164
    "Sublime Grand Lodge of Perfection" established, 16, 20, 22–23, 28, 29, 414–15
childhood learning dysfunctions: treatment of, 280–81, 283, 345, 353–57, 359–60
Children's Language Disorders Centers, 281, 283, 353–56, 359–60
China, 157–58, 254, 279
chivalry, Masonic, 41
Christ Church Mission, Brooklyn, N.Y., 232–33, 244
Christian Coalition, 403, 406
Christian right, 382, 383, 384–85, 397–406, 407–9, 467n10
Christianity and English Scottish Rite ritual, 165, 438n33
church and state, separation of. *See* separation of church and state
Church of Jesus Christ of Latter-day Saints, 429n20
Circular throughout the Two Hemispheres (1802), 20, 29–30
Citizens Flag Alliance, Incorporated, 365–66
civil rights movement, 264–65, 269, 295, 313–14, 315–16

Civil War, 69, 70, 71–73, 76–77
Claudy, Carl H., 191
Clausen, Grand Commander Henry Christian, 217, 289, 303, 319–45, 433n46, 463n18
    Allocutions, 433n46
    background, 319–23
    bust of, 345, 464n78
    and ceremonies, 227, 328
    as Deputy Grand Commander, 316–17, 322
    and George Washington University, 343–45
    and *Grand Constitution of 1786*, 17
    and *History of the Supreme Council*, 324–25
    and House of the Temple, 326
    and international Masonic relations, 339–40
    and C. Fred Kleinknecht, 351–52
    legacy, 345
    and library, 326–27
    and membership growth, 338–39
    and public officials, 332, 333
    and regional Scottish Rite workshops, 323–24
    and rituals, 328–29, 330, 338–39
    and Scottish Rite Foundation, 280–81, 356–57
    and self-help books, 334–35
    and separation of church and state, 332, 341–43
    and Stanford University, 356–57
    and Supreme Council Archives, 323–24
    travel, 339
    writings, 327–31
Clausen's Commentaries on Morals and Dogma (Clausen), 327–28
Clavel, J. F. B., 48, 430n47
Clay, Henry, 35, 37–38, 42, 51–52, 61–62, 332
Clement, Fernand, 254
Clement XII, Pope, 10
Clermont, Duc de, 14
Cleveland, Grover, 111, 116, 124, 129
Clinton, DeWitt, 32–33
Clinton, William J., 333, 362
Cochran, Sam P., 188–89
Coil, Henry Wilson, 13–14, 426n83
Collet, Paul, 279
Colombia, 33, 137
Colon, Colombia, 137
Colonial America, 8–11, 16
Colorado, 355, 356
community service. *See* philanthropy
Compilation of the Messages and Papers of the Confederacy, A (Richardson), 151
concentration camps, 250–56
Concordat of 1855, 53
Confederate States of America, 69, 71–72, 77
Conferences of English-speaking Supreme Councils:
    1954, 279
    1964, 312
Confidential Allocutions. See individual commanders
Connally, Tom, 246, 259
Connery, Charles W., 189
consistories, 52, 53, 64, 276
conspiracy theories, 381, 382, 385, 386–87, 391, 393, 402, 403, 404–5, 406, 454n36, 468n19, 471n58

Constitutions of the Freemasons (Anderson's), 229, 471n57

Converted Catholic, The, 245

Coolidge, August Burt, 229, 452n105

Coolidge, Calvin, 196, 205, 208–9, 213, 220, 221

Cooper, Leroy Gordon, 317

Corbett, William C., 277

cornerstones:
  House of the Temple, 162–63
  Masonic ceremonies for the laying of, 20–21, 50–51, 222, 306, 361
  reenactments of laying of, 361
  Washington Monument, 50–51

Cortissoz, Royal, 175

Cott, Nancy F., 417

Court of Honor:
  ceremonies, 169, 185, 328
  established, 90–91
  Grand Cross of the, 94, 202
  Knights Commander of, 94, 169, 173, 185, 202, 203, 207, 261–62, 284, 328, 351

Cowles, Grand Commander (Capt.) John H., 186, 201–68, 325, 351, 411, 428n49, 433n36, n38, 456n70
  Allocutions, 205–6, 209, 210, 212, 213–14, 215, 216, 218–19, 222, 235, 243, 249, 263, 264–65, 267–68
  and anti-Masonry, 244
  and anti-Masonry in Europe, 238–39, 454n39, n41, n43
  background, 202–3
  bust of, 205–6
  column in *The New Age*, 215
  and consequences of intolerance, 245
  elected Grand Commander, 196–97
  epitaph, 267–68
  and feud with Northern Jurisdiction, 260–61, 262
  funeral, 267
  generosity of, 227, 454n26
  and George Washington University, 456n82
  and *Grand Constitutions of 1786*, 20
  and Thomas Harkins, 272, 274–75
  and history of the Supreme Council, 218–19
  honored by foreign Masonic bodies, 246–47
  and House of the Temple, 176–77, 183, 184–85, 190, 215–16
  and immigration policy, 232, 233
  interment in House of the Temple, 258
  and international Masonry, 185–86, 234, 454n26, n31, 455n39, n41, n43
  and C. Fred Kleinknecht, 464n6
  and Ku Klux Klan, 207–8
  and Masonic lobbying, 195
  and George F. Moore, 177, 190
  and motion picture industry, 244–45
  and non-Masonic philanthropy, 214–15
  and organization of the Supreme Council, 64–65
  and persecution of Masons in Europe, 247–56
  and political involvement, 220, 453n115, n120
  and public education issues, 204, 206, 231–32
  and racial discrimination, 225, 243, 264–65, 457n90
  and recruitment and retention of membership, 214–15, 223–24, 226–27
  and revision of *Statutes*, 226
  and rituals, 216, 226
  and Roman Catholics, 221, 232–33, 244–45
  as Secretary General, 165–66, 170, 180–81, 192, 194, 197, 203–4
  and separation of church and state, 266–67
  and shortcomings of Masons, 243, 245
  sick calls on brethren, 246
  and Social Security, 233, 239–41
  travels, 204, 212, 215, 233–34, 246, 248, 310, 454n22
  and Harry S. Truman, 256–57, 261–62, 263

Cowles Aid Fund, 267

Cowles Benevolent Fund, 267

Cox, Allyn, 307

Cox, Harvey, 405–6

Cox, James M., 196

Cox, Robert W., 326

credit-card programs, 357–59

Crowe, John H., 306–7

Cuba, 33, 136, 234, 279, 294, 311–12

Culver Military Academy, 153–54

Czechoslovakia, 249

Da Costa, Isaac, Sr., 16–17, 22

Dalcho, Grand Commander Frederick, 425n66, 426n83, n5, 427n27
  and Cerneauists, 36
  and formation of Supreme Council, 22–23, 25, 26, 27, 29
  as Grand Commander, 34–37, 428n45
  and *Grand Constitutions of 1786*, 19
  and Northern Jurisdiction, 31, 34
  pilgrimage to grave of, 209

Dallas, Tex., 324–25, 335–37, 354

D'Alviella, Count Goblet, 147–48, 154

Daniels, Ara M., 262

Davies, Robertson, 384

Davis, John W., 209

Davis, Susan Lawrence, 81–82, 435n119

Dawson, J. M., *Studies in Church and State*, Baylor University, 309

Day, Edward C., 192, 197, 207

de Grasse (-Tilly), Alexandre Francois Auguste, 27–28, 30–31, 415

De La Motta, Emanuel, 26, 27, 29, 30–31, 34, 35, 425n66

De La Motta, Grand Commander Jacob, 31, 47–48

de la Rive, Abel Clarin, 469n30

de Ladebat, Charles Laffon, 68

De Lieben, Israel, 27

Decatur, Ga., 181, 207, 280, 354

Declaration of Independence: Masons as signers, 10–11

degrees:
  blue, 83
  defined, 13
  fees for, 79, 152, 228

Knights Templar, 32

Lodge of Perfection. *See* degrees, Rite of Perfection

manual for, 80

paintings representing, 368

sublime. *See* sublime degrees of Masonry

symbols of, 220–21

thirty-third. *See* degrees, thirty-third

See also rituals

degrees, Rite of Perfection:
  conferred by Joseph Cerneau, 32
  origin of, 25

degrees, thirty-third:
  advertising value of, 212, 231
  candidates for, 91, 202, 205, 207, 226–27, 259–60, 261–62
  discipline of holders of, 205
  established, 29–30, 33
  members of Congress, 219
  precursors of, 14
  ritual for, 17, 19–20, 83, 146–47, 368–69
  worth of, 96, 368–69

deHoyos, Arturo, 437n33, 438n36, 439n77, 446n12, 448n53, 451n49, 457n89

Delahogue, Jean Baptiste Marie, 27–28, 33

deMolay, Jacques, 26

DeMolay, Order of, 329, 362

DeMolay Boys' Camp, Tacoma, Wash., 280

Denmark, 78

Denslow, Ray V., 261–62

Desaguliers, Jean Theophile, 7, 8, 422n21

desegregation, 264–65, 313–14, 316

Dewey, Thomas E., 264

Dickens, Charles, 229, 452n105

diploma mills, Masonic, 32, 214

disaster relief aid, 308
  to Charleston, S.C., 113
  to Cuba, 234
  to Dominican Republic, 234
  to Florida, 212
  to Great Britain, 279
  to Jacksonville, Fla., 143
  to Japan, 122, 207
  to Johnstown, Pa., 116
  to the Netherlands, 234, 279
  to San Francisco, Calif., 152–53

District of Columbia:
  Grand Lodge, 50–51, 190
  jurisdictional disputes over, 51, 86
  laying of cornerstones, 20–21, 306
  Lodge of Perfection, 21
  and Pike monument, 130–31, 134, 144–45, 389–96, 443n11
  property exchanges between Supreme Council and local Scottish Rite bodies, 158–59, 182–83
  Scottish Rite membership, 183, 373
  Scottish Rite tax status in, 177, 189–90, 228
  and the Supreme Council, 86, 129, 167, 177, 190

Dole, Robert, 341, 361, 403

Dominican Republic, 234

Drummond, Josiah H., 80, 96, 435n111

Duluth, Minn., 180

Dumenil, Lynn, 177, 194, 195, 204, 223

Dunbar, Ulrich S. J., 210

Duncan, Robert Lipscomb, 59

duty: Masonic concept of, 74–75

Dwight, Timothy, 386–87
Dynamics of Freedom, 324, 329

Eastern Star, Order of, 106
Eastland, James O., 313–14
Eccleston, William E., 339
economic depression of 1893, 124, 131, 133–34
Ecossais Lodges, 30, 427n23
Edinburgh, Scotland, 5
Edstrom, David, 184–85, 189, 215–16
education:
    call for U.S. department of education,
      188, 192, 193, 204, 231, 453n115
    for the deaf, 280
    federal aid for, 281–82, 288, 290–91, 453n115
    Masonic lobbying on, 195, 231–32, 282,
      301, 453n115
    and separation of church and state.
      See separation of church and state.
    special session of the Supreme Council
      on, 190, 192
    See also higher education; public schools;
      scholarships
Eggers, Otto, 184–85
Egypt, 3
Eisenhower, Dwight D., 269–70, 271, 273,
    281–82, 283, 289, 293, 313, 315–16
Eisenson, Jon, 356–57
elderly: care of, 214–15
"Eleven, The," 35–36
Eleven Men of Charleston (Harris), 285
Elliott, F. P., 149
Elliott, Lloyd H., 344–45, 461n54
embezzlement charges (Dallas, Tex.), 335–37
Embury, Aymar, 174
Emerson, Ralph Waldo, 67, 74, 76, 94, 235,
    401, 472n6
Emperors of the East and West, 14–15,
    422n38, 423n47
England:
    early history of Freemasonry in, 3–6, 10,
      421n7, 425n73
    floods, 199, 279
    and international Masonic alliances, 165
English Grand Lodge of France, 14
English Lectures, 6
English-speaking Supreme Councils of
    North America and the British Isles,
    279, 312
Enlightenment, 4, 7, 9, 385–86, 413–14,
    421n18, 422n19
Ervin, Samuel J., 333

Farquhar, Michael, 395–96
Farrakhan, Louis, 388–89, 468n25, 469n26
Fay, Bernard, 244
Fellowship Forum, 193–94, 196, 208
Ferreira, Antonio De S., 95
Feuillard (Feuillas), Lamoliere de, 15
Fleming, Robert J., 126, 128
Fleming, Walter M., 467n1
Flesch, Rudolf, 289
Florence, Billy, 467n1
Florida, 35, 70, 115, 212
Folger, Robert B., 17
Foote, Shelby, 395
Ford, Gerald R., 332, 335
Ford, Henry, 387–88

foreclosures on Scottish Rite temples, 228
Formulas and Rituals (Pike), 63
Forrest, Nathan Bedford, 81–82, 83, 394,
    436n126
Forst, Abraham, 16, 17
Fox, William L., 404–5
Foxman, Abraham, 404, 406
France:
    American Masonic Headquarters in, 189
    development of Freemasonry in, 8, 10,
      14–15
    development of Rite of Perfection degrees
      in, 25
    and early history of Freemasonry, 412–14,
      422n38
    Grand Orient of, 186
    Masonry and atheism, 110
    and persecution of Masons, 252
    and Rite of Memphis, 83–84
    Supreme Council of, 28, 95, 97–98, 252,
      272, 285, 415
    and World War I, 188
Francken, Henry Andrew, 16, 424n49,
    451n48, n49
Franco, Francisco, 247–48, 310–11
Frankland, Abraham Ephraim, 122
Franklin, Benjamin, 10, 11, 278, 380, 422n29
fraternal assistance, 111, 114, 115, 151, 167, 206,
    210, 211, 212–13, 214–15, 226, 228, 243
Fraternal Assistance, Fund for, 111, 114, 115,
    167
Frederick the Great, King of Prussia, 17,
    251, 305, 426n83, 446n12
Fredericksburg, Va., 10
Free and Accepted Masons (F & A M):
    origin of name, 9
Freeman, James Edward, 210–11
Freemasonry:
    in Africa and Asia, 373
    cooperation among the branches of, 377
    in Europe. *See* individual countries
    origins of, 3–4, 5–8
    and religion, 383–87, 396–401, 407–9
    in Russia, 185–87
    social status of, 362
Freemasonry and American Culture 1880–1930
    (Dumenil), 194
Freemasonry and Revolution (Fay), 244
Freemasons: persecution of in World War II
    period, 248–56, 287
    in France, 252
    in Germany, 249, 250–53, 455n39, n41
    in Greece, 247, 253–55
    in Spain, 247–48, 249, 310–11
French, Benjamin B., 50–51, 77–78, 85
French West Indies:
    and early Freemasonry, 414
    Grand Commander of, 28
fund-raising for charitable work, 349, 352–53,
    357–60
funeral services, 66, 83, 118, 126, 138
Furman, Charles M., 49, 54–55, 70–71

Gabriel, Ralph H., 309
Gaines, W. Craig, 71
Gallaudet School for the Deaf, 280
Gamble, William, 16
Garfield, James A., 103

Gems of Thought Encyclopedia (Chris
    Kleinknecht), 325–26
George, King of Greece, 247
George VI, King of England, 246
George Washington Masonic National
    Memorial Association, 150, 163–64, 230
    and John H. Cowles, 163–64, 203, 230–31
    financial support from the Supreme
      Council, 163–64, 180, 184, 230–31
George Washington Masonic National
    Memorial Temple, Alexandria, Va., 230
George Washington University, 263
    donation for school of government,
      217–18, 288, 308–10, 344–45, 461n54
    endowment for scholarships, 193, 290,
      343–45, 372
    Scottish Rite represented on Board of
      Trustees, 218, 343, 456n82
Georgia, 16, 181, 207, 280, 281, 354
Germany, 8, 10
    development of Masonry in, 7–8, 10, 14
    financial aid to, 255
    and Hitler, 234–35
    and persecution of Masons, 249, 250–53,
      455n39, n41
    Scottish Rite in, 251
Gern, Jess W., 368
Givens, William E., 289
Goldsmith, Robert L., 378–79
Goldwater, Barry, 273, 341
Gorbachev, Mikhail, 348
Gould, Robert F., 422n38
Gouley, George Frank, 84
Gourgas, J. J. J., Grand Commander,
    Northern Supreme Council, 43–44,
    45–46, 429n19, 430n31, n34, n37
Grand Commanders:
    Allocutions by. *See* individual commanders
    authority, 146
    duties, 91
    jewel for, 80
    See also individual commanders
Grand Commanders, trips by:
    Thomas Caswell, 131
    Henry C. Clausen, 339
    John H. Cowles, 204, 212, 215, 233–34,
      246, 248, 310, 454n22
    George F. Moore, 176, 188–89, 190
    Albert Pike, 94, 99, 102, 103, 105, 112
    James D. Richardson, 151
    Luther Smith, 286–87, 310, 312
Grand Consistories, 64–65, 102
    California, 134
    Japan, 122
    Kentucky, 52, 203, 433n36
    Louisiana, 52, 433n36
    origin of, 19
    reduced to particular consistories, 157–58
    state, 123, 134, 433n36
Grand Consistory of the United States, 32
Grand Constitutions of 1762, 15, 18, 423n41,
    n42
Grand Constitutions of 1786, 17–20, 22,
    30–31, 34, 45, 47–48, 53, 135, 154, 251,
    305, 330, 425n66, n70, 426n83, 427n27,
    433n38
Grand Council of Princes of Jerusalem, 17,
    20, 33

Grand Lodge According to the Old Institutions, 8
Grand Lodges:
  and African Americans, 264–65, 314–15, 377–79
  California, 322
  civil law and, 115
  Connecticut, 377–78
  Cuba-in-exile, 311
  District of Columbia, 145
  England, 5, 7, 8, 15, 246–47, 254–55, 377, 378
  Florida, 311
  France, 14–15, 413–14
  and George Washington Masonic National Memorial Association, 163–64, 203
  Georgia, 128
  Germany, 251–52
  Idaho, 378
  Iowa, 115, 123
  Israel, 279
  Italy, 210
  Kentucky, 246
  Louisiana, 122, 157
  Maryland, 21, 157
  Massachusetts, 264–65, 377–78, 428n50
  membership, 302, 337, 338, 376–77
  Missouri, 261, 280
  New York, 45
  Oregon, 378
  Pennsylvania, 16
  relationship to Supreme Council, 260
  Scotland, 137, 246, 247
  South Carolina, 34, 43, 46, 48, 49
  system of one for each state, 13, 47
  Utah, 429n20
  Washington, 377
Grand Masters Conference, 1909, 157
Grant, Ulysses S., 85
Great Depression, 221, 222, 224, 227–28, 233, 235, 243
Greece, 247, 253–55
Grub, Phillip D., 343–44
guilds, 3–4, 5–8
Gustaf V, King of Sweden, 246

Haggard, Forrest D., 371
Hahn, Conrad, 9
Hailey, Daniel M., 165
Haiti, 21–22, 414
Hall, Brig. Gen. Robert H., 146
Hallum, John, 122
Hamill, John, 5, 26, 476
Hanauer, Edward M., 229
Handlin, Oscar, 104
Harding, Warren G., 196, 205, 260
Harkins, Grand Commander Thomas J., 255, 272–83
  Allocutions, 279
  background, 271–75, 276
  and ceremonies, 276
  and John H. Cowles, 272, 274–75
  and education issues, 281–82
  and international Masonic relations, 279–80
  legacy, 282–83
  and publications, 276–77
  and relations with Northern Jurisdiction, 276
  resignation, 282

and Scottish Rite Foundation, 280–81, 283, 356
Harris, Ray Baker, 29, 101, 146, 191, 219, 258, 277–78, 285, 305–6, 307, 428n49, 449n93, 458n30, 472n72, 475
Hatch, Thomas Edwards, 125, 126
Hatoyama, Ichiro, 286
Havana, Cuba, International Supreme Council Meeting (1956), 279
Hawaii, 97, 100, 136, 286
Hays, Brooks, 315–16
Hays, Moses Michael, 16–17
Hays, Will H., 244
Henderson, Mary Newton Foote, 160, 162
Hepburn, William P., 153
Herberg, Will, 269
Heredom, 371–72, 475, 477
hermetic theology, 4, 8, 421n18, 422n19
Hicks, Elias, 45
higher education:
  call for a national university in D.C., 192, 204, 206
  dormitories for colleges and universities, 197, 232, 280
  Masonic support for, 151–52, 154, 192, 193, 197, 217–18, 290, 343–45, 461n49
  scholarships for, 151–52, 154, 193, 310, 343–44, 372
  and Scottish Rite, 151–52, 154, 217–18, 308–9, 343–44
  See also education; George Washington University
Hillburn, Sam E., 372–73, 400–401
History of the Supreme Council, The (Carter), 306, 324–25
Hitler, Adolf, 234–35, 251, 263, 453n127, 454n39, n41
Hoban, James, 21
Hobart, Garret A., 130
Hofstadter, Richard, 179, 194, 195–96, 233, 282, 382–83
Hoke, Michael, 181, 207
Holbrook, Grand Commander Moses, 22, 37, 144
  as Grand Commander, 38, 43, 46–48, 429n19, 430n31, n37
  and Northern Jurisdiction, 44–46
Holland, 8, 10, 455n43
Holly, James L., 397, 398, 401
Holmes, Oliver Wendell, 238
Holocaust and Masons, 234–35, 250–56, 311
Holt, Herbert B., 212
Honolulu, Hawaii, 97
Honour, Grand Commander John Henry, 48, 49, 50, 53–55, 63, 70–71
Hoover, Herbert C., 182, 221
Hoover, J. Edgar, 307, 314
House of the Temple: first, at 433 Third Street, NW, 102, 105, 158–59
  dedication of, 111
  expansion of, 128–29, 136, 137
  expenditures for, 105, 126
  as home for the Grand Commander, 102, 103, 118
  Pike memorial room, 144
  remodeling of, 126, 128, 137
  traded to local D.C. Scottish Rite bodies, 158–59, 182–83
House of the Temple: 16th and S Streets, NW

alarm system for, 304
annex added, 372
and archives storage, 324
art for, 368. See also collection of portraits; sculpture for
basement problems, 460n34
caretakers, 277, 304
collection of portraits, 138, 307, 321, 361
cornerstones laid, 162–63, 190
cost, 162, 167, 176–77, 183, 445n90
dedication of, 173–74, 175
design, 174–75, 446n11
enlargement of lot, 188, 305
fire, 304
improvements to, 215–16, 277, 349, 358, 372
inscriptions, 185, 189–90, 191, 196
interment in, 258
memorial plaque to Richardson, 215
opened to the public, 185, 372
Albert Pike Memorial Room, 191, 197
planning for, 158–59, 160–63, 166, 168, 445n107
relationship to its neighborhood, 372
repairs to, 190, 197, 257–58, 326, 372
sculpture for, 184–85, 189, 206, 210, 215–16, 345, 448n45
and Supreme Council sessions, 210
tax-exempt status for, 177, 189–90, 228
House of the Temple Historic Preservation Foundation, 358
Houser, Everett, 338–39
Howard, A. E. Dick, 341–42
Howard, George E., 149
Hudson, Winthrop, 287
Hugo, Trevelyan William, 118, 180, 197, 441n125
Hull, Cordell, 248–49
Humphrey, Hubert H., 295, 297–98
Huntley, Chet, 273
Hurst, Jack, 83, 436n126
Hussey, Ernest B., 192–93
Hutchens, Rex R., 25–26, 76, 367–68, 369, 475
Hymns to the Gods and Other Poems (Pike), 93

Ihle, Earl, 358
Illuminati, Bavarian Society of the, 386, 387–88, 389, 405, 468n15, n21
Illustrations of Masonry: By One of the Fraternity Who Has Devoted Thirty Years to the Subject (Morgan), 39, 40
immigrants, 9–10
  Americanization of, 184, 195, 206
  Catholics, 387
  education of, 184
  Jews, 387
  Masons, 10
  Pike's attitude toward, 62
  restrictions on, 195, 232, 233, 253
  from southern and eastern Europe, 104, 387
immigration:
  and the Holocaust, 253
  and Masons, 184, 195, 206, 232, 233, 253, 287
  quotas, 253
"In the Hearts of Men" (film), 307
Independent Publishing Company, 194, 208. See also Fellowship Forum
Indian Territory, 71–73
industrialization, 139–40, 142, 153

infant care clinics, Masonic:
Duluth, Minn., 180, 441n125
Maryland, 180
insurance policies, 358
inter-fraternal matters: need to keep out of
public forum, 245
International Bureau of Masonic Affairs,
164
International Jew, The, 387–88
international Masonic relations, 65–66, 95,
97–98, 147–48, 154–55, 164–65, 166, 188,
190, 198, 204, 219, 234, 279–80, 305–6,
310–13, 339–40, 373, 454n26, n31, 455n39,
n41, n43. *See also* jurisdictional disputes
Iowa, Grand Lodge of, 115, 123
Iowa Masonic Library, 123, 130, 180
Ireland, William M., 103, 105, 112–13, 114, 116
Ireland, Supreme Council of, 37
isolationism: American, 248–49
Italy, 248–49, 280, 310, 315
attacks on Freemasonry, 210, 234
Grand Lodge of, 10, 210
Supreme Council of, 193–94, 205–6, 210,
279–80
Iversen, Charles S., 390, 392–93, 394–95,
470n31

Jackson, Andrew, 37–38, 42, 142, 332
Jackson, Henry, 341
Jackson, Robert H., 366
Jackson, Thornton A., 457n89
Jacksonville, Fla., 143
Jacob, Margaret C., 4, 414, 416, 422n19
Jamaica, 15–16, 414
Japan, 122, 157–58, 207, 262, 286
Jefferson, Thomas, 11, 22, 23, 35, 42–43,
468n15
Jews:
as Masons, 16, 250–51, 438n33, 454n36
as members of the Supreme Council, 26
persecution of, 250–51, 253, 311
See also conspiracy theories
Jews and Freemasonry in Europe, 1923–1939
(Katz), 250, 251
job placement services, 227, 263–64
Johnson, Andrew, 77–78, 79, 81, 387, 392,
435n102
Johnson, Lyndon B., 296
Johnson, Melvin M., Grand Commander,
Northern Jurisdiction, 259–60, 261, 262,
276
Johnson, Robert W., 85
Johnson, Samuel, 234
Johnstown, Pa.: flood, 116
Joint Scottish Rite Committee on Unity, 379
Jollicoeur, Pamela M., 407–8
Jolsen, Al, 213
"Journeyings of the Grand Commander"
(column), 215
jurisdictional disputes:
over the District of Columbia, 51, 68
with France, 97
over Hawaii, 97
and Mexican cession, 50
involving South America, 137
and Spanish-American War, 44, 136
with the Supreme Council, Northern
Jurisdiction, 31, 43–45, 48, 50, 51, 68,
80, 86, 89, 98, 152, 260–61

with the Supreme Council for the West
Indies, 30–31

Kadosh, Councils of, 64–65
funeral services, 118, 126
membership in, 275
Kah, Gary H., 389, 469n27
Kai-Shek, Chiang, 254, 286
Kammen, Michael, 363
Katz, Jacob, 250, 251
Kennedy, John F., 294–302, 460n23
Kentucky, 52, 64, 100, 202–3
Kerensky, Alexander F., 185–87
Khrushchev, Nikita, 293
Kleinknecht, Grand Commander C. Fred,
Jr., 155, 274, 276, 282, 304, 312, 322–23,
325, 347–80, 411, 412, 470n31
Allocutions, 355, 360–61
and American flag, 365, 366–67
background, 349–52, 379–80, 464n6
and childhood learning disorders, 355
and John H. Cowles, 464n6
and fund raising, 349, 352–53, 357–60
generosity of, 465n13
and George Washington University, 345, 372
and House of the Temple, 358, 372
and international Masonry, 371–73
and Lyndon LaRouche, 391, 392
leadership style, 352–53, 367, 380
and Masonic regalia, 368
and membership recruitment, 376–77
and patriotism, 360–61, 364, 365, 366–67
and philanthropic work, 357, 359
and Pike Monument, 392–93, 396
and possibility of union of Northern and
Southern Jurisdictions, 379
and Prince Hall Masons, 376–77, 378–79
and publications, 367
and Ronald Reagan, 362
and religious right, 398–401, 403
and revision of rituals, 367–69
and Pat Robertson, 403, 472n75
and Scottish Rite Foundation, 357
and Scottish Rite Research Society, 371–72
as Secretary General, 351–52
and Supreme Council accounting system,
351
Kleinknecht, Christian F., Sr., 228, 276,
325–26, 350, 351, 452n80, 464n6
Knights of Labor, 109
Knights of the East, 14, 422n38
Knights Templar:
degrees, 32
Grand Commanders, 125, 128, 422n22
and origin of Scottish Rite, 25–26
and Albert Pike, 61, 84
Knowles, Louis L., 407–8
"Know-Nothing" Party, 62, 63
Ku Klux Klan, 81–83, 193, 194–96, 198–99, 209
and anti-Masonry, 382
and John H. Cowles, 207–8
and Masons, 194, 195, 198, 207–8, 240,
382, 390, 436n124
and Albert Pike, 81–83, 382, 390, 391–96,
435n119, 436n120, n126
ritual, 436n120, n124

La Follette, Robert M., 209
ladies' certificates, 105–6

Lafayette, Marquis de, 37, 411–12, 428n49,
473n2
Lamberth, Royce C., 390, 391
language disorder clinics, 193, 281, 283,
353–57, 359–60
LaRouche, Lyndon, 382, 383, 390, 391–92,
393, 394–95, 401, 407, 470n37
Lasch, Christopher, 330, 418–19
Lassalle, Jean-Pierre, 17
Latin America, 234, 248, 311–12
Lausanne, Switzerland, Congress of
Supreme Councils of the Scottish Rite:
1874, 95
1875, 97–98, 148, 165
1920, 190
1922, 197, 204, 219
Law, Cardinal Bernard, 467n10
Laying of Cornerstones, The (Harris), 306
Lears, Jackson, 131, 132–33
Leazer, Gary, 398
Leffingwell, William Edward, 94
Lehmann, Leo H., 232–33, 244, 245
Lenin, Vladimir I., 171–72, 185, 186–87
Leo XIII, Pope, 106–10, 287–88, 469n30
Leonhardt, Ernest, 249
Let's Celebrate America, 361
Letters to the People of the Northern States
(Pike), 63
Leuchtenberg, William E., 239
Levi, Eliphas, 74
Levin, Nathaniel, 129, 135
Levy, Moses Clava, 28–29, 34
Lewis, Larry L., 400
Lexicon of Freemasonry, A (Mackey), 48–49
Liberty Bonds, 187–88, 193
Library of the Supreme Council:
acquisitions for, 144, 228–30, 277–78
anti-Masonic literature in, 229
appropriations for, 100–101, 125
begun by Albert Pike, 100–101, 104
bequests to, 143, 165, 169, 452n105
Burns Collection, 168–69, 191, 305
catalogues of, 101, 117, 134, 143
classification system for Masonic
materials, 180, 438n52
collection of Masonic medals, 152
Goethe Collection, 191, 228
housing for, 105, 126, 128–29, 175, 277, 371
inventory of, 326–27
librarian's reports, 112, 125, 129, 146, 165,
180, 197
manuscripts, 278
museum, 215, 306–7
open to the public, 305, 326–27
Albert Pike Library, 150, 197, 229
rare books, 229, 326, 327
reading room, 191
renovation of, 371
size of, 105, 113–14, 117, 128, 191, 327
Thatcher Collection, 327
Lichty, Warren D., 371
Life magazine, 284–85
Lincoln, Abraham, 61–62, 63, 67, 70, 77,
92, 229, 392
Lind, Michael, 403–4
Lindbergh, Charles A., 213, 231
Lindsay, R. S., 17
Lippmann, Walter, 171, 187, 189, 259
Lipson, Dorothy Ann, 40

Little Rock, Ark., 59–60, 61, 315–16
Little Rock Advocate, 59, 60
Livingston, Robert R., 13
lobbying, Masonic, 195
Lobingier, Charles S., 17, 211, 218–19, 427n28, 475
Lockwood, R. Lee, 302, 322–23, 336
Lodges of Perfection:
  Albany, N.Y., 16, 20
  Alexandria, Va., 20–21
  attendance at, 224
  authority over, 15, 143, 154–55
  ceremonies for, 66, 83, 224
  Charleston, S.C., 20, 22–23, 28, 29
  charters for, 64–65
  dues and fees, 214–15, 223, 224, 238, 276
  and fraternal assistance and relief, 211
  indebtedness of, 210, 214–15, 302, 373–74
  membership decline, 213–14, 224, 337–39, 375–76
  membership growth, 155, 210, 213–14, 275–76, 302
  numbers of, 155, 210, 275–76
  Philadelphia, Pa., 17, 20
  property of, 302–3, 373–74
  rituals of the, 78, 83
Lodges of Sorrow:
  ceremonies for, 83
  conducted, 85
London, England, 254–55, 257
Long, Odell Squier, 117, 128, 136
Louisiana, 16, 30, 33, 52, 53, 64, 80, 122
Louisville, Ky., 52
Ludendorff, Eric, 235

MacArthur, Douglas, 261, 262
McDonald, Grand Commander Alexander, 46, 48, 49
McKee, John, 335–36
MacKenzie, Maxwell, 358
Mackey, Albert Gallatin, 46–47, 48–49, 52, 68–69, 70, 103, 134, 278
  as Grand Secretary, 79, 80, 86, 101, 112
  and Albert Pike, 49, 52, 53–55, 57, 61, 63, 100, 432n30, 451n49
  publications, 48, 423n47
Mackey, Pauline L., 278
McKinley, William, 130–31, 135, 138, 142, 143–44
McLean, John R., 160
Macoy (publisher), 93
Madison, James, 33, 40
Malcolm, Philip S., 196
Manifesto of 1802 (Scottish Rite), 20, 22, 29–30, 53, 425n70
Manifesto of August 2, 1845, 48
Manker, Orville Paul, 207
Markham, Edwin, 238
Marshall, Thurgood, 265
Marvin, Cloyd Heck, 217–18, 308–9, 344–45, 461n54
Maryland, 86
  and Cerneauists, 114, 115
  Deputy Inspector General for, 16
  Grand Lodge of, 115
  infant care clinic, 180
  and jurisdictional disputes over, 86, 89
Maryland Bank of North America (MBNA), 357–58

Mason, George, 12
Masonic charitable service:
  hospitals for children, 181, 280–81, 353–54
  Scottish Rite as pioneer in, 181
Masonic Information Center, 399–400
Masonic law, 102, 135, 164, 176, 205, 261–62, 335, 336, 416
Masonic medals: collections of, 152, 229–30
Masonic Renewal Committee of North America, 376
Masonic rings, 216–17, 276, 451n48, n49
Masonic Service Association, 257, 354, 361, 399–400
Masonic Service Centers, 257
Masonic titles, 303
Masonic War Relief Association, 180
Masonry Dissected (Pritchard), 40
Masons Company of London, 5
Masons Who Helped Shape Our Nation (Clausen), 329
Massachusetts, 11–12, 33, 44
Massey, William B., 307
Matthews, Reynold J., 133, 371, 462n13
Matusow, Allen J., 300
Mausoleum of Halicarnassus, 160–61, 174
May, Henry F., 468n16
Mayo, Charles H., 231
M'Cosh, Joseph, 428n45
Meese, Edwin A., III, 342
Meese, Norman S., 276–77, 285–86, 314–15, 461n70
Melius, John, 361
membership:
  age of, 373, 466n68
  Catholics, 28, 110, 289
  causes of growth, 153, 164, 371
  costs of, 214–15, 223, 224, 238, 275–76, 339, 44in7
  data, 164, 168, 375, 460n27, 467n68
  declines, 213–14, 222, 223–24, 225, 226–27, 238–39, 242–43, 332, 373–77, 418, 453n6, 467n68
  and educational levels, 159
  growth, 91, 98, 111, 113, 131, 133–34, 136, 142, 144, 151, 153, 155, 193, 198, 201, 205, 210, 213–14, 259, 263, 275–76, 302–4, 337–39, 371, 385, 417
  locations of growth, 142, 159, 183
  Lodges of Perfection, 164, 275, 302, 374–76, 460n27
  and middle-class prosperity, 159
  record-keeping, 325–26
  recruitment of, 214, 339, 376–77
  retention of, 214–15
Memphis, Tenn., 436n126
Mencken, H. L., 179
Meredith, Gilmor, 128, 138
Methodism, 288
Mexican cession, 50, 51–52
middle class:
  and Americanism, 179–80, 195–96
  in Colonial America, 9
  effect of cultural values of on Scottish Rite membership, 131–33, 140–41
  and industrialization, 153
  Masonry as reflection of values of, 131–33, 140–41, 195–96, 199
  Scottish Rite as exemplar of, 172, 223, 232
  and urbanization, 153

military Masonic Lodges, 10. *See also* armed forces
millenarianism, 8, 396–97, 405–6, 471n55
Miller, William M., 333, 378–79
Mills, Wilbur D., 334
Minnesota, Grand Lodge of, 115
Mississippi, 64
Missouri, 280, 307
Mitchell, Grand Commander John, 34, 306–7
  and formation of Supreme Council, 22–23, 25, 26
  and George Washington, 20–21
  legacy, 33–34
  made Deputy Inspector General for South Carolina, 20
  made Sovereign Grand Inspector of South Carolina, 21–22
  and Northern Jurisdiction, 31
Modern Grand Lodge, 8
Moderns:
  Grand Lodge of South Carolina, 33–34
  origin of name, 8–9
Moe, Ronald C., 186
Moley, Raymond, 238
Moore, Grand Commander George F., 135, 149–50, 154, 164, 165, 167
  Allocutions, 173, 175, 178, 180, 182–83, 184, 187, 189, 190, 192, 196
  and Americanism, 194–96, 197
  background, 172–73
  bust of, 193
  and Cerneauists, 156–57
  and John H. Cowles, 180–81, 208
  elected Lt. Grand Commander, 169
  and *Fellowship Forum*, 193–94, 196, 197
  as Grand Commader, 172–99
  and House of the Temple, 175, 184, 185, 189–90, 197
  and international Masonic relations, 187–88
  and Ku Klux Klan, 194–95, 198, 208
  legacy, 198–99
  and need for tax-exempt status for the Supreme Council, 177
  and need to revise *Statutes*, 175–76
  and *The New Age*, 149–50, 156–57, 169, 173, 178–79, 447n26
  papers, 449n93
  rebuffed by the Supreme Council, 189–90, 192
  resignation, 196–97
  and revision of rituals, 169, 175, 185, 190
  statue of, 184–85
  and trip to France, 188–89
  and World War I, 171–72, 182, 187–89
Moore, William D., 132
morality: ceremonies and symbols used to promote, 7
Morals and Dogma (Pike), 73–76, 80, 83, 86, 93, 109, 118, 119, 154–55, 226, 327, 394, 434n78, n81, n85, 435n115, 443n16, 447n24, 470n46
Moray, Robert, 5
Morgan, William, 33, 39–40, 41–42, 229, 428n50, n1, 429n2
Morin, Etienne (Stephen), 15–16, 423n41, n47, 424n48, n49, n50, n53, 451n48
Morison, Samuel Eliot, 51
Mormons, 429n20

Morris, John W., 151, 165–66
Morris, S. Brent, 338, 354, 371, 403, 477
Morse, Jedediah, 386–87
Morton, General Jacob, 13
Mother Council of the World:
  Northern Jurisdiction and name, 260, 276
  origin of name, 20, 145, 279–80
Mother Grand Lodge of the World, 7
Moultrie, James, Sr., 28, 29, 34, 37
Müfflemann, Leopold, 251–52, 454n39, n41
Muhlenberg, Frederick A., 13
Muhlenberg, John Peter, 13
Müller, F. Max, 76
Museum of Our National Heritage,
  Lexington, Mass., 348
music for the Scottish Rite, 104
  at ceremonies, 163, 174
  organs, 184
  for rituals, 184, 443n23
  by Sibelius, 263
Mussolini, Benito, 210, 234, 235, 310
Myers, Joseph M., 16, 17, 20
Mystic Tie, The (Mackey), 49

Nailor, Allison, Jr., 149, 155
National Defense Education Act of 1958, 290
National Education Association, 266
Nations, Gilbert Owen, 194
nativism, 194, 383, 387–88, 402
Nazism, 250–56, 311
Nebraska, Grand Lodge of, 115
Negro Masonry, 225. *See also* Prince Hall
  Masons
Netherlands, 252, 279, 311
New Age, The:
  advertisements in, 151–52
  banned by Nazis, 253
  board of directors, 148–49, 156–57
  board of trustees, 150, 169
  circulation, 307, 329, 452n77
  consultants, 367
  control of, 170, 197
  editors, 156–57, 169, 173, 276–77, 285–86
  format, 276–77, 285–86
  funding for, 178
  Grand Commander's column, 215,
    243–44, 296–97, 298–99, 300, 301,
    314–15, 340
  initiated, 148–50
  and institutional self-esteem, 223
  offices, 156, 169
  as "official organ of the Supreme
    Council," 190, 407–8
  and patriotism, 361
  "Positions Wanted" column, 227
  and presidential campaigns, 221, 296–97,
    298
  and public activism by Scottish Rite,
    192–93
  and scholarships, 151
  and social issues, 178–79, 192, 296–97,
    314–15, 407–8, 447n26, 477
New Orleans, La., 16, 30, 33, 46, 52, 53,
  156–58, 427n23
New World Order, The (Robertson), 401–2,
  403, 404–5, 406
New York City, N.Y., 20, 31, 32–33, 46
New York, 32–33, 42, 45
New York Times, 404, 432n9

Newbury, George A., Grand Commander,
  Northern Jurisdiction, 300
Newton, Isaac, 4, 7–8, 421n18, 422n21
Newton, Joseph Fort, 247–48, 380, 416–17
Nixon, Richard M., 294, 296–97, 299, 333,
  334–35, 408
Noll, Mark, 396
Norcross Brothers Company, 162, 183
North Carolina, 70
North China Language School, 232
Northern Light, The, 366
Norway, 255–56
numismatic collections (Masonic chapter
  or mark pennies), 229
Nunn, Richard J., 149, 150, 151

Obalensky, Prince Vladimir, 186
Odd Fellows, Independent Order of, 49, 61
Odell, William R., 289
*Official Bulletin of the Supreme Council
  for the Southern Jurisdiction of the
  United States*, 90, 123–24, 137, 149
"On the Wings of Words" (film), 359
Order of Colonial Masonic Lodges, 168
Oregon, 193, 206, 209, 232
orients, 45, 49–50, 94, 134
Orlady, George B., 157
Orwell, George, 263
Our Public Schools (Givens), 289, 307
Oxford, Arnold Whitaker, 26

Palmer, Henry L., 123, 144, 149
papal bulls and encyclicals, 245
  Humanum Genus (The Human Race;
    1884), 106–10, 287–88, 469n30
  In Eminenti (1738), 10
  and Masonic response, 245
  Syllabus of Errors, 108
Parfait Maçon, Le (pamphlet), 14, 423n39
Paris, France, 189, 234, 252, 253, 257
Parker, Alton B., 150
Parkhurst, Charles W., 340
parochial schools:
  and compulsory public schools, 193
  Masonic opposition to, 193, 232, 341
  public aid to, 341–43
  as response to Protestant inclination of
    public schools, 106, 109, 439n80
  See also Roman Catholics; separation of
    church and state
Parvin, Theodore Sutton, 123, 130
Passman, Otto E., 296–97, 310
patents:
  to establish a Lodge of Perfection in
    Albany, N.Y., 16
  granted to Joseph Cerneau, 32
  for propagating the Rite of Perfection in
    the Americas, 14–15, 16, 423n47,
    424n48, n50
patriotism:
  celebrations of, 361
  as Masonic value, 168, 361, 363–67, 408
  and Masonic war efforts, 188
  as membership requirement, 281
  See also Americanism
Patton, Frank C., 248
Paul, Francis G., Grand Commander,
  Northern Jurisdiction, 379

Pea Ridge (Arkansas): battle of, 71–73, 77,
  79, 82, 434n70
peace movements: pre–World War I, 164–65,
  168
Peale, Norman Vincent, 269, 270–71, 330,
  398
Pearl Harbor, 320, 321–22
Pelikan, Jaroslav, 106
Penn, James, 70
Pennsylvania, 10, 11, 33
Pershing, General John J., 231
Peru, 95
Pfister, Francis Joseph von, 16
Philadelphia, Pa., 10, 16, 20
philanthropy:
  in American society, 114
  in early guilds, 6
  fund-raising for, 354, 357–60
  Masonic, 114, 177–78, 181, 192–93, 353–54,
    363
  See also philanthropy, Scottish Rite
philanthropy, Scottish Rite:
  care of sick children, 180–81, 207, 353–54
  fraternal. *See* fraternal assistance
  infant care clinics, 180
  milk distribution programs, 180
  origins of, 74–75, 354, 356
  and tax-exempt status, 177–78
  volunteer service, 354, 418
  See also Fraternal Assistance, Fund of
Philippine Islands, 136, 286, 311
philosophical lodges: early development
  of, 3–5
Phylaxis, 393, 394
Pierce, William Frank, 149, 152–53, 154, 158,
  161
Pike, Grand Commander Albert, 411,
  425n66, 432n9, 440n93, 441n125, 473n2
  and African Americans, 62–63, 264–65,
    435n115, 436n140, 457n89, n90, 470n46
  Allocutions by. *See* Pike, Albert, *Allocutions*
  and American Indians, 59, 60, 71–73, 77,
    82, 432n9
  and appeal of the Scottish Rite, 131
  and attendance at Supreme Council
    meetings, 67
  attitude toward immigrants, 62
  attitude toward slavery, 62–63
  background, 57–59, 431n3, n4, n7, 432n9
  becomes Grand Commander, 54–55, 57, 63
  bibliography of writings by, 191
  bust of, 210
  and Catholicism, 107–10
  celebration of 100th anniversary of the
    birth of, 158, 159–60
  and ceremonial rituals, 66
  and Cerneauism, 112, 114–15
  children, 85, 117, 298, 456n68
  and the Civil War, 69, 71–73, 77–78, 79,
    82, 434n70
  and concept of duty, 74–75
  death of, 118
  and expansion of the Scottish Rite, 65
  on formation of the Supreme Council, 29
  and Fund of Fraternal Assistance, 111, 114,
    115
  funeral for, 118
  and Germany, 251

and *Grand Constitutions of 1786*, 17, 19
and *Humanum Genus*, 107–10
interment in House of the Temple, 258
and international conventions of
 Supreme Councils, 65–66, 95, 97–98
and jurisdictional disputes, 44, 51
and the Ku Klux Klan, 81–83, 390, 392–96,
 435n119, 436n120, n126
legacy, 118–19
and Albert Mackey, 49, 52, 53–55, 61, 63,
 100, 103, 451n49
medal of, 123–24, 158
memorial ceremony for, 138, 197
memorials to, 129–30, 191
and Mexican War, 60
and money raised from trips, 99, 105, 112
and need for Sovereign Grand Inspectors
 General in each state, 67–68
and need for temple in Washington, D.C.,
 94, 96
and newspaper publishing, 59, 60, 83, 85
painting of, 129
and Prince Hall Masons, 264–65, 457n89,
 n90
proposal for transcontinental railroad,
 60–61
publications, 134, 191, 443n23. *See also*
 Morals and Dogma
and religious intolerance, 62
and revision of rituals, 52–54, 63, 68,
 73–76, 78, 432n30, 435n111, 438n33,
 443n23
and revision of statutes, 100–101, 102,
 111, 113
salary for, 103
sculpture of, 92
statue of, 134–35, 138, 144–45, 389–96,
 431n3, 443n11, 470n38
and study of ancient religions, 73–76,
 93–94, 437n22, 448n70
and Supreme Council library, 100–101,
 105, 113–14, 115, 117
travels of, 94, 99, 102, 103, 105, 112
visits to the grave of, 130, 138, 146
and women, 92–93, 105–6, 117, 437n20,
 439n77. *See also* Ream, Vinnie
writings, 191, 197, 229, 423n42, 439n77,
 441n121, 443n16, 447n24, 469n30
and York Rite, 52, 61, 84, 96–97, 438n36
Pike, Albert, *Allocutions:*
 1860, 67–68, 69
 1861, 70
 1865, 78
 1866, 79–80
 1868, 83–84
 1870, 90
 1872, 94
 1874, 96, 102
 1876, 96
 1878, 52–53, 100–101
 1880, 102
 1882, 104
 1884, 107
 1886, 113–14
 1888, 115
 1890, 117
Pike, James A., 298
Pike, (Luther) Hamilton, 85, 117

Pike, Mary Ann (Hamilton), 59–60, 73
Pius IX, Pope, 108
Plumbline, The, 371–72
Poland, 10, 454n36
political religious right, 401–6
Pope, John Russell, 162, 185, 215, 445n79
 and base for Cowles bust, 206
 and base for Pike bust, 210
 fee for, 161, 176–77, 183, 447n37
 and House of the Temple, 160–61, 174–75,
 176–77, 183, 184–85, 197, 215–16, 446n11
Populism, 195
Pound, Roscoe, 6–7, 176, 416–17
Power of Positive Thinking, The (Peale), 270
Practice and Procedures for the Scottish Rite
 (Clausen), 330
Prasifka, Paul, 335, 336
presidential campaigns:
 1896, 130
 1900, 142
 1916, 181–82, 272–73
 1920, 196–97
 1924, 208–9
 1928, 220, 221
 1936, 237, 238
 1960, 294–302
 Scottish Rite and, 294–302
Prince Hall Masons, 225, 393–94, 396, 417–18
 and Henry C. Clausen, 340–41
 and John H. Cowles, 225, 243, 264–65
 history of, 377–78
 and C. Fred Kleinknecht, 340–41, 376–79
 and Albert Pike, 264–65, 457n89, n90
 recognition from American Grand
 Lodges, 264–65, 377–79
 recognition from Grand Lodges in other
 countries, 225, 377–78
 and Luther Smith, 314, 315–16
 See also African Americans
Princes of Jerusalem, Councils of, 36, 64–65
Princes of the Royal Secret, 15, 18, 20, 52
Pritchard, Samuel, 40
Progressive Era, 152–53, 161, 195
Prohibition movement, 148
Protestants and Other Americans United
 for the Separation of Church and State
 (POAU), 266–67, 288, 308–9, 342
Protocols of the Elders of Zion, The, 250, 388,
 389
Provincial Grand Master (at Boston), 10
public schools:
 calls for English-only education, 179, 184,
 192, 193, 209
 calls for free, compulsory education, 192,
 193, 204, 206
 compulsory attendance in, 193, 206, 209,
 447n24
 desegregation of, 313, 315–16
 and Masons, 179, 184, 192, 193, 195, 206,
 220, 231–32, 281–82, 289–90, 341–43,
 408, 447n24, n26
 Masons on school boards, 290
 Scottish Rite support for, 178–79, 204
 See also education
Puerto Rico, 33, 136, 158
Putnam, Robert, 418–19
Putney, Albert H., 209

Quebec, Canada, conference, 279
Quisling, Vidcun, 255–56

racial desegregation, 295–96, 313, 315–16
racial discrimination, 225, 261, 264–65, 266,
 313–16, 377–79, 393, 394, 462n70, n71,
 470n46. *See also* African Americans
Ralston, Robert O., Grand Commander,
 Northern Jurisdiction, 359, 379
Ramsay, Andrew Michael, 8, 25
Raymond, Rene, 253
Reagan, Ronald, 273, 342–43, 362, 363–64
Ream, Vinnie, 92–93, 117, 229, 437n20,
 439n77
Reid, H. Wallace, 378–79, 450n26, 478
relief to persecuted Masons abroad, 249,
 253–56
 Czechoslovakia, 249
 Spain, 247–48
 Switzerland, 250
religion:
 civil religion, 384–85
 and European Supreme Councils, 165
 of members of the Supreme Council, 19
 and Scottish Rite, 443n16, 471n63
 and Supreme Council of England, 165
religious prejudice, 383–85, 387–88, 389,
 391, 393, 402, 409
*Revolt of the Elites and the Betrayal of
 Democracy, The* (Lasch), 418
Revolutionary Brotherhood (Bullock), 9
Reynolds, Herbert H., 399
Rhodes, John J., 333
Ribuffo, Leo P., 383
Rich, Clayton, 356
Rich, Frank, 404
Richardson, Grand Commander James D.,
 87, 134, 136, 138, 139, 443n16, n18
 Acting Grand Commander, 138, 139, 142,
 143–44
 Allocutions, 143–44, 147–48, 150–51,
 154–55, 157–58, 161, 164–65, 168–69
 background, 142–43
 Centennial Address, 145–46
 and Cerneauists, 157
 as congressman, 129, 134, 150–51, 162
 and John H. Cowles, 166
 death of, 170
 as Grand Commander, 144, 145–70
 and international Masonic relations,
 147–48, 154, 164–65
 legacy of, 170
 and Masonic charity, 151
 memorial to, 215
 and planning for new House of the
 Temple, 158–59, 160–63, 166
 and Progressivism, 153, 195
 and publications, 148–50, 151, 169
 and scholarships, 151
 and use of drama in rituals, 147
 and use of intoxicants, 148
 rings (Scottish Rite), 216–17, 276, 451n48,
 n49
Rite of Memphis, 83–84, 436n130
Rite of Perfection: origins of, 13–15, 17,
 19–20, 25, 412, 422n38, 423n41, 424n49
rituals, 13–14
 appeal, 370–71

Christian nature of, 165, 438n33
and Henry Clausen, 328
and concept of duty, 74–75
and John Cowles, 216, 226
dedicatory, 145
exposés of, 39–40
factual deficiencies of, 175
for Knight Commanders, 169, 185
as morality plays, 146–47, 368, 371
and mysticism, 133, 214
need for uniformity in degree work, 47,
    226, 369
Northern Jurisdiction, 379, 438n33
and Albert Pike, 52–54, 63, 65–66, 68,
    73–76, 78, 83, 84, 214, 226, 251,
    264–65, 443n23
presentation of, 367–69
and Prince Hall Masons, 264–65, 457n89
revision of, 52–54, 63, 65–66, 68, 73–76,
    78, 83, 137, 146–47, 226, 328, 367–69,
    432n30
Rose Croix, 438n33
secrecy of, 391
Shrine, 467n1
social value of, 131–33, 214, 370–71
Swedish, 455n56
translations of, 94, 158, 251, 367–68
use of drama in, 133, 146–47, 168, 184,
    214, 224, 371, 477–78
use of music in, 184, 443n23
use of painted scenery in, 131–32, 168
and Victorian society, 131–33
York Rite, 41–42, 438n36
Road to Freedom, The, 307
Roberts, Allen E., 11
Robertson, A. Willis, 472n72
Robertson, Pat, 382, 383, 401–6, 407, 468n19,
    472n72, n75
Robinson, Tommie L., Jr., 360
Rogers, Elmer E., 276–77
Rogers, Virgil M., 289
Roman Catholic in the White House, A
    (J. Pike), 298
Roman Catholics, 439n83, 440n85
and compulsory public schooling, 193,
    439n80, n84
to be excommunicated if they join or
    assist Masons, 10
and *Fellowship Forum,* 194
and Masonry, 106–10, 221, 232, 287–88,
    299, 300, 311, 384–85, 422n38, 467n10,
    469n30
as Masons, 28, 110, 288
as U.S. president, 221, 287, 294–98,
    299–302
See also papal bulls and encyclicals
Romania, 249, 255, 312
Roosevelt, Franklin D., 196, 237, 238, 253,
    259–60, 261, 321–22
Roosevelt, Theodore, 142, 146, 150–51,
    153–54, 156, 167, 181, 392
Rose Croix, 84, 149
ceremonies, 66, 227, 276, 303
chapters, 20, 31, 53, 64–65
rituals, 438n33
Rosenbaum, Charles E., 160, 165–66, 167,
    172, 183, 189, 206
Roy, Thomas Sherrard, 399, 471n63

Royal and Select Masters, Councils of, 70
Royal Arch Masonry, 39, 41, 52, 61, 84, 128,
    449n96
Ruskin, John, 222
Russia, 78, 185–87, 372, 448n53, n57

St. Laurent, Count, 45
San Francisco, 152–53, 180, 319–21
Santo Domingo, 14–15
Schiller Society, 390, 470n50
Schirra, Walter M., 318
scholarships:
    for best graduate theses on Americanism,
        289
    colleges and universities, 151, 153–54, 193,
        310, 343–45. *See also* George Washing-
        ton University
    for the deaf, 280
Schooley, William E., 280, 290
Schweigert, William G., 354–55
Schwengel, Fred W., 361
Science of Language (Müller), 76
Scotland, 4, 5, 10
    Grand Lodge of, 246
    Grand Master of, 10
    and origin of Scottish Rite, 25–26, 421n7,
        422n22, n38
Scott, Gary, 395, 470n50
Scottish Rite:
    appeal of, 131–33, 140, 172, 202, 214, 223,
        226–27, 243, 270–71, 362–63, 370–71,
        416–17
    caps, 158, 217
    and conservative political agenda, 407–9
    Creed, 145–46, 443n16, n17
    donations for benevolent work, 197
    feast days, 113
    films, 307
    and France, 412–14, 422n38
    geographic extension of, 70
    history of, 371–72
    lineage of, 13–17
    loyalty oath, 281
    membership, 91, 337–38, 373–77, 466n68
    and membership losses, 373–77
    modernization of, 199
    organization of, 64–65
    property, ownership of, 303
    public activism, 192–93
    regional workshops, 323, 338–39
    and religion, 443n16
    reunions, 328–29
    and social conditions, 139–40, 270–71
    and social equality, 153
    sovereignty of Supreme Council over, 135,
        303
    teaching purpose of, 145
    and women, 105–6
Scottish Rite Endowment, Philanthropic,
    and Educational Foundation, 280
Scottish Rite Foundation, 280–81, 283, 307,
    309–10, 335, 336, 357–59, 418
    Colorado, 355, 356
    fund-raising for, 357–60
    Texas, 335, 336
Scottish Rite Herald, 193–94
Scottish Rite Hospital for Crippled Children:
    Dallas, Tex., 280, 324–25, 335–37, 354

Decatur, Ga., 181, 207, 280, 354
Scottish Rite Institute for Childhood
    Aphasia, 356
Scottish Rite Journal, 366, 367, 398–400, 403
Scottish Rite News Bulletin, 276, 285
Scottish Rite News Bureau, 227
Scottish Rite Research Society, 371–72, 475,
    477
Seale, Ronald A., 378–79
Secret Constitutions of 1761, 14–15, 18
self-help books, 330–31
separation of church and state, 107, 193,
    232, 266–67, 281–82, 287–89, 290,
    294–98, 301, 309–10, 332, 341–43, 386,
    399, 408–9, 439n80, 461n49
Seward, William H., 67, 78–79
Shaffner, Taliaferro P., 78
Shays, Daniel, 11–12
Shepherd, Joshua K., 316–17, 322–23
Shepherd's Tavern, Charleston, S.C.
    (founding place of Supreme Council),
    22–23, 218, 219–20
Sheppard, Morris, 240
Shrine, Imperial Order of the, 373, 374–75,
    376, 381, 465n16, 467n1
Shriners Hospital for Crippled Children, 354
Shryock, Thomas J., 157, 184
Sibelius, Jean, 263
Simmons, William J., 194
Simpkins, Frank, 312
Simpson, Alan K., 361, 362–63
Sizemore, W. Gene, 353, 358, 360–61, 365–66
Skew, John, 10
slavery, 35, 51–52, 62–63, 433n55
Smith, Grand Commander Luther A., 271,
    279, 280, 284–91, 293–318, 322–23,
    351–52, 443n18, 460n19, n23
    and African Americans, 313–16
    Allocutions, 306
    and Americanism, 286–87, 289–90
    background, 284, 290–91
    and Catholicism, 287–89, 294–98
    and charitable endeavors, 308–9
    and George Washington University,
        309–10
    and international Masonic relations, 305,
        310–12, 339
    and library privileges, 305
    and Masonic news center, 285
    and membership growth, 302–4
    and 1960 presidential campaign, 294–302
    scholarships, 310
    and separation of church and state,
        287–89, 309–10
    travels, 286, 310, 312
Smith, Judge Luther A.: Scottish Rite
    Scholarships, Vanderbilt Law School, 310
Smith, Robert V., 280
Smith, William, 278
Smith, William R., 168–69, 305
Smithsonian Institution, 215, 438n52
social equality as Masonic goal, 153
Social Security system, 233, 239–41
social virtue:
    civil religion, 384–85
    lodges as agents of, 41
    women as exemplars of, 41
Somoza, Anastasio, 248, 454n31

Sons of the American Revolution, District of Columbia Society of the, 191
South Carolina, 16, 20, 33, 34, 43, 46, 48, 49, 52
Southern Baptist Convention, 382, 383, 397–401, 407, 461n49, 471n58
Sovereign Grand Consistory, 32–33
Sovereign Grand Inspectors General (thirty-third degree):
  attendance at Supreme Council meetings, 67, 78
  duties of, 18, 20, 134, 190, 192
  one for each state, 49–50, 68, 78
  origin of, 18, 19–20
  title, 135
  for the U.S. Army and Navy, 146
Sovereign Grand Lodge, 15
Spain:
  anti-Masonry attitudes in, 16, 234
  and Florida, 35
  Grand Lodge of, 10
  persecution of Masons in, 247–48, 249, 310–11
Spanish-American War, 44, 136
Spanish Civil War, 247–48
Spitzer, Barend M., 16, 17, 20
Stanford University Medical Center, 308, 356–57
Starr, Kevin, 127
Statue of Liberty, 365
Statutes and Institutions of The Supreme Council, 33d for the Southern Jurisdiction of the United States (1866), 79–80
Statutes of the Supreme Council, 53, 54–55, 64, 65, 67, 70, 100–101, 102, 111, 113, 135, 137–38, 146, 148, 155–56, 169, 175–76, 207, 211, 226
Steele, John, 127
Stevenson, Adlai E., 273
Stevenson, David, 3, 4
Stevenson, Hugh T., 188–89
Still, William T., 381, 468n19
Stogsdill, Russell, 326, 460n34
Story of the Scottish Rite, The (Voorhis), 15
Strong, Josiah, 387
Stukeley, William, 74
sublime degrees of Masonry:
  contested conferrence of, 30–31
  origin and nature of, 29–30
Sublime Princes of the Royal Secret, 91, 94
Sullivan, Mark, 141
"Summer of Decision" (film), 307
Supreme Council of the Scottish Rite, Northern Jurisdiction:
  and anti-Masonry, 45–46
  caps, 451n50
  and Cerneauists, 32–33, 80
  differences with Southern Jurisdiction, 369
  and District of Columbia, 51, 68
  established, 31, 34
  feud with Southern Jurisdiction, 260–61, 262
  Grand Commanders of, 33, 45, 80, 259–60, 298, 312–13, 430n34
  and Warren G. Harding, 205
  and Thomas Harkins, 272, 276
  and jurisdiction for U.S. Army and Navy facilities, 152

jurisdictional disputes with Southern Jurisdiction, 31, 43–45, 48, 50, 51, 68, 80, 86, 89, 98, 152, 260–61
  membership, 453n6
  museum, 348
  and *The New Age* magazine, 149, 150
  philanthropic work, 359
  and Prince Hall Masons, 378–79
  relations with Southern Jurisdiction, 224–26, 379
  rings, 451n48, n49
  rituals, 379, 438n33, 446n12
  and Luther Smith, 298, 300, 301
Supreme Council of the Scottish Rite, Southern Jurisdiction:
  accounting system, 351
  and anti-Masonry, 46
  Archives of the, 323–24, 449n93, 463n13
  attendance at sessions, 67, 69, 78, 79, 115, 124, 128
  budgets, 125–26, 152, 180–81, 307–9
  centennial celebration (1901), 143, 144–46
  and Cerneauists, 31, 34, 36–37
  charitable programs, 280–81, 353–60
  charity fund, 152, 168, 280–81
  charity fund for widows and orphans, 94, 96, 98
  and Civil War, 70–71
  composition of, 18–19, 26–28, 34, 46–47, 64, 67–68
  and Confederate States of America, 69
  Court of Honor. *See* Court of Honor
  disaster relief aid, 113, 116, 122, 143, 153, 207, 234, 279–80
  and Educational Bureau, 188
  election of members, 50, 54
  Emeritus Members of Honor, 247
  and establishment of the Supreme Council, Northern Jurisdiction, 31, 34
  and establishment of Supreme Councils in Europe, 37
  Executive Council established, 79–80
  expansion of membership beyond South Carolina, 50
  expenditures, 79, 90, 105, 123–24, 135, 149, 150, 194, 197, 308
  feud with Northern Jurisdiction, 260–61, 262
  financial status, 64, 93, 100, 101, 112, 114, 122, 133, 135, 137, 144, 155, 159–60, 193, 202, 205, 210, 215, 223, 227, 228, 238, 276, 307–9, 374
  formed, 17, 18–19, 20, 22–23, 25, 26–29, 34, 412–13, 414–16, 426n83, 427n38, 429n23
  frequency of meetings, 226
  Fund of Fraternal Assistance, 111, 114, 115, 168, 206, 210, 211, 212–13
  headquarters moved to Washington, D.C., 86
  history of, 117, 211, 218–19, 285, 305–6, 324–25, 371–72
  honorary membership, 70, 78
  incorporated by Congress, 129
  incorporated in South Carolina, 37, 80
  library. *See* Library of the Supreme Council
  Manifesto of August 2, 1845, 48
  need to build a temple in Washington, D.C., 94, 96, 98

news service, 192, 197, 211–12, 227, 285–86
Pike "In Memoriam," 129–30
Albert Pike memorial service, 138, 197
Pooled Income Fund, 359
possibility of merger with Northern Jurisdiction, 122, 123, 125, 224–25, 379
printing press, 152
public relations, 188, 192, 197, 212, 418
publications, 90, 93, 104, 107, 112, 124, 130, 137, 149, 178, 211–12, 227, 257, 276–77, 285–86, 289, 305, 307, 309, 324, 325, 360–61, 367–68, 441n121. *See also Official Bulletin; New Age, The*
recognition of, 30
records, 34, 35–36, 46, 55, 64, 68, 86, 90, 100, 144
relations with Northern Jurisdiction, 226, 260–61, 360
relief aid for persecuted Masons in Europe, 253–56, 310–11
and scholarships for college. *See* scholarships
social calls at the White House, 79, 138, 146, 261
special sessions, 187–88, 190, 192–93
subordinate bodies, rules for, 125, 260–61
tax-exempt status, 177–78
territorial jurisdiction of, 30, 35, 44–45, 68, 80, 89, 97, 98, 136–37
Transactions indexed, 180, 324
Transactions published, 68, 192
tribunals, 84
visits to Pike's grave, 130
war bonds, 187–88, 193, 257
war relief, 168, 180, 182, 254–55, 257, 456n62
Supreme Council of the Scottish Rite, Southern Jurisdiction: committees, 68
  Centennial Committee, 135, 138
  Committee on Benevolence and Fraternal Assistance, 206, 210, 211, 212
  Committee on Doings of Inspectors and Deputies, 197
  Committee on the Doings of Subordinate Bodies, 95
  Committee on Education, 282, 289
  Committee on Education and Americanism, 307, 341
  Committee on Finance, 128, 169–70, 185, 188, 275–76, 357, 441n121
  Committee on Foreign Relations, 137, 204–5, 255, 256, 260
  Committee on Fraternal Assistance and Education, 185, 197, 204
  Committee on the House of the Temple, 185, 197, 206, 258
  Committee of Jurisprudence, 90
  Committee on Jurisprudence and Legislation, 146, 152, 154, 169, 177, 207, 211, 216–17, 226
  Committee on the Library, 180, 211
  Committee on Library and Buildings, 117, 134, 180
  Committee on Masonic Relations and Masonic Membership Erosion, 339
  Committee on *The New Age*, 197
  Committee on Peace and Arbitration, 164–65

Committee for the Pike Monument, 134–35
Committee on Publications, 277
Committee on the Revision of the Statutes, 125
Committee on Ritual and Ceremonial Forms, 216, 328, 368, 369
Committee on Ritual Revision, 53–54, 63, 137
Committee on Rituals, 130, 146, 147, 173, 185
Committee for Scottish Rite–Masonic Children's Programs, 358–59
Committee on the State of the Order, 122, 123, 302
Committee on Visitations, 276
Council of Administration, 79–80, 90, 126, 176–77, 183, 184
Executive (Building) Committee of Five, 159, 166, 167, 176–77, 183, 184–85, 445n107
Special Committee on Education, 151–52
Special Committee on Fraternal Assistance, 211, 212–13
Special Committee on the Tuberculosis Sanitarium, 210, 211
Supreme Council of the Scottish Rite, Southern Jurisdiction: officers, 18–19, 65
and conflicts of interest, 326, 336
Deputy Grand Commander, 316–17
duties of Secretary-General, 95–96, 170
elections of, 124–25, 135, 169, 172
religion of, 19
responsibilities of, 202
salaries for, 90, 103, 104, 118, 125–26, 150, 166, 169–70, 180–81, 197, 227, 308
Secretaries-General, 79, 80, 86, 101, 103, 112–13, 155–56, 166, 170, 203, 325
terms of, 122, 123, 125, 135
Supreme Council, 33°, Bulletin, The, 211–12
Supreme Councils:
Argentina, 204
Belgium, 147–48, 154, 284
Brazil, 284
Canada, 98, 272
Colombia, 284, 373
conferences of, 65–66, 95, 97–98, 148, 154–55, 165, 166–67, 190, 197, 204, 219, 234, 279, 312, 339
Cuba, 284
Czech Republic, 373
Czecho-Slovakia, 204–5
England and Wales, 65, 98, 154, 165, 272
exchange of representatives, 65
France, 28, 95, 97–98, 252, 272, 284, 415
French West Indies, 28, 30–31, 32
Germany, 251–52, 284, 312, 339, 373, 454n39, n41
Greece, 168, 253–54, 255, 284
Hungary, 373
Ireland, 37, 165
Italy, 193, 205–6, 210, 234, 280
Netherlands, 252, 454n39
New Granada (Colombia), 137
Peru, 95, 312, 339
Philippines, 272, 284
Poland, 204–5, 373
Portugal, 373

proposals for an international organization of, 147–48
recognition of, 204–5
revitalization of, 372–73
Romania, 312, 373
Russia, 372–73
Scotland, 165, 272
Spain, 204–5, 247–48
Spain-in-exile, 312
Switzerland, 454n39
Turkey, 168
Ukraine, 372–73
Yugoslavia, 373
See also Supreme Council of the Scottish Rite, Northern Jurisdiction and Southern Jurisdiction
Susman, Warren, 242–43
Sweden, 78
Sweden, Grand Lodge of, 10, 30, 246
Switzerland:
Grand Lodge of, 10
international congresses in, 95
and persecution of Masons, 249–50
symbolic language as key to ancient wisdom, 6
symbolic lodges:
Inspectors General's authority over, 15
membership, 337–38, 374–77, 453n6
and Prince Hall Masons, 377–78
and the Supreme Council, 113, 137, 276
symbols, Masonic, 4–5
caps, 158, 451n50
as key to ancient wisdom, 6
reevaluation of, 368–69, 370
revision of, 466n50
rings, 216–17, 276, 451n48, n49
used to promote morals, 7

Tacoma, Wash., 280
Taft, William Howard, 156, 167
Taiwan, 286
tax-exemption, 177, 190, 228, 241
Taxil, Leo, 110, 391, 393, 469n30, 470n37, 471n58, 472n75
Taylor, Leroy M., 143
Telepneff, Boris, 186
Teller, Henry M., 134, 136, 165–66, 167
temperance movement, 11
Temple, The, 157
Texas, 324–25, 335–37, 354
Thatcher, Maurice H., 327
theism and Masonry, 312
Thomas, Lowell, 157
"To the Mocking Bird" (Pike), 191
Todd, Samuel M., 78
Tolstoy, Leo, 415–16, 417, 448n53
Tompkins, Daniel, 32–33
Toombs, Robert, 93
Townsend, Francis, 240–41
Trachtenberg, Stephen Joel, 372, 461n54
Transou, Plez A., 371
Trelease, Allen W., 82, 436n120
Trentanove, Gaetano, 134–35
Tresner, James T., 369, 417
Truman, Harry S., 21, 195, 256–57, 259, 260, 261, 263, 264, 273, 296, 299, 313, 333, 399–400, 430n34

tuberculosis sanitarium, 206, 210, 211, 212
Tucker, Grand Commander Philip Crosby, 123, 124–25, 126
Turkey, 255
Turner, Frederick Jackson, 139–40

U.S. Bureau of Education, 179, 184
United States Capitol: laying of the cornerstone for, 20–21, 361–62, 426n79
U.S. Constitution:
bicentennial celebration, 360–61
Masons as signers of, 12
sesquicentennial of, 243–44
U.S. Park Service, 395–96, 470n50
U.S. Supreme Court, 262, 265, 266, 287–88, 295, 341–42, 365–67
University of Texas in Austin, 197, 232, 280
urbanization:
and Masonry, 159, 223
and the middle class, 153, 159
Utah, 429n19

Vail, Charles H., 468n25
van Tongeren, Hermannus, 252
Vanderbilt University, 310
Vaughn, William Preston, 40
Venezuela, 33
Verriere, Ossonde, 424n50, n53
Vincent, William S., 289
Virginia, 11, 16, 64, 100
VISA cards, 357–58
von Hindenburg, Paul, 235
Voorhis, Harold Van Buren, 15, 17

Wacker, Grant, 396
Walgren, Kent, 475
Walkes, Joseph A., Jr., 393–94
Wall Street Journal, 404
war relief aid:
First Balkan War, 168
World War I, 180, 182, 195
World War II, 254–55, 257, 456n62
Warren, Earl, 265, 313
Warren, Joseph, 10
Washington, George, 10, 11–12, 13, 154, 162, 411–12
ceremonial visits to grave of, 68–69
the Mason, 21, 210–11, 217, 229–30, 256, 277–78, 361, 387, 458n30
Masonic memorial to, 150, 163–64, 203, 230–31, 361
and John Mitchell, 20–21
portrait of, 361
statue of for Washington National Cathedral, 210–11, 258–59
Washington, D.C., International Conference of Supreme Councils:
1912, 166–67
1985, 339
Washington Monument, 50–51
Washington National Cathedral, 210–11, 258–59
Washington National Monument Society, 50–51
Washington Post, 135, 160, 305, 392, 395–96
Watergate scandal, 333, 335
Watres, Louis A., 203, 230

Watts, Robert B., 324
Webber, Frederick W., 100
    death of, 155
    as librarian, 125, 128–29, 134
    as secretary general, 112, 124, 131, 134, 138, 145, 146, 149, 151, 152
Weidner, Perry W., 190, 197
Weinman, Adolph A., 185, 216, 447n37
welfare state, 233, 239
West Indies, 15–16, 28, 30–31, 32
Whalen, William J., 467n10
White, George, 361
White, Henry, 161, 162
White, Robert H., 368
White, William R., 399
White House:
    Grand Commander calls at, 332, 362
    laying of cornerstones for, 20–21, 362
    Supreme Council calls at, 79, 138
White House Conference on Children and Youth (1960), 290
White House Conference on Education, 281–82
Why Johnny Can't Read (Flesch), 289
widows and orphans of Masons:
    care of, 111, 114, 115, 168, 206, 211
    visits to by Cowles, 246

Williams, Bert, 225
Williams, Charl O., 266–67
Wills, Garry, 396
Wilson, Charles Reagan, 82–83
Wilson, Woodrow, 165, 167, 171–72, 181, 182, 187–88, 191, 196, 258, 273
Witcover, Hyman W., 207, 219, 227
women:
    and anti-Masonry, 40, 362–63
    and domestic perceptions of Masonry, 166, 362–63
    ladies' certificates for wives, 105–6
    and Masonic chivalry, 41
    rites intended for, 439n77
    role in society, 140, 262
women's suffrage, 196
Wood, Gordon, 9
Woodbridge, Samuel, 276–77, 285–86
Woods, Elliott, 161, 162, 191, 447n37
Woods, Howard L., 394
Woolf, Virginia, 171
"Words Spoken of the Dead" (Pike), 134, 441n121
World War I, 168, 171–72, 173, 179, 181–82, 187–89
World War II, 250–58

xenophobia, 232, 383

Yates, Giles F., 38, 51
York Rite of Freemasonry, 70, 74, 123, 125, 201, 381
    breach with Scottish Rite, 84–85
    and Joseph Cerneau, 32
    members, 128, 173
    membership, 338
    and Albert Pike, 52, 61, 84, 96–97, 438n36
    rituals, 41–42, 84, 438n36
Young, Claud F., 276, 277, 280, 304–5, 351
Yugoslavia, 252–53, 255, 310–11

Ziegfeld, Florenz, 213

The double-headed eagle has been the most distinctive part of the Scottish Rite logo since at least 1801. No other Masonic or fraternal organization has been known by that image. And yet, it has never been exclusively a Masonic symbol, for it dates to the formation of the Holy Roman Empire under Charlemagne. He took the German eagle with its head turned right and the Roman eagle with its head facing left and merged them, so together the eagle looked upon both east and west. The imperial houses of Hapsburg and Romanov used this emblem, too, on their coats of arms. Thus, the Scottish Rite's heraldry has a borrowed and shared past.